THE POLITICAL ECONOMY
OF PRIVATIZATION

Has privatization worked? There is now sufficient empirical evidence available to seriously address this question. Earlier studies of privatization have, by necessity, been largely concerned with a theoretical analysis of privatization policy.

The Political Economy of Privatization draws together substantial evidence and analysis of the experience of privatization programmes in practice over the last ten years. The authors assess the different means of implementing privatization policies and analyse the impact on the economy. The work is an international study of the extensive privatization of the public sector of the advanced industrial countries; the rapid marketization of the East European countries; and the pressures upon developing countries to adopt de-regulation and privatization as the route towards economic growth. The results demonstrate that, far from being a uniform process, privatization can take many forms – from wholesale denationalization to the contracting of competitive tendering. The book is divided into six parts: Part I examines the relationship between ownership and performance; Part II assesses the importance of market structure and regulation; Part III discusses privatization strategies within the public sector; while Parts IV–VI, backed by individual country case-studies, look at the experiences of different countries engaged in the contrasting approaches to privatization. The impact upon government, consumers, managers and employees is also explored and the much vaunted relationship between private ownership and efficiency is critically assessed.

Thomas Clarke is Professor of Corporate Governance at Leeds Business School, Leeds Metropolitan University.
Christos Pitelis is the Barclays Bank Lecturer in Industrial Organisation and Corporate Strategy at the Judge Institute of Management Studies and Official Fellow in Economics at Queens' College, University of Cambridge.

THE POLITICAL ECONOMY OF PRIVATIZATION

Edited by

Thomas Clarke and Christos Pitelis

London and New York

First published 1993
by Routledge
11 New Fetter Lane, London EC4P 4EE

Simultaneously published in the USA and Canada
by Routledge
29 West 35th Street, New York, NY 10001

Paperback edition 1994

© 1993 Thomas Clarke and Christos Pitelis

Typeset in 10 on 12 point September by
Solidus (Bristol) Ltd, Bristol
Printed and bound in Great Britain by
TJ Press (Padstow) Ltd, Padstow, Cornwall

British Library Cataloguing in Publication Data
A catalogue record for this book is available from the British Library

Library of Congress Cataloguing in Publication Data
A catalog record for this book is available from the Library of Congress

ISBN 0-415-12705-X

CONTENTS

CONTENTS

FIGURES

TABLES

CONTRIBUTORS

Peter Anthony   Department of Behaviour in Organisations, the
                      Management School, University of Lancaster.

Alan Bollard   Institute of Economic Research, Wellington, New
                      Zealand.

Trevor Buck   School of Management and Finance, University of
                      Nottingham.

Ha-Joon Chang   Faculty of Economics and Politics, University of
                      Cambridge.

Thomas Clarke   Leeds Business School, Leeds Metropolitan University.

Trevor Colling   Industrial Relations Research Unit, University of
                      Warwick.

Christiane Demers   École des Hautes Études Commerciales, Montreal.

Anthony Ferner   Industrial Relations Research Unit, University of
                      Warwick.

Igor Filatotchev   School of Management and Finance, University of
                      Nottingham.

Taïeb Hafsi   École des Hautes Études Commerciales, Montreal.

John S. Henley   Department of Business Studies, University of
                      Edinburgh.

Nicholas Hooper   Centre for Defence Economics, Institute for Research in
                      the Social Sciences, University of York.

Jomo K.S.   Faculty of Economics and Administration, University of
                      Malaya, Kuala Lumpur.

Trefor Jones   Manchester School of Management, UMIST.

Jan J. Jörgensen   Faculty of Management, McGill University, Montreal.

Yannis Katsoulacos Department of Economics, Economic University of
                      Athens.

Peter Lawrence   Department of Economics and Management Sciences,
                      University of Keele.

David Mayes   National Institute of Economic and Social Research,
                      London.

Francis McGowan   Science Policy Research Unit, University of Sussex.

CONTRIBUTORS

Domenico Mario
Nuti   European University Institute, Florence.
Michael Paddon   Leeds Business School.
David Parker   Business School University of Hertfordshire.
Christos Pitelis   Judge Institute of Management Studies and Queens'
                        College, Cambridge.
Mike Reed   Department of Behaviour in Organisations, the
                        Management School, University of Lancaster.
Bob Rowthorn   Faculty of Economics and Politics, University of
                        Cambridge.
Luisa Segnana   Department of Economics, University of Trento.
Matthew Uttley   Centre for Defence Economics, Institute for Research in
                        the Social Sciences, University of York.
Thomas G.
Weyman-Jones   Department of Economics, University of Loughborough.
Mike Wright   Centre for Management Buy-out Research, University
                        of Nottingham.
Tetsuzo Yamamoto   School of Commerce, Waseda University, Tokyo.

PREFACE

The contributions assembled in this volume originated with a conference held at the University of St Andrews, Scotland. The conference brought together over one hundred delegates from thirty countries to discuss the global phenomena of privatization, which appeared to be one of the major driving forces of industrial and political change with the extensive privatizations of the public sectors of the advanced economies; the rapidly developing marketization of Eastern European countries; and the pressures upon developing countries to adopt privatization and deregulation as routes to economic growth.

The organization of the conference proved more difficult than anticipated, as political events in Eastern Europe became increasingly volatile, resulting in the attempted coup in Russia. At one time it seemed the contingent of delegates from Russia and Estonia might be locked in their countries. In the end they arrived safely in Scotland, as did a large number of other delegates who employed a variety of imaginative modes of transport from the furthest parts of Eastern Europe and from the developing countries.

In these tense but euphoric circumstances the connections between economics and politics were inescapable: restructuring stagnant command economies would require not just economic analysis but political will. After ten years of official and commercial advocacy of privatization as a direct panacea for the problems of both developed and developing economies, it was not surprising that some of the papers contributed at the conference reflected this enthusiasm.

However, at a critical stage in the course of the conference it became clear that privatization in itself could not provide a solution to economic growth, revival or prosperity. The association of markets with efficiency and public ownership with inefficiency was at the very least misleading. The economic malaise of Eastern Europe and the developing countries was much greater than could be resolved in terms of a simple public/private ownership dichotomy. The chapters in this volume reflect many of the empirical questions, intellectual doubts and moral uncertainties expressed during the course of the conference and developed since. We owe much gratitude to Diane Stafford, the desk editor at Routledge who was very patient and resourceful in bringing a manuscript together from several continents, and to Alan Fidler, a copy editor of remarkable ability.

We would like to thank also all of the participants at the conference; Stewart Clegg who as Chairman of the Department of Management at St Andrews University offered unfailing support to our efforts; Maureen Hamilton for doing the initial preparation with her usual commitment to perfection; Paul Vacani and Luka Carloni who in administering the conference gave a new meaning to lean production; and to Sandy Stewart who arranged for the provision of the fine malt whisky which provided a stimulating mist at the height of our deliberations.

Thomas Clarke
Leeds Business School

Christos Pitelis
Queens' College, Cambridge
14 December 1992

1

INTRODUCTION
The political economy of privatization
Christos Pitelis and Thomas Clarke

Privatization of state-owned assets became a major economic policy of many countries in the 1980s, and in some cases amounted to a conscious attempt to roll back the frontiers of the state and return to the market. This was part of a reconsideration of the nature and role of the state sector in developed and less developed market economies that was resolved in favour of the view that government involvement had been excessive. At the end of the 1980s the demise of central planning in Eastern Europe led to an attempt to create markets there and, in a sense, to privatize whole economies. It is tempting to conclude from these developments that state or government failure is the norm, and that the free play of market forces is the solution to such government failures. Much of the neo-liberal theory and ideology, which received wide acclaim and influence during the 1980s, makes exactly this point. However, careful consideration of the theory and evidence of the 'market versus government' issue makes this belief less self-evident.

THE GROWTH OF THE STATE

The state is widely acknowledged to be one of the most important institutional devices for resource allocation (or for others for the division of labour), along with the market (price mechanism), and the firm. In centrally planned economies the state has in fact been the primary such device. However, in market economies too, the role of the state has been increasing steadily since the Second World War. In most OECD countries today government receipts and outlays as a proportion of GDP is very high – in some cases as high as 60 per cent (Mueller 1989). A multitude of theories have tried to explain the growth of the public sector in market economies, the so called 'Wagner's Law', originating from a number of different ideological perspectives. In brief, neo-classical theories tend to consider such growth as a result of increasing demand for state services by sovereign consumers, while public choice theorists regard it as a result of the utility-maximizing policies of state officials, politicians and bureaucrats which tend to favour enhanced state activity. In the Marxist tradition, the growth of the state sector was linked to the 'laws of motion' of capitalism – increasing

1

concentration and centralization of capital, and declining profit rates – which generate simultaneous demands by capital and labour on the state to enhance their relative distributional states, for example through infrastructural provisions and increased welfare services respectively. There are variations on these views within each school, Pitelis (1991) has a detailed discussion.

Besides explaining why states increase their economic involvement over time, many economists in the 1980s focused their attention on why states fail to allocate resources efficiently, and more particularly to the relative efficiency properties of market versus non-market resource allocation. Particularly well known here are the views of the Chicago School, in particular Milton Friedman (1969) and John Stigler (1988). In a number of papers Freidman has emphasized the possibility of states becoming 'captive' to special interests of powerful organized groups, notably rich business people and trade unions. Stigler among others, on the other hand, has pointed to often unintentional inefficiencies involved in cases of state interventions. Examples are redistributional programmes by the state which dissipate more resources (for example, in administrative costs) than they redistribute, suggesting the possibility of direct market-based redistribution as a more efficient solution. For these reasons, and the tendency generated by utility-maximizing bureaucrats and politicians towards excessive growth, rising and redundant costs tend to lead to government failure. Wolf (1990) has a classification of such failures in terms of derived externalities (the Stigler argument), rising and redundant costs due to officials' 'more is better' attitude, and distributional inequities due to powerful pressure groups as in Friedman.

THE CASE FOR PRIVATE OWNERSHIP

On a more general theoretical level, the case for private ownership and market allocation has been based on three well-known theories. First, the neo-classical property rights school, which suggests that communal ownership (the lack of private property rights) will lead to dissipation – the 'tragedy of the commons'. Second, Hayek's (1985) view of 'dispersed knowledge'. According to this, knowledge is widely dispersed in every society and efficient acquisition and utilization of such knowledge can only be achieved through price signals provided by markets. Third, Alchian and Demsetz's (1972) 'residual claimant' theory suggests, much in line with the property rights school, that private capitalist ownership of firms is predicated upon the need for a residual claimant of income generating assets in the absence of which members of a coalition, for example a firm, would tend to free-ride, thus leading to inefficient utilization of resources.

There is now a huge literature on the merits and limitations of these theories – see, for example, Eggertsson (1990) for an extensive coverage. Some significant weaknesses have been exposed in each defence of private ownership and market allocation. Concerning the 'tragedy of the commons', it has been observed that historically communal ownership has often had efficiency enhancing effects. Hayek's critique of pure central planning loses much of its force when one considers choices of degree, which is virtually always the case, at least in market economies. Lastly, the residual claimant theory downplays the potential incentive-enhancing attributes of co-operatives and moreover becomes weaker when applied to modern joint-stock companies run by a controlling management group.

Other well-known mainstream arguments relating to the problem of government failure are Bacon and Eltis's (1976) claim that services, including state services, tend to be unproductive; and Martin Feldstein's (1974) view that pay-as-you-go social security schemes tend to reduce aggregate capital accumulation. The alleged reason for this is the view that rational individuals consider their contributions to such schemes as their saving, and thus reduce their personal savings accordingly to remain at their optimal consumption-savings plans. Given, however, that the schemes are pay-as-you-go (that is, contributions are used by the government to finance current benefits), no actual fund is available, so that the individual's reduction of personal savings represents an equivalent reduction of aggregate saving, equated by Feldstein to capital accumulation.

Some of the above reasoning is reminiscent of (and finds support by) that of some Marxist critics of the role of the state – for example, the view that the state is 'captive' of capitalists' interests (Miliband 1969), and that some state services involve unproductive (that is no surplus value generating) labour (Gough 1979). This is often linked to the falling tendency of the rate of profits, which provides a feedback from government failures to private sector crises. A more specific theory of state failure ('fiscal crisis') in this tradition is that of O'Connor (1973) who identifies a tendency of government spending under advanced capitalism to exceed government receipts for reasons related to demands by both capital and labour on state funds and resistance on both sides to taxation, which are particularly intensified under conditions of monopoly capitalism (see Pitelis 1991 for a critical assessment).

The near universality of the attack on the state, from both ends of the political spectrum, as reflected above, is informative of the general theoretical case underlying the drive to privatize (for one of the few effective attempts to defend public provision in this period see Heald (1983)). Concerning specifically the relative efficiency properties of private sector versus public sector enterprises, the focus of attention has been in the main on issues of managerial incentives, competitive forces and differing objectives. It is alleged that public sector enterprises achieve inferior performances in terms of profits or the efficient use of resources. While private sector managers are subject to various constraints leading them to profit-maximizing policies, this need not be the case with public sector managers it is claimed. Such constraints arise from the capital market, the 'corporate control' (that is the possibility of the take-over of inefficiently managed firms by more efficiently run ones), the market for managers (that bad managers will be penalized in their quest for jobs), and the product market (the view that consumers will choose products of efficiently run firms for their better price for given quality).

Among other factors which tend to ensure that private sector 'agents' (managers) behave in conformity with the wishes of the 'principals' (shareholders), by maximizing profits in private firms, are, for example, the concentration of shares in the hands of financial institutions; the emergence of the M-form organization which tends to ensure that 'divisions' operate as profit centres; the possibility of 'contestable markets', that is markets where competitive forces operate through potential entry by new competitors, given free entry and costless exit conditions. It is assumed public sector enterprises are not subject to such forces, not to the same degree anyway, which implies the possibility that managerial incentives for efficient use of resources and profit maximization may be less pressing in public sector firms.

Many of the above factors are linked to the concept of competition and competitive forces, where again the claim is that public sector enterprises may be more insulated from such forces and thus less likely to pursue efficiency and profit maximization. The latter will also be true if public sector enterprises simply do not aim at such policies – for example, because they are used as redistribution vehicles by the government; and/or for other non-economic reasons such as the need for electoral support; and/or because they aim at correcting structural market failures (for example, the high prices of private sector monopolies). All these factors tend to establish the economic theoretical rationale for the efficiency of private firms and therefore for privatization (Vickers and Yarrow 1988; Kay *et al.* 1986, offer extended discussion on the assumed superiority of private versus state run firms).

THE FAILURES OF THE MARKET

Various limitations can be identified in the case for the relative efficiency of the private sector. One limitation arises from the possibility that the various constraints on private sector firm managers are not as strong as they are often suggested to be. For example, large size may protect inefficient firms from the threat of take-over; it may be hard to tell when a manager has performed well, given the often long-term nature of managerial decisions; and bounded rational consumers may often fail to tell differences in the quality of similarly priced products. Concerning competition, a private sector monopoly is as insulated from it as a public sector monopoly, *ceteris paribus* (assuming no difference in the forces of potential competition). Furthermore, the absence of competition is not *per se*, a reason for privatization; it could well be a reason for opening up the public sector to such forces, for example through competitive tendering and franchising (Yarrow 1986). Such considerations have led serious commentators to the conclusion that the issue is not so much that of the change in ownership structures as it is that of the nature of competitive forces and of regulatory policies (Vickers and Yarrow 1988, Yarrow 1986, Kay and Silberston 1984).

An important issue often downplayed by proponents of privatization policies is that the very reason for public sector enterprises has often been market not government failure (Rees 1986). It is worth reminding ourselves of the issues here. In mainstream economic theory, the first fundamental theorem of welfare economics shows that markets can allocate resources efficiently without state intervention, provided that market failures do not exist. Such failures, however, are widely observed, famous instances being the existence of externalities (interdependencies not conveyed through prices); public goods (goods which are jointly consumed and non-excludable); and monopolies, which tend to increase prices above the competitive norm. The observation among others that efficient government itself is a public good, has led to the idea of 'pervasive market failure' (Dasgupta 1986), which is viewed as the very *raison d'être* of state intervention (Stiglitz 1986). The very reason public sector enterprises are run by the state is that they have been seen as 'natural monopolies' (firms in which the minimum efficient size is equal to the size of the market as a result of economies of scale, leading to declining costs). If private, it is assumed these firms would introduce structural market failure in terms of monopoly pricing. The undertaking of the activities of such natural monopolies (often known as public utilities) by the state could solve the problem through, for example, the introduction of marginal cost pricing policies. Although such policies need not necessarily re-establish a first-best Pareto optimal solution (given imperfections elsewhere in the economy), they could at the very least protect consumers from paying monopoly prices. This in itself would point to the limited value of any claims that public utilities do not maximize profits, given that this was not their objective to start with.

Theory and evidence seem to be less clear-cut on the issue of the relative efficiency properties of different ownership structures than would appear to be the case on the basis of the privatization mania of the 1980s. This is not to say that ownership structures do not matter, but rather that the issue of market versus non-market allocation is far more complex than is often allowed by the proponents of privatization. This conclusion need not be true if the very reason for public enterprise was misplaced to start with. Neo-classical, Chicago and Schumpeterian perspectives point to this conclusion. From the Chicago school it has been suggested by Baumol (1982), for example, that markets may be contestable – that is, characterized by free entry and costless exit. If so, *potential* competition will tend to ensure profit-maximizing behaviour, therefore there is no market failure and no need for public sector ownership. In the same tradition, the Coase (1937) and Williamson (1975) perspective of 'transaction costs', suggests that the growth of firms can often be the result of transaction costs minimizing (efficiency enhancing) strategies. If so, private monopolies are efficiency enhancing and therefore need not be nationalized. In the Chicago perspective, well known is Demsetz's (1973) 'differential efficiency' hypothesis. According to this, it is higher efficiency that allows firms to grow and thus monopolize markets; again, therefore, there is little reason for seeking to nationalize large efficient firms. Lastly Schumpeter's 'differential innovations' hypothesis points to a similar picture. Here, firms grow large because of successful innovations and, moreover, larger firms tend to be more innovative due to access to funds, scientific personnel, etc. For all these reasons, profit should be considered as the just reward and incentive to successful entrepreneurship, therefore the very sources of efficiency should not be removed by nationalization.

The immense literature on the issues of contestable markets, differential efficiency and differential innovation, is at best indecisive however (see Pitelis 1991 for a survey). Furthermore, and importantly, the transaction costs theory is predicated on the existence of firms as solutions to transactional *market failures*, and therefore strongly questions the alleged efficiency of the market. These would appear to question the simple view of the efficient private sector versus the inefficient public sector. Theory and evidence, once again, are indecisive on the issue of the relative efficiency properties of different ownership structures.

The fact that virtually every industrialized country this century has felt the need of a large public sector suggests that public enterprise has served a purpose private entrepreneurship could not fulfil. Moreover, the current enthusiasm for privatization is widespread, most industrial countries have been modest in their transfer of public assets to the market system (Stevens 1992). In the developing world public enterprise was often perceived as the *only* vehicle for economic development in the absence of any effective indigenous market system, and often the push for privatization in the 1980s came from the IMF and World Bank, not the countries concerned (Babai 1988, Ramamurti 1992). The intellectual argument for privatization has often been won by default. The analysis of the relative performance of private versus public enterprises paints a less than clear picture (Vickers and Yarrow 1988, Lay *et al.* 1968). Since privatization, the assessment of the results of privatized enterprises has been very mixed, and most of the early privatizations were of companies that were already relatively efficient and profitable (Curwen 1986). Much of the effort of the privatized companies seems to have gone into fighting off the threat of competition (Swann 1988, Mitchell 1990, Beauchamps 1990), and there is little evidence of the effects of ownership in a truly competitive environment (Stevens 1992). Meanwhile the remaining parts of the public sector – partly under the threat of privatization, partly as a result of a democratic imperative – have been restructuring and reassessing policy and practices in order to achieve greater efficiency and responsiveness to consumer demands (Hambleton 1992, Thomson 1992, Clarke and Grace 1993).

THE REASONS FOR PRIVATIZATION

The explanation of the drive for privatization is more complex, and more political, than pure 'market versus planning' considerations might suggest. Vickers and Yarrow (1988: 157) offer the following classification of the objectives of privatization:

- reducing government involvement in industry;
- improving efficiency in the industries privatized;
- reducing the public sector borrowing requirement;
- easing problems of public sector pay determination by weakening the public sector unions;
- widening share ownership;
- encouraging employee share ownership;
- gaining political advantage.

In the UK, which led the way in the implementation of wholesale privatization, the policy was not originally clearly conceived, but was motivated by political as well as economic reasons. The government's monetarist commitment to lowering taxes and reducing the public sector borrowing requirement (PSBR) was politically easier to achieve by selling public assets than by cutting public expenditure (Brittan 1984). The sales were a means of overcoming the fiscal constraints the government had imposed upon itself (Abromeit 1988). Though primacy was given in government statements to the achievement of the economic aims of enhancing competition and efficiency, when these came into conflict with the immediate political objectives of quickly raising money by successful sales, the political objectives were paramount (Marsh 1991). Thus the policy of promoting competition in liberalized markets was abandoned in favour of the simple transfer of public monopolies into the private sector.

Most industrial countries still maintain substantial public sector assets, despite the burden of public sector deficits. Added to the pressures for privatization is the question of whether domestically based public enterprises can possibly compete in a global economy in which there is vigorous internationalization of production, markets and competition, based on growing political, economic and technological interdependence. The need to achieve scale economies which narrow home markets can no longer provide, such as in telecommunications and computers; the need to establish a presence in foreign markets; and the need to share rapidly mounting research and development costs; present a serious challenge to public enterprise. Few public corporations have ventured into the field of international mergers and acquisitions. However, French public corporations have been as active in cross-border acquisitions as their private sector counterparts, revealing a versatility in the public sector not recognized in most countries (Stevens 1992).

International pressures may well serve to accelerate the pace of privatization in the 1990s, but before the balance of the public and the private sector is decided upon, the evidence concerning the results of privatization should be examined first. Though the scale of privatization in OECD countries by 1991 had amounted to £121 billion,[1] the majority of this was accounted for in the UK and Japan with a combined total of £92 billion (see Table 1.1). Industrial countries may well have been wise to adopt a more cautious approach to privatization than was witnessed in the UK; such scrutiny may well provide a warning to the

Table 1.1 The scale of privatizations in selected OECD countries, 1980–91

Country	Privatization period	Accumulated privatization proceeds absolute (£ equivalent)	As percentage of average annual GDP over the privatization period
Austria	1987–90	Sch 12.7 billion (0.6 b)	0.9
Canada	1984–90	C$3.1 billion (£1.6 b)	0.6
France	1983–91	FF82.4 billion (£8.24 b)	1.5
Germany*	1984–90	DM9.7 billion (£3.34 b)	0.5
Italy	1983–91	L13,500 billion (£6.25 b)	1.4
Japan	1986–88	¥11,000 billion (£47.8 b)	3.1
Netherlands	1987–91	FL4.9 billion (£1.5 b)	1.0
New Zealand	1987–91	NZ$9.0 billion (£3.0 b)	14.1
Portugal	1989–91	Esc364 billion (£1.5 b)	4.3
Spain	1986–90	Ptas207 billion (£1.2 b)	0.5
Sweden	1987–90	SKr14 billion (£1.3 b)	1.2
Turkey	1988–91	TL3,500 billion (£0.3 b)	1.6
UK	1979–91	£44.5 billion	11.9

Source: Stevens 1992: 6.
Note: *Area of Federal Republic of Germany before unification.

Eastern European countries in deciding the degree of market freedom and indicative planning they adopt; and for the developing countries privatization may be seen as no more of an economic panacea than was the unquestioning adoption of central planning decades before.

The objective of this volume on the political economy of privatization is to provide an up-to-date reassessment of the theory and practice of privatization; to offer analyses of the extent of competition and efficiency achieved by privatization; to explore the role and potential effects of the regulatory agencies; and to provide comparative studies of privatization in different countries, with a particular emphasis on the dramatic transformations occurring in Eastern Europe. Policy-making in this area should be informed by greater understanding than has so far been the case.

OWNERSHIP AND PERFORMANCE

The thesis that the transfer of assets from the public to the private sector raises both allocative and technical efficiency is examined by David Parker (Ch. 2). The case for privatization policies is often strong on *a priori* theorizing and weak in empirical confirmation when, as Parker indicates, there is no overwhelming support for the notion that private enterprise is inevitably superior to public enterprise. This study examines the evidence of improved or deteriorating performance with the move towards the private sector and, as importantly, investigates the *causes* of the performance change. How performance is influenced by the degree of competition faced in the product market is considered.

. The transformation in the performance of ten public sector organizations is examined as they move closer to the market, in terms of employment, productivity and financial ratios. In the sample the move from public ownership and control appeared to lead to improved performance in five of the organizations, whereas in the other case-studies there were conflicting results. Critical to improvements in performance were significant changes in the internal organization structures of the enterprises, and many of these changes had pre-dated the privatization process: that is, significant organizational reforms had already occurred within the public sector. '

. The evidence suggests that the move away from public ownership is associated with improved performance, though improvement is not guaranteed. Furthermore, it was not possible to discover whether improved financial performance was at the expense of service quality. The Parker study represents a pioneering attempt at a more rigorous assessment of the performance of privatization, and reveals the stimulating effect of restructuring and decentralization upon the corporations concerned. However, to determine how durable this effect will be, and how powerful the impulse to perform well in future, will require further study as these organizations mature in their privatized status.

Bob Rowthorn and Ha-Joon Chang (Ch. 3) examine theories which equate efficiency with private ownership and argue that they are misleading. They contend the central issue should be the political economy of state intervention rather than ownership *per se*. They examine two dimensions of efficiency: static efficiency in the use of existing resources, and dynamic efficiency in the generation of new resources through sustained innovation and structural change. The economic justification for the superiority of the private enterprise sector relies on residual claimant theory and dispersed knowledge theory. The authors outline the limitations of a model of pure self-interest, and argue that the ideal mix of centralized and decentralized knowledge utilization is a matter of optimum size rather than ownership.

The argument for 'letting the market decide' is not a justification for private ownership but for effective product market competition combined with a 'hard budget' constraint on the enterprises involved, be they public or private. To the contention that performance of public enterprises will inevitably improve by privatization, they respond that the answer lies not in economics but in politics and political economy. Thus privatization may be a way of achieving an outcome which is technically feasible but politically difficult under public ownership.

With reference to the political and economic transformation of Eastern Europe they conclude 'in many ex-Communist countries the scope for rapid privatization, at least of large enterprises, is very limited. Where this is the case, there is simply no alternative, in the medium term, but to concentrate energies on improving the state sector, perhaps either privatizing slowly in the course of time or, following the example of Taiwan, promoting the growth of new private sector enterprises. Moreover, if, contrary to expectation, improvements in the state sector turn out to be adequate, there may be no need for a large-scale private sector at all.'

If problems of resolving questions of competition and regulation are difficult within national boundaries, at the international level they become even more profound. Francis McGowan (Ch. 4) discusses how the European Commission is seeking to introduce competition into sectors traditionally protected by national ownership and regulatory environments. The Commission's task is complicated by the fact that in some countries major industries are organized as competitive private enterprises and in others as regulated public enterprises. McGowan concentrates on two industries – the Electricity Supply Industry, which for many years was a public monopoly throughout Europe; and the air transport industry, which also had monopoly publicly owned operators. He explores the issue of how far public ownership affects the performance of competitively structured markets as the Commission seeks to create a European electricity market and free air transport market.

In 1980 the Commission adopted a directive on the transparency of financial linkages between public enterprises and governments which was aimed primarily at the manufacturing sector, though in 1988 it was used to force a degree of liberalization in the telecommunications market. In electricity, the Commission identified the nationally based arrangements for supply as a source of high costs and began a series of initiatives in 1989 to encourage trade in electricity across national boundaries. In 1991 the Commission declared utility monopolies were contrary to the competition policy of the Treaty of Rome.

Successive efforts have also been made by the Commission to induce greater flexibility in the European air transport market dominated by state-owned carriers and operating in an uncompetitive regulatory regime. However, the close relationship between airlines and governments in most European countries has meant that 'While governments generally welcomed the prospect of lower prices, improved services and greater efficiency as a good thing, they were not prepared to see airlines go to the wall for the sake of these aims. . . . Indeed, as they have had to accept the Commission's reforms over the last few years, the major airlines and their governments have acted to pre-empt the effects of such liberalization.' As yet liberalization has proved ineffective, and it remains to be seen if the Commission's latest initiative, an 'Open Skies' programme which gives all European Community airlines access to all routes dominated by national flag carriers by 1993 and the right to ply any member state's internal routes by 1996, proves any more effective at overcoming perceived national interests in air transport (*Financial Times*, 23 June 1992).

MARKET STRUCTURE AND REGULATION

An unanticipated consequence of privatization is the central significance of the role of the government-appointed regulators who exert efficiency constraints and performance incentives upon enterprises which often enjoy dominant market

positions. Thomas Weyman-Jones (Ch. 5) considers the evolution of the regulatory framework for the electricity supply industry, a possible model for
deregulating the supply of electricity in the rest of the European Community. He
examines different models of regulation suggested in recent years and considers
in detail the implications of price-capping. The inefficiencies of the cost-plus
contracts which governed the relationship between the CEGB and the twelve
area electricity boards prior to privatization are discussed.

In the vain effort to persuade the private capital market to take on the nuclear
power stations within an oligopolistic structure of two competing generating
companies, the chance of creating up to ten competing generating companies was
lost. In addition, transmission and distribution remained natural monopolies
after privatization. This has made the attempt to create a spot market for
electricity more difficult. The National Grid Company (the privatized transmission company) establishes the system marginal price by taking supply from
the generators and bids for load from the regional electricity companies. But the
duopoly in generation allows market power to raise prices sigificantly above
marginal cost, and divesting of generation into smaller companies is a possible
policy option for the future.

Weyman-Jones elaborates Leibenstein's distinction between price efficiency
when firms do not have the market power to exploit consumers, and X-efficiency
when firms irrespective of their dominance in final markets acts to keep costs as
low as possible. The potential of the RPI$-X$ (Retail Price Index minus X) price-
capping formula is explored, relative to other means of regulation. Thus the work
of the regulators is crucial, and with environmental and energy-saving policies
becoming more significant is likely to remain so. 'The initial idea that regulation
of the utilities would wither away as competitive forces emerged has turned out
to be something of an illusion.'

There is in any privatization programme a need to face not only the problem
of how to privatize companies, but also the question of the subsequent market
structure. Trefor Jones (Ch. 6) reveals how in the privatized gas industry
competition has evolved very slowly and how British Gas has been accused of
restricting the growth of competition by its pricing and operational tactics which
have discouraged entry. He argues that privatization of a state enterprise which
generates a market structure without more than one significant competitor,
greatly weakens the economic case for the move. Yet the market structure for
most of the privatized enterprises was either complete monopoly or restrictive
oligopoly (in one of the few cases of complete deregulation, the bus industry, the
results were very mixed).

British Gas was considered to be a natural monopoly in that duplications of
distribution facilities is not an efficient use of resources and makes monopoly the
lowest cost option. Privatized as a monopoly the sale of British Gas was oversubscribed four times and undervalued by £500 million. Criticisms concerning
the performance of the privatized company included the accusation of discrimination in the setting of prices between customers; using control of the pipelines to

prevent potential competitors reaching customers; dominating the North Sea gas market leaving little available for potential competitors; and taking excessive profits because of a light regulatory regime.

Following a report by the Monopolies and Mergers Commission (MMC), British Gas came to an agreement with the Office of Fair Trading (OFT) to implement the MMC proposals. This led to 5.2 per cent of the industrial gas market being claimed by competitors in 1991. A proposal agreed with the OFT is to split British Gas into two companies, with British Gas transmission publishing tariffs offering the same transmission rates to all potential competitors, encouraging entrants into the gas industry. 'The behaviour of the company led to a reference to the Monopolies and Mergers Commission into the contract market which set in process a series of moves which have ended with the company facing dismemberment into two parts.'

The impact of privatization upon management orientations and the conduct of industrial relations in the former public industries is examined by Anthony Ferner and Trevor Colling (Ch. 7). They concentrate upon changes in British Telecom, British Gas, and the water and electricity companies. Some privatized companies have experienced troubled industrial relations while others have adopted a more evolutionary process of change. The regulatory price formulae appear to provide a strong incentive for companies to cut labour costs, though in practice it is uncertain whether the formulae have created a stronger addition spur to labour efficiency than the earlier public sector cost-cutting targets.

Managements' belief in sending the right signals to shareholders has meant operating according to a business logic rather than a public sector one, and privatized corporations have moved quickly to diversify out of their core activity into new sectors. These new activities have been organized as separate businesses, with industrial relations escaping the legacy of the public sector. What could be emerging is a dualism in industrial relations in the privatized concerns with a core business providing a stable utility service of dependable quality, with the retention of consensual industrial relations; and in the new areas of activity an innovative, and more flexible culture reflecting market opportunities.

More general changes in management culture are discernible as management pursue profit-maximizing strategies and attempt to impress regulators and government of their determination to be efficient. Devolution of budgetary responsibility to line-managers, and decentralization towards individual operating units such as telecommunications districts and individual power-stations, is taking place. However, central personnel management remain worried about the systematic effects of local industrial relations difficulties in integrated network industries, and believe in the need for a unified corporate culture. The demand for quality of service restricts the freedom to engage in cost-cutting by major reductions in the labour force, though management are pursuing technological solutions to quality problems.

PRIVATIZATION STRATEGIES WITHIN THE PUBLIC SECTOR

The consequences of another attempt to introduce a degree of privatization within the public services is investigated by Mathew Uttley and Nicholas Hooper (Ch. 8). Compulsory competitive tendering (CCT) legislation by the Conservative Government required local authorities to subject a range of services traditionally supplied in-house to periodic competition from the private sector. The advocates of CCT point to cost-savings and improved technical efficiency through competition; whilst opponents of CCT claim contracting-out leads to deterioration of service quality and excessive costs in enforcing, managing and monitoring the tendering process. Uttley and Hooper examine the scope of current competitive tendering and evidence concerning the impact upon performance in the local authority sector.

Local authorities always relied upon private contractors for some services, though almost all the authorities' statutory services were provided by direct labour organizations in-house: competitive tendering furnishes councils with comparative cost information on alternative sources of supply. The tendering process forces authorities to consider services quality in terms of *outputs* (the effectiveness of the service to local people), rather than in terms of *inputs* (the number of people and amount of resources deployed). Opponents see CCT as an attempt to introduce *efficiency* (the relation of outputs to inputs), rather than *effectiveness* (the quality of outputs in terms of the service to the community).

The data suggests aggregate cost savings are achieved by local authorities engaging in competitive tendering through improved technical efficiency and changes in employment practices, often involving some redundancies and a decline in working conditions for employees. The Audit Commission has stated that the essential factor in cost savings has been the introduction of *competition*, not the handing of the problem to the private sector. CCT has helped to influence the local authorities to become outward-looking organizations concerned with satisfying customers and performing well when measured against potential competitors, and this in turn has brought a realization that local authorities are essentially intermediaries in the supply of services rather than the customers themselves.

Michael Paddon (Ch. 9) explores another dimension of compulsory competitive tendering: the introduction of competition from European contractors for local authority contracts in the UK. European Community public procurement directives will apply to the local government annual expenditure of 614 billion ECUs. This will involve Community-wide advertising of contracts; establishing objective criteria for the award of contracts; and banning the adoption of technical standards which are only needed nationally, discriminating against companies from other countries. Paddon examines the impact of these EC directives upon building works and the purchasing of supplies.

Public purchasing is seen as a particular problem in the completion of the

European single market, though contracts are worth 15 per cent of the GDP of the European Community only a very small proportion (0.14 per cent of the GDP) is awarded to companies outside the national boundaries of the public bodies concerned. The EC directives are being strengthened to liberalize trade in public procurement facilitating greater contracting between member states, as the Cecchini Report stated: 'By not encouraging inter-EC competition, if not by deliberately rejecting it, the public sector pays more than it should for the goods it needs and, in so doing, supports sub-optimal enterprises in the Community' (1988).

However, the directives have a particular significance for the UK since local authorities are larger than in the rest of Europe, and contracts are therefore larger and more attractive to private European firms. So far UK local authorities have often found the EC directives burdensome, with little practical effects and only a tiny number of bids from European concerns; however, Paddon investigates the recent evidence of European multinationals buying UK firms in order to bid for local authority contracts. One company bidding for UK local authority cleaning contracts is the Compagnie Generale des Eaux, with 900 subsidiaries, a global turnover of $20.3 billion and 173,000 employees. Multinationals are able to pursue growth strategies based on loss leader tendering. Such companies pursue vertical integration in single sector markets, for example, water distribution; then foreign investment and overseas subsidiaries, extending the territorial base by acquisition; and finally diversify into new urban service areas, thus achieving the 'encirclement and conquest of new municipalities' (Lorrain 1991). Whether local residents are satisfied by the services of remote multinationals remains to be seen.

Some public services, such as the health service and education, are difficult to privatize even by the most enterprise-oriented government since people require access to them regardless of their ability to pay. In these circumstances other attempts have been made to make services remaining in the public sector adopt private sector practices. The implantation of a commercial management ethos in the National Health Service is examined by Mike Reed and Peter Anthony (Ch. 10). The NHS was subjected to a structural transformation in the 1970s which emphasized an ethos of corporate rationalization and bureaucratic centralization, and in the 1980s has been confronted by the rhetoric of market decentralization and organizational autonomy. As a result, a service previously centrally administered and locally self-managed is now subject to commercial management, external controls and monitoring. This represented a move away from high trust, collaborative work relations towards a low trust control ethos in which directive managerial control became the driving force behind institutional and organizational change.

'NHS general managers ... have become the focal point for the tensions – and resulting conflicts – between a political and economic imperative that demands obeisance to a market-driven conception of economic efficiency and effectiveness and an organizational reality which suggests that these external pressures have to be mediated, and consequently modified, by the organizational contingencies of a highly complex and "politicized" occupational division of labour.' Reed and Anthony present an analysis of the macro-level developments in the NHS, and a case-study of the organizational upheavals in a District Health Authority.

The attempt to deregulate the medical profession, control public expenditure, introduce self-managed units and internal markets, with formalized contracts and a split between purchaser and provider envisaged by recent legislation, projects an organizational dynamic of decentralization and fragmentation. The irony of this approach is that modern production organization is preoccupied with the search for the very flexibility, adaptability, and high-trust work relations characteristic of the traditional organizational practice of the NHS. The future of the NHS is dependent upon the survival of this negotiated order. As Reed and Anthony conclude, all organizations are held together by moral bonds of reciprocal obligations which can prove more effective than the intrusion of market relations.

PRIVATIZATION IN ADVANCED INDUSTRIAL ECONOMIES

Turning to an exploration of the impact of privatization in particular economies, beginning with the advanced industrial countries, it is clear from Table 1.2 that the scale of privatization has varied considerably in different parts of the OECD. Though the policy of privatization may have received substantial public attention in most of these countries, the results of that policy range from minor experiments in privatization as in Sweden, Spain and Holland, to significant programmes as in Japan, New Zealand and the UK. Similarly, the approach to privatization has differed greatly: only in the UK among OECD countries has it been driven by the ideological zeal found in Eastern Europe; in contrast, most OECD economies have remained pragmatic and selective in their implementation of privatization. As Table 1.2 reveals, with the notable exception of the United States, which never developed significant public sector industries, most OECD countries retain significant public sector activities in key industries. Plans may exist for further extensive privatization, but whether these are ever acted upon may depend upon emerging evidence concerning the performance of privatized sectors.

The UK privatization programme has frequently been presented by politicians, industrial consultants, and by some academics as a resounding success and a major contribution to the revival of the economic fortunes of the country. More analytical and critical assessments have emerged, particularly the influential study of Vickers and Yarrow (1988). However, much of the focus within the economics literature has been upon the failure of privatization policy to achieve the efficiency and performance gains possible, due to the failure to introduce effective competition by restructuring public sector monopolies into competing concerns as an essential part of the privatization process. There have been

Table 1.2 Estimated percentage shares of state-owned assets in selected sectors for various OECD countries (about 1990/1)

	Steel	Ship-building	Motor vehicles	Oil/petroleum	Coal/mining	Railways	Airlines	Electricity (production)	Gas	Post	Telecom-munications	Banking	Other
Australia	0	0	0	0	0	100	75	100	0	100	100	a)	
Austria	100	n/a	n/a	85	100	100	52	50	100	100	100	10	b)
Belgium	50	0	0	n/a	n/a	100	52	25	25	100	100	c)	
Canada	0	0	0	n/a	0	75	0	100	0	100	25	n/a	
Finland	90	n/a	100	100	n/a	100	70	n/a	100	100	100	n/a	d)
France	100	n/a	40	n/a	100	100	100	100	100	100	100	n/a	e)
Germany*	n/a	25	0	0	n/a	100	60	n/a	0	100	100	n/a	
Greece	60	70	n/a	n/a	70	100	100	100	100	100	100	70	f)
Italy	60	n/a	n/a	n/a	n/a	100	75	75	80	100	100	40	g)
Japan	0	0	0	0	0	66	0	0	0	100	46	0	
Netherlands	14	n/a	70	n/a	n/a	100	39	n/a	n/a	100	100	n/a	h)
New Zealand	0	n/a	n/a	0	n/a	100	0	94	n/a	100	0	n/a	
Norway	50	n/a	n/a	n/a	n/a	100	n/a	n/a	100	100	100	n/a	
Portugal	100	n/a	n/a	100	n/a	n/a	100	n/a	n/a	100	n/a	75	i)
Spain	60	90	10	50	50	100	100	30	100	100	100	12	j)
Sweden	40	75	0	n/a	n/a	100	30	n/a	0	100	100	k)	l)
Switzerland	0	n/a	n/a	n/a	n/a	100		n/a	n/a	100	100	m)	
Turkey	75	n/a	23	87	100	100	85	40	100	100	100	n)	p)
UK	0	0	0	25	100	100	0	n/a	0	100	20	0	
USA	0	0	0	0	0	q)	0	n/a	n/a	100	0	0	r)

Source: Stevens 1992: 8.

Note: *Former Federal Republic.

Key:

a) State has significant holdings in the banking sector, for example Commonwealth Bank of Australia, which is among the four largest in Australia.

b) Substantial state interests also in metals, chemicals, electrical engineering, electronics and mechanical engineering.

c) Savings banks and credit institutes are semi-public.

d) The country's four largest companies are in public hands. The portfolio includes, among others, base metals, textiles, machinery, petrochemicals, chemicals, and forestry.

e) Substantial state interests in insurance, aerospace, electronics, chemicals.

f) State plays dominant role in manufacturing, including textiles, metals, pulp and paper.

g) Important state interests in, among others, engineering, electronics, chemicals, textiles, metals and cement.

h) State retains some interests in chemicals, aircraft manufacture, banking.

i) Substantial state interests in, among others, chemicals, fertilizers, base metals, breweries, tobacco, cement, pulp and paper, and insurance.

j) State has large holdings in, among others, textiles, chemicals, metals, food and tobacco.

k) Nordbanken, the second largest of the country's banks, is state-owned.

l) Total corporate assets owned by the state are estimated at SKr250 billion (£24 b). The portfolio contains, among others, interests in pharmaceuticals, forestry, mining, and naval shipyards.

m) District banks owned by regional authorities.

n) State interests in four major banks.

p) The state's portfolio includes petrochemicals, textiles, cement, telecommunications equipment, electronics and chemicals. It is estimated to account for 25 per cent of manufacturing capacity and half of total fixed investment.

q) The Amtrak railway is Federally owned.

r) Whilst the Federal government owns very little state and city governments have substantial interests in a wide range of businesses, notably power utilities, airports, water utilities and ports. The value of these is estimated at about $225 billion (£130 b), around 4 per cent of GDP.

comparatively few studies which have questioned the rationale and effects of the privatization policy as a whole, except within the public administration field (Steel and Heald 1984).

A critique of the experience of privatization in Britain is offered by Thomas Clarke (Ch. 11), which contests the usefulness of the UK model for other countries to adopt. There was little coherence or consistency to the UK government's approach to privatization, and although it amounted to a fundamental change in economic direction this was secured at some cost, and the strategy did not achieve what was claimed in terms of transforming the efficiency of industry. The apparent success in creating a shareholder democracy could prove a limited and temporary phenomenon, there is little guarantee consumers will benefit from the switch of public utilities to the private sector, and employees have not enjoyed the benefits from the change which their directors have awarded themselves. If privatization is not as successful a policy as is officially insisted, and if future privatizations in the UK are likely to prove more difficult to implement, then greater emphasis may be placed upon achieving a transformation of the remaining public sector to attain more efficiency and customer responsiveness. The solutions to current economic and organizational problems in the public sector do not lie simply with the resort to private ownership and the market system.

Canada has not engaged in wholesale privatization, but has scaled back and reshaped the state's role in the market. Jan Jörgensen, Taïeb Hafsi and Christiane Demers (Ch. 12) contend that public sector restructuring there has been analogous to divestment in the private sector. They compare privatization at two levels – that carried out by the Canadian Federal Government, and that by the Quebec provincial government. Three general forces made divestment more common in the 1980s: the need for greater external financing; globalization of production and markets; and the recognition of the challenges of managing complex enterprises. Divestment was thus associated with the quest for improved strategic fit between the organization and its changing environment to allow concentration on core skills. Equally, they argue, 'Public sector divestment can also be viewed as a means to achieve better "fit" between the government and its environment. Effective management of the public sector requires that government focuses its scarce managerial resources on critical issues and disengages itself from non-essential activities.'

They explain how at Federal level Canada has used public sector corporations to pioneer new industries, to meet national security goals, to bail-out failing private sector companies, and to promote nation-building by creating East–West links that counter the southern pull of the United States. As a result, Federal public enterprises have been concentrated in three areas – financial; transport and communications; and mining, petroleum and energy. The authors discuss the context, process and outcomes of divestment in seven detailed case-studies, elaborating upon the political problems involved and difficulties of implementation. They emphasize the importance of the involvement of the enterprise participants and identify the risks of imposing a pre-conceived strategy upon complex organizations.

Luisa Segnana (Ch. 13) examines the implications of the structure of owner-ship for the behaviour and performance of firms in Italy. She suggests that a re-evaluation of policy options is possible as some cases of 'failures of the market' are changed in the light of the erosion of natural monopoly by technical progress; and in other cases it is massive demand that now does not justify the monopoly condition. The collusive/competitive nature of private/public sector relationships in Italy is in some respects unique, and the variety of state-owned enterprises is greater than anywhere else in Europe. The Italian public sector comprises a large number of administrative bodies and independent public boards where state companies supply public services at national and local level, and also a large sector of manufacturing and service enterprises owned by public bodies and controlled through three state holding companies.

Segnana explains how after the Second World War state ownership in Italy was viewed not simply as a response to market failures but as a way to promote economic growth. 'The presence of the state was considered inevitable (and tacitly justified by the private sector) in sectors with high financial requirements in order to provide assistance to industrial firms and supporting services, including public utilities and energy sources.' Privatization in the late 1970s was motivated by the need to get rid of financially troubled firms. From 1981, privatization became part of a strategy to reduce the state's control of share-holdings in public enterprises. After 1984 public sector reorganization and rationalization regarding finances and core businesses made further use of privatization. The increasing velocity of changing ownership arrangements were influenced by the capacity to generate internal funds and the search for external funds, and out of this process emerged the widespread utilization of the public enterprise as a joint stock company in Italy.

In New Zealand a different path has been pursued to induce greater commercial efficiency in the public sector. Alan Bollard and David Mayes (Ch. 14) discuss how a corporatization policy has been extensively applied with great speed in an attempt to recreate within the public sector the conditions of private enterprise. The principles of corporatization applied since 1985 are that managers are required to run state-owned enterprises (SOEs) as successful businesses. Responsible for pricing and marketing, managers of SOEs are set performance targets by Ministers which they have to achieve as individual enter-prises without competitive advantages. The clear objective of maximizing commercial performance is encouraged by company boards which have the authority to make strategic decisions.

Differences still exist with the private sector, for the state-owned enterprises have no market for their share, with little threat of take-over or bankruptcy. Government guarantees are still perceived and the potential for political inter-vention still exists, with little freedom to divest and diversify out of the original activity the SOE was established in. Some SOEs have proved transitional stages

19

towards privatization, while others will remain state owned. In terms of performance, labour productivity has generally improved, but financial performance depends upon whether restructuring took place before or after the SOE was established. Some SOEs have been turned round, while others are still loss-making concerns. In a period of difficult macroeconomic circumstances for New Zealand, the corporatization and privatization policies have been part of an attempt to secure control of the public deficit. Whilst corporate restructuring may have been considered essential, unemployment has escalated during the period of liberalization since the mid-1980s from 3 per cent to 10 per cent, with little economic growth.

Japan, also, has not been immune from the drive for privatization, but as Tetsuzo Yamamoto (Ch. 15) reveals, just as the pattern and objectives of state intervention in industry in Japan have been rather different from their western counterparts, so the process of privatization has proved rather different in Japan. As a result of the Shokusun Kohgyoh policy of promoting industry, the Japanese government owned a wide variety of enterprises towards the end of the nineteenth century, some of which were sold off in the 1880s in a first wave of privatization. The US occupation policies from 1949 to 1952 compelled a further round of privatization as the Japanese government scrapped or sold-off many state enterprises, including Japan Electric Power. The third wave of privatizations began in the mid-1980s in response to market and technological changes, which suggested government monopolistic services were no longer permissible in the face of a growing fiscal crisis, the rising cost of the public corporations, and the failure to improve performance in the public sector. In addition there was foreign pressure to privatize as a way of opening up and expanding markets for imports, and the realization that with booming capital markets in Japan sell-offs could be highly profitable for the state.

Japan National Railways (JNR) shared many of the problems of other public enterprises with an ambiguity concerning management responsibility, lack of customer responsiveness, and overmanning. Second, there were problems of regional provision and unstable management/union relations. Opponents of privatization claimed that it would only worsen regional imbalances in transport provision and consequent economic development, and suggested that large-scale redundancies and worse labour relations would only endanger passenger safety. With JNR the second largest contributor to the national deficit with an accumulated corporate debt of 30 trillion yen, privatization was carried in 1987 when the company was dissolved into seven firms; much of the debt was diverted to the JNR Settlement Corporation; recruitment was suspended and redeployment practised.

The result was a slight increase in the volume of traffic, as management pursued more positive operational policies and retrenchment of costs. The number of employees was reduced from 350,000 in 1984 to 200,000 in 1989, most of whom were absorbed in the expanding Japanese economy. Though many local lines were abolished, there was the maintenance of a traditional equitable fares formula, and the Transport Ministry continued to regulate the fares within an integrated transport system in which private companies received public subsidies. However, there was a continuing tension in the effort to reconcile the public interest with efficiency; the share of passenger transport continued to decline; and further restructuring with the possibility of labour militancy lay ahead. In conclusion, rather than being seen as the abandonment of the transport system to market forces, 'JNR's reform should be interpreted as a Japanese-style privatization where the concept of public interest (in particular equity) was thought much of . . .'

In a comparison of different privatization policies appropriate for different countries and cultures, Yannis Katsoulacos (Ch. 16) considers the position of countries such as Greece, which require considerable infrastructural investment. The extension of state activity into many sectors of the economy may have brought failures in efficiency and innovation, but this does not suggest that in all cases a reduction in state involvement will be desirable since the optimal size of the public sector is a complicated issue. However, where in the past there has been over-reliance upon state control of industry for political objectives, privatization can lead to an improvement in efficiency and innovation if there is potential competition and adequate regulation. In examining how to maximize the potential benefits of privatization, Katsoulacos stresses the opportunity of using the proceeds to increase investment in infrastructure to improve overall industrial efficiency in an exploration of different privatization scenarios and strategies.

PRIVATIZATION IN EASTERN EUROPE

The initial rush towards privatization in Eastern Europe as the communist regimes collapsed from 1989 onwards, began to falter as the scale of the problems to be overcome in these dislocated and depressed economies came to be appreciated. Without a legal framework of property rights, or commercial institutions such as functioning banks or stock exchanges, without convertible currencies, or even a culture of market exchange, the process of privatization did not prove an immediate panacea for the structural problems of the economies of these countries as some western advisers enthusiastically promised. Western multinationals cherry-picked the most attractive and profitable state enterprises available, whilst most large state enterprises remained starved of investment, as any prospect of viability, faced with western competition, declined. Governments began to explore ways of transferring ownership, believing in a 'need for ingenious and unconventional mass privatisation programmes designed to help create capitalism without capital' (*Financial Times Survey*, 3 July 1992).

In an energetic analysis Mario Nuti (Ch. 17) considers the drive towards privatization in the transitional economies of Eastern Europe, and the expectation that privatization will inject life into inert traditional social systems, de-politicize economic life and harden budget constraints. Issues raised include the danger of divesting central organs of their power in order to free enterprises, without transferring those powers to other agents. This raises the question of the 're-subjectivization' of ownership prior to privatization, and of what to do with workers' self-management institutions which are widely established. The risk of unfair private appropriation of state assets is discussed, whether by legal means or in the 'wild' exercise of self-interest. Finally, the issue of when should privatization occur in the sequence of reform measures relative to stabilization, demonopolization, and financial and productive restructuring is considered.

In Poland, privatization has been facilitated by the long-standing tradition of private enterprise, but rendered difficult by the necessity to reconcile the sale of shares with the institutions of self-management active in Polish enterprises. Gradually the idealism of the Solidarity movement has been overwhelmed by the concerns of government, and the role of self-management increasingly diminished from perhaps reserving a minority share for employees, to profit sharing, and co-determination. Nuti graphically captures the excitement, confusion, and controversy of the debate over privatization in Poland: revolving around the adverse distributional impact of the process; which sectors to begin with; the small size of the potential market; and how to finance share purchases, with free shares, credit, or foreign capital, and the possibility of debt/equity swaps. These issues reflect an ongoing political struggle, which leaves open the pace and modality of privatization and other forms of economic restructuring but delays further the prospect of significant economic progress.

Examining the problems of privatization in Hungary, Peter Lawrence (Ch. 18) addresses two fundamental issues: the appropriate techniques of privatization (*who buys* the state-owned assets which are sold?), and *control* over the privatization process (on whose behalf is it exercised?). The answers to these questions are by no means self-evident when (a) large-scale state assets have apparently no value attached to them, and (b) there is no chance of western interest confronted by an economy in such a profound state of transition. Lawrence reviews Hungary's economic performance which led to the pressure for enterprise reform and discusses the mechanisms, legal and illegal, for spontaneous or 'wild' privatizations which occurred prior to the establishment of the State Privatization Agency in 1990.

The subsequent programme of government-ordered privatization is examined, as are, given the slow pace of reform, the pressures to return to 'spontaneity' as a means of accelerating the process of state divestment of assets. Public perceptions of privatization in Hungary are alarmed by indications that foreign investment has often involved an asset-stripping of the Hungarian economy, and that even where privatization has occurred the *nomenklatura* (the constraining bureaucrats of the industrial past) have survived in the management of enterprises. To speed the process of divestment up, the State Privatization Agency has resorted to 'privatizing the privatization' – that is, delegating the responsibility for supervising the privatization process to private consultancies.

Hungarian enterprises are certainly in need of fundamental restructuring, and privatization is one route, but Lawrence concludes it may not prove the most appropriate or effective in terms of developing the Hungarian economy. 'For these economies, transforming state enterprises into commercial forms with largely state shareholdings, rationalizing them and stimulating the growth of a small- and medium-size manufacturing and service private sector, may form the most appropriate means of "privatizing" the economy.'

The enormous difficulties of transforming the economies of the republics which once formed the USSR are examined by Igor Filatotchev, Trevor Buck and Mike Wright (Ch. 19). With 46,000 state-owned enterprises producing 90 per cent of total output and employing 92 per cent of the total labour force, dismantling this monopolistic organization of the economy is a herculean task. The fragmentation of the USSR into the constituent republics of the Commonwealth of Independent States (CIS) compounds the legal and institutional complexities involved in privatizing what were formerly 'all-union enterprises', and converting the huge military-industrial complex into commercial purposes presents further challenges. Finally, there is the non-existence of capital markets combined with the small savings of the population: all disposable income and all savings in 1990 amounted to 700 billion roubles, just one-quarter of the fixed and current industrial assets available amounting to 2,700 billion roubles.

Meanwhile, the people of the formerly Soviet republics are deeply suspicious of anything which smacks of the continuation of *nomenklatura* hegemony, and sceptical about the benefits of privatization. Fuelling these fears have been the activities of managers who in a shift towards enterprise autonomy have received the rights of private entrepreneurs without the responsibilities, and have set about plundering their enterprises. In this context, governments have been drawn to radical proposals, such as the issuing of vouchers to the mass of the population, for the purchase of shares. Filatotchev, Buck and Wright suggest a more cautious approach in the development of management and employee buy-outs. In the west buy-outs have proved an effective form of privatization for small- and medium-sized enterprises: concentrating ownership and control in the hands of incumbent managers and their financial supporters, and sharpening the effort–reward relationship. However, the problem of valuation of enterprise assets prior to a buy-out in the west is compounded in the CIS by the existence of artificial state prices, leading to arbitrary profits and losses of state enterprises. Laws passed earlier in the USSR did allow the leasing of assets, which could be the foundation of more extensive buy-outs: in 1990 there were 2,400 leased enterprises. In conclusion, though buy-outs could prove an important means of restoring effective small- and medium-sized enterprises to post-Soviet economies dominated by inefficient giant plants, as with other forms of privatization, forms of regulations of the process of sale are necessary with buy-outs, in order to simulate a competitive outcome and to prevent speculation and corruption.

PRIVATIZATION IN DEVELOPING COUNTRIES

Often, desperate economic circumstances have impelled developing countries towards privatization: serious budget deficits, high foreign debt, and high dependence on international agencies such as the World Bank and IMF. In Latin America and Asia the extensive use of state enterprises is being abandoned in favour of an expanding private sector. In Africa there has been little choice, a privatization policy has usually been imposed by external agencies, which have lost faith in state enterprise in return for continued support (Ramamurti 1992). In the east the growth of the public sector, rather than being associated with social democratic movements, has been under the influence of nationalist movements or ruling elites. Many people resent the waste, corruption, and inefficiency found in the public sector and see privatization as a potential escape. Jomo (Ch. 20) discusses how the Malaysian government embraced and promoted privatization in the mid-1980s, abandoning the commitment to public enterprise. The attempt to stimulate entrepreneurship and relieve the financial and administrative burden of the state has replaced any effort to run the public sector more efficiently with greater accountability.

However, widespread concern has emerged that the privatization process has involved collusion and corruption in the disposal of public assets to private interests. The concern of private investors with short-term profits has effected the availability of basic utilities. Privatization has also been ethnically based, and has not contributed to the declared equity objectives of the state. The transparency of government decision-making has not improved, whilst important sectors of industry have become subjected to the control of politically well-connected private interests. Jomo concludes by detailing a typical case of conflict of interest in the privatization of the North–South highway in Malaysia.

Of all the African states Tanzania has pursued, in the period 1967–86, one of the most strongly interventionist industrialization policies, with the nationalization of the majority of the existing productive capacity and state financing and management of new large-scale projects. The influence of Soviet and Chinese thinking of the post-war period on Tanzanian economic development was reflected in the emphasis on self-reliant industrialization. The attraction of state ownership was the retention of profits from the enterprises rather than seeing them go overseas, and the underlying policy of public enterprise was import-substitution-based industrialization.

However, as John Henley (Ch. 21) graphically portrays, Tanzanian state enterprises became locked in a downward spiral based on insufficient working capital and rates of investment, and low-capacity utilization. Product and process development, and marketing and financial management were neglected in the struggle for survival by keeping production going. The management of the state-owned enterprises was production oriented rather than market oriented, exercising little financial discipline. As a result, rather than securing revenue from the privatization programme, the benefit for the state will be the end of a consistent drain on the expenditure required to support ailing state enterprises. An Economic Recovery Programme commenced in 1986 intent of the liberalization of the economic system but it has encountered considerable difficulties.

Yet again, there is the question of who will hold the equity of enterprises after privatization, and the relationship of the equity holders with the financial institutions which have encouraged a speeding-up of the process without attention to liberalization or competition policy. Privatization with import protection allows the transfer of monopolistic privilege from public servants to private citizens. The key issue in an economy starved of investment is that of finance: the priority is how to develop mechanisms for refinancing illiquid but potentially viable firms and encouraging new inward investment. In this context, a privatization policy alone is likely to abandon this and other African economies to the unrestrained attentions of transnational firms.

CONCLUSIONS

The status and role of public enterprise has been profoundly questioned by the advocates of privatization. In some countries, including the UK, the political rush to privatize neglected the opportunity to develop competition and made more difficult the effective regulation of the privatized companies. This diminishes the likelihood of the achievement of the major efficiency gains promised at the time of privatization. Evidence is now emerging of the performance of the privatized enterprises in the medium term, which suggests that some significant gains in efficiency have been attained. The extent to which such improvements in efficiency were based on restructuring carried out prior to privatization, or were due to reductions in service or quality of products, or asset sales, is not entirely clear.

The question of whether any short- and medium-term efficiency gains are sustained for any length of time remains an open one. Anyway, the frequent intervention of the regulators has clearly been a crucial factor in maintaining the responsiveness of the privatized monopolies to customer concerns. Anxieties concerning the behaviour of privatized monopolies supplying vital utilities to the public have not been entirely assuaged.

The experience of privatization has varied markedly in different economies. Of the advanced industrial economies only the UK and Japan have translated the rhetoric of privatization into massive transfers of public assets into the private sector. Though such wholesale privatization has been discussed in other industrial countries, implementation has been more considered and pragmatic: 'only a handful of countries have implemented privatisation programmes of truly significant proportions' (Stevens 1992: 6). The pressing economic difficulties of Eastern Europe have encouraged the call for the immediate abandonment of state enterprise in favour of mass privatization. In the absence of the gradual creation of the necessary commercial infrastructure, it is possible that such extensive privatization will primarily serve to further dislocate the vulnerable economies of this region. In the developing world, whilst economic change is essential, the imposition of privatization without a fundamental renegotiation of the terms of trade and aid with the developed world is likely to achieve little more than the acute disappointments of central planning.

The wave of privatization over the last decade has been a fascinating phenomenon of deep significance in transforming mainstream political economy. The boundaries between the public and private sector have become blurred, probably for ever. However, in the future it is unlikely that privatization will be adopted quite as unquestioningly as an easy route to economic efficiency as it has been in the recent past.

BIBLIOGRAPHY

Abromeit, H. (1988) 'British privatisation policy', *Parliamentary Affairs* 41(1), 68–85.

Alchian, A. and Demsetz, H. (1972) 'Production, information costs and economic organization', *American Economic Review* 62(5), 777–95.

Babai, D. (1988) 'The World Bank and the IMF: rolling back the state or backing its role?', in R. Vernon (ed.), *The Promise Of Privatisation*, New York: The Council of Foreign Relations.

Bacon, R. and Eltis, W. (1976) *Britain's Economic Problem: Too Few Producers*, London: Macmillan.

Baumol, W.J. (1982) 'Contestable markets: an uprising in the theory of industry structure', *American Economic Review*, 72, 1–15.

Beauchamps, C. (1990) 'National Audit Office: its role in privatisation', *Public Money and Management* 10(2), 55–8.

Brittan, S. (1984) 'The politics and economics of privatisation', *Political Quarterly* 55(2), 109–27.

Buckland, R. (1987) 'The costs and returns of the privatisation of nationalised industries', *Public Administration* 65(3), 241–57.

Chapman, C. (1990) *Selling The Family Silver: Has Privatisation Worked*, London: Hutchinson.

Clarke, T. and Grace, C. (1993) 'Restructuring the public sector: quality assurance, performance measurement and social accountability', in T. Clarke (ed.), *International Privatisation: Strategies and Practices*, Berlin: Walter De Gruyter.

Coase, R.H. (1937) 'The nature of the firm', *Economica*, 4, 386–405.

Curwen, P.J. (1986) *Public Enterprise: A Modern Approach*, London: Wheatsheaf.

Dasgupta, P. (1986) 'Positive freedom, markets, and the welfare state', *Oxford Review of Economic Policy* 2(2), 25–36.

Demsetz, H. (1973) 'Industry structure, market rivalry and public policy', *Journal of Law and Economics*, vol. 16, 1–9.

Eggertsson, T. (1990) *Economic Behaviour and Institutions*, Cambridge: Cambridge University Press.

Fama, E.F. and Jensen, M.C. (1983) 'The separation of ownership and control', *Journal of Law and Economics*, vol. XXVI, 302–24.

Feldstein, M. (1974) 'Social security, retirement and aggregate capital accumulation', *Journal of Political Economy*, 82, 905–26.

Fraser, R. (1988) *Privatisation: The UK Experience and International Trends*, London: Longman.

Friedman, M. (1969) *Capitalism and Freedom*, Chicago: University of Chicago Press.

Gayle, J. and Goodrich, J. (eds) (1990) *Privatisation and Deregulation In Global Perspective*, London: Pinter.

Gough, I. (1979) *The Political Economy of the Welfare State*, London: Macmillan Educational.

Graham, C. and Prosser, T. (1991) *Privatising Public Enterprises: Constitutions, the State, and Regulation in Comparative Perspective*, Oxford: Clarendon Press.

Hambleton, R. (1992) 'Decentralisation and democracy in UK local government', *Public Money and Management*, July–September, pp. 9–20.

Hayek, F.A. (1986) 'The use of knowledge in society', in L. Putterman, (ed.), *The Nature of the Firm: A Reader*, Cambridge: Cambridge University Press.

Heald, D. (1983) *Public Expenditure: Its Defence and Reform*, Oxford: Martin Robertson.

—— (1988) 'The UK privatisation and its political context', *Western European Politics*, II, 31–48.

Helm, D. and Yarrow, G. (1988) 'The regulation of utilities', *Oxford Review of Economic Policy* 4(2), I–XXIX

Kay, J.A. and Silberston, Z.A. (1984) 'The new industrial policy – privatisation and competition', *Midland Bank Review*, Spring, pp. 8–16.

—— , Mayer, C. and Thompson, D. (eds) (1986) *Privatisation and Regulation: The UK Experience*, Oxford: Oxford University Press.

Lorrain, D. (1991) 'Public goods and private operators in France', in R. Batley and G. Stoker (eds), *Local Government in Europe: Trends and Developments*, Basingstoke: Macmillan.

McAvoy, P.W., Stanbury, W.T., Yarrow, G. and Zuckhauser, R.J. (eds) (1989) *Privatisation and State Owned Enterprises: Lessons From the US, Great Britain and Canada*, Boston: Kluwer Academic Publishers.

Marsh, D. (1991) 'Privatisation under Mrs Thatcher: a review of the literature', *Public Administration*, 69 (Winter), 459–80.

Miliband, R. (1969) *The State In Capitalist Society*, London: Quartet Books.

Mitchell, J. (1990) 'Britain's privatisation as myth?', in J. Richardson (ed.), *Privatisation and Deregulation in Canada and Britain*, Aldershot: Dartmouth.

Mueller, D. (1989) *Public Choice II: A Revised Edition of Public Choice*, Cambridge: Cambridge University Press.

O'Connor, J. (1973) *The Fiscal Crisis of the State*, New York: St Martin's Press.

Pitelis, C.N. (1991) *Market and Non-Market Hierarchies*, Oxford: Basil Blackwell.

Ramamurti, R. (1992) 'Why are developing countries privatising?', *Journal of International Business Studies* 23(2), 225–49.

Rees, R. (1986) *Public Enterprise Economics*, Oxford: Philip Allan.

Steel, D. and Heald, D. (1984) *Privatising Public Enterprise*, London: Royal Institute of Public Administration.

Stevens, B. (1992) 'Prospects for privatisation in OECD countries', *National Westminster Bank Quarterly Review*, August, pp. 2–22.

Stigler, J.E. (1988) 'The effects of government on economic efficiency', *Business Economics*, January.

Stiglitz, J.E. (1986) *Economics of the Public Sector*, New York: Norton.

Swann, D. (1988) *The Retreat of the State: Deregulation and Privatisation in the UK and US*, London: Harvester.

Thomson, P. (1992) 'Public sector management in a period of radical change 1979–1992', *Public Money and Management*, July–September, pp. 33–41.

Vickers, J. and Yarrow, G. (1988) *Privatisation: An Economic Analysis*, London: MIT Press.

Williamson, O.E. (1975) *Markets and Hierarchies*, New York: Free Press.

Wolf, C. (1990) 'A theory of non-market behaviour: framework for implementation analysis', *Journal of Law and Economics* 22(1), 107–40.
Yarrow, G. (1986) 'Privatisation in theory and practice', *Economic Policy*, 2, April.

Part I

OWNERSHIP AND PERFORMANCE

2

OWNERSHIP, ORGANIZATIONAL CHANGES AND PERFORMANCE

David Parker

INTRODUCTION

The 1970s saw a resurgence of the notion that transferring assets from the public sector to private enterprise would raise both allocative and technical efficiency, leading to greater economic well-being. The intellectual argument in support of this idea linked performance to ownership:

> privatization involves more than the simple transfer of ownership. It involves the transfer and redefinition of a complex bundle of property rights which creates a whole new penalty-reward system which will alter the incentives in the firm and ultimately its performance.
>
> (Veljanovski 1987: 77–8)

This resurgence in turn led in the UK and elsewhere to privatization and the transferring of remaining state activities from departments to separate governmental agencies. In the UK over £40 billion of state assets have been sold since 1979 and currently huge chunks of the Civil Service are being hived-off to agencies with the objective of 'commercial management' (HMSO 1988). However, the point was made in the mid-1980s that the case for such policies was strong on *a priori* theorizing but relatively weak in empirical confirmation (Parker 1985). Studies in various countries of the comparative efficiency of public and private enterprises have produced mixed results, but certainly no overwhelming support for the notion that private enterprise is always superior to public enterprise. In monopolistic industries such as gas, water and electricity, there is even some suggestion of lower cost production under *public* ownership. This may result from inefficiencies introduced in private firms where there is a need for continued state regulation of prices or profits (Millward and Parker 1983, Parker 1989). Bishop and Kay (1989), in a survey of early post-privatization data for the UK, have suggested that there is no real evidence of major efficiency gains. Lynk (1991) points to the paucity of econometric analysis of production and cost functions prevailing in privatized industries.

There is clearly a need for more studies of the effect of changes in ownership on organizational status, including moving functions into government agencies and transferring them across the public–private divide (privatization and nationalization). This chapter summarizes some of the results of a major research programme, which has been concerned with the validity of public choice and related theories.[1] A number of organizations which underwent relevant status changes in the post-war period were studied. The research was divided into two, albeit related, parts. The first part tested for performance changes at around the time of the status change. Was there any evidence of improved or deteriorating performance? The second part was concerned with attempting to identify the *cause* of performance changes observed or not observed. It explored *where* in the organization performance changes originated. What went on within the organizations which led to changed performance? What were the mechanisms of change?

The structure of the chapter is as follows. The hypothesis on ownership and performance is formally set out under the heading 'Testing for Performance Changes'. The performance measures used are explained and the main results are reported in summary form with comment. The section headed 'Exploring the Internal Environment' discusses the nature of the internal environment of organizations, while 'Changes in the Internal Environment' considers what changes occurred in the organizations studied. The final section provides some general conclusions and outlines the main policy implication.

TESTING FOR PERFORMANCE CHANGES

The analytical framework used for assessing the effect of organizational status on performance has been presented elsewhere (Dunsire *et al.* 1988), hence it is outlined here only briefly. It is summarized in Figure 2.1. On the west-to-east axis are positioned certain organizational forms intended to represent the main types of ownership in the public and private sectors – namely, government departments, governmental agencies (for example, trading funds), public corporations, hybrids (for example, private sector firms highly dependent on government contracts, or co-operatives, charities, etc.), private sector PLCs, and owner managed firms.

Drawing on the conclusions of property rights and public choice theorists (Parker 1985, Mitchell 1988), the central hypothesis is that as organizations in the public sector move away from political control and Exchequer financing towards more independent management their economic and financial performance improve. This should show up particularly when an organization is privatized, but should also be evident when organizations remain in the public sector and achieve an 'arm's length' relationship from government. Quasi-governmental agencies such as trading funds and public corporations were created precisely to reduce political intervention and to introduce more commercially oriented management. Also, the schema suggests that organizational changes can be expected to have their most profound effect on performance the further east organizations travel.[2]

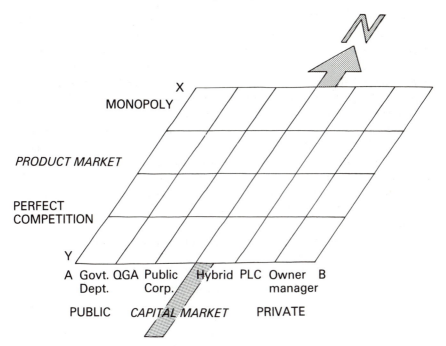

Figure 2.1 The product market and the capital market

According to standard economic theory, performance is also affected by the degree of competition in the product market. While high efficiency is necessary for survival in competitive markets, monopoly provides opportunity for managers and workers to pursue on-the-job leisure and discretionary expenditures leading to organizational 'slack'. In Figure 2.1 changes in the level of competition are represented by movements on the north-to-south axis. Efficiency is expected to rise if firms move southwards but decline with northward moves.

Combining the effects of the product market (north-to-south axis) and the capital market (west-to-east axis) leads to the conclusion that there should be large efficiency gains if organizations move south-eastwards and large efficiency reductions if they move north-westwards. The effect of a movement between south-west and north-east is less easy to isolate because the product market and capital market constraints conflict.

Ten organizations were selected for study on the basis that they had undergone relevant status changes. The sample includes all of the movements within the public sector and between the public and private sectors set out in Figure 2.1. The organizations studied were the postal and telecommunications services; Her Majesty's Stationery Office (HMSO): Rolls-Royce (aero and marine engines); British Aerospace; the National Freight Corporation (NFC); London Transport; the Royal Mint; the Royal Ordnance Factories; and British Airways. Because the research began in 1986/7, privatizations from the mid-1980s were not studied. However, British Airways was included to test for 'anticipation effects'. Although mainly because of outstanding legal disputes it was not privatized until 1987, the intention to privatize was announced in 1980. The organizations, the status changes studied, the dates of the status changes, and the direction of the expected change in efficiency are summarized in Table 2.1. Only three of the organizations studied had clearly identifiable changes in product market competition which might also have impacted on performance in the periods studied – British Aerospace 1977 (the nationalization of three airframe manu-facturers to form British Aerospace reduced competition), London Transport 1984 (tendering for some of London's bus services was introduced) and the HMSO 1982 (loss of the monopoly as supplier to government departments). In all other cases, efficiency changes can be more readily related to the change in organizational status.

Figure 2.2 shows the movements of each of the ten organizations at around

Table 2.1 Organizational status changes

Organization	Type of change	Date	Predicted change in efficiency
Post Office postal	Government department to public corporation	April 1969	Improvement
Post Office telecommunications	Government department to public corporation	April 1969	Improvement
London Transport	Public corporation to (local) government department	Jan 1970	Deterioration
London Transport	(local) government department to public corporation	June 1984	Improvement
British Aerospace	Public limited companies to public corporation	April 1977	Deterioration
British Aerospace	Public corporation to public limited company	Feb 1981	Improvement
National Freight	Public corporation to limited company	Feb 1982	Improvement
HMSO	Government department to trading fund	April 1975	Improvement
Royal Mint	Government department to trading fund	April 1975	Improvement
Rolls-Royce	Public limited company to state owned company	Feb 1971	Deterioration
Royal Ordnance Factories	Government department to trading fund	July 1974	Improvement
British Airways	Public corporation – anticipation effect	1980	Improvement

34

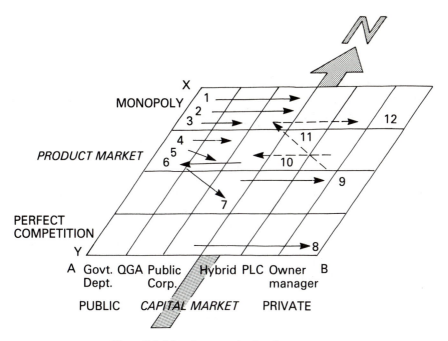

Figure 2.2 Mapping organizational movements

Notes: 1 = PO Telecom 1969; 2 = PO Postal 1969; 3 = Royal Mint 1975; 4 = ROF 1974;
5 = HMSO 1980; 6 = LT 1970; 7 = LT 1984; 8 = NFC 1982; 9 = BA 1980–7; 10 = RR 1971;
11 = BAe 1977; 12 = BAe 1981.

the time of the status change using the schema of Figure 2.1. Since Rolls-Royce and British Aerospace were dependent to a significant degree on government contracts and 'launch aid', the dotted line between the hybrid and PLC categories is intended to reflect the ambiguity about their precise status changes. Two of the organizations – London Transport and British Aerospace – went through two status changes during the period considered. Hence, in total, twelve status changes were studied.

The study was concerned only with identifying changes in production efficiency; wider social welfare effects were ignored, including the implications for efficiency in competing firms (for an insight into this problem see De Fraja 1991). Moreover, because none of the organizations provided data to assess the quality of services before and after the status change it was not possible to test whether economic and financial performance improvements occurred at the expense of service quality.

Three broad measures were used to identify changes in production efficiency – an employment function, productivity measures, and a set of financial ratios.

Employment function

An attempt was made to capture the longer-term effects of a change in organizational status by including a dummy (binary) variable in a standard employment function. Various employment functions were tested (Parker and Hartley 1991a), but the one that provided the most satisfactory fit was based on the function suggested by Ball and St Cyr (1966) and took the general form:

$$L_t = C + b_i V_i + c_i X V_i + DV$$

where L is employment; C is a constant; V is a vector of variables, namely output, a time trend and a lagged dependent variable; X is a slope shift dummy variable for the status change applied to V; and DV is an intercept shift dummy. A negative relationship was predicted for the intercept shift dummy where a west-to-east organizational status change occurred. The dummy variable was used in its slope shift form to estimate any favourable performance effects of status change on output, productivity trends, and on the speed with which employment adjusted to output.

Productivity

Both labour and total factor productivity were estimated for the four years before the status change and were compared with the figures for the four years after. Four-year periods were selected to capture 'leads and lags' in performance changes associated with the status change. The effect of changes in macro-economic factors on productivity was removed by comparing the figures with changes in productivity in the UK economy, UK manufacturing and the public corporation sector.

In the absence of information about hours worked, labour productivity was assessed by calculating the change in each organization's volume of output in relation to changes in the labour input. Total factor productivity was estimated on the basis of the rate of growth of output minus a weighted average of input growth rates, where the weights are the share of each input in total cost (for a more detailed explanation of the procedure and its underlying assumptions, see Milward and Parker 1983: 225–9; and for its precise application in this research, Hartley et al. 1991).

Financial ratios

This part of the study was concerned with changes in the trends of financial ratios associated with an organizational change.[3] The specific financial ratios studied were intended to reflect the quality of management in terms of the efficient use of working capital, labour, fixed assets and profitability. The data came from each organization's annual reports and accounts, supplemented where necessary with information from internal accounts and papers. Six ratios were used:

- Profitability: percentage return on capital employed (ROCE).
- Turnover to average net fixed assets employed.
- Stocks (including work in progress) to turnover.
- Debtors to turnover.
- Labour's share in expenditure.
- Value added per employee.[4]

It might be argued that profitability should be taken as the key measure of financial performance and that the other ratios are subsidiary. However, all of the organizations spent some time in the public sector where other goals may have been more important than profitability. Performance measured simply in terms of the rate of return on capital could, therefore, reflect changes in objectives.

The ratios were studied by taking four-year averages for before and after the status change and were tested using a simple covariance model of the following form:

$$V_{it} = a + bt_i + cXt_i + DV$$

where V_{it} is a vector of performance measures; t is time; X is a binary variable for the status change applied in slope form and DV in intercept shift form. Other factors affecting performance over time are captured in the time trend, t (see Kmenta 1971: 409–30).

The full statistical results using each of the three measures are given in Parker and Hartley 1991a and 1991b, and Hartley *et al.* 1991. Table 2.2 therefore provides only a summary of the results.[5]

On the basis of the sample, west-to-east movements (see Figure 2.2) appear to have led to improved performance in 5 of the 12 status changes studied – that is, the Royal Mint, London Transport (1984), British Aerospace (1981), British Airways and the National Freight Corporation. Interestingly, this includes all three of the organizations which were privatized or being prepared for privatiz-ation. In a further six cases the performance measures produced conflicting results and hence status change had less certain effects – that is, London Transport (1970), the postal and perhaps telecommunications services, the ROF, the nationalization of British Aerospace and the HMSO. However, in one of these cases, London Transport, there was clear evidence of a major loss of efficiency in the mid to late 1970s, which might imply a delayed effect consistent with the central hypothesis. Only one case appeared completely contrary to expectation – the performance of Rolls-Royce *improved* after nationalization. However, this result might well be explained by the 'shock effect' of the bankruptcy in 1971 which led to the government take-over. In support of this view, study of the performance of Rolls-Royce in later years reveals a marked deterioration in all three of the performance measures from the mid-1970s. In

Table 2.2 Performance results of UK organizations

Organization	Employment function	Labour productivity	Total factor productivity	Financial ratios
Royal Mint	Mainly confirmed	Confirmed	Confirmed	See note 3
London Transport (1970 change)	Not confirmed	Not confirmed	Confirmed	Not confirmed
London Transport (1984 change)	Confirmed	Confirmed	Confirmed	Confirmed
British Airways	Confirmed	Confirmed	Confirmed	Confirmed
British Aerospace (nationalization)	Mainly confirmed	Confirmed	Unclear	Not confirmed
British Aerospace (privatization) (1981)	Mainly confirmed	Confirmed	Mainly confirmed	Confirmed
National Freight	Confirmed	Confirmed	Confirmed	Confirmed
Post Office: Postal	Not confirmed	Confirmed	Unclear	Confirmed
Post Office: Telecom- munications	Mainly confirmed	Confirmed	Unclear	Confirmed
HMSO	Confirmed	Confirmed	Not confirmed	Confirmed
Royal Ordnance Factories	Not confirmed	Not confirmed	Unclear	Confirmed
Rolls-Royce	Not confirmed	Not confirmed	Not confirmed	Not confirmed

other words, by the mid-1970s nationalization was having the effect on performance that the central hypothesis predicts.

It appears, therefore, that west-to-east status changes are sometimes associated with improved performance, but that this performance improvement is not guaranteed. Also, one of the cases which clearly supported the central hypothesis was also associated with a change in competition – London Transport (1984) – and the possibility that the change in the product market had some effect on this result should not be ignored. The fact that *all* of the privatization cases were associated with improved performance supports the view that performance improvements are most likely the further eastwards the change in status.

EXPLORING THE INTERNAL ENVIRONMENT

The statement that 'ownership' affects performance says nothing about how this is achieved. In what ways do organizations change when their ownership status alters and what causes/prevents changes in performance? 'The underlying model assumes some stimulus/response mechanism, some form of ecological adaptation' (Woodward 1988). But what is it? To shed light on this requires looking inside organizations – in other words, prising open the economist's 'black box'. An attempt can then be made to observe how the organization adapts to a new external environment; an external environment in which changes in the capital market (and product market where relevant) introduce new threats, while politically imposed constraints (for example, limits on pricing and investment) are removed.

In the subject area of privatization it appears that the least research has been undertaken in this area, which makes it potentially most fertile. If the sources of efficiency gains or the reasons why efficiency did not improve can be identified, this has obvious value to policy-makers, government departments selected for agency status under the 'Next Steps' initiative, and the managements of firms yet to privatize (in the UK, especially London Transport and the coal and rail industries).

An attempt has been made to relate the above findings on organizational status changes and performance to a set of variables, detailed below and collectively referred to as the 'internal environment'. The working hypothesis is that where performance improvement was not found, or where there was ambiguity about the effect on performance, there will be fewer changes in the internal environment than where efficiency clearly increased.

There are special difficulties in undertaking this type of research. What the research is trying to identify in its most general sense is a change in the organization's 'culture' (the organization's meanings, beliefs and values) which impacts on performance. But this requires identifying a number of factors which might reflect or provide some evidence of a cultural change, while bearing in mind the analytical distinction between structures, policies, processes and strategies and the 'cultural system' (Allaire and Firsirotu 1984). Also, it is important to recognize that changes in the internal environment may result from other factors. For example, in the 1980s the 'Thatcher factor' is known to have led to a greater commercialization of the public services independent of changes in their formal status.[6]

According to Peters and Waterman (1982), performance is associated with management clearly signalling the right priorities and providing consistent guidance. Figure 2.3 provides a simple schema linking management, goals, human resources and organizational structure to a firm's performance. The quality and behaviour of management influences performance and is linked to the goals of the firm (dotted line). The management determines the goals the firm pursues (subject to the capital market and product market constraints detailed earlier) and these goals then impinge on performance. At its simplest, a non-profit-making goal can be expected to lead to low profitability! Research suggests that the 'organizational fit' between the organization and its external environment can have an important effect on a firm's performance, while structure is itself linked to management through reporting systems or the effectiveness of the management's 'span of control'. In addition, the organizational structure is linked to the firm's resources, both capital and labour, which in turn impact on performance. For example, the organization structure may be reflected in the type of human resource policy pursued and the quantity and quality (reliability,

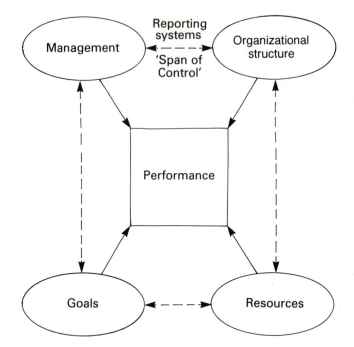

Figure 2.3 Organization and performance

skills and education) of the firm's labour force. Therefore, the following variables appear to capture the important changes in the internal environment which are associated with significant cultural change in an organization:

Organizational structure

According to the organizational theory literature (especially open systems and contingency theories), there is no single structure or mode of control which is optimal for all organizations (optimal here means the form which is best suited to maximizing performance as measured earlier). The optimal form varies with circumstances and is likely, therefore, to change over time (Pugh and Hickson 1976). However, the adoption of a mode of control incongruent with an enterprise's position, internal or external, will lead to reduced performance.

As politically controlled bodies have politically defined structures, these are likely to be non-optimal in the new environments privatization and agency status create. Therefore, we would expect that with a change in ownership (most notably in the case of privatization but also where there is a change of status within the public sector) there will be a change in organization structure. The state sector is popularly perceived as rule-bound and bureaucratic. Although this is no doubt a crude caricature (at least for some parts of the state) and some private sector organizations are bureaucratic (for example, UK commercial banks?), we might expect that privatization and agency status would lead to a less hierarchical, a less centralized and a less rule-bound organizational structure; a movement away from Burns and Stalker's (1961) 'mechanistic' mode of management with a principal concern with 'how things are done' in favour of more 'concern with the outcome'.

More specifically, and building on a theme within the fields of managerial economics and the strategic management literature (for example, Williamson 1970, Johnson and Scholes 1988), we should expect privatization and agency status to be associated with a flattening of the managerial pyramid and an 'M-form' rather than 'U-form' structure. This involves a movement away from a *functional* form of organization, comprising of a large HQ and organization-wide planning, personnel, purchasing, marketing and R&D departments, designed to control inputs and outputs for the whole organization, and usually requiring a developed committee system to co-ordinate the different functions, towards activities arranged in profit or cost centres. The extreme case of this is a holding company form with subsidiary companies having considerable managerial autonomy regarding outputs, prices and employment, subject only to central scrutiny of financial performance and major long-term investments. In a quickly changing environment, competitive advantage requires a speedy response to market signals and hence a centralized and standardized set of procedures (the 'rule book') is inappropriate.

At the same time, a hierarchical structure may sometimes be optimal, if only temporarily, notably where the environment appears to management to be suddenly more hostile and difficult. Increased formalization, including more centralized decision-making, is then a defensive mechanism to protect the whole organization from failure in one part of it. Centralization may also be necessary for a short time so that management can produce, through a top–down programme, a major change in corporate culture. Hence, we would expect in general to see privatization and agency status associated with a move towards more decentralized forms of management, but for short periods the opposite may be true. The ownership change may lead to an attempt by top management to 'get to grips' with long-standing inefficiencies and this may mean a period of more centralized control.

Objectives

Related to the change in organizational structure may be a change in objectives. Although profits are not sufficient for assessing performance, they do provide a concrete objective which may be missing in politically controlled activities. Here goals are more likely to be multifarious and less tangible, concerned more with achieving some vague notion of the 'public interest'. Hence, we might expect west-to-east movements to be associated with more concern with the bottom line. This also implies more stress on meeting the needs of the consumer. In so far as the goals of the organization become clearer with west–east movements, this should reflect itself in the organization's strategy for converting the set of objectives into performance.

Management

Changes in organizational status which lead to discernible performance improvements might be expected to be associated with changes in management. This might be in the form of new managers (entrepreneurs rather than bureaucrats, to use the populist descriptions), changed titles (in the Civil Service top managers are known as permanent secretaries; in private enterprise as chief executives), and new employment contracts (perhaps linking pay and tenure more closely to performance). Civil servants have jobs for life and the pay of public sector managers is rarely related to performance in any meaningful way.

Also, many state enterprises began in government departments and departmental culture takes a long time to change. Managerial behaviour may therefore have an engineering or technical bias and consumer orientation may be weak. A reflection of a change would be the sweeping away of 'controllers' and the establishment of a Marketing Department. As Ramanadham (1988: 3) observes succinctly: 'Analytically, if the essence of public enterprise is that it rests on some kind and degree of de-marketisation of enterprise operations, privatisation implies some kind and degree of re-marketisation.' Serving 'the public' converts to serving 'the consumer'.

Labour relations

A change in organizational status might also be reflected in human resource policy. There might be a reduction in the labour force (switching from labour to capital and reducing over-manning) and a change in labour relations, labour employment contracts and staff training.

The UK public sector has a tradition of 'collective bargaining'. Post-war nationalization legislation included a statutory commitment to 'good labour relations practices' and the Civil Service recognizes unions and has a well-developed tradition of employee consultation through the Whitley Councils. In so far as the public sector is more sympathetic to unionization, collective bargaining and employee participation, a Figure 2.1 west-to-east shift is likely to be associated with some change in human resource policy to create a more 'flexible' (compliant, docile?) labour force. Certainly the unions have anticipated that privatization will lead to major redundancies and worse pay and conditions. As the TUC (1986) has commented: 'there is every indication that it is one of the Government's deliberate objectives; privatisation is *supposed* to undermine workers' conditions. That is one of the ways to make companies more profitable for their new owners.'[7]

Communications and reporting systems

Management success in achieving its goals requires effective reporting systems. Hence, we might expect ownership changes to be associated with the introduction of new reporting structures, including new accounting and other management information systems. What senior management want to know may change as may the way in which lower ranks of management are controlled. Also, a change in the capital market may require changes in the type of published accounts and annual reports.[8]

Nature and location of the business

Finally, public enterprises tend to be heavily restricted by political and administrative constraints (departmental boundaries or geographical areas in the case of local authorities, or, in the case of nationalized industries, by their founding statutes). By contrast, private enterprise is much freer to develop new lines of business (for example, new export markets or sourcing overseas), invest in new locations (including overseas), divest, diversify, and become involved in mergers and take-overs. As Drucker comments:

> Non-profit organizations have no 'bottom line'. They are prone to consider everything they do to be righteous and moral and to serve a cause, so they are not willing to say, if it doesn't produce results then maybe we should direct our resources elsewhere. Non-profit organizations need the discipline of organized abandonment perhaps even more than a business does. They need to face up to critical choices.[9]
>
> (Drucker 1990: 8)

A Figure 2.1 west–east shift might therefore be expected to lead to changes in the nature of the markets served or the sale of some lines of business and the acquisition of others.

CHANGES IN THE INTERNAL ENVIRONMENT

A series of in-depth case studies of the history of the ten organizations studied were prepared based on interviews, published reports and internal data. From these studies an attempt was made to identify changes in the internal environment under the headings outlined above. Space prevents a detailed survey here, instead the following is a summary only. It does, however, provide an indication of the general extent to which the organizations changed when their ownership status changed.[10]

Royal Mint

The Royal Mint began with a functional structure of management and there was little discernible change throughout the period studied. Nor did accounting practices, remuneration or employment conditions appear to alter in a way that was likely to spark a performance change. The source of the performance improvement after the introduction of trading fund status, as discovered in the first part of the research programme, cannot be readily associated with any change in the internal environment variables outlined above. Instead, a likely cause was technological improvements in the production process related to the movement of the Mint from crowded conditions in London to a new, purpose-built plant in South Wales. This sheds doubt on whether the status change was necessary to the improved performance. If it was not, then the Royal Mint ceases to be supportive of the central hypothesis that west to east movements (Figure 2.1) lead to improved performance.

Royal Ordnance Factories

The ROF were organized on a functional basis but with profit centres. However, in 1973, a year before trading fund status, the structure became more functional and Director-Generals were appointed for production, procurement and administration and finance. In 1974 a marketing co-ordinator was appointed for the first time. Hence, there were significant changes in some of the internal environment variables. But the ROF did not support the central hypothesis, with the exception of the financial ratios measure, performance did not seem to improve after the introduction of trading fund status. How might this be explained? One possibility is that the organization became over-centralized, which would not generally be perceived as the optimal structure for a public sector organization wanting to become more efficient. Interestingly, in 1984, immediately before privatization of the ROF, consultants recommended the return to a more decentralized structure by the establishment of four separate operating companies.

Postal service

The movement from government department to public corporation status in 1969 was preceded from the early 1960s by some reorganization and a clearer separation of the postal and telecommunications businesses of the Post Office. However, the postal service management structure continued to be highly functional. With the exception of the Girobank, only in the 1980s were separate organizations formed for each of the main areas of the postal business. In other words, only in the 1980s was there a significant change in the mode of control towards profit centres. This in turn led to long-overdue changes in working practices and a new, more commercially oriented management style. Thus, although its legal status altered in 1969, the Post Office retained its government department structure and culture for a further decade. The 'Thatcher factor' seems to have proved more important in rejuvenating the organization than the move to public corporation status.

Telecommunications

Post Office telecommunications had separate accounts from the postal (and later, Giro) business and its own staffing and management below board level. However, it never really got to grips with defining and managing its various activities. The Post Office's move to public corporation status had apparently no significant effects on the internal environmental variables outlined above. Also, there is evidence of continuing frictions between 'management' and 'technical' staffs. In 1979, ten years after the introduction of the status change, the centre still did not trust its field workers (Beesley and Laidlaw 1989: 21).

In 1981 telecommunications became a separate corporation from the Post Office and three years later the corporation was privatized. The act of privatization, subsequent prodding by the regulatory body OFTEL, and the threat from more competition in the equipment market and in business and long-distance calls (provided by the new operator Mercury Communications), provoked a more aggressive management style. There was a new interest in the 'consumer' and associated marketing of services. However, one less-desirable product of privatization was BT's decision to stop publishing quality-of-service indicators (as required under the 1978 Nationalized Industries White Paper) on the grounds that such information was 'commercially sensitive'. Also, it has taken BT some time to tackle overmanning, especially at management levels. Only after 1989 were large-scale redundancies announced, while at the time of writing the search continues for the optimal organizational structure.

Rolls-Royce

The movement of Rolls-Royce into the state sector was associated with major managerial failures, particularly relating to the RB211 project. The Department of Trade and Industry inspectors' report details major weaknesses in the way the company was being run, particularly in the divisional and corporate accounting functions (DTI 1973). Based on a multidivisional 'profit centres' structure, the main board (overweighted with engineers and long-serving executive members) did not receive the information it needed to keep track of the financial drain coming from aero engines. Following bankruptcy and the state take-over, not surprisingly there were major redundancies and management changes with a completely new board appointed. In the mid-1970s performance began to deteriorate badly again and it may be significant that just before overall profitability was restored, the company restructured towards a more functional form with the management of production and design centralized. This implies that the organization structure under nationalization had remained inadequate to provide effective cost control in the various activities of Rolls-Royce.

British Aerospace

Surprisingly, the nationalization of three firms in the aerospace industry to form BAe led to relatively few organizational changes. Below the new corporation board, the old companies were retained as a multidivisional structure. Nor did there appear to be significant changes in employment terms and conditions, although, in tune with the times, annual reports contained long and enthusiastic commitments to good labour relations.

Privatization in 1981 was followed in 1983 by the appointment of a new managing director and major internal change focused upon centralizing the structure. A whole tier of management was abolished and marketing, research, etc. functions were unified as management attempted to pull together and rationalize the activities of the founder companies. By 1986 the board of BAe was highly functional in nature. Yet in 1987 a new chairman oversaw a reverse process as activities were decentralized and separate limited companies for the divisions were established. Within a year BAe had adopted a 'holding company' form.

Hence, the history of BAe can be broken into three broad periods. The first from 1977 to 1983 containing the short period of state control was associated with a relatively loose affiliation of operations inherited from the nationalized companies. From 1983 to 1987 the management of BAe centralized to take control (and stock?) of its disparate activities. After 1987 the decision was taken that the optimal structural form was separate operating companies. One impetus for this came from the need to assimilate new acquisitions, notably the Royal Ordnance Factories and Rover cars. But it may also have reflected the fashion in the management literature at the time for 'flattening' the management pyramid and sweeping away tiers of middle management.

London Transport

The introduction of control over LT in 1970 by the Greater London Council (GLC) does not appear to have been associated with any significant changes in the internal environment. LT retained a highly centralized and functional board structure. Although bus and rail operations were each given their own managing director, neither had control of planning, engineering supplies, personnel, industrial relations, or finance. Only from 1978 in the face of a deteriorating financial situation, in large part caused by considerable intervention in the management of LT by both Labour and Conservative administrations at County Hall, did a major reorganization take place. A new chairman and deputy were appointed from outside and three businesses were established as profit centres – rail, buses and property management – which absorbed most of the engineering and supply functions. Also, within them management was decentralized into smaller units, each with budgeting and personnel powers. Performance measures were introduced for management at all levels. This trend continued in 1984 when LT became directly accountable once more to central government. Subsidiary companies were formed to manage the bus and underground businesses and this strategy was subsequently extended to most of LT's activities. By 1988 a small central HQ confined itself to corporate planning and financial oversight and was surrounded by subsidiary companies run by 'business boards'. Remaining HQ functions such as computing were contracted out and those which remained, such as architects, now had to charge for their services in order to instil financial discipline.

Broadly, the source of LT's performance improvement after 1984 appears to lie in the reorganization and new management style introduced from 1978. The decline in performance in the mid-1970s largely resulted from the GLC's interference in the corporation's management.

HMSO

Throughout the 1970s there was an ongoing 'commercialization' of the HMSO, which began well before the decision was taken to establish a trading fund. The creation of a trading fund can therefore be seen as a *product of*, rather than the *cause of*, the greater commercialization. In accordance with expectation, the move to trading fund status was associated with a switch from a functional to a profit centre structure during the 1970s. There were also changes in reporting systems, including, in particular, a new management accounting system which, following major teething problems, was operating successfully by the early 1980s. However, there was no input of new senior management and the labour force remained civil servants, with the normal Civil Service terms and conditions.

British Airways

British Airways was formed by the merger of two state owned airlines, BOAC and BEA, in 1973. It took a number of years to successfully create one airline, not least because of the very different management cultures in BOAC and BEA. The initial structure of BA was a loose federation of the two former airlines each retaining considerable managerial autonomy. From the mid-1970s there were repeated attempts to restructure to create a cohesive organization, while in the meantime BA continued to lose market share and the quality of service deteriorated.

By 1981 the corporation was losing £545m a year and its balance sheet showed a negative net worth. Management's response was a 'Survival Plan' which involved large reductions in capacity and employment and the disposal of some businesses. This rationalization contributed to BA's recovery and was sustained by an input of new management talent. Sir John (later Lord) King was brought in from the private sector as chairman with a brief from the government 'to take all necessary steps to restore the group to profitability and prepare it for privatisation' (British Airways 1987: 9). King immediately reconstituted the board. Nine of the existing fourteen members were replaced and there were casualties in the lower tiers of management as he set about destroying the old BOAC and BEA cultures. In the following months King recruited a new financial director and chief executive and senior marketing management. The remaining management, along with all of BA's staff, were put on intensive, consumer-oriented training programmes and the corporation was restructured into product-based profit centres. It was in the area of marketing that the biggest advances were made led by the new management who brought skills from fast-moving, consumer goods industries. By 1985 BA was winning international accolades for the quality of its service and had returned to profit. The resurrection of BA was driven by a determined top management with a clear objective to become 'The world's favourite airline.' The restructuring, management changes and alterations in labour relations and internal communications were all geared to that end.

National Freight Corporation

Like BA, the NFC was a public corporation created by merger. The 1968 Transport Act brought together the haulage activities of the state-owned British Road Services (BRS) and related companies and British Rail. The new corporation managed 28,000 road vehicles and employed around 65,000 staff.

From the outset it was intended that the corporation should adopt a holding company format, leaving day-to-day management to the subsidiary firms, which initially were BRS (the largest), Pickfords, Tayforth and Harold Wood, National Carriers and Freightliner. Under-capitalized and incurring large losses in National Carriers (which in 1968 had lost a staggering £23 million on a turnover of £23 million), by 1975 the NFC was fighting for survival. The management's response was to undertake a major programme of restructuring, appropriately called 'Operation Phoenix', which led to closures and job losses. The government responded with a long overdue capital reconstruction.

During the election of 1979 the Conservative Party committed itself to the introduction of private capital into the corporation. In the early 1980s this pledge was transformed into a commitment to privatization, and in February 1982 this was completed through a management–workforce buy-out. Following privatization the company renewed its efforts to create a unified company ethos through training programmes and improved communications. There was also a further focus on consumer needs which led to the development of new products with higher value added. This meant that the NFC moved away from the low profitability business of general haulage towards higher profitability work in specialized sectors. The mission became to make the NFC 'a company for all seasons' to be achieved by diversification and, more especially, overseas acquisitions.

The NFC is commonly considered to be one of privatization's greatest successes in the UK, and the performance measures (see Table 2.2) confirmed an impressive performance improvement. However, the source of the revival of the NFC occurred from the mid-1970s (long before privatization was mooted), and occurred under broadly an unchanged executive management and organizational structure. For example, Sir Peter Thompson, who was instrumental in designing the buy-out and headed NFC as its chairman for most of the 1980s, had joined the corporation in January 1972 and had become the NFC's chief executive in 1977. The NFC retained its holding company format and even the refocusing of the corporation towards higher value added products was a continuation of a policy begun in the 1970s.

CONCLUSIONS

The research has been concerned with (1) testing the hypothesis that a change in organizational status leads to a change in performance, and (2) with attempting to identify the relationship between performance and the organization's internal environment.

The results confirm that a Figure 2.1 west-to-east (public to private) shift is associated with improved performance, but that this performance improvement is not guaranteed. Thus the link between organizational status and performance is apparently much more complex than many commentators (notably politicians) have assumed.

Turning specifically to the internal environment, the hypothesis that performance improvements are associated with significant changes in organizational structure, objectives, management, labour relations, communication and reporting systems, and the nature and location of the business, is generally confirmed, but again with certain reservations. The performance improvement registered by the Royal Mint cannot be easily related to anything other than the movement of the Mint to a purpose-built site, incorporating the latest technology, for little else seems to have changed. By contrast, the Royal Ordnance Factories did restructure their organization with the granting of trading fund status, but in this case it involved greater centralization of decision-making which was possibly unsuited to the ROFs' needs. This may explain the finding that in general the ROFs' performance did not seem to have improved as expected following the change of status.

The marked performance improvement at British Airways was associated with significant top–down changes across the whole organization affecting *all* of the internal environment variables identified. But while there was also a similar senior-management-driven restructuring at the National Freight Corporation, this began before privatization was on the agenda and did not involve the wholesale changes in executive management found at BA. The mixed performance results for telecommunications and the postal service after the Post Office was granted public corporation status in 1969 are understandable in terms of our discussion of the internal environment. During the 1970s there was no note-worthy change in organization or management style. The Post Office continued to operate much as before.

The performance results for British Aerospace, both after nationalization and privatization, also seem to fit well into our discussion of the internal environment. After nationalization the previous company structure existed largely intact and only after privatization was a real effort made to rationalize the business through a more centralized management structure. BAe provides a good example of a case where temporary centralization was needed to get to grips with the business.

The history of London Transport is not dissimilar to that of the NFC, in that the roots of the improved performance after 1984 can be traced back to well before the decision was taken to provide more management independence by removing the corporation from local authority control. The introduction of local government control in 1970 was not associated with noticeable changes in organization or management and it is therefore not too surprising that there does not seem to have been much change in performance. The poor performance in the mid-1970s is directly related to political intervention in the management of LT.

In the case of the HMSO, becoming a trading fund was part of an ongoing commercialization of the organization which also began a number of years earlier. In addition, the new status did not lead to major changes in the management or labour relations. Hence, it is not altogether surprising that the performance measures failed to provide strong evidence of a marked improvement in performance following the award of trading fund status. Where changes did occur – notably the introduction of profit centres and the new management accounting system – they occurred before the HMSO became a trading fund.

Lastly, Rolls-Royce was unusual because it was the only case where performance changed *contrary* to expectation. Performance improved rather than deteriorated in the first few years after nationalization. This can be traced directly to the wide-sweeping changes at board level in 1971 and the immediate, post-bankruptcy, company rationalization. The fact that performance deteriorated from the mid-1970s suggests, however, that the reorganization was insufficiently deep-rooted to prevent the return of the old, wasteful practices. Only later did Rolls-Royce centralize the important production and design functions and reduce costs.

So what conclusions can we draw from this discussion of the internal environment?

First, the results appear to be congruent with aspects of the organizational theory literature, especially contingency theory, which suggests that performance is the product of many and often subtle forces (Perry and Rainey 1988). In the case of the Royal Mint, the performance improvement can be traced to new investment which was not related to the status change. But in the other cases there were important changes in the internal environment variables where performance improved and very few, if any, changes where the performance results were more ambiguous. British Airways, the National Freight Corporation, and British Aerospace after 1981, all underwent important structural or other reorganizations and in the case of BA all of the internal environment variables studied changed. By contrast, London Transport in 1970, the nationalization of British Aerospace in 1977 and public corporation status for the Post Office in 1969, were all associated with little in the way of internal reform.

Second, in some cases changes in the internal environment occurred independently of the status change. This applied to the HMSO, London Transport before the ending of GLC control in 1984, and the National Freight corporation. In these cases the major restructuring had begun well before the status change, and for London Transport and the NFC well before the status change was planned.

Third, where the structure of management changed, the direction of movement was usually towards a more decentralized, profit centre or holding company structure. This accords with the organizational theory literature which suggests that a more decentralized structure is optimal when the external environment becomes less stable following an ownership change. The clear exception, British Aerospace after 1983, can be explained in terms of a short-term need to centralize so as to take stock of the businesses brought together by the earlier nationalization. Again, such a move finds support in organizational theory.

Last, it has long been recognized that the internal environment needs to be congruent with the external environment. An inappropriate internal environment – for example, an over-centralized structure – will mean that the organization cannot take advantage of the opportunities offered by changes in the external environment. The discussion in this chapter supports this view and implies that critical to the success of ownership changes in improving performance is an appropriate change in internal mechanisms. This provides an important message for economic policy. It suggests that if privatization or agency status within government are to lead to efficiency gains, then there must be contemporaneous changes in the internal environment variables identified in this chapter.[11]

NOTES

1 The research was funded by the Economic and Social Research Council as part of its Management in Government Initiative (Project no. EO925006). Other members of the research team included Professors Keith Hartley and Andrew Dunsire of the University of York. I would particularly like to acknowledge access to Andrew's papers on the history of a number of the organizations studied in this chapter. The usual disclaimer applies. Part of this chapter appeared in the *International Journal of Public Sector Management*, vol. 5, no. 1 (Parker 1992).

2 Stephen Littlechild warns in relation to organizations which retain some government ownership, that: 'as long as ultimate control lies with government, one cannot realistically hope to avoid all the problems' (Littlechild 1981: 14).

3 Owing to the major changes in the Royal Mint's financial records around the time of

the status change, it was not possible to produce reliable financial ratios for this organization.

4   In the absence of detailed information on purchases, this was approximated as $(P + I + W)/N$ where P = profit before tax, I = capital charges in the form of interest on long-term loans, and W = employee wages. P, I and W were expressed in real terms.

5   'Unclear' in Table 2.2 means that the results of the test varied depending upon the precise dates, price deflators or national comparisons used.

6   Research suggests that firms need periodic 'cultural change' and that this occurs at discrete intervals rather than as smooth adaptations to changes in the external environment. Firms also appear to suffer adaptation 'inertia', which events such as privatization may overcome. However, it is important in this line of research to beware of a 'Hawthorn effect' (Roethlisberger and Dickson 1939) – that *any* organizational change creates a shock effect which leads to a questioning of existing practices and beliefs, leading in turn to improved performance (at the same time, of course, major change risks disruption costs which could depress performance). Such an improvement is not likely to be long maintained in the absence of a further 'shock'. An example of this may well be Rolls-Royce, where bankruptcy in 1971 led to improved efficiency, but the improvement was not sustained into the second half of the decade.

7   Many privatized organizations have reduced their labour force in the 1980s as part of their economic restructuring ahead of privatization (for example, the British Steel Corporation and British Airways).

8   In an earlier paper (Dunsire *et al.* 1988) reference was made to the possibility of inferring from the kind of information passed up and down the organization the type of management which exists. Did the information primarily consist of 'controls' or 'news'? Was the information primarily input or output oriented? Unfortunately, it has proved too difficult to obtain the kind of internal data (access to memoranda etc.) to proceed far with this line of enquiry. However, it is potentially a useful area for research where data permit.

9   Drucker's comment was directed at non-profit organizations like charities and non-profit schools and hospitals. However, it appears applicable to all organizational forms where the profit goal is attenuated.

10   There is also a discussion of this part of the research in Dunsire (1991).

11   Although the research did not address the effect of changes of status *within* the *private sector*, the method outlined in this chapter can be adapted to assessing the effects of MBOs, divestments, take-overs, 'going public' and 'going private', etc.

REFERENCES

Allaire, Y. and Firsirotu M. E. (1984) 'Theories of organisational culture', *Organisational Studies*, 5(3) 193–226.

Ball, R. J. and St Cyr, E. B. A. (1966) 'Short-run employment functions in British manufacturing industry', *Review of Economic Studies*, vol. 33, 179–207.

Beesley, M. E. and Laidlaw, B. (1989) *The Future of Telecommunications*, Research Monograph no. 42, London: Institute of Economic Affairs.

Bishop, M. and Kay, J. (1989) *Does Privatization Work? Lessons from the UK*, London: London Business School.

British Airways (1987) *Prospectus: British Airways plc*, London: British Airways.

Burns, T. and Stalker, G. M. (1961) *The Management of Innovation*, London: Tavistock.

De Fraja, G. (1991) 'Efficiency and privatisation in imperfectly competitive industries', *Journal of Industrial Economics* xxxix(3), 311–21.

Department of Trade and Industry (1973) *Rolls Royce Ltd*, London: DTI.

Drucker, P. F. (1990) *Managing the Non-Profit Organization*, Oxford: Butterworth Heinemann.

Dunsire, A. (1991) 'Organizational structure: status change and performance', in K. Hartley and A. Ott (eds), *Privatization and Economic Efficiency*, Aldershot: Edward Elgar.

—— , Hartley, K., Parker, D. and Dimitriou, B. (1988) 'Organisational status and performance: a conceptual framework for testing public choice theories', *Public Administration* 66(4), 363–88.

Hartley, K., Parker, D. and Martin, S. (1991) 'Organisational status, ownership and productivity', *Fiscal Studies* 12(2), 46–60.

HMSO (1988) *Civil Service Management Reform: the Next Steps* (Cmnd. 524), London: HMSO.

Johnson, G. and Scholes, K. (1988) *Exploring Corporate Strategy* (2nd edn), New York: Prentice-Hall.

Kmenta, J. (1971) *Elements of Econometrics*, London: Macmillan.

Littlechild, S. C. (1981) 'Ten steps to denationalisation', *Journal of Economic Affairs* 2(1), 11–19.

Lynk, E. L. (1991) 'Telecommunications divestiture in the UK: a crossed line', *Applied Economics* 23(2), 379–84.

Millward, R. and Parker, D. (1983) 'Public and private enterprise: comparative behaviour and relative efficiency', in R. Millward, D. Parker, L. Rosenthal, M. T. Sumner and N. Topham, *Public Sector Economics*, London: Longman.

Mitchell, W. C. (1988) *Government As It Is*, Hobart Paper 109, London: Institute of Economic Affairs.

Puchi, W. (1981) *Theory 2*, New York: Addison-Wesley.

Parker, D. (1985) 'Is the private sector more efficient? A study in the public v. private debate', *Public Administration Bulletin*, vol. 48, 2–23.

—— (1989) 'Public control of natural monopoly in the United Kingdom: is regulation the answer?', in M. Campbell, M. Hardy and N. Healey (eds), *Controversy in Applied Economics*, London: Harvester-Wheatsheaf.

—— (1991) 'Measuring changes in organisational performance', *Graduate Management Research* 5(4) 8–29.

—— (1992) 'Agency status, privatization and improved performance: some evidence from the UK', *International Journal of Public Sector Management* 5(1), 31–9.

—— and Hartley, K. (1991a) 'Organizational status and performance: the effects on employment', *Applied Economics* 23(2), 403–16.

—— —— (1991b) 'Do changes in organisational status affect financial performance?', *Strategic Management Journal* vol. 12, 631–41.

Perry, J. L. and Rainey, H. G. (1988) 'The public–private distinction in organization theory: a critique and research agenda', *Academy of Management Review* 3(2), 182–201.

Peters, T. J. and Waterman, R. H. (1982) *In Search of Excellence*, New York: Harper & Row.

Pugh, D. S. and Hickson, D. J. (1976) *Organizational Structure in its Context: The Aston Programme*, Farnborough: Saxon House.

Ramanadham, V. V. (ed.) (1988) *Privatisation in the UK*, London: Routledge.

Roethlisberger, F. J. and Dickson, W. J. (1939) *Management and the Worker*, Cambridge, Mass: Harvard University Press.

TUC (1986) *Bargaining in Privatised Companies*, London: Trades Union Congress.

Veljanovski, C. (1987) *Selling the State*, London: Weidenfeld and Nicolson.

Williamson, O. E. (1970) *Corporate Control and Business Behaviour*, Englewood Cliffs, N.J.: Prentice-Hall.

Woodward, N. (1988) '"Managing" cultural change on privatisation', in V. V. Ramanadham (ed.), *Privatisation in the UK*, London: Routledge.

3

PUBLIC OWNERSHIP AND THE THEORY OF THE STATE

Bob Rowthorn and Ha-Joon Chang

INTRODUCTION

During the last decade or so, the question of ownership and economic efficiency – and, on a more practical level, privatization – has become a central issue of policy debate among economists. Privatization has formed the spearhead of the Thatcherite, and other New Right, attacks on the state in the advanced capitalist nations, and has also formed an integral part of the economic reforms implemented in many developing countries with the encouragement of the World Bank and the IMF. Most importantly, the collapse of the Communist system in Eastern Europe and the Soviet Union – where collective ownership was the dominant form of property – has led to various programmes of radical economic reform in which private ownership is supposedly the theoretical linchpin, although in practice the actual pace of privatization has typically been rather slow.

Unfortunately, the participants in this debate are often extremely dogmatic. Those who are strongly in favour of privatization usually take it as self-evident that private ownership is superior to public ownership. Although it may be ideologically useful for those who support privatization for purely political reasons, such an assumption is hardly helpful for those who are genuinely interested in enhancing economic efficiency. In this chapter, we examine some existing theories which equate efficiency with private ownership and argue that they are seriously misleading. We then argue that the central issue should be the *political economy* of state intervention, rather than ownership *per se*. We examine two dimensions of efficiency – static and dynamic – and investigate how political economy relates to the question of efficiency. We then discuss the possibility of 'market socialism' in the light of our discussion. We conclude the chapter with a more general discussion of the political economy of ownership.

WHY PRIVATE OWNERSHIP?

Where justification for the superiority of private ownership is given, this normally relies on the residual claimant theory and/or the dispersed knowledge theory. In the following we examine these theories and see to what extent they provide convincing argument for private ownership.

54

Residual claimant theory

The most widely known variant of this theory is found in Alchian and Demsetz (1972). According to Alchian and Demsetz, modern production is usually organized as team production, and there is an interdependence among the efforts of individual members of the team. In such a situation it is difficult to measure individual effort, and it therefore pays to have a specialized monitor who can ensure that individual members are putting in the maximal amount of effort – that is, that they are not 'shirking'. However, this raises the question of 'who monitors the monitor'. This is because a monitor without a claim on the residual (or surplus) is likely to put in suboptimal monitoring effort. Private ownership guarantees that the 'monitor', as the residual claimant to the profit of the enterprise, has an incentive to maximize profit, whereas public authorities in the form of the state do not have such an incentive.[1] Hence the superiority of private ownership over public ownership.[2]

A more sophisticated variant of the residual claimant theory is found in Barzel (1989: 56–9). Barzel argues, on efficiency grounds, that the claim on the residual income of an enterprise should normally be allocated to a diversity of agents. He argues that the criterion of such allocation should be the degree of *de facto* control which an agent exerts on output. *Ceteris paribus*, the more difficult it is to monitor or direct any particular agent, the greater should be the share of this agent in residual income. Note that this variant of residual claimant theory would not necessarily assign unique or even primary ownership to the top level monitors, as Alchian and Demsetz assume. There is no reason to suppose that monitoring is the only, or even the main, activity in which discretion and responsibility are important. Any agent with a significant degree of effective control over his/her activity should to some degree be a residual claimant.[3]

One important point to note is that the residual claimant theory may justify the owner-managed firm, but it does not lend much support to private ownership in the form of the modern joint stock company. First of all, shareholders in a joint stock company, unlike the owner-manager, do not participate in the production process as members of the 'team', and are therefore at an information disadvantage *vis-à-vis* the managers whom they are supposed to monitor. Second, even where there exists no such informational asymmetry, individual shareholders of a large joint stock company do not have the incentive to devote time and resource to monitoring the managers, given that any improved performance resulting from their monitoring effort is a 'public good', from which those shareholders who do not contribute to such monitoring can also benefit. This point is recognized even by Demsetz himself in his later work (Demsetz and Lehn 1985: 1156). Given such a problem of 'shareholder collective action', it is not clear whether the residual claimant theory allows us to presume anything about the relative efficiency of private firms based on dispersed ownership (Chang and Singh 1992: 17–18).

It is often argued against such criticism that, even though individual shareholders cannot act as ideal monitors, the stock-market will function as a monitoring mechanism (see, for example, Manne 1965). According to this argument, the initial stage of such 'monitoring' will be the 'exit' of dissatisfied customers from a badly performing firm (that is, they will stop buying from the firm). The result will be falling profitability of the firm, which, in turn, will lead to the 'exit' of the shareholders (that is, the shareholders will sell their shares), resulting in a declining share price, which exposes the firm to the possibilities of take-over (Singh 1971, 1975).[4] According to this argument, the managers are forced to manage the firm efficiently, whether the shareholders are monitoring them personally or not. However, this argument is seriously flawed on the following grounds.

First of all, the belief in the efficiency of the stock-market as a monitoring device rests on the belief in the efficiency of the 'exit' mechanism in the product market. However, private ownership *per se* does not guarantee an efficient functioning of the 'exit' option in the product market. Many private monopolies are protected by natural and artificial entry barriers and customers may not in practice have a genuine 'exit' option. And if customers are captive, it will be difficult for the profit figures to fully reflect the enterprise efficiency, and the role of share prices as an indicator of enterprise performance will be seriously limited.

Second, in the real world the selection mechanism in the stock-market is seriously deficient (for details, see Chang and Singh 1992: 23–5). Empirical studies show that selection for survival in the stock-market is based more on size than on efficiency or profitability. Moreover, on average, the profitability of merging firms does not improve after merger. This implies that, to the extent that monopoly power of the acquiring firm in the product market increases as a consequence of take-over, the evidence is compatible with reduced efficiency in resource utilization following merger. Singh (1971, 1975) suggested that instead of disciplining large firms whose managements seek growth for empire building or power motives, the market for corporate control may encourage them to see, a further increase in size precisely in order to avoid being taken over, especially by taking over smaller but relatively more profitable firms. Moreover, the take-over mechanism may encourage, in a number of ways, a 'short-termist' outlook on the part of management to the detriment of long-term investment, economic growth, and international competitiveness (Cosh *et al.* 1990).

Another weakness of the residual claimant theory is that it is based on the behavioural assumption of pure material self-interest. However, individual material interest is not the only thing which motivates human action (McPherson 1984). Paradoxically, the existence of quite different motivations may actually be necessary for the residual claimant theory to hold. In the absence of a well-established and efficiently enforced property rights system, the residual claimant would *not* have the incentive to monitor his 'team-mates', because his claim could not be enforced. However, no legal system, including the property rights system itself, can properly function without some degree of moral commitment – or what North (1991: 55) calls 'ideological commitment to integrity and honesty' – because otherwise the enforcement costs would be prohibitively high.[5] In other words, in practice, the very existence of an efficient property rights system, which is necessary for the residual claimant theory to hold, depends on some departure from the model of pure self-interest.

In the context of public enterprise, we must point out that motives such as nationalism, altruism, and even pride in 'serving the public' can motivate public sector managers towards good performance, although we should also realize that there exists the dangers of bureaucratic self-seeking by the public sector managers (Niskanen 1973). If we adopt the simplifying assumption of fully self-interested behaviour, it becomes difficult to explain why there are many excellent public enterprises even in situations where they enjoy actual or virtual monopoly power (Chang and Singh 1992). Indeed, there are numerous examples throughout the world, where the state, sometimes without even the prospect of privatization, has put enormous pressure on public enterprises to be efficient, through cutting costs, improving quality of output, etc., and the managers of these enterprises have realized these objectives – on a scale which would not have been forthcoming if they were fully rational and self-interested agents. The good performances of public enterprises in countries like France, Austria, Taiwan, and South Korea during the last few decades stand out as examples here (Chang and Singh 1992). The improvement in the UK public sector performance prior to the Thatcherite privatization programme provides another good example (Daring 1989, Rowthorn 1990a).[6]

Dispersed knowledge theory

According to the Austrian School, the nature of human knowledge – including economic knowledge – is such that it can never be fully codified and transmitted to others (Hayek 1949). Given such limited transferability of knowledge, they argue, the state is always more ignorant than individual private owners, as far as the latter's own business is concerned. The failure of central planning, according to this view, is the ultimate proof of the difficulty of centralizing dispersed knowledge through a hierarchical system (Lavoie 1985). Decision-making will, therefore, be more efficient if it is left in the hands of private owners and their agents. Hence the superiority of private over public ownership

This argument is open to several objections. First of all, the difficulty of utilizing dispersed knowledge is ubiquitous, and is not just confined to public enterprise management or other types of state control or intervention. The same problem exists to a similar degree for any large private enterprise, be it multinational or purely domestic in operation. Nevertheless, large private organizations do exist and often function well, at least partly because they have certain other *informational* advantages – for example, economies of scale in information provision or the importance of knowledge embodied in organizational rules and routines. In addition, they may also have advantages of scale and scope in both production and distribution. All these advantages are equally available to large public enterprises. The real question is what is the ideal mix of decentralized and centralized forms of knowledge utilization – that is, between spontaneous interaction among independent units through the market and hierarchical interaction within one organization. And this is primarily a matter of optimum size rather than the ownership.

As the Austrians correctly emphasize, competition, or what they call 'rivalry', plays an important role in the generation of the information necessary for effective co-ordination (Lavoie 1985, Tomlinson 1990). However, this is, strictly speaking, not an argument for private ownership *per se* (Rowthorn 1990b). Product market competition, if effective, will generate the same information regardless of who owns the enterprise concerned. Hence the argument for 'letting the market decide' is not a justification for private ownership *per se*, but for effective product market competition combined with a 'hard budget constraint' on the enterprises involved, be they public or private (see pp. 60–1 for a more detailed discussion of the question of budget constraint).

There are many situations where the introduction of product market competition may increase the efficiency of public enterprises. First of all, competition may come from other public enterprises. For example, in the UK, following deregulation in the early 1980s, the state-owned bus company, National Express, competed vigorously in the area of long distance transport with the state-owned railways (Vickers and Yarrow 1988: 322–5).[7] Second, competition may come from domestic private firms. The good performance of the Italian publicly owned steel-maker, Finsider, and the French auto-producer, Renault, for the last few decades can at least partly be explained by the rather fierce competition from domestic private firms (Ayub and Hegstad 1986: 18). Third, competition may also come from competitors in the export market. The examples here include CVRD of Brazil (iron ore), OCP of Morocco (phosphates), ICL of Israel (chemicals), HMT of India (machine tools) (Ayub and Hegstad 1986: 18).[8] Finally, import liberalization may be another way of increasing competition, although for developing countries this is a limited option since many of the enterprises exposed to such competition are 'infants' and may therefore not be able to withstand it.

Concluding remarks

In this section, we argued that existing theories do not provide a general case for private ownership. Of course, even if private ownership in general may be no better than public ownership, there may be a particular case in which private ownership is preferable. This will occur when the state lacks a particular capability which is available in the private sector and when it is not feasible for the state to acquire this particular capability. For example, a foreign multinational may have superior technology, managerial skills or access to markets, but is not willing to collaborate in joint ventures with the state sector or to administer state enterprises on a contractual basis, or else the terms of doing so are unacceptable. In such a case, the best course for the state and the nation may be to hand over the relevant activities to the multinational in question.

This is only one example amongst many. Such examples do not depend on any intrinsic superiority of private ownership, but on the specific capabilities possessed at any given time by the private and public sectors, and the ability of the public sector to acquire new capabilities on a realistic time-scale. The decision to hive off or leave some particular activities to private enterprises is no different in principle from that of a private company limiting the range of its activities to what it can most effectively manage. The point is that the capabilities of the public sector depend on its past history and must be taken into account when deciding the optimum boundary between private and public sectors. As far as large-scale enterprises are concerned, there is no activity which the public sector cannot in principle perform as efficiently as the private sector. Therefore, for many large-scale enterprises, the decision where to draw the boundary should not be based on general principles concerning the superiority or otherwise of private ownership, but a case-by-case appraisal of the actual and potential capabilities of the public sector.

POLITICAL ECONOMY OR OWNERSHIP?

We have argued above that it is difficult to claim, on purely economic grounds, that private ownership *per se* will guarantee better enterprise performance. The residual claimant theory and the dispersed knowledge theory are great improvements on the traditional neo-classical analysis, where ownership does not matter for efficiency.[9] This is because they take the 'social' nature of the economic process more seriously. The residual claimant theory focuses on conflicts of interest in the production process and warns us against the danger of viewing production as purely an engineering process. The dispersed knowledge theory sees economic co-ordination within and between decision-making units as a 'social' process, where the form of interaction matters because of the problem of knowledge transmission.[10]

Despite their merits, however, these theories do not provide much support for the proposition that private ownership is intrinsically more efficient than public ownership. Why, then, are we so often told that the performance of public enterprises will be improved by privatization? In our opinion, the answer to this question lies not primarily in conventional economics, but rather in the sphere of politics and political economy – that is, in the factors which influence government decision-making and determine how the state apparatus will behave in practice.

The advocates of privatization sometimes admit informally that such a policy might not be required with an ideally functioning state. They concede that an ideal state would impose a suitably tight budget constraint and actively promote competition where required, thereby achieving the efficiency gains they associated with privatization. However, these advocates reject this vision as Utopian, on the grounds that such a state does not exist in reality and that any actual state will not remotely behave in this optimal fashion. On the contrary, it will shield public enterprises from competition and subsidize their inefficiency. Given the supposed inadequacies of any actual state, they conclude that privatization is the second best solution. This, in our view, is an interesting argument which may well be correct in certain cases. Unfortunately, it is rarely articulated explicitly and the argument for privatization is normally based on narrow economic grounds which are often quite spurious.

Before discussing the politics of public enterprise efficiency, we should point out that there exist two concepts of efficiency in the economic literature: static and dynamic. Static efficiency is loosely defined as efficiency in the use of existing resources, whereas dynamic efficiency is loosely defined as efficiency in the generation of new resources through sustained innovation and structural change. In the literature on public enterprise and privatization, as in other conventional economic literature, the uncharted waters of dynamic efficiency are pretty much deserted and the discussion is usually confined to the problem of static efficiency in the form of 'budget constraint'. However, dynamic efficiency deserves more attention, as is increasingly recognized even by economists of more orthodox persuasion who have conventionally concentrated on static efficiency (see Helm et al. 1991, and Newbery 1992, for some examples).[11] In the following discussion, we approach the question of public enterprise efficiency from these two angles.

Static efficiency: budget constraint

The most common argument against public ownership is based on the notion of 'soft budget constraint' as proposed by Kornai (1979). The argument, briefly, is that public enterprises, especially in socialist countries where the state has a large room for manoeuvre for its budget, do not have the incentive to economize on resources because they can almost always claim more resources from the state budget – that is, they face a budget constraint which is not binding enough. How does this relate to the question of political economy?

Think of a situation where a public enterprise is inefficient simply because of open-ended subsidies – or 'soft budget constraint'. The simplest and cheapest solution to this particular problem is to follow the example of Margaret Thatcher in the UK in the early 1980s and establish a 'hard budget constraint' by abolishing or limiting subsidies. This is more efficient than privatization because it avoids the transaction costs incurred by the latter policy (for example, costs for valuation, flotation of the shares, risk premium, etc.). However, under certain conditions, the imposition of a hard budget constraint by the authorities may be politically impractical, because of the opposition from those affected – for example, the managers, workers, consumers, or even other firms who were previously getting their goods at subsidized prices.

In this case, privatization may be the most effective option. With the enterprise in public hands the state may find it impossible to resist demands for subsidization. However, with the enterprise in private hands, the political pressures for subsidization may be greatly weakened, and the enterprise budget constraint correspondingly hardened, although this need not be the case if there is a 'regulatory capture' *à la* Stigler (1975). By privatizing the enterprise, then, the state is in effect 'abdicating' responsibility and thereby insulating itself from interest group pressure (on the theory of 'abdication' of power, see Schelling 1960: ch. 1, and Elster 1984: 411–22).[12]

One must recognize why privatization is the superior option in this case. It has nothing to do with any *intrinsic* superiority of private over public ownership. It is entirely because of the politics of state intervention in the particular case concerned. There will normally exist technically feasible incentive schemes which, in theory, could ensure that public enterprise functions as efficiently as private enterprise – or even more so from the social point of view because of externalities and distributional considerations (see Kaldor 1980, for a more extensive discussion). The problem is that such incentive schemes may be impractical due to political obstacles. In a situation where the ability of the state to enforce its desires is politically limited, or where the state itself has been 'captured' by conservative interests, privatization may be a way of approximating an outcome which is technically feasible but politically impractical under public ownership. It is no coincidence that the public sector has been efficient in countries like Korea, Taiwan and France, where states have been more 'autonomous' from interest group pressures, and therefore more able to impose a hard budget constraint.

Dynamic efficiency: structural change

Dynamic efficiency refers to the ability to generate new resources, in contrast to the good use of the existing resources, which is static efficiency. Outside the fictitious world of steady-state growth, any dynamic economy will go through a series of structural changes. Is there any reason to believe that public enterprises are less capable of achieving such transformation?

Structural change, by definition, involves the transfer of resources from old to new sectors. Such a transfer is not an easy task when the physical and human assets involved are 'specific' in the sense that their redeployment brings about a reduction in their values (on the notion of asset specificity, see Williamson 1985). Such specificity makes the owners of these assets reluctant to accept uncompensated change because of its negative impact on their incomes and wealth. In most cases, the protection of inefficient firms and industries, be they privately or publicly owned, is the result of the political resistance to change by the owners of specific assets whose values are threatened by the change.

Thus, it is not only agents in the public sector who can block structural change but also private sector agents, because what matters here is political influence and not ownership *per se*. As wealth and numbers are important in politics, the owners, managers, and workers in large firms are bound to exert a political influence over the process of structural change, be these firms private or public. In an era of massive structural change, like the 1930s and the 1970s, few states are strong enough to resist pressure to subsidize those who are going to lose out in the process or even to take over ailing large private firms (Ayub and Hegstad 1986: 58). This is testified by the fact that many recent state take-over or rescue operations of large private companies have occurred under political regimes professing ideological allegiance to free market and private ownership – witness the Chrysler rescue operation by the Republican Government in the USA and the nationalization of the shipbuilding industry in the late 1970s by the only non-socialist coalition government since the 1930s in Sweden.

Not only there is no *a priori* reason to believe that public enterprises are worse at structural change than private enterprises, they may actually be a better vehicle for structural change under certain circumstances. In a world where the capital stock is 'interdependent in use but divided in ownership' (Abramovitz 1986: 402), consolidated state ownership may allow a better co-ordination of individual firms' decisions to adapt their capital stock to changing technologies – or, in other words, to internalize externalities arising from the discrepancies between the patterns of interdependence and the patterns of ownership due to technical change.[13] If public enterprises are worse at structural change than private firms, this will be primarily because the state is, for one reason or another, less able to confront the resistance from potentially redundant managers, workers, and others related to the public enterprises concerned (for example, suppliers, consumers) than it would be if these enterprises were private.

Thus seen, ownership is relevant to the question of structural change partly because it may affect the *political* influence of producers and other relevant interest groups to block necessary change. It is tacitly assumed by the advocates of privatization that conservative interest groups have more power in the case of public enterprise than private, but this is frequently not the case. Indeed, policies such as nationalization or the establishment of public enterprise have historically been designed by 'developmental states', which possess what Newbery (1992) calls 'future orientation', precisely to overcome such conservatism in the private sector.[14] Post-war France and Meiji Japan provide good examples in this respect.

ON THE QUESTION OF TRANSITION: MARKET SOCIALISM?

We argued above that the main reason why public enterprises may not function properly lies in the realm of politics, rather than pure economics. This proposition gives us a clue for understanding the crisis of centrally planned economies where the majority of means of production are in public ownership.

In centrally planned economies, economic decisions are normally highly politicized. Of course, this does not mean that economic decisions in capitalist economies are beyond politics – many prices are in fact 'political' even in capitalist economies, as Oskar Lange pointed out long ago. Nevertheless, one important characteristic of capitalism is the often substantial separation of economics from politics which makes it difficult, though not impossible, for those threatened by market forces to organize at a political level to obstruct change. Under central planning, it is hard to insulate economic decision-making from sectional political pressures, because such planning is by its nature a highly politicized activity given the absence of autonomous markets to provide 'objective' information to the planners. In the absence of objective information, there is enormous scope for lobbying and for economic organizations to acquire political influence over decision-making. A major feature of a capitalist economy is not simply the spontaneous discipline of market forces over economic agents, but the related ability of markets to provide objective information, for both the government and other agents, about costs and benefits. In a comprehensively planned economy, such information is almost totally absent and, in consequence, the scope for political manipulation is virtually unlimited (Mises 1935).

In the Communist countries, this conflation of economics and politics did not pose a major problem immediately after the transition to socialism, mainly because the state apparatus was not yet fully 'captured' by specific producer interests. Moreover, many people were initially motivated by the ideal of building a new society and voluntarily subordinated their own sectional interests to this wider goal. With the passage of time, such idealism faded and a multiplicity of coalitions of 'conservative' producer interests, opposed to change, accumulated in a manner suggested by Olson (1982) for capitalist countries. These sectional interests came to dominate state decision-making processes and their activities became increasingly redistributive in nature. When a state is 'captured' by such a multiplicity of sectional interests, policy-making becomes increasingly 'clientelist' in character and the performance of the economy normally deteriorates.

This is the present situation in many ex-Communist countries. In these countries, simple marketization *without* extensive privatization – that is, the establishment of 'market socialism' – may not adequately improve the efficiency of the economy. Without privatization, the dominance of conservative and redistributive coalitions in such economies may persist. These coalitions may inhibit genuine marketization by limiting competition and perpetuating unnecessary state support. And within the state apparatus they may continue to wield a considerable degree of conservative influence. If this is the case, then, extensive privatization may be the only way to break up such coalitions and establish genuine competition. However, the weakness of this argument is that in many ex-Communist countries the scope for rapid privatization, at least of large enterprises, is very limited. Where this is the case, there is simply no alternative, in the medium term, but to concentrate energies on improving the state sector, perhaps either privatizing slowly in the course of time or, following the example of Taiwan, promoting the growth of new private sector enterprises.[15] Moreover, if, contrary to expectation, improvements in the state sector turn out to be adequate, there may be no need for a large-scale private sector at all.

Our discussion so far does not imply that market socialism is *in principle* unworkable. Under market socialism, large industrial and service enterprises are owned either directly by the state or by shareholders of a public nature such as government or co-operative banks, 'not for profit' financial trusts and the like. These enterprises are subject to competition in the product market and there are also arguments for flexible re-assignment of corporate control (but not necessarily through stock-markets of the 'short-termist' Anglo-Saxon variety). Such a system has never been implemented and its feasibility is an open question.[16]

Public ownership *per se* was not the reason for the crisis in socialist economies. If these economies failed, it was partly because of the informational weaknesses of central planning and partly because of Olsonian institutional 'decay', stemming from the failure to contain attempts by public enterprises to exert political influence and obstruct or distort the process of economic change. Such a danger exists in capitalist countries as well. As argued above, large enterprises in capitalist economies are also able to exercise political power due to their size and wealth – if not as much as their counterparts in centrally planned economies. The danger of Olsonian institutional 'decay' exists in any economy, be it socialist or capitalist – as testified by the experience of many developing countries where the domination of clientelist interest groups has led to poor economic performance (Khan 1989). Indeed, the most successful developing economies (for example, South Korea and Taiwan), are precisely those where a strong state has been able to contain such clientelist pressures and thereby avoid such decay. Ironically, the establishment of market socialism may be more feasible in those capitalist economies where there is a strong state able to contain 'clientelist' pressures than in actual or former Communist economies where the political bargaining structure has produced a weak state which has to rely on clientelistic support for its survival.[17]

THE POLITICAL ECONOMY OF OWNERSHIP

We have argued that political economy carries us much further than ownership in explaining the performance of public enterprises. More generally, we would argue that the very definition of ownership itself is a question which can only be fully addressed with reference to political economy.

Much economic analysis starts from the assumption that all property rights are exogenously and clearly defined. Such a practice is unacceptable when we are discussing issues related to ownership *per se*. In reality, existing ownership rights are the product of previous social bargainings, and are constantly being altered because people are constantly attempting to create new property rights, expand the boundaries of existing property rights, eliminate existing property rights, and defend their existing property rights against such encroachments. As a result, most, if not all, ownership rights are 'truncated' in a most complex manner (Demsetz 1988). In reality, there exist very few examples of pure private ownership as envisaged in textbook economics (Barzel 1989: ch. 5).

64

Ceilings (rent control, for example) on floors (the Common Agricultural Policy, for example) are imposed on the prices at which individuals may buy or sell. The ability to dispose of assets or transform them can also be limited. Zoning laws are the best example of this. Many regulated firms have only limited freedom to scrap their physical capital, to set prices, or to decide on the areas they want to serve. Even when there are no such obvious restrictions, the uses to which a resource can be put are bound to be limited. For example, I may own my knife but may not kill someone with it. Or you may own a certain machine but you may not be allowed to operate it with the labour of a child under a certain age. In other words, the delineation of property rights is not independent of what the members of the society believe to be legitimate and are willing to accept. And what is accepted as legitimate depends on the politics of the society concerned. For example, banning child labour may be seen as an encroachment on the fundamental right of the employer in one society, but not in another.

In relation to enterprise ownership in general, it should be pointed out that there does not exist a clear demarcation between public and private ownership, at least as far as large corporations are concerned. First of all, the institution of limited liability in the joint stock company allows people to undertake corporate risks which far exceed what their personal wealth would otherwise allow. This results in what Keynes called 'socialisation of risk'. It is unclear how much we gain, from the point of view of efficiency (if not from the point of view of equity), by regarding such large enterprises purely 'private'. Likewise, managers of public enterprises can wield a certain amount of pseudo-property rights over their enterprises, introducing a certain 'private' element in the network of property rights pertaining to the enterprise. If the demarcation between the public and the private is hazy, what we need to know is who is entitled to what under which rules, and how these items affect enterprise performance, rather than to issue sweeping generalizations as to the optimality or otherwise of pure forms of ownership which hardly exist in real life.

CONCLUSION

In this chapter, we have criticized some purely 'economic' arguments for privatization. In our view, the question of public enterprise efficiency cannot be divorced from politics. Such efficiency depends on the attitude of the state towards items like competition and budgetary policy, which in turn depends, above all, on the ability of the state to insulate itself against conservative pressures from both inside and outside these enterprises. Where the state can insulate itself adequately, public enterprise may be every bit as efficient as private enterprise, whilst offering additional economic and social advantages. Where the state cannot so insulate itself, privatization may well lead to greater efficiency, but this cannot be taken for granted since the same conservative forces previously at work under public ownership may continue to influence state policy even after privatization.

NOTES

1   One related argument is that the team member whose activity is most difficult to monitor should become the owner, since this will maximize the output.

2   An argument related to the residual claimant theory is the theory of open access property (see Eggertsson 1990, ch. 8, for a summary discussion). According to this theory, when the property rights allow an open access to anyone who belongs to the relevant group, there exists a problem of 'tragedy of commons' (Hardin 1968). Since everyone is individually better off exploiting the property regardless of what others do, the collective outcome becomes an 'irrational' one of over-exploitation of the property – the best examples being over-grazing of meadows and improper maintenance of public housing. Analogous to this situation, when an enterprise belongs to a group of people or the whole society, no individual member has the incentive to take care of it. Hence the inefficiency of public enterprise. Like the theory of residual claimant, this theory emphasizes the fact that collective benefit does not motivate people, but, unlike the former theory, because it allows the possibility of communal ownership it does not necessarily endorse private property rights.

3   To the extent that control is based on idiosyncratic knowledge, this variant of the residual claimant theory bears a certain degree of similarity to the dispersed knowledge theory. If knowledge were not idiosyncratic, a complete contract could be written and it would be impossible for anyone to exert control over his/her activity beyond such contract.

4   On the concept of 'exit' and the distinction between 'voice' and 'exit' as disciplining mechanism, see Hirschman (1970).

5   Similarly, Simon (1991) points out that no organization of reasonable size can function without the members developing some organizational loyalty – because otherwise the monitoring cost will be too high. And if there is a certain tendency for organizational loyalty to develop, making the members of the organization conform to the organizational objectives is probably less important than defining the objectives. When the organizational objectives are not clearly defined, the members tend to define them in their own ways, if not in ways to suit their own personal interests. And, as is often pointed out in the context of public enterprises, the lack of clarity in the objectives is one reason behind their inefficiency (see Chang and Singh 1992).

6   It should be noted that most studies of public nterprise performance in the English-speaking academia are confined mostly to examples for Anglo-Saxon countries, where the behavioural assumption of pure self-interest may fit the real world better than in other cultures (see, for example, Vickers and Yarrow 1988). They make no reference whatsoever to evidence from Continental Europe or the newly industrializing countries where examples of successful, highly competent public enterprises abound – especially in the latter group.

7   National Express has since been privatized for no good economic reason.

8   Korea's state-owned steel mill, which is among the most efficient in the world, provides another good example (Amsden 1989: ch. 12).

9   As pointed out by Lavoie (1985), the 'socialist' models of central planning, like the Lange–Taylor model, were fundamentally neo-classical in this sense.

10   For a more generalized critique of the neo-classical view of human rationality, see Simon (1983).

11   One important point to note is that there may be a clash between the pursuit of static efficiency and the pursuit of dynamic efficiency. As Schumpeter (1987) noted, monopoly, which produces static inefficiency in the form of deadweight loss, may (but may not) encourage dynamic efficiency by promoting innovation.

12   Liberalization, in certain contexts, may also be regarded as an attempt on the part of

the state to abdicate itself from power and reduce the scope for private sector pressure on economic policy-making.

13 This does not mean that we necessarily need public ownership for such changes. For example, conglomerates perform a degree of this co-ordinating role in countries like Japan and Korea – of course, with a lot of state intervention if not state ownership – and the banks do it in countries like Germany.

14 Newbery (1992: 8–11) emphasizes that economic development involves an efficient intertemporal allocation of resources in the process of transferring and applying best practice techniques to low factor cost environments. He argues that a successful economic development will require 'future-oriented' institutions which can reduce uncertainties in such a process.

15 After its liberation from Japan, Taiwan had a very large public sector, which was mainly made up of large enterprises confiscated from the Japanese. In 1952, 57 per cent of industrial production in Taiwan was accounted for by public enterprises and the share remained as high as 46 per cent until 1962 (Amsden 1985). Although not a single public enterprise has been privatized since the early 1950s (*Far Eastern Economic Review*, 23 January 1992: 55), the importance of the public sector diminished substantially in Taiwan – by 1980 it accounted for only 18 per cent of industrial production – because of the explosive growth of the private sector.

16 Kornai (1990) has recently claimed that a well-functioning market economy must be based primarily upon private ownership. However, his claims are based on nothing more than the simple assertion that there exists a strong affinity between private (public) ownership and market (bureaucratic) co-ordination, and that therefore market economy based upon public ownership is unstable. His observations are strongly based on the particular experience of Eastern Europe, and contain no general discussion of the feasibility of market socialism *per se*, nor about the possibility of transforming existing capitalist economies in this direction.

17 Przeworski expresses the same opinion in the conclusion to his study of recent reforms in Eastern Europe and Latin America. 'Forget geography for a moment and put Poland in the place of Argentina. Hungary in the place of Uruguay. You will see states weak as organisations; political parties and other associations that are ineffectual in representing and mobilising; economies that are monopolistic, over-protected, and overregulated; agricultures that cannot feed their own people; public bureaucracies that are overgrown; welfare services that are fragmentary and rudimentary. And will you not conclude that such conditions breed governments vulnerable to pressure from large firms, populist movements of doubtful commitment to democratic institutions, armed forces that sit menacingly on the sidelines, church hierarchies torn between authoritarianism and social justice, nationalist sentiments vulnerable to xenophobia' (Przeworski 1991: 191).

BIBLIOGRAPHY

Abramovitz, M. (1986) 'Catching up, forging ahead, and falling behind', *Journal of Economic History* 46(2) 385–406.

Alchian, A. and Demsetz, H. (1972) 'Production, information costs, and economic organization', *American Economic Review* 62(4), 777–95.

Amsden, A. (1985) 'The state and Taiwan's economic development', in P. Evans, D. Rueschemeyer and T. Skocpol (eds), *Bringing the State Back In*, Cambridge: Cambridge University Press.

—— (1989) *Asia's Next Giant*, New York: Oxford University Press.

Ayub, M. and Hegstad, S. (1986) 'Public industrial enterprises', Industry and Finance Series, vol. 17, Washington, D.C.: The World Bank.

Barzel, Y. (1989) *Economic Analysis of Property Rights*, Cambridge: Cambridge University Press.

Chang, H. and Singh, A. (1992) 'Public enterprises in developing countries and economic efficiency – a critical examination of analytical, empirical, and policy issues', United Nations Conference on Trade and Development Discussion Paper no. 48, Geneva: UNCTAD.

Cosh, A., Hughes, A. and Singh, A. (1990) 'Takeovers, short-termism and finance-industry relations in the U.K. economy', Mimeo., Department of Applied Economics, University of Cambridge.

Daring, R. (1989) 'Successful public enterprise: the code of the double paradox', The 1989 Hatfield Lecture, Hatfield Polytechnic.

Demsetz, H. (1988) 'A framework for the study of ownership', in H. Demsetz, *Ownership, Control, and the Firm*, Oxford: Basil Blackwell.

—— and Lehn, K. (1985) 'The structure of corporate ownership: causes and consequences', *Journal of Political Economy* 93(6) 1155–77.

Eggertsson, T. (1990) *Economic Behaviour and Institutions*, Cambridge: Cambridge University Press.

Elster, J. (1984) *Making Sense of Marx*, Cambridge: Cambridge University Press.

Hardin, G. (1968) 'The tragedy of commons', *Science*, 162, 243–8.

Hayek, F. von. (1949) 'Economics and knowledge', in F. Hayek, *Individualism and Economic Order*, London: Routledge & Kegan Paul.

Helm, D., Mayer, C. and Mayhew, K. (1991) 'The assessment: microeconomic policy in the 1980s', *Oxford Review of Economic Policy* 7(3) 1–12.

Hirschman, A. (1970) *Exit, Voice, and Loyalty*, Cambridge, Mass.: Harvard University Press.

Kaldor, N. (1980) 'Public or private enterprise – the issues to be considered', in W. Baumol (ed.), *Public and Private Enterprises in a Mixed Economy*, London and Basingstoke: Macmillan.

Khan, M. (1989) 'Corruption, clientelism, and capitalist development: an analysis of state intervention with special reference to Bangladesh', Unpublished Ph.D. dissertation, Faculty of Economics and Politics, University of Cambridge.

Kornai, J. (1979) 'Resource-constrained versus demand-constrained systems', *Econometrica* 47(4) 801–19.

—— (1990) 'The affinity between ownership forms and coordination mechanisms: the common experience of reform in socialist countries', *Journal of Economic Perspectives* 4(3) 131–48.

Lavoie, D. (1985) *Rivalry and Central Planning*, Cambridge: Cambridge University Press.

McPherson, M. (1984) 'Limits of self-seeking: the role of morality in economic life', in D. Colander (ed.), *Neoclassical Political Economy*, Cambridge: Mass.: Ballinger Publishing Company.

Manne, H. (1965) 'Mergers and the market for corporate control', *Journal of Political Economy*, 73(2) 110–20.

Mises, L. von. (1935) 'Economic calculation in the socialist commonwealth', trans. S. Adler in F. von Hayek (ed.), *Collectivist Economic Planning: Critical Studies on the Possibilities of Socialism*, London: Routledge.

Newbery, D. (1992) 'The role of public enterprises in the national economy', A paper presented at the Asian Development Bank Conference.

Niskanen, W. (1973) *Bureaucracy: Servant or Master?*, London: Institute of Economic Affairs.

North, D. (1991) *Institutions, Institutional Change and Economic Performance*, Cambridge: Cambridge University Press.

Olson, M. (1982) *The Rise and Decline of Nations*, New Haven: Yale University Press.

Przeworski, A. (1991) *Democracy and the Market – Political and Economic Reforms in Eastern Europe and Latin America*, Cambridge: Cambridge University Press.

Rowthorn, B. (1990a) 'The Thatcher Revolution', in F. Green (ed.), *Restructuring the British Economy*, London: Routledge.

—— (1990b) 'Notes on competition and public ownership', Mimeo., Faculty of Economics and Politics, University of Cambridge.

Schelling, T. (1960) *The Strategy of Conflict*, Cambridge, Mass.: Harvard University Press.

Schumpeter, J. (1987) *Capitalism, Socialism, and Democracy* (6th edn), London: Unwin Paperbacks.

Simon, H. (1983) *Reason in Human Affairs*, Oxford: Basil Blackwell.

—— (1991) 'Organisations and markets', *Journal of Economic Perspectives* 5(2) 25–44.

Singh, A. (1971) *Takeovers: Their Reference to the Stock Market and the Theory of the Firm*, Cambridge: Cambridge University Press.

—— (1975) 'Takeovers, economic natural selection and the theory of the firm: evidence from the post-war U.K. experience', *Economic Journal* 85(3) 497–515.

Stigler, G. (1975) *The Citizen and the State*, Chicago: University of Chicago Press.

Tomlinson, J. (1990) *Hayek and the Market*, London: Pluto Press.

Vickers, J. and Yarrow, G. (1988) *Privatization: an Economic Analysis*, London: The MIT Press.

Williamson, O. (1985) *The Economic Institutions of Capitalism*, New York: The Free Press.

World Bank (1983) *World Development Report, 1983*, New York: Oxford University Press.

4

OWNERSHIP AND COMPETITION IN COMMUNITY MARKETS

Francis McGowan

INTRODUCTION

The experience of public enterprise development in the European Community has until recently been one of gradual expansion, almost irrespective of the political identity of the government. Central and local governments have intervened to create, rescue or take over firms in a variety of economic sectors (manufacturing, services and utilities), motivated by a mixture of reasons ranging from ideological conviction through short-term expediency to strategic planning. Countries have for the most part respected one another's different approaches to the issue, as have the institutions of the Community.

In the last ten years, the tendency to extend the role of the state as owner has come under question. A mixture of poor performances, disastrous ventures, financial constraints and new ideological beliefs has undermined the status of public ownership in many countries. As a result many governments have reconsidered their approach to ownership, shifting from a direct entrepreneurial role towards, in some cases, more tactical approaches but, in others, partial or complete reversals through privatization. In some industries and some countries, this reassessment has been accompanied by a debate over the extent to which competition can be introduced into those sectors hitherto dominated by publicly owned monopolies.

Among members of the Community, the current status of the debates on ownership and regulatory reform is uncertain. Some governments are near to exhausting the possibilities of reorganization and denationalization, while others continue to pursue the policy with varying degrees of commitment; action on regulatory reform has been less enthusiastically pursued. Yet the implications of the changes of the last decade are still being felt, nowhere more so than in the development of a number of EC initiatives, particularly in the broad area of competition policy. The organization of industries where publicly owned companies have traditionally dominated is being challenged as are the ways in which governments seek to influence and support firms, particularly those in which they have an ownership stake.

70

The Commission is attempting to introduce competition into sectors which have traditionally existed within protected national ownership and regulatory environments. However, given the divergences in structure and organization between different states, its efforts to develop competitive regimes for utilities impinge on states in very different ways, not least with regard to the question of public ownership. Yet the Commission is not able to address ownership issues directly. How far that position can be sustained may be challenged as the Commission increases the scope for competition in those sectors.

The interaction of these Community initiatives with the measures adopted (or not adopted) at national levels is therefore challenging traditional regimes of ownership and organization. One of the consequences of change has been a new unevenness in the way certain industries are treated: in some countries industries are organized as competitive private enterprises; in others as regulated public services. National differences in such industries mattered little when those sectors were either viewed as country-based monopolies or regulated international cartels. The intensification of trade and competition between such industries which has occurred as part of integration, and the application of new regulatory regimes by the European Commission, however, means that such variations in national treatment become far more important.

This chapter addresses the consequences of new EC policies for publicly owned firms. It briefly reviews the relationship between ownership and market structure before examining the ways in which Community law has dealt with ownership. It then notes the development of public ownership within the Community before focusing on two case-studies where the problems appear likely to become acute. Both of them are industries which can be classified as utilities, where competition has not been a pressing policy concern until the development of new Community policies.

The Electricity Supply Industry (ESI) is a sector where public ownership and monopoly structures have prevailed across much of the Community for many years. Now the industry is undergoing structural reforms in some countries (notably the UK) and is being challenged at the Community level by Commission efforts to create a European electricity market. To the extent that this new regime emerges, the question of public ownership will almost certainly have to be addressed. The question is already being raised in the other sector examined: the Air Transport Industry (ATI). Here too we see an industry traditionally characterized by publicly owned operators (near monopolies in most cases), and where there have been parallel moves to privatize some of these carriers at a national level and to liberalize the market at a European level. As this process of regulatory change has unfolded, so the ownership question is becoming of critical importance.

In both cases the chapter reviews the structure of the industry and the types of reform which are taking place or under consideration. It then notes the development of EC policy, the response of the firms and the wider issues which may arise. The chapter concludes with an analysis of the Community's position on ownership in the light of the difficulties identified and assesses whether its current actions and proposed policies offer a satisfactory resolution of the tension between public ownership and competition.

OWNERSHIP AND MARKET STRUCTURE

The source of the problem for the Commission centres on the difficulties in resolving the pursuit of deregulatory policies in a sector where publicly owned firms play a significant role. The problem is one aspect of a much wider question regarding whether or not public and private companies can coexist in the same markets. In this section we explore briefly some of the issues connected with competition and ownership.

According to which economic theory or political ideology one consults, ownership either is or is not in principle relevant as a factor determining a firm's conduct, affecting its performance and/or conferring strategic advantages on it. At one end of the spectrum, ownership matters from the perspective that public ownership is a good thing, to be promoted because it meets a number of social and economic goals (Holland 1972, or even Lange 1938). At the other end of the spectrum there are those associated with property rights theory who argue that ownership matters because public ownership is fundamentally inefficient (see, for example, Veljanowski 1987). In between there is a body of literature which is, theoretically at least, rather indifferent to ownership. This literature notes that there is no fundamental reason why publicly owned companies should be more or less efficient than private ones, though it often recognizes that public firms are better at meeting some objectives than private ones and vice versa (Rees 1984, Kay and Thompson 1986, Vickers and Yarrow 1988).[1]

As we move from abstract analysis to actual experience, there appears to be rather more evidence to suggest that ownership does matter, though the consequences will vary according to the nature of the market involved, the relationship between public and private sectors overall and, in the case of publicly owned companies, the involvement of the government in the firm. It is possible to categorize the incidence of firms of different ownership characteristics in different market settings, each of which will have different policy and theory implications.

Markets where the product is internationally traded but where participating countries have a single supplier, either public or private (for example, civil aircraft). In these cases, it is extremely difficult to determine whether or not publicly owned companies are more or less efficient than private competitors. Private firms in one country may complain of subsidies and other government-linked advantages given to public firms in another (though the former may be able to obtain equivalent if not similar forms of aid from governments).

Markets where private and public firms compete for supply domestically and internationally (for example, motor vehicles, consumer electronics). Here much will depend on whether government ownership is employed to give active support or is manifest in a more passive 'shareholder' role. Again the same concerns over direct or indirect assistance will prevail and again the possibility that such aid could be extended to private companies exists. There is evidence of such state-owned companies receiving considerable support (as in the case of many UK publicly owned manufacturing companies), but this need not always be the case as the high productivity and competitiveness of other countries' publicly owned companies suggests.

Markets – often international – which are primarily monopolistically structured at a domestic level and which are dominated by either a public or private company but where there may be some smaller participants, normally sanctioned by regulation (for example, airlines). Relations between the two are likely to be tense depending on whether or not private or public entrants challenge the public or private incumbents. Again there are likely to be allegations of favourable support or protection of public companies. However, the forum for debate will be internal: there are unlikely to be international disagreements ensuing.

Domestic markets which are monopolistic but are fragmented regionally or structurally and in which public and private companies coexist rather than compete (for example, electricity or water provision pre-deregulation). There is unlikely to be much tension except to the extent that additional costs stemming from subsidies or taxes are passed on to consumers and lead to trade tensions in those final markets.

Such market relationships moreover may not be static. Not only will there be changes within particular segments (for example, nationalization or privatization) but the characteristics of the market may shift, often as a result of international pressure or national initiative. In these circumstances, where the pace of transition from one market structure to another may vary from country to country, the question of ownership characteristics can become extremely sensitive.

The debate on ownership and market structure, therefore, has considerable analytical and policy relevance. It is difficult to find conclusive evidence on the superiority of public or private ownership in monopolistic sectors though there appears to be some indications that, in practice, private companies perform better in competitive markets.[2] What is certainly the case is that in such markets, public companies will be perceived as enjoying a number of advantages, including preferential access to capital, low risks of bankruptcy and the support of governments in any disputes over trade or regulatory conduct. Even if some of these advantages could be almost equally conferred upon private companies – subsidies is the best example – the absence of the ownership link may make it less likely in practice. Consequently, the presence of public firms in competitive markets is likely to have serious implications for overall conduct within that market (Sikorsky 1986, Vernon 1981).

PUBLIC OWNERSHIP IN THE EC

Defining what is a state enterprise is a difficult task. Not only are there variations in the extent of state shareholdings in companies, but the influence implied by a holding may vary from country to country. Moreover, different countries will treat the same sector very differently both institutionally and on a day to day basis. Accordingly, this chapter takes a pragmatic sector by sector approach to determining whether enterprises are state-owned or not. As a basic requirement, however, state enterprises are defined by a significant shareholding from a central or local government.

There appear to be two clusters of industries in public ownership: those best characterized by the term 'utility industries' (basically communications, energy, transport and water) – these are often owned by local governments as well as central governments; those forming part of a state industrial holding company (a mixture of traditional heavy industries and new technology venture capital-type activities). The former is the one where most countries have retained a large public presence; the latter has been the sector where patterns of ownership have varied most, though in general there has been a trend away from state participation.

There have been three phases to the development of public enterprises: the pre-Second World War era when a limited range of firms or activities were taken into public ownership because of their infrastructural importance. In many regions, utility industries were absorbed in this way (manufacturing firms were less common). The second phase was in the post-war period when a number of countries embarked on substantial nationalization programmes. These were rooted in part in the belief that a large public stake in industry was an essential component of economic management, though other reasons (such as ideological concerns) also played a role. The third phase in the 1970s was a mixture of reactions to economic crisis (with a number of firms facing economic difficulties) and strategic planning (attempting to develop particular industrial capabilities).

Over the 1980s – aside from the initial spurt of nationalizations in the Mitterand government – the mood switched away from the public sector: in some countries this swing away has effectively constituted a backlash; in others such programmes were largely gestures. Programmes of privatization have therefore been pursued with varying degrees of enthusiasm in most member states in the Community. Even so, in many countries, there remains a sizeable space where public ownership has a role to play. Part of the problem in the Community is that the space in question varies quite widely between countries: at one extreme there is the UK where privatization has transferred almost all industrial and most utility sectors out of public ownership; at the other are a cluster of countries – notably Italy and Spain – where state holding companies still play a role in a number of industries.

The related issue of regulatory reform has been addressed much less vigorously by most member states, even by many undertaking privatization. As a result, and possibly more significantly than ownership, there are widening divergences amongst member states regarding the issue of regulation: in particular there are now very different views on how far competition should be a organizing principle of industries hitherto regarded as utilities organized as monopolies. It is within this context of diverging views of ownership and competition that Community policies must operate.

EC POLICY TOWARDS PUBLIC OWNERSHIP

An examination of the treaties which form the basis of the European Community indicates that the Common Market envisaged was one where the principles of the market economy would prevail. In particular the provisions on competition policy point to a regime which would seek to dismantle barriers to access in markets and prevent discrimination. However, the Treaty does not tackle the question of public ownership. More precisely, it addresses the issue of ownership by excluding itself from any opinion on the matter: article 222 of the EEC Treaty states that the Treaty 'shall in no way prejudice the rules in Member States governing the system of property ownership' (and similar provisions are in place in the ECSC and Euratom Treaties). In principle, and as elaborated in various court judgments, the EC is indifferent to whether or not a company is publicly owned or is nationalized. There was, however, considerable debate in the period prior to the creation of the Community and the years immediately afterwards about how far such enterprises could be reconciled with the model of the free market economy envisaged by the Treaty of Rome (Papaconstantinou 1988, Deringer 1964, Marenco 1983, Schindler 1970).

The Commission may be particularly concerned where public participation impinges on the development of a European market – that is, in cases where the way in which a state-owned company behaves, or the way in which the state assists companies, or the way in which it takes over companies, might be considered contrary to the Treaty of Rome. The Treaty indeed addresses this in a number of articles: notably 37 (which covers questions of state monopolies); 90 (which covers public enterprises and particularly questions of the extent of monopoly privileges in sectors which it describes as of general economic interest such as utilities); and 92 (which covers questions of state aids for both public and privately owned firms).

Article 37 states that member states will adjust any state monopolies to ensure that 'no discrimination regarding the conditions under which goods are procured and marketed exists between nationals of Member States'. This provision has been used to constrain the scope of state monopolies and extend the scope of competition. Action on state monopolies has developed over a number of years with a range of industries tackled in many member states. Sectors where governments have had to relax state control over supply include the alcohol and tobacco industries as well as the oil industry. In a number of such cases, state-owned monopolies would be obliged to open up markets to other suppliers.[3]

Article 92 states that, subject to a number of exceptions primarily regarding social and regional policy concerns, aid in whatever form is incompatible with the Common Market. Actions tackling government aids have been long established: the first cases date back to the 1950s under equivalent legislation in the Coal and Steel Community, and since then the rules have been continuously employed with varying degrees of rigour (Lehner and Meiklejohn 1991). In recent years, the policy has received a new impetus. Since 1987 the Commission has published a detailed review of aids to private and public companies (Commission of the European Communities 1989, 1990) and a particular target for investigation has been the public sector.[4]

Article 90 states that for public enterprises and other utility-type industries, member states shall not adopt policies contrary to the Competition rules. Although some scope for exceptions is allowed regarding the extent to which they are necessary for the performance of particular tasks, the article (paragraph 3) also grants the Commission the power to 'address appropriate directives or decisions to Member States' in pursuit of the Treaty's objectives.

While able to utilize its powers under articles 37 and 92, article 90 has potentially the greatest impact on state-owned companies: it provides not only the basis for ensuring that public enterprises comply with the Treaty of Rome but also a mechanism for acting directly, by imposing decisions or directives without the approval of the Council of Ministers. However, in contrast to the other provisions the use of article 90 has been quite limited. The failure to apply it may have been due to factors such as the rather imprecise language used in the article, the lack of interest in tackling the sectors which were covered by it (primarily the utility industries), and the heavy workload of the Commission in developing the other aspects of Competition Policy. However, the failure to apply it may also have been due to the highly sensitive nature of the article and its implications (Pappalardo 1991, Hancher and Van Slot 1990).

Outside of the issue of state monopolies, and to a lesser extent of state aids to public firms, the issue of public enterprises (including utilities), and the actual and potential advantages which they might enjoy, has been raised only sporadically in the history of the Community. In the 1960s and early 1970s, the issue was occasionally addressed by the Commission, often on the prompting of the Parliament. After a number of studies, the Commission concluded that greater transparency was required in the relationship between governments and state enterprise. From the mid-1970s on, the Commission was engaged in reviewing a number of distortions linked to public enterprise and developing its proposals for action. The opposition of most governments to its efforts meant that concrete measures were adopted only slowly. None the less, the Commission insisted on its powers to act in this area, and though it stressed its indifference to ownership under article 222 it noted that,

the undeniable liberty of a Member State to choose the system of property ownership it prefers does not diminish its responsibility to ensure that both its administration of the public sector and the market behaviour of its public undertakings are in accordance with Treaty rules.

(Commission of the European Communities 1979)

In 1980 the Commission adopted its directive on transparency of financial linkages between public enterprises and governments, utilizing its powers under article 90.3 to impose the legislation in the face of member state opposition (Commission of the European Communities 1980). This obliged member states to supply information to the Commission upon request on the nature and effect of their financial links with public undertakings, pimarily in the manufacturing sector. The use of article 90 to pursue this was opposed by a number of governments who took the Commission to the Court; the Court upheld the Commission's right to intervene. Governments continued to resist the Commission's initiative (for example, by giving only partial responses to Commission requests for information on financial aid). The scope of the directive was extended in 1985 to cover the utility industries (Commission of the European Communities 1985).

In 1988, the Commission also used its powers under article 90.3 to force a degree of liberalization in the telecommunications sector, principally the opening of supply arrangements for equipment (later followed by similar moves on service provision). Again the action was challenged by a number of states, but again the Commission's actions were upheld by the Court. This decision was seen as having widespread implications for other utilities, demonstrating the Commission's preparedness to challenge existing structural relationships within such industries (Platteau 1991).

Latterly, the Commissioner has again tackled the issue of state enterprises by making further reforms of the transparency directive (making reports on financial relations between government and such companies mandatory), despite the opposition of many state enterprises (*Agence Europe*, 11 May and 26 July 1991). Although the response of the state companies has been generally hostile, the Commission has argued that its actions do not infringe its obligations under article 222. Together, the actions taken by the Commission in this and other areas (such as the scrutiny of shareholdings and aid to public companies) open up the question of the extent of monopoly privileges and the terms on which those monopolies are operated and bring into question the ways in which governments can use public ownership.

OWNERSHIP AND THE NEW COMMUNITY REGIME

How far does public ownership affect the performance of competitively structured markets? It is perhaps worth noting that the bulk of the tensions on this issue have been focused on specific sectors and raised at times of general or sectoral economic upheaval. For the most part, the areas where the complaint over ownership has been raised have been in capital intensive oligopolistic sectors often under regulatory reform or increased foreign competition. In the industrial sector, there have been disputes concerning the steel industry where aid to public companies was an issue in the 1980s and the 1990s, most recently in the case of Usinor, which received a capital injection from the French state bank Banque National de Paris. The move was widely condemned by private steel operators, though the Commission eventually supported it (*Economist*, 14 September 1991). State aids to public and private enterprises have also been a long-running concern in the car industry (Bhaskar 1990). Here, however, we focus on two classes in the utilities sector where the implications are potentially even more controversial.

THE EC ESI

Before examining how Community policy might affect the ownership of the electricity supply industry (ESI) it is best to review briefly the structure of the industry, the changes that are under way in member states and the policies which the Commission has begun to introduce. The EC ESI exhibits a wide variety of structures in terms of ownership and organization. Technologically, too, there has been considerable diversity in terms of plant choices and fuels used. Both institutionally and technically, the diversity owes much to variations in geography, economic development, resource endowments and political culture. Table 4.1 presents the broad characteristics of the industry's ownership and the extent of changes introduced in the sector.

In terms of structure, there is a cluster of utilities which are largely publicly owned centralized monopolies. Other countries have a largely decentralized structure but with public ownership dominant in the system. A few are dominated by private companies and appear to be more decentralized in their organization. In all cases, however, the industry has been characterized by monopolistic structures: competition has been perceived as wasteful and ineffi- cient whereas centralization was seen as the best way of obtaining the benefits of developments in technologies and scale economies. Indeed, for the most part utilities have consolidated horizontally and vertically with the number of firms decreasing in almost all countries over the last century, while the growing concentration of the industry has been accompanied by higher public partici- pation, whether at a national or a regional level (Bouttes and Lederer 1990). As recently as the 1970s, a system was nationalized (in Portugal) and since then governments have sought greater control of the largely private Spanish and Belgian industries.

The reason for growing public participation in the industry has been a mixture of political and economic factors. The political rationale has generally been linked to the fact that most nationalizations have been carried out by socialist or social democratic governments: France, Portugal and the UK fall into this category. But such an orientation has not always been necessary. Even in those cases where the motivation was partly political/ideological, there was also a need to rationalize the industries. To that extent there was a clear case for integrating

Table 4.1 The structure of the Community electricity supply industry

Country	Ownership	Reforms and restructuring
Belgium	Largely private, dominated by Electrabel. Small state-owned production company, some locally owned distributors	Consolidation of private production companies into Electrabel in 1990
Denmark	Mixture of co-operative and locally owned distributors, owning production companies which in turn own two power pools, Elsam and Elkraft	Moves to increase independent generation from renewables
France	Dominated by Electricité de France, state-owned monopoly	Internal restructuring; possibility of partial privatization for financing needs
Germany	Eight large 'private' companies (with local and regional government shareholders). Several hundred public and private distribution and production companies	Moves to increase independent generation from renewables. Federal government sold stakes in industry in 1980s
Greece	One state-owned vertically integrated company, PPC	Possibility of large independent power projects
Ireland	One state-owned vertically integrated company, ESB. Also state-owned peat producer	Possibility of privatization
Italy	Dominated by ENEL, but a number of municipal distribution companies and some independent power production	Possibility of privatization. New rules for independent power production
Luxembourg	One mixed ownership transmission and distribution company and a number of local distributors	No significant changes
Netherlands	Approximately forty distributors owning four production companies, owning one transmission company. All municipally/locally owned	Major reform in 1980s to rationalize industry and to a lesser extent, open up to competition
Portugal	Dominated by Electricidade de Portugal; some distributors	Plans to split up the industry and encourage new production by independents. Possibility of privatization
Spain	Dominated by five producers (one public, four private) and jointly owned transmission company	Partial privatization of public company Endesa in 1980s but Endesa also buying into private producers
UK	Dominated by four privatized producers and twelve privatized distributors. Nuclear power has remained in public hands	Industry privatized in 1990/1

and consolidating the sectors; bringing them into public control was one way of achieving this.

The pattern of co-ordination and co-operation at a national level has been reflected in the international aspects of electricity supply. Within Europe, utilities have respected one another's autonomy and have formed organizations to promote technical co-operation. In most cases their interests have converged – for example, in the promotion of specific technologies such as nuclear. The most important aspect of co-operation has been the development of trade amongst utilities. Electricity trade has been a feature of the industry for much of this century with utilities willingly co-operating to exploit resources (such as hydro-electricity) and to take advantage of different patterns of demand and power-plant capacity. Such trade has always been carried out by utilities alone, however. The utilities have retained their national monopolies, arguing that the need to ensure security of supply and the technical stability of the system requires that trade be conducted on this basis (Finon 1990).

The shift in the last few years has been twofold. On the one hand, there has been the increasing criticism of existing structures and the convergence of this with plans for reform of the industry. On the other, there has been an intensification of trade and changing interests in that trade. The former is prompted by a mix of factors (consumer, economic and environmental criticisms) but it has raised the issue of reform (itself a mixture of ideological and financial motivations). Divergences in the performance and price of utilities has coincided with increased trade, raising the issue of whether or not the benefits of trade should be absorbed by utilities.

Claims that the public ESI has failed have been strongest in those countries with neo-liberal governments (though they are not unique to them). In this context, it is hardly surprising that the industry came to be regarded as part of the reform agenda. Ideas which were applied to other regulated industries were considered for the energy sectors, including the ESI. The types of reform have focused in internal reorganization, the introduction of competitive mechanisms into the industry, and privatization (McGowan and Mansell 1992).

The UK has apparently been the most radical in its approach to reforming the ESI. This is hardly surprising given the government's apparent commitment to radical pro-market policies, particularly in the sphere of privatization. The government had privatized a number of industrial and utility companies throughout its time in power and had, less successfully, attempted to introduce a more competitive regime in many. When the government announced it would privatize the ESI following its 1987 re-election, it was obliged to adopt a more radical pro-competitive approach. It planned to privatize the industry at the same time as restructuring the production and transmission aspects of the industry and introducing competition throughout the system (Department of Energy 1988, Vickers and Yarrow 1991).

Other countries' policies have been less ambitious, focusing on either the transfer of ownership or access for non-utility suppliers. In Germany, the federal government has sold its shares in the industrial holding companies Veba and Viag, thereby relinquishing its stakes in the German ESI, while in Spain a partial privatization of the state-owned utility Endesa has been carried out (following a major restructuring of the industry in the mid-1980s). In The Netherlands, the government has secured a major reform of the structure of the industry, involving some consolidation of the industry and a limited market for power; the industry remains municipally owned, however. A number of countries have introduced legislation designed to encourage independent production of power (either through renewables or industrial cogeneration), though as much for environmental and energy efficiency, as for pro-competition, reasons.

The pattern of trade has also undergone significant changes in the last ten years. The relative share of traded power has grown (up to 7–8 per cent of total consumption), and the distribution of trade has changed from one of broadly balanced exchanges to one where net importers and net exporters have emerged. Moreover, the problems of the 1980s and the increasing divergence in the performance and prices of ESIs has increased the scope for tension between the utilities and between them and their customers over the trade issue (as in the dispute between the French and Portuguese utilities on the one hand and the Spanish transmission company on the other over electricity trade, and between the German ESI and the French government over access to German industrial customers).

What has been the role of the EC in these internal and international developments? Until recently, EC policy on electricity has been practically non-existent. From the beginning, the Commission has faced an uphill struggle to develop a competence in the energy areas *per se* let alone in electricity. Attempts to develop a common energy policy from the 1950s to the 1980s came to very little, due to governments' and industries' desire to retain autonomy in this area. Such an attitude was even stronger in the case of the electricity industry.

However, in recent years things have begun to change. In cases of internal reform, the Commission has been able to intervene (most notably during the UK ESI privatization where it was able to secure changes to the way the nuclear industry is protected), thereby establishing its importance in decision-making. Where utilities and consumers have been in dispute, they have in some cases looked to the Commission as a means of settling these disputes. Such cases have coincided with a growing activism on the part of the Commission, particularly since the reforms of the Single Act and the Single Market. The two trends coincided with the publication of the Commission document *An Internal Market for Energy* (Commission of the European Communities 1988). In this document, electricity was a particular target. The Commission accepted the sector's special characteristics (technical complexity, monopoly components and the non-storability of electricity) but argued that these need not hinder the emergence of an internal market for electricity. According to the Commission, the obstacles to such a market stemmed less from the special nature of the ESI than from the wide divergences in the conditions which the industry faced: financial, fiscal and planning conditions varied widely (not least because of different ownership characteristics).

While each of these factors is likely to distort the costs of producing power and to raise prices for consumers, the Commission identified a further source of high costs – the nationally based arrangements for the supply of electricity itself. By being organized on a national or regional basis, existing planning and purchasing arrangements did not fully exploit the scope for trade with neighbouring countries and integrated planning of investment across borders. The organizational structure of the ESI (and particularly the close links between production on the one hand and transmission and distribution on the other) in most member states also worked against an internal electricity market. In the report, the Commission indicated that it sought a radical transformation of the industry when it suggested that 'a change in the operational (as distinct from the ownership) system would be conducive to further opening of the internal market' (Commission of the European Communities 1988: 72).

The Commission began to put the Internal Market for electricity into practice at the beginning of 1989. A series of initiatives covering the purchasing arrangements between national electricity and coal industries, transparency of electricity prices and trade in electricity were introduced. Its approach to the latter issue was incremental. Initially it adopted a pragmatic approach and sought to establish the right of utilities across the Community to trade electricity (Council of the European Communities 1990). While securing agreement on these issues was difficult, the most controversial aspect of its programme has always been its plans to increase the scope of the EC electricity markets, allowing open access to the electricity system for non-utility generators on the one hand and large consumers and distribution companies on the other. After a lengthy consultation process, during which most of the industry and most governments maintained their opposition, the Commission pressed ahead with its plans.

In 1991, the Commission announced that utility electricity import monopolies were contrary to the Treaty and in 1992 it followed this up with plans to implement the principle of greater competition. Its proposals involve access for large consumers and independent producers, the restructuring of existing utilities' management and organization to restrict cross subsidies and controls on state aids to national industries (Agence Europe, 22 January 1992). The proposed directive does not use the option of article 90 due to the extreme political sensitivity surrounding its application. However, if the Commission is unable to get the agreement of member states to its proposals, there is every chance that the option of article 90 would be reviewed.

If the Commission is successful in obtaining the changes it seeks, then the EC ESI will operate in a very different way from before. Competition rather than coordination will prevail and the intensification of competition that could arise from such changes will expose a number of the distortions which different national systems have enjoyed. This has already happened in the area of fuel purchasing (for example, subsidies for German coal and British nuclear); further competition would probably bring into focus less direct forms of protection and support. Amongst these indirect supports, the influence of public ownership will be of importance. In the Internal Energy Market report, the Commission identified such factors as financial controls as potential obstacles to a fully developed market and in its recent proposals for reform it is seeking a disaggregation of accounts for publicly owned utilities.

Further complications might arise from different utilities competing for markets. Where one is publicly owned, the other may argue that it is discriminated against. Something like this has already occurred in the Franco-German tensions of the 1980s: in defending itself against what were perceived to be French pressures to enter the German market, elements in the industry argued that French exports were subsidized by a publicly supported nuclear power programme. Proving that French nuclear power is subsidized is extremely difficult; none the less, the accusations reflected a wider perception that the apparent cheapness of French electricity was due to the state's guarantee for Electricite de France's massive nuclear programme.

Whether these issues become contentious is of course open to question. It may be that something short of a fully competitive regime will emerge in the European electricity market. It is also possible that the major utilities will act to pre-empt the most drastic consequences of greater competition (through the establishment of joint ventures). However, the UK experience of privatization and competition shows how such changes can affect attitudes to investment and strategic planning. How would such myopic firms fare in competition with other operators playing by the old rules? If the Commission were to intervene to tackle such distortions, its actions would effectively restrict the ways in which governments use publicly owned utilities.

THE EC ATI

The tension between public and private firms is already apparent in the case of the Community's air transport industry (ATI). This sector has been dominated by government-owned carriers for most of its history (see Table 4.2). These airlines are responsible for the bulk of scheduled air transport both internationally and internally. In some cases the origins of the airlines themselves are in the public sector, in others they were brought under state ownership, principally in the 1930s and 1940s. The rationale for state ownership hinged on questions of national security and sovereignty. While private companies did exist (for example, UTA, British Caledonian, the charter market) they were for the most part second-order carriers. Needless to say the public operators have been protected by governments in the international regulatory framework (Gidwitz 1980).

Like most international air transport, European civil aviation is regulated by a combination of bilateral treaties, airline agreements and IATA fare-setting procedures. The bilateral agreement covers the range of terms and conditions of

Table 4.2 The structure of the Community air transport industry

Country	Ownership	Reforms and restructuring
Belgium	Dominated by Sabena, majority owned by government. Some private charter operators	Air France takes stake in Sabena
Denmark	Dominated by SAS, partially state owned (with Swedish and Norwegian interests). Some private regional and charter operators	No significant changes, but SAS investigating links with other operators
France	Dominated by Air France, 99 per cent owned by state. Some private scheduled and charter operators	Air France acquired stakes in other major French carrier UTA in 1990. Possibility of partial privatization
Germany	Dominated by Lufthansa which also has stakes in a number of other carriers. Some independent regional and charter operators	Partial privatization over the 1980s
Greece	Dominated by Olympic, 100 per cent state owned	No significant changes
Ireland	Dominated by Aer Lingus, 100 per cent state owned	Some liberalization in 1980s
Italy	Dominated by Alitalia, largely state owned	Partial privatization in 1980s
Luxembourg	Dominated by Luxair, partially state owned	No significant changes
Netherlands	Dominated by KLM, partially state owned (also has stakes in most other Dutch carriers)	Liberal policy throughout 1980s. Partial privatization of KLM over 1980s
Portugal	Dominated by TAP, 100 per cent state owned	Privatization proposed
Spain	Dominated by Iberia, 99 per cent owned by state. Some private airlines	No major changes
UK	Dominated by BA, but a number of significant private operators on domestic and international routes, scheduled and non-scheduled	Liberal policy throughout 1980s. Privatization of BA in 1986

air services between countries, in particular issues of market entry, tariffs, routes and capacity. Such agreements reflect the balance of the two countries' aviation policies (though they can include elements which stem primarily from considerations of foreign policy). The bilateral structure also means that competition on most routes is confined to the airlines of the two countries involved, normally

84

one from each country. Its very structure means that international aviation services are not freely traded international goods. In addition to these governmental agreements, which are of course subject to extensive discussions with national airlines, there are agreements between the airlines themselves which effectively iron out whatever differences in revenue are permitted by the bilateral. These pools share out the revenue and allocate capacity, sometimes on a 50–50 basis, but generally in a way that compensates the airline which carries less passengers (McGowan and Trengove 1986).

Traditionally, therefore, European air transport has been dominated by state-owned carriers operating within an effectively uncompetitive regulatory regime. This structure has been increasingly criticized by consumers and second-order carriers (spurred by the apparent success of deregulation in the US domestic aviation industry), and over the 1980s a number of countries have begun to liberalize their industries: within the EC, only Ireland, The Netherlands and the UK have pursued liberalizing policies independent of the Commission's reform programme. At the same time, the airlines themselves have been variously constrained for finance and criticized for inefficiency, concerns which have triggered moves towards privatization or partial privatization of national airlines in many countries (ITA 1988). As with the ESI, however, neither the moves to privatize nor the moves to liberalize have been carried out uniformly. Consequently, as the European Community has begun to address the issue of reform, national positions have varied quite strongly.

The prevailing regime was clearly at variance with the rules of the Community. The Treaty of Rome specifically outlaws the types of practices which constitute everyday life in the conduct of civil aviation. The competition provisions apply to all sectors of the European economy unless they are specifically exempted in the Treaty or in the course of making a particular sectoral policy. However, the architects of the Treaty left the formulation of a common air transport policy to a later date.[5]

The reason for the slow pace of reform was the same as the reason for the existing pattern of regulation: the close relationship between government and airlines in most European countries. While governments generally welcomed the prospect of lower prices, improved services and greater efficiency as a good thing, they were not prepared to see airlines go to the wall for the sake of these aims. The fact that many airlines were state owned and/or were perceived as vital national interests ruled out the possibility of any radical change that might have endangered their position.

The Commission began to tackle airline regulation seriously in 1984 with the publication of the Second Memorandum on Air Transport (Commission of the European Communities 1984). This included a number of proposals designed to reform the existing system, including greater flexibility on fare and capacity setting. Further measures were introduced in follow-up packages of reforms in 1989 and 1991, and taken together these reforms go a long way to obtaining an open market for air services in the Community. That it will have taken more than seven years for liberalization to be introduced is a reflection of the opposition of the industry and most governments. Indeed, as they have had to accept the Commission's reforms over the last few years, the major airlines and their governments have acted to pre-empt the effects of such liberalization. A number of mergers and joint ventures have taken place or been proposed while governments have for the most part supported their flag carriers against too competitive an environment. This latter point can be seen by reference to the contrasting experience of two airlines, one private the other largely public.

Air Europe was a privately owned charter airline which entered the main-stream scheduled market on the back of the UK government's liberal policy. It proved to be reasonably successful in offering a low-cost, low-fare service to a number of European destinations. However, it expanded its operations too quickly and accumulated financial problems over the course of 1990 and 1991 (*Avmark Aviation Economist* 1991). It collapsed in 1992 in the midst of the recession and the Gulf crisis. Other carriers which entered the scheduled market in the late 1980s/early 1990s also experienced serious difficulties.

Sabena World Airways is the Belgian flag carrier which, despite its dominance of the local market, has faced persistent financial and operating problems. In 1989, it sought to merge with BA and KLM but reservations from the Commission forced the venture to be abandoned. Facing further financial problems in 1990 and 1991, it received a substantial cash injection from the Belgian government earlier this year and continues to operate. The aid was approved by the Commission, which also approved aid to Air France (*Agence Europe*, 26 July 1991, 21 November 1991). Nor are such air programmes likely to be the last for publicly owned flag carriers in the Community.

Such a pattern of events, combined with the consolidation of the industry (often involving the purchase of stakes in smaller operators by flag carriers), threatens the development of competition in the Community ATI. The experi-ence of US deregulations (where all the carriers were privately owned) was of severe bouts of bankruptcies and mergers. In the European framework the process of rationalization might involve private airlines disappearing and publicly owned ones surviving. It is scarcely surprising, therefore, that the largest private airline in the Community, British Airways, has complained that a deregulated European market will be rigged against it.

What can the Commission do in these circumstances? From the time of the Second Memorandum it made clear that it thought state assistance to airlines and state ownership of carriers could be a problem, fearing that deregulation would only result in a subsidy race unless it was controlled. However, so far its proposals for controlling state assistance have been rather weak as witnessed in these recent cases. Until a coherent policy towards state ownership and state aids is developed there is a risk that liberalization will prove to be ineffective.

CONCLUSIONS

This chapter has sought to identify some ways in which ownership may become a problem which the European Community will have to tackle, despite its formal indifference to the issue. Many of these difficulties were envisaged in the early days of the Community and a number have been addressed, notably in the area of state monopolies and to some extent state aids to public firms. Other more fundamental problems, focusing on the interaction of state-owned and private companies in markets, were left unresolved and largely dormant for the first thirty years of the EC. Now as the process of making a truly Common Market unfolds, and as policies of privatization and deregulation are carried out in some – but not all – member states, those tensions are becoming more apparent.

This is particularly true for the utility industries, given their special characteristics. The scope for subsidy between government and enterprises are for cross subsidy within the enterprise is considerable, particularly given the opaqueness of the industries involved. The capital intensiveness of the sector means that the relationship between their performance and such issues as terms of access to capital are also important. How can the Commission encourage trade and competition in markets where there are both state utilities using low discount rates and private utilities with much tougher profitability requirements and risk exposure? Moreover, there may well be more fundamental 'distortions' revolving around the issue of ownership, most importantly the strategic advantages conferred by government ownership. It is likely that tackling the myriad of distortions and ensuring transparency will, if successful, almost certainly reveal major imbalances in treatment between governments and enterprises and particularly between public and private enterprises. Many of these imbalances are likely to focus on questions of structure and ownership, not least the fact of public ownership. How these sectors can be opened up and the imbalances addressed is likely to present the Commission with a difficult task.

In many cases these questions may transcend ownership issues. They may revolve round the question of specific characteristics of national industries – German private utilities do not behave like UK private utilities – but the more general factors of ownership and the organizing principles of the market are likely to be of considerable importance. Where divergences in national treatment 'converge' in liberalized markets, reconciling the differences will be difficult.

The chapter has indicated some of the ways in which the Commission will be able to tackle these difficulties. Accountancy transparencies, obligations to provide access in certain market segments, and strict controls on the types of investment arrangements are all instruments which potentially the Commission could apply. But, quite apart from the political and practical difficulties of implementing these measures, will they not be seen as constraining the ability of utilities to reap full economies and of governments to manage their own economic development? There is a risk that in meeting the obligations to the market place, the broader objectives of utilities and governments may be sacrificed by the Commission's decisions on how such publicly owned firms are allowed to operate. (A similar point is made on more general terms in Monnier 1990.)

To a great extent, therefore, the autonomy of governments in terms of overall economic strategy may well be eroded. This is an inevitable concomitant of greater interdependence in a Single Market, but it does come close to the heart of the abilities of governments to choose the ownership characteristics of their industries. In such circumstances, it would be surprising if governments accepted such developments lying down (and the evidence from the article 90 cases is that they will not). In the manner of increased resort to non-tariff barriers post-trade liberalization, this may prompt governments to look to subterfuges to retain some control and influence. From the Community's point of view it would therefore be better to indicate that these issues will be dealt with in a coherent policy and thereby restrict the scope for such policies.

Of course, it may be that the issue will not become a sticking point. There are a number of cases of state firms and private firms coexisting and competing in international markets: tensions exist but they are not insurmountable. Perhaps the same coexistence will be possible in deregulated utility industries. This begs the question of how far actual competition takes place in such markets; some have suggested (though not proved) that it may be more likely that private and public firms will opt for cartel-like behaviour (Vernon 1981).

Nor is it clear how the Commission will react to developments, particularly where firms' or utilities' operations are put at risk. The political costs of bankruptcy (let alone being seen to preside over it) may be too high for the Commission. It may be that the experience of the airline industry (and of a number of manufacturing industries) will be the norm; the Commission's bark on aid to public firms may be worse than its bite.

Besides, the apparent logic of deregulation and privatization may lose its momentum: the pendulum may be swinging away from market solutions and the diminution of state responsibilities. If so, the rationale for a debate on increasing scrutiny of state enterprises might evaporate. At the moment, it is too early to say whether this will happen. One possibility is a potentially more conflictual phase where some countries seek to defend their sovereignty, both against other countries seeking greater liberalization and the Commission desperately trying to level the playing field. This is probably more likely than a *de facto* privatization of such enterprises under the purview of the Commission.

This chapter has reviewed the development of public ownership and the attitude of the Commission. It has argued that, despite formal disengagement from the issue, there is an inevitable interaction between the rules of the European Community (particularly after the Single Market) and the character of ownership and the conduct of firms. Part of the motivation for this comes from the formal provisions of Community treaties but more recently it is a by-product of changes in specific markets and of broader EC policies for reform in those sectors. The aim of the chapter has not been to argue against public ownership nor even public ownership in competitive economic sectors (as distinct from monopolistic or socially based concerns); rather it has sought to point out the existing and potential difficulties which may emerge as the Community policies restructure such industries in isolation from ownership concerns.

NOTES

1   While this literature often offers a critical account of the record of public enterprise, there is no presumption that the system is inherently flawed.
2   A good summary of the performance debate is given in Millward (1982). Estrin and Perotin (1991) provide interesting insights into the way in which the relationships between 'management' and 'shareholders' in private and public firms also affect performance.
3   Such cases are regularly dealt with in the Commission's Annual Reports on Competition Policy.
4   Over the last few years there has been a body of research conducted for the Commission on issues such as the extent to which state shareholdings can be regarded as a form of state aid. See Belcredi et al. (1988) and Bhaskar (1990).
5   The debate on air transport reform has taken place since the earliest days of the Community but most efforts failed to get off the ground, as in the case of energy and electricity. See McGowan and Trengove (1986).

BIBLIOGRAPHY

Belcredi, M., Caprio, L. and Ranci, P. (1988) *The Aid Element in State Participation to Company Capital*, Report to the Commission, Luxembourg: Office for Official Publications of the European Community.
Bhaskar, K. (1990) *The Effect of Different State Aid Measurers on Inter-Country Competition*, Report to the Commission, Luxembourg: Office for Official Publications of the European Community.
Bouttes, J. P. and Lederer, P. (1990) 'The organization of electricity systems and the behaviour of players in Europe and the US', Paper to the CEPRIM Conference on Organizing and Regulating Electricity Systems in the Nineties, Paris.
Commission of the European Communities (1979) *Annual Report of Competition Policy*, Luxembourg: Office for Official Publications of the European Community.
—— (1980) Commission Directive 80/723/EEC of 25 June 1980 on the transparency of financial relations between Member States and public undertakings, *Official Journal*, L195, 29 July.
—— (1984) *Progress Towards the Development of a Community Air Transport Policy*, Civil Aviation Memorandum No. 2, Brussels: Commission of the European Communities, COM(84) 72.
—— (1985) Commission Directive, 85/413/EEC of 24 July 1985 amending Directive 80/723/EEC on the transparency of financial relations between Member States and public undertakings, *Official Journal*, L229, 28 August.
—— (1988) *An Internal Market for Energy*. Brussels: Commission of the European Communities, COM(88) 234.
—— (1989) *Survey of State Aids*, Luxembourg: Office for Official Publications of the European Community.
—— (1990) *Second Survey of State Aids*, Luxembourg: Office for Official Publications of the European Community.
Council of the European Communities (1990) Council Directive of 29 October 1990 on the transit of electricity through transmission grids (90/547/EEC).

Department of Energy (1988) *Privatising Electricity*, London: HMSO.

Deringer, A. (1964) 'The interpretation of article 90(2) of the EEC Treaty', *Common Market Law Review* 2(2), 129–38.

Estrin, S. and Perotin, V. (1991) 'Does ownership always matter?', *International Journal of Industrial Organisation* 9(1), 55–72.

Finon, D. (1990) 'Opening access to European grids – in search of common ground', *Energy Policy* 18(5), 480 *ff.*

Gidwitz, B. (1980) *The Politics of International Air Transport*, Lexington, Massachusetts: Lexington Books.

Hancher, L. and Slot, P. (1990) 'Article 90', *European Competition Law Review* 11(1), 35–9.

Holland, S. (1972) *The State as Entrepreneur; New Dimensions for Public Enterprise*, London: Weidenfeld & Nicolson.

ITA (1988) *Airline Privatisation in Europe*, Paris: ITA.

Kay, J. A. and Thompson, D. J. (1986) 'Privatisation: a policy in search of a rationale', *Economic Journal* 96(1), 18–32.

Lange, O. (1938) *On the Economic Theory of Socialism*, Minneapolis, Minnesota: Minnesota University Press.

Lehner, S. and Meiklejohn, R. (1991) 'Fair competition in the internal market: Community state aid policy', *European Economy*, no. 48, 7–49.

McGowan, F. and Trengove, C. (1986) *European Aviation – A Common Market?*, London: IFS.

—— and Mansell, R. (1992) 'EC utilities: a regime in transition', *Futures*, 24(1), 65–82.

Marenco, G. (1983) 'Public sector and Community law', *Common Market Law Review* 20(3), 495–527.

Millward, R. (1982) 'The comparative performance of public and private ownership' in E. Roll (ed.), *The Mixed Economy*, London: Macmillan.

Monnier, L. (1990) 'Prospective de l'Entreprise Publique dans le Marche Unique', *Annals of Public and Cooperative Economy* 61(1), 9–23.

Papaconstantinou, H. (1988) *Free Trade and Competition in the EEC*, London: Macmillan.

Pappalardo, A. (1991) 'State measures and public undertakings: article 90 of the EEC Treaty revised', *European Competition Law Review* 12(1), 29–39.

Platteau, K. (1991) 'Article 90 EEC Treaty after the court judgement in the telecommunications (1991) terminal equipment case', *European Competition Law Review* 12(3), 108–12.

Rees, R. (1984) *Public Enterprise Economics*, London: Weidenfeld & Nicolson.

Schindler, P. (1970) 'Public enterprises and the EEC Treaty', *Common Market Law Review* 7(1), 56–71.

Sikorsky, D. (1986) 'Public enterprise (PE): how is it different from the private sector', *Annals of Public and Cooperative Economy* 57(4), 477–511.

Veljanowski, C. (1987) *Selling the State*, London: Weidenfeld & Nicolson.

Vernon, R. (1981) 'Introduction', in R. Vernon and Y. Aharoni (eds), *State-Owned Enterprises in Western Economies*, London, Croom Helm.

Vickers, J. and Yarrow, G. (1988) *Privatisation – An Economic Analysis*, Cambridge: MIT.

—— —— (1991) 'The British electricity experiment', *Economic Policy*, no. 12 (April), 187–231.

Part II

MARKET STRUCTURE AND REGULATION

5

REGULATING THE PRIVATIZED ELECTRICITY UTILITIES IN THE UK

Thomas G. Weyman-Jones

INTRODUCTION

The privatization of the previously state-owned public utilities in the UK has been proceeding for several years, but the largest of these privatizations, and the most complex in terms of the regulatory framework, is one of the most recent. This is the privatization of the electricity supply industry in the UK.

The evolution of the regulations for electricity supply is the most controversial aspect of the privatization, and forms the core of this chapter. These regulations are likely to serve as one possible model for deregulating the supply of electricity in the rest of the European Community (EC), and they therefore have international implications.

This chapter is structured as follows. It begins by setting out the structure of the industry before and after privatization. This is followed by an examination of the different economic models of regulation which have been suggested in recent years and their influence on the construction of the UK regulatory framework. The third section considers the regulatory instruments used in practice, and four are highlighted: the pool auction, new entry and access, RPI$-X$ price-capping, and yardstick competition. Fourth, the implications of price-capping are considered in detail. The fifth section considers the question of regulatory review of the X-factor in the price-cap. Finally, some conclusions are drawn about the progress of the privatized industry so far and the role of the regulator.

STRUCTURE OF UK ELECTRICITY SUPPLY

The electricity supply industry in the UK is a complex organization, and we should first distinguish between the industry in England and Wales with about 52,000 megawatts (MW) of capacity prior to privatization, and the industry in Scotland with about 10,000 MW of capacity before privatization. This chapter concentrates on the industry in England and Wales for two reasons: its structure as well as its ownership has changed significantly in the privatization programme, while the industry in Scotland remains structurally unchanged

93

despite the change of ownership, and, in addition, the regulatory framework is likely to be a much greater instrument of change in the larger system in England and Wales.

Before considering these changes in detail, it is critical to understand what the term 'privatization' means in the UK economy. Privatization is defined as the sale to the general public of shares (equity) in at least 50 per cent of the assets and earning power of previously nationalized or state-owned public corporations. The government may, and does in fact, retain ownership of large fractions of the industry, though it may offer these for sale in instalments at later dates, as is currently the case with British Telecommunications.

Privatization is not synonymous with deregulation or market liberalization. Deregulation means the removal or loosening of government restrictions on pricing, output and investment decisions of both public and private industries. For example, independent television has been *deregulated* by the removal of the quality of programme content as a condition for obtaining a broadcasting franchise, and its replacement by a highest bidder auction. The supply of many public services in the fields of health and education have been *liberalized* by allowing private companies to compete for the contracts previously limited to publicly owned bodies. On the other hand, some nationalized industries – for example, British Gas – have been privatized with a framework of new regulations, and without any market liberalization in the form of competitive new entrants to the marketplace. The essence of privatization remains the change of ownership, but in the case of electricity supply in England and Wales this has been accompanied by a change in the regulations relating to pricing and quality of supply, and by a liberalization in the encouragement of new entrants, and the removal of previous barriers to entry at different stages of the output process.

Figures 5.1 and 5.2 illustrate the industry in England and Wales before and

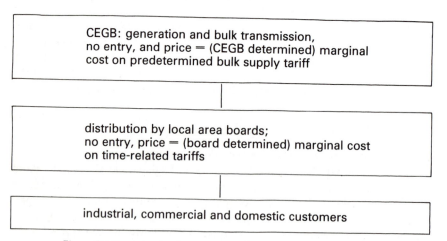

Figure 5.1 Pre-privatization structure of the UK electricity industry

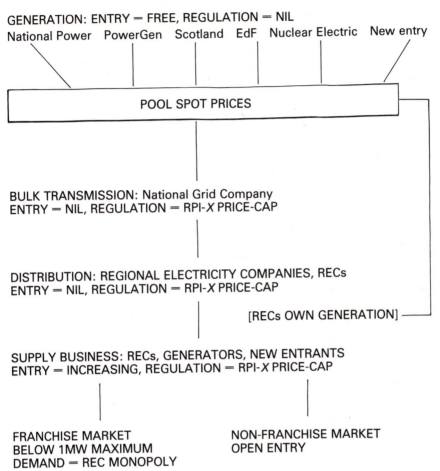

GENERATION: ENTRY = FREE, REGULATION = NIL
National Power   PowerGen   Scotland   EdF   Nuclear Electric   New entry

POOL SPOT PRICES

BULK TRANSMISSION: National Grid Company
ENTRY = NIL, REGULATION = RPI-*X* PRICE-CAP

DISTRIBUTION: REGIONAL ELECTRICITY COMPANIES, RECs
ENTRY = NIL, REGULATION = RPI-*X* PRICE-CAP

[RECs OWN GENERATION]

SUPPLY BUSINESS: RECs, GENERATORS, NEW ENTRANTS
ENTRY = INCREASING, REGULATION = RPI-*X* PRICE-CAP

FRANCHISE MARKET   NON-FRANCHISE MARKET
BELOW 1MW MAXIMUM   OPEN ENTRY
DEMAND = REC MONOPOLY

Figure 5.2 Privatized structure of the UK electricity industry

after privatization. The thirteen nationalized corporations (Central Electricity Generating Board (CEGB) and the twelve area electricity boards), have been replaced by fifteen privatized companies, and one nationalized corporation, Nuclear Electric.

However, the restructuring goes much deeper than a simple change of ownership, since a completely new pattern of horizontal relationships has replaced the vertically organized pre-privatization structure. Prior to privatization there was a single monopoly (the CEGB), responsible for all generation and bulk transmission of electricity at high voltage. This corporation had the statutory responsibility for maintaining the system's reliability – that is, freedom from blackout, brownout, or other interruptions to supply. Consequently, it dominated the demand forecasting and investment decisions of the whole industry. The twelve local low-voltage-distribution corporations largely behaved as passive conduits of CEGB initiatives.

The CEGB, as well as the distribution boards, was instructed to set prices proportional to marginal cost, but since the CEGB possessed a monopoly of cost information this amounted to a cost-plus contract. The inevitable inefficiency manifested itself in two ways: an excessively reliable system in which interruption costs were not evaluated, and an investment programme that was heavily pro-nuclear and nationalistic in its technology choice. This inefficiency was further compounded by the use of a risk-free social discount rate which grossly underestimated the private capital market's opportunity cost of capital for long-lived high-risk projects. Finally, in the absence of competitive information sources, the CEGB appeared to greatly underestimate the costs of decommissioning nuclear power-stations at the end of their active life.

Early in the privatization debate, the idea of opening generation up to competition was widely canvassed, with statistical studies of US generation suggesting that up to ten viable generating companies could be constructed from the CEGB. However, in its initial attempt to privatize existing nuclear power-stations in the privatization programme, the government realized that a significant degree of cross-subsidization would be needed to sell nuclear power to a sceptical private capital market. Consequently it opted for an oligopolistic rather than a competitive structure, and split the CEGB into only two competing companies of unequal size – the larger to carry the uneconomic nuclear component. The capital market remained unconvinced, and nuclear power had to remain in the public sector, but by then it was too late to reorganize the proposed duopoly in generation. Entry into generation is unrestricted, and so is trade with Scotland and Electricité de France, but the size of the duopolists remains a significant barrier to entry.

Transmission and distribution clearly fulfil the conditions of natural monopoly industries, so that competition was never a likely outcome. Instead, these parts of the industry became the focus of regulation and control. In addition, responsibility for system reliability has passed to the new distribution companies; this has implications for the contractual relationships with the generators.

The restructuring of the privatized industry partly resulted from the criticism of the earlier UK privatizations, especially that of British Gas, in which the nationalized monopoly was privatized intact. In the case of British Gas this reflected the bargaining power of the industry in the pre-privatization negotiations.

Generation, now open to unrestricted entry, has been vertically separated from the rest of the industry, and an attempt has been made to establish a competitive spot market. Transmission remains a monopoly in the form of the National Grid Company which acts as a spot-market auctioneer and load despatcher with authority over the operation of generating stations in the spot market.

The National Grid Company's wires are, however, open to common carriage by third parties and a set of regulated prices is published for this service. The regulations are in the form of a price-cap.

The buyers in the pool are the twelve regional electricity companies (RECs), but unlike their nationalized predecessors, the area boards, their activities are separated into two distinct businesses: distribution and supply, with distribution charges being incorporated into supply charges as transfer prices. Both sets of charges are price-capped.

Entry to distribution is not permitted, in order to retain the benefits of non-duplication of the natural monopoly network, but the network wires are also open to common carriage under regulated charges.

All these common carriage provisions are designed to facilitate entry to the supply market where distribution companies, generators, and industrial cogenerators may be in competition for contracts to supply final consumers. Initially the supply market is subdivided into a monopoly franchise and an open sector, but this is scheduled to disappear by 1998.

At each stage of the production process where entry is at least partially restricted – that is, all except generation – there is a regulatory cap on prices and charges.

THE ECONOMICS OF REGULATION

From the time of Adam Smith onwards, economists have operated with a variety of different regulatory models, but there is a primary distinction between positive and normative approaches. Broadly, the positive approach asks how and why do regulators *really* act in practice, while the normative approach asks how *should* regulators act to achieve certain political and economic ends? It is much too early to establish any results in the former positive approach in the privatized UK industries, so our attention is presently confined entirely to the normative approach. This is also the area of most recent theoretical and practical developments, and, in part, these reflect the privatizing–deregulating ethos of the 1980s and 1990s.

An early, and in retrospect naïve, approach which characterized economists' prescriptions for the nationalized industries in the UK and in much of Europe, was based on the search for pricing and investment rules or guidelines which would bring about an optimal allocation of resources in the economists' traditional Pareto-based framework of value judgements. This led to the recommendation to use marginal cost pricing together with investment decision-making using a government-determined, risk-free social discount rate. As described above in the case of the CEGB, this in effect was a cost-plus regulatory framework, which removed the industries' ability to make and keep monopoly profits, but was an invitation to act inefficiently, especially where the industry had a monopoly of information about how costs were determined. This model had been abandoned in all but name by the time of the first Thatcher government in 1979.

97

Following a brief attempt to use cash-limited budgeting on the nationalized industries, emphasis shifted to privatizing the utilities, and this required the construction of a completely new regulatory framework. Concurrently in the US, the traditional rate of return or cost of service regulation of the investor-owned utilities was also being construed as a cost-plus contract (see Joskow and Schmalensee 1986). In this light, considerable attention has been given to the possibility of moving away from cost-plus regulation, and shifting towards some form of incentive-based regulations that would encourage utilities to improve their efficiency.

This shift of emphasis raises two fundamental questions. First, what do we mean by efficiency? Second, how can a regulator provide an efficiency incentive if the utility knows more about the industry's critical cost information than he or she does?

Economists have several different concepts of efficiency, each of which is optimized by the theoretical ideal of perfectly competitive markets without unpriced spillovers or external effects. A primary distinction used by Leibenstein (1966) is that between price efficiency and X-efficiency. Under price efficiency, firms do not have any market power to exploit consumers, and prices are set by competitive forces (or by government instruction) to be equal to marginal costs. Firms appear not to make excessive profits. X-efficiency, however, means that firms, irrespective of their dominance in final markets, act to keep costs as low as possible. It is perfectly possible for firms facing limited competition to appear not to make excessive profits, yet to have inefficiently high costs. This is likely to occur when the firms' managers are not the ultimate owners or shareholders or when firms operate under cost-plus regulations. Both sets of conditions, of course, characterized the nationalized public utilities.

X-efficiency can be further divided into allocative and technical efficiency. Firms which are allocatively inefficient have not used the cheapest production process open to them, while firms which are technically inefficient could produce more output from the set of inputs they have currently adopted. A basic principle is that by leaving the firm's managers some residual claim on the firm's profits, they have an incentive to increase those profits by operating with less X-inefficiency. The opportunity cost is that cost-plus regulatory contracts are abandoned, and so is the ability to confiscate all the profits of a monopoly public utility for the consumer or the Treasury.

For those industries where the perfectly competitive model cannot be roughly applied, there is no escape from this dilemma for the regulator. His or her difficulties are compounded if the utility has an information as well as a market monopoly.

Economists have devised two broad approaches to answering this second difficulty of how to regulate for efficiency when the utility knows more than the regulator. Both adopt what is now called the Principal–Agent Game Theory approach. The principal in the contract is the regulator with some policy objective based on minimizing the welfare losses to society from price and X-

inefficiency. He must devise a regulatory contract which meets two constraints. First the utility must want to participate in the game. This requires that it achieves a minimum level of profit. Hence the UK regulators all have as a basic objective the aim of ensuring that each of the privatized utilities remains financially viable. New entrants to an industry may be allowed to go bankrupt, but privatized incumbents cannot. Without this, the privatization programme would not have got off the ground. The second constraint is one of incentive compatibility: it must be possible for the utility to respond to its regulations in a way that allows it to increase its own profits by altering its behaviour in a way that reveals the unknown information to the regulator. This incentive-compatible revelation will require that the utility receives a reward for giving up its monopoly of information.

Within this broad Game Theory model, economists either assume that the regulator can develop some probabilistic estimators for the missing information, or, alternatively, must rely only on outdated cost and sales information published by the utility.

The first set of assumptions leads to a set of very abstract but insightful policy prescriptions known as Bayesian regulatory theory. Such models can distinguish different types of information asymmetry, such as *moral hazard*, in which the firm needs an incentive to carry out some cost-reducing effort, and *adverse selection*, in which the firm needs some incentive to reveal whether it has access to a low-cost technology. In general, fixed price or residual claimant contracts provide the optimal incentive to meet moral hazard problems, since the firm retains the additional profits of cost-reducing activity – for example, that required to beat a price-cap.

For adverse selection problems, some form of cost-sharing contract is needed as an incentive for the firm not to pretend that it is always a high-cost producer. This works by ensuring that firms are offered a menu of contracts according to the level of cost technology that they report to the regulator. High-cost firms are allowed to share their costs with the regulator – for example, by being allowed high prices in excess of marginal cost – but consequently having low outputs and break-even profits. Optimally designed contracts will ensure that low-cost firms will always choose the low-cost contract that allows for low prices and high outputs, and consequently larger profits. Under an optimal regulatory mechanism, it will never be incentive-compatible for a low-cost firm to opt for a high-cost firm's contract. The nature of the precise menu of contracts offered to the utility depends on which of the two types of problem is dominant, together with the regulator's prior beliefs about the probability distribution of costs, and his or her subjective weights attached to consumer welfare as opposed to managers' incomes. These weights are important because the regulator will wish to trade off efficiency gains against the equity objective of confiscating excess profits. With equal weights, equity is no longer an objective, and the regulator will decentralize all decisions to the firm in a fixed-price residual claimant contract. This literature is surveyed in Besanko and Sappington (1987).

In practice, most economists would argue that the second set of assumptions is a more useful guide to policy-making – that is, the regulator has no prior beliefs about the probability distribution of the firm's costs, but must rely on outdated historical accounting information published by the utility itself. Such non-Bayesian regulatory models have received a huge interest in recent years, particularly from proponents of price-capping regulation. In particular, the non-Bayesian price-capping model forms the cornerstone of the UK approach to regulating the privatized utilities, especially in the field of electricity supply.

REGULATORY INSTRUMENTS IN THE UK ELECTRICITY SUPPLY INDUSTRY

The UK approach to regulation is normally called RPI–X price-capping, but this conceals several complexities. In UK electricity supply, there are at least four primary areas where the regulator takes an especial interest. Briefly these can be characterized as:

- the spot-market pool;
- entry and access to markets;
- RPI–X price-capping;
- yardstick performance.

The pool is a new mechanism in UK electricity supply although it replaces an informal load-scheduling mechanism based on merit ordering of power plant by marginal operating cost that the CEGB used.

Each day the new privatized transmission company, NGC, requests offers to supply load to the system from generators: National Power, PowerGen, EdF, Scotland, Nuclear Electric, and any other private generators who have entered the market. Ranged in ascending order of the offer price, these form the supply schedule for bulk electricity in the pool. Simultaneously, the privatized distribution companies or RECs bid for load at different prices. These bids form the demand schedule. There is, for each half-hour of daily demand, a single market clearing price established by the intersection of the instantaneous supply and demand schedules. This is the system marginal price (SMP).

At times when the system is near to capacity, the NGC can ration demand by adding a peak-related quality of supply premium determined by the probability of excess demand (loss of load probability, LOLP), and the predetermined opportunity cost of interrupted load (value of lost load, VOLL). The latter is currently set at 35–40 times the average daytime price of electricity. This gives the following result for the pool price of electricity load at any given half-hour:

$$P = SMP + LOLP[VOLL - SMP]$$

In a competitive market such a market clearing price is equal to both the marginal opportunity cost of supply in any period and the marginal willingness to pay for the last unit consumed. The quality of supply premium added at peak periods is a signal of the marginal willingness to pay for new capacity, and is designed to cover the capital costs of generation. Note that this spot-pricing mechanism still implies significant regulatory intervention because of the centrally imposed figure for the value of lost load. It would appear, therefore, to be an ideal pricing mechanism, superior to the old Bulk Supply Tariff which was preset one year ahead and open to manipulation by the monopolistic CEGB.

However, this optimistic inference ignores the fact that there is effectively a duopoly on the supply side. Were the duopolists to recognize their market power they could gain by strategically limiting the offers to supply load at any time. The duopolists do not set price, this is done by the NGC auctioneer. However, by recognizing their individual market power, each duopolist will only bid capacity in such a way that the NGC's clearing price corresponds to that at which, after taking into account the probable supply of the other, marginal revenue for each equals marginal cost. Green and Newbery (1991) have simulated a similar model. This suggests that even without explicit collusion, the duopolists, by establishing a Nash equilibrium in supply schedules which take account of the other's reaction and the market power of each of them, could raise price above marginal cost by about 50 per cent, unless significantly deterred by the threat of punitive regulation or new entry. Since regulation is concentrated on the transmission and distribution functions, and there are significant barriers to entry in the way the industry has been privatized, it may appear that the government has significantly overestimated the benefits of the current structure of the privatized generation of electricity. The simulated welfare losses associated with the duopoly largely disappeared when the Green and Newbery simulations allowed for a non-competitive outcome with five producers.

The possibility of encouraging entry to generation remains one of the regulator's other policy instruments. It is a little too early yet to conclude on the likely possibilities here. Several private generation projects are under consideration or approaching fruition, but the bulk market power of the incumbent generators remains very large, and further divesting of generation assets into smaller companies remains a possible policy option for the future. In addition, Vickers and Yarrow (1991) point out that strengthening the national grid can provide an unpriced social benefit ('pro-competitive externality'), by reducing the costs for new entrants to generation. The regulator will therefore need to consider the detailed investment and line reinforcement decisions of the National Grid Company as well as its charges.

PRICE-CAPPING

The best-known regulatory instrument in the UK economy is RPI−X price-capping. RPI is the Retail Price Index or consumer price index for the UK economy, and its role in the formula is to focus our attention on prices in real terms. This is a policy instrument that has been in operation in all of the privatizations since 1984, and its use raises several important economic questions:

- What incentives does it offer to efficiency?
- Can it lead to excessive profits?
- What is its impact on quality of supply?
- How is X determined and reviewed?
- How does it differ from rate of return regulation?

The essential principles of any price-capping mechanism are quite simple. In general, the industries in question are multiproduct in nature – in other words the output has many dimensions. In the case of electricity, a single output unit, 1 kilowatt hour, differs by time of day, season of the year, class of consumer, and place of consumption. Each separate category has an impact on the marginal cost incurred and the price elasticity of demand, and consequently a large range of unit prices is determined by the different supply and demand characteristics of each of the many markets in which any particular electricity utility is involved.

The utility will therefore have a large range of prices or tariffs: $[p_1, \ldots, p_n]$. The regulatory mechanism allows the utility to choose the optimal structure of these multiproduct prices itself and, to maximize profits, it can determine them on the basis of the individual product elasticities of demand while removing any cross-subsidization that was implicit in the pre-privatization guidelines. All of the privatized utilities have used this freedom to rebalance their price structures after privatization. The price-cap refers to an index of these prices, and its change from year to year. For example, the price-cap will isolate a particular basket of the utility's products and identify a quantity weighted index of those prices:

$$P = \Sigma q_i p_i.$$

The price-cap mechanism then requires that this index should change in a pre-determined pattern from year to year.

One initial suggestion for a regulatory price-cap mechanism that has attracted much interest amongst economists is that of Vogelsang and Finsinger [V–F] (see Vogelsang 1990). In order to capture a natural monopoly's economic rents or excess profits when the utility has an information monopoly, V–F suggest that the price index, using the quantity weights from the base year, should fall each year in real terms by the previous year's ratio of profits to turnover. In the absence of inflation this gives:

$$P_t/P_{t-1} = 1 - [\text{profits/turnover}]_{t-1}.$$

There are two principal arguments for the V–F mechanism. First, its information requirements are very low: it only needs historical accounting information published by the utility. Second, it improves consumer welfare in a simple mechanistic way. Since prices on average are being held at the previous year's published costs, a natural monopoly utility with decreasing unit costs will attempt to increase profits under the price ceiling by expanding output. But since output expansion at fixed prices increases consumer satisfaction, the mechanism moves the utility in the direction of a (second best) Pareto optimal allocation of resources.

The principal argument against the mechanism is that since it confiscates all of the utility's previous profits one year later, the utility has an incentive to engage in strategic behaviour. By wasting resources, and incurring extra costs this year, it can raise the ceiling on next year's prices, and profits. Unless its discount rate is very high, this trade-off may well be worth while for the utility. This returns us in a different way to the efficiency dilemma that arose under marginal cost pricing guidelines in nationalized industries.

The RPI$-X$ mechanism suggested by Littlechild for the UK privatizations proceeds differently (Beesley and Littlechild 1989). In the absence of inflation the utility's price index must fall by a fixed amount, X, each year:

$$P_t/P_{t-1} = 1 - X$$

Rather than confiscate all of a utility's profits, this is a fixed price contract that allows the utility to keep the profits from any cost reductions in excess of X which it can achieve in any given year. It is clearly directed at the problem of X-inefficiency, unlike the V–F mechanism whose focus is price efficiency.

The arguments for and against the mechanism have already made themselves very clear in practice. There is a strong incentive to rebalance the structure of prices to remove cross-subsidization, and to reduce costs to increase profits. Both features have characterized the privatized utilities. However, there is only a weak attempt to capture monopoly profits, and all of the industries have shown startling profits growth following privatization. This has led to misplaced calls to require the industries reporting large profits to reduce prices to the consumer. Such calls simply amount to a form of retrospective V–F mechanism, and if taken seriously would simply lead the utilities into strategic wasting of resources and cost increases.

Finally, it is important to note that neither form of price-capping mechanism tests the quality of supply. In trying to move away from a regulatory framework based on legal processes towards a price contract, the privatization programme has largely ignored quality of supply considerations. These are to some extent to be addressed in the future in the recently announced Citizen's Charter, which includes compensation to customers for poor delivery of services; but this clearly is a form of afterthought rather than a central part of the regulatory framework.

The mechanism applies differently in the electricity industry's different markets. Three components of the final weighted price of electricity are outside the control of the transmission and distribution companies; these are the electricity component, E, based on the pool prices, the administrative pool settlement costs, S, and the fossil fuel levy, F. (The last is a subsidy from fossil fuel inputs to nuclear and renewables.)

Three regulated market components remain, each representing a different stage in the supply of electricity, and each with its own separate RPI$-X$

regulatory formula. These give rise to transmission charges, T, distribution charges, U, and supply charges, P_s.

Therefore the final price of electricity is:

$$M = \{P_s + U + T\}^* + [E + S + F]^{**}$$

where * = regulated; ** = unregulated.

The distinction between the different markets in the regulated components is crucial. Clearly, entry to bulk transmission is not permitted since the social costs of duplicating the national grid are too large to be outweighed by the benefits of competition. The regulator is therefore likely to be particularly concerned, not only with the level but also with the structure of access charges to the bulk network since many companies are expected to be involved in wheeling electricity into different final competitive markets.

Similarly, the localized distribution network is a natural monopoly where single firm operation is optimal. Once again access charges for use of the wires by third parties is a critical focus of the regulator's attention. The distribution business of the RECs is, however, separated from their supply business, and the government at least expect strong competitive elements to emerge here.

The supply of electricity essentially consists of the contract between final consumer and supplier in which the supplier delivers electricity which it may have bought from a generator, or from another regional distribution company, or which it may have generated itself. Participants in the supply market therefore include the major independent generators, and all of the regional distribution companies, together with any small localized producers which may emerge in particular areas. They will all use the national and local grids for common carriage, hence the importance of the structure of access charges. Entry to the supply market is to be liberalized in two stages over the period 1991–8, with only those consumers with a maximum demand of less than 100kW remaining under the local REC monopoly after 1994.

Entry conditions to both this market and that of bulk generation are likely to be contentious, and may possibly be the area where legal processes enter the regulatory framework. At present, there are threats and counterthreats amongst rival generators and British Gas over gas price contracts for generation. Any such disputes are in the public domain, as are all of the regulator's actions, and therefore may become the subject of judicial review.

REGULATORY REVIEW AND THE X-FACTOR

Initial determination of the X-factor in the UK privatizations has been largely concerned with establishing the viability of the industries and the marketability of their shares in the initial flotation. However, each industry knows that it faces a review of its X-factor after a, possibly random, number of years.

How is this review determined? Here all of the fundamental questions of regulation are reopened.

Four possibilities have been suggested for setting the revised X-factor:

- the rate of profitability over the previous regulatory period;
- the rate of return on capital over the previous period;
- the regulator's exogenously fixed target for increased efficiency;
- yardstick comparisons of efficiency from other comparable utilities.

The first two suggestions imply a form of cost-plus regulatory review, while the last two are more in the spirit of fixed-price contracts.

For example, X may be determined for the next five years on the basis of the utility's rate of profit over the previous five years. This would give us a form of V–F mechanism with regulatory lag. The regulatory lag (with prices effectively fixed within the five-year period) may be enough to overcome the strategic incentive to waste resources, and allow the regulator to improve price efficiency.

More likely, given the experience with British Telecommunications, is the use of the utility's rate of return on capital to determine X. Many economists – for example, Vickers and Yarrow (1991) – would argue that this is simply US-style rate of return regulation by another name. Beesley and Littlechild (1989), however, have disputed this argument. They acknowledge that where entry is difficult and technology evolves steadily and slowly – for example, in the case of the National Grid Company – then RPI−X will probably reduce to US-style rate of return regulation, though the regulator will also be interested in the structure of prices as well as their level.

However, the regulator seeking to encourage efficiency using a fixed-price contract is expected to take a more proactive role by setting X exogenously on the basis of some target productivity improvement. This could be achieved for example by using the regulatory review procedure to examine the profit opportunities for each utility which may emerge over the future. This means that regulatory review will focus on tariff structure and its entry incentives, on the diversification activities of utilities and the cross-subsidization implications, and on the comparative performance of other utilities.

In this context, yardstick competition can be an effective policy instrument. Initially the draft regulations envisaged that electricity costs would be based on long-term contracts, and that the regulated supply charges would be based for each utility on the average contract terms negotiated by other utilities. This form of automatic yardstick was abandoned in the pre-privatization negotiations. However, empirical studies suggest that prior to privatization there were widespread differences in efficiency between the different distribution corporations. When reviewing each utility's future X-factor, the regulator will want to compare efficiency performance, especially in those areas where objective comparison is possible and collusion on costs is difficult. The comparability issue may be troublesome since the cost performance of a utility may depend on many market characteristics outside its control, and allowing for these may involve the regulator in a large information-gathering and processing exercise – all of which defeats the objective of regulation with a light hand, which was an early purpose of the UK system.

Yardstick competition has a strong appeal as a form of fixed-price contract. For example, if the regulated price is based on the mean unit cost of a group of identical producers, each has a profit incentive to produce below the previous mean unit cost of the group in order to retain the additional profits. This eliminates the moral hazard problem of X-inefficiency. To be incentive-compatible for the utilities, and optimal for the regulator, a detailed cost model of the utilities must be formulated. For example, a utility's unit costs may be determined by the following model:

$$c = f(q_1, \ldots q_n, w_1, \ldots w_n,) + \Sigma \alpha_i S_i + u$$

where the q's are the different outputs produced, the w's are the prices of inputs, the S's are particular variable characteristics that distinguish each utility but are not under its own control, and u is a random error. The appropriate unit cost to be calculated for each utility is $[c - \Sigma \alpha_i S_i]$, and a regression approach based on a sample of the utilities can be used to eliminate random differences between their measured costs.

Establishing such a model is no easy task. If an econometric approach is used the regulator has to determine a particular functional form for the regression model, and adopt a consensus view of the appropriate S characteristics. An alternative that has been used successfully to measure relative efficiencies is some form of non-parametric mathematical programming technique such as data envelopment analysis, but this cannot in general allow for the distinguishing characteristics of each utility. This activity is a primary candidate for the utilities to seek judicial review of the regulator's decisions. Unfortunately, if the regulator is unable to establish that the firms are homogeneous, or that he or she can successfully devise the correct handicapping scheme that accounts for their separate characteristics, then yardstick competition cannot deliver an optimal regulatory policy. The chief conclusion in this area is that fixing an exogenous X-factor at the regulatory review increases rather than reduces the difficulty of the regulatory problem. Fixed-price contracts therefore do not offer as easy a way to establish efficiency improvements as might seem at first sight.

CONCLUSIONS: THE ROLE OF THE REGULATOR

The UK privatization programme has had one consequence not foreseen by its initial advocates who sought market liberalization. That is the emergence of a powerful group of industry regulators. Most of the privatizations, and the electricity industry is no exception, underestimated the complexity of the new market structures which would emerge. In addition most were carried out rather quickly, and with an emphasis on the fund-raising involved in the initial flotation of shares. This has put the regulators in the position of having a powerful and immediate impact on the evolution of the industry. It is difficult to see, for example, how the regulator can forever ignore the duopolistic nature of the generation of electricity, and therefore this liberalized market is likely to see either more regulatory intervention in future or more divestment of the existing firms.

The regulator is likely to face demands for detailed regulation of environmental and energy-saving policies as fears about global warming increase. He or she is also likely to have a major ongoing role as the regulatory review procedure becomes an increasingly important part of the industry's evolution. The initial idea that regulation of the utilities would wither away as competitive forces emerged has turned out to be something of an illusion.

Nevertheless, we can see that a bold experiment has been undertaken, and that a revolutionary new form of regulatory framework is delivering efficiency gains and innovations that were totally absent from the old nationalized industry performance. It is not clear however that the economic issues facing the regulator are any easier to resolve than those which faced the government in the days of the nationalized industries.

REFERENCES

Beesley, M. and Littlechild, S. (1989) 'The regulation of privatized monopolies in the United Kingdom', *Rand Journal of Economics* 20(3), 454–72.

Besanko, D. and Sappington, D. (1987) *Designing Regulatory Policy with Limited Information*, London: Harwood Academic Publishers.

Green, R. and Newbery, D. (1991) 'Competition in the British electricity spot market', *Discussion Paper 557*, London: Centre for Economic Policy Research.

Joskow, P. and Schmalensee, R. (1986) 'Incentive regulation for electric utilities', *Yale Journal on Regulation* 4(1), 1–49.

Leibenstein, H. (1966) 'Allocative efficiency vs. X-efficiency', *American Economic Review*, 56 (June), 392–415.

Vickers, J. and Yarrow, G. (1991) 'The British electricity experiment', *Economic Policy*, no. 12 (April), 187–232.

Vogelsang, I. (1990) *Public Enterprise in Monopolistic and Oligopolistic Industries*, London: Harwood Academic Publishers.

6

PRIVATIZATION AND MARKET STRUCTURE IN THE UK GAS INDUSTRY

Trefor Jones

... the Conservative Party has never believed that the business of government is the government of business.

N. Lawson 1980

INTRODUCTION

Privatization of publicly owned productive enterprises has been a key element in the economic policy portfolio of the Conservative Government in the UK in the 1980s. Such a policy fitted closely with their professed beliefs in the efficacy of markets and private ownership compared to the failures of government resource allocation and state ownership (see Wolf 1990 for a critique). The process of privatization, however, is not always complementary to the promotion of competition. Indeed, it might be argued that in the UK, the method and execution of privatization positively hindered the development of competitive market structures in a number of cases. This resulted from the emphasis of policy upon changing ownership for reasons other than the promotion of competitive markets, which might have led to greater gains in both allocative and productive efficiency than were actually achieved. Thus, publicly owned monopolies become privately owned monopolies thereby depriving the economy of many of the claimed benefits of private ownership, which are dependent upon the presence of competition in the product market.

The proponents of privatization argue that the change from public to private ownership will bring about improvements in both productive and allocative efficiency. These will be achieved in two ways. First, the private ownership of enterprises would make them more efficient organizations in that they would achieve lower costs per unit of output than as public sector enterprises. This is thought to be the consequence of their private owners following more specific goals – for example, profit unconstrained by social concerns, and the processes and disciplines of the capital market which allow inefficient firms to be taken over. The latter process involves private shareholders selling their shares in the company to someone prepared to offer a higher price in the belief that they would be able to make better use of the assets of the enterprise. Public enterprises are, however, largely immunized from the consequences of competition and the fear of bankruptcy (see Dunsire *et al.* 1991). Second, privatization presents opportunities for restructuring industries to create competitive market structures by breaking up existing state-owned firms into smaller-sized enterprises, and by removing entry barriers to allow new entry competition.

The extent to which the twin aims of promoting private ownership and competition can be simultaneously achieved depends upon the role of other government objectives in influencing the nature of the privatization programme. The UK government were keen to balance the government budget, to lower income tax rates and promote wider ownership of shares. Receipts from the privatization of enterprises became an important source of marginal revenue so that maximizing the capital market valuation of a privatized company became a major concern, modified only by the desire to ensure the successful sale of the shares. However, maximizing revenue and the introduction of competition are in some sense opposites because the more monopolistic the position of a company in a market the higher its potential profits and the higher the receipts from the sale of the enterprise. The break-up of an enterprise or the encouragement of entry would generate greater uncertainty about future potential profits and lower the level of revenue realized.

The experience of British Gas illustrates these difficulties. It was moved from the public to the private sector unchanged as an organization accompanied by limited changes in the business environment. It was granted a monopoly of supply for domestic customers but the possibility of competition evolving was allowed for in the industrial market where potential entrants were given the right to use the company's pipeline system to access customers. Competition has evolved very slowly and British Gas has been accused of restricting the growth of competition by its pricing and operational tactics which have discouraged entry. Five years after privatization, the company now faces a period of considerable uncertainty as the competition authorities press for changes in the way the company conducts its business and for its possible break-up to encourage competition to develop at a faster pace. The objective of this chapter, therefore, is to examine the consequences of these conflicts in policy upon the subsequent market structures and regulatory problems that have arisen following the privatization of British Gas.

MARKET STRUCTURE AND PRIVATIZATION

Privatization of state monopolies presents a unique opportunity to shape the future market structure of an industry. The typical pattern of public ownership in the UK was an institutional monopoly for each industry irrespective of its underlying structural characteristics. Thus, the National Coal Board (now British Coal) was given a virtual monopoly of coal production despite the fragmented nature of the production process which would have allowed a large number of competing enterprises. In other sectors, for example, electricity, gas, telephones, water, and rail, where integrated networks are operated and duplication of facilities is considered wasteful, public monopolies were established in the belief that in part a publicly owned enterprise is a better solution to the monopoly problem than a privately owned one (see Parker 1989).

The privatization of publicly owned enterprises holding statutory monopolies immediately leads to questions as to whether the subsequent market structure can or cannot be made competitive. If an enterprise is returned to the private sector as a profit-maximizing monopolist, then according to economic theory it would be expected to have positive consequences for the productive efficiency of the enterprise but to have adverse consequences for allocative efficiency, whereas public enterprises, it might be argued, are better for allocative efficiency (they are encouraged to pursue marginal cost pricing) but less good for productive efficiency. Many studies have been made comparing the performance of public and private enterprise but the results are indecisive in that private enterprise is not invariably more efficient than public enterprise; more significant may be the environment and constraints within which they both operate (Millward 1982, Millward and Parker 1983, Wolf 1990).

If monopoly public enterprises can be broken up to create a number of competitive enterprises then competitive forces, threats of take-over, bankruptcy, and profit-maximizing behaviour on the part of the firms will encourage both allocative and productive efficiency. If monopoly public enterprises cannot be broken up into competitive enterprises, then the absence of enterprise restructuring from a privatization programme is likely to be a major cause for concern. Thus, a privatization programme needs to face not only the problem of how to privatize companies but also the question of the subsequent market structure. In the UK, for example, in the privatization of gas supply this problem was ignored, while in others, most notably electricity, it was tackled.

The potential relationships between ownership and market structure were explored by Kay and Thompson (1986). For ownership the following questions were asked:

- Can the firm go bankrupt?
- Can the firm be taken over?

and for product market structures:

- Are there incentives to allocative efficiency?
- Are there incentives to productive efficiency?

The answers to all these questions in the benchmark model of perfect competition is 'yes', and in addition allocative and productive efficiency are maximized to achieve a Pareto optimal position. For public enterprises the answers to the first two questions are generally 'no' in that they cannot be taken over or go bankrupt without government permission, whereas for private firms the answers are 'yes' because they can go bankrupt and be taken over, though the large size of some firms may make them virtually immune to the take-over process. In terms of the incentives provided by market structures, it might be argued that as these increase for both public and private firms the more competitive the market, which is generally considered to be a positive function of the number of firms. However, the development of contestable market theory (Baumol *et al.* 1982) has placed the emphasis not so much upon the present number of participants in a market but more upon the threat of potential entry and its impact upon firm behaviour, and the limits it places upon the exploitation of a monopolistic position since excessive profits and/or high costs of production will encourage entry.

The above analysis (summarized in Table 6.1) suggests that the privatization of a state enterprise, which generates a market structure without more than one significant competitor, greatly weakens the economic case for privatization. Generally, the more competitive a sector the greater are the expected benefits.

Markets can also be classified by ownership and number of enterprises. Table 6.2 presents such a schema. Thus, the typical position for a UK public enterprise prior to privatization, assuming a narrow definition of the market, would be in cell E with no private competition. The preferred move in terms of a policy of privatization aiming to increase economic welfare would be, if feasible, a move from cell E to cell D, combining ownership and market structure changes

Table 6.1 Ownership and market structure

Ownership	Monopoly		Competition	
	Public	Private	Public	Private
Can firm go bankrupt?	No	Yes	No	Yes
Can firm be taken over?	No	No	No	Yes
Are their incentives to:				
Allocative efficiency?	?	No	Yes	Yes
Productive efficiency?	No	No	No	Yes

Source: Based on J. A. Kay and D. J. Thompson (1986) 'Privatisation: a policy in search of a rationale', *Economic Journal* 96(1), 18–32.

Table 6.2 Market structure and ownership

		Number of private enterprises			
		None	One	Two	Many
Number	None	A	B	C	D
of	One	E	F	G	H
public	Two	I	J	K	L
enterprises	Many	M	N	O	P

with three or more firms competing. The change most open to question is that from cell E to B, the straight switching of a public monopoly to a private one.

How to move from cell E to a competitive market structure with a significant number of privately owned enterprises is the problem to be solved. The choices facing the government were to:

- transfer the public enterprise to the private sector intact but with no initial or expected change in market structure;
- transfer the public enterprise to the private sector intact but remove all legislative barriers to entry so that new firms, other barriers to entry permitting, can enter the market which thus might slowly evolve into a more competitive one;
- accept that monopoly market structures are inevitable but break up the public enterprise – before transfer to the private sector – so that a number of regional monopolies are created and competition by emulation can take place;
- break up the public enterprise before transfer to the private sector so that a number of competitive enterprises are created.

The decisions taken in the UK in relation to privatization, enterprise restructuring and subsequent market structure are summarized in Table 6.3 with more detail given in the Appendix (see p. 123).

In general terms the managements of the state enterprise argue the case for the company to be transferred to the private sector unchanged. The case for breaking up the enterprise and producing a new market structure has to be made by critics of the enterprise. In proposing restructuring considerable attention has to be given to the feasibility of breaking up the enterprise, given the technological nature of the sector which might favour the continuation of a single national operator or at best a small number of regional monopolies. Even where the desire to restructure an industry into a more competitive one is strong, it may still not be feasible. Factors to be considered include whether the technology is changing,

Table 6.3 Privatization: market and enterprise restructuring

Enterprise structure	Domestic market structure		
	Monopoly	*Oligopoly*	*Competition*
Unchanged	Gas	Telecoms	Amersham ports
	Electricity	Airways	
	Regional Co.	Aerospace	
	Scottish Water	Aero engines	
	London Airports		
Changed	Electricity grid	Electricity	Buses
		generation	

Source: Author.

whether the process involves closely linked networks/pipelines that are expensive to duplicate, and whether the market is large enough to support two or more firms of optimal size. Similar factors would have to be considered in terms of whether a market will naturally evolve into a competitive one, together with a consideration of barriers to entry and firm behaviour which may deter entry even where it appears feasible.

Thus, the major activities where no attempts were made to alter the market structure were in gas, London airports, water and regional electricity. In telecommunications, the duopoly policy introduced some competition in long distance telephone calls but left local calls as a monopoly. The performance of these companies and their regulatory regimes have been subject to considerable criticism. Foreman-Peck and Manning, for example, argue on the basis of a comparison of the performance of BT and European companies that BT should have been broken up since 'smaller telecom organisations appear to be more productive than larger ones, and networks that have private equity capital do not invariably perform better than state owned enterprises. Privatisation as such is apparently no panacea, as yet' (Foreman-Peck and Manning 1988: 54). The system seems to have promoted the well-being of BT and Mercury rather than the promotion of competition.

THE PRIVATIZATION OF BRITISH GAS

The pre-privatized gas industry in the UK could be divided into two parts: the production and the distribution of natural gas. Natural gas was produced in the North Sea by a number of consortia generally involving one or more major oil companies. All gas produced was sold to the UK or, to be more precise, to the state-owned British Gas Corporation (BGC) which then distributed it through its own pipeline network to regional divisions which then sold the gas to domestic, commercial and industrial consumers. The distribution of gas is considered to be a natural monopoly in that duplication of distribution facilities is an inefficient use of resources and makes monopoly the lowest cost option. Some attempt at liberalizing the gas industry was made through the Oil and Gas (Enterprise) Act of 1982 which ended BGC's statutory monopsony, although all gas still had to be delivered to the UK, and allowed the Secretary of State to give permission to other companies to use BGC's pipelines to transport gas to customers purchasing at least 25,000 therms. These changes had little or no impact upon the dominant position of British Gas (Vickers and Yarrow 1988a: 345–81).

The British Gas Corporation was privatized as a single entity in November 1986 and as a monopsonistic buyer of natural gas, a monopolistic supplier of gas to the UK market, and a dominant retailer of gas appliances. British Gas (BG) is also a dominant player in the broader energy market and at the time of privatization it was estimated to control some 60 per cent of the domestic energy market, 75 per cent in areas where gas is available, and 36 per cent of the industrial market (Price and Gibson 1989: 162).

The argument for transferring the corporation to the private sector intact was put strongly by the then chairman Sir Dennis Rooke on the basis that to break up a successful organization would be destructive, that its integrated operations were able to offer a high degree of security of supply, and an efficient and low cost distribution system as a result of economies of scale. These arguments were accepted by the government and the then Secretary of State for Energy, Peter Walker, who is reported to have said: 'I decided the breaking up of the corporation was lunacy ... for ... I wanted a powerful British company that would compete around the world.' In addition the government also wished to obtain as high a price as possible for the shares subject to a successful sale. It was felt that purchasers would be happier to buy shares in a company with a record rather than create uncertainty by restructuring the enterprise. The flotation was successful. The price per share was set at 135p with a first instalment of 50p. At the end of day 1 the price was 68p, a capital gain of 36 per cent. The sale raised £5.6 billion, and overall the issue was oversubscribed by four times and under-valued by £500 million.

The decision not to take the opportunity to restructure BGC was criticized by Hammond *et al.* (1985) who argued that the gas industry in its nationalized form was characterized by allocative inefficiency in its charging policies and by productive inefficiency, and that improved performance would depend less on a change in ownership and more on the structure of the privatized industry.

The consequence of the government's decision was that a state monopoly enterprise was transferred to the private sector accompanied by no initial change in market structure, a limited amount of liberalization and a significant change in the regulatory regime. Unfortunately, monopolies do not change their nature merely as a result of a change in ownership, given that the existing management remains in place. Gabb (1989) has argued that British Gas had shown few signs of an effective metamorphosis from slow-moving monopolistic utility to fleet-footed operator in the private sector. In a similar vein Price and Gibson comment that, 'The impression was sometimes given by staff that the corporation could do no wrong, that its interest and the public interest were necessarily synonymous' (Price and Gibson 1989: 162). They also argue that the most important criticism of the privatization of gas was that no attempt was made to alter the industry's structure or to effectively liberalize its operating conditions. Thus, the expectation in terms of the relationships set out in Table 6.1 would be for the sector to become less efficient in allocative terms as the private monopoly would make greater use of its market power than when state owned, and for improvements in productive efficiency to be small because of the absence of product market competition and take-over threats. Therefore, unless a strong regulatory regime could be established to counter the absence of competition, it would seem that the government were expecting British Gas not to behave as the monopolist it had become – serving the interests of its shareholders – but to be public-spirited and forgo the use of market power.

REGULATORY CHANGE AND PRIVATIZA`

Under nationalization the corporation was subject to overall
sponsoring department who set financial and performance ta
control over price levels. There was a considerable political
behaviour of nationalized industries so that in a number of ye
1980s, for example, gas price increases were announced by the Chancellor of the
Exchequer in his budget speech.

Following privatization, a new regulatory regime was established. It involved
granting to British Gas (BG) a licence or authorization to be a public gas supplier
and the establishment of an Office of Gas Regulation (Ofgas) to oversee the
regulatory regime. The regulator may with BG's agreement modify the conditions of its authorization. In addition, Ofgas is responsible for the implementation and oversight of the regulatory regime based on the RPI−X formula and its
adjustment from time to time. If BG is alleged to have abused its monopolistic
position then its regulated activities may be investigated by Ofgas and its non-
regulated activities, which are subject to the general rules of competition policy,
by the Monopolies and Mergers Commission. The RPI−X structure was based
on the recommendations of Littlechild who envisaged such a regime to be of a
temporary nature, saying: 'Regulation is essentially a means of preventing the
worse excesses of monopoly; it is not a substitute for competition. It is a means
of "holding the fort" until competition arrives' (Littlechild 1983: para. 4.1). The
regulatory regime was, therefore, to be of a temporary nature whilst the market
structure evolved to make regulation unnecessary. Therefore, at the time of privatization it is necessary to establish market and regulatory structures conducive to
the development of effective competition − otherwise the notion that the regulatory regime would be of a temporary nature would be misguided.

MARKET STRUCTURE

The privatization of gas followed the conventional wisdom which argues that in
activities characterized by large capital-intensive and industry-specific investments with long lives, the industry will typically consist of a single firm or of a
small number of territorial firms each with its own pipeline network. Where then
in this kind of industry is there room for competition which, critics have argued,
should have been introduced along with privatization? There are at least two
possible approaches. The first is to establish a number of regional companies
each with their own distribution network but with access to North Sea gas
through pipelines jointly owned with gas suppliers or with gas distributors.
Individual gas consumers would have no choice of gas supplier, but the
performances of the separate companies could be compared and alternative
competitive strategies might be adopted by the companies instead of the one all-
pervasive philosophy of a single operator.

The second alternative solution, which avoids duplication of distribution

⹁cilities, is for all pipelines to be compelled to operate as common carriers, thus allowing the possibility of a greater number of natural gas suppliers participating in the distribution industry and for individual gas consumers to have a choice of gas supplier. However, potential entrants must have access not only to potential customers but also to supplies of gas. While the idea is theoretically appealing it raises many practical problems, particularly if the network owner is also a supply competitor. Problems arise in terms of tariffs, point of entry terms, back-up supplies and use of storage. To apply the latter alternative in the UK would require alterations to BGC's licence or the reorganization or break-up of the company.

A combination of these two alternatives was favoured at the time of privatization by Hammond *et al.* (1985), who considered it the most practical alternative structure to a unitary enterprise. They proposed the creation of twelve separate regional distribution companies and a separate grid company which would own and operate the national pipeline and storage system. The advantages of such a system would have been to create twelve competitive buyers of gas instead of one; it would have made the job of regulating the distribution monopolies easier because of the additional information and the ease of making comparisons; the smaller distribution companies would have faced a more realistic threat of take-over, though probably not of bankruptcy; and potential entry would have been easier as a result of all companies having to use an independent pipeline system.

The continued criticisms of the performance of British Gas since privatization have led to a revived interest in the possible alternatives to a single enterprise and alternative ways and means of allowing the market structure to evolve towards a more competitive structure. Some of the reasons for dissatisfaction with the market structure and performance of BG are now explored.

ABUSES OF MARKET POWER

The creation of a monopoly supplier with a regulatory regime only applying to domestic consumers and considered by critics to be 'weak', has led to British Gas being criticized for abusing its monopoly position and to calls for a reappraisal of the structure of the industry. The criticisms have included assertions of:

- discrimination in the setting of prices;
- using its control of the pipeline network to prevent potential competitors from reaching their customers;
- its monopsonistic position in buying natural gas from the North Sea on long-term contracts, backed by the government's unwillingness to allow imports, means little gas is available to potential competitors;
- excessive profits because of the light regulatory regime.

Price discrimination

Being in a dominant position British Gas can operate a number of potential pricing practices that allow it to exploit consumers and also prevent entry of potential competitors. Following complaints about its pricing policy, particularly in the contract market, BG was referred to the Monopolies and Mergers Commission (MMC) in November 1987 by the Director-General of Fair Trading concerning the supply of gas to non-tariff customers – for example, industrial and commercial customers who use more than 25,000 therms of gas per year. These contract customers total only 21,000 compared to some 17 million tariff customers, but they represent 38 per cent of gas sales by volume and 26 per cent by revenue. Some 1,000 contract customers have interruptible contracts, allowing interruptions of supply on up to 63 days with notice of interruption of 2–4 hours; and these represent 37 per cent of contract sales by value and 49 per cent of contract sales by volume (MMC 1988: 11).

In the contract market BG had been given a free hand to set prices, and individual agreements are made with each customer. Both the government and BG argued in evidence to the MMC that there was sufficient competition in the contract market for regulation to be unnecessary, yet BG supplies over one-third of the industrial energy market, and it clearly has substantial monopoly power over parts of the market. BG's policy was to price according to the market circumstances of each customer, thereby expropriating consumer surplus, which leads to wide variations in the prices charged for the same product.

The MMC, however, judged that 'the extensive discrimination in prices of firm gas is attributable to the existence of the monopoly situation since it would not be sustainable if there were competition from other gas suppliers' (MMC 1988: para. 8.37). The reasons given by the MMC for reaching this conclusion were:

- Price discrimination involves charging those customers with the least alternatives higher prices. This imposes arbitrary higher costs on some customers and distorts competition.
- BG relates prices to the alternatives available to each customer. This gives it the power to selectively undercut potential competing gas suppliers which may deter entrants and inhibit the development of competition in the market.
- The lack of transparency in pricing creates uncertainty in the minds of customers about future prices and renders the business environment more risky.

The MMC concluded that BG should publish a schedule of prices at which it is prepared to supply firm and interruptible gas to contract customers and not to discriminate in pricing or supply.

Pipelines and common carrier rules

Earlier it was argued that a competitive market structure in gas may only be feasible where pipeline access is open to a number of gas suppliers. In theory BG's pipelines have been open to use by others since the Oil and Gas (Enterprise) Act 1982 and the Energy Act 1983 made it possible for other suppliers to sell gas to industrial users and provided for such a supplier to have access to BG's distribution system provided the Secretary of State for Energy approved. However, in the pre-privatization period only a few contracts were signed.

To overcome the disappointing response, the Gas Act 1986 set new ground rules for the use of BG's pipelines. Section 3 of the Act removed BG's previously privileged position in that the Secretary of State could authorize other public gas suppliers, and give third parties the right to use gas pipelines subject to the approval of a common carriage tariff. Section 19 of the 1986 Act laid down the principles for charging. Prices must cover an appropriate proportion of the operating, administrative and maintenance costs of the system, as well as a rate of return on the capital value of the system including depreciation equal to the appropriate proportion of the rate earned by BG (Ofgas 1987, MMC 1988: Appendix 3.1).

If the potential user cannot reach an agreement with BG he can apply to the Director-General of Ofgas who may specify terms on which the gas should be transported. Ofgas intervened in the first few cases to impose terms for transmission when BG set prices that would have made it impossible for new entrants to compete with BG. The charge related to replacement cost of the system plus a reasonable rate of return to BG. However, North Sea gas producers who are potential users of BG's pipelines still have to negotiate with a company which is currently the only buyer of its gas. This places the supplier in a difficult negotiating position in terms of exchange of information and BG's reaction in future supply negotiations with that company. The MMC recommended that BG should publish further information on common carriage terms in sufficient detail to put a potential customer in a position to make a reasonable estimate of the charge that would be sought by BG.

In addition the MMC was keen to encourage the availability of gas for sale to the contract market by encouraging new entrants to enter the market. To encourage this the MMC recommended that BG contract initially for no more than 90 per cent of any new gas field, leaving 10 per cent available to others. This would allow competitors to take a small but increasing proportion of the contract market, depending on the growth of the market and the amount of new gas becoming available. This development may proceed more quickly as a result of the privatization of electricity. All new proposals for power-stations appear to wish to use gas as the fuel, substantially adding to the demand (8–10 per cent in 1992/3 and perhaps 20 per cent by 1995/6). Other gas producers have contracted to supply 3 billion therms of gas compared to 1 billion therms for BG. This gas will have to reach their customers through BG's network.

Profits and the regulatory regime

The basic regulatory rule for BG's supply of gas to tariff customers is based on the formula RPI$-X$ $+/-$ y, where RPI indicates movements in the retail price index in a given period, X is a negative number (initially 2 per cent) which puts pressure on the company to reduce its non-gas operating costs, and Y refers to movements in the price of gas supplies which can be passed directly to the customer. This has been criticized as 'too easy' for the corporation to meet. A review of the formula was instituted by Ofgas in 1990 and published in April 1991. It proposed increasing the X factor from 2 to 5 per cent for a period of five years. In addition the new regime places a ceiling on the passing on of gas costs. This, it is hoped, will give the company a greater incentive to negotiate lower prices for its gas supplies from third parties and encourage it to operate its own fields more efficiently. The agreement also sets standards of service which cannot be reduced in the pursuit of cost savings. BG's profit record for the period 1984/5 to 1990/1 is shown in Table 6.4. It shows the return on capital employed to be on a rising trend.

The new formula, according to Ofgas, envisages a rate of return of between 5 and 7 per cent in current cost terms on its regulated activities. Table 6.4 shows this to be more or less within its historic range. To maintain profits with the tougher, regulatory rule, BG must operate more efficiently and reduce its cost levels. It has been estimated that this implies a reduction in its workforce of 7,500 for each year of the five-year period (*Financial Times*, 30 April 1991).

COMPETITION REVIEW

Following the recommendations of the MMC, British Gas came to an agreement with the Office of Fair Trading (OFT) in February 1990 for the implementation

Table 6.4 British Gas turnover and profitability

Year	Turnover (£m)	Current cost operating profit (£m)	Rate of return current cost (%)	Rate of return historic cost (%)	Dividends per share	Return on turnover (%)
1984/85	6,914	662	4.1	15.5	–	9.6
1985/86	7,687	706	4.2	15.3	–	9.2
1986/87	7,610	1,010	5.8	18.2	6.5p	13.2
1987/88	7,364	1,063	6.3	19.4	8.0p	14.3
1988/89	7,526	1,131	6.4	19.0	9.0p	15.0
1989/90	7,983	1,107	5.7	16.1	10.5p	13.9
1990/91	9,491	1,655	7.7	20.1	12.5p	12.4

Source: Company accounts.

of the MMC recommendations. British Gas agreed to publish price schedules for firm and interruptible contract gas customers; to abide by the Ofgas recommendations on pipeline pricing; and that they would not contract for more than 90 per cent of any new gas coming from UK North Sea fields between June 1989 and May 1991, thus, making gas available to potential competitors. (This is known as the 90/10 rule.) The government also promised that a review of the agreement would be undertaken in July 1991 to see whether British Gas had kept to its undertakings and to review progress in the development of the market.

The regulatory system as developed by Ofgas and modified by the MMC is seen by some to be a perfectly adequate framework in which competition can emerge and develop in order to be effective in terms of constraining the market behaviour of the dominant enterprise. Supporters of this view draw attention to the pace of change and the progress made by the independent gas marketers in the two years following the MMC report. *The Financial Times* (13 October 1991) reported that in the 12 months ending June 1991, 15 per cent of the new gas sold had come from companies competing with BG; that this was double the amount sold in the previous 12 months; and that eight competitors now supply 553 large corporate customers with 350 million therms per year – some 5 per cent of the industrial market. In addition it has been argued that UK gas prices are not too out of line with those in Europe. With published price schedules and published transport schedules there are in reality no barriers to the entry of independent companies into the UK gas market. This view was supported by British Gas whose chairman drew attention to the unusual nature of what the competition authorities expect of BG to help dismantle their monopoly position. He was reported in July 1991 as saying:

> Few companies, I suspect, have had to take the apparently bizarre challenge which British Gas has faced over the past two years. Having built up a thriving market for gas in industry and commerce we are seeking every opportunity to give a substantial proportion of that market to competitors.
>
> (*Financial Times*, 24 July 1991)

The review undertaken by the Office of Fair Trading of the impact of the MMC recommendations was published in October 1991 (OFT 1991). It found that British Gas had kept to the agreement it had made, but that competition had not developed to a stage where it could be regarded as self-sustainable. After five years of privatization the share of the industrial gas market held by competitors was 0.4 per cent in 1990 and 5.2 per cent in 1991, thanks largely to British Gas agreeing to swap deals – that is, letting competitors have access to gas currently contracted to BG subject to repayment at some time in the future. The report identified three factors which would hinder the development of future competition: the availability of gas, problems in balancing supply and demand, and discriminatory practices by British Gas.

Gas available to competitors will depend upon the coming-on-stream of new fields, and the removal of restrictions on imports and their availability. None of these sources is likely to be significant before 1995, therefore in the short to medium term the OFT recommended that British Gas release gas it has contracted to buy to its competitors to be repaid in the future. In addition the 90/10 rule should be replaced with a requirement that BG contracts for no more than the quantities necessary to allow competition to develop in this market.

The ability of BG to balance supply and demand for any given pattern of demand, because of its extensive storage facilities which are not available to competitors, is a substantial hindrance to new entrants. To deal with this problem and those of common carriage, the report recommends the creation of a separate subsidiary, responsible for transmission and storage, which deals in a non-discriminatory way with both BG and it competitors and sets charges related to costs, overseen by the regulator. In addition the report recommends the removal of the tariff threshold which limits competition to those consumers buying 25,000 therms or more per year, thus creating a larger pool of potential customers.

The Director-General concluded that he would wish to make a further reference to the MMC, but proposed a delay to the end of 1991 before activating the recommendation to see whether BG would be willing to give meaningful undertakings. Meanwhile the government were asked to consider strengthening the powers of Ofgas, modifying planning rules for pipelines and liberalizing trade policies for gas.

The period following the report saw intensive bargaining between British Gas and the competition authorities with BG attempting to gain concessions on the regulatory regime, particularly a lowering of the X-factor of 5 per cent, whilst avoiding a far-reaching reference to the MMC. In December 1991 BG announced it had reached a provisional agreement with the OFT to split the company into two separate companies in 1993 both with separate accounts; that BG transmission would publish tariffs so that it was clear it was offering the same transmission rates to BG as to its competitors; and to open up the industrial market to more competition by agreeing to limit its supplies to the market to 40 per cent by 1995. In return it expected a downward revision of the X-factor agreed earlier in 1991 – that is, higher charges for domestic customers in compensation for the loss of market share in the industrial market. The consequences of no agreement, BG argued, would be upward pressure on prices, lower service standards, a reduction in investment, and a slow-down in extensions to the pipeline system. These arguments were rejected by Ofgas and consumer bodies who argued that there could be no justification for revising the regulatory regime and charging consumers higher prices.

Final agreement between British Gas and the government was reached on 15 January 1992 with the only concession being a promised review by Ofgas of the regulatory control agreement. The Energy Secretary has given assurances that the government wishes the market for gas to proceed in a way 'fair to the company, its customers, employees, its shareholders and competitors' (*Guardian* 16 January 1992). The agreement thus creates a framework in which British Gas will strive to lose market share and make entry a relatively costless affair by making its pipeline operation into an 'arm's-length' operation thereby limiting the financial commitment of entrants. The agreements do not, however, guarantee entry, they merely make it feasible. The cost barriers to entry are greatly reduced but may still deter some companies, while customers may prefer to stay with British Gas and their guarantee of security of supply.

CONCLUSIONS

This chapter has explored the relationship between privatization and market structure. It illustrates the failure of government policy towards British Gas which placed the main emphasis upon privatization without paying much attention to the subsequent market structure and the development of effective competition. The result was a failure to achieve the expected results of privatization in that competition failed to develop, and the newly privatized monopoly abused its market power in its non-regulated activities thus attracting considerable criticism of the privatization process.

The behaviour of the company led to a reference to the Monopolies and Mergers Commission into the contract market which set in process a series of moves which have ended with the company facing dismemberment into two parts. The MMC suggested the introduction of published prices, the 90/10 rule for new gas becoming available, and a clear set of prices for use of the pipeline. These have led to a reduction in price discrimination, encouraged the development of competition from other suppliers of gas, produced greater transparency in the prices charged to customers and competitors, removed the previous uncertainty surrounding prices, and to Ofgas imposing a tougher regulatory regime. OFT, in their review of the effectiveness of the MMC prescriptions, suggested further revisions of policy which have been accepted by British Gas. The expectation is that providing entrants and consumers behave in the appropriate way, that competitor companies will have 60 per cent of the industrial market by 1995.

If the opportunity had been taken in 1985 to change the structure of the gas industry to a grid company and a number of distribution companies, a more efficient industry might have emerged sooner. The lesson to be learnt from the British experience of privatizing the gas industry is that an ownership change without at the same time developing a more competitive environment will fail to deliver the expected gains in economic efficiency. Therefore, before a state-owned enterprise is privatized serious consideration should be given to the subsequent market structure to be created if the full benefits of the change are to be achieved.

APPENDIX: MAJOR PRIVATIZATIONS AND MARKET STRUCTURES

A **Enterprise unchanged and monopoly market**
British Airports Authority (London)
British Gas
Regional electricity distribution (12 companies)
National electricity grid (Gridco)
Scottish electricity (2 companies)
Water (regional companies with monopolies)

B **Enterprise unchanged, dominant firms in domestic market but facing international competition**
British Aerospace (BAe)
British Airways
Rolls-Royce

C **Dominant firms in domestic market but some competitors**
British Telecom (competitor Mercury)
Electricity production (National Power and PowerGen plus small number of independent producers)

D **Competitive domestic market**
Buses but regional firms may be in a dominant position
Associated British Ports
Amersham International
British Leyland (owned by British Aerospace)
Britoil (now BP)
Enterprise Oil
Jaguar (now Ford)
British Petroleum

BIBLIOGRAPHY

Arthur, C. (1989) 'The gas man', *Business*, August, pp. 88–90.

Baumol, W. J., Panzer, J. and Willig, R. D. (1982) *Contestable Markets and Industrial Structure*, New York: Harcourt Brace Jovanovich.

Beesley, M. E. and Littlechild, S. C. (1989) 'The regulation of privatised monopolies in the UK', *Rand Journal of Economics* 20(3), 454–72.

Bradley, I. and Price, C. (1988) 'The economic regulation of private industries by price constraints', *Journal of Industrial Economics* 37(1), 99–106.

Dunsire, A., Hartley, K. and Parker, D. (1991) 'Organisational status and performance: summary of the findings', *Public Administration* 69(1), 21–40.

Foreman-Peck, J. and Manning, D. (1988) 'How well is BT performing? An international comparison of telecommunications total factor productivity', *Fiscal Studies* 9(3), 54–67.

Gabb, A. (1989) 'British Gas explores its future', *Management Today*, August, pp. 32–33.

Hammond, B., Helm, D. and Thompson, D. (1985) 'British Gas: options for privatisation', *Fiscal Studies* 6(4), 1–20.

Helm, D. and Yarrow, G. (1988) 'The regulation of utilities', *Oxford Review of Economic Policy* 4(2), i–xxix.

Kay, J., Mayer, C. and Thompson, D. (eds) (1986) *Privatisation and Regulation: The UK Experience*, Oxford: Oxford University Press.

—— and Thompson, D. J. (1986) 'Privatisation: a policy in search of a rationale, *Economic Journal* 96(1), 18–32.

Lawson, N. (1980) Parliamentary Speech, *Hansard* Eighth Series, vol. 1, col. 921, January.

Littlechild, S. C. (1983) *Regulation of British Telecommunications Profitability* London: HMSO.

McKinnon, J. (1991) 'Office of gas supply: regulation of gas', in C. Veljanovski, *Regulators and the Market*, London: Institute of Economic Affairs.

Millward, R. (1982) 'The comparative performance of public and private enterprise', in E. Roll (ed.), *The Mixed Economy*, London: Macmillan.

—— and Parker, D. (1983) 'Public and private enterprise: comparative behaviour and relative efficiency', in R. Millward, D. Parker, L. Rosenthal, M. T. Sumner and N. Topham (eds), *Public Sector Economics*, London: Longman.

Monopolies and Mergers Commission (MMC) (1988) *Gas*, Cm 500, London: HMSO.

Office of Fair Trading (OFT) (1991) *The Gas Review*, October, London.

Office of Gas Supply (1987) *Competition in Gas Supply*, London.

Parker, D. (1989) 'Public control of natural monopoly in the UK', in M. Campbell, M. Naroy and N. Healey (eds), *Controversy in Applied Economics*, Hemel Hempstead: Harvester/Wheatsheaf.

Price, C. (1985) 'Competition in UK gas distribution', *Energy Policy* 13(1), 37–50.

—— and Gibson, M. (1989) 'Privatisation and regulation: British Gas', in A. Harrison (ed.), *Reshaping Nationalised Industries*, Newbury: Policy Journals.

Rost, P. (1988) 'Towards a competitive market-related energy policy', *Energy Policy* 16(5), 450–4.

Stern, J. (1986) 'After Sleipner: a policy for UK gas supplies', *Energy Policy* 14(1), 9–14.

Veljanovski, C. (1989) 'Privatisation: experience with regulation', *Energy Policy* 17(4), 351–5.

Vickers, J, and Yarrow, G. (1988a) *Privatisation: An Economic Analysis*, London: MIT Press.

—— —— (1988b) 'Regulation of privatised firms', *European Economic Review* 32(2), 456–72.

Wolf, J. (1990) *Markets or Governments: Choosing Between Imperfect Alternatives*, Cambridge, Mass.: MIT Press.

Wright, M. (1987) 'Government divestments and the regulation of natural monopolies in the UK: the case of British Gas', *Energy Policy* 15(3), 193–216.

7

PRIVATIZATION OF THE BRITISH UTILITIES

Regulation, decentralization and industrial relations[1]

Anthony Ferner and Trevor Colling

INTRODUCTION

A central tenet of Conservative policy in the 1980s was that public enterprises would be managed much more efficiently in the private sector, not least because the power of the public sector unions would be reduced. In the public sector, the unions' hand was strengthened by the absence of the threat of bankruptcy, and they had been able to involve governments 'in the interests of their political objectives if not in the interests of their members' (Moore 1986: 89). Even where public monopolies were turned into private ones, it was claimed, privatization would have a beneficial effect since private ownership itself would increase 'X-efficiency': that is, management and shareholders would have an incentive to increase efficiency since they could hope to appropriate the resulting gains, regardless of any pressures to efficiency from competitive market structures.

Thus privatization was expected by its advocates to have important consequences for industrial relations. This chapter explores what has happened in practice. It attempts to answer the basic question: Does privatization make any difference to industrial relations? For despite some well-publicized signs of new industrial relations in the privatized companies, notably in telecommunications and the water industry, the question remains as to how far these changes are due to privatization rather than to processes that would have taken place anyway. The chapter concentrates on the regulated privatized companies – BT (formerly British Telecom), British Gas, the water companies and the electricity distribution companies, though it also covers other areas such as electricity generation.[2]

The problem may be illustrated by the 1986 TUC report on the consequences of privatization. It painted a dire picture of employment cuts, deteriorating conditions, the reduction of collective bargaining and unionization and so on, in a climate of 'macho management'. These things can still be observed in the privatized companies. BT, for example, cut almost 19,000 in 1990–1, a third of

l staff (*NCU Journal*, June 1991: 1), while British Gas has
10,000 over the last four years.

nces, it is possible to draw a direct link between privatization and
ons changes. This is the case where a subsidiary unit of a public
hived off' as an independent unit within an industrial sector with
very different private industrial relations traditions. An example is that of British
Rail's hotels, sold off from 1983 onwards into a private sector where problems of
union organization of the workforce and of obtaining collective bargaining
recognition are common. The protection afforded to the workforce as employees
of BR, with its long-standing public enterprise bargaining traditions, was
removed, and as a result unionization declined sharply – 80 per cent of members
had left the NUR (as it then was) within two years of privatization (Terry 1990:
1). With new owners claiming that they could not afford the taxpayer-subsidized,
lengthy and costly negotiating procedures (TUC 1986), collective bargaining was
undermined.

But the fact is that in general the same phenomena of industrial relations
change have been observed in the public enterprise sector as in the privatized
companies. In some cases this is clearly due to the intention to privatize, as with
the rationalizations in the steel industry (Blyton 1990), or in British Airways,
marked down for privatization since 1981. Similarly, the break-up of national
bargaining in the water industry was triggered by the government's privatization
plans (Ogden 1990). But it has to be remembered that the privatization
programme developed gradually, almost by chance; the first major privatization of
a core public corporation, that of British Telecom in 1984, was largely seen as a
way of resolving problems of raising finance under tight Treasury rules for the
public sector. The ideological coherence came later. The privatization of the
water industry would have seemed improbable before being put on the agenda in
1985, while electricity privatization was proposed at the time of the 1987
election. Before 1987, the privatization of the railways was not an issue.[3] Thus
much of the industrial relations change observable in the nationalized industries
during the 1980s had nothing to do with preparing the corporations for privatization. Yet indications of 'macho' management were as visible in the public
enterprises as in privatized ones: employment was slashed in coal, steel and the
railways; there were major strikes during the 1980s in steel, the railways, the Post
Office, the water industry and, of course, the coal industry; traditional collective
bargaining arrangements were challenged by management and groups of
managerial staff were removed from collective bargaining (Ferner 1989).

Another problem with sweeping generalizations about the effects of privatization is that there has been considerable variety among the privatized companies.
Whereas BT has had a rocky record of troubled industrial relations, with a major
strike by telecommunications technicians in 1987 and the first ever national
action by managerial and professional staff in 1990, BG by contrast has had
relatively peaceful relationships and a more evolutionary process of change (see,
for example, IRRR 1989). BT's employment has fluctuated, with cuts followed

by increases in staff in the late 1980s, followed by maj
employment reduction in the early 1990s. This suggests that
privatization may be at work in explaining some of the cha
munications, the introduction of advanced microelectronic exch
with profound implications for employment levels and for the
work, is likely to have been a major influence on patterns of ind
regardless of changes in ownership.

Such problems in interpreting the effects of privatization mean t..at an analysis
must do more than merely catalogue the changes in industrial relations of
privatized companies: there is a need to explore in more depth the processes
specific to privatization and their consequences for industrial relations. It may
well be that behind the similarity of industrial relations phenomena in the public
and private sectors like quite different causal processes. In short, the chapter does
not offer a comprehensive review of the consequences of privatization, nor an
exhaustive analysis of the content of the changes themselves, but rather an
exploration of some of the forces behind observable changes.

THE CONSEQUENCES OF PRIVATIZATION

Under state ownership, public corporations were subject to direct political
control. This meant that their role was statutorily defined, and that the
responsible minister had formal powers to set financial performance and other
objectives, vet and approve spending plans and investment programmes, regulate
borrowing, appoint board members, and issue directives to management on
matters affecting the national interest. But in addition, political control gave
ministers more diffuse means of exerting informal pressures on management, to
engage in 'arm-twisting' and to intervene directly (whether openly or behind the
scenes) in management decision-making over a range of issues. Since many
industrial relations questions such as pay, productivity, closures and redundancy,
strikes and industrial conflict have such important repercussions for other aspects
of public policy, governments have had ample motive for exerting their statutory
and less formal political powers. Both management and unions learned to
operate in this environment (Ferner 1988). During the Thatcher years, the access
of the unions to 'political exchange' with the government was, of course, severely
restricted if not eliminated. But the government continued to intervene frequently
(despite its rhetoric of leaving management to manage) in a range of issues from
pay determination to closure decisions and the conduct of industrial disputes.
For example, many of the major public sector disputes of the 1980s, in coal,
steel, water and the railways, reflected direct political pressure on management to
force through change by means of confrontation if necessary (see Ferner 1989).

After privatization, however, the formal political link is broken. Ministerial
control is replaced by shareholder control and, in the case of the regulated
utilities, by regulator control as well. This section will explore the consequences
of regulation and of stock-market pressures for industrial relations.

The industrial relations consequences of regulation

BT and the utilities in water, gas and electricity, all of which continued to enjoy a large degree of market power after privatization, have been subject to a framework of regulation.[4] Each of the industries has a regulatory agency – Oftel, Ofwat, Ofgas and Offer respectively – responsible for setting formulae for price increases, as well as overseeing the development of competition and monitoring service quality.

The companies are provided with a price formula that limits price increases for core services (for example, domestic gas prices, water supply, telephone calls) to a set amount below (or, as in the water industry, above) rises in the retail price index. This means that in order to increase profitability, companies have an incentive to cut costs. Since labour forms a high proportion of total controllable costs (about half in electricity distribution, 60 per cent in gas, 40 per cent in water, and just under half in telecommunications), the regulatory price formula thus appears to provide a strong incentive for companies to cut labour costs.

In practice, however, it is uncertain whether the formula has created a strong additional spur to labour efficiency. Prior to privatization, the utilities had been working to government-imposed cost reduction targets, which they had achieved fairly easily. The gas, electricity and water utilities had all been consistently shedding labour for several years, although BT had been fairly static at just under quarter of a million employees. The pricing formula set by the regulator was usually no more onerous than the earlier public sector cost-cutting targets (cf. Vickers and Yarrow 1988). It was perhaps not surprising given that the formulae were set, not by some transparent technical mechanism, but on the basis of hard bargaining between government, corporation and regulator. Consultants advising the regulator on setting the formula were usually dependent on far from transparent cost information from the companies themselves. According to one manager interviewed:

> Those in the industry were sceptical about the consultants' ability to get to the bottom of things – as an example, the significance of overtime. Also management pushed a picture of gloom and doom, for example stressing the potential significance for costs of the equal value claims. The consultants went round with a 'minder'. But they had a free hand to ask for anything. There was genuinely no co-ordinated attempt to thwart them. But there was an instinctive feel right the way down that it was in everyone's self-interest not to spill the beans. They were given no incorrect information, it was just a question of what they made of it, since for every piece of information they had, they would have needed so much more to make sense of it.

None the less, it seems that the rigour of formula-setting is increasing. The current BT pricing formula is more stringent than the previous one, and the regulator has shown an interest in extending price regulation to the previously unregulated international telecommunications business. In gas, too, the new pricing formula announced in April 1992 holds prices to 5 percentage points below the rate of inflation, compared with 2 percentage points under the previous formula; given current inflation trends, reductions in gas prices are therefore likely in the next few years. The water regulator has hinted that permitted price rises will be curtailed if promised capital expenditure levels in the industry are not maintained (*Financial Times*, 19 June 1991). One of the major concerns of the regulators, particularly in gas, has been to force management to create cost information for different activities, where often none existed at the time of privatization. This would make it more difficult to transfer costs between regulated and unregulated activities. In sectors where regional monopolies operate, as in water and electricity supply, the regulator will use 'yardstick competition', comparing the performance of different regional companies, to help judge appropriate price targets.

The pricing formula is perhaps as important for its symbolic role in management–union relations as for the real pressure it exerts. It has acted, according to one respondent, as a way of 'focusing existing cost pressures', and management has been able to use it as a *legitimation* for cutting labour costs. It has become part of the ritual posturing of negotiation.

A second area in which regulation is influencing industrial relations is that of quality of service. Quality in the privatized monopolies such as gas and telecommunications has been a highly sensitive issue politically, since deteriorating standards of service would be likely to tarnish the image of the government's privatization programme as a whole. Companies such as BT have been conscious of the effects of service quality on government judgements concerning the future structure of the industry, as in the recent review of the telecommunications duopoly.[5] The regulator has intervened directly in the area of quality, by forcing companies to offer compensation to customers receiving poor service, pressurizing them to publish more informative quality-of-service statistics, and linking quality performance with the pricing formula. In 1991, the gas regulator reached an agreement with British Gas under which performance on quality indicators such as response times to gas leaks would be monitored, and if standards were not met, the company could be referred to the Monopolies and Mergers Commission which would have the power to impose further price cuts as a penalty (*Financial Times*, 30 April 1991).

The quality-of-service issue has had conflicting consequences for industrial relations. In the short term, it has forced management – notably in BT – to retreat from a cost-cutting strategy. Following the major strike in early 1987, employment in BT rose by 10,000 in response to a devastating chorus of criticism from users and the regulator about the poor service, and in 1989 the workforce was more or less the same size as in 1981. BT also introduced a wide-ranging programme of 'Total Quality Management' in an ambitious attempt to build concern for quality and 'customer-led attitudes' into the organizational culture. Based on the idea of 'right first time, every time', TQM was implemented through the use of workshops and 'facilitators' reporting to district general managers, and supervisors were trained to solve practical problems of service provision using techniques such as brainstorming and critical path analysis. TQM provided a rationale for both unions and managers to demand more resources in order 'to do a quality job'; but it also gave management the opportunity to erode traditional union influence over working practices by providing a forum for devising 'solutions' to work organization issues outside conventional management–union arrangements.

In the longer term, however, cost reduction and quality improvement are likely to be made compatible through the introduction of new technology, especially in the case of BT through microelectronic exchange equipment which could slash the need for telecommunications technicians. Indeed, the trend to increasing employment in BT has been reversed with a vengeance since 1989. In addition to the 38,000 jobs shed between 1990 and 1992, BT planned to cut a further 24,000 in 1992/3. The concern with quality of service has also prompted management to search for increased flexibility in work organization in order to improve service provision. Both BT and British Gas, for example, have reached agreement with their unions on flexible working hours to enable customer service to be provided by telephone engineers, gas meter readers, and so on during a greater portion of the working day.

The industrial relations consequences of the City

As with the effects of regulation, the impact of 'shareholder control' on industrial relations is ambiguous. On the one hand, there is increased pressure from City investment analysts for cost-cutting and for 'paring away the fat' believed to have accumulated under public ownership. In 1990, for example, James Capel was reported as saying that electricity generators had 'substantial scope for efficiency improvements' that would flow through into profits, and that many power-stations could cut staff by 40 per cent (*Financial Times*, 3 May 1990). BT was likewise publicly lambasted by the analysts. In 1987, brokers Wood MacKenzie saw scope for cuts of 70,000 employees, about one third of the workforce. Moreover, analysts drew comparisons (not always appropriate given the difficulty of comparing like-with-like) between the productivity of privatized companies and that of their equivalent overseas. BT, for example, was said to be 'terribly inefficient' by comparison with foreign telephone companies (cited in *Financial Times*, 27 September 1990); a study by Robert Fleming Securities showed BT as having far fewer lines per employee than major telephone companies in North America, Japan and even Italy or Spain (reported in *Financial Times*, 1 November 1991). Similarly, during the privatization process in the electricity industry, one respondent spoke of institutional advisers 'poking their noses through the door', comparing manning levels with those in the United States or West Germany. After privatization, managers in the largest generating company, National Power, were conscious of the need to match the productivity performance of their main rival, PowerGen, and this appears to have been one motive behind National Power's decision to halve its overhead staff from 4,000 to 2,000 between 1991 and 1992. Fear of the City's penchant for making external comparisons may well also be a factor in the desire of companies like BT to subcontract areas of work, such as catering or printing services, previously performed by direct employees.

The 'expectations' of the City extended not only to staffing levels, but also to the 'culture' of industrial relations. Management believed in 'sending the right signals' to investors. This was one factor in the impending break-up of the electricity supply industry's national bargaining machinery following the decision of several companies to issue notice of withdrawal in December 1991: individual companies were perceived to need their own tailor-made industrial relations arrangements appropriate for their particular business strategy and competitive situation. In one privatizing company, a senior personnel manager spoke of the need to reduce the power of an influential managerial and professional union, because 'the shareholders wouldn't accept it that the unions were running the company'. A major element of public sector managerial unionism, the widespread phenomenon of collective bargaining for management and professional staff, was seen as 'inappropriate' in private sector companies. 'It was widely clear to all concerned', said one respondent, 'that shareholders would not expect senior managers' terms and conditions to be set by collective bargaining in the future.' In much of the privatized sector, managers' terms and conditions were increasingly determined through personal contract rather than collectively bargained, and pay linked to individual or corporate performance was widely introduced.

However, there is anecdotal evidence that some of the external pressure from the City was deliberately fomented and encouraged by management in order to provide it with an external legitimation for cost-cutting drives and other industrial relations changes. The analysts' judgements relied on information on overstaffing 'fed' them by corporate management itself. The resulting report could then be used as a card in negotiations with the unions.

On the other hand, some managements played down the need for change, arguing that it was precisely the industry's history of stable industrial relations under public ownership that was the attraction for investors, and that the stability should not be endangered by abrupt challenges to the *status quo*. The emphasis, therefore, was on *controlled* change. Even where managers were pursuing a robust strategy of cost reduction, they were anxious to avoid industrial relations problems, especially in the period prior to flotation 'because City confidence will be damaged because it'll show in stark silhouette how much industrial relations power is vested in ... staff'. Certainly, shareholders were perceived to dislike the idea of 'ideological' confrontation with staff merely in order to demonstrate management's willingness to 'face down' the unions, as had been occurring in the public enterprise sector during the 1980s. The dangers were pointed up by the 1987 telecommunications strike and its consequences which had such detrimental effects on the quality of BT's service. Service problems were especially acute in the financial services sector in the City of London, where they were compounded by BT's inability to cope with the explosive growth in demand caused by financial deregulation. In general, investors were as likely to be concerned about poor quality as about overstaffing: the former was likely to affect profitability not only through loss of sales and market share, but also because it was likely to lead eventually to demands for tighter regulation and greater competition in the core services. In the short term at least, raising quality would mean easing the reduction in labour costs.

Thus shareholder 'perceptions' were not some pure objective datum for management, and to the extent that they really did exert influence on management behaviour, the pressures did not all point in the same direction.

DIVERSIFICATION OUT OF 'CORE' SERVICES AND ITS IMPLICATIONS FOR INDUSTRIAL RELATIONS

Privatization and the ending of political control have provided both the opportunities and the incentives for companies to diversify out of their 'core' utility activities into new areas: the question of 'what business are we in?' can again be placed on the management strategy agenda. First, the former statutory restrictions on the public enterprises' area of business, laid down in the nationalization Acts that created them, have been lifted. Freed from their statutory shackles, the newly privatized companies, operating according to a business logic rather than a public sector one, have moved swiftly to diversify out of their core activity into new sectors. Second, the possibilities of the core have been restricted by the regime of regulation, by sluggish long-term growth prospects for core services, especially in utilities such as gas supply, and by increasing competition in the core. As already mentioned, BT faces new entrants in the market for fixed-link telecommunications services as a result of the 1990–1 'duopoly review'. British Gas has been prodded by the regulator to open up its transmission network to rival gas suppliers: under the regulator's threat of a 'Draconian' solution involving breaking the company up into a gas transmission network and different regional businesses, BG has been asked to surrender 30 per cent of its main industrial gas market by 1993 (*Financial Times*, 31 January 1991). However, the pressures for increased competition in core services appear to be intensifying rather than abating: an October 1991 report from the Office of Fair Trading recommended opening up British Gas's household customer business to competition and selling off the pipeline division; and the Conservative government is preparing to enforce these changes through further legislation, as well as increasing competition in water supply (*Financial Times*, 17 October 1991, 1 November 1991). Electricity generation has been broken up into rival companies and the way has been opened for new entrants, especially taking advantage of modern gas turbine technology, to build new capacity relatively cheaply and quickly.

The upshot has been a marked diversification of activities, both geographically and sectorally, British Gas and BT see themselves as 'the world's first global gas business' and as a 'Top Telco' respectively, and both have been investing in overseas capacity. British Gas has been buying up major foreign utilities and moving into oil and gas exploration. At home, it has been planning to take advantage of electricity privatization by moving into power generation. BT has been looking at the massive US market, planning global alliances with IBM, establishing an international joint venture network ('Syncordia') to supply worldwide services to multinational corporations, and buying stakes in the mobile phone and data communications sectors. The water and electricity companies have also been engaged in more modest but still significant diversification, into plumbing and water treatment services, telecommunications, waste treatment and so on; Welsh Water saw it as logical to purchase a stake in one of its major customers, South Wales Electricity.[6]

Diversification is likely to have profound consequences for industrial relations. New activities are organized as separate business units or subsidiaries, and their industrial relations can be managed as a clean slate, free of the public sector industrial relations legacy that continues to influence relationships in the core sectors. Early indications are that management has tried to adopt a much more individualized approach to employee relations, playing down the collective aspect and the role of the unions and introducing individualized payment schemes. According to one senior manager in a utility, 'as far as the unions were concerned, we are not seeking to destroy the older relations but have told them that as [new activities] increase, there will be chunks of activity the unions would have no locus in'. In some BT subsidiaries, management has refused to recognize unions for bargaining purposes, and the National Communications Union has fought unsuccessfully for union recognition at several of BT's subsidiaries. The union claimed, despite management denials, that refusal of recognition at subsidiaries was a centrally co-ordinated management policy in the company. Even where unions continue to be recognized, single union deals may well become more common, and terms and conditions are likely to diverge increasingly from those of the core; in BT, for example, unions have been reluctantly forced to recognize that pay in the company's subsidiaries will vary according to levels of profitability.

Unions also fear that in the longer run, management will use non-core activities as test beds for developing new industrial relations policies which could then be imported into the main organization, and they are also worried that increasingly, management may transfer activities away from the centre to subsidiaries, where the unions would have little control over working practices, new technology, grading structures or terms and conditions. There is some evidence in the water industry that diversified new activities are the prime targets for the introduction of non-standard employment relations. For example, in one privatizing water authority, the new plumbing service relied entirely on sub-contracted self-employed workers, reflecting management perceptions of the

133

commercial risk involved (O'Connell Davidson 1990: 534–5). In electricity, the generators appear to be exploiting the introduction of power-stations using new 'combined cycle' gas turbine technology to erode traditional demarcations between technical and skilled blue-collar staff, and to extend the use of sub-contracting.

In some cases, diversification has been occurring through the hiving off of particular kinds of work from the core into separate organizations. For example, in the water authority studied by O'Connell Davidson (1990: 534) the prospect of privatization led management to consider ways of exploiting the commercial potential of maintenance by setting up independent profit centres. By measuring performance against short-term profit targets, the new structure provided managers with strong additional incentives to cut labour costs (see also next section), especially given the high labour intensity of the maintenance function.

If these developments turn out to be an accurate portent of the way things are moving, then it may be possible to posit an increasing 'dualism' in the industrial relations of the major privatized corporations. In the core business, the concern with the provision of a reasonably stable utility service of uniform quality may favour the retention, perhaps with some hiccups, of familiar patterns of stable, relatively consensual industrial relations. Strong unions remain, and despite the *de facto* derecognition of management unions in many instances, they are likely to retain an influential role in determining terms and conditions through collective bargaining within fairly traditional and elaborate negotiating machineries. In the new areas of activity, management will see as desirable an innovative, more flexible culture of industrial relations reflecting the dynamism of new market opportunities, and the opportunities for experimentation with new patterns. With the relative expansion of new activities and the decline of the core, employment in the subsidiaries is likely to rise proportionately and their industrial relations likely to lead gradually to a significant shift in the climate of industrial relations in the privatized corporations as a whole.

One may question how far this picture corresponds to reality. There seems to have been considerable variation even within the core activities between the relatively consensual, relatively stable industrial relations strategies of a British Gas, and the more fluctuating and change-oriented approach of a BT. Indeed, in BT there seems to have been something of an oscillation between traditional patterns and a new more aggressive hard-line approach (see Ferner and Colling 1991) in which management responded to the conflicting external signals from regulator, investors and government. A more conciliatory phase following the service disasters of 1987 appears once more to have given way to a strategic exploitation of the NCU's weakness revealed in the 1987 strike. Thus management has adopted an assertive change-oriented approach and implemented rapid and large cuts in employment.

Even at its most 'macho', BT has not fundamentally challenged institutional arrangements of collective bargaining (except for the top 6,000–7,000 managers). There are indications, however, that some companies believe that they can break free of the public sector heritage of the negotiation machinery. The clearest case is that of Northumbrian Water, which has decided to set up a company council to determine pay and other employment-related matters (Smith 1991). Remarkably, the new set-up will not have direct union representation. Four of the eleven-member council will be appointed by management and seven elected by local employee councils directly elected by the workforce; the unions will only be able to elect a representative to advise the council. Such a scheme, developed by management to encourage a 'team' approach and to break with 'the them and us attitude', potentially represents a profound challenge to the traditional union-dominated collective relations that characterized the core activities under public ownership. One question is the effect that such structures will have on the role of the unions in a traditionally heavily unionized sector. Another is the extent to which Northumbria's plan will provide a model that other privatized utilities will copy.[7]

CHANGING MANAGEMENT CULTURE AND INDUSTRIAL RELATIONS: THE EXAMPLE OF DECENTRALIZATION[8]

Industrial relations have also been affected by the internal changes in managerial structure that privatization has brought in its train. The managements of privatized companies have striven to adapt organization 'culture' to a more market-driven environment, by making it more responsive to customer demands, and more innovative and flexible in the face of competitive pressures (Colling 1991, Ferner 1990). The primary motivation for changing management culture was that the former public corporations now had shareholders to satisfy, and profitability was the major preoccupation of management strategy. Similar pressures for greater 'commercialism' also faced the nationalized industries in the 1980s. But public sector commercialism was primarily driven by political concerns, sending signals to the government that the corporations were shaking off the supposed lethargy and bureaucracy of public sector management for models more inspired by the private sector. It seems likely that the privatized utilities also had a subsidiary *political* motive for changing their culture, given the 'quasi-political contingency' facing them: they saw a need to convince the government and the regulators about their intentions to be more dynamic and efficient, and by doing so avoid any tightening of the regulatory framework, and also ward off pressures for the introduction of greater competition.

Within the process of change, line managers have been assigned a key role. Budgetary responsibility and greater decision-making powers have been devolved to lower organizational levels, both to enable line managers to 'get close to the customer', and to encourage them to deploy resources more efficiently. Local managers are being encouraged to pursue growth opportunities, and adopt more 'entrepreneurial' attitudes, concerning themselves with running 'mini-businesses' rather than primarily seeing themselves as concerned with the minutiae of service delivery.

In several privatized companies, decentralization was intended to lead eventually to a structure of profit centres at 'business' level or even at the level of individual operating units such as telecommunications districts or power-stations. Unit managers would then have direct responsibility for the 'bottom line' profit performance of their unit. In practice, the concept was difficult to implement because in most cases unit managers could not have control over major elements of cost or revenue. But it was seen as useful for causing 'us to think differently about how we are managed compared with when we were cost-centre-orientated', according to one senior respondent.

Even a limited degree of decentralization was likely to have significant consequences for industrial relations. Indeed, in some cases, the unions believed that one motivation for decentralization was management's desire to bypass unions at the central level where they were traditionally strongest. For example, in BT, the NCU *Journal* (March 1986: 33) produced a leaked training document in which district managers were encouraged to take advantage of their 'current power position' to impose change rather than negotiate it, and to distinguish between those national collective agreements that were 'sacrosanct' for strategic reasons and those that local managers could take their own initiatives on.

In general, devolution meant a transfer of functions from central personnel departments to line managers. Local managers were expected to take the initiative on industrial relations issues (although not in general on pay determination which has continued to be centralized at corporate level or at least within broad business divisions). The emphasis was placed on the propagation of the new cultural assumptions through line leadership and motivation of staff, involving direct communication. Without implementing major reforms of the machinery of industrial relations, managers were able to engineer changes in the way in which it operated in practice. In some instances, the local machinery was gradually being turned from a traditional local consultative mechanism into a tool of management communication and culture change. Elsewhere management's move to direct communication marginalized the traditional union-dominated machinery of local joint consultation. There was also a change in the relationship between the different hierarchical levels of the machinery. With managers being encouraged to deal with industrial relations matters more at local level, it was the perception both of managers and union respondents that the traditional flow of issues from the bottom up to higher stages was being cut back. At a higher organizational level, there has been some decentralization of national bargaining machinery. In the water industry, of course, this has meant that major pay-bargaining has been taken over by the individual water plc's, with the same happening in electricity from the end of 1992 as companies withdrew from the national agreement to go their own way. Within telecommunications, several sets of negotiations, often with different settlement dates, are being conducted with BT's different businesses.

With or without encouragement from the top, it was likely that the devolution of managerial authority would lead line managers to question nationally negotiated arrangements that restricted their decision-making flexibility. There was evidence that in practice this sometimes brought them into conflict with the broad thrust of corporate personnel strategy. In one company, where custom and practice traditionally allowed a later retirement age than that formally laid down in the national agreement, line managers' attempts to impose the lower age brought intervention by the central personnel function because of fears that uncoordinated local action by managers could lead to a national conflict with the union. In another instance, business sector managers in a privatizing company interpreted their new freedom too liberally and urged their line managers to implement change in working arrangements without agreement if necessary; again, central personnel was forced to defuse the situation and bring the 'errant' managers into line.

The concern of central personnel and industrial relations management for the wider impact of local managerial action partly reflects its traditional reliance on, and familiarity with, a public sector model of centralized, formalized 'strong' bargaining relationships with national union officials. This created strong 'micropolitical' interests for the retention of central control over many aspects of devolution, despite the rhetoric of decentralization. In some instances, there appears to have been an *ad hoc*, tacit alliance between personnel and union leaders to dampen the effects of decentralization. For example, in one company, national union officers protested forcefully about the corporate personnel director being bypassed in a major plant closure decision. This union intervention was regarded by personnel managers as 'manna from heaven', and in the words of a national union official, 'because of the unions' reaction, Personnel has been able to re-establish its influence' (personal communication).

Beyond the micropolitics, there were more structural concerns that limited the extent of decentralization. First, central personnel worried about the systemic effects of local industrial relations difficulties in integrated network industries. What happened in one part of the system could have technical 'knock-on' effects elsewhere. Moreover, since the core services were usually fairly homogeneous, identifiable products requiring a specific set of skills across the organization, there was a case for a unified corporate culture and a corporate internal labour market, and these were likely to be compromised by too great a local latitude in terms and conditions, grading structures and so on. In such circumstances, leap-frogging claims between units within the same system were not a prospect that management would wish to contemplate.

There were also external constraints on the extent of decentralization. In the regulated utilities, the regulator's insistence on consistent service standards, and the proposals for compensation for service failures, led companies like BT to reconsider their strategy of 'getting close to the customer' through devolution to districts. Such a strategy was perceived as leading to unacceptable variation across districts in a situation in which comparative performance was being scrutinized by external agencies. There were also pressing commercial motives for limiting decentralization of responsibility for service provision. Large industrial customers provided the lion's share of revenue. In BT, for example, the top 15 per cent of customers provided 85 per cent of revenue. Business customers were seen as expecting a uniform standard of service. But in addition, especially in the case of network industries such as large banks, they required a service that was properly coordinated across the country. Finally, even in the absence of direct political control, the managements of large privatized utilities were alert to the repercussions of issues of low commercial priority but high political sensitivity – the service standards of public coinboxes, for example, or certain aspects of the residential telephone service – that were likely to shape public perceptions and hence the pressures for strengthening the regulatory framework.

The network industries, therefore, have been viewed as vulnerable to the repercussive effects of local events. In the words of one senior operations manager, 'there is no such thing as a "local situation"'. This vulnerability has been increased in some ways with privatization. For example, an electricity generating company is now more at risk from industrial action at a large station, since it would endanger a larger proportion of revenue and carry the risk of a permanent loss of business to a competitor. Decentralization increases the risk of local incidents by devolving responsibility to local managers, and encouraging them with a rhetoric of entrepreneurial initiative and proactive decision-making. By providing managers with incentives such as performance-related pay, devolution may also encourage a business unit 'outlook' rather than a corporate perspective, leading to a concern for the performance of the unit in isolation from the overall needs of the company.

These tensions have been behind a certain recentralizing of managerial control and at best an uneasy cohabitation of decentralizing and recentralizing forces. Overt recentralization has been most apparent in BT, which has recently been moving to abolish the district as the basis of management organization and to rearrange its activities around 'market segments', primarily business and domestic services. Companies have retreated, too, from the full-blooded implementation of the profit centre idea. The likelihood is that local managers will continue to receive confused signals as to their autonomy and responsibility and that this will spill over into a certain amount of industrial relations instability.

CONCLUSIONS

Privatization has produced such a wide range of industrial relations phenomena, such a variety of style and substance, that it is necessary to explore the underlying processes that are driving them, rather than merely catalogue the changes. It has been argued that privatization has changed the context in which managerial strategies are formulated. Direct ministerial control has either been removed entirely or has been replaced by arm's-length control via the regulator. This has been referred to as the 'quasi-political contingency' (Ferner 1991). The regulator sets the boundaries within which 'responsibility to the shareholders' is to be discharged. Privatization also triggers reform of organizational structures,

managerial control systems, and corporate culture. An emphas
preneurial, market-responsive behaviour has prompted the devolutic
authority, over resources and over the conduct of industrial relatic
managers.

These elements create pressures, some of which appear to balance
requirements of the regulator and the expectations of investors both point in the
direction of cost reduction, particularly in labour costs. But they also make
demands about quality which may constrain labour-cutting, at least in the short
term. Investors are also seen to be worried about industrial relations stability; if
change is pushed too vigorously, the resulting industrial relations tensions are
likely to have a detrimental impact on stock-market perceptions. Managers thus
perform a balancing act between countervailing forces, assessing which is
dominant at a particular time. The need to arbitrate between these forces – the
quasi-political agenda, one might call it – sets up a tension with the business-
oriented agenda of devolved decision-making and responsibility structures. One
tension is that discussed above, between decentralization and recentralization.
Another is that between the internal logic of managerial planning, and the logic
of responding to external pressures. For example, the City may judge long-term
prospects on the basis of short-term 'proxies' such as immediate cuts in labour or
visible changes in industrial relations structures (such as the ending of managerial
collective bargaining or the introduction of single table bargaining). Management
may therefore feel obliged to satisfy these expectations even where the measures
taken are not optimal from the point of view of the internal logic of resource
deployment and planning. On the other hand, while these external pressures
undoubtedly represent real objective constraints on management, the evidence
also suggests that, to an extent, they are manipulated by management in order to
influence other actors. For example, 'investor expectations', or the 'demands of
the regulator' can be seen as levers deployed by management to help it to achieve
its own agenda of cutting costs and increasing efficiency and profitability.

It is not surprising that the industrial relations consequences of privatization
fluctuate according to which set of pressures predominates at a particular time.
One pattern has been a veering between hard-line, aggressive industrial relations
policies centered on job-cutting and a frontal challenge to the conventional
assumptions of collective relations, and a more conciliatory approach designed to
restore workforce commitment and service reliability. In the longer term,
managements may be able to reconcile some of the tensions through the introduction of new technology, allowing labour to be reduced without affecting the
quality of services. They may also be able to develop new forms of attaining
workforce commitment based on some of the current tenets of human resource
management – Total Quality Management, for example – rather than on the
'public service ethos' on which industrial relations traditionally rested under
public ownership. One of the tasks for the unions will be to adapt their strategies
to the new management agendas on quality.

Despite the changes in the core services, the degree of industrial relations stability is likely to be higher than that in new areas where the public ownership heritage is absent and where the dynamism of markets is the key determinant of managerial personnel and industrial relations strategies. However, there are some signs of more radical readjustments to collective relations in the core, and these too may eventually diverge profoundly from the old public sector pattern.

A final comment concerns the differences between privatized companies. One broad difference is that between the regulated utilities and those unregulated companies, such as British Steel, operating in competitive markets. In their case, the end of political control has brought a sharp reduction in the general political influence over managerial decision-making, as illustrated by the failure of ministers to overturn a management decision to close the Ravenscraig steelworks (see Ferner 1991). Within the regulated companies, however, there are still marked differences of tone or style between a BT and a British Gas. How are these to be explained? One element is the structural difference between companies: BT exploits a rapidly evolving, 'leading edge' technology with dramatic long-term implications for employment levels, while British Gas's technology is slowly evolving and less radical in its industrial relations implications. British Gas, to a far greater extent than BT, has to be aware of the public safety consequences of its operations, and this is seen by its managers as a factor of stability and caution in the handling of its collective relations. But beyond these factors, there would appear to be space for management to exercise a degree of 'strategic choice' over the kind of industrial relations that are developed.

NOTES

1   This chapter is based on research into the industrial relations consequences of privatization in electricity, gas, water and telecommunications, conducted at the Industrial Relations Research Unit by the authors, and funded by the Economic and Social Research Council. It brings together many of the findings and analyses of a number of articles: Ferner 1991, Ferner and Colling 1991, and Colling and Ferner 1992. The main primary source of research data is around a hundred in-depth interviews in the above industries, conducted mainly between 1988 and 1990. Interviewees included personnel and industrial relations management at industry, company (including board), regional and local level, and union officials, again at national and local level. Operational managers at different levels were also interviewed.

2   British Telecom was privatized in 1984, with the sale of 51 per cent of the shares. A further tranche was sold in November 1991. British Gas was floated in 1986, the water companies in 1989, electricity distribution companies in 1990, and the electricity generators in 1991.

3   The Conservatives are currently planning legislation to introduce competing private rail services on a state-owned track system, rather than privatizing the railways as a whole.

4   In the electricity industry, it is the regional supply monopolies which are price-regulated. On the generation side, an element of competition has been introduced. The old Central Electricity Generating Board was broken up into three competing suppliers, and the scope for new generating ventures has been greatly widened.

5   During the 1980s, only one company, Mercury, was licensed by the government to run a fixed-link telecommunications network in competition with BT. In late 1990 the government published recommendations for the opening up of competition in this area.

6   It should be noted that the water industry regulator has expressed concern that diversification may lead to the neglect of the core water supply activity (Ofwat 1991: 9).

7   A straw in the wind is the 1991 agreement at Yorkshire Water for a novel 'single-table' bargaining arrangement to replace separate negotiations for craft, manual and white-collar workers (*Financial Times*, 10 May 1991).

8   This section draws heavily on Colling and Ferner 1992.

REFERENCES

Blyton, P. (1990) 'Steel: a classic case of industrial relations change in the 1980s,' Paper presented to Conference on 'Employment Relations in the Enterprise Culture', University of Cardiff Business School, 18–19 September.

Colling, T. (1991) 'Privatization and the management of IR in electricity distribution', *Industrial Relations Journal* 22(2), 117–29.

——— and Ferner, A. (1992) 'The limits of autonomy: devolution, line managers and industrial relations in privatized companies', *Journal of Management Studies* 29(2), 209–27.

Ferner, A. (1988) *Governments, Managers, and Industrial Relations. Public Enterprises in Their Political Environment*, Oxford: Blackwell.

——— (1989) 'Ten years of Thatcherism. Changing industrial relations in British public enterprises', Warwick Papers in Industrial Relations, no. 27, University of Warwick, Industrial Relations Research Unit.

——— (1990) 'The changing influence of the personnel function: privatization and organizational politics in electricity generation,' *Human Resource Management Journal*, 1(1), 12–30.

——— (1991) 'Privatization and industrial relations: the end of politics?', Paper presented to the 10th Egos Colloquium, Vienna, 15–18 July.

——— and Colling, T. (1991) 'Privatization, regulation and industrial relations,' *British Journal of Industrial Relations* 29(3), 491–409.

IRRR (Industrial Relations Review & Report) (1989) 'Industrial relations after privatization', *IRS Employment Trends* 439, 10 May, 12–14.

Moore, J. (1986) 'Why privatise?', in J. Kay, C. Mayer and D. Thompson (eds), *Privatization and Regulation: The UK Experience*, Oxford: Clarendon.

O'Connell Davidson, J. (1990) 'The commercialization of employment relations: the case of the water industry', *Work, Employment and Society* 4(4), 531–50.

Ofwat (1991) *1990 Report of the Director General of Water Services*, London: HMSO.

Ogden, S. (1990) 'The impact of privatization on industrial relations in the water industry', Paper presented to Conference on 'Employee Relations in the Enterprise Culture', University of Cardiff Business School, 18–19 September.

Smith, M. (1991) 'Northumbrian takes the steam out of bargaining', *Financial Times*, 26 April, p. 20.

Terry, M. (1990) 'Public sector trade unionism: the rediscovery of self-confidence,' Unpublished paper, University of Warwick.

Trades Union Congress (TUC) (1986) *Bargaining in the Privatised Companies*, London: TUC.

Vickers, J. and Yarrow, G. (1988) *Privatization. An Economic Analysis*, Cambridge, Mass./London: MIT Press.

Part III

PRIVATIZATION STRATEGIES WITHIN THE PUBLIC SECTOR

8

THE POLITICAL ECONOMY OF COMPETITIVE TENDERING[1]

Matthew Uttley and Nicholas Harper

INTRODUCTION

Since 1979, the introduction of competition for public service provision has been a central feature of the Conservative government's microeconomic policy. By 1988 the method of policy implementation for local authorities was through 'compulsory competitive tendering' (CCT): central government legislation requiring authorities to subject a range of services traditionally supplied in-house by direct labour to periodic competition from the private sector. Though local councils continue to pay for the services, through the competitive tendering (CT) process they could subsequently be provided by private contractors. The range of activities currently subsumed under CCT legislation are building and highway construction and maintenance (Local Government Planning and Land Act 1980), and refuse collection, street cleaning, building cleaning, schools and welfare catering, other catering, vehicle maintenance, and the management of sports and leisure facilities (Local Government Act 1988). Indications are that the government intends to extend mandatory competition to include various professional activities (architecture, buildings inspection, etc.) in future legislative initiatives (HM Treasury 1991: 24).

Competitive tendering policy has generated a highly politicized debate. On the one hand, advocates point to considerable cost savings and improved technical efficiency through competition (see, for example, Hunt 1990). On the other, opponents claim that competition and contracting-out to private firms lead to a deterioration of service quality, worker exploitation (SCAT 1985), and excessive costs in enforcing, managing and monitoring the tendering process (see, for example, SCAT 1989). Of the limited number of academic studies that have emerged, attention has tended to focus on the main issues arising from the political debate: whether CT leads to cost-saving (Hartley and Huby 1986), and the sources of purported efficiency gains (see, for example, Cubbin et al. 1987).

This chapter attempts to contribute to a broader understanding of competitive tendering and its implications for the supply of publicly-funded services. The first section addresses three issues: the scope of current tendering legislation; the arguments surrounding the likely outcomes of CCT; and the existing empirical evidence of the performance of CT in the UK local authority sector. The primary conclusion reached is that though CT appears to result in aggregate cost savings, a number of important questions still remain unanswered. The second section introduces a theoretical framework premised on the concept of 'corporate culture', and briefly outlines the application of the model to the available data on local authority competitive tendering.

CCT AND LOCAL AUTHORITIES: THE LEGISLATION

Local authorities have always relied on private and voluntary organizations to provide goods and services. Prior to 1979, however, the vast majority of authorities' statutory service functions were provided as a matter of course by direct labour organizations (DLOs): in-house units organized according to service role (for example, refuse collection, catering, etc.). Furthermore, the dominant political ethos that in-house public sector organization was naturally the most 'effective' type of service provision meant that DLOs were immune from private sector competition.

During the 1980s, as Parker points out: 'Legislation on compulsory competitive tendering arose ... because of the failure of most local authorities to react to what the Government saw as overwhelming evidence of efficiency gains from competition' (Parker 1990: 654). On the one hand, the Conservatives entered office with a declared policy of efficiency in public services, the reduction of union influence and an expanded role for the private sector (Key 1988: 65). Early implementation of reform was through the Local Government Planning and Land Act (1980), and an explicit commitment to further rounds of legislation (see Table 8.1). The political impetus for compulsory competitive tendering and contractorization was further reinforced by evidence of cost savings elsewhere in the public sector, notably the Ministry of Defence (hospital cleaning) and the NHS.

On the other hand, a number of Conservative authorities including Wandsworth and Southend-on-Sea, had voluntarily extended competitive tendering to services beyond those contained in the 1980 Act and obtained significant economies. Despite these demonstrable cost savings, however, the

Table 8.1 The range of local authority services currently subjected to mandatory competitive tendering

---

Local Government Planning and Land Act 1980
The introduction of CCT for building and highway construction and maintenance.

Local Government Act 1988
The introduction of CCT in refuse collection, street cleaning, building cleaning, schools and welfare catering, other catering, vehicle maintenance, and the management of sports and leisure facilities (added by Parliamentary Order in November 1989).

---

majority of authorities were reluctant to extend CT on a unilateral basis. Consequently, three factors – central government ideological objectives, proven efficiency gains, and the unwillingness of authorities to implement CT on a voluntary basis – were precursors to the Local Government Act 1988.

The scope and provisions of the 1988 Act (see Table 8.1) reflect the political environment surrounding its implementation. In addition to defining the services to be subjected to competition, clear stipulations are incorporated to avoid 'anti-competitive' behaviour by authorities. A summary of the main stipulations of the 1988 Act are contained in Table 8.2.

Though the legislation is designed to prevent authorities favouring DLOs in the selection process, scope still exists for anti-competitive behaviour. For instance, authorities may attempt to package contracts in sizes which preclude private companies from bidding, or release selective information to DLOs to enhance their bids in relation to private companies.

ARGUMENTS SURROUNDING COMPETITIVE TENDERING

Advocates of market processes in publicly-funded service supply *per se*, and CT in particular, point to potential benefits from periodic contestability. Central is the claim that competition leads to cost savings through increased efficiency, both technical and allocative. This argument is premised on three propositions:

First, cost savings and efficiency improvements result from CT because tendering makes the market for the provision of services periodically contestable (Parker 1990). The economic case for CT arises because local authorities have traditionally been monopoly service providers, and in the absence of competition there has been no yardstick for assessing the efficiency of in-house units. Competitive tendering, it is argued, furnishes councils with comparative cost information on alternative sources of supply (Hartley 1984). In addition, periodic competition – low entry costs and the threat of substitution by rival

Table 8.2 Provisions of the Local Goverment Act 1988

- The authority must advertise its intention to let a contract.
- The authority is required to invite at least three companies to tender from those who express an interest.
- DLOs are required to tender on the same grounds as private organizations.
- The specification of minimum and maximum contract periods.
- If DLOs are awarded tendered contracts the authority is required to keep a separate trading account.
- No cross subsidy between, or subsidization of trading accounts is allowed.
- Authorities should not act in a manner likely to distort competition.
- Timetables specifying when services should be subject to competition.
- The exemption of services which had a contract value less than £100,000 in the year prior to CCT legislation.

---

organizations – serves to drive down tender bids and encourage operating efficiency.

Second, cost savings occur through CT because it counteracts inherent inefficiencies in public sector bureaucracies. Tendering, according to 'New Right' and 'public choice' economists, reduces the tendency of bureaucrats to over-supply services by directing resources to the demands of consumers rather than where 'they would best serve the needs of producers' (Pirie 1988: 6). Oversupply, it is argued, emanates from bureaucratic monopoly of cost information, and objectives of budget-maximization and economic rents (see, for example, Hartley 1980). Advocates of CT claim competition releases alternative cost information to clients (local councils), whilst providing a mechanism for reform of working practices. It is important to note, however, that though CT may indeed lead to increased technical efficiency it still falls short of *consumer* choice: the public are still unable to express specific service preferences since local councils still act as purchasing agents.

Third, CT leads to more efficient service provision because implementation requires improved management procedures and oversight. The claim is made that CT divorces service provision from quality control and regulation, removing the potential 'conflict of interest' associated with traditional monopoly-based in-house provision. Furthermore, statutory CCT legislation enables sanctions to be applied to contractors, either DLOs or private, if performance is inadequate in terms of contract specifications. In addition, the tendering process forces authorities to consider services quality in terms of *outputs* (effectiveness of service to local Community Charge payers), rather than the quantity of inputs (for example, number of personnel employed). Finally, with the emphasis on service output that CT implies, authorities will be more inclined to consider alternative *levels* of service, facilitating possible improvements in allocative efficiency (reducing undersupply and oversupply problems by allocating outputs more in accordance with the patterns of 'consumer' (local authority) preferences).

Opponents of CT, mainly located in the trade union movement, have focused their claims on what they identify as the undesirable consequences of 'commercializing' local government. Specifically, they point to purported costs associated with: 'the dominant use of efficiency and financial criteria and simply trying to follow private contractors' unit costs, productivity levels, wage rates and conditions of service, rather than basing services on local needs' (SCAT 1990: 7).

CCT is seen as an attempt to introduce 'efficiency' (the relation of outputs to inputs) at the expense of 'effectiveness' (the quality of outputs in terms of their impact on the community) – effectiveness which is best provided by public service employees rather than profit-maximizing firms. The case against CT can be summarized as follows:

First, contrary to the claims of advocates of tendering and competition, CT leads to a clear decline in service quality. Critics cite numerous cases where contractors have defaulted on contracts leading to poor standards of cleaning and other services (see, for example, SCAT 1989, and TUC 1985). It is important to note, however, that the point that CT leads to a decline in service quality has not remained unchallenged. The conclusion of a recent Audit Commission report points out that 'there is no need for competition to lead to a deterioration in service' (Audit Commission 1989) as the onus of contract specification – the definition of service requirements including quality – remains with local councils. Furthermore, there is no logical reason why 'contractor' failure should necessarily be restricted to the private sector.

Second, another argument cited against CCT is that cost savings achieved are at the expense of large-scale redundancies and a decline in working conditions. Though comprehensive data are unavailable on cumulative job losses from CT to date, recent estimates indicate that since 1985 UK council blue-collar employees fell from 631,000 to 539,000, with 'some' of the difference attributable to contracting to the private sector (*Financial Times*, 28 August 1991). Further, job losses, it is argued, have a multiplier effect on local economies: a recent study notes that in Sheffield, 'for every four jobs lost through contracting-out one further job would be lost in private services in the local economy' (SCAT 1989: 16). In addition, it is claimed that new working practices resulting from CT have been at an unacceptable social cost – a reduction in workers' living standards (see, for example, *Financial Times*, 28 August 1991). Employment practices and CT have thus introduced a distributional element to the debate because of the potential for 'winner' and 'loser' groups.

Third, critics point to the possibility of private sector corruption in the tendering process and the dangers of replacing in-house units with private cartels, for service quality.

Fourth, a further criticism of CT is that unacceptable administrative costs are incurred in tender. Writing specifications, analysing tendering documents and monitoring contracts, it is argued, incurs excessive manpower and financial expenses by councils. In support of this claim, a study for Manchester City Council estimated that administration expenses approximately halved anticipated CT savings in an analysis of 448 tendered contracts (SCAT 1989: 54). Though costs are incurred in tendering, proponents of CT have responded by pointing out that these expenses should always have been incurred by efficient authorities in monitoring in-house units.

Finally, in contrast to the claims of trade unions and the 'broad left', some have claimed that current CCT legislation does not go far enough. As Parker and Hartley note, a 'New Right' criticism of authorities is that they have sometimes provided too high a level of service, oblivious of the marginal cost to provide a little more or less of a given service output (Parker and Hartley 1990). Because CCT policy leaves questions of service levels to local politicians, and services are funded out of general taxation, 'competitive tendering does not introduce consumer choice and allocative efficiency. In this respect it falls short of complete privatisation' (Parker and Hartley 1990: 12).

Certainly, CCT falls short of a number of 'New Right' policy objectives (user specific charges etc.) – objectives which may also have attendant implementation problems (see, for example, Stoker 1990). However, it is important to note, as subsequent sections illustrate, that questions of *consumer* choice have largely been marginalized in the mainstream debate over CCT.

As this section demonstrates, competitive tendering is a highly controversial area of economic policy. The myth and emotion that surrounds CT provides a case for analysing the various claims and counter-claims as testable hypotheses.

ANALYSING THE DATA

Since the Local Government Planning and Land Act 1980 a number of empirical studies have assessed the effects of CT in the local authority sector and elsewhere (see, for example, Hooper and Whitbread 1992). It is important to note that these studies have focused in the main on the parameters of the broader political debate. That is:

- the proportion of contracts won by DLOs and private companies after the tender process;
- the aggregate (overall) and average (by service and authority) cost savings resulting from CT where contracts have been won either by DLOs or private contractors;
- the sources of efficiency gains (changes in management structure, technical efficiency improvements, new working practices, etc.);
- the relative effect of ownership (private vs DLO) on service cost.

For ease of presentation, the results of these studies will be presented as answers to major questions in the political debate:

What proportion of contracts have been retained by DLOs after CT?

Indications are that since the introduction of CCT, the vast majority of contracts have been won by local authority DLOs. According to a report commissioned by the Local Authority Associations (Local Government Management Board 1992), DLOs have won approximately 80 per cent of tendered contracts, a figure broadly confirmed by the Centre for Local Economic Strategies (1990) and the Audit Commission (1989).

A number of interpretations have been applied to the distribution of contracts in recent tendering rounds. Groups opposed to CT in principle have heralded the success of DLOs (SCAT 1985). In contrast, however, according to a recent report by the Audit Commission (1987), the limited extent of contracting out reflects aspects of authority work which are unattractive to the private sector. Specifically, the report identifies:

- anxiety on the part of firms over the highly 'visible' nature of local authority work: performance short-falls lead to immediate and unfavourable publicity;
- no opportunity to build a pre-emptive local position;

- emphasis on cost rather than value; and
- the lack of suitable local facilities or capital equipment available within specific authority boundaries.

Furthermore, evidence suggests that some firms have been reluctant to bid in early tendering rounds, preferring instead to monitor the practical implementation of the tender process (Walsh 1991). In other cases, firms claim to have been dissuaded from competing following accusations of particular authorities favouring in-house bids.

Does CT result in cost savings?

Empirical studies do suggest that CT has led to *aggregate* cost savings for local authority services. Existing analyses fall into two broad categories: early studies, largely cross-sectional in nature, comparing costs of authorities which voluntarily contracted out with those retaining services in-house; and more recent studies analysing identical services before and after competition (see Table 8.3).

Work by Hartley and Huby (1986), based on a survey of 410 authorities, identified *average* savings of 26 per cent from CT. In addition, using a computer model developed by the Local Authorities Management Service, the Audit Commission concluded that authorities with privatized refuse collection tended to have lower than average costs. It is important to note, however, that both studies highlight average cost savings: in the Hartley and Huby survey, for example, figures ranged between 68 per cent savings to extra costs of 28 per cent from tendering. Furthermore, the Audit Commission noted that: 'The most competitive DLOs have costs that are lower than the prices quoted by the average private suppliers; but on average DLO's costs are more expensive to ratepayers than private suppliers' (Audit Commission 1987: 2).

Table 8.3 Cost savings resulting from CT

Study	Date	Service	Findings
Audit Commission	1984	Refuse collection	Estimated savings of 20 per cent from CT
Hartley and Huby	1986	Range of services	Average percentage savings of 26 per cent per annum from competition
Domberger *et al.*	1986	Refuse collection	Savings of 20 per cent from CT
Walsh	1991	Range of services	Average savings of 5.7 per cent from CCT

In a case study of refuse collection based on 1984/5 CIPFA statistics, Domberger *et al.* (1986) concluded that costs were about 22 per cent lower for authorities where contracting-out was taking place after tendering. This study also indicates that similar cost savings were obtained where tendered contracts have been won by in-house DLOs. Again, these findings appear to confirm the proposition that CT leads to average cost savings whether contracts are placed with DLOs or with firms, with savings broadly in line with other research.

In a more recent analysis, Walsh (1991) compared estimated annual costs of a range of services before and after the Local Government Act 1988. Surveying forty authorities, Walsh found average cost saving of 5.7 per cent after competitive tendering. Though CT led to overall post-tendering cost reductions, figures ranged from savings in one authority of 48.9 per cent (building cleaning) to an increase of 25.9 per cent (street cleaning).

What are the sources of cost savings?

Economies from CT could arise from two sources. On the one hand, as advocates claim, tendering may have led to improved technical efficiency: the same service outputs with fewer inputs, or the same inputs with higher outputs. Other factors may include improved management processes, better factor mix and the introduction of new technologies. On the other hand, as opponents claim, cost savings may be attributable to lower input prices or the increased intensity of input use (reductions in wages and benefits and large-scale redundancies offset by increased working hours).

From the existing data sets the main conclusion is that cost savings have been obtained from a mixture of technical efficiency improvements and changes in employment patterns/practices. Academic research indicates that the bulk of savings are attributable to more efficient factor mix (Domberger *et al.* 1986) and improved management structures (Walsh 1991). However, job losses have by no means been absent from the introduction of competition: Audit Commission figures, for example, indicate that private contractors in authorities which have voluntarily contracted-out typically use 35 to 45 per cent fewer employees (Audit Commission 1989: 23).

Does ownership (private or public) affect performance in the CT process?

The issue of privatization and the effect of ownership on organizational performance has generated a body of literature, the detailed analysis of which is beyond the scope of this chapter. The germane facts on the ownership issue, based on the existing data sets on CT, are best summed up by Domberger *et al.*: 'It is the introduction of competition, rather than awarding contracts to private firms, which is the critical factor in lowering costs' (Domberger *et al.* 1986: 79–80). Consequently, as the Audit Commission have pointed out: 'authorities would be unwise to assume that all the benefits of enhanced competitiveness will be realised easily by handing the problem to the private sector' (Audit Commission 1987: 5).

In general terms, though arguments in favour of both private and public provision (see, for example, Audit Commission 1987) *in a competitive framework* remain in principle, the experience of actual CCT policy provides no conclusive evidence either way.

A FRAMEWORK FOR ANALYSIS

It becomes apparent from existing data on CT that a number of important questions remain unanswered. Specifically, ambiguity still exists about:

- Why CT only leads to *aggregate* cost savings in service provision. That is, why is there no one-to-one relationship between competition and increased technical efficiency/cost savings?
- How the mechanism by which competition affects performance can be explained.

To provide an explanation of why introducing contestability into local authority services might be expected to improve their provision it is necessary to consider the nature of competition, and in particular the notion of competition as a search process. This characterization of competition is perhaps best expressed by Hayek, as 'a method of discovering particular facts relevant to the achievement of specific, temporary purposes' (Hayek 1978: 181). It is not the extent to which markets conform to some predetermined criteria which determines whether the outcome is competitive. Competition is successful if it leads to information which enables goals to be achieved which could not be achieved by any other method. As a result, it is difficult if not impossible to assess how effective competition is, as the facts which are essential for success are only discovered after the process of competition. Other facts leading to alternative outcomes which may or may not be preferable remain unknown. In other words, the opportunity cost against which outcomes can be measured is unknown and unknowable (see, for example, Langlois 1986, Wiseman 1990). Indeed, outside researchers face the additional task of second-guessing the forecast or expected (unknowable) outcomes which influenced which alternative was selected.

The notion of competition as a process allows for organizations to determine the objectives they will pursue and the relative importance they will attach to various factors when making decisions in the face of uncertainty. Such decisions are the essence of entrepreneurship – the choice of market and product (issues of allocative efficiency) and of factors of production (technical efficiency). But entrepreneurship also involves decisions as to how choices are made within the organization – not only the formal structure of the decision-making process, but also the relative importance given to the various factors which enter into each decision. In other words, entrepreneurship involves establishing, maintaining and operating the mechanism by which the competitive process is operated. The essence of this mechanism is a series of relationships within the organization, and between the organization and other entities. This set of relationships can be referred to as the culture of the organization. Thus, one of the entrepreneurial functions is to establish, maintain and operate the culture of the organization as a set of relationships which determine the decision-making process.

The set of relationships established by the entrepreneur, and the importance and emphasis given to each, will vary. Indeed, seeking and establishing relationships is part of the search process of competition. However, the types of relationship involved can be internal or external.

Internal

Objectives of the enterprise;
managerial structure and responsibility;
organization and methods of production;
personnel policy;
nature and role of trade unions;
motivation of workforce;
structure and determinants of rewards.

External

An organization has many external relationships, some of which will be more important at any one time. Examples include: customers, suppliers, competitors, and regulatory and other constraints.

1   *Customers* Whether customers are viewed as an essential part of the business, providing goals and objectives for the business to meet, or essentially as external to the business, providing a hole into which the output determined by the organization disappears. In the case of local authorities there is an issue as to who the customer is – whether local authorities are themselves the customer for services such as refuse collection, street cleaning, etc. or are agents acting on behalf of the residents who form the actual customers.

2   *Suppliers* Whether suppliers are treated as adversaries to be exploited or as partners in the production process.

3   *Competitors* Whether competition is to be avoided, or seen as a part of the process of determining customer demands.

4   *Regulatory and other constraints* The paradigm set of relationships which are accepted as permissible ways of operating at the time.

These are not one-way, isolated relationships. By their nature, relationships are two-way, and are influenced by both parties. They also vary over time; indeed change and development may be at the heart of the culture of an organization (see, for example, Peters 1989).

The concept of culture, defined as a set of relationships, leads to the expectation that organizations competing by a search process may choose different cultures, leading to different learning paths and hence adopting alternative approaches and solutions to the search for success. Indeed, it is unlikely that two organizations would adopt identical paths, unless their cultures included a deliberate objective to mirror each other's choices.

In the context of contracting-out by local authorities, differences between the culture of public sector and private sector providers can be postulated. When public sector bodies act as procurement agencies, a similar pattern of differences from the behaviour of private consumers may occur. The impact of contestability may thus be on the public sector as procurement agency, rather than on the public or private sector as supplier. The empirical stage of this study is concerned with testing for the existence of such differences on both the supply and demand sides, by analysing the provision of services before and after the introduction of contestability, and by comparing the experience of local authorities with that of the NHS and MoD which are also dominated by public sector procurement.

The main differences postulated between the cultures of public sector and private organizations as suppliers of services (or agents), relate to the relationships which determine objectives, the assessment of performance, and the relationship with the customer.

The hypothesis to be explored is that organizations fall on a continuum between two broad types which can be stylized as *inward-looking* and *outward-looking*, examples of their characteristics being given below.

Inward-looking

1 *Objectives*: determined by reference to the organization, not to the customer.
2 *Motivation*: related to achieving bureaucratic objectives (for example, size of department).
3 *Performance*: assessed by comparison with predetermined and fixed norms set by the organization itself; little incentive to exceed or improve norms.
4 *Customers*: customer needs determined by organization and providers, rather than by search process and customer response.

Outward-looking

1 *Objectives*: determined by reference to the customer through a search process.
2 *Motivation*: related to criteria which reflect satisfying customers' needs as customers see them.
3 *Performance*: by comparison with achievement of competitors; every incentive to exceed or improve norms.
4 *Customers*: customer needs determined by search process and customer response measured against alternatives offered by competitors.

The central hypothesis is that local authorities acting as procurement agencies are predominantly inward-looking organizations; introducing contestability is a way of moving them along the continuum towards outward-looking organizations.

It is not that public sector organizations are of necessity less efficient, better or worse than private providers. Indeed, focusing on culture suggests there is no one-to-one between ownership and performance (as found empirically). If public sector organizations were allowed to determine their own set of relationships, they could adopt an outward-looking culture seeking to identify and meet the needs of customers as perceived by the customers, rather than as predetermined by the suppliers or agents. In the case of local authorities, this may entail recognizing that they are intermediaries or procurement agents in the supply of services to the public, rather than customers themselves, and allowing the customer to determine objectives.

Similarly, private companies may adopt a culture similar to that which characterizes the stylized public organization, provided that they can also find a way of maintaining customers in the face of alternatives offered by competitors. This may be achieved either by making internally based decisions which mirror customers' perception of their demands, or by monopoly control of the market.

By divorcing the provision from the determination of the service to be provided the opportunity is introduced for alternative solutions, both technical and allocative. This is the essence behind the expectation that contestability will lead to improved performance.

Empirical analysis

The above approach is being used as the framework for an empirical analysis of the effect of introducing contestability into the provision services. The study involves analysis of contracting by the MoD for defence services, the NHS for ancillary services and local authorities' services. Comparisons are made over time within each service and between the three agencies.

The study aims to test the following propositions:

1   That introducing contestability improves the performance of suppliers, irrespective of whether the contract is issued to a public or private sector contractor.

2   That the experience of contestability changes the behaviour of procurement agencies, and in particular shifts the objectives and performance criteria of agencies towards external (customer) determined factors. Evidence that has emerged so far on this question indicates that such shifts do occur (see, for example, Walsh 1991).

3   That there will be an initial attempt to resist the introduction of contestability, to maintain the role and power of the parties likely to lose by the change.

Specific questions which are being considered include:

- What are the limits to contracting out?
- How is bidding organized and is the process really competitive?
- Are competitions for a given level of service (technical efficiency) or for different levels of service (allocative efficiency)?
- Does contestability result in cost savings?
- Are there any differences between performance on contracts won competitively by in-house units compared with those won by outside contractors?
- Are there any differences between performance on contracts won competitively by in-house units compared with their performance before the introduction of competition?
- What happens to quality after competition, and is the comparison being made on a like-for-like basis?
- How does the structure and application of managerial incentives compare before and after competition, and between the three bureaucracies?
- What are the transaction costs of introducing and enforcing contestability?
- Which groups oppose the change, and what types of barriers are introduced?
- Does the introduction of contestability lead local authorities to view themselves as intermediaries or procurement agents rather than customers, or does the distinction between procurement and finance by the authority and provision of a service by a contracted party reinforce the view of local authority as customer?

NOTES

1   This research was directed by Professor Keith Hartley with project funding from the GSRC (Project R000232464). The usual disclaimers apply.

BIBLIOGRAPHY

Audit Commission (1984) *Securing Further Improvements in Refuse Collection*, London: HMSO.
—— (1987) *Competitiveness and Contracting Out of Local Authority Services*, p. 4, London: HMSO.
—— (1989) *Preparing for Compulsory Competition*, London: HMSO.
Centre for Local Economic Strategies (1990) *Seconds Out, Round Two: The First Round of Compulsory Competitive Tendering*, Manchester: CLET.
Cubbin, J., Domberger, S. and Meadowcroft, S. (1987) 'Compulsory competitive tendering and refuse collection', *Fiscal Studies* 8(3), 49–59.
Domberger, S., Meadowcroft, S. A. and Thompson, D. J. (1986) 'Competitive tendering and efficiency: the case of refuse collection', *Fiscal Studies* 7(4), 69–87.
Evans, S. (1990) 'Ensuring efficient local services', in *Tender Traps*, London: Adam Smith Institute.
HM Treasury (1991) *Competing for Quality: Buying Better Public Services*, Cm 1730, London: HMSO.

Hartley, K. (1980) 'The economics of bureaucracy and local government', *Institute of Economic Affairs Readings*, 25, 105–22.

—— (1984) 'Policy towards contracting-out: the lessons of experience', *Fiscal Studies* 5(1), 98–105.

—— and Huby, M. (1986) 'Contracting-out policy: theory and evidence', in J. Kay, C. Mayer and D. Thompson *Privatisation and Regulation: The UK Experience*, Oxford: Clarendon Press.

Hayek, F. A. (1978) 'Competition as a discovery procedure', in Hayek, F. A. *New Studies in Philosophy, Politics, Economics and the History of Ideas*, Chicago: University of Chicago Press.

Hooper, N. and Whitbread, C. (1993) 'Contracting-out in the NHS', in A. Harrison (ed.), *From Hierarchy to Contract*, London: Policy Journals.

Hunt, D. (1990) 'Compulsory competitive tendering: the government's view', in *The Tender Traps*, London: Adam Smith Institute.

Key, T. (1988) 'Contracting-out ancillary services', in R. Maxwell (ed.), *Reshaping the National Health Service*, Newbury: Policy Journals.

Langlois, R. N. (ed.) (1986) *Economics as a Process: Essays in the New Institutional Economics*, Cambridge: Cambridge University Press.

Local Government Management Board (1992) CCT *Information Service: Survey Report No. 5*, London: LGMB.

Parker, D. (1990) 'The 1988 Local Government Act and compulsory competitive tendering', *Urban Studies* 27(5), 653–68.

—— and Hartley, K. (1990) 'Competitive tendering: issues and evidence', *Public Money and Management*, Autumn, pp. 9–16.

Peters, T. J. (1989) *Thriving in Chaos: Handbook for a Management Revolution*, London: Pan Books.

Pirie, M. (1988) *Privatisation*, Aldershot: Wildwood House.

SCAT (Services to Community Actions and Trade Unions) (1989) *The Price of Winning: Lessons from the First Round of Competitive Tendering*, Manchester: Manchester City Council.

Stoker, G. (1990) 'Government beyond Whitehall', in P. Dunleavy, A. Gamble and G. Peele, *Developments in British Politics 3*, London: Macmillan.

TUC (1985) *Contractors' Failures: The Privatisation Experience*, London: TUC.

Walsh, K. (1991) *Competitive Tendering for Local Authority Services*, London: HMSO.

Wiseman, J. (1990) *Cost, Choice and Political Economy*, Aldershot: Edward Elgar.

9

EC PUBLIC PROCUREMENT DIRECTIVES AND THE COMPETITION FROM EUROPEAN CONTRACTORS FOR LOCAL AUTHORITY CONTRACTS IN THE UK[1]

Michael Paddon

INTRODUCTION

Virtually all contacts awarded in European Community member states by public bodies or by organizations (public or private) which undertake their functions will be covered by an EC legal framework by 1993. This regime of Public Procurement Directives originated in the 1970s but has been substantially revised and extended as part of the programme for the Single European Market. Purchasing of goods and services by public bodies constitutes a substantial potential market. Public purchasing in the EC in 1986 was estimated to total 530 billion ECU, equivalent to 15 per cent of the Gross Domestic Product of the Community (Cecchini 1988). The largest markets in individual countries are in Germany and France where the total value of procurement by local government alone in each case nears £20bn, as shown in Table 9.1.

However, for services in particular, procurement from the private sector only provides a relatively small proportion of all the work undertaken for public bodies. An estimated 20–25 per cent of service requirements are bought from private sources (that is, covered by procurement) (Booz Allen and Hamilton 1991). The bulk of services are provided by in-house or from centralized government service units. The Procurement Directives, therefore, fit into a wider discussion about the most appropriate ways for central and local governments and other public bodies to cover their service requirements. Hence, they are part of that wider debate about contracting-out and other forms of 'privatization'.

This chapter focuses on the local government sector which has a total annual expenditure in the Community of around 614bn ECU (Booze Allen and Hamilton 1991). The Directives have implications for local authorities in their three roles as purchasers of goods and services from the private sector; deliverers

159

Table 9.1 The value of local government public procurement in Europe

Member state	Spending (£m)
Germany	19,602
Italy	19,563
France	18,690
UK	10,905
Spain	4,909
Netherlands	4,140
Denmark	3,686
Belgium	909
Portugal	269
Luxembourg	142

Source: L. Digings (1991).
Note: 1 Figures refer to 1985 or 1986. Comparable figures not available for Greece and Ireland.

of services to their communities; and contractors, in their own right, for the delivery of these services through, what in the UK are termed, their direct service and direct labour organizations. These roles are also covered in the UK by domestic legislation which has compelled local authorities to tender competitively for building work and other 'defined services' when they wish to use their own in-house organizations to undertake work. For building construction work and in several services, the activities of local authorities are therefore covered by two legislative frameworks; one from the EC, the other domestic. The UK legislation is now in the process of being extended. The result would be that by 1993 when the relevant EC Directive is likely to be in place, this dual legislation will cover most of the major service areas in local government.

This chapter looks at the different starting points of UK and EC legislation on public purchasing in relation to local authorities. Two major areas of local government activities are already covered by EC Directives; works and purchasing of supplies. From the information now available, the chapter assesses the limited impact of these Directives in attracting competition from other EC member states. It suggests that in building works, which are also covered by UK competitive tendering, European contractors interested in gaining access to UK public markets have used acquisitions and joint arrangements rather than the routes offered by procurement competition.

A similar process already seems to be underway in the service areas which will not be covered by EC Directives until 1993. A number of European multinational corporations have used the opportunities arising from privatization in the UK and competitive tendering legislation to establish UK operational bases and acquire a market share. The Directives are likely to have only limited impact on the strategies of these corporations. The likelihood of small- and medium-sized enterprises in these areas using the avenues opened by the Directives are likely to be limited both by the market strategies of the established multinationals and by the quite proper ways in which local authorities operate their tendering procedures.

PUBLIC PROCUREMENT LEGISLATION AND UK LOCAL AUTHORITIES

The establishment of a 'Common Market' through the removal of trade barriers, to allow the 'free movement of persons, services goods and capital' has been the defining aim of the European Community since the signing of the Treaty of Rome in 1957 (CLES 1990). Spending by public bodies has always been regarded by the Commission as an important component of and a potential impediment to this 'freedom of movement'. The articles of the Treaty, which prohibit public restrictions on tenderers from other EC countries, were therefore specifically augmented by EC Directives to cover the award of contracts for public building works (in 1971) and public supplies purchasing (in 1977). The Directives had three basic elements. First, the Community-wide advertising of contracts. Second, establishing objective criteria for the award of contracts. Third, banning adoption of technical standards which are only used nationally and, hence, have the effect of discriminating against contractors based in other EC states (Barnes *et al.* 1989).

By the time of the Commission's review of progress towards a common market in the mid-1980s and the preparation of the White Paper *Completing the Internal Market* in 1985, Public Procurement was deemed to be a particular problem area. While total public purchasing in the EC was estimated to be 530 billion ECU in 1986, equivalent to 15 per cent of the Gross Domestic Product of the EC, only a very small proportion (less than 0.14 per cent of the GDP) was awarded to European companies from outside the national boundaries of the public bodies concerned (Cecchini 1988). The existing Directives were presumed not to have achieved their objective, so the White Paper set out a legislative programme for Public Procurement as part of the steps for a Single Market to be implemented by 1992. The Directives were to be tightened and extended. The extensions were intended to close what were seen to be loopholes in procedures; to make procedures more easily monitored; and to bring both public services and contracts awarded by public bodies not previously included into the coverage of Directives (Digings 1991).

At the European level, this legislative programme is close to completion. Revised Works and Supplies Directives came into effect in 1989 and 1990 respectively. A 'Remedies' Directive, providing a framework for administrative or judicial review, triggered by contractors' complaints, was to be implemented in each member state by December 1991. A 'Utilities' Directive was passed in 1990 to cover works and supplies contracts awarded by public water, energy, transport and telecommunications bodies. Directives are in the final stages of the EC decision-making processes which will provide legislative 'remedies' for non-compliance with the Utilities Directives, and cover, in separate Directives,

Table 9.2 EC Public Procurement Directives

Directives covering local authorities

Already agreed by EC	*Implementation date*
1 Works Directive: originally passed in 1971 amended in 1989 by 89/440/EEC	Amended version July 1990
2 Supplies Directive: originally passed 1977 amended in 1988 by 88/295/EEC	Amended version January 1990
3 Compliance Directive: passed in 1989 as 89/665/EEC	By 21 December 1991

Directives not yet agreed

4 Services Directive: final proposal COM (91) 322	By late 1993

Directives covering utilities: water, transport, energy and telecommunications

Directives already agreed by EC	*Implementation date*
1 Utilities Directive: covering works and supplies passed 1990 as 90/531/EEC	By July 1992 but can opt for January 1993

Directives not yet agreed

2 Utilities Compliance: final proposal COM (91) 158	By July 1992 but can opt for January 1993
3 Utilities Directive: covering services final proposal COM (91) 347	By July 1992 but can opt for January 1993

---

contracts for services in the utilities and in all other public bodies (see Table 9.2).

Local authorities in the UK should have been implementing the Works and Supplies Directives since they first came into force. Both Directives have now been codified into UK Law through the Statutory Instruments in December 1991 which also fulfilled the requirements of the Remedies Directive.[2] All of the elements of the '1992' programme will have implications for councils, including the two 'Utilities' Directives, since many authorities have interests in ports, airports, etc. They will be significant for them in carrying out three roles. First, they are major purchasers of manufactured items, basic materials and other supplies. Second, they are responsible for providing services such as education, housing, street cleaning, etc., to their communities and must undertake for these services to be delivered either by the authority's own workforce, or by outside contractors or providers. Third, they are deliverers of services, in which role they may find themselves in competition with other agencies and contractors for contracts to provide the service.

The distinction between the second and third of these roles has been one of the products of the various measures introduced by the four Conservative governments in the major areas of UK public policy to distinguish the responsibility for making and co-ordinating policy from the operational responsibility for day-to-day delivery of services (Savage and Robbins 1990). The intention has been to break up the public sector, to privatize major parts of it and to introduce a diversity of non-public agencies into the delivery of major services. For UK local authorities a distinction is now made conceptually, and in many councils departmentally, between what are now conventionally described as their separate 'client' and 'contractor' functions. In the former guise, they decide upon service requirements, draft contractual documentation and award contracts. In the latter, they prepare tender bids for contracts, operate the contracts they have won, and keep separate accounts of their trading activities. This distinction has largely been a product of the two pieces of legislation which have made competition with private contracts compulsory for certain services.

The Planning and Land Act in 1980 introduced the principle of compulsory competitive tendering for categories of construction work associated with building, road, and sewerage systems. Establishing the pattern later to be followed for other 'defined' services, the legislation laid down advertising and contract award procedures which had to be followed if an authority wanted to consider offering work to its own in-house departments or direct labour organizations (DLOs). These were intended to give access to such work to outside, private contractors, but did not apply if the authority intended to use such contractors and not an in-house workforce. The legislation also set financial targets, or rates of return, for DLOs which were to use a required framework for their internal accounting.

The Local Government Act 1988 extended the same principles and general procedures to a set of services which the Minister was empowered to 'define', bringing the term 'compulsory competitive tendering' (CCT) into common use in UK local government.[3] But it went further in setting out a general, but loosely defined, obligation on authorities not to act 'anti-competitively' in awarding contracts. And for *any* contracts for goods and services awarded by authorities it prohibited consideration of 'non-commercial' considerations, another vaguely specified term which in practical terms includes employment conditions, trade union membership, and many aspects of equal opportunities practice.

In working within this domestic legislation, British authorities in their 'client' roles have largely attempted to maximize the extent to which they can continue to specify the type and quality of service they require, including, where possible, consideration when awarding contracts of wider policies on issues like employ-ment. In their 'contractor' roles they have tried to devise organizations and procedures which can successfully compete with outside contractors, and then generate the required financial surplus when delivering the service. This domestic response provides the key to the way in which the EC Directives are now viewed and evaluated by British local authorities. As purchasers and clients, the concerns of UK councils are with the potential costs, in resources and time, of following an additional set of procedures when awarding contracts. And there are consider-able doubts about the apparent benefits in terms of the price and quality of goods and services which will result. As contractors, the concerns are with the potential for the Directives to generate further competition through the access they may offer to UK markets for European private contractors, on terms that most of them feel are weighted heavily by domestic legislation in favour of the private sector.

DIFFERENT STARTING POINTS FOR EC AND UK LEGISLATION

Whether or not these views are either accurate or legitimate, UK local authorities certainly now face dual obligations under the respective legislation. In broad terms, the revised programme of EC directives and UK legislation on CCT covers similar aspects of the award of contracts: advertising, award procedures, criteria for selection of contractors, etc.[4] The coverage of construction work in the case of several of the defined services is the same, hence the concerns about the potential for further unwanted competition. However, the detail attached to each stage of the process of awarding contracts differs significantly, which is why there are fears about the additional costs. What may be of greater significance in the longer term is the fundamental difference in intention between the two sets of legislation. As a result each is triggered at a different stage in the decision by local authorities about how service should be delivered. The EC Directives take effect only once an authority has decided that it wishes to outsource supply or to use a private contractor. Its obligations cease once a contract has been awarded. UK CCT legislation intercedes in this first decision by requiring competition with private contractors, and the obligations on local authorities continue for the whole of the contract period.

Consistent with the central aim of the EC and the progress towards a Single Market, the intention of the Directives is to 'liberalize' trade in public procurement by facilitating greater contracting *between* member states. The research commissioned to provide 'objective' justification for the 1985 EC White Paper on the completion of the Single Market estimated that in 1984 the total level of public purchasing was 440 billion ECU, equivalent to 15 per cent of the EC's GDP. Of this, between 170 and 250 billion ECU was subject to contract procedures, approximating to 6–10 per cent of GDP. Local authority purchasing accounted for between 15 and 40 per cent of total public purchasing, depending on the individual EC member state. The Cecchini report claimed that 'By not encouraging intra-EC competition – if not by deliberately rejecting it – the public sector pays more than it should for the goods it needs and, in so doing, supports sub-optimal enterprises in the Community' (Cecchini 1988). Looking at five countries in 1984, the background research claims that the macroeconomic effect of removing these 'inefficiencies' would be potential public expenditure savings of between 8–19 billion ECU. These savings were estimated to be made up of three elements (European Commission 1988):

1   A *static trade effect* – that is, the savings to be made by buying from the cheapest supplying country in the EC – would save 3–8 billion ECU or 1–2 per cent of public purchasing.

2   A *competition effect* would save a further 1–3 billion ECU (about 0.5 per cent of public purchasing) by putting downward pressure on the prices charged by domestic firms in sectors which have not previously been open to international competition.

3   A *restructuring effect* would save 4–8 billion ECU (1–2 per cent of public purchasing), through the economies of scale achieved as industries reorganized under pressure from the new competitive conditions. These savings were likely to be concentrated in certain high technology industries like defence, computers, telecommunications and in railways.

Adjusting the figures to cover all twelve EC member countries, and averaging the results, the research estimated that total savings of 17.5 billion ECU, about 0.5 per cent of total EC GDP, would be made by opening up public procurement Community-wide.

This analysis and the projected savings cannot easily be translated into figures for local government. The industries identified by the research as most likely to be affected by restructuring are not significant for local government. There is also wide variation between EC member states in the degree of centralization of government, and the size and functions of local government. And for individual authorities, the research acknowledges that there may remain positive benefits from buying within national boundaries.

Overall, the analysis is really concerned with inter-EC member state trade. The Directives which have derived from it thus come into play at the point at which a public body, such as a local authority, decides to purchase goods or services and to award a contract. They do not apply if an authority chooses to undertake work itself, in-house. The intention of the Directives is not necessarily to increase the amount of local authority or other public sector work put out to tender. Nor do they concern themselves with how the decision is made within an authority to award work in-house rather than go out to tender. This is spelt out in the memorandum which accompanies the draft Directive to cover Services.

Commenting on the use of in-house organizations, the memorandum observes that 'Many contracting authorities are in a position to satisfy their needs for certain services by performing the activities concerned *with their own means*' (my emphasis). It continues 'In such cases the choice between buying the relevant services from outside and in-house performance is relatively open. Community procurement rules do not interfere with public authorities' decisions as to buying in the market place or satisfying their needs with their own means' (European Commission 1990).

It is possible that this emphasis may change in the future. The Services Directive contains a commitment to a review after three years which will include an appraisal of the effects of in-house performance on the opening up of the market. The concern is that the degree of in-house provision may affect the total size of the market to be competed for. A consultant's report commissioned by the EC to investigate in-house services suggests that it may be difficult for the Directives to move from this present position. First, because it estimates that at least 50 per cent of the total of internally provided services in the Community could never be outsourced. Second, because 'currently there is no overwhelming evidence that outsourcing results in significantly better value-for-money in the long term and across a full range of services which are procurable' (Booz Allen and Hamilton 1991). The same consultant's report claims that even in the UK there is no convincing evidence of potential savings from the enforced 'challenging of in-house service units'.

The rationale for CCT in UK legislation is precisely to intervene in decisions about buying in the market place or providing service using their own means. Both the 1980 and the 1988 Acts in Britain were intended to do either or both of two things. First, to put more of the provision of specific local authority services out to private contractors – that is, to privatize service provision. Second, to introduce the mechanisms of the market into the direct labour and direct service organizations which local authorities operate as their own contracting services.

Similar arguments were used to those which have accompanied the EC Directives – that increased competition would produce substantial savings to the public sector. The arguments have never been backed by undisputed research evidence. They were contested before the 1988 Act was introduced.[5] Researchers commissioned by the Department of the Environment to monitor the effects of the Act whilst producing an aggregate figure of potential savings of 6 per cent have warned that the methodological difficulties were so great and the degree of variation in the findings between services and authorities so diverse that it is unsafe to claim definite conclusions.[6] While the consultant researching the use of in-house services by public bodies for the EC has also concluded that the findings from CCT in the UK do not suggest significant savings nor greater value for money (Booz Allen and Hamilton 1991).

British CCT legislation comes into effect when an authority is making the decision between using its in-house service or awarding a contract to an outside contractor, and makes competition procedures compulsory. If an authority does not intend to use in-house services the procedures do not apply. EC Directives, alternatively, are not directed at the decision to use in-house services or contractors. But they do apply whenever an authority is putting work out to contract even where only external contractors are involved. For British local authorities the Directives will only impact on decisions about the award of contracts to DLOs or DSOs, rather than private contractors, because of the obligation to follow two sets of procedures. Were CCT to be removed in British law the compulsion to put work out to tender, and hence this aspect of the compulsion to use EC procedures, would also be removed.

ATTRACTING EUROPEAN CONTRACTORS TO UK LOCAL AUTHORITY MARKETS

The anticipation that the EC Directives will attract particular interest to the UK local authority market from European contractors, which is shared by a number of commentators as well as the authorities themselves, is based on five factors.

First, the relative size of the total market for local authority goods and services. Britain stands fourth in the 'league table' of the total spending by local authorities on public procurement. With spending in 1986 of £10.9 billion, UK local authorities spent approximately only half as much as the three largest spending member states, Germany, Italy and France, but more than twice as much as the next three, Spain, the Netherlands and Denmark (see Table 9.1).

Second, individual authorities in the UK are larger than many of their counterparts elsewhere in the EC. Thus, over half the local authorities in England serve populations of over 100,000 while less than 0.5 per cent of French councils have populations of this size. Over 98 per cent of French councils serve populations of less than 2,000 (Digings 1991). The detailed research carried out on public procurement for the Cecchini report claims that the purchasing and contracting in the UK is more concentrated than in any other member state with around 700 contracting bodies (including local government) compared with 1,000 in Belgium, 50,000 in France and 20,000 each in Germany and Italy (European Commission 1988). As a result, contracts for goods and services awarded by individual authorities are likely to be larger. They are more likely, therefore, to fall above the thresholds set by the EC at which the Directives take effect. And large contracts are also likely to offer greater inducement to contractors to incur the expenditure necessary to be able to compete and operate at a European level.

Third, since 1979, the UK labour market has been substantially 'de-regulated' by Conservative governments. The Fair Wages Resolution, which since 1947 imposed a requirement on contractors to pay employees appropriate rates in their occupations and areas, was removed in 1983 and with it Convention 94 of the International Labour Organization which requires that 'While producers should be free to compete on matters of price, design, quality of product and service, it is unfair for competition to be based on a bidding down of workers'

Table 9.3 The size of European municipalities

	% of municipalities	
Population served	England	France
More than 100,000	52%	<0.5%
10,000–100,000	48%	2%
Less than 2,000	<0.5%	98%

Source: Digings, 1991.

wages' (Parker 1990). Changes in employment law have restricted the activities of trade unions. These, and other moves, seem to offer contractors greater latitude in the labour market to lower or change terms and conditions of employment. Elsewhere in Europe, five EC member states – France, The Netherlands, Spain, Portugal and Luxembourg – have a minimum wage fixed by government, while in Greece and Belgium a national minimum wage is agreed between employers and unions (Labour Research 1991).

Fourth, and perhaps most important, the UK is alone in the EC in having legal compulsion on local authorities for compulsory or enforced competitive tendering. While other EC member states have elaborate legal codes to govern the procedures for awarding contracts, such as the French Codes des Marches on which the EC regime is largely based, they only come into play, as do the EC Directives, once an authority has taken the decision to contract work out. Only in the UK is competitive tendering imposed on local authorities as a compulsory requirement by central government.

Fifth, and related to the last point, CCT is one of a number of changes which Conservative governments in the UK have made to the role, size and organization of the public sector. Other measures, to either reduce the role of the public sector or to introduce private companies into its operations, have provided development opportunities for private firms, including European contractors. Privatization of the water industry in 1989, the introduction of competitive tendering for ancillary service in the health services from 1982, and the reorganization of the local authority operation of waste management, in particular, have enabled some contractors to devise associated strategies for entry into UK public sector markets.

THE EC DIRECTIVES AND COMPETITION FOR LOCAL AUTHORITY CONTRACTS

In the remainder of this chapter, an assessment will be made of the extent to which the Directives have introduced greater competition from European suppliers or contractors for UK local authority contracts. There has, as yet, been little time for the new regime of Directives to have an effect. The revised Works Directive came into operation in July 1990 and the Supplies Directive in January 1989, while the Services Directive will be in force in 1993. There are signs, however, that while the formal impact of the Directives may be limited, processes of concentration and restructuring are underway at a European level which will have significance for the nature of future competition in construction and many services.

Local authority construction and the EC Works Directive

EC Directives have covered building works since 1971. The revised Works Directive, which took effect in 1990, covers public works contracts with extensions to cover 'works concessions', the rather more complex arrangements common in Continental Europe by which contractors first build and then operate facilities. It also raised the threshold of contracts values at which the Directive automatically applies from £662,000 to £3.31 million (at the exchange rates operating in 1991).

The new value threshold takes many local authority contracts outside the coverage of the Directives. The capital and other restrictions under which local government has been operating have dramatically reduced the value of new building undertaken and contracted out, particularly new house building. UK official statistics for all public bodies indicate that in 1989 only 1.9 per cent of contracts for new house building were over £3 million in value and 2.1 per cent contracts for other new building work (see Table 9.4). The two areas of building work more likely to fall within the remit of the Directives are contracts for maintenance work to existing buildings and construction work funded in whole or part by EC grants.

Many of the larger metropolitan councils in the UK certainly package their building maintenance work in contracts which exceed £3.3 million and now use the prescribed EC procedures in advertising and awarding contracts. Others, however, have taken a view, on legal advice, that the Directive as presently drafted does not cover the maintenance of buildings, so do not use the procedures. Once the complete framework of Directives is in place, it will be extremely difficult for any authority to argue that such contracts are not covered by any of them, given the Commission's intention that all public contracts for any good or services will be included somewhere in their remit. And within EC law judicial rulings are based on the *intention* of legislation, rather than a detailed reading of specific clauses (Bennett 1991).

Since March 1989 local authority projects financed from the EC structural funds or other EC lending bodies have been obliged to follow the Procurement Directives. Compliance is monitored through questionnaires with the possible

Table 9.4 Value of new public sector construction orders in the UK

£'000	Public sector new housing (%)	Public sector other new work (%)
Under 500	75.4	88.1
500–1,000	11.9	5.5
1,000–2,000	8.4	3.1
2,000–3,000	2.4	1.2
Over 3,000	1.9	2.1
Total	100	100

Source: DoE housing and construction statistics.
Note: Figures are for value of new orders to contractors in 1989.

sanction of non-payment of funds if the Directives have not been complied with in the award of contracts.

Through whatever mechanism the Directives are applied, the evidence suggests that little additional interest in UK contracts has been generated from European-based contractors. The local authority Association of Metropolitan Authorities (AMA) recently surveyed its member authorities on their experience of using the EC Works Directive. The thirteen authorities which responded had between them awarded only six contracts over £3.31 million in value in the year since the amended Directive came into effect. EC funding conditions on projects resulted in a total of forty-six contracts being awarded using the EC procedures. However, no responses to advertisements in the EC official journal were received from European contractors and no authorities had awarded contracts to non-UK-based firms (Association of Metropolitan Authorities 1991b).

This apparent lack of response through the formal EC procedures suggests two things. The first is that UK legislation already offers significant access to tendering in local authority markets for contractors. Extensions to the Planning and Land Act 1980 now effectively mean that all local authority building work is subject to CCT under terms which are more restrictive on them than the European Directives. The second is that those European contractors with an interest in competing for UK local authority markets will do so through acquisitions in the British construction industry or joint ventures with domestic contractors rather than tendering for work from a base and in the name of a Continental contractor.

French, German, Dutch and Italian contractors have been pursuing strategies of geographical expansion and industrial diversification since the mid-1980s. The French multinational conglomerate, Compagnie Generale des Eaux, discussed in greater detail below because of its contracting interests in other local authority services, bought the UK building contracting firm Norwest Holt through its own construction subsidiary SGE in 1989–90. It has a strategy of acquiring a medium-sized construction company with experience in the public sector in every EC member state before the Single Market is achieved (Paddon 1990). The other comparable French conglomerate, Lyonnaise des Eaux, diversified its activities in 1990 by merging with one of the largest French construction companies Dumez, which holds a small stake in the British contractor McAlpine. The Dutch HGB Group acquired the British contractor Nuttalls in 1984 and bought Kyle Stewart at the end of the decade, while another Dutch firm, Ballast Nedam, bought Rush and Tomkins contracting. The opportunity to buy into UK companies in the late 1980s appears to have been provided by the slump in the property market and resulting low stock-market value of British construction firms. And similar patterns of European integration are evident in the closely related building services sector (Swiss Bank Corporation 1990, Digings 1991). The impetus for these strategies may come from an intention to establish European-wide contracting bases in preparation for the Single Market. But they are unrelated to the procedures of the Directives and point to the need for a more comprehensive and contemporary assessment of the actual patterns of concentration in these sectors so that the real likelihood of increasing competition for contracts can be evaluated.

Local authority supplies purchasing and the EC Directives

Like building work, the general purchasing of supplies by local authorities has been governed by EC Directives since the 1970s. As with works, the earlier Supplies Directive, passed in 1977, has been revised in an amended Directive which took effect in January 1989. Local authority professional purchasing officers, therefore, have some years' experience, both of working with the initial Directive and with the amended version. Some of them have been amongst the most vocal sceptics about the impact of the Directives in attracting interest from European suppliers whilst emphasizing the potential additional costs for local authorities in carrying out the EC procedures. Speaking in 1989, the Director of East Shires Purchasing Organization reported that he had advertised in the EC official journal for eleven years without a single tender from a European supplier (CLES 1990: 64). Initial indications are that the amendments to the Directive in 1989 have not produced major changes.

The AMA's Purchasing and Supplies Group conducted a survey of the first two years of operation of the revised Directive in early 1991. The thirty-one authorities studied awarded 315 contracts each year under the Supplies Directive. In response to advertisements in the EC official journal they sent out 6,699 tender documents to suppliers expressing interest. Only 186 were from non-UK, EC-based suppliers. They received a total of 3,844 bids for the contracts, only sixteen of these from EC suppliers. Only three of the 315 contracts were finally awarded to EC-based suppliers (this information is summarized in Table 9.5 as average rates per 100 contracts). Just over half the authorities reported that the additional time taken and costs incurred in complying with the Directive were negligible – though thirteen authorities said that the additional time spent ranged from 10–70 hours of officer time each

Table 9.5 Supplies contracts awarded to UK and European contractors for each 100 contracts

For each 100 contracts	UK-based suppliers	Other EC-based suppliers
Tender documents set out to		
interested enquirers	2,084	59
Tenders received	1,220	5
Contracts awarded	99	1

Source: Association of Metropolitan Authorities (1991a).
Notes: 1 Figures are taken from an AMA survey of contracts awarded under the EC Supplies Directive. The thirty-one authorities surveyed award an average of 315 contracts each year which fall within the thresholds of the Directive.
2 This table expresses the replies to the survey in terms of average numbers per 100 contracts.

month, and fifteen estimated their additional costs at over £100 per month. Overall, the authorities concerned seem to think that the 'costs outweigh the benefits' and they could see little additional impact, with greater interest from EC-based contractors from 1992 (Association of Metropolitan Authorities 1991a). The CLES survey of the implications of all the '1992' EC policies for local authorities has reached similar conclusions: 'The Supplies Directive … appears to be somewhat burdensome. It is costly and in Britain at the beginning of the 90s frequently irrelevant. Significant administrative burdens have been placed on local authorities with no apparent gain' (CLES 1990: 66).

There may be one qualification to this final assessment. Without doubt, local authorities offer substantial markets to potential suppliers in areas like information technology. For these suppliers the key issues may be standards which are adopted in supplies and equipment as the European standards, since the Directives place some onus on authorities to use these where possible in specifying their requirements. Competition between suppliers may therefore be fought out in terms of designation of standards at the European level, rather than on the basis of pricing for supply tenders to individual authorities.[7]

Service industries and the EC Directives

The Services Directive was formally adopted by the European Council of Ministers in 1992 to take effect in 1993. Its proposed coverage makes it potentially the most significant of the Public Procurement Directives for UK authorities. Its drafting is such that virtually all remaining services not covered elsewhere will fall within one of the two categories identified in the Directive. As a result, and even though the product classification used by the EC has yet to be properly interpreted, there will be important overlaps between the services covered by the draft Directive and those 'defined' for CCT under the Local Government Act 1988.[8] There are two services which fall in the priority services in the draft Directive (to which the full range of advertising and tendering procedures therefore apply) which are also 'defined services' under the UK Legislation: vehicle maintenance and building cleaning. A third priority service, sewage and refuse disposal, is closely related operationally to refuse collection and street cleansing which are 'defined' services in the UK. Two of the service categories named in the EC's residual services (restaurant services, recreational cultural and sporting activities) also have a close affinity to UK-defined services. So, the more limited technical and publicity requirements will apply to these. Since the stated intention of the Public Procurement programme is that all purchases of supplies and services will eventually be covered, the Commission will undoubtedly find a home for the remaining defined services in one of the Service Directive categories.

It is in these services that the pursuit of Europe-wide development and acquisition strategies by a number of EC-based multinational service companies, with particular targeting of the UK public sector, is most evident (see Table 9.6). From the mid-1980s a group of European multinationals has established its presence,

Table 9.6 Main European-based companies contracting for work with UK local authorities

Parent Co.	Country	Contracting Co.	Services
Bougyes	France	Stalwart Env. Services	Refuse/SC
		Cambrian Env. Services	Refuse/SC
		Fosse Group	Refuse/ground m.
Electrolux	Sweden	Electrolux Con. Services	Cleaning
		Greenfingers	Ground m.
FOCSA	Spain	FOCSA	Refuse/ground m.
Compagnie Générale des Eaux	France	Onyx	Refuse/SC
		Wistech	Refuse/SC
		L&C Waste Tech.	Refuse/SC
		UK Waste Control	Refuse/SC
		Norwest Holst	Building
ISS Servisystem	Denmark	ISS Servisystem	Cleaning
		Mediclean	Cleaning/portering
Krinkels	Netherlands	Krinkels	Ground m.
		Continental Landscapes	Ground m.
Lyonnaise des Eaux	France	Sitaclean	Refuse/SC
		McAlpine	Building
Sodexho	France	Sodexho	Catering

providing services to the UK public sector using the related opportunities of enforced tendering in the NHS; the government's privatization programme for nationalized industries, notably in the water industry; compulsory competitive tendering in the defined services of local authorities; and changes in the organization and delivery of other local authority responsibilities in areas such as waste management.

Since 1988 several databases have collected systematic information on the award of contracts by local councils. These enable us to identify the European multinationals which have gained access to UK markets before the Directive, and the development strategies they have used.

At first sight, private contractors have gained only limited access to contracts awarded in the 'defined services' under the terms of UK 1988 legislation. Up to January 1991, DSOs had won, overall, 70 per cent of the number of contracts awarded under CCT and 84 per cent of the value of contracts (see Table 9.7). This suggests both a relative 'competitiveness' of local authority in-house services (though a more measured assessment would have to look at how this was achieved) and the fact that private contractors are more likely to win smaller contracts. The patterns vary significantly between the defined services. Local authority DSOs have been most successful in education and welfare catering where they have won just under 99 per cent of contracts and just over 99 per cent

Table 9.7 Outcome of UK contract awards under CCT by defined service area

	Per cent of contracts by number of contracts		Per cent of contracts by value of contracts	
	DSO	*Other contractors*	*DSO*	*Other contractors*
Building cleaning	57.2	42.8	84.1	15.9
Refuse collection	71.6	28.4	78.5	21.5
Other cleaning	74.8	25.2	81.4	18.6
Vehicle maintenance	79.4	20.6	86.7	13.3
Education and welfare catering	95.3	4.7	98.7	1.3
Other catering	77.4	22.6	81.6	18.4
Ground maintenance	68.5	31.5	81.7	18.3
Overall	74.9	25.1	84.7	15.3

Source: Figures taken from Local Government Management Board CCT Information Service Survey Report (no. 4), December 1991.
Notes: The survey covers 3,021 contracts awarded in England and Wales up to 1 August 1991.

of the value of work. Private contractors have been most successful in building cleaning where they have won four out of every ten contracts, though the fact that this amounts to only 14 per cent of the total value of contracts awarded indicates that they have won a substantial number of small contracts. The three services in which private contractors have won the largest proportion of contracts are also those in which European contractors have been most active: building cleaning, refuse collection and ground maintenance. In each of these areas also, they are starting to accumulate a significant share of the market won by private contractors.

Building cleaning

Two European multinationals have been competing for contracts in building cleaning: the ISS Servisystem subsidiary of the Danish multinational ISS and the Contract Services subsidiary of the Swedish manufacturing and service group Electrolux. Between them they have won 4 per cent of the contracts won by the private sector which amounts to 13 per cent of the total value of contracts awarded (see Table 9.8). In both cases, the entry into local authority markets through CCT has followed and been associated with the contractors' successful attempts to win contracts in the areas of the health service which have been opened up to enforced tendering since 1983. Electrolux established its Contracts services subsidiary in the UK in 1985, aiming initially at the Health Service markets in cleaning, catering and portering. It also at that time picked up a small number of contracts from local authorities, generally Conservative controlled such as Kent County Council and keen to contract-out services before the

Table 9.8 European contractors tendering success under CCT: building cleaning

Parent company	Contractor	Contract wins	Average contract (£m)	Per cent of market value*	Per cent of contracts[†]
Electrolux	Electrolux	2	0.771	5	1.0
ISS Servisystem	ISS Servisystem	6	0.391	8	3.1
Total European contractors		8		13	4.1

Source: Local Government Management Board (1991a). All information is taken from LGMB database and covers up to Apriil 1991.
Notes: *Market per cent refers to share of the total market in value terms won by private contractors.
[†]Per cent of contracts refers to the total number of contracts won by private contractors.

compulsion of the 1988 Act. Under the 1988 Act Electrolux has been awarded contracts in building and cleaning and other cleaning on the basis of which its turnover and employment doubled between 1988 and 1989. However, at the end of 1990, the subsidiary, which changed its name to Electrolux Environmental Services, was reporting losses. And Electrolux's other subsidiary seeking to enter CCT markets in grounds maintenance, Greenfingers, had yet to win a contract.

ISS Servisystem has been a more aggressive entrant into UK public service contracts, albeit using a similar initial route through the Health Service. ISS established its own Hospital Services Subsidiary in the UK in 1982 to offer a full range of domestic services to the NHS. Through its Servisystem Subsidiary, operating in commercial and industrial cleaning services, it also won contracts for central and local government bodies. These were in areas of central government being pushed in the direction of contracting out (such as cleaning contracts for the Ministry of Defence), in Conservative-controlled local authorities seeking to contract-out (such as Lincolnshire County Council) or initiatives 'on the borders' of the public sector as traditionally defined in the UK (such as cleaning in the newly built Tyne Wear Metro). In the late 1980s, ISS commenced a rapid expansion programme centring its European focus on the UK and using acquisitions to enhance its market shares. The government commitment to further extensive privatization was a significant consideration. Outlining the expansion programme in 1989, the ISS Chief Executive remarked that 'the UK is one of our most exciting markets by virtue of privatisation and the use of private service companies in the public sector, so it was natural for us to base our European HQ in London' (*Financial Times*, 1989). The parent company acquired cleaning contract firms in the US, Germany and Scandinavia. In the UK, it bought Mediclean in 1989 with the intention of developing its European-wide hospital service interests from a UK base. The acquisition gave ISS over 100 contracts for the NHS. At the end of the decade, ISS Mediclean, based in Slough, had an annual turnover of £16 million and employed nearly 4,000. Under CCT, ISS

Servisystem was reported to have won six building cleaning contracts up to 1991 (see Table 9.8).

Refuse collection and street cleaning

There is an even more marked pattern of accumulation of market share by European contractors through a targeted programme of expansion in refuse collection and street cleaning. Four EC-based conglomerates have gained access to these CCT-defined service markets through establishing UK subsidiaries, acquisitions and joint ventures. Between them, by April 1991, they had accumulated 28 per cent of the total value of work won by private contractors in refuse collection; 69 per cent of the work won by the private sector in street cleaning; and 24 per cent of private sector work won where refuse and street cleaning were combined into single contracts (see Table 9.9). And these figures do not include the two large and well-publicized contracts, each valued at over £1m per annum, awarded to the Onyx subsidiary of Compagnie Generale des Eaux in early summer of 1991 in the London Borough of Camden and in the City of Liverpool. The routes for the expansion of interests in the UK have been through associated ventures and acquisitions in water privatization, waste management, construction and civil engineering. Leaders in these processes have been subsidiaries of the two French-based conglomerates Compagnie General des Eaux and Lyonnaise des Eaux–Dumez.

Compagnie Generale des Eaux operates through nearly 900 consolidated firms in the water industry, building and public works, energy, cleaning services and other service industries such as health and property. In 1991 it was the 43rd largest company in Europe with an annual turnover of $20.3 billion and over 173,000 employees world-wide.[9] Its refuse collection and street cleaning subsidiary CGEA, with an annual turnover of over £100 million, has been seeking to expand in Europe (Spain and Germany as well as the UK) and in Asia. To take advantage of CCT legislation, it jointly set up Cory CGEA/Cory Onyx in 1988, with a 50 per cent share. Having sold out its share to the other partner, CGEA continued to tender as Onyx and in 1990 bought a majority share in UES in 1990 through which it acquired UK Waste Control, a company set up in 1988 by UES to compete for refuse and cleansing contracts. UK Control had contracts with fourteen local authorities. CGEA also acquired two refuse collection contracts through its acquisition of control of Wistech and L. & C. Waste Tech. The growth programme built on company acquisition is said, by those working in local government with a knowledge of pricing structures in the industry, to be accompanied by a 'loss leader' tendering strategy, though the dubious legality of such practices in EC law makes this difficult to substantiate. The parent has also bought stakes in nine of the statutory water companies during the water privatization programme. Its expansion programme in construction, and civil engineering, described above, provides the group with a potential presence in public works in the UK to mirror its significant interests in French public road

Table 9.9 European contractors tendering success under CCT: refuse collection and street cleaning

Parent company of	Contractor	Contract bids	Contract wins	Per cent of market*
Compagnie Générale des Eaux	Onyx UK Waste-control Wistech	Refuse –	8	10.0
		Street cleaning –	11	37.6
		Combined contracts –	4	7.0
FOCSA	FOCSA	Refuse 19	4	5.5
		Street cleaning 18	2	13.5
		Combined contracts –	2	12.4
Lyonnaise des Eaux-Dumez	Sitaclean	Refuse 92	8	9.4
		Street cleaning 16	1	9.0
		Combined contracts –	1	4.1
Bougyes†	Stalwart Cambrian Fosse	Refuse 11	4	3.0
		Street cleaning 13	4	9.0
Total EC contractors		Refuse 122	24	27.9
		Street cleaning 49	18	69.3
		Combined contracts –	4	23.5

Source: Local Government Management Board (1991a). All information is taken from LGMB database and covers up to April 1991.
Notes: *Market per cent refers to share of the total market in value terms won by private contractors.
†Figures for the Bougyes Group cover the contracting companies jointly owned by the Bougyes subsidiary, Saur, and Southern Water (Stalwart) and Welsh Water (Cambrian).

building and public contracting through its SGE and Fougerolle companies.

Lyonnaise des Eaux–Dumez has a similar range of international industrial interests to CGE, though on a smaller scale. It was the 110th largest European firm in 1991 with a turnover of $12.5 billion. It has followed a similar route into the UK through water privatization, construction and CCT, but has appeared to pursue a less aggressive acquisition policy. The parent company set up Lyonnaise

UK in 1988 as a holding company for its interests in the UK water industry. These have amounted to take-overs of several statutory water companies before privatization, including Bristol, East Anglia and Essex, together with substantial investment since 1988 including interests in the Anglia, Wessex and Severn–Trent Companies. Sitaclean Technology was set up in the UK in 1988 as a British base for the SITA Group, Lyonnaise's waste services, collection and treatment section which collects rubbish and cleans streets in a number of major French towns and cities. It has bid extensively for CCT contracts as Sitaclean (its tenders for refuse collection numbering nearly 100) and has won nearly 10 per cent of the private sector market in refuse collection and street cleaning. Its success rate in only one in ten of the tenders it has submitted partly explains why the company has been the most vociferous complainant to the Secretary of State under the provisions of the 1988 Act, that contract award procedures have not been properly followed.

The Spanish company, FOCSA, through its fifty or more subsidiaries, has a similar portfolio of activities to the two French-based conglomerates in construction, water and sewerage, refuse and waste disposal. It is itself a subsidiary of the major Spanish conglomerate Con-y-Con. FOCSA has a substantial base in Spanish public service markets, with 50 per cent of the waste and sanitation market and over seventy contracts for refuse collection, and fifty for street cleaning. FOCSA UK was established in 1989 to provide a UK base for tendering for defined services. Eight refuse collection contracts have been won, including the contract in Brighton worth almost £2 million and a £3 million contract in Stockpot.

The fourth EC conglomerate is not directly competing for defined services. The Bougyes Group, the largest French building and civil engineering contractor, operates worldwide, particularly in road building, including a major involvement in the Channel Tunnel. It is the 283rd largest European firm, with an annual turnover of $9.8 billion and employing 73,000 people worldwide. It is involved in the UK defined service market through two joint ventures with newly-privatized British Water Companies. Bougyes' water treatment and distribution subsidiary 'SAUR' acquired in 1984, set up Stalwart Environmental Services in 1989 jointly with Southern Water to compete for refuse and cleaning contracts in the South East. The company had won the refuse contract in the London Borough of Harrow. Also established in 1989 was the joint venture with Welsh Water, Cambrian Environmental Services, which had won two street cleaning contracts by early 1991. Cambrian Environmental Services also took over two further contracts in 1991 when it bought out the FOSSE Group, which, as a management buy-out of Stratford-on-Avon Technical Services, had been awarded contracts in Stratford and the Cotswolds.

The three French multinationals are merely extending the practices that have long since established them in a number of urban utilities during this century. First, vertical integration in a single sector market, such as water distribution. Second, foreign investment and the establishment of overseas subsidiaries. Third, extending the 'territorial basis of their market' by a mixture of taking over companies which already have contracts and/or 'a process of encirclement and conquest of new municipalities'. And fourth, diversification into new urban service areas from their initial base (Lorrain, 1991).

Grounds maintenance

The third defined service under the 1988 Act in which European contractors have established an identifiable market share is grounds maintenance (see Table 9.10). The contractor involved, Krinkels, is different in structure to those previously described, and partly as a result of this has appeared to be pursuing a less strategic and extensive development programme than the multinational conglomerates. Krinkels, a Dutch-based horticulture and landscaping company, is not extensively diversified either in product/service terms or geographically, though it has contracts elsewhere in North West Europe and in the Middle East. Having, apparently, discovered the potential for expansion into the UK Local Authority market under CCT while working as landscaping subcontractor on a golf course building project, Krinkels has tendered for work first from its Dutch base, and then from its UK subsidiary, Continental Landscapes, established in 1989. It has won an increasing proportion of contracts in each successive tranche of grounds maintenance contracts under CCT.

Multinationals in the service sector

From a review of the involvement of European-based multinationals and conglomerates in tendering for contracts in service areas which are defined for CCT legislation in the UK and also likely to be covered by the EC Directives, we can draw a number of conclusions with implications for the effect of the Directives. First, in these particular service areas what has been evident are strategies of concentration and diversification as a *prelude* to the Single European Market which has been evident in other industries. Second, that the processes have been underway since the mid to late 1980s and they have used as routes the associated channels offered by privatization, CCT and the other extensions of contracting for public services in the UK. Third, they have strategically combined company acquisitions, joint ventures and the establishment of subsidiaries to provide a contracting and operational base within the UK. These have been intended to overcome the operational, technical and legal difficulties contractors have found in trying to compete for contracts form bases on mainland Europe. Allied to a pricing strategy, that has probably included loss leaders, they are strategies to build up market shares in these service industries. We can probably conclude that those European multinationals with an interest in the UK local authority and public service markets have used the opportunities available through the Conservative governments' restructuring of the UK public sector. They are already in a position to tender for work on public contracts before the EC Services Directive has been implemented, and it is unlikely that the Directives will offer any additional avenues of information or procedures to those which have been available to them under domestic UK legislation. The exception is that the enforcement procedures to be implemented for all the EC Directives on Public Procurement will offer access to civil courts for those contractors who feel that the Directives have been transgressed. Since several of the multinationals have been major complainants about non-compliance with UK law when they have failed to win contracts, it is to be anticipated that they may take up these procedures in pursuit of damages or annulment of contract decisions. In terms of market access to those services covered by CCT, the EC Services Directive is unlikely to provoke interest from multinational service contractors who have not already made their way into the UK market.

Less predictable is the impact of the Service Directive in attracting competition from small- or medium-sized contractors who have not previously competed for work in the UK market, and which do not have the resources for the company strategies of the multinationals. This is the major area of concern both for the Commission and for those in the UK who seek positive benefits from the international opening-out of the public service market. The Commission has been trying to promote small and medium firms into the Public Procurement market through public procurement fairs, schemes encouraging firms to work together in competing for contracts, and through proposals to public bodies that contracts be divided into smaller units (*Financial Times*, 1990; European Commission 1990b). In the UK the National Economic Development Council established a working party part of whose brief was to consider how European small- and medium-sized contractors could be attracted to compete for contracts under the EC Directives.[11] However, it seems questionable whether either the Directives or these initiatives will result in a significant entry of new, smaller contractors competing for local authority contracts in the services which have been analysed thus far. There is no comprehensive analysis available on how services are delivered in other EC member states. But what information there is suggests that only in France is more than a third of public sector work carried out

Table 9.10 European contractors tendering success under CCT: grounds maintenance

Parent company	Contractor	Contract wins	Average contract (£m)	Per cent of market value*	Per cent of contracts†
Krinkels	Krinkels	10	0.587	17.0	5.5
	Continental Landscapes	3	0.286	2.8	1.6
Bougyes	Stalwart Fosse	1	n/a	n/a	0.5
Total EC contractors		14		19.8	7.6

Source: Local Government Management Board (1991a). All information is taken from LGMB database and covers up to April 1991.

Notes: *Market per cent refers to share of the total market in value terms won by private contractors.

†Per cent of contracts refers to the total number of contracts won by private contractors.

by private contractors employing less than 500 people. This probably reflects the small size of many French local authorities with 98 per cent of them covering populations of less than 2,000 people. Overall, then, large firms, such as multinationals, predominate in the markets for public service throughout most of the EC. The EC Directives themselves will also produce a contracting regime which is relatively complex and will carry quite significant administrative costs for potential contractors. The size of contracts that UK authorities conventionally award in these service areas is likely to exclude small contractors. And small or medium contractors are less likely to be able to pass the standards of financial stability which authorities will continue to set, quite legitimately under UK and EC legislation.

THE FUTURE: TENSIONS AND EXTENSIONS

Of necessity, these conclusions are tentative. The analysis covers only a limited range of industrial sectors which are distinctive in that they are covered by both sets of legislation and, in the case of construction and refuse-related activities, they have been regarded as complementary in the acquisition and development strategies of a number of European multinationals. For an assessment of the longer term, we also need to be aware of two things. First, the additional implications of imminent extensions in the coverage of both UK domestic and European legislation. Second, the fact that, despite the attempts of the Commission to produce detailed legislation which suggests otherwise, there is an apparent tension between two of the key dimensions of the Single European Act programme: the Single European Market and the social dimension.

In the UK, the government has introduced further legislation to extend the scope of CCT and, in an accompanying consultation paper, has identified the services which might be encompassed (LGIU 1991, DoE 1991b). Most significantly this could mean that a number of white-collar and professional services would be covered by CCT legislation and by all of the requirements of the EC Services Directive by 1994 and 1995. These include architectural services, financial services, computing services, accounting, and management consultancy. The nature of these services and the technologies employed may make them both more mobile and amenable to trans-European development by medium and small businesses, as may the scale of contracts likely to be offered. However, there is already evidence of the considerable presence of the multinational consultancy and accounting firms in the international extension of privatization (Howard 1990). This might suggest that, as in the 'blue-collar' services discussed here in greater detail, the availability of market opportunities through CCT will become considerations in the commercial and acquisition strategies in European and international restructuring. The legislation to enable implementation of this additional programme of CCT will be in place from early 1992.

The geographical boundaries of restructuring are also likely to be renegotiated. The European Commission has been actively trying to extend the public procurement framework through agreements with the EFTA and GATT trade blocs. In October 1991, the EC and EFTA reached agreement on a European Economic Area which, from 1993, will start to extend EC rules, including public procurement, to the seven EFTA member states: Sweden, Norway, Iceland, Switzerland, Austria, Finland and Liechtenstein. An immediate agreement with the GATT trade bloc seems less likely, since the areas of public procurement where there might be some common ground are overshadowed in these discussions by issues such as agricultural policy where there are major differences between North America and Europe.

In the practical application of the EC Directives, and hence in their real impact for public bodies like local authorities, public procurement is also one of the policy areas in which there appears to be a tension between two of the major dimensions of the Single European Act: the Single European Market and the 'social dimension'. The question, in a sense, is whether the Procurement Directives allow public bodies to 'regulate' or monitor compliance with social and employment regulations by contractors through the contracts they award. And, whether public bodies can pursue wider social and economic policies through such contracts. The major piece of European case law on public procurement, the ruling by the European Court of Justice in the 'Beentjes' case, arose when a contracting body attempted to put a clause into contracts requiring the successful contractor to recruit a proportion of the workforce from the local unemployed. The Court's ruling seems to imply that such clauses in contracts are not prohibited by EC Directives provided that they do not, in principle, disadvantage contractors from other member states. This argument has been more widely applied by the Commission to suggest that clauses in contracts on employment, health and safety at work, and sex and race discrimination issues are permissible provided they do not contravene the cardinal rule of not disadvantaging contractors from other member states (European Commission 1989). But the application of this rule in practice is less clear cut and much will depend on how it is interpreted. This is all the more so in the UK where the CCT legislation precludes consideration of some of these issues in the award of contracts and prescribes the way in which others may be taken into account.

NOTES

1   The detailed material on European contractors contained in this chapter has been taken from material collected by the Public Services Privatization Unit, a database jointly funded by the public sector unions COHSE, NALGO, NIPSA, NUCPS, NUPE, TGWU. Thanks are due to the Unit for access to this material with the agreement of the funding unions. The views expressed in the chapter are not necessarily those of the Unit or the funding unions.

2   In December 1991, the British government introduced two Statutory Instruments which both enact, in formal terms, the Works and Supplies Directive into UK law, and set out the remedies to be available in civil courts, thus fulfilling the requirements of the Remedies Directive.

3   The initial 'defined' services were refuse collection; other cleaning (street cleaning); school and welfare catering; other catering; vehicle maintenance; building cleaning; grounds maintenance. The management of sports and leisure facilities was added to the defined services in 1989 with the first phase of CCT to be completed by January 1992. In Spring 1991, the Conservative government commissioned a consultant's report on the feasibility of extending CCT to all the white-collar services in local government, including financial and legal services.

4   Lee Digings (1991), compares the requirements of the Directives with UK legislation, as do papers presented at two seminars organized in 1991 by the AMA and Leeds Business School's Policy Research Unit (Association of Metropolitan Authorities 1991c).

5   For rather different summaries of the arguments and empirical evidence see, for example, Manchester City Council (1988) and David Parker (1990).

6   Department of the Environment (1991a: Ch. 13). This particular comment was made by the report's author, Kieron Walsh, at a seminar in February 1991 organized by the AMA.

7   I am grateful for this point to Gary Herman who is researching into the restructuring of IT systems and manufacturing in the EC.

8   The Services Directive divides services into two categories: priority services, to which all the requirements of the Directives apply, and residual services to which only a selective number apply covering advertising procedures etc. Lee Digings (1991: 178–9) gives a complete list of services in both categories.

9   All the 1990 figures quoted for turnover and employment of European companies quoted in this section are taken from *The Financial Times*, January 1992.

10 The EC's proposals to encourage small- and medium-sized businesses are set out in European Commission (1990a). See also *Financial Times*, June 1990.

11 The NEDC has commissioned a consultant's report into the 'opportunities and threats facing the SME (small and medium enterprises) segment and to devise appropriate strategies for overcoming or removing barriers' (*Financial Times*, May 1991).

BIBLIOGRAPHY

Association of Metropolitan Authorities (AMA) (1991a) Report by AMA Purchasing and Supply Group, February.
—— (1991b) *Public Works and Europe*, A Report to the AMA's Public Works Committee, 9 July.
—— (1991c) *An Introduction to EC Public Procurement Directives*, Papers of a Seminar jointly organized by the AMA and the Policy Research Unit, Leeds Business School.
Barnes, I., Campbell, J. and Pepper, C. (1989) 'Local authorities, public procurement and 1992', *Local Government Studies*, November/December, pp. 10–16.
Bennett, J. (1991) 'EC Directives and European law', in Association of Metropolitan Authorities, *An Introduction to EC Public Procurement Directives*, Papers of a Seminar jointly organized by the AMA and the Policy Research Unit, Leeds Business School.
Booz Allen and Hamilton (1991) *Study of Inhouse Performance of Services in the Public Sector: Executive Summary*, Advisory Committee on the Opening Up of Public Procurement, CCO/91/87, Brussels: European Commission.
Cecchini, P. (1988) *The European Challenge* (The Cecchini Report), Wildwood House, Hants.
Centre for Local Economic Strategies (CLES) (1990) *Local Authorities and 1992*, Manchester: CLES.

Department of the Environment (DoE) (1990) *Housing and Construction Statistics*, London: HMSO.

—— (1991a) *Competitive Tendering and for Local Authority Services*, London: HMSO.

—— (1991b) *Competing for Quality: Competition in the Provision of Local Services: A Discussion Paper* London: DoE.

Digings, L. (1991) *Competitive Tendering and the European Communities: Public Procurement, CCT and Local Services*, London: Association of Metropolitan Authorities.

European Commission (1988) *Research on the Cost of 'Non-Europe'*: vol. 5A, *The Cost of 'Non-Europe' in Public Sector Procurement*, Luxembourg: Office for the Official Publications of the EC.

—— (1989) *Public Procurement: Regional and Social Aspects*, COM (89) Final, Brussels.

—— (1990a) *Promoting SME Participation in Public Procurement in the Community*, COM (90) 166 Final, Brussels.

—— (1990b) *Proposal for a Council Directive on the Award of Public Service Contracts*, COM (90) 372, Brussels.

Financial Times (June 1990) 'Why EC efforts face a variety of hurdles', June 19.

—— (May 1991) 'Small companies may lose in EC deals race', May 14.

—— (January 1992) 'European Top 500', January 13.

Howard, M. (1990) *The Use of Consultants by the Public Sector in Australia: Recent Evidence and Issues*, Public Sector Research Centre Working Paper, PSRC, University of New South Wales.

Labour Research (1991) 'Minimum wage and setting the rate', September, vol. 80, no. 9, pp. 9–10.

Local Government Information Unit (LGIU) (1991) *The Local Government Bill*, Special Briefing Number 38, December, London.

Local Government Management Board (LGMB) (1991a) *CCT Information Service*, Survey Report Number 3, April, London.

—— (1991b) *CCT Information Service*, Survey Report Number 4, December, London.

Lorrain, D. (1991) 'Public goods and private operators in France', in R. Batley and G. Stoker (eds), *Local Government in Europe: Trends and Developments*, Basingstoke: Macmillan.

Manchester City Council (1988) *Contractors' Audit* (vols 1–3), Manchester.

Paddon, M. (1990) 'Last pieces in Euro-jigsaw', *LA Week*, May 17.

Parker, D. (1990) 'The 1988 Local Government Act and compulsory competitive tendering', *Urban Studies* 27(5), 653–68.

Savage, S. and Robbins, L. (1990) *Public Policy under Thatcher*, London: Macmillan.

Swiss Bank Corporation (1990) *The European Contractors*, London.

Whitfield, D. (1992) *The Welfare State: Privatisation, Deregulation and commercialisation of Public Services*, London: Pluto.

10

BETWEEN AN IDEOLOGICAL ROCK AND AN ORGANIZATIONAL HARD PLACE

NHS management in the 1980s and 1990s

Mike Reed and Peter Anthony

INTRODUCTION

Since the mid-1970s the British National Health Service has gone through a series of structural transformations in which the desire to implant a 'managerial' discourse and practice within a service that had previously been 'administered' has played a strategic role. The attempt to introduce a managerial discourse and practice has taken very different ideological forms and produced varying programmes of structural reform. While the 1970s were dominated by the ethos of corporate rationalization and bureaucratic centralization, the 1980s have been shaped by the rhetoric of 'market decentralization' and organizational autonomy (Harrison *et al.* 1990, Small 1989). The era of corporate rationalization was based on an ideology of bureaucratic centralization and control which left 'professional power' – particularly the power and authority of the doctors – relatively untouched. The political drive to design and administer a health service which was more efficient and effective in structural – rather than *operational* – terms left medical power largely unscathed. However, the major shifts in ideological and political context experienced in the British National Health Service in the 1980s *necessarily* entailed a more substantial assault on the professional privileges and collaborative networks that had directed and legitimated the *provision* of health care practice from the inception of the NHS in 1948. A service which had previously been centrally administered and locally self-managed was now deemed to be in need of management, and all the paraphernalia of external controls and monitoring which this radical transformation in organizational and ideological rationales entailed (Clark and Starkey 1988).

Both at the level of managerial philosophy/structure and at the level of a 'negotiated' work organization within the NHS, these wider shifts in ideological momentum and political expediency demanded a move away from the relatively high-trust, collaborative work relations characteristic of the service (Burns 1982) pre-Griffiths – backed by a supportive (some would say indulgent) managerial practice – and towards a low-trust control ethos in which directive managerial control became the driving force behind institutional and organizational change.

The purpose of this chapter is to review and assess these longer-term transformations in managerial ideology and organizational design, with particular regard to NHS general managers or their progeny under the latest legislation. The latter have become the focal point for the tensions – and resulting conflicts – between a political and economic imperative that demands obeisance to a market-driven conception of economic efficiency and effectiveness and an organizational reality which suggests that these external pressures have to be mediated, and consequently modified, by the organizational contingencies of a highly complex and 'politicized' occupational division of labour. Indeed, NHS managers seem to be situated at the epicentre of an ideological storm, and consequent organizational upheaval – in which most of the political 'fallout' – in 'big P' and 'small P' terms – from the cultural revolution entailed in a shift from morally grounded collaboration to managerially directed control is generating a wide range of unresolved (and unresolvable?) contradictions.

The ideological and political dynamic underlying the major cultural and political changes taking place in the NHS during the 1980s has undoubtedly strengthened the organizational apparatus of managerial control at the expense of negotiated order and morally grounded multidisciplinary collaboration within a highly complex occupational division of labour. Yet this has left NHS managers in a highly ambiguous position in which they have to strike a constantly changing balance between the political imperatives of tighter external control and the organizational realities of negotiated compromises and incremental changes (Thompson 1987).

This chapter is divided into two major parts. The first part reviews and analyses the most significant macro-level developments that have occurred in NHS organization – and their underlying rationales – between the mid-1970s and the early 1990s. It indicates that the long-term movement from an ideology of collaboration, and its organizational correlates, to an ideology of control is the overriding political and ideological reality to which NHS personnel have been forced to adapt during this period. It also suggests that the new cadre of NHS general managers which the DHSS Griffiths Report of 1983 (HMSO 1983) created, has been placed in a position where the managers are forced to play a major role in contending with the unresolved, or unfinished, business which this permanent 'organizational revolution' produced. The second part of the chapter grounds this macro-level exposition and analysis within a more detailed, empirically based, case-study of a district health authority undergoing the organizational upheavals of the Griffiths proposals. It also presumes to offer an overall analysis of the attempted cultural transformations and organizational transitions which the NHS has undergone over the last decade or so in terms of a deep-seated conflict between the values of institutional growth and expansion on the one hand and the social (and managerial) practices associated with community building and maintenance on the other (MacIntyre 1981; Anthony 1986). In short, it suggests that general managers are the products of a series of cultural and organizational transitions that have located them within a web of contradictory pressures and demands that oscillate between the priorities of economic survival in an increasingly competitive health care 'marketplace' and the maintenance of internal moral order. They have become the key actors responsible for formulating policies and implementing practices which will inevitably exacerbate the fundamental conflict between the imperatives of externally determined organizational survival and the internal needs for moral settlement and social integration. This conflict is likely to become even more acute within an ideological context and political setting dominated by the rhetoric of market rationality and the severe organizational pressures which it necessarily imposes on a highly complex, and often fragile, 'negotiated order' at the level of work organization and service delivery.

FROM CORPORATE RATIONALIZATION TO MARKET DECENTRALIZATION

The quest for a more 'rational' – and hence efficient and effective – organizational structure and managerial control strategy has been a perennial theme in the historical development of the NHS since its founding in 1948 (Clark and Starkey 1988, Small 1989, Harrison *et al.* 1990, Pollitt 1990, Cox 1991). While the particular ideological and economic imperatives driving this search for the 'nirvana' of sustained organizational rationality and entrenched managerial control have changed considerably over the years, the aspiration to construct and maintain a more coherent and unified institutional framework through which health care services could be effectively allocated and efficiently rationed is a leitmotif of the system's evolution.

However, from the late 1960s onwards the pace and momentum of this drive towards a 'managed', rather than an 'administered' service quickened. By the 1980s, managerialism – of one sort or another – had become 'the dominant intellectual framework within which the health service thinks about itself and its role in society' (quoted in Small 1989: 159). This related not only to questions of resource allocation and operational performance, but also to the broader social values and moral considerations which were thought to underpin the system's existence and its legitimate role within society. Thus, the shift from a primarily medical service organization, undergirded by various administrative support systems, to a market-led commodity managed by managerial experts (Coombs and Green 1989) entailed transformations in ideological and ethical foundations – as well as power relations and occupational politics – which are only now becoming more visible.

The 1960s and 1970s were dominated by a combination of rational positivism and scientific management which translated into a set of organizational imperatives that stressed centralized planning and bureaucratic control (Barnard 1989, Small 1989, Harrison *et al.* 1990). In general terms, this wave of organizational restructuring and managerial development left 'medical power' relatively untouched. It did not question the power of doctors to exercise 'clinical autonomy' unfettered by considerations of incremental resource utilization and the unplanned priorities which it implicitly established. Instead, it looked for an overall administrative structure within which some degree of national or regional planning and local co-ordination could be realized.

> An essentially managerial ideology of reform permeated the public sector as a whole throughout this period.... The 1960s and 1970s were characterized by a general belief in the efficacy of organization structure and management training as a means of producing better management in the public sector; better management career structures were seen as the answer to the problem, almost irrespective of what the problem was.
>
> (Harrison *et al.* 1990: 77)

Yet the new emphasis on centralized co-ordination and more detailed administrative planning underpinning the reforms of the 1970s didn't question or erode the power and authority of the major professional groups within the service – at least, not in any obvious or open way. Indeed, it tended to reinforce the powers of self-regulation and autonomy which they had traditionally enjoyed. This was true to the extent that it legitimated organizational reform in terms of an ideology of corporate rationalization which would enhance 'consensus management' within the service by clarifying and codifying existing occupational relations and practices (Cox 1991). The producer cartels or co-operatives which are often seen as the organizational hallmark of public sector services (Ackroyd *et al.* 1989) would continue to be protected in the sense that the 1970s reforms were framed within the tradition of 'custodial management' that left the former relatively unscathed. This tradition of 'custodial management':

> sees its role purely in terms of perpetuating existing standards of provision ... it tends to have an exaggerated respect for practitioner autonomy and is ill-equipped to adjudicate between the demands of different services or to form general policies.... Management sees itself primarily as the custodian of standards of service provision. It is, in self-conception, if not practice, management of the stable state ... and is almost invariably *wedded to the conceptions of practice held by service providers themselves.*
>
> (Ackroyd *et al.* 1989: 612–13, our italics)

As Clark and Starkey have argued, the 1970s' reforms were based on a model of change parasitic on the assumed technical–rational expertise of bureaucratic management. The organizational solution to perceived 'operational drift' was based on a philosophy of change which emphasized the advantages to be derived from 'a unitary, hierarchical, centralized structure based on area health authorities and the emphasis put on co-ordination and efficiency under central control' (Clark and Starkey 1988: 163–4). However, this move towards a more highly integrated and hierarchically co-ordinated structure had to be accommodated to the existing power and privileges of established occupational politics – particularly 'medical power'. Consequently: 'A political deal was struck with the medical profession as the price of change. This was the incorporation of the clinician into the managerial process through consensus management teams *where decisions were taken by collegiate professional groups*' (Clark and Starkey 1988: 164, our italics).

By the early 1980s, the highly complex and multi-tiered administrative structure which the 1970s' reforms had produced was increasingly seen as unwieldy and prejudicial to a more 'customer oriented' service, and the inherent push towards innovation and change which that ethos was thought to generate. Thus the 'Patients First' proposals which formed the basis of the second major phase of reorganization in 1982 adopted a rather different line to the 1974 restructuring. This was true in the sense that the ideology of rational positivism and scientific management was incrementally giving way to a very different kind of emphasis on 'patients, local autonomy and simplicity of managerial arrangements based on moving the locus of decision-making closer to the community' (Clark and Starkey 1988: 166). While the central issue of medical power and its hold over the operational allocation of resources was left untouched, the 1982 reorganization implied a move away from an obsession with bureaucratic centralism and a synoptic rational planning towards a rationale for change in which the need for a much more decentralized market-oriented, service provision, *subject to much tighter managerial control at the point of delivery*, became the overriding theme.

In this respect, the Griffiths Report of 1983, and the organizational changes arising out of it, signalled the arrival of an ideological rationale and organizational logic in which the inevitable conflict between medical – even 'professional' – power and authority and the growing demand for effective managerial control could no longer be fudged. As such, the Griffiths-initiated reforms seemed to herald the imminent imposition of a new, non-negotiable order on health care professionals in general – and doctors in particular – in which the management of intra-organizational conflict in the interest of market efficiency became the dominant political and organizational demand (Cox 1991). While the rhetoric of scientific management and rational cost control permeated the Griffiths Report and the implementation of authority-level reforms that followed, the sub-text of the report anticipated a relatively short and traumatic cultural revolution within the NHS in which commercially oriented priorities and practices would become implanted within the service's organizational ethos.

Under the Griffiths rubric, a new cadre of general (line) managers were given the strategic role of 'change agents' in initiating this cultural metamorphosis within the NHS. Thus, the structural reforms which the Griffiths Report generated were underpinned by an ideology – often spoken *sotto voce* – of cultural change in which the new, customer-oriented, efficiency driven doctrines which general managers carried in their organizational knapsacks were as important, if not more so, than the formal administrative reforms that they were meant to secure. If this rhetoric was to become an organizational reality, then the issue of professional autonomy – and its powerful symbolic resonances with a value system which emphasized internally legitimated moral commitment and involvement over externally imposed managerial efficiency and effectiveness – could not be indefinitely postponed.

In this way, the Griffiths reforms simultaneously built on previous phases of organizational change pressing in the direction of enhanced managerial power and control. But they also implied the search for a rather different kind of strategic vision and organizational practice in which the certainties of corporate consensus and bureaucratic muddling-through would be superseded by the uncertainties of effective resource utilization in an increasingly competitive and unforgiving economic environment (Gabbay and Dopson 1987). Thus, the call for more sophisticated information systems consequent on the implementation of the Griffiths reforms should not be seen simply as a matter of technical fine-tuning and rational planning. It also symbolized a rupture with medical dominance and the shift towards a fundamentally different framework of values and attitudes directing the development of more advanced information systems 'in which fundamental issues concerning the quality of the service, the effectiveness of delivery, the balance of types of activity and the appropriate devices for measurement of these concepts are continually being raised and contested' (Coombs and Green 1989: 284).

What these developments reveal is that the ramifications of the Griffiths Report and reforms were far greater than those encapsulated in the specific structural innovations which it initiated. Indeed, the introduction of a cadre of general managers at all levels of the restructured service signalled the arrival of a countervailing source of organizational power and ideological legitimacy that directly questioned the automatic right of professional groups to speak for the general moral ends to which the service was deemed to be directed (Strong and Robinson 1990, Cox 1991). For the first time in the history of the NHS, there was an increasingly influential, not to say powerful, group of *managers* with political patronage and administrative support who represented a rather different legitimatory rationale to that projected by the key professional groups – and particularly by the doctors. As Cox maintains:

> Griffiths can be seen as part of the desire to deregulate professions, control public expenditure, introduce market discipline and commercial and industrial models of management.... The expansion of public services is seen as being in part driven by the ambitions of those professionals and administrators whose careers and prospects derive from that expansion.... Competition is the spur to good management and there was an expectation

that many of the new general managers would be attracted in from industry and bring in appropriate standards and techniques.

(Cox 1991)

The most recent changes brought in by the *Working for Patients* White Paper of 1989 take this ideological rationale of market-led managerialism – and the need to impose a much more powerful and effective regime of external controls on professional decision-making – to its logical organizational conclusion. In direct contrast to the belief in a form of bureaucratic centralism and administratial rationalization subordinated to the dictates of 'bottom-up' professional autonomy and control over day-to-day service provision and consequently longer-term resource allocation priorities, the present reforms owe their ideological allegiance to a philosophy in which market-determined prices become the prime consideration in deciding what services will be provided, when, where and how. The market may be rigged, or at least regulated, in various ways, and certain administrative checks and balances on the most severe distortions in the overall distribution of service provision may be checked or moderated to some degree. But the move towards self-managed units, internal markets, formalized contracts, and the 'purchaser/provider' split envisaged by the recent legislation signifies the political acceptance of an organizational dynamic that presses in the direction of decentralization and fragmentation – at least at the level of service provision, if not at the level of service contracting and monitoring. In the case of the latter, a move towards greater co-ordination and merger between enlarged purchasing units – mainly the district health authorities and budget-holding general practices – would seem to counterbalance the organizational drift towards more intense competition, rivalry and fragmentation between provider units. The longer-term effects of these moves towards a much more market-led and decentralized, not to say fragmented, pattern of service provision on internal organizational order and morally grounded collaboration between the bricolage of occupational groups and interests which constitute the 'work organization' of the NHS, seems to be a relatively low political priority. As usual, it is the managers – in the widest sense of that term, encompassing both 'line' (that is, general) and 'professional' management – who are left to pick-up the organiz-ational bits and pieces and assemble them into a reasonably coherent pattern of standardized service provision.

However, a more penetrating analysis of the position and role of general managers within the NHS – whatever their particular current organizational designation – requires a deeper appreciation of the underlying transformations in managerial ideology and organizational culture which have both informed and issued from the series of structural changes reviewed in the previous section.

FROM COLLABORATION TO CONTROL

Previous discussion has indicated that the post-Griffiths reforms of the 1980s within the NHS pose a much more serious threat to the ideologica hegemony and established occupational power of entrenched professional interests than anything emanating from the previous decade of organizational restructuring. It is also suggested that the normative foundations of 'negotiated order' within the NHS are likely to be eroded, if not totally undermined, by the implementation of a managerial strategy of intensified external control over work performance and the specific organizational practices associated with it. As such, the reforms of the 1980s – undertaken within the ideological rubric of an encompassing political programme of market-led deregulation of public sector services (Cousins 1987, 1988) – can be interpreted as entailing a 'pincer movement' on two of the axial principles on which the organization of the NHS had previously been based. First, the recognition and legitimacy which the latter gave to the need for a relatively high – if not totally unconstrained – degree of professional autonomy. Second, the need to preserve an extremely complex and subtle form of work organization which was crucially dependent on internalized beliefs and values emphasizing the importance of 'normative commitment' (Etzioni 1975) to organizational goals and moral involvement in occupational roles (Burns 1982). Both of these principles – a form of professional autonomy which 'rubbed off' on the wide range of occupational groups which contribute to health care delivery and a 'high trust' set of work relations emphasizing the centrality of comparatively broad discretion in task performance – were challenged by the imposition of a form of managerialism clothed in the rhetoric of consensus and collaboration, but practising the techniques of tighter control and accountability.

Indeed, the rapid demise of the philosophy and practice of 'consensus management' – and the myriad of decision-making networks and teams that it had engendered and legitimated – was one very clear sign that a very different kind of managerial ideology and technique was now in the organizational driving-seat (Strong and Robinson 1990). However, the *operational realities* of managerial practice in the post-Griffiths era placed the new cadre of general managers, which the former had created (as well as their professional advisers or hybrid 'medical managers'), in a position where the old 'collaborative system' was under severe attack, but there was no viable alternative to replace it as a moral foundation for work organization – except the imposition of an extremely rigid and restrictive regime of task controls and cost reductions. While the former had been grounded in a normative commitment to organizational goals and the externally flexible 'negotiated' agreements between occupational groups which generalized high trust work relations fostered, the latter merely offered a form of 'industrial' or 'business' authority based on a combination of Taylorism and Fordism. This was set in motion at a time when certain industries and businesses were showing very clear signs of rejecting the strategy of 'direct control' associated with Taylorite rationalization and Fordist bureaucracy (Reed 1991).

Indeed, current debates about the organization of production in advanced industrial societies seem to be preoccupied with the search for the very flexibilities, adaptability and high trust work relations characteristic of *organizational practice* within the NHS (Anthony 1986, Reed and Anthony 1992).

Consequently, general managers seem to find themselves in a situation where 'the powerful pressures exerted on the NHS to use resources more economically and to justify its activities have created an impetus towards measurement, calculation, analysis and cost control' (Coombs and Green 1989: 293). Yet this movement towards direct control over work organization and task performance seems to have robbed them of – or at least substantially eroded – the 'core' moral principles and organizational practices on, and out of, which a highly diversified, not to say fragmented, occupational division of labour could be co-ordinated to provide a reasonably efficient and effective standard of service delivery. General management – and the organizational innovations which seem to have been stimulated by *Working for Patients*, such as 'chief executives' and 'clinical directorates' – are bereft of the crucial ideological framework and cultural cement which previously held together an extremely fissiparous work organization. The drive for a much more rigid form of 'direct control' seems to have irreparably damaged the moral order underpinning work organization on which previous generations of administrators and managers could usually depend and draw on to secure a 'negotiated order' between occupational groups, and the crucial contributions which it made to effective service delivery.

However, recently published research on the organizational realities of the post-Griffiths reform indicates that the situation may be somewhat more complicated then this rather bleak assessment of driving control and incipient moral anomie conveys (Alleway 1987, Thompson 1987, Cousins 1988, Johnston 1988, Strong and Robinson 1990, Cox 1991). The imposition of a quasi-market discipline on professional decision-making, and work performance more broadly defined, has proved to be more difficult than was originally anticipated – particularly by government ministers and senior administrators/managers. As Coombs's research on the implementation of activity accounting and cost accounting systems in two Swedish hospitals reveals:

> the collegial or clan control mechanisms internal to the medical profession are not easily conformable with any bureaucratic control mechanisms which may be attempted by administrators. This results in part from genuine difficulties in relating inputs to outputs in medical practice, and partly from the ability of the medical profession *to use this uncertainty to promote their own collective and individual autonomy.*
>
> (Coombs 1987: 392, our italics)

Professional, and more broadly based worker resistance to the implementation of more direct bureaucratic controls and rigid financial templates has proved to be a major obstacle to the *effective operational imposition* of quasi-market relations and the logic of commercial enterprise on health care organization and delivery.

More crucially, the strategically located managerial agents charged with initiating and sustaining this ideological/cultural transformation from self-administered service to market-determined commodity find themselves struggling with the political intricacies and ethical complexities deeply embedded within the very organizational fabric of the NHS. As Strong and Robinson argue:

> Griffiths, then, was not simply a revolution; a mighty upheaval to be followed when the dust had settled and the bodies buried, but a new status quo. It offered instead a very different scenario; not Lenin but Trotsky – the possibility, indeed the necessity, of permanent revolution. This was doubly ambitious: both a mission into unknown territory and, simultaneously, an attempt to define organisational methods so flexible and yet so robust that they could cope with any unforeseen eventuality. The future, so it was hoped, was built into the structure ... [but, in practice] Griffiths was fundamentally a compromise; a new model of management which nevertheless made many striking concessions to traditional methods of organising health care ... the NHS might, at last, have leaders but, to the doctrinally pure at heart, they remained trapped within inflexible hierarchies and still subject to the massive countervailing power of medical syndicalism.
>
> (Strong and Robinson 1990: 100–49)

There are some indications of groups of managers within the newly reformed NHS beginning to think and act as a distinctive political coalition which will establish and advance its own innovative decision-making agenda (Thompson 1987, Alleway 1987). Nevertheless, they are confronted by a unique culture and an extremely complex set of organizational relationships which makes the transition from ideological doctrine and political programme to operational reality extremely difficult to deliver. The post-Griffiths reforms were, and are, directed to implementing a non-negotiable organizational order on health care professionals to the extent that they are intended to expose them to a degree of market constraint and managerial control previously unheard of in the history of the NHS. While the ideological and economic imperatives pushing in the direction of managerial solutions may be substantially modified by the restraining influence of intra-organizational politics and extra-organizational publicity and political pressure (Cox 1991), there is little doubt that the post-Griffiths changes entail the move to a radically different ideological paradigm and managerial rationale as a basis for organizing and delivering health care provision in the UK.

This attempted transformation in organizational culture and operational practices signifies an underlying conflict between two, radically opposed, moral orders as a basis for organizing the management and delivery of health care services. On the one hand, a philosophy of health care provision in which market-determined price and its managerial correlates are uppermost or, on the other, a rationale for service organization and delivery in which the traditional values of collective provision and 'negotiated order' are the prevailing operational principles. The new managerial leaders which the post-Griffiths reforms have created are precariously situated within the vortex of the political upheavals and organizational conflicts that these changes have initiated.

The second half of this chapter examines the specific, 'local', details of this resulting 'culture conflict' in greater depth and outlines an overall interpretation in which its underlying dynamics may be more clearly appreciated.

MANAGERIAL CULTURE AND ORGANIZATIONAL ORDER

This section is based upon an investigation of management roles and relationships in a large district health authority. Our conclusions confirmed a view of managerial organizations which, although substantial and authoritative, challenges both the paradigmatic assumptions and the descriptions of reality associated with classical management theory and the 'Neo-Taylorian' control strategy that it legitimates (Pollitt 1990). We set out to listen to, rather than to interrogate, a substantial number of clinicians, administrators, nurse managers and general managers and what we heard revealed a view compatible with the negotiated order and task-related co-operation that is to be found running through the work of Dalton (1959), Mintzberg (1973), Stewart (1983) and Kotter (1982). The managers – all of whom exercised managerial responsibility, whatever their job titles – particularly at the level of the hospital, did not deny the existence of a formal system of controls maintained by chains of command and functional divisions; they simply regarded it as irrelevant to the unbounded co-operative networks in which they worked and which they had to maintain. In more extreme cases, and there were many, they saw the formal system as relevant only because it was a threat that had to be overcome in order to accomplish tasks, the value and importance of which were shared by members of a community extended well beyond the confines of the NHS and, therefore, outside the control of its formal authority (Anthony and Reed 1988).

The vocabulary of nurse managers and clinicians revealed an unarticulated distinction between management and 'management'. Management was an important part of their jobs and both groups were involved in the direction and leadership of subordinates, the co-ordination of peers and anyone else whose co-operation was necessary in the control of complex processes of care and treatment and in the exercise of discretionary judgement; they were not modest in their claim to great managerial ability. But 'management' as they understood the formal exercise of managerial authority, was an alien and threatening activity imposed upon them and to be resisted: 'Managing? I haven't done much in the way of "managing" – particularly present day "managing". But I think I manage all right,' was a typical response.

This represents one of the real difficulties in promoting, training for, or developing management, at least in the health service; it represents different activities, ends and values. We distinguish between four usages or forms:

1   *Crisis management*: the unpredictable reaction to emergency, 'keeping the show on the road'.
2   *Administrative chores*: the routines imposed by the monitoring and control systems.
3   *Task or craft-based management*: the development, application and co-ordination of skills and effort to achieve intended consequences – in this case, diagnosis, treatment and care.
4   *Corporate management*: the unified, central and accountable direction of the whole organization's resources directed at the achievement of corporate goals, as they are identified by senior managers.

The rational system or corporate conception of management as an ideal towards which the NHS should strive, by the time the movement reached its greatest momentum, has become outmoded. Despite the persistence of Taylorite methods of control of work and of bureaucratic patterns of organization, by the 1980s the theoretical assault on bureaucracy had reached fashionable proportions. Loose structures were to be held in place by tight cultural commitment to shared values, and the greater discretion required from employees in the 'core' labour sector demanded that they should be treated more like professionals (Sadler 1988). Professional-like judgement was not only necessary, it would also ensure the more whole-hearted co-operation of all in the pursuit of the organization's objectives. The new model of imitation by the centralized corporations was something like a university, or a hospital. In the circumstances, the determination, in the face of post-Fordism and the arrival of disorganized capitalism (Reed 1991), to bring the NHS into the twentieth century would seem to be perverse in its intention to destroy a normative basis of compliance so much the envy of Ford. One is tempted to find an explanation for this 'organizational pathology' in a *zeitgeist* derived either from Marx or from Weber, which finds professional autonomy antithetical to modernity. There are more mundane explanations.

Corporate management is the model to which the NHS has been hesitatingly but, since Griffiths, more determinedly, moving. The change in pace and in will is explained by a change in the strategy of innovation and control. Reorganizations prior to Griffiths were described by NHS managers (in the general sense) as having little significant impact on their work or their objectives: reorganizations come and go – with remarkable regularity – but the work goes on unhindered. With, as we have argued earlier, the increasing incorporation of the clinicians came a necessary belief in the abiding value of some degree of consensus management, but that must remain a problem within the corporate model. Some post-Griffiths managers see consensus as merely transitional; an evolutionary survival on the way to central direction and control when the clinicians, turbulent priests, are faintly subdued or don the mantle of 'managers'. Others see it as a useful means of accommodating the autonomy and importance of different groups and cultures to their corporate control. The fact that the matter is or was, still *sub judice* signals the perceived inadequacy of reorganization as a method of strategic and cultural change. So far, change has been attempted by fiat and by exhortation and it has been contested to the extent that it has been open to participation, if not consensus. After Griffiths, who at least assured that the managerial *nomenclature* was in place, the change would follow from involuntary and inevitable response to a change in the environment in the relationships of production and exchange. The success or failure of the current proposals for the NHS will demonstrate the dependence of a Conservative government upon a Marxist analysis of social change.

It reveals this dependence, at least in the short term, in the fact that, while other attempts at reorganization changed the organizational structure, this one marginalizes the structure, assuming that it will be conditioned in some valuable but unpredictable way by a change in the market context to which it will have to adapt. The division between purchase and provision, and the creation of an internal market, is not accompanied by any planned or strategic formal reorganization; an acknowledgement, perhaps, that formal reorganization is irrelevant because organization will follow the material requirements of the situation.

Our own recent investigations of management practice in the NHS suggest that this is an accurate observation and that it is likely to be as true of the future as it has been of the past. Formal organization always was irrelevant in the NHS or, at least, it was perceived to be irrelevant by its managers up to and including hospital level. What determined the roles and relationships of managers, to continue an analogy, was the relationships of production and exchange which subordinated all to the tasks to be undertaken within a prevailing culture dominated by those with the greatest authority in task control – an essentially syndicalist structure. The comparison between Conservative and Marxist analysis breaks down, however, in terms of the preferred nature of the market that is to condition behaviour. The NHS was constructed in imitation of something like a command economy; the model for its proposed reconstruction is an enterprise economy. From this distinction very different but equally involuntary consequences are expected to follow. It is the values associated with enterprise, with competitive success, reward for performance preferred by the customer, unerringly chosen by value for money, rather than professional judgement that are to prevail. Two questions arise: whether what is proposed for the NHS can be done and whether it should be done?

There is little question that the provision of health care could be determined by market demand, the objection is that the result would be socially unjust. Keat argues that the extension of market decision to service provision rests upon utilitarian theory and that it is open to the objection that the aggregation of need is, consequently, undiscriminating:

> since the operation of market economies tends to generate major inequalities of income and wealth, the relative ease of people's access to these

services (and indeed the relative quality of the services thereby received) would then broadly reflect these inequalities, and hence be unrelated to people's need for them. Whatever the merits of market economies, their distributive consequences clearly do not satisfy need-based criteria of justice, and hence their obvious unsuitability for the provision of goods and services where such criteria are regarded as relevant.

(Keat 1991: 217–18)

The argument from the market can defend itself by proposing necessary modification, a floor of care below which no one sinks and above which the market reigns, but the concern obviously remains; my ingrowing toe-nail is more important than your hip replacement because I can afford treatment. The argument is likely to be interminable and the evidence to be confusing: it is not our present concern (as it is neither Keat's). Whether or not the NHS can be turned into provision for society's care as a whole, the immediate question is whether it can be turned into an *internal* market – that is, a service whose overall funding is determined by a political process, not by economic competition, but in which the available funding is divided internally by competition between providers. Is it conceivable to imagine a near monopoly service – the Conservative party is resolute in its commitment to the NHS – the internal distribution of which is determined by competition?

The difficulties in the way of importing entrepreneurial values into the service while it is protected from their external influence are formidable. It would be contrary to its culture, its history and the principles upon which it was founded and, we are told these days, such matters are difficult to overcome, particularly in organizations where strong cultures reside. More particularly, the containment of entrepreneurial activity in an organization that rests on a foundation of normative compliance, negotiated order and intimate co-operation between a rich diversity of groups, some of which enjoy power and prestige, would seem to present problems. Even in an enterprise dedicated simply to the manufacture and sale of beefburgers, the prospect of survival for an employee who entrepreneurially pursued his or her own interest at the expense of corporate good might be poor. The dangers of interdepartmental and functional border warfare are sufficiently acknowledged to make it unlikely that they should be enlarged by the encouragement of entrepreneurial advantage for purchasing at the expense of production – or, in this case, service provision.

The difficulties reside in the fact that even the most commercially directed organizations are entrepreneurial and competitive on the outside and as co-operative or collaborative as they can be on the inside. The whole thrust of generations of consultant and academic advice to managers has been to reach a nirvana of harmony and co-operation. All complex organizations would break up in anarchic disorder if they were not maintained by some degree of trust (Fox 1974). Some of them are more particularly the reserves of activities and values deemed largely antithetical to self-seeking and competition.

INSTITUTIONAL MANAGEMENT AND HEALTH-CARE PRACTICE

In *After Virtue*, MacIntyre (1981) distinguishes between 'institutions' and 'practices': the former concerned with the production of goods which are the object of competitive and distributive exchange, the latter with internal goods, with standards of excellence and with human conceptions of ends and values. Practices are inherently different from institutions but they depend upon them to sustain them and are at the same time threatened to be overcome by them (MacIntyre 1981, Anthony 1986, Keat 1991). In these terms, the clinical and nursing values and internal 'goods' represent a practice sustained in an uneasy relationship with the institution of the NHS. But the traditions of autonomous professions are sufficiently strong to have influenced the institution, at least to have held it at bay. It may require a change in the market environment to reverse this relationship so that it is the practice and its concern for internal goods, valued by the wider community, that is weakened.

As the professionals of health care see it, the institution of the NHS exists to resource and facilitate the delivery of a service the quality of which must be determined by them. Clinicians, in particular, believe that they, and only they, can control the quality of a service which the institution must serve to deliver. Clinicians and nurse managers share a task-based view of their duties to which they see the organization as subordinate or secondary, existing so as to ensure that those duties can be carried out. This is a perfectly defensible and rational view of an organization, a view which regards it as secondary or instrumental to the performance of a task or the provision of a service. It is not readily compatible with the belief that it is the organization that must be paramount and that it is the authority of its managers that must be advanced, to the point when it is those managers' own 'professional' status that needs to be secured. The task-based perception of a practice *would* seem to be compatible with much of the current concern with the maintenance and, in particular, with the embedding of quality into organizational culture (Pollitt 1990). It seems paradoxical that, where it has been established and nurtured by a tradition of collaboration through 'negotiated order' and autonomous (or at least semi-autonomous) control, it is deemed to be necessary to subject it to an examination by entrepreneurs to be conducted in the market place. That the latter require a much more elaborate and constraining system of bureaucratic management and control to realize the 'marketization' of health care provision is an added paradox, not to say contradiction.

We have suggested, however, that the prospects for success of the current plans are not certain. One of the difficulties is the inappropriateness of the bureaucratic techniques of measurement and control to the discretionary practice of the professional – a difficulty which has been identified within bureaucracy itself before it was exported to health care (Scott 1981). Universities have also experienced the banal attempts to apply discredited industrial techniques to the measurement and reward of scholarship and teaching. But in the practice of education, the inadequacy of techniques can be replaced by the adjudication of the market without too much visible damage, at least in the short term. That may not be the case in the health service.

A more real but less imminent danger is that such innovations may represent a confrontation between cultures, between practices and institutions, in which an essentially moral fabric of relationships is gradually eroded by a new vocabulary of performance-related reward, human asset accounting, and a constant concern for the bottom line. All organizations that succeed in persisting over time are communities and all communities are held together by moral bonds of reciprocal obligation underpinned by trust relationships that have some significance and meaning in shaping work performance (Gouldner 1959, Salaman 1986). The extent of that truth has been obscured by a tendency to exaggerate the systematic and rational aspects of organization at no great general cost other than in misunderstanding. The cost of introducing inappropriate methods and values to the NHS could be borne by its patients and by the literal demoralization of those members of its staff in whom resides the responsibility for sustaining those values which it exists to embody.

CONCLUSIONS

Broadly speaking, the analysis which we have provided in this chapter supports Pollitt's view that health service reorganization in the 1980s and early 1990s has been driven by a neo-Taylorism management ideology and practice (Pollitt 1990). This has entailed the widespread imposition of a generic model of management organization which bureaucratizes the structure of control and simultaneously debureaucratizes the employment relationship (Pollitt 1990: 16). While the former process entails a strengthening and tightening of external controls on internal task performance, the latter 'frees' established employment relationships and practices from institutional regulation and subordinates them to the dictates of the labour market.

The widespread diffusion of neo–Taylorism management ideology and practice has been legitimated by the search for 'a single version of a more tightly focused, financially disciplined, performance conscious management' (Pollitt 1990: 112). It has undoubtedly led to a weakening of the complex, and often fragile, processes of 'negotiated order' through which 'high-trust' collaborative work organization and culture has been nurtured and sustained within the NHS. Yet managers are left in a position where they are forced to draw on the moral capital which the latter has accumulated if the new tenets of the 'internal market' are to be translated into organizational reality. They have to be sensitive to the political, social and ethical dilemmas and conflicts which confront the *practice* of management in health service organizations, if they are to have any chance of success in achieving their operational and strategic objectives (Thompson 1987).

At the very least, this analysis identifies the limitations, not to say dangers, of imposing a market-oriented model of bureaucratic management on health service organizations which largely ignores their historical, culture and organizational distinctiveness. It also highlights the theoretical and practical importance of developing an informed understanding of the 'peculiarities' of management practice within health service organizations, given that the latter still have the *potential* to combine the qualities of operational effectiveness, structural adaptability and strategic flexibility so ardently sought after by the current crop of 'management gurus'. However, it is unlikely that any of these qualities will be preserved, much less enhanced, if a relatively crude and largely outmoded theory of management practice is implemented in such a way that it virtually destroys the moral foundations of organizational effectiveness. The need to be more responsive to external wants and expectations, and to oblige professional providers to be more aware of changing patient requirements, is unlikely to be met unless the complex problem of securing a proper balance between institutional demands and organizational practice is more sensitively addressed. It is certainly an issue which health service managers will have to confront whatever the make-up of the institutional framework and organizational setting in which they operate.

BIBLIOGRAPHY

Ackroyd, S., Hughes, J. and Soothill, K. (1989) 'Public sector services and their management', *Journal of Management Studies* 26(6), 603–19.

Alleway, L. (1987) 'Back on the outside looking in', *The Health Service Journal* 16 July, pp. 818–19.

Anthony, P. D. (1986) *The Foundation of Management* London: Tavistock.

—— and Reed, M. (1988) 'A study of management roles and relationships in a district health authority', unpublished report: University College, Cardiff.

—— —— (1990) 'Managerial roles and relationships: the impact of the Griffiths Report', *International Journal of Health* 3(3), 20–31.

Barnard, K. (1989) 'National Health Service management', in I. Taylor and G. Popham (eds), *An Introduction to Public Sector Management,* London: Unwin Hyman.

Burns, T. (1982) 'Rediscovering organisation: aspects of collaboration and managerialism in hospital organisation', Social Science Research Council, Unpublished Research Paper.

Clark, K. and Starkey, K. (1988) *Organisation Transitions and Innovative Design,* London: Pinter Publishers.

Coombs, R. (1987) 'Accounting for the control of doctors: management information systems in hospitals', *Accounting, Organisations and Society* 12(4), 389–404.

—— and Green, G. (1989) 'Work organisation and product change in the service sector: the case of the UK National Health Service', in S. Wood (ed.), *The Transformation of Work?,* London: Unwin Hyman.

Cousins, C. (1987) *Controlling Social Welfare: A Sociology of State Welfare Work and Organisation,* Brighton: Wheatsheaf.

—— (1988) 'The restructuring of welfare work', *Work, Employment and Society* 2(2), 210–28.

Cox, D. (1991) 'Health service management: a sociological view', in J. Gabe, M. Bury and M. Calnon (eds), *Sociology of Health Services,* London: Routledge.

Dalton, M. (1959) *Men Who Manage*, New York: Wiley.

DHSS (1983) *NHS Management Inquiry* (The Griffiths Report), London: HMSO.

Etzioni, A. (1975) *A Comparative Analysis of Complex Organisations* (2nd edn), New York: Free Press.

Fox, A. (1974) *Beyond Contract: Work, Power and Trust Relations*, London: Faber and Faber.

Gabbay, J. and Dopson, S. (1987) 'The search for a shared vision', *The Health Service Journal*, vol. 10, September, pp. 1042–3.

Gouldner, A. (1959) 'Organizational analysis', in R. K. Merton, L. Broom and C. Cotterell (eds), *Sociology Today*, New York: Basic Books.

Harrison, S., Hunter, D. J. and Pollitt, C. (1990) *The Dynamics of British Health Policy*, London: Unwin Hyman.

Johnston, L. (1988) 'Controlling police work: problems of organisational reform in large public bureaucracies', *Work, Employment and Society* 2(1), 51–70.

Keat, R. (1991) 'Consumer sovereignty and the integrity of practices,' in R. Keat and N. Abercrombie (eds), *Enterprise Culture*, London: Routledge.

Kotter, J. (1982) *The General Managers*, New York: Free Press.

MacIntyre, A. (1981) *After Virtue: A Study in Moral Theory*, London: Duckworth.

Mintzberg, H. (1973) *The Nature of Management*, New York: Harper & Row.

Pollitt, C. (1990) *Managerialism and The Public Services: The Anglo American Experience*, Oxford: Blackwell.

Reed, M. (1991) 'The disorganised society: a theme in search of a theory?', in P. Blyton and J. Morris (eds), *A Flexible Future?*, Berlin: Walter de Gruyter & Company.

Reed, M. and Anthony, P. D. (1992) 'Professional management and managing professionalization', *Journal of Management Studies*, 29(5), 591–614.

Sadler, B. (1988) *Managerial Leadership in the Post-Industrial Society*, Aldershot: Gower.

Salaman, G. (1986) *Working*, London: Tavistock.

Scott, W.H. (1981) *Organizations: Rational, Natural and Open Systems*, Englewood Cliffs, N.J.: Prentice-Hall.

Small, N. (1989) *Politics and Planning in the N.H.S.*, Milton Keynes: Open University Press.

Stewart, R. (1983) 'Managerial behaviour: how research has changed the traditional picture', in M. J. Earl (ed.), *Perspectives on Management*, Oxford: Oxford University Press.

Strong, P. and Robinson, J. (1990) *The N.H.S. Under New Management*, Milton Keynes: Open University Press.

Thompson, D. (1987) 'Coalitions and conflict in the N.H.S.: some implications for general management', *Sociology of Health and Illness* 9(2), 127–53.

Working for Patients (1989) Department of Health White Paper.

Part IV

PRIVATIZATION IN ADVANCED INDUSTRIAL ECONOMIES

11

THE POLITICAL ECONOMY OF THE UK PRIVATIZATION PROGRAMME

A blueprint for other countries?

Thomas Clarke

INTRODUCTION: UK PRIVATIZATION – A BLUEPRINT FOR OTHER COUNTRIES?

The policy of privatization now sweeping through the world commenced in Britain in the early 1980s. Although it began as a limited programme of returning some major utilities to private ownership, it quickly gathered pace and became an apparently unstoppable movement to restore the market system and 'roll back the frontiers of the state'. The political consensus in Britain that there is an appropriate balance of public and private industries, upheld by all post-war governments, was deliberately shattered. The impression was created that the public sector was inherently inefficient and wasteful, and that the release of entrepreneurial energies with the escape to privatization would quickly transform any sluggish public sector enterprise into a competitive, dynamic concern.

Before firm evidence was available as to the success in practice of the privatization policy in Britain, or what the wider implications and effects of the programme might be, an enthusiastic drive for privatization has occurred in most other advanced industrial countries; and there has been much pressure upon the developing countries to adopt privatization as a way out of their intractable economic problems. Similarly, in Eastern Europe the democratic transformation of the Communist states has been accompanied by a call for immediate and universal privatization of public assets. This programme of privatization, were it ever implemented, would have much deeper consequences than in Western Europe because the state sector represented almost the whole of significant economic activity in most of the former command economies.

The political drive for privatization has often been accompanied by almost euphoric pronouncements of the achievements so far attained by the programme in Britain; for example John Moore, a Minister in Margaret Thatcher's cabinet for ten years, and as Financial Secretary to the Treasury from 1983–6 responsible for the initial stages of the privatization programme, celebrated the phenomenon in the following less than measured terms in the pages of the *Harvard Business Review*:

> Privatisation has shown itself capable not only of rescuing individual industries and a whole economy headed for disaster but also of transforming public attitudes towards economic responsibility and the concept of private property. Begun as a radical experiment, privatisation works so well that it has become a practical process by which a state-owned industry can join the free market with visible, often dramatic gains for the industry, its employees, its customers, and for the citizens who set it free by purchasing its shares. More important, privatisation has become an education process by which the people of a country can grasp the fundamental beliefs and values of free enterprise.
>
> (Moore 1992: 115–16)

Each of these claims merits some inquiry: has privatization in the UK really led to 'dramatic gains' for industry, and precisely what are those gains? Second, have shareholders, consumers, and employees benefited in quite the way described? First, though it is useful to examine the development of privatization policy and how it was implemented in the UK.

POST-FACTUM POLICY-MAKING

Though the scale of privatization in the UK since 1979 under four consecutive Conservative governments has proved massive, there is little evidence of any initial declared policy commitment to this goal. The 1979 Thatcher administration was wedded to monetarist beliefs, and the emphasis in manifesto commitments was to controlling the money supply, reducing public expenditure, and cutting income tax. Specific commitments were given to return aerospace and shipbuilding to private ownership; sell shares in the National Freight Corporation and deregulate the bus industry; finally there was the promise to sell council houses to their tenants. But this was little more than other former Conservative administrations had proposed, and it was only in the second and third Thatcher governments that the commitment to sell major public enterprises was made.

In the first term the government had experienced a series of disappointments in economic policy: unemployment rose, the recession deepened, inflation increased, manufacturing output declined, interest rates rose, and most embarassingly of all, public expenditure continued to grow. In this context privatization was seized upon by a government in economic difficulties as a way of apparently reducing the public sector borrowing requirement, without engaging in politically unpopular serious cuts in public expenditure (Marsh 1991: 460–1). The contradictions of the government's policy have been highlighted by Abromeit:

The privatisation policy marks a decisive U-turn in the Government's monetarist policy, of which it was meant to form an integral part; the sales have turned into an easy means to circumvent the fiscal constraints, following from restrictions of the money supply which ought to be the core of monetarism. Monetarism is clearly in tatters when, as *The Economist* has noted, state assets are sold because 'State treasurers want to raise money without printing it.'

(Abromeit 1988: 84)

Thus privatization proceeds disguised the fact public expenditure had risen to pay increased levels of social security payments to the unemployed. As receipts from privatization sales rose dramatically in the late 1980s, government policy began to change also:

The Government turned towards more overtly supply-side policies. In this context the proceeds from the privatisation programme could be used to offset other expenditure and finance the government's tax-reduction aspirations – all this and the PSBR continuing to be reduced or becoming a surplus. Thus, the financial objectives changed somewhat, to providing room for desired tax cuts in the name of their supposed supply-side incentive effects.

(Thompson 1990: 144)

Privatization was pursued for political reasons related to the government's troubled attempt to manage the economy and stay in power, rather than to the economic pursuit of efficiency in the industries concerned. This explains many other inconsistencies in the way in which privatization was approached and undertaken.

A PRIVATIZATION STRATEGY?

Before the question of whether there ever was a consistent privatization strategy in the UK is examined, it is necessary to inquire about the origins and development of the public sector, to explore whether privatization was as inevitable as the government subsequently insisted. In Britain and other West European countries the public sector was not the result of the oppressive intervention of a malign highly centralized state apparatus. On the contrary public intervention occurred in a widespread, decentralized way in recognition of the inadequacies of market provision. In the early nineteenth century local commissions were established to provide street lighting, cleaning, road building, sewers, water supply and public health. Later, local authorities began to build low-cost public housing to get the urban population out of the slums, and local education authorities were set up to provide mass education to those neglected by the private schools. Finally, to ensure a low-cost, reliable service, public utilities were established by local councils providing public transport, water, gas and electricity supply.

The post-1945 expansion of the nationalized industries was pursued by a Labour government which stressed the essential irresponsibility of private capital, the failure of the market system to provide the investment necessary to sustain the efficiency of industry, or to provide even essential services (such as health care) to those who could not afford to pay. The Welfare State was designed, it was thought, to protect the rights of individuals without wealth or property. Cross-subsidy could ensure a comprehensive service was available to all. The purpose of nationalization and the Welfare State therefore, rather than the narrow pursuit of profit maximization, was the creation of a stable economic infrastructure and reliable social provision. This policy was built into the pricing structure of the public industries, which often meant they made losses. However, losses in the public sector were conceived as a vital subsidy to the private sector of the economy, providing low-cost utilities and a healthy, well-educated workforce. Though this difference should have been widely understood, it was rarely acknowledged in more recent years when public sector enterprises were often subjected to critical comparison with the profit-motivated private sector, despite the fact that, 'Simple comparisons of the efficiency and effectiveness of private sector and public sector management cannot readily take account of their very different objectives. This fact confounds comparative assessments of public and private sector efficiency' (Lapsley and Wright 1990: 49).

As the scale of the public sector continued to grow in the 1970s and public expenditure consumed a higher proportion of gross national product, criticisms of the performance of the public sector began to increase. In one sense these were inevitable, since the public sector was providing goods for which there was an ever-expanding demand – for example, in education and health care, which it was impossible to fully satisfy. However, many of the complaints concerned how the public sector used the resources it did have to satisfy consumers. Moreover the centralized bureaucratic mode of the public sector began to be recognized as not only inefficient and inflexible but as oppressive and unresponsive to both employees and consumers alike. Managers in the public sector complained of tight control of their finances and of recurrent, undue political interference which made strategic planning difficult. Necessary investment in public industries was denied by governments faced with external constraints upon their growing borrowing requirements, and mounting losses were experienced by industries such as the railways which found they were increasingly unable to compete with private transport due to a lack of modern infrastructure and trains.

Successive governments recognized the need to improve the efficiency of the public sector, and introduced a series of reforms to attempt to ensure efficiency and value for money in the public sector. These included applying strict cash limits to the expenditure of public sector industries, rather than allowing them to draw indefinitely on the public purse; limiting employment levels within public companies; introducing the assessment of staff at regular intervals; establishing periodic reviews of functions and organizations; having regular internal and external audits; regular studies of comparative costs and outputs; contracting-out work to competitive tender which could not be done efficiently in-house; and setting performance indicators and performance measurement (Pliatzky 1988). The belief that the public sector was synonymous with inefficiency was therefore a little unfair, and there is much evidence which suggests the private sector is not inherently more efficient (Millward and Parker 1983, Vickers and Yarrow 1988). A reading of western economic theory, which suggests all that has to be achieved is a transition from the public to the private sector in order to attain efficiency, is rather misleading (Grosfeld 1990).

The drive of the three Thatcher governments of the 1980s towards the commercialization and privatization of the public sector had much more to do with ideological belief than economic analysis and comparative assessment of performance. The government regarded privatization *a priori* as serving a multiplicity of self-reinforcing objectives. *Economic freedom*: the management of the privatized corporations would be free to invest in market opportunities and the consumer free to choose; *efficiency*: the disciplines of the product and capital market and the profit incentive would enhance the pursuit of enterprise efficiency; *wider share ownership*: privatization would promote popular capitalism by dispersing shares widely. Though the government has confidently proclaimed the achievement of each of these objectives, when the results of privatization are examined more closely, serious questions begin to emerge about what exactly has been achieved.

Different forms privatization has taken in Britain include:

1   Asset sales, which may involve denationalization, as in the case of British Gas, British Airways, and British Telecom; the sale of public sector companies earlier transferred from the private sector such as Jaguar and Rolls-Royce; or the sale of government holdings in private companies such as BP.
2   Deregulation, or the relaxing of state monopolies, which exposes public sector industries to competition as in bus deregulation and the parcel delivery service.
3   Contracting out work, previously done in-house by direct labour, as in local government, the NHS and the Civil Service.
4   The private provision of services, allowing the private sector to provide services to the public, as in nursing homes.
5   Investment projects designed to encourage private sector involvement, as in projects in deprived areas, and special units in public sector organizations devoted to commercial returns.
6   The reduction of subsidies and the increase in charges for public sector services such as health and welfare (Young 1986: 238–44).
7   Council house sales (Forrest 1988).

The privatization programme in Britain began in a tentative way, with the postponement of the privatization of British Airways, British Shipbuilders, and the National Freight Corporation in the early 1980s due to the recession and the poor state of the finances of the companies concerned. Only after the further injection of public funds and the restructuring of these companies were they offered for sale. Instead the most successful companies of the public sector were privatized, including British Aerospace and the high technology company Amersham International. The price of the shares was set so low by the government that the sales were oversubscribed many times and speculators made quick profits from immediately selling the stock they bought. By 1984 privatization revenue was over £1 billion per annum, but with the sale of British Telecom more than £2.5 billion had to be found. The government looked to two new markets for shares: the wider population, most of whom had never contemplated owning company shares; and overseas investors. Shares were acquired by 2.3 million people in the UK, encouraged by a subsidy of their telephone account, and 230,000 British Telecom employees. However, a substantial tranche of the shares went overseas, and when trading opened with the shares at a 90 per cent premium above the price they had been sold by the government, overseas speculators were in a position to make a killing.

Fixed-price share launches had created a speculator's dream rather than the encouragement of long-term investment by small shareholders. The British Airways and subsequent launches were therefore designed as a combination of tender and fixed price, encouraging public participation whilst maximizing the proceeds from institutions. Another weakness in the government's privatization strategy was revealed in 1987 with the attempt to sell the remaining 31.5 per cent government stake in British Petroleum valued at £5.7 billion, the world's biggest-ever stock-market sale. All of the former privatizations had succeeded in a bull market in which investors assumed they would receive an immediate gain. The BP sale coincided with the biggest global stock-market crash since 1929. Share prices in the *Financial Times* Share Index dropped by 21.7 per cent on 19 and 20 October 1987, spreading panic. The BP offer price of 330p was faced with a stock-market price of 266p, which meant the underwriters of the launch would end up with most of the shares issued. They urged the government to abandon the sale, and though it went ahead, the Bank of England agreed to buy back some of the unwanted shares. Some of the dangers associated with massive sales of vital utilities on the market had been exposed, and from this point the government proceeded more cautiously in the sale of the water and electricity industries. None the less, the privatization programme continued, and by 1992 sales of state assets had reached £44.5 billion (see Table 11.1), together with a further £36 billion from council house sales.

Those who opposed the policy were worn down. Public sector managers who had doubts about privatization found that life in the public sector was made unbearable by tight Treasury-imposed limits upon external financing:

> When they complained, they were told that such 'public sector constraints' were an inevitable consequence of their nationalised status and the only way to relax them would be to set the industries 'free in the market place.'

Table 11.1 Public asset sales in the UK, 1979–91

Company	Financial year of initial flotation	Golden share	Net proceeds to HMG (£ millions)	Times oversubscribed (under-subscribed)	Discount on share price (%)
British Petroleum	1979/80	No	6,149	n/a	–
British Aerospace	1980/81	Yes	390	n/a	–
Cable and Wireless	1981/82	Yes	1,024	5.6	17
Amersham International	1981/82	Yes	60	24.0	26
Britoil	1982/83	Yes	53	(0.3)	n/a
Associated British Ports	1982/83	No	97	34.0	21
Enterprise Oil (British Gas subsidiary)	1984/85	Yes	382	(0.4)	n/a
Jaguar (British Leyland subsidiary)	1984/85	Yes	–	8.3	6
British Telecom	1985/86	Yes	3,681	3.0	21
TSB	1986/87	No			
British Gas	1986/87	Yes	7,731	4.0	11
British Airways	1986/87	Yes	850	23.0	29
Rolls-Royce	1987/88	Yes	1,028	9.4	25
British Airports Authority	1987/88	Yes	1,183	8.1	12
10 Water Companies	1989/90	Yes	3,480	2.8	17
Electric Companies	1990/91	Yes	5,200	10.7	21
2 Electricity Generating Companies (PowerGen and National Power)	1991/92	Yes	2,000	4.0	37

Source: Marsh 1991.

Making life unnecessarily unpleasant for the nationalised industries thus became a convenient spur to a change in management attitude towards denationalisation.

(Steel and Heald 1984: 17)

The process of pre-privatization restructuring prepared the ground – for example, at British Steel this involved a cut in workers from 166,000 to 52,000, a reduction in government external funding from £1,119 million to £24 million, achieving a net profit of £178 million instead of a net loss of £1,784 million on a similar £3,000 million turnover.

Most nationalized industry directors were prepared to do anything the government required, as long as their corporations were allowed to retain their monopoly position. Leo Pliatzky, who was a senior civil servant at the Treasury and the Department of Industry, has insisted:

At top management level, the industries were mainly concerned to keep their enterprises intact on privatisation and to resist fragmentation into competitive elements; once this had been secured, the Boards looked forward to escaping from government control and joining the ranks of the self-perpetuating corporate oligarchies which dominate the modern industrial scene. Public versus private ownership (as distinct from public expenditure versus tax reliefs) has ceased, for good or ill, to be a live issue in British politics for the foreseeable future, though acute problems remain about the accountability and regulation of privatised monopolies.

(Pliatzky 1988: 44)

COMPETITION AND EFFICIENCY?

If competitive efficiency had been the primary objective, then restructuring the nationalized industries into competing corporations and divisions would have been essential, though this would have greatly reduced the attractiveness of the privatized share offers on the stock-market, may have jeopardized some sales, and the government would have received less in revenue. 'Where a successful disposal at a good price conflicts with liberalisation, it is liberalisation which loses out' (Prosser 1986: 81). The transformation of public monopolies into private monopolies was a safer and easier option, though it undermined government's claims concerning the future efficiency of the companies, and contradicted the economic theory government propounded: 'allocative efficiency is a function of market structure rather than ownership. Thus, in the absence of competition, denationalisation is unlikely to result in major gains in efficiency performance' (Kirkpatrick 1988: 240). Though the water and electricity industries were broken up into constituent regional companies partly in response to the criticism of earlier privatizations, and in 1991 the decision was taken to further liberalize the telecommunications market to encourage other companies to compete with BT and Mercury, this is still a long way from creating effective competition in the industries concerned.

(The contortions of the government and the Central Electricity Generating Board (CEGB) concerning the future of the nuclear power-stations after privatization reveal that neither the privatization of electricity nor the investment in the nuclear industry itself from its origin, were based on grounds of competitive efficiency, and that political considerations still take precedence over the market. The attempt was made to include the nuclear industry in the privatization of electricity by inserting it within a duopoly of two large generating companies that would have secure profits, and providing it with a privileged pricing structure. Even the promise of tranches of up to £2.5 billion at a time to assist with decommissioning costs did not reassure financial investment specialists (Estrin *et al.* 1990: 46). As a result, the government had to privatize National Power and PowerGen without the nuclear industry. Nuclear Electric remained as a public company, supported by a nuclear levy, the Non-Fossil Fuel Obligation (NFFO), which adds 11 per cent to the cost of power produced by burning fossil fuels. Around 99 per cent of this levy is used by the government to support the nuclear power industry; and the 1 per cent remaining used to support wave and wind power development. When Stephen Littlechild, the Offer regulator, in September 1992 questioned the need for a £1.3 billion annual subsidy for the nuclear industry he was met by a furious response from Nuclear Electric. Yet if the planned new generators come on stream, there will be overcapacity of 11,700 MW by 1998. Nuclear Electric produces 12,000 MW, and it is likely that as government support for an expensive and dangerous industry wanes, the nuclear power industry will become a waste disposal service, slowly disposing of the radioactive waste created by itself for many years to come.)

It is difficult to imagine any advantages of a private monopoly compared to a public monopoly. If leaner, fitter and more responsive industries were to emerge from the privatization process there had to be some incentive or restraint to become so (Woodward 1988). The private sector is as prone to the erection of large-scale, complex and remote bureaucracies as the public sector, as Max Weber and many other organization theorists have argued (Clegg and Dunkerley 1980). Schumpeter has stressed the inevitability of bureaucracy in private firms, and many economists since have acknowledged the problem. Periods of restructuring inevitably cause significant further effects, and the experience of privatization would have a sharp effect in any organization. But to assume this will invariably lead to sustained attention to performance and quality is unfounded when a monopoly position allows the pursuit of very different orientations. Kaletsky made this point bluntly in *The Financial Times*: 'The new system will tend to settle down and the natural lassitude of any huge monopolistic enterprise is likely to reassert itself ... the natural frictions between any monopoly and its customers will come to the fore again' (13 February 1986).

The subordination of the objective of achieving economic efficiency in the industries to be privatized to the government's immediate political priorities to raise short-term revenue and secure quick sales of public assets, has not only undermined the logic of the government's case for privatization, but more seriously has provided vital sectors of British industry with a comfortable private monopoly it will now be extremely difficult to break, as Vickers and Yarrow conclude in their study:

> In the long run the British privatisation programme will be judged in terms of its effect on economic efficiency. By failing to introduce sufficiently effective frameworks of competition and regulation before privatising such industries as telecommunications and gas, the Government has lost a major opportunity to tackle fundamental problems experienced in the past under public ownership.
>
> (Vickers and Yarrow 1988: 425–9)

Though corporate bureaucracies may survive almost intact with privatization, the direction in which they are driven has altered, with the substitution of the goal of profit maximization and growth for the government definition of the public good. The potential problems caused by this change in orientation have been recognized even by the supporters of privatization such as Beesley and Littlechild who advised the Department of Industry concerning BT privatization:

> Privatisation is intended to change motivations of management towards profit-making. A privately owned company will have greater incentive to exploit monopoly power commercially. To the extent this is not limited, consumer benefits from privatisation will be less than they might be. Second, a privatised company will be less willing to provide uneconomic services. The resources so released will be used more productively, but particular sets of consumers will lose by the change. This raises the question of how such losses, often thought of as social obligations, should be handled.
>
> (Beesley and Littlechild 1989)

In the absence of competition, the creation of regulatory agencies was the only means to rescue the consumer from the possibility of naked exploitation. The establishment of regulatory agencies for each of the privatized industries – including Ofgas, Oftel, Ofwat and Offer – was a remarkably unexpected result of privatization:

> In the case of the major utilities such as BT and British Gas, the Government rolled back the boundaries of the State as far as the immediate responsibility for the supply of services was concerned. However ... they immediately rolled them forward again by setting up regulatory bodies to ensure fair play between the industries and the consumers on the one hand, and between the industries and their potential competitors on the other.
>
> (Gretton *et al.* 1987: 17)

Though the RPI − X formula used by the regulatory bodies to restrict price increases in the privatized utilities to the rate of inflation minus X per cent provides an incentive to reduce costs and innovate (and is less discretionary than the rate of return regulation practised in the US, and less open to the behaviour of the firm manipulating the outcome), it still has important limitations. The formula only applies to those services offered in non-competitive markets so, for example, about half of BT's revenue is not subject to price control. Second, the regulator can never achieve the information available to the company management, and will inevitably err on the side of caution for fear of damaging the company with an unrealistic target.

Thus the first years of the regulatory regime were rather lax considering the potential profitability of the companies concerned, with X set at 3 per cent at BT, with the price-cap set in a way BT could discriminate against domestic consumers; and X set at 2 per cent at British Gas and applied only to domestic consumers though it supplies 35 per cent of the industrial energy market (Estrin *et al.* 1990: 41). After water privatization of the RPI + K formula, designed to assist in the extensive investment necessary in the industry, permitted price increases of 13–16 per cent in 1991–2. The regulators are aware they are the only real line of defence of the public, and have in one or two instances attempted to rise to public expectations. In 1992 Ofgas engaged in open pressure upon British Gas to reduce its prices, which resulted in two successive price reductions for domestic and small business customers of 3 per cent and 2 per cent. This was achieved against the protests of British Gas which took the unusual step for a monopoly supplier of asking the Monopolies Commission to carry out a full inquiry into the industry! (*The Guardian*, 26 August 1992).

As the agencies have attempted to exert influence over the companies they are intended to regulate they have exposed the necessary limitations upon the freedom of monopolies in essential industries. Almost inevitably, government has been drawn into discussions concerning the cost bases, pricing policies, and investment programmes of the industries concerned: 'Ministers and MPs will continue to be the recipients of complaints about performance – and rightly so, since if competitive markets do not provide an opportunity for consumers to register dissatisfaction the political process is all that is left (Kay and Silberston 1984: 15). The continuing responsibility of the government for the industries concerned is formally recognized in the retention of a 'golden share' to prevent developments in the ownership of these vital industries judged antithetical to the national interest. Equally, it would be wrong to suppose that the Conservative government's belief in the infallibility of the free market is sufficiently strong to allow essential industries such as water, gas, or electricity to go bankrupt. 'De-coupling the state and the economy' is not as easy as it might at first appear.

PRIVATIZATION IN PRACTICE?

The long-term costs and benefits of privatization in practice are yet to be discovered, but evidence is merging of the short- and medium-term consequences.

First, the impression that privatization has proved a spectacularly successful means of raising government revenue must be contested. Virtually all the privatized concerns now have a market capitalization far greater than the amount raised by the government in the sale of the assets. It might be suggested that this difference represents a significant loss to the public purse of valuable assets which were sold off cheaply in order to ensure the privatization programme succeeded. On the contrary the government would insist the higher value of the privatized industries now acknowledged represents the results of a remarkable transformation in these companies' commercial performance. Such an optimistic view neglects some important considerations. First, much of the restructuring of the corporations took place as a preparation for privatization with the injection of massive amounts of public money. For example, the water authorities had £5 billion of debts written off and received a further £1.6 billion 'green dowry'. The National Audit Office subsequently noted, 'the Department [of the Environment] took considerable care to establish financially stable companies that would achieve the profitability and cash flow requirements necessary for flotation' (National Audit Office 1992: 8). Thus in addition the privatized water companies received costs-pass-through concessions relating to new legal requirements including EEC Directives, the possible costs of installing domestic water meters, and beneficial corporation tax treatment which means that no water company is likely to pay mainstream corporation tax over ten years because of the billions of pounds of unused capital allowances available to be offset against pre-tax profits (Richardson *et al.* 1992: 171).

Second, privatization shares were consistently deliberately undervalued at the launch, and the moment the shares began dealing the government recorded losses, which amounted to billions of pounds, including an immediate loss of £1,300 million on the day of the British Telecom sale (TUC 1987). Large discounts on share prices were consciously provided by the government to entice subscribers, but this was done in an unnecessarily extravagant way as successive sales were consistently subscribed several times over (see Table 11.1). In addition the government had paid hundreds of millions in fees to the merchant banks, accounting firms, stockbrokers, and advertising agencies who prepared the companies for privatization (see Table 11.2). The National Audit Office calculated that by the time of electricity privatization in 1991 the process would have cost the government £2,375 million, more than half of which was spent on the recent electricity and water privatizations (Beauchamps 1990). As Buckland has concluded, 'by every yardstick, [this] policy has been costly to the tax-payer' (Buckland 1987: 255).

Finally, to the extent that the public corporations have been successfully turned around in terms of profitability since privatization and earned a higher market capitalization, this may not have been through the hard work of reducing costs, improving quality and expanding sales. Cruder, but effective devices such as increasing prices, selling off assets, reducing manpower, and cutting unprofitable services were available as these companies capitalized on their monopoly

TAble 11.2 Five UK companies: the costs of privatization*, 1984–7

	British Telecom (1984)	British Gas (1986)	British Airways (1987)	Rolls-Royce (1987)	British Airports (1987)
Direct costs:					
Underwriting, broking, etc.	74*	60	7.8	12.5	13.6
Commissions	13	9	2.9	4.2	4.2
Bank costs	20	45	7.5	11.0	13.2
Marketing	14	40	6.2	4.0	10.0
Fees to advisers	6	5	4.3	2.2	2.4
Total	127	159	28.7	33.9	43.4
Cost of employees' preferential treatment: Free and matching					
shares	51	33	13.1	12.0	3.3
Discounted shares	5	4	1.6	2.4	
Total	56	37	14.7	14.4	3.3
Cost of direct incentives to investors:					
Bonus shares	88	122	13.1		53.9
Bill vouchers	23	63			
Total	111	185	13.1		53.9
Cost of indirect incentives to investors: Premium as % of					
issue price†	91	28	63	70	37

Source: Price Waterhouse.
Notes: *Million of pounds.
†The premium is computed as the percentage change in share price from the paid issue price to the closing price after one week's dealing.

positions. Thus one survey of the literature concludes, 'a common consequence of privatisation is increased prices to customers' (Marsh 1991: 469). If they had abandoned their commitments to social responsibility, the former public corporations could have recorded higher profits by precisely these means at any time, though whether this would have benefited the wider economy or society is open to question.

A thorough cost–benefit analysis of the long-term consequences of the government privatization programme remains to be conducted, but any claims concerning the revival of the fortunes of the industries concerned would have to be balanced against other less attractive results. Elements of these would include the high cost of redundancy payments and unemployment benefits to the workers who lost their jobs as a result of pre-privatization restructuring; the loss of revenue from the public industries which were profitable (in 1983/4 public industries generated £4,600 million in funds and paid £2,700 million in interest, tax and dividends to the Exchequer) (Labour Party 1986: 1); the loss of the capacity to meet directly social and economic priorities through cross-subsidization; the increase in the retail price index and the resulting inflationary pressures caused by those privatized industries that increased their profitability largely by increasing prices, or failing to reduce prices by what efficiency gains allowed; and the harmful effects upon the performance of the rest of industry of having to pay higher prices for basic utilities. On the benefit side the government could record the use of privatization proceeds to lower taxes, and sustain public expenditure, and the longer-term benefit of the revenue raised in tax from the privatized company profits.

A SHAREHOLDER DEMOCRACY?

The privatization programme did initiate a huge and unprecedented expansion in the number of shareholders, which the government has claimed created the foundations of a 'shareholders' democracy'. The City Editor of *The Observer* has indicated that:

> The Government ... had, through the marketing of one counter, British Telecom, captured the imagination (and savings) of more members of the public than had previously been drawn into the entire 2,000 strong spectrum of UK registered companies quoted on the London Stock Exchange.

> (*Observer*, 25 October 1987)

By attaching incentives to the privatization shares, not simply the immediate premium but in the cases of Telecom, gas and electricity an individual temporary subsidy for the shareholders of the cost of using the utility in question, an explosion in the number of shareholders in Britain did occur. But the massive inflation of the number of shareholders appears to be a very temporary phenomenon. As Table 11.3 reveals the percentage of original shareholders who retained their shares is on average significantly below the 66 per cent claimed by the government, and since this data was compiled by Bishop and Kay in 1988 has drifted down towards 40 per cent retention overall. The majority of these new shareholders quickly disposed of their investment having secured the benefit of the initial discount, and the government realized that the number of shareholders could only be sustained at this inflated level by the repeated issue of massive amounts of shares in new privatizations. At a rate of loss of several million shareholders each year, eventually the government would run out of public assets to privatize, at which point there was a real danger the number of shareholders would gradually collapse back over a period of years in the direction of the original figure (Clarke 1990: 500).

Table 11.3 Size of privatized company share registers in the UK

Company	Successful applicants	Number of shareholders: end first year	latest	Percentage of original number
Amersham Int'l	65,000	8,601	6,048	9.3
British Telecom	2,300,000	1,692,979	1,311,139	57.0
BAA	2,187,500	1,064,815	1,064,815	48.7
British Gas	4,407,100	3,111,872	2,903,416	65.9
British Airways	1,100,000	420,526	347,897	31.6
Jaguar	125,000	54,104	42,790	34.2
Britoil	35,000	39,558	*	*
Assoc. Brit. Ports	45,000	15,500	n/a	n/a
Enterprise Oil	13,700	14,146	10,714	78.2
Rolls-Royce	2,000,000	924,970	924,970	46.2

Source: M. Bishop and J. Kay, (1988) *Does Privatisation Work – Lessons from the UK*, London Business School.
Note: *Acquired by BP.

Behind the expensively erected facade of privatization there was little real change in the distribution of property ownership in Britain: 70 per cent of shareholders had a modest investment of £3,000 or less. As indicated by Tables 11.4 and 11.5, the great majority of personal shareholdings are extremely modest and could not be claimed to provide a real stake in the system. As Howard Hyman of Price Waterhouse, seconded to the Treasury, put it:

> Although the percentage of adults owning shares has dramatically increased the proportion of the total equity market controlled by individuals rather than institutions continues to decline. Between 1963 and 1981 the proportion of the stock market directly owned by individuals fell from 54% to 28%. Statistics available for 1986 indicate that out of a total equity market valued at £368 billion, some £88 billion was owned by individuals or 24 per cent.
>
> (*Observer*, 25 October 1987)

Despite appearances to the contrary, the impact of privatization has not served to reverse this trend: the great majority of privatized shares have ended up with the financial institutions. As a result of privatization there has been a *widening* but not a *deepening* of personal share-ownership in the UK (Marsh 1991: 475). As Buckland concludes:

> The privatisation programme, therefore, is unlikely to be making much impact upon equity ownership in the UK. The deregulation of share trading and marketing in October 1986 and the expansion of decentralised information systems are likely to have more far-reaching and durable effects. What the programme has undeniably done is shift the median line

Table 11.4 The number of companies invested in by individual shareholders in the UK, 1987

Shares in:	Shareholders (%)	Approximate number
1 company	56	5.4 million
2 companies	22	2.1 million
3 companies	9	0.8 million
4 to 9 companies	8	0.8 million
10 plus companies	3	0.3 million

Source: Dewe Rogerson Marketing Consultants 1986.

of the UK's public sector and redistribute large amounts of public sector wealth to share purchasers particularly the financial institutions.

(Buckland 1987: 255)

Nigel Lawson, as Chancellor of the Exchequer, was a major architect of the privatization policy, and stated confidently in 1987, 'The Government has no plans to abandon its previous policies of offering state assets at a material discount to the private sector to encourage its dreams of an ever-widening share-owning democracy' (*Observer*, 21 June). Confronted by the sale of privatized shares by the mass of new shareholders, it must have become apparent, even to the government, that what in fact it was achieving was: first, introducing people to the mechanics of share ownership with which they were previously unacquainted, while giving them a very small financial stake in the dismember-ment of the public sector, and an interest in electing future Conservative govern-ments; and, second, concealing the transfer of very substantial assets from the public sector to large financial and multinational companies under the camou-flage of 'popular capitalism'.

A CONSUMERS' DEMOCRACY?

A third claim of the government is to have established a consumer democracy with freedom of choice where before there had been dull uniformity. However,

Table 11.5 Value of shareholdings (for positive respondents) in the UK, 1986

Value of shareholdings	Percentage of shareholders
Less than £500	34
£ 501–£1,000	19.4
£1,001–£3,000	18
£3,000+	30

Sources: Grout 1987, Stock Exchange Survey 1986.

behind the explosion of profits in the newly privatized industries, there is not necessarily a host of delighted customers. Some economists applaud the enhanced profitability of the privatized companies without inquiring too closely where the extra profits came from (Mathews and Minford 1987). In fact, consumer complaints increased markedly in almost all the privatized companies as consumers found they were paying more for services which often had been reduced. For example, price increases of 13 per cent in electricity charges in 1992 were expected to push profits up to £1.43 billion – up 43 per cent on 1991. Similarly in the water and telecom industries rapidly escalating prices were accompanied by an explosive growth in profits. In the mid-1980s BT faced mounting public complaints about quality of service, and only made hurried efforts in 1987/8 to repair the 23 per cent of phone boxes out of order when Mercury Communications were offered entry into the phone box network, though they were only interested in the prime city centre sites. Public disillusion with BT spread when it increased domestic tariffs where the likelihood of competition was slight due to the extent of sunk investment, in order to reduce business tariffs, a market Mercury were interested in.

The promise of privatization was a dramatic improvement in consumer choice as corporations were set free to respond to market demands rather than political constraints. The worry about privatization was the effect upon the quality and range of provision, and access to it, as the elimination of cross subsidization undermined a comprehensive service. These tendencies have reached an extreme in the market-based society of the United States, where as Goodman and Loveman suggest,

> Private sector managers may have no compunction about adopting profit-making strategies or corporate practices that make essential services unaffordable or unavailable to large segments of the population. A profit-seeking operation may not, for example, choose to provide health care to the indigent or extend education to poor or learning disabled children.
>
> (Goodman and Loveman 1991: 27)

The fear of consumer bodies is that privatization of vital utilities of water, gas, electricity and telephone, will seriously threaten the most vulnerable sections of society as directors demand higher profits and shareholders higher dividends, both taking precedence over service, with falling standards, higher prices, and greater numbers of disconnections. As the evidence of the National Association of Citizens' Advice Bureaux regarding disconnections stated to the Department of the Environment, 'If financial interest takes precedence over social considerations now, how much greater will the pressures be when the Water Authorities must account to their shareholders?' (1987). The worst fears of the Association were realized in 1991/2 with an increase in water disconnections of 177 per cent. With evidence of dysentery breaking out among those without a water supply for washing and toilet facilities, Ian Gregory has claimed,

It is clear why the 1985 Housing Act dubs any house without a water supply as being 'unfit for habitation.' But with Ofwat and the DSS doing too little too late the water companies, monopoly suppliers of the most essential commodity, seem set to extend the drought to more of Britain's poor.

(*The Guardian*, 2 September 1992)

WORKER OWNERS?

Finally the position of employees in the privatized companies should be considered. Any impression that these are now invariably happy worker–owners should be dispelled. Though in most privatizations there were facilities for workers to buy shares, and almost all did, the value of the total worker shareholding remained at a derisory level. At BT in 1989 1 per cent of share capital was held in trust for employees. Whereas the top five BT executives held 1.3 million BT shares worth £5 million, an average employee held 270 shares. At British Gas in 1991 the top seven executives owned 1.5 million shares worth £3.5 million, whilst an average employee held 850 shares worth around £2,000 (Nichols and O'Connell Davidson 1992: 107). British Aerospace sold 3 million shares to its workforce, which amounted to 1.3 per cent of the total. In the privatization of British Steel workers with 20 years' service received just a few hundred pounds of shares each. A Minister responsible for this distribution, John Moore, has claimed, 'Most people own very modest numbers of shares, but whatever they own often represents their first source of income beyond an otherwise total and, for many, frightening reliance on their weekly pay' (Moore 1992: 119). Nearer to reality is that, 'In circumstances such as these, even dramatic shifts in profits will have a negligible impact on the income of most employee shareholders. . . . Attitudinal differences between participants and non-participants in share schemes are marginal' (Nichols and O'Connell Davidson 1992: 108–12). As with earlier exercises in employee shareholding the object seemed to be to bind workers into an identification with their companies rather than allowing them a genuine share in the ownership of them. Any hope these tiny holdings could be built into something more substantial is largely illusory: the tendency has been for workers, conscious of the impossibility of ever achieving any real stake in their companies, to simply sell the shares off.

Nevertheless, one group of employees has benefited massively from privatization. Salary increases of up to 352 per cent in the income of top company executives have been recorded in the three years after privatization (see Table 11.6). Whilst paying ordinary workers annual increases of 6 per cent or 7 per cent, senior executives have happily awarded themselves up to ten times this figure, free of the constraints of any real form of public accountability. As each industry has been privatized in turn, executives have been more blatant in their greed as the electricity industry, privatized in 1990, indicates (see Table 11.7).

Not only wages, but job security and conditions did not fare quite so well in

222

Table 11.6 Increase in UK directors' salaries after privatization

Company	Before privatization	After privatization Year 2	After privatization Year 3	After privatization Year 4	After privatization Year 5	Increase (%)
Amersham International	£30,360 (1981–2)	£88,983 (1983–4)	£130,178 (1984–5)			329
Associated British Ports	£35,196 (1982)	£58,749 (1984)				67
British Aerospace	£44,467 (1980)	£73,378 (1982)	£87,260 (1983)	£100,790 (1984)	£125,000 (1985)	181
BP	£120,385 (1979)	£158,151 (1981)	£172,770 (1982)	£183,134 (1983)	£241,547 (1984)	101
British Telecom	£67,900 (1983)	£111,399 (1985)	£160,000 (1986)			136
Britoil	£72,000 (1982)	£98,000 (1984)				36
Cable & Wireless	£30,277 (1981)	£111,952 (1985)	£136,881 (1986)			352
Enterprise Oil	£28,560 (1983)	£90,000 (1985)				215
National Freight Consortium	£51,046 (1982)	£98,292 (1984)				93
British Airways	£52,000 (1987)	£178,000 (1988)				242
British Gas		£184,000 (1988)				68

Sources: TUC, *Privatisation and Top Pay*, London: TUC, 1985; British Institute of Management Survey on Top Salaries, 1988; *Financial Times*, 14 July 1988.
Note: The average increase in earnings during the period 1980–6 in the UK was 7.5 per cent per annum.

Table 11.7 Chairman's pay and price increases in the UK electricity industry, December 1990 to June 1991

Company	Chairman's salary (£)	Chairman's share options (£)	Changes since December 1990 (%)	
			Salary	Prices
Southern	220,000	219,000	+253	+13
Eastern	210,000	79,000	+237	+14
East Mids	205,000	147,000	+229	+15
Seeboard	190,000	124,000	+205	+13
Manweb	185,000	169,000	+197	+13
Midlands	181,790	247,000	+191	+12
Norweb	175,000	103,000	+181	+11
London	162,000	188,000	+160	+11
South West	158,595	274,000	+155	+14
South Wales	155,000	177,000	+149	+13
Northern	141,511	95,000	+127	+13

Source: *Sunday Times* (London), 7 June 1992.

these industries, and the impact upon morale of directors looking after themselves, whilst neglecting the welfare of other employees should not be underestimated. Invariably these were the same directors who had managed the public enterprises prior to privatization. Commenting on similar directoral salary increases in the water industry, the management guru Henry Mintzberg has argued:

> How can you have any real sense of commitment to a company when, as we have seen recently, top management takes huge salary increases at the same time as everyone else is being cut back. People keep saying it's the market, the market. Well, I think that is complete nonsense. Those guys in the water companies in the UK were willing to hold the top jobs before they were privatised: why do they now need twice the salary to do the same job? Why did they take the job in the first place? It is a disease. There are lots of good honest, devoted people. But acts like this ... are a reflection of a deep malaise in organisations.
>
> (Lloyd 1992: 103)

Meanwhile life has not been so comfortable for the rest of the employees in the privatized companies. In a number of privatizations, such as at British Gas, the pressures to change (and often worsen) conditions have not been so great. But in other cases trade union bargaining and consultation rights have been restricted; benefits, too, have been eroded, including index-linked pensions (TUC 1986).

Along with reductions in manpower, accident rates have often risen. Those workers who have been subjected to the harshest changes have been the ones affected by contracting out of work from the public to the private sector. Often they have found they have had to compete with others for the work they were already doing, and the only way they have been able to remain in employment is by accepting much lower wages, more work, and worse conditions.

Contracting-out has been practised in the past in order to reduce operating costs; minimize the use of capital; meet peak work loads; and provide a specialist capacity not available in-house. However contracting-out as now imposed in Britain is quite different as the services being contracted out are already being performed in-house, leaving the workers concerned redundant if they fail to win the contract. In a government review *Using Private Enterprise in Government* published by the Cabinet Efficiency Unit in 1986, five main reasons are given for promoting contracting out of services: to save money; to save management time; to obtain expertise not available in-house; to retain flexibility; and to re-establish management control (from the unions). Such arguments either ignore or have no concern for the contrary view that in-house services often provide better quality; are more reliable and flexible; that private contractors cut corners to increase profits; private employees often have little training or loyalty to the job; and contracting-out undermines wages, conditions, and manning levels and trade union rights. With reference to National Health Service competitive tendering a House of Commons Social Services Committee report stated in June 1985:

> The whole exercise, which has now been underway for around four years, has involved a considerable amount of management time and effort; has caused disruption and discontent, not exclusively among NHS staff directly employed in these services, and to date has not brought home the bacon.
>
> (IPM 1986: 16)

Contradicting the extravagant claims of government regarding cost savings is often evidence of contractors, as they have been introduced, inflicting lower standards in the public services.

THE STRUCTURAL LIMITS TO PRIVATIZATION: UP AGAINST THE BUFFERS?

As the privatization programme relentlessly advanced in the UK, the industries remaining in the public sector have proved more difficult for the government to tackle. First, public opinion has been left behind by the ambitions of the government, as the impetus towards privatization came from the government not the electorate (McAllister and Studlar 1989). Initially the government plans were greeted by 'bewilderment in the population as a whole', as John Moore confesses (Moore 1992: 116); then the lavish advertising campaigns for specific privatizations and the extravagant incentives attracted a good deal of popular interest; but increasingly there is a widespread sense in the public at large that privatization has gone far enough. Gallup and NOP surveys suggested that 57 per cent opposed privatization of British Gas; 56 per cent were opposed to privatization of BT; and 72 per cent expressed opposition to the privatization of water and electricity (Crewe 1988: 42–3). A Harris opinion poll carried out in June 1989 indicated that 79 per cent believed that water should not be privatized (Meredith 1992: 80).

Evidence of extensive public disquiet did not deflect the government from its course in the privatization of water and electricity, but public anxieties remain. Fears concerning the environmental consequences of water privatization are considerable, and were not alleviated by the water authorities campaign to regulate themselves after privatization. It was European Community influence that insisted that 'the competent (regulatory) authority has to be completely separate and independent from the recipient of its authorisations' (Richardson *et al.* 1992: 164). In Scotland in 1992 the announcement of the intention to introduce water privatization was greeted by a public outcry. Opposition to what was called the 'tap-tax' was promised to be as great as to the poll tax. Water was considered a natural resource in Scotland, which people would not pay more for. A leading Conservative councillor stated that the 'Government will drown in the opposition to water privatisation'. As one disconsolate salmon fisherman said, 'They've taken everything else from us, the water is the last thing we've got left!' (BBC TV, *Newsnight*, 9 September 1992).

The intention to privatize the coal industry was widely seen as a further episode in the tragic decline of a once great industry. From 170 pits with 180,000 miners in 1984, by 1992 the industry had been forcibly contracted to 49 pits with 43,000 miners. Productivity had increased from 2.5 tons per man shift in 1986, to 6 tons per man shift in 1992. However a government brokered five-year deal with the privatized electricity industry reached in 1992 proposed a reduction from the 65 million tons supplied in 1992 to 40 million tons in 1993 and 30 million tons from 1995. The direct result of this deal would be to force a reduction to 12 mines and to make redundant 75 per cent of the remaining miners (*The Guardian*, 11 September 1992). This was despite the fact that Britain has among the richest seams of deep-mined coal in Europe, and that other members of the EC were keeping open mines which were far inferior to the ones set for closure in the UK. A furious public outburst at the proposal to run down the pits caused the government to retreat and examine the problem again. But the Secretary of State for Industry, Michael Heseltine, was unable to move the electricity companies from their intention to build new gas-fired power-stations, to import coal from overseas, and to import French electricity. All that was offered in the new government policy announced in March 1993 was the temporary reprieve of half the threatened coal mines, which seemed unlikely to halt the catastrophic collapse of the UK coal industry. This reveals the difficulty of achieving any kind of rational integrated energy policy in a privatized context where generators and suppliers are primarily interested in the profitability of their own companies.

rational, integrated energy policy in a privatized context where generators are primarily interested in the profitability of their own companies.

The publication of the government White Paper on the privatization of British Rail, *New Opportunities for the Railways* (HMSO 1992) was greeted by a heartfelt groan from the long-suffering travelling public. Whilst dismay with the standard of service on offer from BR after years of underfunding was profound, there was little public confidence that privatization would bring any great improvement, and serious concerns were expressed regarding the continuation of rail services of doubtful profitability, the consequences for commuters of increased cost of fares, and the implications for safety of a fragmented rail service. The only major attempt at determining whether BR could be profitable had envisaged a rail network reduced to 1,630 route miles from 11,000 route miles, and even this entailed subsidy (Serpell Report 1983). Whilst the injection of entrepreneurial spirit in the railways might be welcomed, the difficulty of the government proposals to split BR into two parts, one owning the tracks, signalling, stations, etc. and the second running the trains in competition with new companies granted operating licences, is one of cost allocation which may have a significant impact on the assessment of relative profitability. 'The problem of cost allocation in railway services: the high proportion of fixed costs from track and signalling; the high degree of joint and common use of assets and people; and the network effect which results in a high degree of interdependence of assets and services' (Lapsley and Wright 1990: 53), make the government proposals a recipe for commercial conflict and travelling chaos.

The final privatization, which even the government dare not breathe the name of, is that of the health service. Whilst consistent promises have been made by the government that it is entirely committed to a national health service, free at the point of delivery; faced with an ever-expanding demand for health care, the principles and practices of the NHS have been subjected to a steady process of erosion. The activity of the private medical sector has been encouraged to grow, and the creation of the NHS hospital trusts a move in the direction of independent organizations operating on a more commercial basis. Yet the most significant model of a market-based system of health care is a nightmare. In the US where medical bills are the primary cause of bankruptcy, there are 37 million people without the cover of medical insurance.

> America may have the best doctors and certainly has the best medical equipment in the world, but because of the built-in inequities of the system, overall standards are abysmal. Although the US spends more per capita on health than any other country, it ranks twenty-second in infant mortality and comes a shameful last in its treatment of breast cancer.
>
> (*Observer*, 6 September 1992)

PRIVATIZATION AND THE REFORM OF THE PUBLIC SECTOR

The emphasis upon privatization in recent years has distracted attention away from the possibility of reform and restructuring *within* the public sector. The highly centralized, often authoritarian models and sometimes inefficient practices of the public sector are no longer widely tolerated. Clearly fundamental transformation of the public sector is necessary, the question is whether the only way to achieve this is through privatization (and given the foregoing analysis the question can be posed whether privatization is at all an effective means of attaining efficiency objectives). In what remains of the public sector in Britain, partly spurred by the realization that if significant changes are not achieved then privatization will be imposed, there has been attention to abandoning out-dated monolithic and rigid structures, and replacing them with greater customer responsiveness, product quality, and employee professionalism. As Hambleton suggests, a sea change is occurring in conceptions of public sector management:

> From an emphasis on internal procedures to a concern for outcomes. From an emphasis on hierarchical decision-making to an approach stressing delegation and personal responsibility. From a focus on the quantity of service provided to one concentrating also on quality. From a culture that values stability and uniformity to one that cherishes innovation and diversity.
>
> (Hambleton 1992: 10)

Widespread concern about the quality of services has focused attention upon methods of quality assurance which are being pursued as energetically in the public sector as in the private sector. Local authorities have pioneered the introduction of customer contracts and quality audits. The awakening of customer care in the public sector with a clear sense of responsibility to be responsive to client needs and the protocols through which these should be identified and satisfied, is a major step forward for the parts of the public sector which have realized it. The Citizen's Charter introduced by the government, whilst long on rhetoric and short on the resources with which promises would be fulfilled, still captured some of the changing consciousness in the organization and management of the public sector.

> An overt and articulated commitment to quality in standards of service delivery. Clear and agreed criteria by which such quality can be measured. The increased visibility of people engaged in the public service at all levels. The overt and articulated commitment of the public sector to a climate of continuous improvement.
>
> (Thomson 1992: 36)

Others have suggested that underlying much of the consumerist agenda is the familiar model of society drawn from neo-classical economics. 'A world of perfect information and sovereign individual consumers, a world in which the only incentives are monetary and only discipline that of competition' (Mulgan 1991: 17). An alternative approach which may transcend the narrow individualist bias of the market model, is to balance the empowerment of the consumer with some assessment of the needs of the community and the interests of the providers. The market fragments, and the cost of an individualistic market-driven society is mutual indifference. Mulgan calls for a revitalization of community ethics, reconstructing the democratic case for collective provision; revitalizing a sense of mission of the people working in the public sector; and engaging fully in organizational reform. In this work rather than applying the inappropriate model of centralized control by accountants, there should be an emphasis upon the importance of human resources, organizational culture, and non-monetary incentives. Risk, enterprise and innovation can all exist within a structure of universal provision (Mulgan 1991).

In contrast, far from transforming the public sector in the direction of efficiency the Fordist commercial model imposed by government in many services could prove counter-productive. Thus the objective of much of the Thatcher governments' intervention in the public sector was to use financial controls to extend Taylorism in the control of public sector workers; to centralize management control; and to replace locally provided public services by mass-produced commercial ones:

> The Thatcher Government has had an impoverished concept of management as revealed by several telltale signs: a mechanistic view of control, the disregard for civil servants' morale, and a 'costs' mentality. For this government the most basic elements of management – people, dynamic organisation, motivation, leadership – often have been left out, replaced by costs and an archaic command and control mystique of leaders and docile followers, coupled uneasily with the belief that recalcitrant civil servants must be brought to heel.
>
> (Williams 1988: 123)

The difficult work of rebuilding an efficient, flexible and responsive economy may not be assisted by a simple reliance on the one technique of privatization in a free market system: there is much scope for reform and transformation *within* the public sector (Clarke and Grace 1993).

CONCLUSIONS

It is a curious historical irony that as Eastern Europe has rejected the deceit of the economic dogma of central planning, the west has simultaneously been seduced by the ideology of the market:

> Some evocations of the market achieve an almost lyrical quality in which it stands revealed as a thing of terrible beauty and awesome symmetry, and

no myth has proved more persistent than the belief in a lost Golden Age in which true competition existed.

(New Statesman, 12 February 1988)

There is an assumption abroad that Margaret Thatcher engineered an economic renaissance in Britain (Walters 1985), when it is capitalism which has been restored not the British economy. The belief that monetarism and privatization together rescued the British economy conceals a modest performance relative to industrial growth in the rest of Western Europe, despite the enormous advantage Britain had in the expansion of North Sea Oil. Though the British economy is undoubtedly now a great deal more efficient than it was in the 1970s, performance has improved in the public as well as in the private sector, and this is due to a very wide range of factors. Kirkpatrick observes that privatization is a 'confluence of ideology and pragmatism' (Kirkpatrick 1988: 237). Despite many claims to the contrary it is not directly concerned either with economic democracy or efficiency.

Privatization is a contradictory policy and the resulting industrial structure is unstable. The private monopolies in essential industries created by privatization in Britain have a built-in tendency to become less socially responsible and possibly less commercially efficient than was tolerated in the public sector, potentially exposing the population to monopolistic exploitation. In this situation consumer interests, if they are to be protected at all, will be protected by the operation of the regulatory agencies, not the privatized monopolies themselves. Privatization has caused the loss of much of the legacy of fifty years of patient social democratic construction of the public sector in Britain. The manifest deficiencies in large parts of the public sector laid it open to attack, deficiencies which are now being seriously attended to in what remains of the public sector.

In reconstructing economic efficiency and social democracy within the public sector, there is the stimulus of considerable organizational innovation attempted around the world to create flexible, adaptive and responsive institutions, when in earlier decades it was often thought the Soviet central command economy was the only relevant model. It is now comprehended that public ownership is not simply state ownership, but represents a multiplicity of potential forms in which the active participation of producers and consumers is the guarantee of social responsibility and economic effectiveness.

BIBLIOGRAPHY

Abromeit, H. (1988) 'British privatisation policy', *Parliamentary Affairs* 41(1), 68–85.
Beauchamps, C. (1990) 'National Audit Office: its role in privatisation', *Public Money and Management* 10(2), 55–8.
Beesley, M. and Littlechild, S. (1989) 'The regulation of privatised monopolies in the UK', *Rand Journal of Economics* 20(3), 454–72.
Bishop, M. and Kay, J. (1988) *Does Privatisation Work – Lessons from the UK.*
Buckland, R. (1987) 'The costs and returns of the privatisation of nationalised industries',

Public Administration 65(3), 241–57.

Bosanquet, N. (1984) 'The "social market economy": principles behind the policies', *Political Quarterly* 55, 245–56.

Cabinet Efficiency Unit (1986) *Using Private Enterprise in Government*, London: HMSO.

CBI (1984) *Efficiency In the Public Services*, London: CBI.

Caiden, G. A. (1991) *Administrative Reform Comes of Age*, Berlin: Walter de Gruyter.

Chapman, C. (1990) *Selling the Family Silver: Has Privatisation Worked*, London: Hutchinson.

Clarke, T. (1990) 'Socialised industry: social ownership or shareholding democracy', in S. Clegg, *Organisation Theory and Class Analysis*, Berlin: Walter de Gruyter.

——— and Grace, C. (1993) 'Reconstructing the public sector: quality assurance, performance measurement and social accountability', in T. Clarke (ed.), *International Privatisation: Strategies and Practices*, Berlin: Walter de Gruyter.

Clegg, S. and Dunkerley, D. (1980) *Organisation, Class and Control*, London: Routledge & Kegan Paul.

Cook, P. and Kirkpatrick, C. (1988) *Privatisation In Less Developed Countries*, Brighton: Wheatsheaf.

Crewe, I. (1988) 'Has the electorate become more Thatcherite?', in R. Skidelsky (ed.), *Thatcherism*, London: Chatto & Windus.

Curwen, P. J. (1986) *Public Enterprise: A Modern Approach*, Brighton: Harvester Press.

Dewe Rogerson (1986) *Survey Conducted for Trustee Savings Bank*, London: Dewe Rogerson Consultants.

Estrin, S., Marin, A. and Selby, M. J. P. (1990) 'Conflicting aims in electricity privatisation', *Public Money and Management*, Autumn, pp. 39–47.

Fama, E. F. and Jensen, M. C. (1983) 'The separation of ownership and control', *Journal of Law and Economics*, XXVI, pp. 302–24.

Forrest, R. (1988) *Selling the Welfare State: The Privatisation of Public Housing*, London: Routledge.

Fraser, R. (1988) *Privatisation: The UK Experience and International Trends*, London: Longman.

Gayle, J. and Goodman, J. (eds) (1990) *Privatisation and Deregulation in Global Perspective*, London: Pinter.

Goodman, J. B. and Loveman, G. W. (1991) 'Does privatisation serve the public interest?', *Harvard Business Review*, November–December, pp. 26–40.

Graham, C. and Prosser, T. (1988) 'Rolling back the frontiers: the privatisation of state enterprises', in C. Graham and T. Prosser, *Waiving the Rules*, Milton Keynes: Open University Press.

——— ——— (1991) *Privatising Public Enterprises: Constitutions, the State, and Regulation In Comparative Perspective*, Oxford: Clarendon Press.

Gretton, J., Harrison, A. and Beeton, D. (1987) 'How far have the frontiers of the state been rolled back between 1979 and 1987?', *Public Money*, December, pp. 17–25.

Grosfeld, I. (1990) 'Reform economics and western economic theory: unexploited opportunities', *Economics of Planning* 23(1), 1–19.

Grout, P. (1987) 'The wider share ownership programme', *Fiscal Studies* 8(3), 59–74.

——— (1988) 'Employee share ownership and privatisation: some theoretical issues', *Economic Journal*, no. 98, pp. 97–104.

Hambleton, R. (1992) 'Decentralisation and democracy in UK local government', *Public Money and Management*, July–September, pp. 9–20.

Heald, D. (1988) 'The UK privatisation and its political context', *Western European Politics*, II, pp. 31–8.

Helm, D. (1987) 'Nuclear power and the privatisation of electricity generation', *Fiscal Studies*, 8(4), 69–73.

Hepworth, N. (1988) 'Measuring performance in non-market organisation, *International Journal of Public Sector Management* 1(1), 16–28.

HMSO (1992) *New Opportunities for the Railways*, Department of Transport.

IPM (Institute of Personnel Management and Incomes Data Services) (1986) *Competitive Tendering In the Public Sector*, London: IPM/IDS.

Kay, J. A. and Silberston, Z. A. (1984) 'The new industrial policy: privatisation and competition', *Midland Bank Review*, Spring, pp. 8–16.

——— , Mayer, C. and Thompson, D. (1986) *Privatisation and Regulation*, London: Institute of Fiscal Studies.

——— and Thompson, D. (1986) 'Privatisation: a policy in search of a rationale', *Economic Journal* 96(1), 18–32.

Kirkpatrick, C. (1988) 'The UK privatisation models: is it transferable to developing countries?', in V. Ramanadham (ed.), *Privatisation in the UK*, London: Routledge.

Labour Party (1986) 'Social Ownership', Statement by the NEC to the 85th Annual Conference, Blackpool.

Labour Research (1987) 'Big fish grab sell-off shares', in vol. 76, no. 9 (7 September).

Labour Research, (1988) 'Public assets going for a song', in vol. 77, no. 6 (14 June).

Labour Research Department (1982) *Public or Private: The Case Against Privatisation*, London: LRD.

——— (1985) *Privatisation: The Great Sell-Out*, London: LRD.

Lapsley, I. and Wright, H. (1990) 'On the privatisation of British Rail', *Public Money and Management*, Autumn, pp. 49–53.

Letwin, O. (1988) *Privatising the World*, London: Cassell.

Lloyd, B. (1992) 'Mintzberg on the rise and fall of strategic management', *Long Range Planning* 25(4), 99–104.

McAllister, I. and Studlar, D. (1989) 'Popular versus elite views of privatisation: the case of Britain', *Journal of Public Policy* 9, 157–78.

McAvoy, P., Stanbury, R., Yarrow, G. and Zeckhauser, R. (eds) (1989) *Privatisation and State Owned Enterprises: Lessons from the US, Great Britain, and Canada*, Boston: Kluwer Academic Publishers.

Marsh, D. (1991) 'Privatisation under Mrs Thatcher: a review of the literature', *Public Administration* vol. 69 (Winter) pp. 459–80.

——— and Rhodes, R. A. W. (1992) 'Implementing Thatcherism: policy change in the 1980s', *Parliamentary Affairs* 45(1), 33–50.

Mathews, K. and Minford, P. (1987) 'Mrs Thatcher's economic policies 1979–87', *Economic Policy*, October, pp. 57–102.

Meredith, S. (1992) 'Water privatisation: the dangers and the benefits', *Long Range Planning* 25(4), 72–81.

Millward, R. and Parker, D. (1983) 'Public and private enterprise: comparative behaviour and relative efficiency', in R. Millward, D. Parker, L. Rosenthal, M. T. Sumner, and N. Topham (eds), *Public Sector Economics*, London: Longman.

Mitchell, J. (1990) 'Britain: privatisation as myth?', in J. Richardson (ed.), *Privatisation and Deregulation in Canada and Britain*, Aldershot: Dartmouth.

Moore, J. (1992) 'British privatisation: taking capitalism to the people', *Harvard Business Review*, January–February, pp. 115–24.

Mulgan, G. (1991) 'Power to the public', *Marxism Today*, May.

Murray, R. (1991) 'The state after Henry', *Marxism Today*, May.

National Audit Office (1992) *Department of the Environment: Sale of the water authorities in England and Wales*, London: HMSO.

Nichols, T. and O'Connell Davidson, J. (1992) 'Employee shareholders in two privatised utilities', *Industrial Relations Journal* 23(2), 107–19.

NOP (1987) *Shareholder Survey*, London: Stock Exchange.

Observer, Privatisation Survey, 25 October.

Parker, I. D. (1987) 'The New Right, state ownership and privatisation', *Economic and Industrial Democracy*, vol. 8, 349–78.

Parris, H., Pestieau, P. and Saynor, P. (1987) *Public Enterprise In Western Europe*, London: Croom Helm.

Pera, A. (1989) 'Deregulation and privatisation in an economy-wide context', *OECD Economic Studies*, 12, Spring, pp. 159–204.

Pliatzky, L. (1988) 'Optimising the role of the public sector: constraints and remedial policies', *Public Policy and Administration* 3(1), 35–44.

Posner, M. (1984) 'Privatisation: the frontiers between public and private', *Policy Studies* 5(1) (July), 22–32.

Prosser, T. (1986) *Nationalised Industries and Public Control*, Oxford: Basil Blackwell.

Pryke, R. (1987) 'Privatising electricity generation', *Fiscal Studies* 8(3), 75–88.

Ramanadham, V. V. (ed.) (1988) *Privatisation In The UK*, London: Routledge.

Richardson, J. J., Maloney, W. A. and Rudig, W. (1992) 'The dynamics of policy change: lobbying and water privatisation', *Public Administration* 70(2), 157–75.

RIPA (1984) *Contracting-Out in the Public Sector*, London: Royal Institute of Public Administration.

Roberts, J., Elliot, D. and Houghton, T. (1991) *Privatising Electricity: The Politics of Power*, London: Belhaven Press.

Schumpeter, J. (1950) *Capitalism, Socialism and Democracy* (3rd edn), London: Allen & Unwin.

Shackleton, J. (1984) 'Privatisation: the case examined', *National Westminster Bank Quarterly Review*, May, 59–73.

Steel, D. and Heald, D. (1982) 'Privatising public enterprise: an analysis of the government's case', *Political Quarterly*, no. 53, 333–49.

——— ——— (1984) *Privatising Public Enterprises*, London: Royal Institute of Public Administration.

Stock Exchange (1986) *The Changing Face of Share Ownership*, London: London Stock Exchange.

Thompson, G. (1990) *The Political Economy of the New Right*, London: Pinter.

Thompson, P. (1992) 'Public sector management in a period of radical change: 1979–1992', *Public Money and Management*, July–September, pp. 33–41.

Tivey, L. (1973) *Nationalisation in British Industry*, London: Jonathan Cape.

TUC (1986) *Bargaining in the Privatised Companies*. London: TUC.

——— (1987) *The UK Privatisation Programme*, London: TUC.

Vickers, J. and Yarrow, G. (1988) *Privatisation: An Economic Analysis*, Cambridge, Mass.: MIT Press.

Walters, A. (1985) *Britain's Economic Renaissance – Margaret Thatcher's Reforms 1979–1984*, Oxford: Oxford University Press, for the American Enterprise Institute.

Williams, W. (1988) *Washington, Westminster and Whitehall*, Cambridge: Cambridge University Press.

Woodward, N. (1988) 'Managing cultural change on privatisation', in V. V. Ramanadham (ed.), *Privatisation In The UK*, London: Routledge.

Young, S. (1986) 'The nature of privatisation in Britain, 1979–85', *West European Politics* 9, 235–52.

12

CONTEXT AND PROCESS IN PRIVATIZATION:
Canada/Quebec

Jan. J. Jörgensen, Taïeb Hafsi and Christiane Demers

Privatization in Canada has occurred on a less dramatic scale than in Great Britain, New Zealand or France, far less than that under way in Eastern Europe. Canada has not embarked on a wholesale change in the economic order, although it has mirrored the 1980s' fashion of scaling back and reshaping the state's role in the market. It is perhaps because of the mildness of the Canadian shift that we have found it useful in our own research[1] on the privatization process to subsume the many forms of privatization under the more general phenomenon of divestment. As Coyne and Wright (1986) observe, public sector restructuring through privatization is analogous to divestment in the private sector (Ellsworth 1979, Gilmour, 1973, Hamermesh 1976, Hayes 1972, Nees 1981, Porter 1976). The phenomena covered by private sector divestment are also diverse.

Divestment in either the public or private sectors can be broadly defined as any reduction in the scope of the parent organization's activities or control over a sub-unit. This includes the following phenomena:

1   Sale of the company or a subsidiary unit, whether by private sale, sale to a government, public share offering, or leveraged buy-out by managers or workers.
2   An organizational restructuring that reduces top management's control, such as a shift from a wholly owned subsidiary to a joint venture, creation of a more autonomous subsidiary from a former department,[2] or commercialization of a sub-unit so that it is more subject to market forces and less subject to administrative control (Ramanadham 1988, Sexty 1987).
3   Contracting out or franchising services and intermediate products formerly produced internally.
4   Retrenchment, either internal, as in employee lay-offs, or external, as in the abandonment of a product/market or closure of a subsidiary unit.

In Canada privatization encompasses the closure of state firms (Canagrex and Loto Canada) and transfer of control from one government to another, as in the federal sale of Northern Canada Power to the Yukon government, or the sale of CDC Life Sciences (Connaught) to Institut Mérieux, controlled by the French government. Moreover, the sale of a state firm to private owners is often preceded by commercialization or restructuring that reduces direct government control. For example, the addition of 'contemplation of profit' to Air Canada's mandate in 1977 proved to be an important step on the road to its eventual public share offering. A reorganization such as the establishment of Canada Development Investment Corporation (CDIC) in 1982 presaged the sale of its holdings in Teleglobe Canada, De Havilland, Canadair, Eldorado Nuclear and other interests.[3] A shift from a wholly owned subsidiary to a joint venture with another level of government was one step in the ongoing process of privatizing of Eldorado Nuclear (now CAMECO). Finally, firms such as De Havilland and Canadair have twice moved into and out of the public sector.

This chapter compares privatization at two levels: the Canadian federal government and the Quebec provincial government.[4] After reviewing the context and process of privatization at these two levels, we focus on context and process in each of seven cases. The first case is an example of retrenchment through closure, Sidbec-Dosco's divestment of its mining affiliate, Sidbec-Normines (SN) in Quebec. Two cases involved the sale of the firm through a public share offering. These were Air Canada, the national airline, and Cambior, formed from SOQUEM, a provincially owned mining company. Finally, four cases were divestments through the private sale of the firm or subsidiary units: the sale of Canadair to Bombardier, the sale of Teleglobe Canada to Memotec, the sale of Québecair to Nordair-Metro and the abortive attempt by the Société des alcools du Québec (SAQ) to sell its retail outlets (see Appendix for details).

Three forces have made divestment more common in both the public and private sectors in the past decade: (1) greater external financing, (2) globalization, and (3) recognition of the challenges of managing complex organizations (Hafsi and Jörgensen 1992, Prichard 1983, Ostry 1990).

In response to these forces, the motive to divest has shifted. In the 1970s divestment was associated with poor performance and the stigma of failure. Today divestment is as likely to be associated with the quest for improved strategic fit between the organization and its changing environment. Divestment has thereby acquired a more positive connotation, as a means to focus on core skills that contribute to the organization's competitive advantage (Coyne and Wright 1986, Duhaime and Grant 1984, Hamermesh 1975, Harrigan 1982, Montgomery and Thomas 1988, Tuzzolino 1988). The volume of divestment activity has increased.[5]

Public sector divestment can also be viewed as a means to achieve better 'fit' between the government and its environment. Effective management of the public sector requires that government focuses its scarce managerial resources on critical issues and disengages itself from non-essential activities (Hafsi and Jörgensen 1990). Privatization is one such form of disengagement. Public sector firms might be divested due to lack of fit with the prevailing political agenda in order to refocus government activity towards current as opposed to past policy goals.

Even so, the rationality of the forces for divestment and the search for strategic fit may be overstated. These forces influence but do not determine outcomes. In both private and public sectors, what happens in each case results from a process in which competing rationalities, cognitive limitations, emotional attachments, 'lessons' from the past (Miller 1990), and internal politics also play a role (Gilmour 1973, Kingdon 1984).

CONTEXT: ORIGINS AND SCOPE OF PUBLIC ENTERPRISE IN CANADA

At the federal level, Canada has used public sector corporations to pioneer new industries, to meet national security goals, to bail out failing private sector firms, and above all to promote nation-building by creating east–west links that counter the southern pull of the United States, as in Air Canada (Trans-Canada Airlines) and the Canadian Broadcasting Corporation. During the Second World War, the government set up thirty-three new public enterprises to co-ordinate and supply needed inputs ranging from synthetic rubber to housing. Although these enterprises were mostly divested after the war (Borins 1983), the number of public enterprises later increased, especially in the 1960s and 1970s, often to address regional disparities, to rescue failing private firms, to prevent foreign take-overs, or to address sectorial problems.

Overall, government-owned and controlled enterprises accounted for 26 per cent of net fixed assets of all Canadian corporations in 1983, and for over 35 per cent of all public sector employment (government plus public agencies and enterprises) but for less than 5 per cent of total employment in the economy (Economic Council of Canada 1986: 7). Public enterprises dominated the electrical power sector with 95 per cent of all assets, and were major participants in transportation (50 per cent of assets), communications (25 per cent), and mining and petroleum (22 per cent) (Economic Council of Canada 1986).

The number of parent public enterprises at the federal level in 1985 totalled 73 with another 81 subsidiary firms (Economic Council of Canada 1986, Knubley 1987).[6] As shown in Table 12.1, federal public enterprises were concentrated in three sectors: *financial* with 31 per cent of assets (Federal Business Development Bank, Canada Deposit Insurance Corporation, Farm Credit Corporation, Canada Mortgage and Housing Corporation); *transport and communications* 25 per cent (Canadian National Railway, Canada Post, Air Canada, St Lawrence Seaway, VIA Rail, Canadian Broadcasting Corporation, Teleglobe Canada, Canada Ports, etc.); and *mining, petroleum and energy* 18 per cent (Petro-Canada, Atomic Energy of Canada, Eldorado Nuclear, etc.). Total assets were 60 billion Canadian dollars in 1983, while budgetary funding for public enterprises was $5.5 billion in fiscal 1983/4.[7]

At the provincial level (ten provinces and two territories) transportation and communications needs also fuelled the creation of public enterprises. A Conservative government in Ontario started a hydro-electric enterprise in 1906, which was copied by other provinces (Economic Council of Canada 1986: 13). After prohibition ended in the 1920s, provinces acquired a monopoly on sale of alcoholic beverages, and in the 1970s established a monopoly on gambling through lotteries. In the 1950s several provinces set up development corporations which became holding companies. Finally, provinces formed public enterprises as tools in jurisdictional disputes with other provinces or the federal government. Examples include British Columbia's 1961 take-over of electric power and Alberta's 1971 purchase of Pacific Western Airlines (Economic Council of Canada 1986: 19–20).

The number of parent public enterprises at the provincial level in 1985 totalled 228 with 187 subsidiaries (Economic Council of Canada 1986: 7). As shown in Table 12.2, assets were concentrated in *mining, petroleum and energy* with 58 per cent (Hydro Québec, Ontario Hydro, British Columbia Hydro and Power, New Brunswick Electric Power, Manitoba Hydro-Electric, etc.) and *finance* with 25 per cent (Caisse de dépôt et placement du Québec, Treasury Branches Deposit Fund (Alberta), Alberta Home Mortgage Corporation, Régie de l'assurance-automobile du Québec, Alberta Housing Corporation, Insurance Corporation of British Columbia, Société générale de financement du Québec, etc.). The provincial $129 billion of provincial public enterprises assets were twice those of the federal government.[8] Public sector enterprise accounted for a larger share of the economy in Saskatchewan than elsewhere, but Quebec led in the total number of public enterprises: forty-nine enterprises with total assets of $52 billion (see Table 12.3).

The financial performance of the largest 171 federal and provincial firms varied greatly: 17 enjoyed returns on assets higher than 20 per cent while 21 suffered negative returns exceeding −20 per cent. Nearly half the returns (83) were clustered in the +5 per cent to −5 per cent range.[9] The overall return on assets for 62 federal public enterprises was −1.4 per cent, with key losses in transport and communications.[10] The return on assets for 198 provincial enterprises was 2.8 per cent, thanks to positive returns for electrical utilities, and high profits for alcoholic beverage and lottery monopolies (see Tables 12.1 and 12.2).[11] For Quebec's public enterprises, the overall return on assets was 3.9 per cent (see Table 12.3).

The Quebec government owned few Crown corporations prior to the 1960s. Moral as well as fiscal concerns led to government control of wine and liquor sales in 1921. During the Second World War, government established a sugar-beet refinery and an embryonic Hydro-Québec to produce and distribute electricity. When Quebec nationalists strove to become 'masters in their own house' during the 1960s' 'Quiet Revolution', the public sector grew. Under the Liberal government, major private electric utilities were nationalized in 1963 and incorporated into Hydro-Québec. The government established new government enterprises in key sectors: integrated iron and steel complex, SIDBEC 1964; pension funds, Caisse de dépôt et placement du Québec 1969; mining, SOQUEM 1969; petroleum, SOQUIP 1969; forestry, REXFOR 1969; industrial

Table 12.1 Sectorial distribution of federal government public enterprises in Canada, 1983

	Number of firms	Firms with full data	Adjusted assets C$'000	Assets by sector (%)	Return on assets (%)	Debt C$'000 1983	Budgetary funding C$'000 1984
Agriculture, fishing, forestry	5	3	4,338,465	7.2	13.4	2,527,253	120,682
Mining, petroleum, energy	7	6	11,079,612	18.4	1.1	1,856,636	526,859
Manufacturing	6	5	3,338,695	5.5	-2.2	6,353,183	0
Transport and communications	33	29	15,359,770	25.5	-7.4	4,362,145	2,256,729
Commerce	3	3	7,363,519	12.2	-0.0	4,887,347	17,168
Banking, insurance, etc.	6	6	18,603,918	30.9	-1.2	17,267,178	1,692,394
Construction, real estate, land	8	6	78,647	0.1	-64.0	–	97,665
Other services	5	4	38,731	0.1	-42.8	241	16,613
Total	73	62	60,201,357	100.0	-1.4	37,253,983	4,728,110

Source: Calculated from data in Economic Council of Canada (1986) Minding the Public's Business (Ottawa), Table B-1, Statistical Summary, pp. 157–64.

Table 12.2 Sectorial distribution of provincial government public enterprises in Canada, 1983

	Number of firms	Firms with full data	Adjusted assets C$'000	Assets by sector (%)	Return on assets (%)	Debt C$'000 1983
Agriculture, fishing, forestry	18	15	1,373,936	1.1	-4.1	993,447
Mining, petroleum, energy	31	28	75,338,150	58.3	2.2	57,069,689
Manufacturing	21	17	2,691,756	2.1	-9.0	1,773,441
Transport and communications	30	26	7,351,518	5.7	-4.0	5,810,810
Commerce	18	16	747,206	0.6	218.3	68,439
Banking, insurance, etc.	36	32	32,932,893	25.5	3.6	16,861,987
Construction, real estate, land	21	19	7,635,221	5.9	-8.9	6,482,424
Other services	53	45	1,127,149	0.9	33.7	485,177
Total	228	198	129,197,829	100.0	2.8	89,545,415

Source: Calculated from data in Economic Council of Canada (1986) *Minding the Public's Business* (Ottawa), Table B-1, Statistical Summary, pp. 157–64.

Table 12.3 Sectorial distribution of Quebec provincial government public enterprises, 1983

	Number of firms	Firms with full data	Adjusted assets C$'000	Assets by sector (%)	Return on assets (%)	Debt C$'000 1983
Agriculture, fishing, forestry	6	3	256,152	0.5	−1.6	103,535
Mining, petroleum, energy	5	5	26,020,796	49.8	2.8	17,785,099
Manufacturing	5	2	1,076,657	2.1	−13.7	594,544
Transport and communications	6	4	174,375	0.3	−33.5	93,630
Commerce	2	1	154,593	0.3	167.2	24,887
Banking, insurance, etc.	10	9	21,592,991	41.3	6.5	12,560,670
Construction, real estate, land	3	3	2,685,288	5.1	−10.9	2,125,453
Other services	12	11	266,237	0.5	49.9	138,532
Total	49	38	52,227,089	100.0	3.9	33,426,350

Source: Calculated from data in Economic Council of Canada (1986) Minding the Public's Business (Ottawa), Table B-1, Statistical Summary, pp. 157–64.

development financing, SDI 1971, and SGF 1973; housing SHQ 1971; and broadcasting, Radio-Québec 1969. Other Crown corporations were created for energy, transport, agri-business, asbestos mining, and fishing.

A key holding company was the Caisse de dépôt et placement du Québec, the pension fund for all private and public employees in the province. Unlike the Canada Pension Plan or Social Security in the United States, the funds in the Quebec plan are invested in shares of private firms as well as in conventional treasury bills and interest-bearing deposits.[12] The Caisse de dépôt had a stake in 42 private and public firms in 1984, and 53 firms in 1990, while Société générale de financement du Québec (SGF) had a stake in 11 firms in both 1984 and 1990.

Under the nationalist Parti Québécois (PQ) elected in 1976, Crown corporation investment accounted for as much as a quarter of total investment in the province (1978), most of it concentrated in the hydro-electric sector. A rapidly growing francophone business elite in the public and private sectors filled any void created by anglophone private firms exiting to Toronto.

Against this background, we turn to a comparison of the privatization programmes undertaken by the federal and Quebec governments.[13]

PROCESS: IMPETUS FOR PRIVATIZATION

There have been striking differences in goals, structures, and processes of privatization between the Canadian federal government and the Quebec provincial government. Divestment through privatization became a solution to somewhat different problems on each government's agenda, as each undertook multiple divestments from 1984 onward.

Canada: problems of control and accountability

High public confidence in Crown corporations was shaken in the mid-1970s by allegations of mismanagement at Air Canada (Estey 1975) and of improper payments by Polysar and Atomic Energy Canada (Economic Council of Canada 1986). The Auditor-General issued a scathing report in 1976 on the government's financial management and the weak accountability framework for Crown corporations. Combined with the Trudeau government's passion for rational centralization, these events gradually led to two 'solutions': (1) a tighter control and accountability framework for Crown corporations, and (2) a review of holdings for possible rationalization. Realization of the first solution proceeded more swiftly, smoothly and deliberately than the second.

The key point is that divestment of federal Crown corporations and holdings became a solution to a perceived problem of control and accountability that has occupied the federal government agenda from 1975 to the present. Managerial complexity was the issue.

The Privy Council Office issued a report on control of Crown corporations in 1977, followed by recommendations on Crown corporations by the Lambert

Royal Commission in 1979 (Canada, Privy Council Office 1977, Canada, Lambert Commission 1979). Amendments to the Financial Administration Act (FAA) in 1984 altered the control framework by requiring Crown corporations to submit annual business plans to Treasury Board, to seek government approval for new subsidiaries, and to undergo a 'value for money' audit every five years to determine whether the firm had carried out operations effectively and managed its resources economically and efficiently (Hanna 1987). As of 1987, the number of parent corporations had been pared to 54, of which 46 were subject to the new rules (Ryan 1987). Mixed ownership firms such as Telesat Canada were exempt from the more stringent FAA reporting requirements.

Although more centralized control rather than divestment was the initial government response, there was agreement, at least among economists and the Liberal and Progressive Conservative parties, if not the New Democratic Party, that the number of Crown corporations was unwieldy, that some had outmoded or fuzzy mandates, and that policy goals might be achieved by other means: regulation, incentives, or increased competition.

During the 1979 Conservative minority government, Sinclair Stevens emerged as a strong privatization advocate. In targeting Petro-Canada as the key privatization candidate, the government encountered unexpected financial, legal and political problems that led to its downfall. On the initial round, the government failed to link the privatization solution to the perceived problem of control and accountability. Privatization was a solution in search of a problem (Kingdon 1984).

Under the following Liberal government, privatization remained on the agenda but its ranking slipped during the 1981/2 recession. The founding of CDIC was a form of divestment: a restructuring that reduced direct government control over certain Crown corporations and holdings.

On 30 October 1984, Sinclair Stevens, as minister responsible for CDIC in the new Conservative government, unilaterally resolved CDIC's goal ambiguity by announcing that all CDIC holdings were to be privatized by sale to the British Columbia Resources Investment Corporation (BCRIC), which had earlier been privatized by its provincial owner (Schultz 1988). Stevens forecast completion of the deal within six to twelve months. But rival buyers emerged demanding open bidding, especially for Teleglobe Canada.

Stevens's proposed solution preceded the formal statement of the problem. The policy rationale underpinning Stevens's proposal arrived a full month later in Finance Minister Wilson's manifesto (Wilson 1984). The primary theme was better management of the government's $50 billion assets in Crown corporations rather than privatization itself. By May 1985 the criterion for divestment broadened, when the ministerial task force on privatization recommended that government divest any corporation for which there was no strong policy argument for retention.

The ebb and flow of careers of individuals was thus a major factor in the expansion and contraction of Crown corporations. Just as C. D. Howe's presence guided the post-Second World War establishment of Crown corporations, it was Sinclair Stevens who championed the cause of privatization, first as President of the Treasury Board in 1979, and later in 1984 as the Minister for Regional Industrial Expansion (DRIE). When his career tumbled amid charges of impropriety, the Department of Regional Industrial Expansion lost its leadership role on the privatization issue.

Quebec: problems of changed goals and large losses

Near the end of its mandate, the PQ government became involved on an *ad hoc* basis in several divestment initiatives: Sidbec Normines, SAQ, Québecair (see Appendix), plus a strategic retrenchment at Hydro-Québec (Hafsi and Demers 1989). As Premier René Lévesque stated:

> The state apparatus' legitimacy is now based on its ability to abstain, to disengage itself from social responsibilities, to reduce its 'non productive' expenses, to model its operations on private sector practices, to renew with the principles of productivity, profitability and competitiveness, to prefer market mechanisms for a more automatic regulation of social exchanges.
>
> (Lévesque 1981)

The 1985 return of a Liberal provincial government signalled that the nationalists' success in commerce momentarily overshadowed the political dream of sovereignty for Quebec.

The new government outlined its motives for privatization in 1986 (Quebec, Minister Responsible for Privatization 1986). First, the original need for state firms to fill an entrepreneurial void had been met. Quebec had developed a dynamic managerial class, many of whom first served in the Crown corporations. Second, increasing global competition weakened some Crown corporations, and the government could no longer afford to sustain their losses. Thus divestment by Quebec was linked to mounting losses of some Crown corporations and the desire of private entrepreneurs for new investment domains.

PROCESS: MANAGING PRIVATIZATION

Federal Level: decentralized divestment and learning over time

Initially divestment of federal holdings was handled by the parent organization: the relevant governmental department or the parent Crown corporation. Thus, the sale of Northern Transportation, begun under the Liberal government, was carried out by the Department of Transportation. The Canada Development Corporation handled the sale of AES Data; Canadian National Railways (CNR) managed the sale of its trucking, hotel, and telecommunications subsidiaries; and the Post Office the franchising of new postal outlets.

243

The largest of these decentralized divestment programmes was at CNR, which had been pressured by the government-owner to shed non-rail subsidiaries to become more focused. Here the government's role in the divestment process was minimal. As ultimate shareholder, it provided the catalyst for divestment, and the divested CNR entities were included in the government's tally of privatization achievements published by the Office of Privatization and Regulatory Affairs.[14]

A second pattern emerged from Sinclair Stevens's push to divest CDIC holdings. He appointed businessmen such as Paul Marshall from Westmin Resources to head CDIC and alter its tone. There was a deliberate effort by privatization champions to keep management of the process out of the hands of public servants.[15] For example, although DRIE retained a formal leadership role for privatization, it was CDIC which hired the financial advisers to do the preparatory work on each firm: Teleglobe Canada, Canadair, De Havilland, Canadian Arsenals and Eldorado Nuclear.

The flaw in contracting out the divestment process to CDIC and its advisers was that this side-stepped industry policy issues that had to be resolved before divestment could proceed. As Doern and Atherton (1987) point out, public enterprises are not free-standing firms but are enmeshed in layers of sectorial policy commitments, regulatory frameworks, subsidies, community obligations and expectations, contractual commitments to domestic and foreign suppliers and buyers, and in the case of Canadian Arsenals and Teleglobe Canada the baggage of indexed public service pension plans. When it became clear that buyers were reluctant to bid until policy issues were resolved, co-ordination of the privatization process shifted back to joint management by CDIC and responsible departments. Here the process became embroiled in interdepartmental policy disputes (Schultz 1988).

So a third pattern emerged: a central authority for privatization established in August 1986 under the Cabinet Committee on Privatization, Regulatory Affairs and Operations, with Barbara McDougall as minister. This led in December 1986 to a new central agency responsible for privatization to resolve conflicting departmental goals and to act as a repository for learning about the privatization process: the Office of Privatization and Regulatory Affairs (OPRA). Despite centralization, the OPRA's reporting authority was itself diffuse, coming at times and in varying degrees under Finance, Treasury Board, and the Prime Minister's Office, depending on changes in the minister responsible for OPRA.

The federal process for privatization under OPRA had five formal stages (Canada OPRA 1990, McDermid 1989):

1 *Preliminary analysis* co-ordinated by OPRA to determine the candidate's commercial viability, public policy role, feasibility of privatization, and approval by Cabinet.

2 *In-depth review* by a team consisting of government and Crown corporation managers and private sector advisers, reporting to the Minister of State responsible for privatization and regulatory affairs to examine the mode of

sale, participation by foreign buyers, bilingual policy issues, and decision by Cabinet.

3 *Passage of legislation* including review of the sale by Parliament and drafting of covenants[16] to meet policy goals.

4 *Preparation for sale* including the managerial, legal and financial steps required for divestment.

5 *Implementation of sale* according to the mode of sale: share offering, employee buy-out, or third party sale.

These stages were weighted towards the mechanics of divestment as a goal in itself rather than viewing divestment as one of several means to solve problems. Although the formal process made no mention of commitment-building, OPRA came to recognize that 'soft' implementation aspects such as public communications and employee morale were often more challenging than 'hard' issues such as valuation (Canada OPRA 1988). In practice, privatization cases varied considerably at stage two in the degree of consultation with managers of the divestment candidate. The OPRA privatization process was not formally linked to the extensive Crown corporation assessment procedures laid out in the 1984 amendments to the Financial Administration Act, which remained the responsibility of the Treasury Board Secretariat.

Participants in the Canadian divestment process often pointed to organizational learning:

- 'In retrospect the 1985 bidding process [which was aborted] was not useless. For the 1986 round we merely had to update documents. Moreover in the 1985 round we were able to see what government saw as feasible and likely' (Teleglobe).
- 'We were able to apply much of what we had learned from the De Havilland sale directly to Canadair' (DRIE).
- 'We owe a debt to Teleglobe for sorting out the government policy on privatization' (Air Canada).
- 'The aborted 1987 privatization effort was a good dress rehearsal for the real thing' (Air Canada).

As OPRA became more like a central agency and less like a co-ordinating task force, what was learned became orthodoxy. Boasts by OPRA officials that Canada could become the first country to sell its postal corporation suggest that the spillover-effects from previous divestments had become very strong. In 1991 the government dissolved OPRA as part of its streamlining efforts, and handed the co-ordinating role for privatization to the Department of Finance.

Quebec level: learning from others

To determine a method for privatization, the Quebec government compared the ongoing British and Canadian experiences and concluded that public support was a key element for success. It felt the public was more interested in the 'why' of the process and the consequences of divestment than in technical and financial details. In its policy statement, the government emphasized that privatization was not an end in itself and that privatization would be carried out pragmatically on a case by case basis. The structural objectives of strengthening the economy and ensuring a continued Quebec presence in key sectors would take precedence over maximizing financial returns from sale of Crown corporations (Quebec, Minister Responsible for Privatization 1986).

Management of the divestment process was entrusted to a ministry for privatization within the ministry of finance. The ministry reviewed the role of Crown corporations within a socio-political climate where the state sought a reduced economic role because of deficits and general confidence in a viable francophone private sector.

The new formally structured process was as follows (Quebec, Minister Responsible for Privatization 1986):

1 *Review of the Crown corporation's dossier* by the Standing Cabinet Committee on Economic Development (CMPDE).
2 *Analysis of four options* – total or partial privatization, reorganization followed by later privatization, reorientation or turn-around, and the *status quo* – for the firm by a joint committee consisting of (a) the minister responsible for the firm, (b) the Minister of State for Privatization, (c) one or more representatives from the firm, and (d) representatives from other departments.
3 *Development of consensus and plan* for realization of the chosen alternative.
4 *Joint submission of the plan* by the Minister for Privatization and the responsible minister for the firm to the CMPDE and then the whole Cabinet for review and approval.
5 *Implementation* by the Ministry for Privatization assisted by an operational task force, with legislative scrutiny and approval where needed.
6 *Formal review of the programme* as a whole by the Minister for Privatization.

In most cases, the divestment proceeded quickly and relatively smoothly with little public controversy, apart from opposition charges that the selling price of some firms was too low. More turbulent cases included the abortive SAQ outlet sale and the Québecair saga. Some firms like Domtar (construction materials and forestry products) failed to attract buyers.

To assuage concerns that privatization might extend to key assets such as Hydro-Québec, the government announced in October 1988 that the main goals in privatization had been attained and that the future pace would be slower.

CONTEXT AND PROCESS IN SEVEN CASES:

The findings from seven individual cases of divestment in the appendix are discussed comparatively in three areas: context, process, and outcomes.

Context

The general context for the cases appears similar to that suggested by the traditional literature on private sector divestment.[17]

First, these divestments occurred in *difficult economic times* for the parent and/or the unit being divested. At both the federal and provincial levels, the government-owner perceived itself to be financially weak with huge deficits and strong popular resistance to increasing the tax burden. The Quebec government strongly wished to stem the haemorrhage of funds to state-owned enterprises. The federal government declared itself unable to finance the fleet renewal strategy of Air Canada. The government also found it anomalous to be in the executive jet business (Canadair) in the midst of difficult economic times. As for the divested units, Sidbec-Dosco, Canadair, Québecair and SOQUEM were financially and competitively fragile. Air Canada was financially constrained by its inability to obtain new equity injections from its owner for fleet renewal. However, there were two exceptions: Teleglobe and SAQ were financially strong. It so happens that managing the divestment process for the latter two was problematic.

Second, as in the private sector *emotional attachments* often played a key role in delaying the decision to divest. Air Canada had a strong symbolic value that was difficult to disentangle from the national identity, an attachment reinforced by the Prime Minister's 1985 pledge not to sell. While Québecair did not have time to acquire a similar symbolic role within Quebec, structuring its divestment required avoiding the appearance of a direct take-over by the Calgary-based PWA/Air Canadian. Decision-making on Canadair and De Havilland was haunted by the lingering symbolism of the 1959 Arrow cancellation. Decision-makers wished to avoid a 'second' Arrow debacle. Teleglobe Canada's links to post-Second World War Commonwealth telecommunications policy helped shield it from scrutiny for sale until the British government announced its intention to divest British Telecom. Hydro-Québec is so closely linked with modern Quebec nationalism and the provincial Liberal leader's economic strategy that it was excluded at the outset from the list of investment candidates.

Third, substantial *links with existing units* could delay divestment. For Sidbec-Normines, a long time was devoted to understanding and working out the impact of a possible divestment. In the Cambior, Québecair, Canadair, and Air Canada cases, links to industry policy goals drew careful attention. In the SAQ case, links were postulated as weak, and no further consideration was given to the effects of divestment on both the outlets and the remaining SAQ. Similarly in the Teleglobe case, Stevens postulated no significant links with Telesat Canada or other players in the industry and gave limited consideration to industry effects of the divestment. In both cases the links proved to be stronger.

Fourth, the privatization programmes at the federal and provincial levels were associated with *changed leadership*: the new Progressive Conservative government (1984) and the new Liberal government (1986). At the micro-level, in five

247

of the seven cases divestment started being considered as a possible solution only with the appointment of new chief executives or new ministers, who were not committed to existing structures. In the Sidbec case, the appointment of Leboutillier, in 1982, coincides with the first contemplation of closing the Fire Lake mine. In the SAQ case, Lord announced the privatization project soon after being appointed. In the Québecair and Cambior case, the new Liberal government gave the go-ahead. In the Canadair case, the divestment was preceded by new management and by a new government. In two cases, leadership changes were not a significant factor. In the Air Canada case, management gradually came to favour privatization after passage of the Air Canada Act 1977 and airline deregulation in the 1980s. In the Teleglobe Canada case, existing management faced privatization under a new government, but the divestment process had in a sense been initiated in a different form by the former Liberal government in 1982 with the transfer of responsibility for Teleglobe to CDIC.

The influence of newer forces for divestment and strategic fit was as follows.

External financing, which is closely linked to the financial difficulty context of the traditional divestment literature, was a strong factor in the Quebec decisions to divest. At the federal level, divestment was linked to deficit reduction through scaling back new commitments to state-owned firms: for example, by refraining from financing Air Canada's fleet renewal or Canadair's future research and development efforts.[18]

Globalization was an important factor in the Sidbec-Normines, Cambior, Canadair, Teleglobe Canada, and Air Canada divestments. It was indirectly important for Québecair in that globalization had prompted industry deregulation, but unimportant for the SAQ. Even when important, the consequences of globalization could be ambiguous. Globalization made telecommunications a competitive tool for businesses, which demanded more varied services and lower costs, but there were trade-offs between deficit reduction and communications cost reduction.[19] For Air Canada divestment was linked to the need for more flexible management and financing to meet competition arising from deregulation and globalization, but these forces also threaten the very existence of Canadian-based air carriers, as shown in the 1991 'open-skies' talks with the United States.

Reduction of *managerial complexity* was a strong force for the federal divestment programme and a moderate factor for Quebec. At the micro-level it was very important in the case of Air Canada, and moderately important in the case of Canadair and Cambior. Its importance for SAQ and Québecair was ambiguous. At Teleglobe Canada, managerial complexity increased following divestment because it came under tariff regulation by the Canadian Radio–Television and Telecommunications Commission (CRTC).

Finally, divestment for *improved strategic fit* was important. The federal government's divestment criterion was that a firm should be divested unless there still existed policy reasons for government ownership. In the Québecair, Canadair, Teleglobe and Air Canada cases, the government decided that current policy goals could be met more effectively by regulations and covenants imposed on the new owners. This relieved the government burdens of ownership and monitoring day-to-day management. The Quebec government's decision framework for divestment embodied more options than divest or retain, but the overall purpose was to reassess goals and determine what changes in policies and ownership structures were needed to realign government activities with current goals. At Sidbec-Normines divestment for improved strategic fit was essential for survival. At SOQUEM, realignment resulted from government's diminished ability and the private sector's improved ability to undertake expensive mining development costs. In the case of SAQ, the stated lack of fit between government ownership and retail operations had some merit, but cross-subsidization within SAQ's retail network meant that only half the outlets attracted bidders.

Process

Across the cases studied, we found processes similar to those identified by Gilmour (1973) and Kingdon (1984):

1 *Problem recognition*: perception of an anomalous condition or a discrepancy.
2 *Proposal formation*: development and examination of solutions.
3 *Political processes*: support gathering, bargaining, commitment building.
4 *Implementation processes*: packaging, valuation, enabling legislation (unique to public sector), marketing assets and handling bids, and coping with stakeholder obligations.
5 *Learning processes*: perceived lessons, spillover effects, and consequences for other cases.

From a 'rational' decision-making perspective, there is a natural sequence from 1 to 5. In practice the processes are independent and may not follow the 'natural' order. Processes overlap; and processes may be protracted, compressed or intermittent. In addition, cases are interdependent so processes interact across cases. The processes are emergent as well as deliberate (Mintzberg and Jörgensen 1987).

Taking Air Canada as an example, the problem recognition process identified management problems and lack of autonomy as anomalies in the 1970s. The proposal formation process led to the Air Canada Act 1977, with autonomy from CNR plus a profit goal. Meanwhile, generic recommendations for Crown corporations went in two directions: increased oversight and control by Treasury Board (1977–84) and privatization (1979 and 1984). The generic privatization solution and the problem of Air Canada's autonomy did not get linked until an appropriate window of opportunity arose in the mid-1980s: the juncture of industry deregulation and fleet renewal on Air Canada's side and mounting deficits and a commitment to privatize on the government side.

Initially, in the Québecair, Cambior and Canadair cases, divestment was not the first solution proposed. At Sidbec, closing the mine was an emergent solution; initially the plan was to sell the entire firm. For Sidbec and Canadair the problem-solving process was lengthy and open. In the Cambior, Sidbec and Air Canada cases, the government had no preconceived solution or at least did not push for divestment at the outset. Generally, it identified the key stakeholders, and pushed them to find a solution. Their solution finally became the government's. The political process and proposal formation processes were intertwined.

At Air Canada, Canadair, Cambior, Québecair and Sidbec, the problem recognition process led to a widely shared perception of the nature of the discrepancy between actual and desired performance. At Teleglobe Canada and SAQ the nature and magnitude of the discrepancy was debatable. Both companies were very profitable. They were generally well perceived (or almost unknown in the Teleglobe case) by the public. Criticism levelled at the SAQ related to its fiscal role rather than the quality of its service or management. In the case of Teleglobe, minor criticism was levelled at its monopoly status rather than its performance. Without agreement on the existence of a problem, there was no shared rationale for divesting either SAQ or Teleglobe.

The political process involved significant negotiation and commitment-building in all cases except SAQ. Even at Teleglobe there was an effort in the second round to allay concerns of managers and employees. In most cases commitment-building was linked to shared recognition of the problem and how divestment could help. In the Sidbec, Cambior, Québecair, Canadair, and Air Canada cases, consensus emerged from the problem recognition process; (a) the need to stop Sidbec's financial losses, (b) the need to reduce the firm's debt burden in the case of Cambior and Canadiar, (c) Air Canada's need to finance fleet renewal and compete under deregulation, and (d) the eventual recognition that fleet renewal was not enough to solve Québecair's competitive problems.

Political processes often overlap with both proposal formation (Sidbec-Normines, Québecair, Canadair, Air Canada) and implementation (Teleglobe Canada). Proposal formation can re-emerge during implementation: counter-proposals by SAQ employees continued during the bidding process; at Teleglobe Canada abortive implementation in the first round was followed by renewed problem recognition, proposal formation and political processes. Canadair and De Havilland illustrate cases that are interdependent across all processes.

In the absence of rational process sequences, what does it mean to manage the divestment process other than in the technically narrow implementation sense? For Air Canada's management, it entailed being a political broker (Kingdon 1984). Rather than simply going from its problems to seek government solutions, management matched its preferred solution – privatization – to government problems. For example, it commissioned opinion polls to demonstrate how privatization could enhance the government's popularity prior to an election. It performed the legwork for government: authorizing feasibility studies, identifying key political issues, drafting answers for the legislative process, and designing the employee share-ownership plan. It placed a key official in Ottawa to monitor and facilitate the co-ordination efforts of the Office of Privatization and Regulatory Affairs. Management engaged in background work when windows of opportunity were closed, as after the Prime Minister's 1985 'no sale' pledge, and seized open windows of opportunity, as prior to the 1988 election.

Managers of public enterprises can advise on the appropriateness of divestment for the organization, on the options available for such a divestment, and on what form the divestment might take to be acceptable to key stakeholders. Managers who want more autonomy must emphasize how divestment through privatization would enable the government to achieve its social goals by other means. Managers who are comfortable with existing government ownership must mobilize stakeholders to focus government's attention on the continued public policy role of the firm.

Outcomes at the federal level

The primary goals of government programmes are often revealed in the way results are reported. No study of British privatization is complete without totalling the returns realized by the Treasury from the sell-off. For the Canadian government, what appears most important is the number of firms divested. Between 1984 and mid-1992, the Canadian government sold fifteen wholly owned or indirectly owned firms, divested its stake in six mixed ownership corporations, and partially divested two (CAMECO and Petro-Canada) (see Table 12.4). Another eight Crown corporations (five inactive, one start-up and two lotteries) were wound up (Doern and Atherton 1987). Simplifying government management through divestment appears to be a major goal. When asked in 1988 if they monitored the performance of divested firms, OPRA officials seemed surprised. Getting out of the monitoring task was central to the goal of reducing managerial complexity. The proceeds from the sale of federal government holdings totalled C$3.67 billion, half of which went to pay down the government's debt, the remainder to the firms themselves or parent Crown corporations to pay off debts.

Despite ideological statements by some members of the Conservative government, divestment goals have continued to be a rationalization of holdings and better management of resources. Borins and Boothman (1985) claim that Canadian Crown corporations, unlike the British, did not suffer from significant operational inefficiencies, especially those in competitive environments. Even so, two went bankrupt soon after their sale (AES and CN Route[20]), while shares of Air Canada and Petro-Canada traded well below their issue price in 1992.

Thanks to privatization, the federal government has reversed the previous trend of expanding commitments to Crown corporations: annual budgetary funding has levelled off at below $5 billion. Because of inflation, this represents a real decline. In relative terms, funding for public enterprise has declined from 6.9 to 3.4 per cent of the total budget between 1982 and 1991.[21] Yet some of the privatized firms continue to be dependent on government contracts and support,

Table 12.4 Canadian federal government: public sector divestment, 1984–92

Crown corporation or holding	Crown status	Employees	Divestment date	Buyer or divestment mode	Proceeds from sale	
					Reported by govt. ($ mill.)	Calculated net proceeds # ($ mill.)
AES	CDC	1,400	87-09-01	Kinburn Technology	Excl.	14.0*
Air Canada	†Canada	22,640	88-10-13	Public share issue (43%)	246.2	225.8*
			89-07-19	Public share issue (57%)	493.5	471.9
Canada Development Corp.	Canada (47%)	17,808	86-09-16	Public share issue	246.0	246.0
			87-06-12	Private placement	15.8	15.8
			87-10-27	Public share issue	99.0	99.0
Canadair Ltd	†CDIC	5,431	86-12-23	Bombardier Inc.	143.3	143.0
Canada Post Corporation	†Canada	52,760	87-00-00	Franchising of postal outlets	Excl.	–
Canadian Arsenals Ltd	†Canada	924	86-05-09	SNC Group	92.2	92.2
CDC Life Sciences	CDC (67%)	1,136	86-11-00	Public share issue (42%)	Excl.	133.2*
CN Hotels	†CNR	3,400	88-01-29	Canadian Pacific Hotels	265.0	265.0*
CN Route	†CNR	2,227	86-12-05	Route Canada Holdings	29.0	29.0*
CNCP	CNR (50%)	3,120	88-12-16	Canadian Pacific	235.0	235.0*
De Havilland Aircraft	†CDIC	4,405	86-01-31	Boeing Company (US)	–90.0	90.0
(settlement)			90-02-09	Settlement of claims against govt.		–63.0
Eldorado Nuclear	†CDIC	1,013	88-10-05	Joint venture CAMECO (38% Federal govt; 62% Saskatchewan govt.)	Excl.	–444.1
(CAMECO)	CDIC (38%)		91-07-11	Partial public share offering	128.9	39.0*
	CDIC 19%		92-02-05	Private sale of warrants	83.9	83.9*
Fishery Products Int.	Canada (63%)	8,650	87-04-15	Public share issue	104.4	104.4
Nanisivik Mines	Canada (18%)	195	86-10-28	Mineral Resources Int.	6.0	6.0
Nordair	†Air Canada	1,317	84-12-01	Innocan	Excl.	34.0*
Nordion International	†AECL division	550	91-06-11	MDS Health Group consortium	165.0	165.0*

Company	Owner	Date	Employees	Buyer / Description		
Northern Canada Power	†Canada	87–03–31	34	Yukon government	75.5	35.5
		88–05–05		Govt. of Northwest Territories	75.5	10.0
Northern Transportation	†Canada	85–07–15	389	Inuvialuit and Nunasi Dev. Corps	53.0	27.0
NorthwestTel	†CNR	88–08–08	450	BCE	200.0	140.0*
Pêcheries Canada Inc.	†Canada	86–04–18	575	La co-operative agro-alim. Purdel	5.0	5.0
Petro-Canada	†Canada	91–07–03	7,373	Partial public share offering (19.5%)	520.4	506.6*
Teleglobe Canada	†Canada	87–04–03	1,110	Memotec Data	611.5	611.5
Telesat Canada	Canada (& CNR) (53%)	92–03–24	675	Alouette (iv: Telecom Canada/Spar)	154.8	154.8
Terra Nova Tel	†CNR	88–08–08	400	Newfoundland Tel (BCE)	170.0	170.0*
Varity (M-F warrants)	CDIC	87–12–31	16,330	Sale of purchase warrants	3.2	3.2
(settlement)		90–10–00		Settlement of claims against Varity	Excl.	7.8
(Varity shares)		91–00–00		Sale of Varity shares	6.0	6.0
VIA RAIL	†Canada	90–01–15	7,300	Retrenchment cuts 2,761 jobs	Excl.	–
EMPLOYEES TOTAL (excludes Varity, Can.Post, double-counting and holdings below 40%; includes VIA Rail cuts)			85,252	TOTAL PROCEEDS		3,666.3
				OF WHICH, FEDERAL GOVERNMENT		1,738.9

Sources: Data supplied by the Office of the Privatization and Regulatory Affairs (1989) and the Privatization Branch, Department of Finance (1991 and 1992); W. T. Stanbury, 'Privatization in Canada', *Privatization and State-Owned Enterprises*, eds. Paul W. MacAvoy, W. T. Stanbury, George Yarrow, and Richard J. Zeckhauser (Boston: Kluwer Academic Publishers, 1989), p. 286; CDIC Annual Reports 1985–91; *Financial Post Daily*, 30 August 1988, p. 44; and the prospectus for the following issues: Air Canada (September 1988 and July 1989), Cameco (June 1991), Fishery Products International (March 1987), and Petro-Canada (June 1991). *Notes*: Divestments in progress (June 1992): CN Exploration (CNX); Theratronics International (320 employees; ex-Atomic Energy Canada Ltd [AECL] division); and remaining shares in CAMECO and Petro-Canada.

\# Sale price plus dividends and royalties, less underwriters' fees, other expenses, asset write-downs and loans written off.

† Crown corporation or wholly owned subsidiary.

* All or majority of proceeds kept by the corporation or its parent (generally to reduce debt).

Excl. Excluded or not reported by OPRA as part of privatization program.

notably De Havilland (Boeing) and Canadair (Bombardier). Unlike Britain (Hall 1986), privatization in Canada has not been accompanied by major improvements in the performance of remaining public enterprises.[22]

One can point to examples where divestment has increased industry concentration. Canada's largest polyethylene producer, Nova Corporation, won control of Polysar, also a major polyethylene producer, after Polysar-CDC was privatized. A big winner in Canada's telecommunications deregulation and privatization is BCE (Bell Canada). On the one hand, it has thwarted potential competitors by vigorously fighting deregulation of entry into long-distance services; on the other hand, it has aggressively taken advantage of privatization, taking a key stake in Teleglobe Canada (through Memotec) and buying CNR's regional telecommunications subsidiaries (Jörgensen 1990: 407).

Outcomes at the Quebec level

In its published assessment of the privatization programme, the Quebec government emphasized the stemming of losses by state corporations, the general retention of control of divested units in Quebec, the use of funds from the divestment exercise, and the restored ability of slimmed-down parent Crown corporations to undertake new socio-economic initiatives (Québec, Ministre délégué 1988). Quebec divested completely its holdings in Québecair, la Raffinerie du sucre du Québec in sugar refining and Madelipêche in fisheries. It sold off three subsidiaries of SOQUEM, four holdings of SOQUIA in food processing and distribution, three of REXFOR in forestry, four of SNA in asbestos, and one each of SGF and SOQUIP (see Table 12.5). Proceeds totalling C$826 million were largely used to reduce the debt of parent corporations. SAQ, Loto-Qúbec and Hydro-Québec were explicitly excluded from the divestment exercise.

Despite privatization and claims that the new managerial class tilted the state-market boundaries to the private sector, the Quebec government continues to have a major indirect role in key economic sectors through the Caisse de dépôt et placement du Québec and SGF, its own alternative policy instruments. The Quebec government divested in order to intervene more effectively and at a lower cost. Slimmed-down Crown corporations have been given redefined mandates, as illustrated by SOQUEM.

Conclusion: comparing the federal and provincial divestment programmes

Divestment illustrates the challenge of designing administrative structures for non-routine policy implementation. Three troublesome cases, Teleglobe, SAQ and Québecair, occurred near the start of a programme of multiple public sector divestments by their respective governments.

Despite the emphasis on rational management of government assets and letting managers manage, the federal government's divestment programme has

Table 12.5 Quebec provincial government: public sector divestment, 1984–8

Crown corporation or holding	Governance status	Employees	Transfer date	Buyer or divestment mode	Proceeds ($m)
Cambior Inc.	*SOQUEM	412	86-08-14	Public share offering (69%)	170.0†
Crustacés-des-Iles Inc.	*Madelipêche	1,045	87-12-31	Groupe Delaney	3.1
Diatex-SNA	SNA (50%)	470	86-07-17	Echlin inc.	3.2†
Donohue	*SGF	2,025	87-07-07	Mircor (51%)	320.0
Filaq-SNA	SNA (66.7%)	n/a	88-02-10	Industries 3-R Inc.	0.1†
Grande-Entrée	*Madelipêche	320	87-08-14	Groupe Hubert	0.5
Industries 3-R Inc.	SNA (30%)	n/a	88-02-10	Industries 3-R share repurchase	0.1†
J. E. Landry Inc.	SOQUIA (42%)	n/a	87-01-19	Provigo	2.9†
La société minière Louvem	SOQUEM (22%)	110	87-11-05	Ressources Sainte-Geneviève	8.4†
Lupel-SNA	*SNA	n/a	86-07-30	Cascades Inc.	5.6†
Madelipêche Inc.	*Quebec	1,000	87-11-19	Groupe Delaney	1.1
Mines Seleine Inc.	*SOQUEM	200	88-04-29	Société canadienne de sel Ltée	35.0
Ministry of Public Works	Govt Department	n/a	84-10-01	Transformed into Crown corporation	–
Panofor Inc.	Rexfor (33%)	n/a	87-10-29	Normick-Perron (assets only)	14.0†
Papier Cascades Cabano	Rexfor (30%)	n/a	87-08-31	Cascades Inc.	11.0†
Pêches Nordiques Inc.	SOQUIA (92%)	n/a	87-03-04	Fruits de mer de l'Est du Québec	2.5†
Provigo	SOQUIA (6.7%)	23,000	86-03-17	Unigesco (26%)	48.4
Québecair	Quebec	827	86-08-01	Nordair-Metro (CP Air 35%)	21.0
Raffinerie du sucre	*Quebec	94	86-09-18	Sucre Lantic Ltée	43.2
Scierie des Outardes Enr.	Rexfor (60%)	n/a	88-03-31	Cie. de papier Québec & Ontario	11.0†
Sidbec-Normines	Sidbec-Dosco (50.1%)	940	84-12-31	Mine closed; pellet plant leased to QC	-67.5
Soc. des Alcools du Québec	*Quebec	(2,459)	(1985)	Privatization of outlets aborted	–
Soc. des pêches de Newport	SOQUIA (39%)	600	88-02-08	Fishermen	3.5†
SOQUIP-Alberta	*SOQUIP	n/a	87-12-23	Sceptre Resources Ltd	188.8
Total (excludes SAQ and double counting)		31,043		Total proceeds	825.9
				Of which, provincial treasury	102.9

Sources: Quebec, Ministre délégué aux Finances et à la Privatisation (1988) Privatisation des sociétés d'état; rapport d'étape, 1986–88; Les Affaires 500, June.

Notes: *Crown corporation or wholly owned subsidiary.
†All or majority of proceeds kept by Crown corporation.

experienced repeated changes in structure and uneven participation by Crown corporation representatives. Quick exit has occasionally overshadowed socio-political goals such as fostering competition. The emphasis on the mechanics of divestment rather than the post-divestment policy framework for each sector follows from the desire to reduce managerial complexity and the challenge of achieving consensus on sectorial policy goals in a federal structure.

Conversely, notwithstanding messy cases such as SAQ and Québecair, the Quebec divestment programme has been characterized by greater consensus. It has emphasized continuing government policy goals for each sector rather than maximizing the number of divested firms. The Quebec government retains its socio-economic role even as it divests.

Management of divestment demonstrates the importance of having a widely shared perception of the problem to resolve, the desirability of having clearly understood goals, the importance of commitment building, the desirability of involving managers, employees and other stakeholders in the problem-solution, the importance of the post-divestment framework, and the risks of imposing a preconceived strategy in complex organizations.

Apart from showing the contrast between an approach emphasizing quick exit (federal government) and one stressing socio-political goals (Quebec), the Canadian experience may have limited relevance for privatization in Eastern Europe or developing countries. At the micro-level there may be more relevance. Future research will examine how privatization necessitates changes in core competencies (Prahalad and Hamel 1990) within the privatized firms and how new organizational capabilities are acquired.

APPENDIX: CONTEXT AND PROCESS IN SEVEN SELECTED CASES

Seven public sector divestment cases from the 1980s were chosen from the Canadian federal government and the Quebec provincial government for detailed study of context and process. A synopsis of these cases follows.[23]

Sidbec-Normines(SN)[24]

SN was established in the 1960s as the mining core of an integrated steel industry based on Quebec's iron ore and hydro-electric resources in partnership with foreign firms. The partners agreed to purchase at the prevailing North American (Great Lakes) price the 6 million ton annual output of ore, in proportion to their interest in SN. The steel-making side, Sidbec-Dosco, was added in 1968. By 1981 the Great Lakes ore price was twice the international price due to new entrants like Brazil. Sidbec-Dosco produced about 600,000 tons of steel, but was committed to buy 3 million tons of iron pellets at a $20 per ton premium over the international price. Its steel operations could never be profitable and the annual deficit reached $81 million in 1983.

A new president took over, and a committee of the Quebec National Assembly was appointed to search for a solution. Québec Cartier (a 100 per cent subsidiary of US Steel) offered to take over the pelletizing plant, to keep it running, and supply the partners with pellets at the international price, if SN were closed. Sidbec-Dosco executives believed that there was no other solution and pushed for acceptance. SN's managers were by now aware of the need to close the mine and could offer no alternative. The key aspect was allowing time for everyone involved to be convinced that there was no other choice. Officials went to great lengths to show their concern for the employees and their families, and to stress their determination to reduce their hardship. All parties were asked to propose a better solution, and the government appeared to be genuinely ready to accept any other reasonable alternative. The transfer of the pellet plant was delicate, because it could be seen as a sell-out of a 'national asset' to foreigners. The unions were essentially concerned with jobs, and sought to ensure that the transfer would minimize job losses. Because of early retirement and transfers of pellet plant workers and some miners to the Québec Cartier Mining Company, the number of permanent lay-offs was kept to 300 miners and 35 office staff among the 940 employees of Sidbec-Normines (Canada Energy Mines 1985). Freed from the losses incurred by mining, Sidbec-Dosco was able to show some profits.

La société des alcools du québec (SAQ)[25]

The SAQ is Quebec's monopoly for importation, bottling, and distribution of wine, spirits, and other alcoholic beverages, except beer. In the fiscal year ending 31 March 1985, SAQ's sales were $889 million, a 5.3 per cent increase over the previous year's performance, and its profits were $340.5 million, a 12.2 per cent increase. The profitability of SAQ was perceived to be the result of fiscal monopoly effects and tight management practices. There was, however, a lot of tension between management and the union. On average, the employees had been on strike 10 per cent of the time for the previous twenty years. In October 1983, Jean-Guy Lord, a vice-president of a major Canadian wine-maker and distributor, was appointed SAQ Chief Executive Officer, with a mandate 'to eliminate the monopolistic tendencies, which have been the hallmark of SAQ activities, and ensure the firm's operations [were] in accordance with rules and principles in use in the private sector'. In November 1983, Lord announced in a newspaper interview (Nadeau 1983), that SAQ retail outlets were for sale. The project, approved by both the minister responsible for SAQ, and by the Minister of Finance, was to be implemented quickly over a few months.

The SAQ employees and managers were taken by surprise. Top SAQ management suggested that some outlets might be converted to co-operatives owned by employees.[26] Union leaders denounced the proposed plans as an attempt to liquidate the union. Store managers also expressed discontent, and asked to be allowed to participate by buying into their stores. The union obtained a temporary injunction to prevent the company from continuing with the co-op plan, but the Superior Court later ruled that the SAQ could go ahead with the sale of outlets. The union proposed an alternative project to sell up to 49 per cent of the shares of the entire SAQ (including wholesale and bottling operations).

The government decided to go ahead with the sale of Montreal-area outlets to private investors and co-ops. Nearly half the 129 outlets were unprofitable, and so only 56 tenders came in, including 31 from co-ops. New legal battles followed, and the whole project collapsed in late 1985 amid Cabinet disagreement on the desirability and feasibility of the privatization project. Under the subsequent Liberal government, the SAQ was not on the Ministry of Privatization's list of state-owned firms to be divested. Indirect privatization occurred as the government allowed grocery shops and supermarkets to sell wines bottled in Quebec, including popular wines imported in bulk. This has reduced wine sales through the SAQ retail outlets, and some outlets have therefore moved into smaller premises.[27]

Québecair[28]

Québecair was a regional airline serving the Quebec North Shore and Labrador. Because of former federal policies reserving trunk routes for Air Canada and CP Air, only in 1981 did Québecair gain permission for a Montreal–Toronto route. Suffering losses half the years between 1966 and 1981 and accumulating a consolidated deficit of $13.2 million, Québecair was poorly positioned to take advantage of domestic air transport deregulation in the 1980s. Apart from marginal routes, problems included a disparate fleet of 80 aircraft of 15 different types plus weak management. Earnings were volatile, with profits linked to hydroelectric construction projects in northern Quebec and Labrador. By contrast, its anglophone-owned rival Nordair, founded in a 1957 merger, operated in the profitable Montreal–Ottawa–Hamilton–Windsor corridor plus Pittsburgh, Thunder Bay, northern Quebec, and the Arctic. With good routes and a jet fleet, Nordair enjoyed growth and profits.

Initially it was thought that Québecair's problems could be solved through acquisition of a modern jet fleet and, possibly, a merger with another carrier to gain economies of scale and a larger route network. From 1978 to 1986 there were multiple attempts by Québecair and Nordair to acquire each other and changes in ownership of each firm. In 1981 the Quebec government injected new capital into Québecair for updating its fleet and promised to match within two years a bid for Québecair offered by Nordair and Air Canada. In 1983 the Quebec government was obliged to carry out its offer to acquire the shares of Québecair, and set up Société Québécoise des Transports (SQT) as its Crown holding company. The state take-over had popular support. Meanwhile, in 1984, the venture capital firm Innocan acquired a controlling interest in Nordair from Air Canada, with Québecair holding an indirect 34 per cent share through SQT. Québecair's losses continued: $8.4 million in 1985.

After investing more than $80 million in the airline, the Quebec government announced its intention to privatize Québecair in January 1986. Soliciting bids, the government set four policy objectives: (1) maintaining adequate regional service; (2) keeping the base of operations and headquarters in Quebec; (3) keeping as many employees as possible; and (4) obtaining a reasonable price. Three competing groups emerged as potential buyers. The first two groups proposed major restructuring to replace jets with smaller turbo-props for more frequent service and lower crew costs. The third group, consisting of Québecair employees and pilots, faced problems assembling a bid. Lacking business experience, it approached bidding like a collective bargaining exercise, tenaciously defending the *status quo* (Morisset 1986). After unsuccessful attempts to get financial backing from the Quebec Federation of Labour (FTQ) and the Mouvement Desjardins (a major financial co-operative), it turned to Air Canada for support. The government accepted instead the bid from Nordair-Metro in late July 1986. Public support for the sale was high in the summer but declined in autumn as employee lay-offs started.[29]

Québecair became profitable as Inter-Canadian, the feeder airline in the Canadian Regional Airlines network of PWA, which had purchased CP Air from CP and renamed it Canadian International.[30] When friction later developed between PWA and Michel Leblanc, Inter-Canadian's chief executive officer, the subsidiary was purchased by Leblanc and his partners for $16.5 million and renamed Intair. Intair was unable to survive the industry downturn of 1990. The Quebec government resisted a major bail-out, and Intair returned to the PWA fold after Leblanc resigned in March 1991 (Leconte 1990, McGovern 1991).

Cambior[31]

Cambior was formed from the Société québécoise d'exploration minière (SOQUEM), created in 1965. Apart from stimulating exploration and mining development consortia, SOQUEM's goal was to promote Quebec francophone entrepreneurship in the sector, reduce foreign ownership of critical national resources, rationalize infrastructure services provided to mining firms, and promote downstream development (processing, fabrication). It participated in joint ventures involving forty private firms that contributed about $85 million for their part. By 1986 SOQUEM seemed to have exhausted its usefulness as a stimulant to the Quebec mining industry. New tax incentives and other fiscal policies had proved effective in accomplishing at a lower cost what SOQUEM had been set up to do. Its 'market share' in new exploration had fallen from 13 per cent in 1972 to 1.6 per cent in 1985 (Québec, Ministre délégué aux Finances 1988: 56). Despite having achieved most of its original objectives, it was heavily in debt, over $100 million in 1985, a level that the government was no longer comfortable sustaining.

The firm's managers started looking for solutions. Selling assets to pay down SOQUEM's debts appeared to be the route to go. Its main salt mine went on the auction block, but a change in government thwarted the sale.

The new Liberal government developed its framework for privatization and decided that the SOQUEM case could be used to test it. In April 1986 the Minister for Privatization and the Minister for Mining declared that the very success of SOQUEM in developing a francophone mining industry in Quebec made it less essential than before. A committee was appointed, comprised of SOQUEM managers, representatives from the Minister for Mines and the Minister for Privatization, to develop several privatization scenarios. One of these was the creation of a new company, Cambior, that would take over the most valuable gold-producing properties of SOQUEM. There was little internal resistance to this privatization. The managers themselves helped develop the proposal. Laid-off engineers were in a market where they had little problem finding new assignments. The separation packages finally agreed upon were generous enough to soothe any resistance. Cambior's initial public share offering met with great enthusiasm, yielding gross proceeds of $157.5 million, of which $92 million came from outside Quebec.[32] SOQUEM retained 30.7 per cent of the outstanding shares, intending to sell them gradually, as is commonly done in Europe. Furthermore, most of the employees and managers of SOQUEM became shareholders of the newly created company. Cambior share prices shot up soon after the issue and kept going up the following year. The slimmed-down SOQUEM was given a new mandate: fostering mineral exploration in remote areas not yet developed while avoiding costly development.

Canadair[33]

Canadair started in 1920 as the Aircraft Division in Montreal of Canadian Vickers. When Canadian Vickers decided to concentrate on shipbuilding during the Second World War, the division was sold to the federal government and renamed Canadair Ltd in 1944. Soon after the war, the government decided to return its aircraft firms to the private sector. Canadair was sold to the Electric Boat Company of Connecticut, which became General Dynamics (Borins 1983: 468). Canadair prospered during the Korean War peaking at 13,500 employees in 1953. But the government's 1959 cancellation of A. V. Roe's Arrow project signalled a switch in both Canadian and US military procurement policy. Henceforth Canadian firms would be subcontractors to the American defence firms rather than prime contractors (Laux and Molot 1988: 90). Apart from subcontracting, Canadair produced water bombers and military surveillance drones.

When the aircraft industry slumped in the 1970s, General Dynamics retrenched by divesting Canadair. Fearing a permanent loss of Canadian aerospace expertise, the federal government purchased Canadair for $46 million in late 1975. The government faced three options for Canadair: (1) closing the firm and selling its land to developers to recoup the purchase price; (2) expanding the firm's aerospace subcontracting business; or (3) returning

Canadair to its former status as a first-tier aircraft designer, developer and manufacturer (Borins and Brown 1986: 18). Canadair President Frederick Kearns championed the third option, based on a Lear-designed executive jet aircraft, and won government backing for what was to become the Challenger jet. Canadair employment rose from 1,500 employees in 1975 to nearly 7,000 in 1981.

By the end of 1982 the cumulative cost of the Challenger programme reached $1.9 billion versus revenues of $0.6 billion. Parliament was forced to make an emergency equity infusion of $200 million in December 1982 (Austin 1983). At the end of 1982, control of Canadair was handed over to the newly formed Canada Development Investment Corporation (CDIC).

CDIC was created to address two very different problems. One problem consisted of firms with significant losses, notably the aerospace firms, De Havilland and Canadair. The other was government disenchantment with its lack of policy control over the mixed ownership CDC, a diversified holding company.[34] Some politicians viewed CDIC as a vehicle for industrial policy to use the earnings from Teleglobe to promote job creation in aerospace; others viewed it as a half-way house on the road to privatization.

The crisis at Canadair and De Havilland (purchased in a 1974 government bail-out) sparked reconsideration of their status. Officially both firms had been for sale since acquired by the government. A merger of the two firms was explored around 1983 to create a critical mass for design, development and production to survive in the aerospace industry. Canadair, despite its problems with the Challenger, had a good reputation in manufacturing and some marketing flair but was weak in complex design, while De Havilland was strong at design but weak in production and marketing. But the two firms had very different organizational cultures, and there was the delicate problem of where to put the head office to avoid offending Ontario or Quebec. The merger proposal languished.

Canadair's $1.2 billion debt was transferred to CDIC, and consultants helped it on cost control, operations, and market forecasts. Simultaneously the Liberal government reaffirmed its faith in the Challenger products, reminding critics of the industry consequences of the 1959 Arrow termination (Austin 1983).

When Sinclair Stevens, Minister for Regional Industrial Expansion (DRIE), announced that all CDIC holdings would be privatized within six months, DRIE officials sought buyers with strong financial resources and knowledge of the industry. Early on it became clear that the De Havilland sale could be expedited because there was a serious reputable buyer, Boeing Corporation. The stark December 1985 announcement of De Havilland's sale to a United States buyer turned into a political bombshell, especially in Ontario.

Meanwhile, the Canadair sale lagged, and uncertainty battered employee morale. In February 1986 Bombardier, which had not been on the original list of prospects, stepped forward as a bidder, advised by Donald Lowe, who had been on the Canadair board under the Liberals and who had proved himself in turnaround situations at Pratt & Whitney and Kidd Creek Mines. According to industry sources, Bombardier did not believe the federal government's commitment to privatization until De Havilland was actually sold and the government weathered criticism of that sale. Bombardier's bid for Canadair won in August 1986 and the final agreement was signed in December. The low sale price of $120 million drew some criticism. Canadair has prospered with Bombardier, winning a much disputed F-18 fighter maintenance contract and Airbus subcontracts while developing a regional jet based on stretching the Challenger, with loans of $86 million from government.

By contrast, Boeing experienced great difficulties getting De Havilland's production pace up and costs down. In 1991 Boeing sought to sell De Havilland to a state-owned consortium, Aerospatiale of France and Alenia of Italy, in order to focus on its traditional large jet market (Valorzi 1991). The take-over was blocked by European Community authorities. Subsequently Bombardier emerged as the buyer in partnership with the Ontario government.[35]

Teleglobe Canada[36]

Teleglobe Canada was established after the Second World War as a Crown corporation to control the overseas links of Canadian Marconi Company and Cable and Wireless Ltd. It enjoyed unusual autonomy as a Crown corporation. It was not subject to the regulatory authority of the Canadian Radio–Television and Telecommunications Commission (CRTC), but reported to Cabinet through the Department of Communications (DOC). Because it was profitable and self-financing, it was left very much on its own. It averaged over 40 per cent return on equity from 1975 to 1985; achieving net income of $53 million on revenues of $679 million in 1985. Critics argued that its overseas rates were 33 to 43 per cent higher than in the United States. With global competition, higher telecommunications costs could put Canadian-based firms at a disadvantage. When the Liberal government gave responsibility for Teleglobe Canada to the CDIC, the enabling legislation was never passed. Teleglobe Canada was CDIC's main cash-cow.

Around this time, Teleglobe management developed its own privatization scenario, consisting of a merger with Telesat Canada, the Canadian satellite carrier, 50 per cent owned by the government. The merged entity would be owned one-third by public shareholders, one-third by Telecom Canada (the trans-Canada association of domestic carriers) and one-third by the government. Teleglobe's championing of the proposal was unsuccessful. Teleglobe went on the selling block with Sinclair Stevens's 1984 declaration. If the policy rationale for divesting Teleglobe was unclear, so was the rationale for keeping it as a Crown corporation. The British government's announced intention to divest British Telecom eroded the original Commonwealth rationale for state owner-ship of external telecommunications.

Privatization of Teleglobe proved to be an unexpectedly long and complex process, largely because of unresolved policy questions: telecommunications policy, the post-divestment regulatory framework, potential foreign ownership and potential by-pass via foreign carriers, and potential concentration of ownership. Teleglobe managers were excluded from the process to resolve these issues. An incomplete policy framework was set before bidders in August 1985. Eleven formal bids were received, but conflict within the federal government over ownership by domestic carriers stalled the sale for a year. Two factors restarted the process. First, chance events removed the two key leaders of opposing policy factions. Second, dissatisfaction with the pace of privatization led to the creation of the Ministry of State for Privatization. Teleglobe was the first to go through the new centralized process. In November 1986, the government issued its second call for bids, this time setting forth a detailed policy framework on restricted domestic carrier and foreign ownership, employee shares, asset valuation, regulatory framework, tariff reduction, and a five-year continuance of a monopoly on overseas telecommunications. On 5 February 1986, CDIC recommended acceptance of Memotec Data's bid, worth $488 million. The sale was closed on 3 April 1987, 29 months after Stevens's initial announcement of intent to privatize CDIC holdings. Subsequently 30 per cent of the shares in Memotec were purchased by Bell Canada Enterprises (BCE), a member of the losing Telecom Canada team. While privatization of Teleglobe Canada ended federal ownership, provincial government ownership increased. The Quebec provincial pension fund, Caisse de dépôt et placement du Québec, acquired a direct 8 per cent in Memotec Data in addition to its existing 5 per cent stake in BCE (Ravensbergen 1991). Teleglobe has found adapting to rate of return tariff regulations unexpectedly bureaucratic at a time when deregulation of entry into telecommunications requires that it becomes more flexible to satisfy the diverse global communications needs of major clients. In 1991 and 1992 BCE tried to increase its effective control over Teleglobe through alliances with other parties, and displaced the original Memotec managers. Teleglobe's monopoly on overseas calls was renewed for five years.

Air Canada[37]

Air Canada was created in 1937 by an Act of the federal Parliament as a subsidiary of the Canadian National Railway. Between 1970 and 1976, top management tasks were divided between a chairman–chief executive officer (CEO) and a president–chief operating officer (COO). The firm shifted from an operations to a market orientation with emphasis on strategic planning. Simultaneously, it underwent massive decentralization and divisionalization. Morale suffered from heavy-handed reorganizational efforts. Allegations of mismanagement led to appointment of the Estey Commission to examine the airline. Justice Willard Estey found that the absence of key managers during crucial decisions contributed to poor communications, mismanagement and loss of control (Estey 1975).

The inquiry generated the political momentum needed to restructure the airline through the Air Canada Act 1977. The airline was separated from CNR and required to operate on sound business principles 'in contemplation of profit'. Government assumed $329 million of Air Canada's debt in return for 329,000 shares. Divestment from CNR and the commercialization of Air Canada's goals under the new Act legitimized management's drive for more autonomy.

This new phase coincided with Air Canada veteran Claude Taylor's term as CEO/COO. The period was marked by confrontation between management and government, notably over aircraft purchases and acquisition of subsidiaries such as Nordair in 1978 (Hafsi 1981). In 1984, Liberal Transport Minister Lloyd Axworthy announced that the industry would be deregulated and that Air Canada would no longer be the sole national carrier. Simultaneously, the airline began lobbying for government funding to finance a new fleet of fuel efficient aircraft to compete in the proposed deregulated environment. The request never got high priority from government. Faced with slow government decision-making in an industry undergoing deregulation and increased competition, Air Canada management suggested in its 1985 Annual Report that partial privatization could be an alternative source for its fleet financing (Ouellet 1989). Rival CP Air supported divestment to level the playing field. One possibility discussed in 1984/5 was to split Air Canada, retaining government control of the international side and selling the domestic operations to a rival. Sale of domestic routes to its rival was anathema to Air Canada managers, so the idea was dropped.

The momentum towards privatization halted in January 1985 when Prime Minister Brian Mulroney, emerging from a meeting with Louis Laberge of the Quebec Federation of Labour (FTQ), declared that Air Canada was not for sale (Langford and Huffman 1988: 122). No government decision to proceed could be made as long as the 1985 declaration remained fresh in the public mind. The Economic Council of Canada issued a report in 1986 recommending privatization of the airline. Air Canada set up an internal task force on privatization in 1987 and moved a key manager with Treasury Board experience from Montreal to Ottawa to work closely with OPRA. Months of preparation ended in summer 1987 when the federal Cabinet shied away from the go-ahead on privatization.

Meanwhile fare deregulation on competitive 'southern routes' in Canada went into effect. Pressure on government to act increased. Agreement was reached in January 1988, and in April Air Canada was allowed to announce an initial public share offering for autumn, amounting to 43 per cent of outstanding shares. The airline kept the $233.8 million proceeds to pay down debt and finance its new fleet.

The airline itself managed much of the divestment process, while government controlled the timing. Air Canada ordered feasibility studies to demonstrate that Air Canada could be sold and could be profitable, and commissioned three public opinion surveys to demonstrate that privatization could be politically popular. The company lobbied Members of Parliament and officials in government departments. It published an internal newsletter on privatization for employees and commissioned an in-depth survey of employees to assess support and identify areas of concern. Stakeholders' attitudes were analysed and fears allayed. Foreign ownership was capped at 25 per cent. Responding to union concerns on safety, management noted that safety rules were not being deregulated. The Finance Department needed convincing that a share issue the size of Air Canada could be absorbed by the market. Employees were assured that pensions would be unaffected by privatization. Skilfully switching issues to allay job security concerns, the firm devised a generous subsidized employee share purchase plan in which 17,000 of its 23,000 employees participated (Ouellet 1989: 22). To Atlantic Canada communities that feared a loss of service under privatization, the company argued that any change from jet service to feeder service would be due to competitive pressures caused by deregulation rather than privatization.

A second share issue in July 1989 privatized the remaining 57 per cent of Air Canada shares, with $474 million in proceeds going to the federal government. Since then, Air Canada's fortunes have mirrored those of the North American airline industry – the euphoria of 1989 giving way to the 1990 recession and lay-offs. Air Canada and PWA/Canadian Airlines confront the challenge of proposed 'open skies' airline competition within North America (Canada, House of Commons 1991) and predictions that the world airline industry will become concentrated around only six or seven giant carriers. Both seek larger American partners, and Air Canada also proposed a merger with its Canadian rival.

NOTES

1 The research has been supported by funding from the Canadian Centre for Management Development and the Social Sciences and Humanities Research Council. It is part of a larger study of managing divestment that is comparative across the public and private sectors and across countries, including Canada (federal and Quebec), France, Malaysia, The Netherlands, the United Kingdom, the United States, Senegal and Mexico. Thanks are due to other curent and former members of the HEC-McGill Public Sector Divestment Research Project: Ameur Boujenoui, Joelle Piffault, Pascal Beaudoin, Fang He, Roch Ouellet, Roberto Fachin, M. Shahid Bhatty, Michel Labelle, and Loralie Barker for their assistance and intellectual support.

2 For example, in 1984 the Quebec government dismantled a department, the Ministry of Public works (MPW), and transferred its activities to a new Crown corporation, Société Immobilière du Québec (SIQ) to promote efficiency, effectiveness and accountability (Dumas 1986).

3 Other CDIC interests included the government's shares in Canada Development Corporation (CDC), and holdings in portions of Massey-Ferguson/Varity, the agricultural equipment maker that the federal government bailed out in 1981.

4 Although much has been written about management of Crown corporations in Canada (Berkowitz and Kotowitz 1985, Boothman 1987, Brooks 1983, Hafsi et al. 1987, Kirsch 1985, Knubley 1987, Laux and Molot 1988, Sexty 1980), less is known about the privatization process (Doern and Atherton 1987, Hardin 1989, Hart 1985,

Richardson 1990, Schultz 1988, Sexty 1987, Stanbury 1989, Tupper and Doern 1988).

5   The increasing importance of divestment is illustrated in a sample of 50 United States firms covering the period 1960–86 (Taylor 1988). The total divestments undertaken by these firms numbered 41 for 1960–9, 141 for 1970–9 and 219 for 1980–6. Even more striking, the ratio of divestments to acquisitions rose from 0.09 in the era of conglomerates (1960–9), to 0.28 in the more turbulent 1970s and 0.59 from 1980–6. The trend in Canada is less pronounced. In 1988 there were 310 divestments and 1,301 acquisitions reported in Canada, for a ratio of 0.24; see Venture Economics Canada (1989: 2.1 and 2.42).

6   The key federal holding companies were the Canada Development Corporation (CDC) with more than a dozen key subsidiaries and the Canada Development Investment Corporation (CDIC) with six different holdings in 1984, including the government's shares in the mixed enterprise CDC. Other enterprises such as Petro-Canada and Canadian National Railways (CNR) had many subsidiary firms; CNR had holdings in hotels, trucking, real estate, ferries, and telecommunications. Enterprises with mixed public and private sector ownership included CDC and Telesat Canada.

7. Calculated from data in Canada, Treasury Board (1991) *Estimates 1991–92*; Part I: *The Government Expenditure Plan* (Ottawa: Minister of Supply and Services) 62. Note that the US billion (a thousand millions) is used throughout this chapter.

8   The smaller municipal public enterprises in transportation and utilities are excluded from these figures.

9   The calculation of return on assets was calculated by dividing the difference between gross revenues and expenses averaged over 1980–3 by the adjusted assets in 1983, using data found in Economic Council of Canada (1986: 157–64, Table B-1).

10 Earnings for large federal enterprises such as the Canadian National Railways and the Canadian Wheat Board are highly cyclical, depending on world wheat markets and general economic conditions, while VIA Rail and the Canadian Broadcasting Corporation require large subsidies for their operations.

11 In Tables 12.1–12.3, the sale of alcoholic beverages is classified under 'Commerce'; lotteries under 'Other services'. The federal government's attempt to enter the lottery business was derailed by provincial protests in the 1980s.

12 Hence the Caisse de dépôt operates like a private pension fund, with two major differences. First, it has aggressively used its status as government-owned enterprise to bypass security exchange regulations on trading and ownership. This has led to conflict with the Ontario securities regulatory body, when the Quebec fund acquired a large stake in firms listed on the Toronto Stock Exchange without notifying Ontario regulatory authorities. Second, although it seeks to maximize returns and enjoys operational autonomy from government intervention, it pursues socio-political as well as financial goals in its private investments, often in collaboration with SGF.

13 Studies of other provincial divestment programmes exist including the pioneering privatization programme in British Columbia in 1979 (Vining and Botterell 1983, Spindler 1980, Pitsula and Rasmussen 1990, Molot 1988, Maule 1987, Fotheringham 1989).

14 OPRA information kits include material on CNCP, Terra Nova, Northwestel, CN Route, and CN Hotels, although OPRA had no role in their sale, which was handled by the parent CNR.

15 A similar desire to relieve the public service of as much of the detail of the divestment process as possible can be seen in the Air Canada privatization, where management feared that leaving implementation details to the public service would cause unwanted delays.

16 Covenants were Canada's alternative to the British practice of government retaining a golden share. In cases requiring legislation to effect the sale, such as Air Canada, Teleglobe Canada, and Canadian Arsenals, detailed covenants covered items such as extent of foreign ownership, bilingual status, location of headquarters, and limits of sales of assets. By contrast, in the Canadair case the covenants were not in legislation but in the letter of intent for the sale to Bombardier.

17 See Ellsworth 1979, Gilmour 1973, and Tuzzolino 1988.

18 Ultimately the federal government subsidized part of both, giving Air Canada the proceeds of the first privatization phase and arranging a $86 million package for Bombardier for the development of Canadair's regional jet. Neither subsidy shows up on the budget as a contribution to a Crown corporation.

19 A high selling price for Teleglobe Canada to reduce the deficit would inflate the asset value on which CRTC-approved tariffs were based.

20 The bankruptcy of CN Route is under criminal investigation by the Royal Canadian Mounted Police (RCMP).

21 Calculated from data in Canada, House of Commons (1991) *Main Estimates, 1991–92*, Part I: 62. The decline is partly due to growing expenditures on public debt servicing. As a percentage of *programme* expenditure, public enterprise allocations declined from 8.6 to 4.8 per cent between 1982 and 1991.

22 For example, restructuring efforts at VIA Rail have been undermined by the continued stacking of the board with weak patronage appointees and indecision on the future role of government in rail passenger service.

23 Additional details of the cases and sources used may be found in Hafsi and Jörgensen 1992, and Hafsi and Demers 1990.

24 Taïeb Hafsi, Christiane Demers, and Roberto Fachin conducted the research on Sidbec-Normines. The main sources used were the following: Québec, Commission permanente de l'industrie, du commerce et du tourisme (1982); SECOR (1982); Farah (1982); Canada, Department of Energy, Mines and Resources (1985); Canada, Department of Regional Industrial Expansion (1985); Massobrio (1985); Sidbec, *Annual Report*, 1977, 1981, 1982, 1984, 1986; Sidbec-Dosco, Inc. *Annual Report*, 1987, 1988, 1989; and interviews with John Le Boutillier, President and Chief Executive Officer, Sidbec, 20 November 1985; Terence Dancy, former VP Technology, Sidbec-Normines, 22 April 1986; Georges H. Laferrière, VP Supplies and Engineering, Sidbec-Dosco, 23 April 1986; Paul E Landry, VP Finance and Administration, Sidbec, 23 April 1986; and Pierre Miville, former Treasurer, Sidbec-Normines, 29 April 1986.

25 Research on SAQ was conducted by Christiane Demers and Taïeb Hafsi and is based on newspaper accounts, and an interview with Ronald Asselin, head of the union for SAQ employees, June 1986. Officials of SAQ and the government declined to be interviewed because of litigation regarding the sale of SAQ outlets.

26 The Conseil de la Coopération du Québec (CCQ), which oversees the implementation of co-operative regulations, expressed some concern that the franchise system would not allow 'the autonomous and democratic operation of the co-op, nor the voluntary membership of workers' – basic tenets of the co-op movement.

27 The gradual shift in wine sales from provincially owned shops to grocery stores and the shift in postal services federal post offices to agents located in pharmacies are examples of what Eastern Europeans call 'privatization from below'.

28 Research on Québecair was conducted by Christiane Demers. Primary sources include interviews with a former manager of Québecair, a vice-president of Intair, two union representatives, and an official in the Quebec Ministry of Privatization plus the following: Québec, Comité conjoint sur la privatisation de Québecair (1986); Québec, Ministre délégué aux Finances et à la Privatisation (1986a, 1986b, 1988: 47–50).

267

29 Among the hardest hit were the 110 pilots who faced either lay-offs or a one-third cut in salary because of the change over from large jets to small Convair turbo-props.

30 PWA was itself a privatized regional carrier, formerly owned by the Alberta government.

31 Research on the Cambior case was conducted by Ameur Boujenoui. The main documents and primary sources include the following: SOQUEM, *Rapport d'activité de SOQUEM*, 1984, 1985, 1986, 1987; Québec, Ministre délégué aux Finances et à la Privatisation (1986c, 1986d and 1988); Raby (1987); Bernard and Gaudet (1988); Laurin (1988); and interviews with Raymond Raby, VP SOQUEM, 18 May 1988, and with Gilles Mercure, President of Cambior, 7 October 1988.

32 Some $100 million of the proceeds were applied to SOQUEM's debt.

33 The Canadair case was compiled by Pascal Beaudoin, Joelle Piffault, and Jan Jörgensen. Main documents and primary sources include the following: Canadair, *États Financiers Consolidés*, 31 December 1979; Canadair Ltd, *Consolidated Financial Statements*, 31 December 1982; Canadair, *Annual Report*, 1983, 1985; Shieldings Investments Ltd (1982); Austin (1983); Canada, Office of Privatization and Regulatory Affairs (1986 and 1988); and interviews with Robert Brown, Bombardier, 24 August 1989 and 12 October 1989, and Peter Sagar, Department of Industry, Science and Technology, Ottawa, 21 February 1990.

34 Because private investors held 14 per cent of common and all CDC preferred shares, CDC won significant autonomy and ceased to be subject to policy direction from the government.

35 Drew Fagan 'De Havilland rescue near', *Toronto Globe and Mail*, 8 January 1992, p. B-2.

36 The Teleglobe case was compiled by Jan Jörgensen. The main documents and sources include the following: Teleglobe Canada, *Annual Report*, 1980, 1985, 1986; Memotec, *Annual Report*, 1987; Ontario, Communications Division, Ministry of Transportation and Communications (1985); Canada, Department of Communications (1986); Canada, Office of Privatization and Regulatory Affairs (1987); and interviews with Leo Konomis and Richard Lebec, Office of Privatization and Regulatory Affairs, Ottawa, 25 May 1988; André Lapointe, Executive Vice-President Corporate Affairs, and Robert Séguin, Vice-President, Policy Planning and International Affairs, Teleglobe Canada Inc., 18 July 1989; and Simon Addey-Jibb, Executive VP, Finance and Administration, Teleglobe Canada Inc., 10 August 1989. An indispensable secondary source was Schultz (1988).

37 The Air Canada case study was compiled by Jan Jörgensen and Taïeb Hafsi. The main sources used include the following: Wood Gundy (1987); Air Canada, *Annual Report*, 1984, 1985, 1988, 1989, 1990; Air Canada, *Prospectus for Initial Public Offering*, 26 September 1988; Air Canada, *Prospectus for Secondary Offering*, 5 July 1989; and interviews with Howard Whitton, VP Corporate and Financial Planning, Air Canada, 1 September 1989; Claude Taylor, Chairman, Air Canada, 21 September 1989; Donald E. Ingham, Director of Investor Relations, Air Canada, 21 September 1989, and 19 July 1990. A vital secondary source was Langford and Huffman (1988).

REFERENCES

Austin, J. (1983) 'Canadair Ltd.', Report to the Standing Committee on Public Accounts of the House of Commons, Ottawa, 7 June, Ottawa, Senate Debates, 5755–72.

Berkowitz, M. K. and Kotowitz, Y. (1985) *The Organization and Control of Crown Corporations*, Discussion Paper No. 285 (July), Ottawa: Economic Council of Canada.

Bernard J. T. and Gaudet, G. (1988) 'SOQUEM: son mandat, contraintes et rentabilité', SOQUEM Doc. le 299, internal document, March.

Boothman, B. E. C. (1987) 'Strategy formation in Canadian government corporations in business', in Frank Hoy (ed.), *Academy of Management Best Papers Proceedings, 1987,* New Orleans: Academy of Management.

Borins, S. F. (1983) 'World War II Crown corporations: their functions and their fate', in R. Robert S. Prichard (ed.), *Crown Corporations in Canada: The Calculus of the Instrument of Choice,* Toronto: Butterworth & Co.

—— and Boothman, B. E. C. (1985) 'Crown corporations and economic efficiency', in D. G. McFetridge (ed.), *Canadian Industrial Policy in Action,* Toronto: University of Toronto Press for the Royal Commission on Economic Union and Development Prospects for Canada.

—— and Brown, L. (1986) *Investments in Failure,* Toronto: Methuen.

Brooks, S. (1983) 'The state as entrepreneur: from CDC to CDIC', *Canadian Public Administration* 26(4), 525–43.

Canada, Department of Communications (1986) *Canadian Telecommunications: An Overview of the Canadian Telecommunications Carriage Industry,* Ottawa, FS-86-3824E.

—— Department of Energy, Mines and Resources (1985) *Canadian Minerals Yearbook, 1983–1984,* Ottawa: Supply and Services.

—— Department of Regional Industrial Expansion (1985) 'The Canadian steel industry – past, present and future', Paper delivered at the Canadian Steel Trade Conference, Sault. Ste. Marie, 5–7 May.

—— House of Commons (1991) *Open Skies: Meeting the Challenge: Report of the Special Committee on Canada–United States Air Transport Services* (Robert Corbett, Chairman), Ottawa: Second Session of the Thirty-fourth Parliament, January.

—— Lambert Commission (1979) *Royal Commission on Financial Management and Accountability: Final Report,* Ottawa.

—— Office of Privatization and Regulatory Affairs (OPRA) (1986) *Information* (folder on Canadair), Ottawa, August.

—— —— (1987) *Information* (folder on Teleglobe), Ottawa.

—— —— (1988) *Privatized Corporations: Performance and Process,* Ottawa, January.

—— —— (1990) *Information* (folder), Ottawa.

—— Privy Council Office (1977) *Crown Corporations: Direction Control, Accountability,* Ottawa.

Coyne, J. and Wright, M. (1986) 'An introduction to divestment: the conceptual issues', in J. Coyne, and M. Wright (eds), *Divestment and Strategic Change,* Oxford: Philip Allan.

Doern, G. B. and Atherton, J. (1987) 'The Tories and the Crowns: restraining and privatizing in a political minefield', in M. J. Prince (ed.), *How Ottawa Spends, 1987–88; Restraining the State,* Toronto: Methuen.

Duhaime, I. M. and Grant J. H. (1984) 'Factors influencing divestment decision-making: evidence from a field study', *Strategic Management Journal* 5(4), 301–18.

Dumas, P. (1986) 'Nouvelle stratégie de l'administration publique québecoise: le cas de la création de la SIQ', Unpublished Master's Thesis, Ecole des Hautes Etudes Commerciales, Montreal.

Economic Council of Canada (1986) *Minding the Public's Business,* Ottawa.

Ellsworth, R. (1979) 'A note on the decision to divest', Boston: Harvard Business School, Case No. 9-379-167.

Estey, W. Z. (1975) *Air Canada Inquiry Report,* Ottawa, October.

Farah, S. E. (1982) *L'industrie du mineral de fer au Québec-Labrador; Etat de la situation,* Quebec: Ministère de l'energie et des ressources, November.

Fotheringham, A. (1989) 'Failed BCRIC has become a fallen brick', *Financial Post*, 23–5 December, p. 6.

Gilmour, S. C. (1973) 'The divestment decision process', Unpublished Doctoral Dissertation, Harvard University.

Hafsi, T. (1981) 'The strategic decision-making process in state-owned enterprises', Unpublished Doctoral Dissertation, Harvard University.

—— and Demers, C. (1989) *Le changement radical dans les organisations complexes: le cas d'Hydro-Québec*, Montreal: Gaëtan Morin.

—— —— (1990) 'Strategic divestments by government: a management process perspective', *Canadian Journal of Administrative Sciences* 7(3) 37–46.

—— and Jörgensen, J. J. (1990) 'L'état en mutation: désinvestir pour mieux agir', *Gestion* (Montreal) 15(3): 111–20.

—— —— (1992) *Managing Public Sector Divestment*, Ottawa: Canadian Centre for Management Development.

——, Kiggundu, M. N. and Jörgensen, J. J. (1987) 'Strategic apex configurations in state-owned enterprises', *Academy of Management Review* 12(4), 714–30.

Hall, P. (1986) *Governing the Economy: The Politics of State Intervention in Britain and France*, New York: Oxford University Press.

Hamermesh, R. (1975) 'Fuqua Industries (A)', Boston: Harvard Business School, Case No. 9-375-189.

—— (1976) 'The corporate response to divisional profit crises', Unpublished Doctoral Dissertation, Harvard University.

Hanna, J. A. (1987) 'Bill C-24 and Crown corporations', *CGA Magazine* Part I (February), pp. 18–23; Part II (March), pp. 24–9.

Hardin, H. (1989) *The Privatization Putsch*, Halifax: Institute for Research on Public Policy.

Harrigan, K. R. (1982) 'Exit decisions in mature industries', *Academy of Management Journal* 25(4), 707–32.

Hart, J. W. (1985) 'The process of privatization', in W. T. Stanbury and T. E. Kierans (eds), *Papers on Privatization*, Montreal: Institute for Research on Public Policy.

Hayes, R. H. (1972) 'New emphasis on divestment opportunities', *Harvard Business Review* 50 (July–August), 58–67.

Jörgensen, J. J. (1990) 'Managing privatization and deregulation: the telecommunications sector in Canada', in D. J. Gayle and J. N. Goodrich (eds), *Privatization and Deregulation in Global Perspective*, New York: Quorum Books.

Kingdon, J. W. (1984) *Agendas, Alternatives and Policy Choices*, Boston: Little, Brown.

Kirsch, E. (1985) *Crown Corporations as Instruments of Public Policy: A Legal and Institutional Perspective*, Discussion Paper No. 295 (December), Ottawa: Economic Council of Canada.

Knubley, J. (1987) *The Origins of Government Enterprise in Canada*, Discussion Paper No. 329, Ottawa: Economic Council of Canada.

Langford, J. and Huffman, K. (1988) 'Air Canada', in A. Tupper and G. B. Doern (eds), *Privatization, Public Corporations and Public Policy in Canada*, Halifax, Nova Scotia: Institute for Research on Public Policy.

Laurin, A. F. (1988) 'Allocution à l'occasion de Séminaire Andrien Pouliot', SOQUEM, March.

Laux, K. J. and Molot, A. M. (1988) *State Capitalism: Public Enterprise in Canada*, Ithaca, N.Y.: Cornell University Press.

Leconte, C. (1990) 'L'homme qui vole à contre-courant', *L'Actualité* (Montreal), June, pp. 45–7.

Lévesque, R. (1981) 'Le Québec economique dans un deuxième mandat', Colloque 1981, L'Ecole des Hautes Etudes Commerciales, Montreal, 31 October.

McDermid, J. (1989) 'Privatization: the purpose, the process' *Canadian Business Review*, 16 (Winter), 16–18.

McGovern, S. (1991) 'Leblanc resigns as president of Intair', *Montreal Gazette*, 8 March, D-1, D-3.

Massobrio, G. (President of Québec Cartier Mining) (1985) 'Iron ore: restructuring to meet the competition', Canadian Mineral Outlook Conference, Ottawa, 14 May.

Maule, C. J. (1987) 'Privatization – the case of the Urban Transportation Development Corporation Ltd', *Business Quarterly* 52(2), 26–32.

Miller, D. (1990) *The Icarus Paradox: How Exceptional Companies Bring About Their Own Downfall*, New York: Harper Business.

Mintzberg, H. and Jörgensen, J. T. (1987) 'Emergent strategy for public policy', *Canadian Public Administration* 30(2), 214–29.

Molot, A. M. (1988) 'The provinces and privatization: are the provinces really getting out of business?', in A. Tupper and G. B. Doern (eds), *Privatization, Public Policy and Public Corporations in Canada*, Halifax, Nova Scotia: Institute for Research on Public Policy.

Montgomery, C. and Thomas, A. R. (1988) 'Divestment: motives and gains', *Strategic Management Journal* 9(1), 93–7.

Morisset, P. (1986) 'Radiographie d'une privatisation', *L'Actualité* (Montreal), November, pp. 26–7.

Nadeau, M. (1983) 'Un réseau de franchises prendra la relève des 360 succursales de la SAQ; la "privatisation" ne serait plus qu'une question de mois', *Le Devoir* (Montreal), 30 November, p. 1.

Nees, D. (1981) 'Increase your divestment effectiveness', *Strategic Management Journal* 2(2), 119–30.

Ontario, Communications Division, Ministry of Transportation and Communications (1985) *The Privatization of Teleglobe Canada: Issues and Concerns*, Toronto.

Ostry, S. (1990) *Governments & Corporations in a Shrinking World; Trade & Innovation Policies in the United States, Europe & Japan*, New York: Council on Foreign Relations Press.

Ouellet, F. V. (1989) 'The privatization of Air Canada', *Canadian Business Review* 16 (Winter), 19–22.

Pitsula, J. and Rasmussen, K. (1990) *Privatizing a Province: The New Right in Saskatchewan*, Vancouver: New Star Books.

Porter, M. (1976) 'Please note location of nearest exit: exit barriers and planning', *California Management Review* 19(2), 21–33.

Prahalad, C. K. and Hamel, G. (1990) 'The core competence of the corporation', *Harvard Business Review* 90(3) (May–June), 79–91.

Prichard, R. S. (ed.) (1983) *Crown Corporations in Canada; The Calculus of the Instrument of Choice*, Toronto: Butterworth & Co.

Quebec, Comité conjoint sur la privatisation de Québecair (1986) *La privatisation de Québecair: L'état du dossier*, October.

—— Commission permanente de l'industrie, du commerce et du tourisme (1982) 'Audition en vue de la révision de l'orientation de Sidbec', *Journal des Débats*, Third Session, 32nd Legislature, nos 192 and 195, 10 and 11 November.

—— Minister Responsible for Privatization (1986) *Privatization of Crown Corporations: Orientation & Prospects*, Quebec: Ministry of Finance.

—— Ministre délégué aux Finances et à la Privatisation (1986a) 'Dossier Privatisation, Québecair:, 3 vols, Quebec: Ministry of Finance.

—— —— (1986b) 'Quatre offres pour Québecair', Communiqués de presse, no. 86-17.

—— —— (1986c) 'Les ministres Pierre Fortier et Raymond Savoie annoncent le processus de privatisation partielle de SOQUEM', Communiqués de presse, no. 86-09.

—— —— (1986d) 'Cambior – Symbole d'excellence du monde minier et des affaires', Communiqués de presse, no. 86-10.

—— —— (1988) *Privatisation des sociétés d'état' rapport d'étape, 1986–88*, Quebec: Ministry of Finance.

Raby, R. (1987) 'The role of state enterprises in the solid mineral industry of developing countries; headaches and successes of a state-owned mining exploration company', United Nations Inter-regional Seminar, Budapest, Hungary, 1–10 October.

Ramanadham, V. V. (1988) 'The concept and rationale of privatization', in V. V. Ramanadham (ed.), *Privatisation in the United Kingdom*, London: Routledge.

Ravensbergen, J. (1991) 'McKenzie's bitter struggle for control at Memotec', *Montreal Gazette*, 27 May, p. 3 (Business Section).

Richardson, J. J. (ed.) (1990) *Privatization and Deregulation in Canada and Britain*, Aldershot: Gower.

Ryan, M. G. (1987) 'Crown corporations: is the fog clearing'?, *Canadian Business Review* 14 (Summer), 31–4.

Schultz, R. (1988) 'Teleglobe Canada: selling the jewel in the Crowns', in A. Tupper and G. B. Doern (eds), *Privatization, Public Corporations and Public Policy in Canada*, Halifax, Nova Scotia: Institute for Research on Public Policy.

SECOR (1982) 'L'avenir de Sidbec-Normines: Un dossier d'analyse; une étude commanditée par Ville de Port Cartier, Ville de Gagnon, et La Corporation de développement économique de la région de Port Cartier, Gagnon et Fermont', Montreal, November.

Sexty, R. W. (1980) 'Autonomy strategies of government owned business corporations in Canada', *Strategic Management Journal* 1(4), 371–84.

—— (1987) 'The commercialization process in public enterprises', Academy of Management Association Meeting, New Orleans.

Shieldings Investments Ltd (1982) *Canadair Analysis* (public version), Toronto, October–November.

Spindler, Z. A. (1980) '"Bricking up" government bureaux and Crown corporations', in T. M. Ohashi and T. P. Roth, *Privatization: Theory & Practice*, Vancouver: Fraser Institute.

Stanbury, W. T. (1989) 'Privatization in Canada: ideology, symbolism or substance', in P. W. MacAvoy, W. T. Stanbury, G. Yarrow, and R. J. Zeckhauser (eds), *Privatization and State-Owned Enterprises*, Boston: Kluwer Academic Publishers.

Taylor M. L. (1988) *Divesting Business Units; Making the Decision and Making It Work*, Lexington, Mass.: Lexington Books.

Tupper, A. and Doern, G. B. (eds) (1988) *Privatization, Public Policy and Public Corporations in Canada*, Halifax, Nova Scotia: Institute for Research on Public Policy.

Tuzzolino, F. A. (1988) 'A contingency model of exit choice behavior of divesting firms', Unpublished Doctoral Dissertation, Arizona State University (Tempe).

Valorzi, J. (1991) 'Aircraft maker couldn't turn profit', *Montreal Gazette*, 16 April, D-8.

Venture Economics Canada (1989) *Mergers and Acquisitions in Canada; 1989 Edition*, Toronto: Venture Economics Canada Limited.

Vining, A. R. and Botterell, R. (1983) 'An overview of the origins, growth, size and functions of provincial Crown corporations', in R. R. S. Prichard (ed.), *Crown Corporations in Canada: The Calculus of the Instrument of Choice*, Toronto: Butterworth & Co.

Wilson, M. H. (1984) *A New Direction for Canada: An Agenda for Economic Renewal*, Ottawa: Department of Finance.

Wood Gundy (1987) *Air Canada Privatization Study*, 15 January.

13

PUBLIC–PRIVATE RELATIONS IN ITALY

The experience of the 1980s[1]

Luisa Segnana

INTRODUCTION

This chapter will attempt to describe the relationship between private and public sector companies in Italy as a basis for the following:

- comparison of dynamic processes of adjustment by private and state-owned enterprises during the 1980s.
- framing and measuring the privatization processes currently in progress in this country.

The public/private relationship, as well as the structure of the public sector in Italy, is crucial to an understanding of the nature and the characteristics of these national privatization processes.

Apart from the obvious point that privatization is high on the political agenda in Italy, this chapter has at least two reasons for re-examining the implications of the structure of ownership for the behaviour and performance of firms. First, over the past decade there have been significant advances in economic theory which are of relevance to the ownership question, including principal–agent theory, imperfect competition and regulatory theory. Second, technological and structural changes in a number of industries where public ownership is common indicate that a revaluation of policy options is in order. Some cases of 'failures of the market' are changed in the light of the frequent erosion of natural monopoly by technical progress; in other cases it is massive demand that no longer justifies the monopoly condition. Even the strategic role of some industries (for instance the steel industry) can nowadays be questioned. But there is a third reason, one that is now in the public domain in Italy and concerns the present passage taking place from a spontaneous approach to privatization pursued in the 1980s to a different, more planned programme of privatization induced by the overall Italian public deficit. And this passage requires evaluation of the nature and the relative importance of *government-led and enterprise-led privatization* processes,[2] especially where comparisons with other countries' experiences are concerned.

This chapter is organized as follows: the second section reviews some institutional features of the Italian system, focusing on the *sistema delle partecipazioni statali* (system of state-owned holdings or public agencies). Attention is drawn to two current features of state property rights and their significance for privatization policy: the diffused nature of these property rights and their indirectness. These two features are the key explanation of the difficulties and differential norms and procedures that state holdings and other public authorities had and have to face in pursuing privatization. They suggest that privatization processes should be analysed at different levels: those, for instance, of the privatization of state holdings and within state holdings. They also shed light on the present overcoming in Italy of the traditional dichotomy between *ente pubblico* and joint-stock company, the country's move towards a more frequent and widespread utilization of the *ente pubblico* organized as joint-stock company. The third section summarizes the development of the private and public sector companies in Italy, paying specific attention to the new characteristics that emerged during the 1980s. The fourth section examines these new characteristics from the point of view of the sources and applications of funds. On this basis, the fifth section outlines the evolution of privatization processes and proposes a measure for the relevance of the phenomenon during the 1980s for state holdings and industrial affiliates.

Inspection of the relationships between private and public sector companies shows the following. From the point of view of applications, whereas in private firms financial investment (and among them acquisition policy) was crucial in the 1980s for governing growth, this was not the case for state-controlled enterprises. This seems to be the basic distinction between private and public behaviour and it apparently qualifies recent economic results, both in terms of net financial expenses and in terms of external growth. From the point of view of financial sources, until 1988/9 both private and public sector companies displayed progressive substitution between external and internal sources of financing and, within the external sources, debts were substituted by equity. In this case, too, there were significant differences between state-owned firms and private enterprises: the former showed delayed adjustment both in terms of their generation of cash flow and for the differential nature of their shareholders' equity (endowment funds).

These results have a twofold significance: first, they mean that private and public firms drew closer in the 1980s, giving more financial autonomy to public sector companies. Second, they highlight two crucial points of difference between private and public sector companies in terms of financial investment and the differential ranking of financial sources. These results are important when related both to the identified nature and diffusion of property rights and to the government-led approach to privatization that is now emerging.

As regards the results of privatization, more detailed results at the group and company level are given which measure privatization processes for the three public agencies and their industrial affiliates. They show a generally increasing process for IRI, a changing tendency for ENI as a group but a constantly increasing privatization in its industrial affiliates, and erratic behaviour by EFIM. At the group level this indicates a negative correlation between the privatization of state holdings and its capacity to generate cash flow: the search for funds through privatization seems to be still high on the agenda of public agencies. At the same time, these results show that in the years 1989 and 1990 privatization processes shifted from the industrial affiliates level to the state-holdings level, which gives a quantitative evaluation of the characteristics of the processes currently in progress in Italy.

SOME INSTITUTIONAL FEATURES: THE DISTRIBUTION AND THE INDIRECT NATURE OF STATE PROPERTY RIGHTS

Italy provides an interesting case for a qualitative and quantitative assessment of private public relations for two essential reasons: her long historical and institutional background in private–public relationships dating back to the rescue operations conducted in the 1930s,[3] and the more recent debate on the nature and characteristics of national privatization processes. The scale (and the variety) of state-owned enterprises in this country is greater than anywhere else in Europe.

Some specifications are necessary regarding the Italian industrial system, because the notion of the state-owned sector is used in this chapter in the Italian sense.

The Italian public sector[4] comprises not only a large number of administrative bodies and independent public boards where state companies supply public services, both at national and local levels,[5] but also a large sector of manufacturing and service enterprises owned by public bodies. The Italian government controls this large sector through three holdings – IRI, ENI and EFIM – co-ordinated by the Ministry of State Holdings. These entities *manage* state shareholdings in industrial enterprises (joint-stock companies) like, for instance, those inherited through IRI, and in several service monopolies. These state holdings have a different legal status from that of the state: the term 'state-owned firms' in this case indicates the direct interest of the state in a firm, not direct legal ownership by the state.[6]

We therefore have two forms of diffusion of state property rights: the first relates to enterprises integrated into a government department; the second refers to enterprises and assets that are not held by the state itself but by distinct public legal persons. This second form[7] (which is the rule rather than the exception in some western countries), and specifically the case examined in this chapter of *enti di gestione di partecipazioni azionarie*, is quite peculiar to the Italian case: first, these entities act as public shareholders in wholly or partially owned joint-stock companies; second, they are characterized by features of *public law* whenever the relationship between the state itself and the state holdings is considered, and other features of *private law* when the relationships between state holdings and

275

third parties (employees, users) are taken into account.

These two forms of state property rights create three notions of 'public enterprises' typical of the Italian system: the public firm as an entity without a legal status; the public firm as a public holding agency (the holding, not the state, being the entrepreneurial agent); and the public firm as a joint-stock company, where the notion of 'public' is somewhat peculiar as it does not represent the legal *private* status of the joint-stock company.

From the standpoint of property rights, these three notions of public enterprises comprise a further implicit distinction between the diffusion of property rights among different public bodies and the indirect holding of such rights, through shareholdings by public entities in companies constituted under the ordinary forms of company law. This indirect holding system means that such subsidiaries, whether wholly or partly owned, are of course the property of the relevant enterprise, not of the state.

This chapter uses the expression 'public sector companies' or 'state-owned enterprises' to refer specifically to this set of enterprises, companies and firms, indirectly owned by the state through the state holdings, at different levels and in different ways. Therefore only the specific form of diffusion of property rights typical of the Italian state holdings system, and the latter two notions of public enterprises, are of relevance here.

The privatization process relates closely to these institutional aspects. It is well known that the same term, 'privatization', covers several distinct and possibly alternative ways to change the relationships between the government and the private sector. Among the most important of these are denationalization (a sale of publicly owned assets), deregulation (the introduction of competition into statutory monopoly), and contracting out (the franchising to private firms of the production of state-financed goods and services). This chapter takes privatization to be the sale of assets and therefore the transfer of ownership (total or partial) from 'public hands' to 'private hands', with particular reference to asset sales[8] by public sector enterprises.

Given Italy's peculiar institutional features, this may involve:

- The issue of state-holding shares, making room – when necessary – for the preliminary institutional and organizational passage from public entities to companies and their sale to the public.
- The share-trading of assets of joint-stock companies wholly or partly owned by state holdings.

These 'two levels' of privatization have different economic and political meanings: the privatization of state holdings ('cold privatization') and privatization within state holdings.[9]

The main point that emerges when the institutional analysis of state property rights is applied to the privatization debate is the present evolution towards the more frequent and widespread creation and utilization of the *ente pubblico* organized as joint-stock company. This evolution stems from at least two factors:

276

(1) the enlargement of the notion of *ente pubblico*, and (2) the progressive neutralization of the notion of joint-stock company. The chief characteristic of *ente pubblico* is that it is an entrepreneurial agent.[10] The joint-stock company does not find its distinguishing profile in its pursuit of profit maximization but in its distinction between the organization and goods of the company and the personal activity of the owner.[11] This 'neutralized' joint-stock company can therefore be utilized for a variety of objectives.

The privatization debate began in Italy in the context of industrial restructuring during the early 1980s under various different names; years in which even the Ministry of State Holdings drew attention to the fact that government was losing control of the financial and management situation of state enterprises. Various forms of privatization were then devised and introduced as *spontaneous and enterprise-led* processes concerning the share-trading of assets of joint-stock companies wholly or partly owned by state holdings and ranging from the complete sale of firms to the sale of minority stakes on the market. The framework for this process was mainly the effort to reorder the 'public' industrial system undertaken in the 1980s. The problem of the Italian overall deficit has now changed this framework, and it constitutes a strong incentive to privatize as a measure intended to reduce the government or public sector deficit. This implies a shift towards a more *planned and government-led* programme of privatization; one that not only seeks to define a programme for privatizing industrial affiliates but also initiates statutory changes in state holdings in order to proceed with the issue and trading of their shares.

DEVELOPMENT OF PRIVATE AND PUBLIC SECTOR COMPANIES IN ITALY

Four basic historical periods can be identified:[12] the first covering the years 1950–64 (the period of post-war reconstruction and the so-called 'economic miracle'); the second, the years 1964–75; the third, the years 1975–83; and the fourth from 1983 till now (see next section). Only the last three periods are considered here because it was with the beginning of the 1960s that state intervention became more intense and widespread. The oil-shock crisis marks the end of the second period, and the second major recession of the Italian economy marks the end of the third.

After the Second World War, state ownership was viewed in Italy as a way to promote economic development and balanced economic growth not as a simple and direct response to the failure of private markets to secure efficient outcomes. The presence of the state was considered inevitable (and tacitly justified by the private sector) in sectors with high financial requirements in order to provide assistance to industrial firms and supporting services, including public utilities and energy sources.[13]

The electricity industry was nationalized in 1962, a measure which deeply affected the economic system and which led to a widespread 'fear of nationalization', as well as to the significant reinvestment of financial resources by firms relatively poorly endowed with strategic management.

During the years 1964–75 there was an expansion of public intervention in pursuit of planning objectives, the most important of these being intervention for the modernization of agriculture and infrastructure in the south of Italy.[14]

The government's 1966–70 programme, on the one hand, used the public firms as instruments to accomplish its aims, while in the other there was a clear requirement to safeguard the entrepreneurial function and to operate according to rigorous criteria of cost-effectiveness.[15] At the same time the powers of control exercised by the Ministry of State Holdings were increased.[16] These guidelines translated into increasing political control combined with conflicting objectives assigned to public firms, at least in terms of the above-mentioned rigorous economic criteria to safeguard. Financial incentives generated a negative real interest rate and the growth of firms was basically debt-oriented. Tax relief and credit facilities for investment made it more advantageous to locate the petro-chemical and steel industries – both capital intensive – in the south of the country.

These elements produced their effects at the beginning of the 1970s through the following developments in the public sector:

- the progressive abandonment of benchmark accounting data and cost-effectiveness constraints for evaluation of their performances;
- the beginning of an intense process of acquisition of troubled private industrial firms,[17] mostly undergoing through productive and financial crisis;
- the start of increasing requirements for endowment funds in order to meet their increasing financial requirements;[18]

These points summarize the private-public relationship in the period: collusive on one side, as far as real transfers of firms in the hands of public sectors are concerned, and competitive on the other as competition for available financial assistance increased.

This was certainly not an easy period for private sector firms. After the postwar stage of private sector acceptance and justification for state-owned industry, the seventies were difficult years for Italian private industry. The weakness of the

Table 13.1 Public and private sector companies in Italy

	Public companies			Private companies		
	1968	1975	1983	1968	1975	1983
Financ./expenses/sales (%)	6.9	9.4	4.6	2.4	4.7	2.1
Net profit, (loss)/sales (%)	0.0	−6.0	−3.9	1.5	−2.3	0.0
Debts/net worth (no. of times)	2.3	9.0	1.8	0.9	2.7	1.0

Source: Based on Mediobanca (1990), *Dati cumulativi di 1743 società italiane.*

Table 13.2 Employment by major Italian private and state-owned groups

Private	1979	1983	1985	1989
Fiat*	357,836	263,760	226,222	286,294
Montedison	117,943	76,890	69,653	22,049
Pirelli	72,867	67,275	62,314	70,566
Olivetti	59,070	48,781	48,944	56,937
Zanussi	32,650	28,000	19,417	15,263
Snia	30,737	19,653	17,800	10,834
Bastogi	25,494	15,183	10,808	1,387
Philips	18,046	14,658	13,085	5,172
Michelin	15,036	13,565	11,683	10,101
Falck	16,108	12,608	9,497	7,987
Piaggio	11,915	11,706	7,552	7,805
Rizzoli[†]	10,415	9,092	7,378	5,430
State owned				
Agip	3,796	5,426	5,613	5,990
Stet	132,908	133,100	133,200	122,653
Agip Petroli	5,168	5,934	5,966	4,058
Snam	11,745	13,308	14,866	15,876
Finsider	110,333	15,898	–	–
SME	22,519	19,174	15,365	20,056
Saipem	10,662[‡]	10,898	10,051	7,898
Rai	13,790	14,626	14,636	14,738
Fincantieri	32,854	25,564	24,643	21,579
Breda	6,015	7,929	7,669	6,915
Agusta	9,043	10,561	9,776	9,826
Nuovo Pignone	6,438	6,674	6,490	5,833

Source: Ricerche & Studi, *R&S* (various years).
Notes: *Includes foreign subsidiaries.
[†]RCS Editori since 1986.
[‡]Data for 1980.

ownership structures of the main industrial groups, due in many cases to cross-participation and the strength of industrial relations in 1969–1973, led to an increase in labour costs and to inflexibility in the use of labour. Profits also declined and financial indebtedness rose significantly (see Table 13.1).

The mid-1970s[19] saw the following elements reach maturation:

- the limitations of the debt-oriented growth of Italian firms, giving rise, in 1975, to a sort of 'liquidity crisis' among some traditional and leading Italian groups;
- the limitations of the productive decentralization policies pursued by large Italian firms at the beginning of the seventies in order to maintain a better control over contractual relationships.

The first oil shock occurred in a situation of relative financial fragility and industrial rigidity in Italian industry, at both the private and public levels. Real

Table 13.3 Balance sheet structures of leading Italian groups, 1975

						Composition of total assets (%)								
	a	b	(a+b)	(*)	(**)	c		d	e	(d+e)	(***)	f	Oth.	(b+c−f)
Fiat	42.8	38.3	81.1	8.3	0.0	10.6	100.0	25.6	26.2	51.8	24.8	19.5	3.9	29.4
Montedison	55.5	25.7	81.3	6.0	7.3	5.5	100.0	9.0	13.4	22.4	34.5	39.5	3.6	−8.3
Olivetti	23.8	59.2	82.9	16.0	0.0	1.0	100.0	18.5	24.6	43.1	28.7	27.9	0.3	32.3
Pirelli	47.1	49.9	96.9	3.1	0.0	0.0	100.0	42.4	7.4	49.8	29.7	13.6	6.9	36.3
Snia	55.2	24.2	79.4	12.8	7.2	0.6	100.0	16.0	12.8	28.8	45.1	26.1	0.0	−1.3
Sir/Rumianca	90.8	−6.6	84.2	5.3	4.7	5.8	100.0	15.6	1.7	17.3	67.0	15.5	0.2	−16.2
Liquigas	80.7	11.3	92.0	4.3	0.0	3.7	100.0	3.4	3.9	7.4	61.7	30.6	0.4	−15.6
Monti	70.1	22.2	92.3	6.6	0.7	0.5	100.0	20.2	5.7	25.9	26.5	47.3	0.3	−24.6
Pesenti	50.1	6.1	56.2	41.1	0.3	2.4	100.0	25.3	7.7	32.9	11.5	51.2	4.4	−42.7
Falck	49.1	39.1	88.1	11.3	0.0	0.6	100.0	32.5	29.1	61.6	16.8	21.4	0.2	18.2
Burgo	69.9	18.7	88.6	10.5	0.6	0.3	100.0	28.4	14.8	43.2	22.2	34.7	0.0	−15.7
Zanussi	42.6	47.7	90.3	7.3	0.0	2.4	100.0	22.5	17.3	39.8	16.1	44.1	0.1	6.0
Marzotto	57.2	36.2	93.4	4.4	0.5	1.8	100.0	41.0	16.7	57.8	32.9	9.3	0.1	28.7
Galbani	38.1	30.5	68.6	2.3	2.3	26.8	100.0	46.6	44.0	90.5	9.5	0.0	0.0	57.3
Barilla	47.2	41.0	88.3	7.8	0.0	3.9	100.0	46.0	20.5	66.5	21.5	5.1	6.8	39.8
Total	56.3	28.0	84.2	7.9	2.6	5.1	100.0	20.3	14.1	34.4	35.2	27.5	2.9	5.7

Source: Coltorti (1988).

Notes: a = net fixed assets; b = working capital; c = cash in hand and with banks and fixed interest securities; d = shareholders' equity; e = staff severance indemnity fund; f = short-term financial debts; (*) = equity and financial investments; (**) = other assets; (***) = medium- and long-term debts; Oth. = other liabilities; (b+c−f) = balance of current assets and liabilities.

restructuring was to constitute – in the second half of the 1970s – the answer and the turning point.[20] The aim of this restructuring was to increase the flexible utilization of the labour force via plans for the substitution and modernization of capital equipment,[21] and, at the end of the 1970s, to achieve productive reorganization, mainly of private Italian groups.

The outcome was the increased flexibility[22] of the industrial system. The private sector was the first to take this opportunity: state enterprises were principally involved in staple industries in which the decentralization of production and reorganization processes were more difficult to accomplish. These firms faced longer-term constraints in the form of trade union inflexibility and their traditional role as an employment buffer during recession (see Table 13.2).[23] The 1970s also revealed the effects of previous purchases of businesses by the private sector. Thus public sector firms continued to post heavy losses, reaching an all-time low during 1981–3; private sector large firms were the first to give more favourable balance sheet results, after 1983/4.

However real restructuring does not account for another aspect – sometimes called financial restructuring – which proceeded quite slowly after 1975 but with important consequences. Again it was the private sector that seized the opportunity first. Restructuring plans, apart from their productive purpose of increasing flexibility, developed at two levels: organizational–hierarchical, and the financial.[24]

Providing behavioural detail of these aspects necessarily requires a shift of analysis to the group level, the most adequate unit of analysis. The results are anticipated now and will be fully explained in the next section: on the one hand, new forms of real and entrepreneurial decentralization with wide managerial autonomy were realized and, on the other, there was strong centralization of financial flows management.

The situation of leading Italian groups in 1975 (see Table 13.3) shows that strong inflationary pressure had amplified the structural financial fragility of the industrial system, especially among large-sized groups, which were the most heavily indebted. This exacerbated the already-mentioned weaknesses of property control, with the result that the most heavily indebted groups were removed from the market. This process involved the three groups that had achieved the most growth in the post-war period, mostly debt-financed. Other groups either had to sell large amounts of their assets or were compelled to undertake a complete change of ownership.

At the group level, a positive correlation can be drawn from Table 13.3 between the 'liquidity crisis' and the change in property rights (which had also entailed a change from national to foreign control). Behind the organizational and financial lines of restructuring there lay a stringent selection process, which pressed for the reorganization of production processes in order to safeguard against similarly severe and explosive liquidity crises.

The reasons for the recovery of surviving groups in the second half of the 1970s can be summarized in terms of financial resources,[25] as follows:

Table 13.4 Balance sheet structures of leading Italian groups, 1986

						Composition of total assets (%)							
	a	b	(a+b)	(*)	(**)	c		d	e	(d+e)	(***)	f	Oth.	(b+c−f)
Fiat	36.2	13.3	49.5	7.5	19.6	23.5	100.0	43.2	10.5	53.8	19.9	19.8	6.6	17.0
Montedison	50.2	9.7	59.8	11.3	5.5	23.3	100.0	28.1	8.1	36.2	39.2	20.4	4.3	12.6
Olivetti	18.0	30.6	48.6	2.2	–	49.1	100.0	44.3	9.1	53.5	34.1	9.6	2.9	70.1
Ferruzzi	30.8	30.9	96.9	3.1	0.0	0.0	100.0	16.6	1.5	18.1	38.7	37.8	5.4	9.1
Pirelli	52.7	33.0	79.4	12.8	7.2	0.6	100.0	45.5	8.2	53.7	21.0	23.1	2.2	20.7
Cir	9.5	11.3	84.2	5.3	4.7	5.8	100.0	44.7	2.4	47.1	40.7	9.3	3.0	47.2
Snia	41.9	28.1	92.0	4.3	0.0	3.7	100.0	47.7	7.4	55.1	26.4	18.1	0.3	32.0
Pesenti	26.6	12.6	92.3	6.6	0.7	0.5	100.0	67.2	4.5	71.7	16.1	12.2	0.0	39.8
Falck	46.7	41.8	56.2	41.1	0.3	2.4	100.0	47.7	6.1	53.8	21.2	16.7	8.3	29.8
Burgo	56.2	31.1	88.1	11.3	0.0	0.6	100.0	55.5	8.9	64.5	26.8	7.4	1.4	34.3
Marzotto	43.6	38.6	88.6	10.5	0.6	0.3	100.0	42.8	11.3	54.1	31.0	11.5	3.5	39.8
Galbani	16.7	8.7	90.3	7.3	0.0	2.4	100.0	82.6	13.3	95.9	0.3	0.0	3.8	82.1
Fininvest	59.9	−7.6	93.4	4.4	0.5	1.8	100.0	24.7	4.5	29.2	22.5	6.8	41.6	24.5
Barilla	35.2	18.1	23.8	23.8	1.5	21.4	100.0	56.1	14.8	70.8	5.4	18.1	5.6	21.3
Total	36.6	19.0	55.6	9.6	8.8	26.0	100.0	40.1	8.2	48.3	27.8	19.0	4.9	26.0

Source: Coltorti (1988).

Notes: a = net fixed assets; b = working capital; c = cash in hand and with banks and fixed interest securities; d = shareholders' equity; e = staff severance indemnity fund; f = short-term financial debts; (*) = equity and financial investments; (**) = other assets; (***) = medium- and long-term debts; Oth. = other liabilities; (b+c−f) = balance of current assets and liabilities.

Table 13.5 Balance sheet structures of Italian private and public sector companies, 1990

	a	*b*	*a+b*	*(*)*	*c*	*(*)+c*	*Oth.*	

	a	*b*	*a+b*	*(*)*	*c*	*(*)+c*	*Oth.*	
1770 co.	31.7	29.3	61.0	21.6	6.3	27.9	11.1	100.0
Private	21.0	29.0	50.0	27.9	8.9	36.8	13.2	100.0
State owned	45.4	29.7	75.1	13.6	3.0	16.6	8.3	100.0
Manuf. co.	20.9	36.5	57.4	24.6	6.5	31.1	11.5	100.0
Service co.	77.8	−1.3	76.5	8.9	5.2	14.1	9.4	100.0
	d	*e*	*(***)*	*f*	*(***)+f*	*Oth.*		
1770 co.	36.3	6.1	23.4	9.5	32.9	24.7	100.0	
Private	42.8	6.7	18.2	12.5	30.7	19.8	100.0	
State owned	28.1	5.3	30.0	5.7	35.7	30.9	100.0	
Manuf. co.	36.6	6.0	19.9	11.2	31.1	26.3	100.0	
Service co.	35.0	6.4	38.7	2.1	40.8	17.8	100.0	

Source: Based on Mediobanca (1991).
Notes: *a* = net fixed assets; *b* = net working capital; *(a+b)* = industrial assets; *c* = cash in hand and with banks and fixed interest securities; *d* = shareholders' equity; *e* = staff severance indemnity provisions fund; *f* = short-term financial debts; *(*)* = equity and financial investments; *(*)+c* = financial assets; *(***)* = medium- and long-term debts; *(***)+f* = financial debts; *Oth.* = other assets or liabilities.

- a progressive increase in shareholders' equity, initially correlated to short-term financial equilibrium and later aimed at the consolidation of previous, relatively fragile, controlling shareholding;
- a strong reduction in net working capital;
- a substantial increase in cash in hand and with banks and marketable securities.

This increased attention paid to short-run financial equilibrium in fact indicated a closer concern for liability management.

The other level of restructuring – organization–hierarchical – continued between 1975 and 1983,[26] enabling corporate restructuring towards a form of private group which was quite often reorganized by a central holding (the parent company) and by autonomous industrial affiliates. This freed some industrial enterprises from very large industrial investments by sharing these out and orienting new industrial groups towards more flexible structures.[27]

Both these lines basically represented a disintegration process within Italian private industry which took place during the second half of the 1970s.

RECENT ECONOMIC RESULTS

The last period considered starts in 1983, the year when the 1980–3 recession of the Italian economy came to an end.

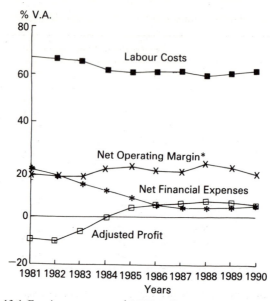

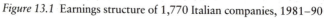

Figure 13.1 Earnings structure of 1,770 Italian companies, 1981–90

Source: Based on Mediobanca (1991).
Note: *Net of ordinary depreciation.

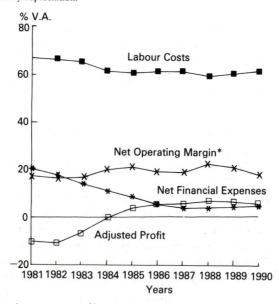

Figure 13.2 Earnings structure of large private and state-owned companies in Italy, 1981–90

Source: Based on Mediobanca (1991).
Note: *Net of ordinary depreciation.

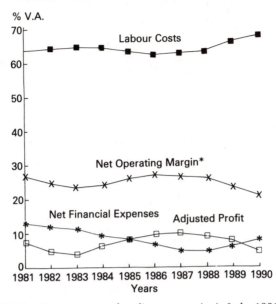

Figure 13.3 Earnings structure of medium companies in Italy, 1981–90

Source: Based on Mediobanca (1991).
Note: *Net of ordinary depreciation.

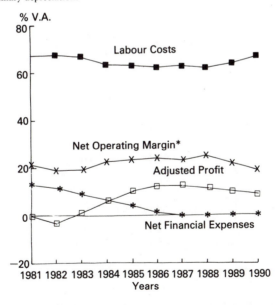

Figure 13.4 Earnings structure of private companies in Italy, 1981–90

Source: Based on Mediobanca (1991).
Note: *Net of ordinary depreciation.

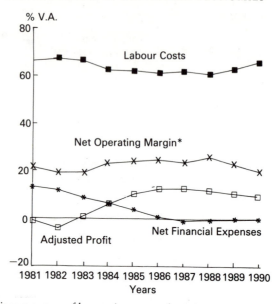

Figure 13.5 Earnings structure of large private manufacturing companies in Italy, 1981–90

Source: Based on Mediobanca (1991).
Note: *Net of ordinary depreciation.

Figure 13.6 Earnings structure of medium private manufacturing companies in Italy, 1981–90

Source: Based on Mediobanca (1991).
Note: *Net of ordinary depreciation.

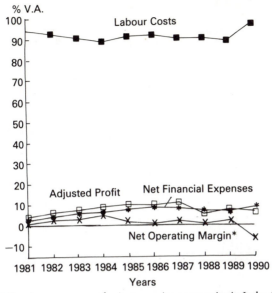

Figure 13.7 Earnings structure of private service companies in Italy, 1981–90

Source: Based on Mediobanca (1991).
Note: *Net of ordinary depreciation.

Figure 13.8 Earnings structure of state-owned companies in Italy, 1981–90

Source: Based on Mediobanca (1991).
Note: *Net of ordinary depreciation.

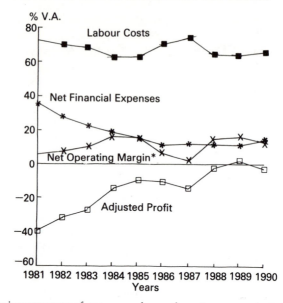

Figure 13.9 Earnings structure of state-owned manufacturing companies in Italy, 1981–90

Source: Based on Mediobanca (1991).
Note: *Net of ordinary depreciation.

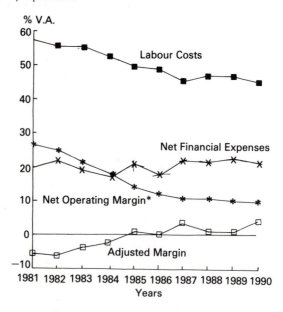

Figure 13.10 Earnings structure of state-owned service companies in Italy, 1981–90

Source: Based on Mediobanca (1991).
Note: *Net of ordinary depreciation.

The private group situation is well summarized by Table 13.4 for 1986 and can be compared with Table 13.3 for 1975. The situation of private and public sector companies can be also compared for year 1990 in Table 13.5.

State-owned groups and firms underwent the kind of delayed readjustment processes that have been depicted since the beginning of the 1980s. At the same time the Planning Report for State Holdings Enterprises for 1987 tried to redefine the complex interactions among the goals of state-owned enterprises considered to be crucial and their operating conditions.[28] This redefinition revived the old post-war evaluation of the weakness of private human and financial resources and the need for direct state intervention in order to support productive operations that no other single private agent could undertake on an appropriate scale. And this happened in the presence of a private sector in good shape, with no similarities to its immediate post-war conditions.

The aggregation between private and state-owned firms shows this delay. Starting with the 1,770 companies (private and state owned) selected by the Mediobanca sample (see Figures 13.1, 13.2 and 13.3), it is possible to show the processes of adjustment[29] of private vs state-owned enterprises. Note, on the one hand, the disaggregation of the private sector among large and medium manufacturing companies (Figures 13.4, 13.5 and 13.6) and, on the other, the disaggregation of public sector companies between manufacturing companies and service enterprises (Figures 13.7, 13.8, 13.9 and 13.10).

The differences between private and state-owned firms at the beginning of the 1980s are striking with respect to the relative incidence of both net financial expenditures and net operating margin. The recovery is impressive as well: after 1984 private companies drastically reduced their net financial expenses and increased their margin of profit, which they maintained – after 1986 – at a 10 per cent average level. The recovery of state-owned enterprises was much slower, although it shows a trend towards improved net operating margin and profits. When disaggregations are examined, they show that most private performances come from large private industrial firms, and most state-owned adjustments from service companies.

When these results are evaluated by means of a source/application framework (see Table 13.6), two tendencies emerge. First, the restructuring of assets: the weight of industrial assets (net fixed assets and net working capital) progressively decreased from an average of 80–90 per cent of total assets in the 1970s to an average of 55 per cent.[30] This tendency was also stronger at the group level than at the company level.[31] Again the distinction between private and public sector companies is important, since private companies reduced their share of industrial assets quite drastically in line with the groups' results; state-owned firms, by contrast, increased them by more than 10 percentage points.[32]

The other tendency is the recomposition of the financial resource structure, showing an increasing role of internal resources matched by a decreasing share of the debt to equity ratio.

Examination of the 1980s with particular reference to the state-holding

Table 13.6 Sources and applications of funds in 1,770 Italian companies (per cent of composition)

	1770 companies			Private companies			State-owned companies		
	1982–84	1985–87	1988–90	1982–84	1985–87	1988–90	1980–82	1983–85	1986–88
Capital expenditure	54.8	63.2	56.9	45.1	45.1	40.9	65.7	94.6	81.9
Financial investments	12.1	24.1	31.4	11.0	33.2	43.4	13.3	8.2	12.6
Increase in liquid assets	13.3	7.8	0.9	23.4	9.9	0.7	2.1	4.0	1.4
Increase in net working capital	19.8	4.9	10.8	20.5	11.8	15.0	18.9	–6.8	4.1
Total funds	100.0	100.0	100.0	100.0	100.0	100.0	100.0	100.0	100.0
Cash flow	32.2	67.5	55.4	53.9	71.1	58.9	7.9	61.2	49.9
Funds provided by shareholders	23.0	13.5	9.2	7.4	8.1	7.0	40.5	22.9	12.6
Grants	6.4	5.7	4.8	3.7	3.0	2.4	9.4	10.4	8.2
Increase in financial debts	30.3	9.4	24.5	26.7	11.9	24.8	34.3	5.1	24.2
Increase in other liabilities	8.1	3.9	6.1	8.3	5.9	6.9	7.9	0.4	5.1
Total resources	100.0	100.0	100.0	100.0	100.0	100.0	100.0	100.0	100.0

Source: Based on Mediobanca (1991).

system can be framed by these two tendencies. The following subsection focuses on two flows of assets: capital expenditure and financial investment. The differences between these two forms of growth seem to be a distinctive feature of private versus the public behaviour in Italy. The next subsection draws attention to the recomposition of financial flows of resources.

Investment activity by leading groups in Italy: state-owned versus private groups?

Attention focused on acquisition activity during the 1980s could be the necessary completion to analysis of industrial restructuring[33] for two reasons: first, the temporal correspondence between the completion of restructuring programmes and the acquisition activity is clear; second, it helps to clarify the changing perspectives for industrial structure that emerge from restructuring.

Accordingly, this subsection identifies expenditures on acquisitions by the leading groups operating in Italy through quantification of their weight and relative importance with respect to capital expenditures, and by outlining their main qualitative aspects.

This requires the solution of various problems:[34] first, from an historical perspective because we are dealing with a changing structure of groups; second, from a methodological point of view since the possibility of data comparison among groups is very limited.

Although the approach utilized here[35] is mainly methodological in nature, it can be used to give a first quantitative analysis of a phenomenon – the external growth of industrial groups in Italy – that has had a profound effect on both Italy and other industrial countries. When this methodology and its implementation is applied at a disaggregated level, it allows adequate inter-firm and sectoral comparison; comparison that, as far as I know, has not been conducted to any significant extent in Italy.[36] At the same time, when this methodology is applied at the aggregate level as well, it can provide the basis for analysis of changing ownership structure and of financial concentration. It also enables us to make comparisons among the data that emerge – on different bases – from national accounts and balance of payments. The methodological approach reconstructs panel data on expenditures on tangible fixed assets and acquisitions of leading business groups operating in Italy in the years 1981–8. A new methodology is therefore introduced in order to make a comparable data reconstruction. On this basis, the conclusions raise a number of issues concerning the results presented here with respect to aggregate and firm-level analysis.

The method of analysis suggests shifting from a take-over approach to external growth, to an acquisition approach. Only in this way is it possible to include that huge number of operations that do not necessarily entail control by an external firm but which may sometimes sum up the many forms of intra-firm agreement that can create a 'community of interest', like sharing technology information, tacit collusion, co-operative control.

The set of groups analysed was first obtained by ranking the eighty leading

Table 13.7 Percentage share of expenditures on fixed assets and acquisitions by
63 industrial groups according to ownership characteristics

Year	1981	1982	1983	1984	1985	1986	1987	1988
Privately owned								
Total	100.0	100.0	100.0	100.0	100.0	100.0	100.0	100.0
Investment	86.9	87.3	86.0	86.6	75.8	54.9	80.2	76.7
Acquisition	13.1	12.7	14.0	13.4	24.2	45.1	19.8	23.3
State-owned								
Total	100.0	100.0	100.0	100.0	100.0	100.0	100.0	100.0
Investment	84.8	83.3	87.7	74.1	70.4	89.9	85.3	92.7
Acquisition	15.2	16.7	12.3	25.9	29.6	10.1	14.7	7.3
Foreign-owned								
Total	100.0	100.0	100.0	100.0	100.0	100.0	100.0	100.0
Investment	98.9	94.3	99.3	93.6	92.0	94.6	83.5	82.7
Acquisition	1.1	5.7	0.7	6.4	8.0	5.4	16.5	17.3
63 groups								
Total	100.0	100.0	100.0	100.0	100.0	100.0	100.0	100.0
Investment	86.8	85.2	97.9	79.0	73.4	72.9	83.0	84.7
Acquisition	13.2	14.8	12.1	21.0	26.6	27.1	17.0	15.3

Source: Author's calculations on *R&S* data (various years).

groups in Italy on the basis of their 1984 sales, the period considered being
1981–8. Some specific constraints on the possibility of data reconstruction
allowed the analysis of those sixty-three groups listed (methodological details of
this subsection are in Segnana (1990)).

The methodological approach adopted here isolates capital expenditure and
acquisitions which are, respectively, additions to tangible fixed assets and
purchases of equities from third parties. There are three steps involved: first,
analysis of the group structure; second, identification of expenditures on tangible
fixed assets and on acquisitions; and third, quantitative and qualitative
comparison between the two series.[37]

The acquisitions and capital expenditures of sixty-three groups in the period
1981–8 are now examined (see Table 13.7). Two sets are considered: the first
includes all groups. This is the main datum-point, as it refers to leading groups
whose 1988 investment amounted to 71 per cent of the investment in the Mediobanca sample.[38] Within these sixty-three groups, a second set is considered which
comprises all the groups characterized by a holding[39] for which it was possible to
reconstruct the whole series 1981–8: twenty-one holdings are therefore given full
consideration for the period.[40]

The results provide a first quantitative analysis of the flows at aggregate and sectoral level, and a qualitative and quantitative analysis of the behaviour of holdings.

Two comments are in order.

The first concerns the size of acquisitions and their share. The positive aggregate dynamics of this flow is clear enough, since it reaches its maximum in the years 1984–6. In these aggregate dynamics, public (state owned) and private-owned groups behave very differently: private groups show positive rates of growth at least from 1982 onwards, while an alternate dynamic characterizes public (state owned) and foreign groups.[41] This can be fully specified when one observes that the share of acquisitions is remarkably different among different types of groups (see Table 13.7). Although at the aggregate level the share of these two flows of resources does not seem to have changed very much, the relative importance of acquisitions for private groups increased by about 10 percentage points between 1981 and 1988 and, in parallel, the weight of invest-ment decreased. By contrast, public groups still continued to increase their share of expenditures on fixed assets, reaching a share of more than 90 per cent in 1988.

From these observations it is possible to draw a first conclusion which links the two flows. By examining the ratio of investment to acquisitions one can approximate the rate of turnover of private and public groups. If it were possible to take the size of yearly investment as indicating the value of the group's ownership, then the ratio between investment and acquisitions would indicate the rate of turnover of this hypothetical ownership – in other words, the number of years required for a complete change of ownership. Therefore, even though in the aggregate case this turnover does not seem to change a great deal, inspection of Table 13.7 shows two different tendencies in public and private groups. This hypothetical number of years decreased rapidly for private groups, from an average of 6–7 years from 1981–2 to an average of 2–3 years from 1986–8, whereas it increased for public groups, falling from an average of 5 in the period 1981–2 to an average of 8 in the years 1985–8.

The second observation concerns the evolution of expenditures on fixed assets: in the low phase of the cycle, the investment evolution is characterized by negative changes. In the group case this holds even for 1984, which is usually indicated by the national accounts – and also by Mediobanca's sample results – as the year of recovery of the investment cycle. At the same time, in the years 1985 and 1986 the rates of change in investment by groups were larger than the Mediobanca sample, and were generally quite larger than national accounts results.

Overall, these results suggest a likely substitution effect between investment and acquisitions in the year 1984, although the period 1985–6 contradicts this by showing a clearly complementary effect between expenditures on fixed assets and acquisitions. There are no more indications of possible substitution between the two flows after the moment when they start increasing together.

These considerations reveal the basic tendencies emerging from group behaviour in recent years. The increased share of acquisitions characterizing private Italian groups therefore shows their predominant tendency to pursue their objectives through methods of external growth – that is, by buying firms

Table 13.8 Annual percentage changes in the acquisitions of 21 holdings

Year	82/81	83/82	84/83	85/84	86/85	87/86	88/87
Acquisitions	40.3	40.7	15.7	277.5	311.7	−58.9	−4.5

Source: Author's calculations on *R&S* data (various years).

Table 13.9 Temporal distribution of 322 acquisitions by 21 holdings

Year	1981	1982	1983	1984	1985	1986	1987	1988
No. of operations	18	28	22	34	46	63	58	63

Source: Author's calculations on *R&S* data (various years).

already operating on the domestic and foreign markets. This method does not crowd out internal growth, at least in the upward phase of the economic cycle. Both forms of growth increased together in the years 1984–6.

When the level of the analysis is changed from the sectoral/aggregate perspective to the holding companies level, their acquisition and investment decisions also generate increasing activity in equity purchases. Table 13.8 shows the annual percentage variations of this flow, and Tables 13.9 and 13.10 show the principal characteristics of these acquisitions in the years 1981–8.

The increased importance of external growth is evident in this case too, with rates exceeding 200 per cent in 1985–6: this evolution is therefore greater than both that of the groups and that of the aggregate Mediobanca sample of Italian companies. The parent companies of industrial groups certainly constitute the section most closely involved in this process. This is essentially an *ex post* check of the working hypothesis, according to which all external operations have passed through holdings.

Further confirmation would emerge if holdings were again differentiated by the ownership characteristics of their groups, since in this case too an even more evident difference among the group types would arise.

Other qualitative features emerge in the case of holdings. The temporal distribution of operations performed from 1981–8 shows a significant dynamic, especially in the more recent years, with 322 acquisitions involving 158 firms (see Tables 13.9 and 13.10).[42] On this basis it is possible to provide a better specification of the strategies pursued by holdings.

Around 30 per cent of the acquisitions were made during 1981–4 and almost 70 per cent in the years 1985–8. This flow was directed towards firms almost equally distributed between the manufacturing and the non-manufacturing sectors. By associating operations, firms and sectoral destination of resources, one notes a very heterogeneous distribution of firms and share of resources

Table 13.10 Sectoral distribution of target firms and of acquisitions by 21 holdings, 1981–8 (% Composition)

	Number of target firms	*Acquisitions*
Manufacturing	48.7	45.9
Services	12.7	1.0
Financial	22.7	32.4
Banking	5.1	4.1
Insurance	7.0	16.3
Other	3.8	0.2
Total	100.0	100.0

Source: Author's calculations on *R&S* data (various years).
Note: Rounding may affect totals.

outside the manufacturing sector. In the services sector many target firms are associated with a relatively low amount of utilized resources, while the opposite occurs in the financial, banking and insurance sectors. The case of financial and insurance sectors are the most striking examples.

The most striking feature in this case is the non-homogeneity of holdings' behaviour: even apart from the different propensities to grow by public and private holdings, they behave differently with respect to acquisitions in manufacturing and non-manufacturing. The concentration of acquisitions in financial banking and insurance is the result of a few major acquisitions, which certainly do not involve a large number of holdings.

Financial resources of private–public sectors

The aggregate balance sheet structures of private and public sector companies were characterized by two different circuits at the beginning of the 1980s.[43] After 1983, the private sector showed a ranking of financial sources that comprised 45 per cent of debts, 40 per cent of cash flows and 11 per cent of shareholders' equity. Public sector companies showed a ranking of financial sources which comprised debts (45 per cent), shareholders' equity (36 per cent)[44] and cash flow (12 per cent). The differential capability to generate cash flow is probably the most striking feature here, together with the complementarily differential relative importance of external sources.

Financial resource recomposition in the 1980s displayed two main characteristics: the first was substitution *between* external and internal source of financing, the second was *within* the external sources and consisted of a progressive substitution of debts.

In private groups (see Tables 13.3 and 13.4), the coverage of total assets by debts decreased drastically from 63 per cent in 1975 to 46 per cent; at the same time, the coverage by shareholders' equity rose by almost 20 percentage points.

The rescheduling by industrial affiliates differs from that undertaken by the group as a whole: in the case of industrial entities, the role of shareholders' equity is smaller and debt reduction rather bigger.

Before we go into private–public differences,[45] a point must be made: at the group level there is, throughout the 1980s, strong substitution between debts and shareholders' equity: that is, a substitution of financial sources *within* the external source of financing. At the company level there is clear substitution *between* the external and internal source of financing.

As well as state-owned companies, private companies (see Table 13.6) show this strong process of substitution between external and internal sources: in this case, the share of cash flow increased from 50 per cent in years from 1982–4 to more than 70 per cent from 1985–7. However, this financial rescheduling shows that even state-owned companies reached a more balanced financial structure in the 1980s by increasing their capacity to generate cash flows, passing from 8 per cent to more than 50 per cent. This process slowed down in the years 1989 and 1990 and shows two critical points: the decreased generation of internal financial sources by both private and public enterprises, and the slowdown of the substitution within external sources of financing: in 1988 both private and public sectors started to increase their financial debts (see Tables 13.5 and 13.6).

The basic difference between private and state-owned lies not only at the source level (financial investment) but also at the application level.

ITALIAN PRIVATIZATION PROCESSES

Italian privatization cannot be viewed independently of the above framework of readjustment processes within Italian industry and the characteristics of public–private relations in the 1980s.

Table 13.11 Purchases and sales of enterprises by the IRI group, 1951–87

	1951–60	1961–70	1971–80	1981–85	1986	1987
Enterprises						
Purchases of enterprises (no.)	19	30	128	29	2	5
Sales of enterprises (no.)	9	17	34	81	10	59
Balance	10	13	94	−52	−8	−54
Employees						
Acquired	22,632	24,422	81,423	10,214	125	956
Lost	5,324	9,601	15,820	25,833	1,057	47,986
Balance	17,308	14,821	65,603	−15,619	−932	−47,030

Source: Based on data published in Del Canuto (1991).

Table 13.12 IRI: per cent equity interest in affiliated companies listed on the Stock Exchange, 1983 and 1990

	Dec. 1983 (%)	Dec. 1990 (%)
Banca Commerciale Italiana	88.4	54.7
Banco di Roma	88.6	87.5
Banco di S. Spirito	97.6	(sold)
Credito Italiano	76.8	65.4
Aeritalia	100.0	80.4*
Alitalia	99.1	86.0
Cementir	67.9	53.6
Dalmine	89.3	78.0
Italcable	57.7	46.4
Sme	77.5	64.7
Sip	90.2	59.4
Sirti	50.0	49.1
Stet	93.5	64.1

Source: Based on Annual Reports.
Note: *Alenia (ex Aeritalia).

The privatization operations effected in the post-war period were almost irrelevant. Public sector companies grew with a successive stratification of goals, operating conditions and operative sectors in a way that Saraceno (the most important theoretician in this respect) in 1975 admitted to be contingently motivated.

In the years 1959–75, sales of firms covered approximately 4 per cent (in 1959) and 0.9 per cent (in 1975) of the financial requirement of the state-holding system. Marginal enough, they were ways to get rid of 'heterogeneous firms', and financial reasons had no relevance at all.

All the cases of privatization in the second half of the 1970s were motivated by the need to get rid of troubled firms with heavy financial disequilibrium and sectorial troubles. The year 1981 was probably the turning point: from then onwards privatization was instrumental to a strategy of state-owned enterprises – a strategy that started because of financial sources reorganization; became the abstention from the traditional rescue of private firms in trouble; and was then implemented as a flexible strategy, ranging from the total sale of firms to partial privatization through a decrease in the state's controlling shareholding. After 1983/4 public sectors were affected by slow reorganization processes which, although they lagged behind private industry, marked the beginning of a managerial rationalizing effort regarding both financial resources and core business: privatization strategy was part of this effort.

In 1983, IRI started an effective privatization policy by drawing up a taxonomy of privatizing firms and by pursuing various privatization techniques.

Two features should be mentioned: the sale of enterprises and the reduction of shareholding control.

As regards the first, in Table 13.11 the negative signs of both the balance of purchases–sales of enterprises and the acquired–lost employees indicate the outset of this strategy. Many of the firms sold off were initially small enterprises, marginal to the main interest of the group. The most striking cases were the attempts to sell Maccarese, Sme (a food industry subholding), Lanerossi and Alfa-Romeo. These encountered many difficulties – indeed the sale of Lanerossi and Alfa-Romeo were only completed in 1987.[46] Each, however, followed a different course, assuming different prerequisites and setting too many different targets.[47]

Regarding the second feature of IRI's privatization policy, Table 13.12 clearly shows the progressive reduction in equity interests in affiliated companies – banks and industrial enterprises showing a progressive decrease of public control. These attempts and their difficulties demonstrate the problems involved in privatization. When privatization involved the sale of marginal firms (as Table 13.11 shows, in 1986 the average size of the firms sold was approximately of 100 employees), this was simply part of internal industrial restructuring and a reinforcing of the core business. Since privatization strategy involved large firms,

Table 13.13 Privatization by leading Italian state-owned groups and affiliated enterprises

	Minority interests/shareholders' funds + minority interests (%)						
	1984	*1985*	*1986*	*1987*	*1988*	*1989*	*1990*
IRI	**14.5**	**19.2**	**23.3**	**27.8**	**33.2**	**35.9**	**42.8**
Finmeccanica	28.1	26.0	28.8	27.9	20.8	33.8	26.6
Finsider	13.8	4.0	10.2	12.2	(*)	–	–
Ilva	–	–	–	–	(*)	4.2	7.2
Sme	12.8	1.6	3.0	3.2	5.8	4.2	16.3
Italstat	17.9	17.7	4.7	3.8	31.1	39.1	34.5
Alitalia	2.0	1.6	2.0	2.0	2.6	4.4	3.6
Stet	13.8	28.6	30.4	32.5	34.9	33.5	36.0
Rai	0.0	0.0	0.0	0.0	0.0	0.0	0.0
ENI	**13.4**	**10.7**	**11.5**	**8.7**	**8.9**	**8.4**	**13.8**
Agip Petroli	–	–	18.0	27.1	24.3	21.8	32.4
Agip		1.9	7.8	2.7	10.7	12.0	10.9
Nuovo Pignone	–	–	–	–	3.5	3.5	2.5
Saipem	4.6	4.5	7.2	8.2	10.9	19.2	20.7
Snamprogetti	20.1	2.0	21.0	21.0	23.2	24.2	24.4
Snam	–	19.5	22.2	21.0	25.1	22.8	21.7
EFIM	**30.4**	**23.9**	**17.5**	**22.3**	**25.5**	**35.6**	**61.6**
MCS (Alumix)	20.5	30.8	27.0	29.0	19.4	16.8	48.5
Breda	–	0.0	0.0	0.0	24.8	16.7	21.3

Source: Based on Mediobanca, *Le principali società italiane* (various years).
Note: (*) Reorganization from Finsider to Ilva.

the identification of procedures and norms to follow showed the doubtful extent of managerial autonomy in public enterprises[48] as well as the difficulty of identifying the procedures and the industrial objectives of privatization.[49]

During the 1980s, Italian privatization could be seen as a selection procedure by means of the sale of small firms and the reduction of the public controlling stake in banking, manufacturing and service joint-stock companies. At the same time, the failures of privatization decisions involving large firms, and especially the failure of the Enimont joint venture involving private and state-owned chemical enterprises, are the most important evidence for both the difficulties in redefining the public presence in industrial sectors open to international competition and the transparency of the procedures that should have governed such processes.

After 1988, what was a spontaneous industrial selection within the state-holding system became a more planned and government-led process, motivated by more binding financial constraints. These are the official reasons of the privatization plan, defined by financial law, setting 15,000 billion lira as the return from partial privatization of the state-holding system in 1992: a plan that defines only the procedures to follow in order to transform public agencies in joint-stock companies.[50]

Table 13.14 Minority interests by leading Italian state-owned groups and affiliated enterprises

	1985	1986	1987	1988	1989	1990
IRI	4,992	6,511	7,589	8,946	10,682	12,638
Finmeccanica	384	466	400	392	968	859
Finsider	187	404	303	(*)	–	–
Ilva	–	–	–	(*)	102	207
Sme	9	16	20	40	39	198
Italstat	507	823	1,109	1,256	1,303	1,392
Alitalia	14	21	22	33	43	52
Stet	3,440	4,110	4,635	5,305	5,385	6,267
Rai	0	0	0	0	0	0
ENI	973	1,250	994	1,226	1,269	2,505
Agip Petroli	–	369	552	548	488	876
Agip	68	109	785	615	721	782
Nuovo Pignone	–	–	–	7	8	8
Saipem	28	30	71	117	189	146
Snamprogetti	36	47	50	51	56	60
Snam	617	825	832	956	912	1,050
EFIM	173	169	189	253	435	451
MCS (Alumix)	70	57	61	49	49	64
Breda	2	2	1	57	90	111

Source: Mediobanca, *Le principali società italiane* (various years).
Note: (*) Reorganization from Finsider to Ilva.

A measure of privatization processes

A measure of privatization processes is proposed here in order to assess the size of the phenomenon in the years 1984–90, as far as state-owned enterprises (state holdings and industrial affiliates) are concerned.[51] The results for the major state groupings, holdings and enterprises are collected in Tables 13.13 and 13.14 at the two levels identified in the second section (see pp. 275–7).

Inspection of the ratio of the minority interests over total worth can show, year after year, the increasing or decreasing interests of the 'external' shareholders. An increasing ratio can be taken as a proxy for increasing privatization; a decreasing ratio as a concentration of interest around the traditional main shareholder or, in other words, a further process of nationalization. The rate of growth of these ratios can be interpreted as an index of privatization, but this should be done carefully: first, *its increase or decrease may be due to both effects, decreasing net worth and an increase in the share of minorities*; second, its aggregation in order to build up a general index may be ambiguous because of the mixed situations of increasing (decreasing) shareholding equity and minority interests.

The figures in Tables 13.13 and 13.14 show a process of privatization within IRI, especially through its sectoral subholdings, although this does not apply to public service enterprises like Alitalia and Rai.[52] ENI appears first to reduce and then to increase its rate of privatization. However, a more careful inspection shows that, at the industrial company level, enterprises increased their minority interest,[53] while, at the holding level, it was the increase in shareholders' funds that gave rise to a decreasing rate of privatization in the years 1985–9. EFIM's privatization rate followed an erratic pattern: its final increase in the privatization rate was surely due to its decrease in total worth.

Two principal points can be made here: first, there is a negative correlation between the privatization processes shown by the peculiar but useful indicator used here and these holdings' capacity to generate internal financial sources. Therefore the search for funds seems to qualify the incentive to privatize as an alternative way to generate the funds needed to cover losses that were previously cleared by increasing flows of endowment funds.[54] Second, the state holdings show a tendency to increase privatization processes in the years 1989 and 1990 in a more marked manner than their industrial affiliates.

CONCLUDING REMARKS

The purpose of this chapter has been to use the historical institutional background of private–public relationships in Italy in order to check more recent economic results and the size of privatization processes in Italy during the 1980s.

The long history of Italian private–public relationships shows an interweaving and complex interaction between the roles and the paths followed by the private and public sectors in the Italian economy. Historical perspectives have been of help in framing the collusive/competitive nature of private–public relationships, and the nature of decision-making within Italian public sector companies. The relative autonomy of these two sectors seems to be the main result of the dynamic evolution during the 1980s.

Recent economic results have been analysed from two perspectives: the external growth and financial ranking by private and public sectors, firms and groups. The first and most important difference to emerge is the crucial difference in their propensities to grow externally; this differentiation is distinctive of recent economic results, both in terms of financial expenses and in terms of acquisition policy. Second, the convergence between the public and private sector companies in terms of utilization of financial sources during the 1980s slowed in 1989 and 1990, so that the differential ranking and the differential nature of funds provided by shareholders in the public case have been the main points at issue.

These results are important when related both to the differential approach of managing growth and to the difficulties and various degrees of freedom that state holdings have had to face in order to pursue privatization.

In terms of industrial structure, the analysis has suggested a possible way to examine that huge number of operations that do not necessarily entail control by an external firm but which could sum up the many forms of intra-firm agreements capable of creating a 'community of interest' (sharing technology information, tacit collusion, co-operative control, for example). The changes described in governing growth have shown an increasing velocity of changing ownership structures and its sectoral effects, both for industrial and financial concentration and for the relevant unit of analysis. These changes determine the prospects for increased turnover by private groups and decreased turnover in state-owned groups, and they generate prospects for the constantly developing unit of analysis – the group. Although not captured by national accounts, they lie simultaneously at the origin of the revival and good performances of the Italian large-firms system in the second half of the 1980s.

The main features of a spontaneous and enterprise-led privatization process during the 1980s within the Italian system of state holdings have been described. Detailed results measuring privatization processes for the three state-controlled holdings and their main industrial affiliates highlight two emerging tendencies: a negative correlation between privatization processes and the generation of internal sources so that the search for funds by privatizing seems to be still high on the political agenda – a shift in the years 1989 and 1990 from industrial affiliates to state holdings of the level of privatization. At the same time this chapter has outlined the present passage taking place from the spontaneous approach to privatization to a different, more planned programme for privatization induced by the overall Italian public deficit. This does not necessarily mean a shift to a more slowly directed programme of privatizaton similar to the English experience, but rather evaluation of the relative importance and the nature of *government-led and enterprise-led privatization* as well the objective of these processes. Financial objectives are now dominant even though the effectiveness of the 1992 privatization programme by the Italian government has been questioned. In this context, the following has been outlined:

- the institutional tendency to overcome the traditional dichotomy between *ente pubblico* and joint-stock company, by the more frequent and wide-spread utilization of the *ente pubblico* organized as joint-stock company;
- the slow-down of the convergence process between private and public sector companies in 1989 and 1990, showing that the nature of funds provided by shareholders in the public case is now the main point at issue, both at national and EEC level;
- the 'silent' privatization processes that took place in the 1980s at sectoral and industrial affiliates level in the Italian system of state holdings;
- the shift in 1989 and 1990 to privatization processes at state-holdings level, a shift that does not in fact reflect a rationalizing effort by overlapping activities but simply a search for funds.

Indeed, the industrial policy objectives behind these processes have yet not emerged.

NOTES

1 The results presented here are based on the findings of a research project on 'European economic integration' conducted by a group in the Department of Economics, University of Trento, and on those of a research project on 'Transition and the measurement of economic activity in Central-Eastern Europe: the contribution of the private sector', sponsored by the World Bank.

2 For an international law comparison see Daintith (1991).

3 Ever since the unification of the country in 1861, the state has frequently intervened to prevent the collapse of banking and industrial groups. A common feature of these interventions has been – during recessions – handling the collapse of the banking system controlling the industrial system. The mot important intervention was the setting up of IRI (The Industrial Reconstruction Institute) in January 1933 as temporary public body and later – since 1937 – as a permanent body. IRI held a majority share in the three major Italian banks as well as shares in industry, agriculture and services, together with the rescue shares that have been taken out by a special section since 1923. IRI's employees numbered over 200,000 in 1938, and it had enterprises in almost every sector of industry and finance, predominating in steel and iron, ship building, maritime transport and heavy engineering.

4 General indications about the size of the public sector can be drawn from the *Relazione sulla situazione economica del paese* presented to the Parliament on 6 April 1990 by the Ministries of the Treasury and the Budget. In 1989, total investment by the Italian system was approx. 256,000 billion lira, further subdivided as follows: investment by the 'enlarged public sector' was approx. 25 per cent (60,000 billion lira), comprising investment by the public administration – 40,000 billion lira – and firms (*aziende autonome e di stato*, 18,000 billion lira). The investment by state holdings amounted to 20,000 billion lira. When these are added to those of previous state firms, the result (38,000 billion lira) indicates the amount of investment by enterprises directly or indirectly owned by the state. Note that Italian national accounts consider the contribution of state holdings to be part of marketable goods and services, thus distinguishing it from the contribution of the public administration.

302

5   One should add a large number of services run by companies under the control of various ministries and local administrations.

6   Thus there is an important difference between firms in the hands of state holdings, and a firm or entity under direct legal ownership of the state, which is the case of several public service enterprises.

7   This is the case of the Italian *enti pubblici economici*. These can be further classified in *enti a struttura istituzionale* (or institutional entities like, for instance, Ina, Enel and Ente ferrovie dello stato), *enti-impresa* (entities acting directly as firms, often organized as joint-stock companies), *enti di gestione di partecipazioni azionarie* (IRI, ENI and EFIM), which act as holdings of public shareholdings in companies constituted under the ordinary forms of company law. For further details see Rossi (1991).

8   This, of course, is a very reductive and partial meaning of privatization (see Vickers and Wright 1988 and Vickers and Yarrow 1991) not only because in this way all forms not involving a sale of physical assets are omitted – for instance, cases of contracting out where the assets sold are a service contract or a franchise agreement, but also because no attention is paid at this stage either to the role of market structures (see Kay and Thompson 1986) or to the very important interaction with industrial policy and regulatory policy.

9   See Levante (1991). See also the shift from the proposal of the law of 25 July 1990 which excluded state holdings from transformation into joint-stock companies to the present law where the state holdings are actually candidates for transformation into joint-stock companies.

10   See Rossi (1991: 157) for a legal evaluation of the holding as an entrepreneurial agent, independently of its objectives (which may also be public objectives).

11   Rossi (1991: 172–3).

12   See Coltorti (1990).

13   A point needs making here: the explicit reference to the role of public initiative and to private entrepreneurship in the Italian constitution was the result of long debate and many comprises between the adoption of a development model of 'liberal protectionism' and its Keynesian criticism. The result of this compromise has been the central position of the state for development purposes without, however, its performing a specific directive role and with the focus on the supporting role of the state. This is the reason for the puzzling co-presence in the post-war period of many public institutions and instruments framed according to liberal logic. State intervention was therefore intervention without direct dirigism. Some forms of industrial directive protectionism were to be introduced later, in the planning years. For details see Amato (1972).

14   Since 1957, with the passing of law no. 634, direct governmental intervention in the southern areas has required that 40 per cent of publicly owned firms' investment should be directed to the south of the country.

15   This is the basic dual nature of state-holding enterprises in Italy which has given rise to an historical stratification of goals, monitoring processes and operative sectors. This would be reinterpreted in the 1980s.

16   The investment programmes of publicly owned companies were subject to the approval of *Cipe*, another body established in 1967 with a monitoring purpose. In these years one notes a growing involvement of the 'hidden political shareholder'.

17   For the period under consideration see the following cases: acquisitions of textile firms by ENI, the absorption of Motta, Alemagna, Cirio and Star by Sme (already under IRI control), the passage of Montedison aluminum sector to Efim, the founding of Egam, the holding company for mineral-metall. firms which after 1971 started a massive acquisition policy.

18 See Coltorti (1990).
19 Barca-Magnani (1989) call the period 1973–77 a period of 'uncertainty'; I take 1975 to be a crucial year because of the liquidity crisis of major industrial groups; see the two following footnotes.
20 As specified in Barca and Magnani (1989) there were two social preconditions for the later successful adjustments of the industrial system: the social co-operative plan among employers–unions–employees aimed at contractual moderation, and an accommodating monetary policy. These both contributed to a redistribution in favour of profit with increasing margins for private firms in the years 1977–80.
21 The years 1975–8 can be further subperiodized as follows: 1978–80 were principally years of the modernization of capital equipment, and 1981–3 were years when adjustments mainly affected labour forces. The capital substitution remained almost unchanged till 1977, while after 1978 private large firms activated substitution-disinvesture processes such as to reduce the average life of technical equipment from 18.1 to 15.8 years in three to four years (see Barca and Magnani 1989).
22 At the aggregate level, there is an important difference between the purposes of investment activity in the years 1979–81 (mainly of intensive nature) and the previous investment cycle (mainly of extensive nature); in the period 1980–2 the hourly productivity started to show anticyclical behaviour for the first time since the war, thus introducing a variant of the Okun–Verdoorn empirical law.
23 See data in Table 13.2, especially for the years 1979 and 1983.
24 The unified treatment of corporate government and corporate finance literature, as in Williamson (1988), can be very helpful in this respect.
25 From Table 13.4, the results of private groups' financial reorganization in 1986 can be compared with the 1975 situation illustrated in Table 13.3.
26 By-laws no. 576/1975, no. 904/1977, no. 72/1983.
27 See the three cases of 'new' groups in Table 13.4: Feruzzi, Cir and Fininvest.
28 The following quotation is translated from The Planning Report (1986): 'the following strategic areas may be focussed upon as those where the need for a decisive contribution, such as that which the state holding enterprises are called upon to ensure, is indispensable: development of the South: defence of and contribution to an increase in the employment level; decreasing dependence on foreign nations; technological innovation' (pp. 18–19). As regards operating conditions: 'It should, however, be emphasized that the basic condition necessary for ensuring that state holdings are run suitably is to restore economic management conditions' (p. 19). For operating sectors, priority was given to the following: large networks and related plant and system engineering, advanced technology manufacturing sectors, traditional plants in basic and manufacturing where the return to competitive conditions cannot be undertaken without the support or collaboration of the private sector. As we can see, these recommendations comprise a wide range of goals and sectors, roughly divided into two groups: operations for maintaining a presence in traditional sectors, or for entering innovative sectors where there is no possibility of a suitable level of private operators being present; operations for setting up and running service networks.
29 The data on operating margin and financial expenses are calculated in order to make meaningful comparison between state-owned and private companies. This does not imply any evaluation on the efficiency or the relative performances of the two sets of companies: the accent is on processes of adjustment rather than on static comparison. For the debate on performance and efficiency see, among many others, Domberger and Piggot (1986), Borcherding et al. (1983), and Boardman and Vining (1989).
30 These figures derive from comparison between Tables 13.3, 13.4 and 13.5.

31 This can be drawn comparing results for groups and companies, respectively, in Tables 13.3, 13.4 and 13.5.

32 See the cases in Tables 13.5 and 13.6.

33 For the Italian case see – among others – Giavazzi and Spaventa (1989) for a macroperspective, and the papers collected in Banca d'Italia (1988) for micro and financial perspectives.

34 Solving these problems will answer various questions: on a theoretical level the solution can provide an adequate unit of analysis – the group – which will suit the organizational and managerial perspective in analysis of industrial structure. Another question to be answered originates from the difficulties in empirical assessment. Examples of this difficulty arise in the reconstruction of historical series on flows of resources by industrial groups. This allows such limited confrontation and ambiguous comparison in the Italian case that it is no coincidence that Italian business groups are omitted from international comparisons on merger and take-over activity; on this omission see Frank and Mayer (1990), among many others.

35 For further details see Segnana (1990).

36 For some recent quantitative findings and databases in the Italian case see the references quoted in Segnana (1990).

37 The methodological approach adopted here isolates investment and acquisitions which are, respectively, additions to tangible fixed assets and purchases of equities from third parties. As regards the *first step*, its importance is already common knowledge: the evolution of a group's structure in its organizational and institutional forms has such a 'country specific' character that it is only possible to proceed with the help of historical and institutional elements. But it is even more important in the Italian case where, on the one hand, fiscal law in the years 1975–81 had profound effects on the organizational structure of groups, and on the other, the assembly of standardized accounting records of groups' balance sheets and profit and loss data is not a major public concern.

38 Expenditures on tangible fixed assets by Mediobanca's aggregate sample refer to assets of Italian companies only.

39 The reference is to groups whose organizational structure is characterized by a parent company which does not engage in industrial activity.

40 The reasons for this disaggregation lie mainly in the actual possibility of identifying target firms. This cannot be done when the group does not have a parent company, or when the holding is industrial in character, and is probably less relevant anyway. In any case, for all these groups with this characteristic the value of the expenditures on acquisitions directed towards target firms have been identified.

41 Because the presence of foreign and publicly owned groups is not very significant, such subsets are very sensitive to specific operations.

42 The difference between the data on Table 13.9 and 13.10 is due to acquisitions directed towards the same firm.

43 See Tables 13.3, 13.4 and 13.5.

44 There is a basic difference between shareholders' equity for private and public firms, since the latter case includes endowment funds.

45 For more details on the nature, purposes and characteristics of financial resources in state-owned enterprises, with specific information on endowment funds and debt financing, see Di Stefano, in AAVV (1986: 208–69).

46 Lanerossi was sold by ENI in 1987 for 166 billion lira; the net value of Alfa-Romeo was set at 1,085 billion lira, to be paid to Finmeccanica from 1993 onwards in five-yearly instalments without interest. The other failures were typical examples of the conflict between the authorization power of the Ministry of State Holdings in disinvesture processes, and the autonomy of state holdings. Solved in favour of the

Minister, this case has shown the lack of a uniform discipline providing norms and procedures for the three state holdings.

47 The lack of a coherent strategy can be conveyed by observing that EFIM sold all its activities in the food industry: ENI gradually withdrew from the textiles, glass and aluminium industries; but EFIM withdrew from one sector (food industry), and IRI was forced to stay in the same sector (the SME case) by political disagreements.

48 Note that the uncertainty and flexibility of the prescriptive framework made it possible to pursue the mentioned spontaneous process (Cassese 1988). Different constraints bind state holdings in case of divestiture: they go from the hypothetical lack of authorized procedures for IRI (see, by contrast, the SME case) to authoritative intervention by the Ministry for divestiture under 51 per cent by ENI, to authorized intervention by the Ministries of State holdings and Treasury for EFIM. These differential constraints are puzzled by the fact that several public enterprises have special statutory norms imposing a public majority: this is the case of *società di interesse nazionale*. Some examples are the following cases: Rai, Finmare, Autostrade, Italposte for IRI, the art. 3 in the statutory profil for ENI, and some telecommunication firms held by Stet.

49 See Aronica (1990).

50 See law no. 35, 29 January 1992.

51 Some examples are in papers collected in Di Majo (1989).

52 See note 48 on statutory profile for Rai.

53 There is a peculiarity here because of the cross-holding of minority interests among industrial affiliates.

54 For data on endowment funds see Coltorti (1990). See also the debate about transfers and aided grant at both national and international level in Forti, Pezzoli and Ranci (1992: ch. 5). This tendency is reinforced by the public sector deficit and by the debate on transfers to public firms at EEC level and the ongoing debate about the nature of these funds.

REFERENCES

AAVV (1986) *Risanamento e riordino delle partecipazioni statali*, Milano: Franco Angeli.

Amato, G. (ed.) (1972) *Il governo dell'industria in Italia*, Bologna: Il Mulino.

Aronica, A. (1990) 'Privatization and industrial policy', Presented at Conferencia 'O Mercado e no estado no desenvolvimento economico nos anos noventa', São Paulo, 25–26 October.

Banca d'Italia (1988) *Ristrutturazione economica e finanziaria delle imprese*, II voll., Roma.

Barca, F. and Magnani, M. (1989) *L'industria tra capitale e lavoro*, Bologna, Il Mulino.

Boardman, A. E. and Vining, A. R. (1989) 'Ownership and performance in competitive environments: a comparison of the performance of private, mixed, and state-owned enterprises', *Journal of Law and Economics*, April.

Borcherding, T. E. Pommerehne, W. W. and Schneider, F. (1982) 'Comparing the efficiency of private and public production: the evidence from five countries', *Zeitschrift fur Nationalokonomie*, suppl. 2, pp. 127–56.

Brioschi, F. and Buzzacchi, C.-Colombo (1988) 'Risk capital financing and the separation of ownership and control in business group', Presented at the 9th Conference on Input–Output Techniques, Keszthely, Hungary.

Cassese, S. (1988) 'Le privatizzazioni in Italia', *Rivista Trimestrale di diritto pubblico*, no. 1.

Coltorti, F. (1988) Note sulla modificasioné della strutture finansiaria delle imprese italiane regli ultimi venti anni, published in *Banca d'Italia* (1988), vol. 2, pp. 594–655.

Coltorti, F. (1990) 'Phrases of Italian industrial development and the relationship between the public and the private sectors', *Rivista di Politica Economica*, vol. LXXX, 65–131.

Daintith, T. (1992) 'The legal techniques of privatisation', *International Privatisation: Strategies and Practices*, University of St Andrews Research Conference, 1991.

Del Canuto, U. (1991) 'Mutamenti nella struttura occupazionale del gruppo Iri negli anni 1937–1987', *Economia Pubblica*, no. 4–5, 191–209.

Di Majo, A. (ed.) (1989) *Le politiche di privatizzazione in Italia*, Bologna: Il Mulino.

Domberger, S. and Piggot, J. (1986) 'Privatization policies and public enterprises: a survey', *The Economic Record*, June, pp. 145–62.

Forti, A., Pezzoli, R. and Ranci, P. (eds) (1992) *Una politica industriale per la nuova legislatura*, Bologna: Il Mulino.

Franks, J. and Mayer C. (1990) 'Capital markets and corporate control: a study of France, Germany and the U.K.', *Economic Policy*, no. 10, 189–231.

Giavazzi, F. and Spaventa, L. (1989) 'Italy: the real effects of inflation and disinflation', *Economic Policy*, no. 8.

Kay, J. A. and Thompson, D. J. (1986) 'Privatization: a policy in search of a rationale', *Economic Journal* 96(1), 18–32.

Kingh, M. (1989) 'Economic growth and the life cycle of firms', *European Economic Review*, no. 2/3, 325–34.

Kumar, M. S. (1984) *Growth, Acquisition and Investment*, Cambridge: Cambridge University Press.

Levante, R. (1991) 'Pubblico e privato nell'economia italiana', *Economia pubblica*, no. 6, 279–302.

Mediobanca (1990) *Dati cumulativi di 1743 società italiane*, Milano.

—— (1991) *Dati cumulativi di 1770 società italiane*, Milano.

Ricerche e Studi (1990) *R&S* (3 voll.), Milano.

Rossi, G. (1991) *Gli enti pubblici*, Bologna: Il Mulino.

Segnana, L. (1990) 'Acquisitions and investment activity by leading groups in Italy', Paper given at the Conference 'Mergers, Oligopoly and Trade', Aix en Provence, 21–22 June.

Vickers, J. and Yarrow, G. (1988) *Privatization: An Economic Analysis*, Cambridge, Mass.: MIT Press.

—— and Yarrow, G. (1991) 'Economic perspectives on privatization', *Journal of Economic Perspectives*, no. 2, 111–32.

Williamson, O. (1988) 'Corporate finance and corporate governance', *Journal of Finance*, no. 3, 567–91.

14

CORPORATIZATION AND PRIVATIZATION IN NEW ZEALAND[1]

Alan Bollard and David Mayes

Many countries have undertaken programmes of corporatization or privatization in recent years, but New Zealand's programme is one the most valuable for study because of its large scale, speed and rate of evolution. New Zealand started in the mid-1980s with a heavily protected economy and a scale of government intervention and ownership in the economy which was among the greatest of the industrialized countries. By the end of the decade much of that protection had been removed, there had been wholesale abandonment of internal intervention, and large portions of the public sector had been either corporatized or transferred into private ownership. This is rapidly switching New Zealand from one end of the spectrum to the other.

The consequences of such a drastic programme of reform have been felt throughout the economy: land prices have slumped with the ending of support for agriculture, and major unemployment has been experienced in heavily protected industries and in public sector activities – both in government departments whose role of intervention has been reduced and in the enterprise sector that has been corporatized or privatized. All this has taken place in a difficult macroeconomic context. The period began with a problem of rapidly mounting internal deficits, external debt and inflation. The microeconomic reform we describe in this chapter was matched by a programme of macroeconomic reform, floating the dollar, bringing the money supply under control and squeezing the budget. That process is not complete but inflation is now down well below the OECD average and likely to remain there, and the internal and external deficits are greatly reduced (see the New Zealand Institute's latest *Quarterly Predictions* for a full picture of the economy and its prospects). The reform does not end there because there has been comprehensive tax reform as well: the introduction of a flat rate value added tax covering all goods and services; the shifting of the income tax schedule to only a couple of rates thus giving the country one of the lowest top rates in the world; and a general reorganization of the rest of the tax system to remove distortions.

This whole process has not been without cost. Unemployment, traditionally negligible in New Zealand, has reached European levels, and growth since 1985 has been very limited, placing the country at the bottom of the league table. The fact that it was a Labour rather than a National government which implemented such a programme meant that the government dominated the political scene in its early years and was easily re-elected in 1987. However, the underlying political and economic pressures were always present, resulting ultimately, as unemployment mounted and the economy failed to pick up, in divisions within the Labour Party and a resounding defeat at the polls.

One of the most interesting features, on which we focus, is the separation of the ideas of 'corporatization' and 'privatization'. At the outset of the programme the major emphasis was on reforming publicly owned enterprises so that they operated efficiently and provided a proper rate of return to their owner. It was not regarded as necessary to transfer enterprises to the private sector to achieve that. The pressing need to close the fiscal deficit rather than failure to achieve performance objectives within the enterprises was the prime stimulus. One of the most exciting questions, which the New Zealand experience will be uniquely qualified to answer, is: Is it possible to get state-owned enterprises to perform as well as their private sector counterparts? In most countries companies are in state ownership because governments wish to set them further objectives in addition to those which private sector companies set themselves. The most common is to remain in unprofitable activities or locations for social or strategic reasons. These objectives therefore usually conflict, resulting in the need for ownership. Privatization of public utilities in the UK has attempted to find a formula to recombine them. However, if the New Zealand experience can show examples of where the state as owner has withdrawn these extra constraints it will be possible to compare the results of ownership separately from the contrast between objectives.

As this chapter goes on to show it is too early to draw firm conclusions, and the extent of privatization has meant that it is the state-owned enterprises with the best prospects of private sector performance that have been privatized, thus confusing the comparison. As it is, there is a rich variety of arrangements and routes which have been employed to achieve the transfer to the private sector. As the process is extended to local government as well, New Zealand will continue to provide one of the richest examples to study. This chapter is only an introduction; we hope it will encourage further research.

THE SETTING FOR GOVERNMENT REFORM

In 1984, after the change to a Labour government at the general election, New Zealand commenced down a path of radical structural economic reform. That process of change is still continuing today despite the return to power of the National party in 1990.[2] A number of factors contributed to the decision to make that major step:

- New Zealand's poor productivity and growth performance since the mid-1970s;

- an increasingly *ad hoc* and restrictive set of regulatory interventions by government in the 1970s;
- the record of devaluation, inflation, and mistimed stabilization attempts during the 1970s, and a realization of the structural problems facing the government;
- a western world increasingly embracing the theory and practice of economic liberalization; in addition the more recent economic breakup of Eastern Europe and some of the East Asian centrally planned economies spelt the failure of highly interventionist systems;
- a new government relatively free from producer and labour group lobbying links;
- a thin political system (single chamber, two party, no significant splinter groups, no important state or local government economic policies, no written constitution, no proportional representation, and a three-year term which accelerated reform);
- evidence of the failures of direct government intervention during some major public investment programmes in the 1970s, which alienated many civil servants from having a direct role in productive activity;
- the rapid dissemination of some recent microeconomic theoretical developments (public choice, contestability, property rights) to key parts of the New Zealand bureaucracy.

It is a feature of New Zealand economic deregulations, in comparison with other countries, that from 1984 radical changes were made across a wide range of fronts rapidly and simultaneously. The Appendix lists the major reforms that took place.[3]

The regulatory reform programme was built on a number of strands:

- factor markets were a key area for reform, including financial sector deregulation, reform of energy and transport, and more recently labour market deregulation;
- product market reform was less important: price support on agricultural products and exports was terminated;
- industry regulatory reform was carried out including business law reform, and the ending of price and entry controls;
- the exchange rate was floated, international capital controls removed, foreign investment liberalized, import licences abolished, and tariffs reduced.

The reforms were heavily microeconomic in character. On the macro-economic side a tight monetary policy was put in place to achieve price stability, and the tax revenue system was placed on a broader base with regional rates flattened. However, government spending, especially on social services, remained high, and a persistent fiscal deficit was incurred. As part of this programme of reform, the role of the government sector was placed under the spotlight. By western standards the New Zealand government had always played a very active role in providing core administrative and social services. In addition, over the years they have owned and operated a wide range of traded services. By 1984 government spending constituted over 40 per cent of GDP.

THE POLICY OF CORPORATIZATION

Traditionally most government trading activity was carried out through government departments, subject to tight central controls, their funds scrutinized in considerable detail by Parliament, and with separate controls of over capital works, other investment, staffing and activities. In the mid-1980s as part of the programme of liberalization, the government began a comprehensive programme to improve efficiency in departmental trading activities, initially through corporatization. In 1985 the Minister of Finance published five general principles for the reorganization of state trading activities. These were:

- non-commercial functions would be separated from major state trading organizations;
- managers would be required to run them as successful business enterprises;
- managers would also be responsible for using inputs, for pricing, and for marketing their products within performance objectives set by ministers;
- the enterprises would be required to operate without competitive advantages or disadvantages, so that commercial criteria would provide an assessment of managerial performance;
- enterprises would be set up on an individual basis depending on their commercial purposes, under the guidance of boards modelled on the private sector.

In 1987, the government further announced that public trading enterprises would be required to fund spending from unsubsidized private sector capital sources, and that they would also be required to pay tax and dividends to the government. In addition the intention was to split off regulatory and policy objectives of government departments into different organizations.

The main vehicle for this reorganization was the State-Owned Enterprises Act 1986:

to promote improved performance in respect of government trading activities and, to this end, to
(a) specify principles governing the operation of state enterprises; and
(b) authorise the formation of companies to carry on certain government activities and control the ownership thereof; and
(c) establish requirements about the accountability of state enterprises, and the responsibility of ministers.

The Act stated that the principal objective of every state enterprise should be to operate as a successful business, being:

Table 14.1 State-owned corporations in New Zealand

	Original activity	Current status (1991)
Various corporate forms pre-1987		
NZ Railways Corporation	Train, bus, ferry services	Non-core assets hived off into separate disposal SOE
Housing Corporation	Concessional mortgages and rental properties	Mortgages due for sale
Development Finance Corporation	Development bank	Sold, under statutory management
Bank of New Zealand	Trading bank	Part privatized
Air New Zealand Ltd	Domestic and international air services	Privatized
Petroleum Corporation of New Zealand	Oil and gas production	Privatized
Tourist Hotel Corporation of New Zealand	Hotels	Privatized
Shipping Corporation of New Zealand Ltd	Shipping services	Privatized
Rural Bank	Agricultural bank	Privatized
Established under 1987 Act		
Airways Corporation of New Zealand Ltd	Air traffic control	SOE
Coal Corporation of New Zealand Ltd	Coal mining	Setting ownership claims before likely sale
Electricity Corporation of New Zealand Ltd	Electricity generation and transmission	Transmission into separate SOE: likely sale
Government Life Insurance Corporation	Life insurance	Now owned by policy-holders
Government Property Services Ltd	Government property holdings	Selling assets
Land Corporation Ltd	Government rural land holdings	Mortgages sold
NZ Forestry Corporation Ltd	Forests and sawmills	Some forests sold
NZ Post Ltd	Postal services	Preparing for possible sale
Post Office Bank Ltd	Savings bank	Privatized
Telecom Corporation of New Zealand Ltd	Telephone services	Privatized
Established in 1988		
Works and Development Services Corporation	Civil engineering	SOE
Government Computing Services Ltd	Computer systems	SOE
Government Supply Brokerage Corporation	Government purchasing company	Preparing for sale
Radio New Zealand Ltd	National radio services	SOE
Television New Zealand Ltd	Two national TV channels	SOE

Uncorporatized Bodies		
Health Computing Services	Health computing	Privatized
Government Print	Printing	Privatized
National Film Unit	Film-making	Sold to SOE
Communicate New Zealand	Publicity services	Privatized
Local Authorized Corporations		
13 Port Companies	Port operations	Minor share privatizations
24 Airport Companies	Airport management	Possible privatizations
49 Electrical Supply Authorities	Local electricity distribution	Preparing for privatizations, possibly by voucher
Local Authority Trading Enterprises	Buses, rubbish collection, other services	Some contracting-out

(a) as profitable and efficient as comparable business that are not owned by the Crown; and

(b) a good employer; and

(c) an organisation that exhibits a sense of social responsibility by having regard to the interests of the community in which it operates by endeavouring to accommodate or encourage these when able to do so.

(State-Owned Enterprises Act 1986, section 4)

The Act provided for the appointment of a board of directors, accountable to the Minister of Finance, and a further responsible Minister who would hold the shares and who in turn would be responsible to Parliament for the performance of the enterprise. The Ministers could not sell or allot these shares. If the Crown wished the state-owned enterprise (SOE) to provide non-commercial activities, it would need to contract it specifically to do so. The enterprise was to compose a Statement of Corporate Intent including corporate objectives, the scope of activities, accounting policies, performance targets, estimated returns, commercial valuations, and other information. The Act also specified that the SOE would deliver annual, half-yearly and other information to the Shareholding Minister.

The Act subjected SOEs to the same antitrust and company legislation as the private sector. In addition the State Sector Act 1988 essentially overrode the old State Services employment conditions, bringing SOEs into line with the private sector labour legislation. On 1 April 1987 nine SOEs, as specified in the Second Schedule of the SOE Act, were formally established, with others set up in the following year. By 1989 there were fifteen SOEs in existence. It should also be noted that some central government trading activities took a number of other corporate and quasi-corporate forms. These included:

- Departments of State (for example, Ministry of Energy);
- Public Corporations with the Public Service subject to the State Services Act 1962 (for example, Housing Corporation);
- Public Corporations within the State Services subject to the provisions of the State Services Conditions of Employment Act 1977 (for example, NZ Railways);
- Corporations in the public sector (for example, Development Finance Corporation);
- Government-owned limited liability companies under the Companies Act 1955 (for example, Air New Zealand).

In later years many of these organizations were converted to state-owned enterprise status. The list of state trading operations is detailed in Table 14.1.

UNDERLYING THEORETICAL THINKING

The underlying theoretical rationale for corporatization was relatively clear cut: it was felt that efficiency could be improved by approximating a private sector model. The argument drew heavily on the literature on property rights and principal–agent theory. In particular, it was argued that managers' responsibilities and incentives had to be redefined so as to bring them into line with the principal's (that is, the Crown's) objectives.[4]

In line with this theoretical approach, Deane identifies four key objectives of the corporatization process in New Zealand:[5]

1   SOE managers are meant to have a single clear objective: the maximization of commercial performance. This is intended to provide a direct and unambiguous focus, facilitate monitoring, improve accountability and prevent inconsistent political objectives.
2   SOE boards of directors are meant to have the authority to make the decisions necessary to meet these objectives. They are responsible for major investment, recruitment and other strategic decisions. Ministers retain overall responsibility for the firm's performance but should not be more closely involved.
3   Management performance should be closely monitored – by Ministers, the Treasury providing advice – against the objectives achieved; some private sector monitoring also occurs.
4   There is an improved system of managerial rewards and sanctions to reinforce the incentives for performance. Salaries and employment should be linked to performance.

At the same time Deane noted two further reforms to ensure that SOEs compete with other business on more neutral terms:

1   In the factor markets, SOEs now raise funds in capital markets rather than at subsidized rates from the state, without explicit government guarantees on debt (and indeed the government has tried to remove any implicit guarantees). They must earn a rate of return on equity capital in line with the market, and pay dividends and taxes to government. In most cases they employ labour on a similar basis to the private sector, with comparable union coverage. They can purchase material and other inputs from any source rather than be required to use other government services.
2   Most SOEs no longer have statutory monopoly protection or preferential access to government business. Therefore in those markets where potential competition exists, they are exposed to it.

Figure 14.1 summarizes some of the salient differences between the three main types of trading organization. There are key differences in ownership, strategic role and operational management. In all but ownership, the SOE model approximates more closely the publicly listed company model. Note that the

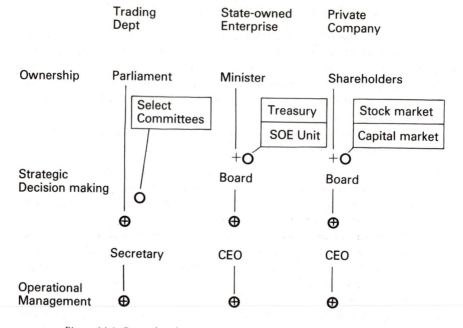

Figure 14.1 Control and monitoring of organizations in New Zealand

Notes: + implies a control point; o implies a monitoring point.

trading department relationship is difficult to represent accurately in this way. Formally the Crown owns the assets, Parliament buys the outputs of the department, and the Minister is responsible for supplying them.

Accompanying this new approach to trading organizations, there had also been widespread reform of the core government sector. This was strongly influenced by public choice theory with its emphasis on budget-maximizing behaviour by bureaucrats and producer capture. It led to a focus on separation of policy advice, policy implementation, and regulation, plus a concentration on transparency of objectives.[6]

THE PROCESS OF CORPORATIZATION

Government trading organizations in New Zealand come from a range of backgrounds. Some originated from state development of utilities and public works in the nineteenth century. Some were set up with statutory monopolies in order to crowd out private sector organizations, while others were established because the private sector was not seen to be meeting requirements. Mascarenhas reports that in 1981 it was estimated that public enterprises contributed 12 per cent of GDP and 20 per cent of gross investment in New Zealand.[7]

By the early 1980s most were government departments accountable to a

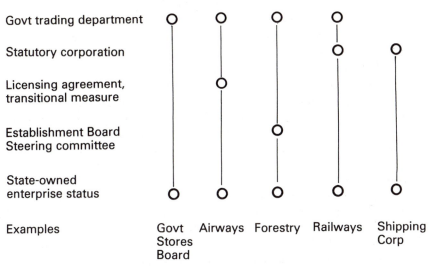

Figure 14.2 Transition paths to SOE status in New Zealand

Minister, or divisions of a department accountable to the departmental head. A few were already established as limited liability companies under their own legislation; these reported directly to Ministers, were tightly constrained in their operations, and often had to fulfil political objectives such as employment generation.

The record of corporatization in New Zealand is best viewed as a variety of processes rather than a single predefined step. The standard intended technique was to set up an establishment board or steering committee to oversee the transitional arrangements in an orderly way, and prepare the ground for the SOE. In some cases, due to prior departmental restructuring, the jump was made directly from department to SOE. In other cases, where a statutory corporation was already in existence, the step to SOE or equivalent status was made by removing various operating restrictions (for example, State Services employment conditions). In a couple of cases, extraordinary transitional arrangements had to be made to ensure continued operation. Figure 14.2 shows some different paths used to reach SOE status.

Just as the transition paths differed case by case, so has the speed of transition: some simpler or already reorganized organizations completed the transitions reasonably easily within two years, and in other cases this might have happened but for problems beyond their control (for example, Maori land claims under the Treaty of Waitangi).

More often the transition was slow and indirect, mainly because of changes of mind by politicians and bureaucrats as to the appropriate organizational forms, and difficulties over valuation. In several cases various transitional mechanisms were experimented with, making transitional operations very difficult for the

317

management. In other cases privatization was announced and preparations made, only to see sales postponed. There was often a gap between formal SOE status and the transfer of assets, during which the organizations had to operate with unclear balance sheets.

A further important aspect is the order in which the corporatization took place. One key question was whether radical restructuring occurred before or after corporatization. Where the establishment boards carried out early restructuring of employment, finance and operations, the Crown assumed the cost of redundancy and debt, leaving the new SOEs to start with a clear balance sheet. However, in most cases the SOE had to deal with this restructuring after corporatization, and sometimes the costs of doing this held up the restructuring.

Another important issue was whether industry deregulation took place before or after transition. Again the experience differs: where trading departments had to restructure as SOEs and face competition immediately, there were considerable adjustment problems. In most cases the ultimate regulatory framework was at least worked out in advance; in particular this would affect the SOE valuation. Most government trading departments had operated with mixed objectives, including provision of commercial services, policy advice, regulation and social objectives. In general the corporatization process gave the SOEs clear consistent commercial objectives that would be measurable and not easily interfered with by politicians. Corporate objectives were drafted by SOE boards, approved by the Minister and incorporated into the statements of Corporate Intent reviewable each year. The principal objective was to operate as a successful business, this usually being expressed in terms of criteria such as rate of return on capital employed or net profits and the need to maintain an agreed capital structure – although some other objectives were also stated. In addition, the scope of activity undertaken by the organization is also specified. Generally SOEs are encouraged or instructed to concentrate on core activities. In the final event the Minister has the power to define the nature and scope of the business.

An important step before corporatization was reaching an agreed valuation of the assets and liabilities to be transferred to the corporation. This was a hotly contested exercise that forced a complete rethinking of the value of certain activities and assets; in a number of cases these were found to be zero or negative. Under old trading structures many enterprises had long periods of losses and entered the transition burdened by debt payments or lack of capital. In some cases the government wrote off these debts during the transition. SOEs with still unrestructured debt complained that this has put a constraint on their reinvestment abilities.

In return for the transfer of state assets, SOEs were intended to achieve target rates of return on assets (at levels approximating equivalent private sector returns). They were expected to pay dividends to the government for the use of these assets, and also pay taxes.

Under their old status all departmental ministers of government trading operations had a close involvement in policy and sometimes in operational matters. Consequently, operations like Railways were vulnerable to instructions to take on staff in key constituencies for employment-generation reasons. Under the SOE structure the Ministers of Finance and State-Owned Enterprises become the joint shareholders. They are expected to monitor returns but not be actively involved in business strategy. Nevertheless considerable ministerial involvement has continued especially in SOEs that are still restructuring.

The SOE accounts no longer form part of the government's estimates to be debated by the House of Representatives each year. They are, however, tabled in the House, which has the opportunity to bring the relevant Ministers to account for their duties under the Act (which does not generally occur). However the SOE's statutory statements and reports delivered to the shareholding Ministers must be placed before the House and these are still examined by Parliamentary Select Committees. With corporatization, some, but not all, bureaucratic monitoring involvement has disappeared. An SOE Unit monitors performance, as also does the Treasury and the Government Audit Office. The Auditor-General has taken the view that SOEs should remain subject to Parliamentary Select Committees' scrutiny as are government departments. SOE boards have opposed this view arguing that, far from following the private model, SOEs are over-scrutinized and monitored.

The SOE Act requires the board of directors to be accountable to the share-holding Ministers. Most board members have been drawn from the business sector with few political or interest-group appointments. There is little use of executive directors. Chief executive officers have probably been the single most important element in the transitional process of change. Some have been selected from state trading organizations, while the majority have been brought in from outside. In addition there has been considerable change in senior management, with fewer recruits from engineering and other trades backgrounds in the organizations, and many new Treasury, accounting, public relations and marketing recruits. There is now much more mobility amongst senior and middle management, and between SOEs and the private sector.

A wide range of management structures have been set up, generally with decentralized control functions and clearly defined profit centres. In general SOEs have become less unionized and many have renegotiated staff conditions to achieve more flexible work conditions and pay arrangements.

Table 14.2 summarizes these organizational and operational changes. The actual process of corporatization was a drawn-out one that differed in each case.[8] Some of the problems that arose in the corporatization process were:

- circularity in the valuation process and the setting of profit targets;
- delays and disruption in clearing titles and other property rights;
- wide variability in the timing and degree of restructuring;
- some tendency to continued political and/or bureaucratic interference;
- problems with performance monitoring yardsticks;
- continued principal/agency problems between executives and SOE boards.

Table 14.2 Operational and organizational differences in New Zealand, by type of institution

	Government department	Statutory corporation	State-owned enterprise	Privatized enterprise
Ownership				
Legally responsible to:	Parliament	Parliament	Minister	Private shareholders
Shareholders	n/a	Crown	Crown/bondholders	Private
Dividends	None	Not usual	To Crown	To shareholders
Liability	Unlimited	Unlimited	Unlimited but private insurance	Limited
Gov't guarantee	Explicit	Explicit	Implicit	Implicit
Discretionary behaviour				
Board autonomy	n/a	Limited	Moderate	Considerable
Ultimate threat	Reorganization	Corporatization/ privatization	Privatization	Merger/bankruptcy
Managerial autonomy	Little	Moderate	Considerable	Considerable
Setting dividends	None	Not usual	Treasury/Minister	Board
Constraints on operation				
Statutory monopoly	Probable	Possible	Mainly removed	Removed
Source of finance	Consolidated funds	Specific fund allocation	Private capital markets	Private capital markets
Operational scope	Limited	Limited	Wider	Comprehensive
Organizational flexibility	None	Minor	Some	Complete privatization
Objectives				
Commercial	Mixed	Mixed	Single	Single
Other objectives	Regulatory/policy/social	Social	Only when contracted	None
Incentives/sanctions				
Management	State Services Commission	State Services Commission	Board	Board
Employees	State Services Act	State Services Act	Employment Contracts Act	Employment Contracts Act

Internal monitoring				
Board	n/a	Minister/Treasury	Minister/SOE Unit	Private shareholders
Top management	SSC/Minister	Board	Board	Board
Middle management	Secretary	GM	CEO	CEO
External monitoring				
Spending plans	Parliament	Parliament/Minister	Minister/capital markets	Capital market
Financial accounts	Audit office	Audit office	Audit office	Private auditor
Overall performance	Treasury/SSC/Select Committees	Treasury/SSC/Select Committees	SOE Board/Treasury	Capital and stock markets

THE POLICY OF PRIVATIZATION

In designing the SOE framework, the government has tried to approximate the conditions of the private sector in a politically acceptable way. However it has not proved possible to replicate private conditions, and in addition the private sector itself may suffer competitive problems. A number of commentators (NZ Business Roundtable 1988, Economic Development Commission 1989, Treasury 1987, Deane 1989) have pointed to strategic operational weaknesses in the SOE model.[9]

1   There is no (share)market for ownership: this means that much of the monitoring by sharebrokers, banks, etc. that occurs for the publicly quoted part of the private sector, does not take place. The incentives for owners to monitor management performance may be relatively weak, and non-tradeability of equity leads to major problems in valuing the business and establishing the appropriate capital structures.

2   There is little threat of take-over or bankruptcy for an SOE, an ultimate motivation or improved performance by managers and directors. (There is however threat of privatization, departmentalization, regulation or break-up.)

3   Directors will not hold shares in the company and may therefore have reduced incentives to perform; also the replacement of directors must take a different form from the private sector.

4   In our view there is still a perceived implicit government guarantee on SOE debt notwithstanding official disclaimers; consequently there is less pressure exerted on management from cost of funds or threat of financial failure.

5   Despite the more hands-off approach in the SOE structure, the possibility of political intervention in managerial or directorial responsibilities still exists. Interest groups have incentives to lobby for special benefits, and government may be tempted to use SOEs to deliver such benefits at the expense of overall efficiency.

6   The statutory requirements to be a 'good employer' displaying social responsibility (the Official Information requirements, the ability to be subjected to ombudsman scrutiny, and the Treaty of Waitangi provision) are not faced by the private sector, giving them a competitive advantage.

7   The position of the Treasury and the State-Owned Enterprises Unit in monitoring performance and advising the Minister can be an uneasy one, without parallel in the private sector.

8   The SOE Act sets the organizational form of these businesses in concrete at a certain time (although there continues to be internal flexibility). In practice, private sector organizations have the flexibility to divest, diversify, acquire, merge, go out of business, or reorganize themselves in a wide range of ways denied to SOEs.

9   The provision of a commercial activity which has natural monopoly elements, by a state-owned enterprise is subject to the same problems as

when provided by a private natural monopolist; it is difficult to design a light-hand regulatory structure satisfactorily to reduce the costs of monopoly behaviour. The proponents of these arguments generally consider that the only way around (all but the last of) these difficulties is complete privatization by one of a number of mechanisms.

Between 1987 and 1991 the New Zealand government took this further step and carried out a series of privatizations, mostly (but not all) being of state-owned enterprises. The privatizations carried out to date are listed in Table 14.3. The predominant motives for their sale were mixed. To the Treasury the important motive was to transfer assets to the private sector to address the efficiency shortfalls of corporatization. To some politicians the need to reduce public debt and avoid future SOE financing requirements was more important.

THE PRIVATIZATION PROCESS

In contrast with the corporatization programme of trading activities which is now nearing completion, the privatization process has been a partial ongoing process. A range of techniques has been used, depending on the demand for the assets in the marketplace, the goverment's fiscal requirements, and the political implications of different types of sales. Table 14.4 shows some of the methods of privatization used.

In some cases the intention to sell was announced and then retracted. In many others some underused assets were deemed to have little value and were closed or realized. Many SOEs have divested some of their non-core activities or financial assets prior to full privatization. Of the non-privatized SOEs, some are already in the transitional phase where privatization is possible; others could sell off all their assets over future years; while a few look likely to remain state owned. Whether the SOE regards itself as in a long-term operational mode or as a transitional body preparing for future sell-off, clearly affects its investment attitudes and performance.

As shown in Table 14.4, privatizations followed one of two main routes, either selling assets or selling shares. To generalize, the equity route was followed in the case of the more clearly defined commercial operations, whereas the asset route had to be followed in the case of the more unwieldy less commercial operations: many of these latter needed to redefine their focus, rid surplus assets, and prove their commercial viability before privatization. The first step for many of these SOEs was to improve their balance sheet, and this meant divesting physical or financial assets. In the case of SOEs holding Crown property it was not difficult to split up the assets. These partial privatizations proved relatively easy to carry out, being less contentious and more easily absorbed by the markets.

The other form of partial sale used was to sell a proportion of shares in the SOE, either by floating on the stock-market, or by private contract with single

Table 14.3 Sales of state-owned enterprises and assets in New Zealand

Business	Sale price ($m)	Settlement date	Purchaser
NZ Steel	327.2	1988	Equiticorp NZ investment company (90%) (resold to BHP *et al.*)
Petrocorp	801.1	1988	Fletcher Challenge, NZ Conglomerate
Health Computing Services	4.3	1988	Paxus Information Services, NZ Computing company
Development Finance Corporation	111.3	1988	National Provident Fund, NZ superan. company (80%) Salomon Bros (20%) (DFC now under statutory management)
Post Bank	678.5	1989	ANZ, Australian trading bank
Shipping Corporation	33.6	1989/90	ACT (NZ) Ltd, Committee, UK shipping company
Air New Zealand	660.0	1989	BIL, NZ investment company (65%) Qantas (19.9%) Japan Air Lines (7.5%) American Airlines (7.5%) (30% of BIL's holding now on-sold)
Landcorp (financial instruments)	77.0	1989/90	Mortgagees
Rural Bank	550.0	1989	Fletcher Challenge, NZ conglomerate
Government Print	35.0	1990	Rank Group, NZ printer
National Film Unit	2.5	1990	TVNZ, NZ SOE
Communicate NZ	0.1	1989	DAC Group
State Insurance	735.0	1990	Norwich Insurance, UK company
Telecom NZ Ltd	4,250.0	1990	Bell Atlantic, Ameritech (US telecomms companies) (90%) now sold, Fay Richwhite, Freightways (NZ companies) (5% each) (now publicly floated)
NZ Liquid Fuel Investments Maui Gass & Synfuel stocks	80.2*	1990	Fletcher Challenge *et al.*
Export Guarantee Ltd	15.1	1990	State Insurance an ex SOE
Tourist Hotel Corporation	73.8	1990	Southern Pacific Hotels, US company
Forestry Corporation (cutting rights)	Not known	1989/90	Not known
NZ Railways Corporation (bus services)	Not known	1991	Co-operative of NZ operators

Bank of New Zealand	†	1988	Fay Richwhite, NZ merchant bank (13%) (63% still government-owned)

Sources: SOE Office, *NZ Yearbook*, R.C. Mascarenhas, The Treasury.
Notes: There have also been sales of usage rights to oil, gas, minerals, water, airwaves and fish.
* Government to receive further profit-sharing and clawback arrangements.
† BNZ not formally sold: issues of new shares diluted government's shareholding.

buyers. This technique proved more contentious because of disputes arising between the minority owner(s) and the Crown over liabilities and over minority rights following subsequent full privatization. In several cases shares were sold with implicit assurances of minority shareholder rights that were later brought into conflict.

In a speech in 1990 the then Minister for SOEs argued a number of reasons why partial privatization was not a good idea:

- management capture by the minority shareholder causing problems with further sell-downs;
- the potential to take a higher risk approach than the government wants;
- problems with the conflict over the government as regulator;
- problems with capital for expansion.[10]

The Minister also argued that sale by tender has a number of advantages over share market floats:

- the thin local markets have limited ability to absorb significant amounts of shares;
- many of the businesses for sale are financially immature and difficult for non-corporate buyers to assess.

A number of techniques have been used to transfer complete ownership: sale of all assets, sale of the complete corporate entity, or sale of all the shares. In

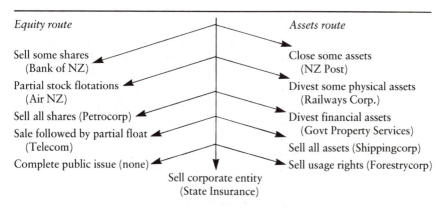

Figure 14.3 Privatization techniques in New Zealand

practice there has not been a lot of difference between these three methods. A more restricted transfer of property rights has been to sell usage rights: so far this has involved cutting rights to forests, extraction rights to gas and oil, and fishing rights. A major reason for this has been concern to protect Maori resource rights under the Treaty of Waitangi.

In practice a number of problems arose in the sale process, especially in the earlier years. With little experience of privatization in government, the bureaucracy and the New Zealand financial sector, much rapid learning had to take place and some mistakes were made. The use of advisers was contentious, and some potential conflicts of interest came to light partly as a consequence of the relatively small interlocking New Zealand corporate structure.

Just as valuation of SOEs proved complex, so also pricing for privatization was difficult. The government generally believed that sale by treaty (tender followed by negotiation) was the best method, though in at least two cases (Petrocorp and Air New Zealand), this led to allegations of political preferment of particular bidders. In two cases (Air New Zealand and Telecom) the government held a 'kiwi share' (giving the shareholder a veto over changes to the Articles of Association) to keep some control over the privatized entity, and in some other cases operating restrictions were placed on the sale.

To date there have been no full market flotations such as the UK government have used. The main reason has been the argument that a higher premium will be paid for total control and that this should be reflected in more efficient use of the asset. Privatizations have not been seen as an exercise to increase share ownership (already reasonably widespread among the New Zealand public, especially following the boom share-market years of 1984–7).

Furthermore, in comparison with Eastern Europe there has been no use of voucher systems (although they have been considered for electricity supply authority reform). In several cases partial management or employee buy-outs have been considered, but it is recognized there are some problems here: the fact that managers may know more about the real value of an SOE than the shareholder does, and the dangers of undervaluing for the benefit of employees at the expense of taxpayers.

With hindsight, some of the asset prices agreed turned out to be too low: the most controversial case was the Rural Bank which delivered very large profits during its first year in private ownership. The markets would also consider that several surprisingly high prices were reached. On the other side of the account, several assets were sold with very little equity. In the case of the Development Finance Corporation, the newly privatized company went into statutory management within a year of sale, sparking a legal argument about the information provided to the seller.

Another problem facing the government was the state of the markets for assets. By 1988 when the first sales began, New Zealand's stock-market had suffered a fall in value of over 50 per cent, and the economy was in recession. New Zealand markets for substantial assets would be expected to be thin at any time, and this raised major problems about whether to proceed with the sales. At one time the New Zealand government was simultaneously trying to sell interest in four government banks plus some other financial assets. This was made more difficult by the fact that the financial sector had recently been deregulated, that entry was effectively open, and that a large number of new banks had been set up. Privatization in New Zealand was helped by the radical deregulation of the capital markets during the preceding few years. The markets expanded rapidly between 1985–7, and were able to provide advice and finance for relatively large purchases. The main capital constraint was the weak state of the New Zealand share-market after the 1987 crash.

One way to lessen these problems of thin local markets was the New Zealand government's willingness to accept foreign buyers for what many countries continue to think of as reserved 'strategic' industries. For example, the national airline Air New Zealand was sold to a consortium including Australian, US and Japanese airlines. Since deregulation of capital controls, foreign investment in New Zealand has been effectively rubber-stamped by the regulatory authority. Though the sale process was reasonably independent of political influence, pressure was applied in a couple of sales to assist local buyers.

Following the change of government in 1990, the National government has reviewed its privatization strategy.[11] It has committed itself to continue sales of those businesses that 'will perform better within the framework of market disciplines'. It aims to sell businesses with clearly defined assets and regulatory frameworks, avoiding the need for warranties or indemnities. It has announced that it may continue to use the 'kiwi share' to be viable. It favours complete sale even if this takes a number of years, and it does not expect to retain part share-holding in the long term.

Funds raised from sales to date total about $9 billion. To put this in some perspective it represents about 12 per cent of GDP or 45 per cent of total public sector debt. The New Zealand Public Accounts 1986/87 just prior to the privatization process listed wholly financed public enterprise investments totalling $12.2 billion. However, this figure does not reflect the capital injections that have had to be made before sale.

THE OPERATING ENVIRONMENT

Government departments used to supply a large proportion of government needs and often dominated wider markets for services. In some cases, after several years of operation as SOEs or private companies, they still hold complete monopolies over at least part of their markets. However, today these market positions are frequently being eroded. This is partly due to government deregulation, which has included the removal of entry barriers to allow others to compete and required government departments to buy their supplies and accommodation requirements from the cheapest suppliers in the market rather than restricting themselves to government purchasing. The general effect is to break down internal market barriers and allow SOEs to operate more widely.

In some cases SOEs compete with one another (for example, Coalcorp now competes with Electricorp and Petrocorp in wider energy markets). Only in the case of NZ Post and Airways Corporation has full deregulation not yet taken place, with the SOE retaining a monopoly of letter post (not courier) mail and in return meeting certain social obligations. This is now being reviewed.

Despite these deregulations, about half the SOEs must still be judged as dominant firms in their industries, although only a few might claim to constitute natural monopolies. Most of the rest face increasing competition and will probably lose market share over the next few years. Many dominant SOEs claim to be constrained by the countervaling power of their major clients and in addition they are subject to the constraining power of the Commerce Act 1986. The operation of SOEs and privatized entities, even in natural monopoly areas, are generally not constrained by official regulation other than general anti-trust law. There are no consumer watchdogs other than the Commerce Commission. The Commission does receive a large number of SOE-related consumer complaints, and they are increasingly focusing on dominant SOEs or privatized utilities.

The wider process of economic liberalization has impacted directly on many SOEs. For example agricultural sector deregulation affected the Rural Bank, waterfront deregulation impacted on the New Zealand Shipping Corporation, and local authority deregulation has hit the Works and Services Corporation. Other SOEs report that they are constrained by regulations relating to environment protection and Treaty of Waitangi issues which have slowed down asset valuation, corporatization or sale. The Crown has taken over the responsibility of compensation for any Maori claims on SOE resources, but SOEs still suffer costs from consequential delay and uncertainty in transferring their assets.

The performance of SOEs obviously depends on the strength of the markets they operate in. Some are cyclical (for example, Railways, depending on agricultural and business cycles). Many operate in mature industries and cannot expect major growth without diversification. Some operate in markets that have been heavily affected by structural change (for example, Forestrycorp and Rural Bank). In broad terms, business conditions have been very tight in New Zealand since 1984 (the rate of growth of profits averaged only about 1 per cent per annum over this period). This tight market environment has heavily constrained SOE and private sector performance.

COMPANY RESTRUCTURING

In the light of their changed corporate status and the background operating environment discussed above, how did these transformed organizations order their commercial behaviour? Compared to the pre-corporatization period most enterprises have more clearly defined their core activities, and most are concentrating on this core, setting up non-mainstream operations as subsidiaries, selling them off or closing them down. Dissatisfaction with the limitations on their current operating scope and awareness of new opportunities has led to some expansions into related areas of activity. Some enterprises have extended their customer base to the private sector (for example, Government Computing Services), expanded into overseas markets (for example, Works Corp designing new stations on the London Underground), or produced new products. A few SOEs have asked to invest in more radical diversification, and in most cases Ministers have refused permission.[12]

One exception was NZ Railways' joint venture (using fibre optics cabling alongside the rail track) with an alternative long-distance telecommunications company. Attempts at vertical integration (for example, Airways Corp wanting to buy into airports, Coalcorp wanting to buy into electricity generating capacity) have been vigorously discouraged by Ministers. Applications for horizontal take-overs are judged by the Commerce Commission on normal commercial merger principles.

Divestment strategies have been more notable than expansion strategies: most SOEs have reviewed what can be efficiently done in-house and have ended up contracting-out services, selling off peripheral businesses and disposing of unused assets. The valuation process clearly revealed for the first time the extent of departmental holdings of lands and buildings, indicating a huge unused stock of capital assets.

Government trading departments were frequently overmanned due to poor management, union pressure, mixed objectives, or political pressures to take on staff. All SOEs have reviewed staff requirements, and most of the large ones have made many employees redundant. In the case of Railways, Coalcorp and Forestrycorp, up to 65 per cent of staff were laid off with little resulting reduction of output. Cuts of 10 to 25 per cent of staff numbers were common in SOEs. Most of these staff reductions took place at the time of corporatization rather than during subsequent privatization. Cuts were borne most heavily by blue-collar workers. Redundancy costs were considerable (though following new labour legislation in 1991 they will be cheaper in the future).

Enterprises restructuring in the early 1980s at the time of low unemployment, found it easier to get voluntary severance agreements, and labour force reductions were more easily achieved. Linked to the lay-off programmes were new manning and productivity agreements (for example, a two-man crewing agreement made by Railways in 1985, followed by a one-man crewing agreement in 1987). From 1987 unemployment rose rapidly in New Zealand, and SOEs have found it more difficult to reduce workforces after this time. SOE lay-offs were responsible for a significant proportion of the increase in unemployment.

In terms of capital investment, many SOEs felt there had been over-investment in the past, and in some cases grandiose plans from departmental days have been cut back. There has been considerable new spending on computing, account-ing, and other operating systems, but a marked change in long-term investment plans. Generally SOE boards are using tighter criteria than in the past to judge investment plans. Returns are judged on shorter paybacks than previously. For example, Forestrycorp has cut back on the planting of trees, Coalcorp has cut back on planned large expansions, and R&D has been trimmed in many SOEs. However, it is still noticeable that during the depressed business conditions of 1986–91 many of New Zealand's larger business investments involved SOEs or ex-SOEs.

Pricing policies have changed markedly. Many enterprises used to be under direct or indirect price control but this has now ceased. In a few cases prices have actually fallen. The most outstanding example would be Railways, where average real freight rates fell by 46 per cent between 1983 and 1989. Low pricing for social objectives has been terminated, as have cross-subsidies between different activities and other indirect subsidies. In some cases this has affected other industries. For example, wood for local sawmills used to be subsidized; recent increases to export price levels have resulted in a number of sawmill failures. In the past many prices were published; more often today SOEs negotiate individually with large customers, keeping contracts confidential. This transition to discriminatory competitive pricing has not proved easy; there has been considerable negative customer response and some legal actions. In only perhaps four cases has intense competition actually reduced prices.

Another change relates to marketing strategies: in the past sales relationships were stable, assured, and effectively 'in-house'. Many SOEs talk about changing production or engineering cultures into a marketing mode, now seeing themselves as 'client-driven'. In practice this had meant appointing marketing managers and sales forces with advertising budgets, and paying more attention to long-term client relationships.

In the past many enterprises paid relatively little attention to financial management. Monitoring was primarily to show that spending had met departmental vote requirements rather than being commercially effective. There has been considerable investment in establishing financial management, treasury functions, foreign exchange management, debt management and new accounting systems.

THE PERFORMANCE OF STATE ENTERPRISES

It is extremely difficult to measure improvements in performance as a result of corporatization and privatization. This is because of the relatively short period of corporatization to date, the difficulty of separating out the effects of institutional change from other background factors, and because it is difficult to obtain data on a consistent and comparable basis pre- and post-corporatization/privatization. In addition, it has been difficult to remove the financial effects of balance sheet restructuring and to measure changes in quality of inputs and outputs. Furthermore, differences in market outlook, competition, and regulation, all affect performance.

As a generalization, physical indicators of performance such as labour productivity have improved sharply since corporatization. However, financial measures such as profitability and return on assets have depended crucially on whether or not balance sheets were restructured before corporatization, with appropriate capital injections from the Crown. It is possible to group the organizations into broad categories according to their performance so far:

1 *Long-term basket cases*: There are a small number of SOEs that have been categorized by losses or poor returns, declining equity ratios, and little progress in reducing labour costs. These have typically been capital intensive, with militant and strategically placed unions or with nationalistic motivations for getting into an industry where New Zealand had few competitive strengths. One example was Shipping Corp. Corporatization did not solve these problems till an emergency restructuring took place immediately prior to sale. Since then performance has been on commercial lines.

2 *Gradual turnaround from loss-making*: Other organizations such as New Zealand Rail have inherited major operating constraints, with heavy capital structures in mature or declining industries. This category of SOEs was able to achieve major down-sizing over time, but they have suffered from protracted restructuring of their balance sheets. Railways has achieved remarkable improvement in productivity and small operating profits (without subsidies) but are still running overall losses. Alongside any other freight rail operation in the world this is a remarkably good performance, but it is still judged harshly by New Zealand SOE standards.

3 *Sharp turnarounds*: A number of SOEs successfully met new commercial objectives during corporatization and managed to turn around both physical productivity and financial performance, with profitability improving since the first year as an SOE (for example, Coalcorp, Forestrycorp and New Zealand Post).

4 *Increasingly profitable SOEs*: Bodies like Electricorp, aided by their natural monopoly in some areas of operation have operated successfully as an SOE, making commercial decisions on investment, pricing, marketing, and consequently maintaining or increasing profitability. This category includes a small number of highly profitable SOEs, partly as a result of favourable demand conditions and market positions. These would include Petrocorp and State Insurance.

LOCAL AUTHORITY TRADING ENTERPRISES

In New Zealand local government provides a range of local services. In 1989 the government made an attempt to extend the principles of corporatization and privatization to cover the trading activities of local government. The 1989 (No. 2) amendment to the Local Government Act created companies to be called Local Authority Trading Enterprises (LATEs). The Act required that in order to qualify for central government subsidies, passenger transport and public works operations had to be made into LATEs by 1991, and these would only remain in business if they proved competitive with the private sector, this to be tested by open tendering. This was an attempt to force commercial principles on these operations, many of which had existed on ill-defined cross-subsidies for years.

Local authorities have generally been unenthusiastic about this corporatization. In tendering bus routes the incumbent local authority operators have often been the favoured contractors. These authorities continue to operate many other businesses such as zoos, abbatoirs, water and sewage operations, refuse disposal and golf courses. Few of these activities have been set up as LATEs or even as profit centres. The authorities are also able to privatize their operations, but there has been a marked distaste to actually doing this.

As part of the restructuring of transport operations in New Zealand local authorities now hold part or full shares in port companies and airport authorities. The government has expressed dissatisfaction with the way these are being run, and is threatening to force authorities to sell at least a partial share. In addition local authorities own some electricity distribution operations, but these are likely to be restructured in the form of consumer trusts. To generalize, local authorities (while not highly politicized) have shown little enthusiasm for the government's programme of restructuring, and there has been little voluntary corporatization or privatization. With their ability to increase local rates, these authorities have largely been cushioned from the business recession and also from the financial pressures central government has faced as a result of its fiscal deficit. However, these pressures to change are now slowly reaching local government.

BROADER ECONOMIC EFFECTS

The size of the corporatization and privatization programme in New Zealand has been such that there have been significant effects on other aspects of the macroeconomy. This section reviews some of these.

The transfer of state trading functions into SOEs led to a large number of work lay-offs. During the period of liberalization, unemployment in New Zealand rose from 3 to 10 per cent, and SOEs contributed a significant part of this. Another impact has been through price increases: once corporatized, SOEs have been free to set their own prices. New Zealand has been going through a period of tight monetary policy to reduce the high levels of inflation (18 per cent in 1984, now 3 per cent). During this period the government had been occasionally embarrassed by sizeable price increases announced by SOEs that were outside its control. These have been justified by the SOEs' need to restructure their pricing following interventions and ineffective management during their trading department days. There have, however, also been significant price cuts, and in net terms the sector has probably not contributed to inflation. Several larger public utility SOEs have undertaken to restrict price rises to less than the overall rate of inflation.

A more noticeable effect has come from capital restructuring. After the exercises of valuing assets and assessing the viability and marketability of SOEs, it became clear that some government trading operations required either new capital investments or else the writing off of uneconomic assets. In addition many SOEs needed a restructuring of their balance sheets. These capital injections put the government financial accounts under some stress during the period 1986–90. Upon corporatization some SOEs went directly to capital markets to fund restructuring, and for several years they were the dominant source of business investment. This strong demand for funds probably contributed to the continuing high interest rates in New Zealand and may have exacerbated private sector crowd-out in the capital markets.

The macroeconomic indicator of most concern in New Zealand is currently the overseas debt. The heavy SOE borrowing has certainly contributed to the increase in gross market debt between 1988 and 1991, although this has been part matched by repayments of public debt. In 1990 total overseas liabilities held by SOEs totalled some $8 billion, in contrast to New Zealand's total (public and private) overseas debt of $49 billion.

To some degree these effects have been countered by the privatization programme. One reason given for the programme of sales was government's need to reduce its debt. In general the funds earned from sales have been committed to debt reduction (with the exception of an allocation from the sale of Telecom made to health and education spending for political reasons). However, the impact of this has been offset by continuous financial deficits through the period.

Different regimes have been followed with respect to the balance of domestic and overseas debt repayments. In an attempt to reduce the exchange rate effects of large capital movements a policy of repaying debt in the currency of the sale was adopted. In 1989/90 government policy was to retire domestic debt. This has now changed: in its 1991 Budget the government announced that it would specifically retire overseas debt from asset sales. Overall, the sales have raised about $9 billion in revenue to date, and most of this has been committed to debt retirement. The net public sector debt now stands at about $48 billion.

However, the main hoped-for effects of corporatization and privatization were not on the government's balance sheet, but rather on improvement in production efficiency and consequently in allocative efficiency. As noted above, it is easy to illustrate this anecdotally, but not yet possible to technically measure much operational improvement.

It is important to view corporatization and privatization in New Zealand in the context of wider structural reform. There was a radical restructuring of private sector trading conditions (partly through an appreciation of the real exchange rate that impacted on the traded sector). After that it was easy to argue that the large government sector also had to suffer its share of the pain. Corporatization was regarded as an early phase reform as can be seen in Figure 14.3. Privatization was a middle–late phase reform, still being only part underway.

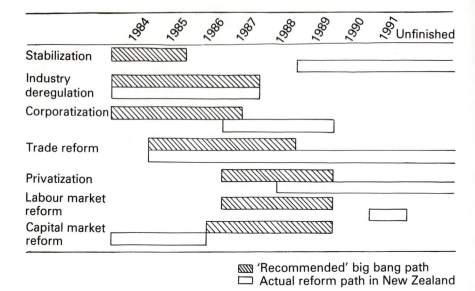

Figure 14.4 'Recommended' and actual phasing of reforms in New Zealand

Source: The 'recommended' phasing is derived from a generalized proposal for speedy reform in H. Genberg, *On the Sequencing of Reforms in Eastern Europe*, WP/9/13 (IMF, 1991).
Note: This diagram is conceptual in nature only.

The financial demands of corporatization exacerbated the structural fiscal deficit in New Zealand. This meant that stabilization has taken longer to achieve than would otherwise have been the case. This in turn has exacerbated the capital inflows that have contributed to high interest rates and high exchange rates and the crowding-out effect on the traded sector. On the other hand corporatization/privatization on this scale would not have been possible without liberalization of the financial sector and capital controls.

In terms of future policy, the corporatization process is now nearly complete, with no wholesale reversal possible. About a half of the SOEs have been privatized. The process is likely to continue, though the government has said it will in future be guided by the ability of the market to absorb assets and will no longer issue a timetable of expected sales and earnings. In the meantime the process of corporatization and privatization is being extended to local authority trading activities in a more vigorous way. In addition the 1991 Budget announced that a watered-down form of corporate reorganization would be applied to government science organizations ('Crown Research Institutes') and to reorganized hospital services ('Crown Health Enterprises').

APPENDIX: LIST OF NEW ZEALAND ECONOMIC LIBERALIZATION MEASURES

Closer economic relations with Australia	1983+
Deregulation of land freight transport	1983–85
Removal of foreign exchange controls	1984
Deregulation of entry licensing in industry	1984+
Removal of other operating barriers in industry	1984+
Removal of concessions for favoured investment (for example, R&D)	1984+
Removal of subsidized agricultural prices	1984
Removal of financial controls (interest rate ceiling, reserve ratio requirements, priorities for various sectors)	1984–86
Removal of most price control	1984–88
Removal of import licensing	1984–89
Liberalization of foreign direct investment	1985
Floating of the exchange rate	1985
Partial deregulation of occupational licensing	1985–90
Significant decrease in import tariffs	1985–92
Deregulation of milk industry	1986
Deregulation of financial services sector	1986
Removal of concessional funding for agricultural exports	1986–88
Partial deregulation of energy sector	1986–91
Removal of monopoly rights on state trading	1986–88
Revision of corporate, personal and direct taxation	1986–88
Corporatization of state trading activities	1986–90
Review of competition regulation Commerce Act	1986–91
Abolition of many quangos and quasi-government organizations	1987
Review of role of producer marketing boards	1987+
Reorganization of core government departments	1987+
New entry to air transport	1987–90
Revision of town and country planning	1987–90
Programme of sale of state assets	1987–90
Business law reform (Companies Act, Securities legislation)	1988+
Review of education and health provision	1988–90
Deregulation of harbours and wharves	1989
Removal of shop trading hours restrictions	1989
Corporatization of some local authority trading activities	1989
Reform of local government	1989–91
Deregulation of land passenger transport	1989–90
Restructing of science funding	1989–92
Partial deregulation of shipping	1990

Reform of intellectual property law	1990–92
Resource management law reform	1991
Deregulation of the labour market	1991
Restructuring of guaranteed retirement income	1991
Complete health sector restructuring	1991–93

NOTES

1   The chapter represents the views of the authors, and does not necessarily represent those of the New Zealand government. No liability is accepted for errors of fact or opinion in this chapter whether or not due to negligence on the part of the Institutes, their contributors, employees or Boards of Trustees. This work is based on a larger project on state trading organizations in New Zealand. The authors wish to acknowledge the work of Ian Duncan and Brendan O'Donovan, and helpful comments from Stan Vandersyp, Bruce Carrie and James Templeton.

2   National's most radical steps have been in moving away from a general system of social provision towards one targeted more on those in greatest need. As this will shift the finance of activities from the public to the private purse rather than affect the ownership or operation of enterprises it is not considered in this chapter. We therefore deal with this whole process of corporatization and privatization from 1984 to the present day as a single evolving experience.

3   For a fuller account of the economic issues see A. Bollard and R. Buckle (eds), *Economic Liberalisation in New Zealand*, Allen & Unwin, 1987. For an account of the political/economic interface, see B. Easton, *The Making of Rogernomics*, Auckland University Press, 1989; M. Holland and J. Boston, *The Fourth Labour Government*, Oxford University Press, 1990; A. Bollard, *Economic Liberalisation in New Zealand: It was the Best of Times, It was the Worst of Times*, Working Paper 91/5, NZ Institute of Economic Research, 1991. Note also that in the late 1970s the National government did put in place some early deregulatory reforms, and it is a generalization to suggest the process started with the 1984 Labour government.

4   See, for example: R. L. Cameron and P. J. Duignan, *Government Owned Enterprises: Theory, Performance and Efficiency*, The Treasury, 1984.

5   R. Deane, *Corporatisation and Privatisation: A Discussion of the Issues*, Electricorp, 1989.

6   For a detailed review see J. Boston *et al.* (eds), *Reshaping the State: New Zealand's Bureaucratic Revolution*, Oxford University Press, 1991.

7   For a more detailed background, see R. C. Mascarenhas, *State-Owned Enterprises*, chapter 2 in J. Boston *et al.* (eds), *Reshaping the State: New Zealand's Bureaucratic Revolution*, Oxford University Press, 1991.

8   For an inside account by the then Minister of Finance, see R. Douglas and L. Callen *Towards Prosperity*, David Bateman, 1987.

9   *State-Owned Enterprise Policy: Issues in Ownership and Regulation*, NZ Business Roundtable, 1988; *Privatising State Owned Enterprises*, Economic Development Commission, 1989; *Commercial Performance of State-Owned Enterprises*, The Treasury, 1987; R. Deane, *Corporatisation and Privatisation: A Discussion of the Issues*, Electricity Corporation, 1989.

10   'The case for complete rather than partial privatisation and for economic deregulation', Address by the Hon. R. W. Prebble, World Bank, 24 October, 1990.

11   See 'Privatisation strategy', Annex 5 in *Budget 1991*, Publication B6A.

12   See, for example, B. Wheeler, *Diversification Issues for State-Owned Enterprises*, SOE Advisory Unit, 1989.

15

AN ANALYSIS OF THE PRIVATIZATION OF JAPAN NATIONAL RAILWAY CORPORATION[1]

Tetsuzo Yamamoto

INTRODUCTION

The period from 1981 to 1987 could be defined as the age of administrative reform in Japan. This period began with the creation of the second *ad hoc* Council on Administrative Reform (Rincho) and ended with the privatization of Japan National Railways (JNR).

Rincho, chaired by Toshiwo Doko, raised two basic ideas of reform – namely, building a revitalized welfare society, and contributing positively to the well-being of the world. It aimed at drastic reforms concerning: the replacement of a paternal and protective administration by a new one which would require the people to be more independent and self-supportive; the promotion of deregulation and privatization instead of an increase in government control; a re-adjustment of relationships between the central and local governments, especially with respect to the transfer of power or jurisdiction to the local self-autonomies.

Rincho submitted five reports during 1981–3. The Third Report in July 1982 was very important: it recommended that the so-called three public corporations (JNR, NTT – the Nippon Telegraph and Telephone Public Corporation, JTSPC – the Japan Tobacco and Salt Public Corporation) should be privatized and opened up to competition. In particular the privatization of JNR was the most controversial and symbolic of the range of regulatory reforms in respect of its scale and overall significance for the Japanese economy.

In this chapter, we will first of all consider the background and factors which acted as a catalyst to privatizations in Japan, especially that of JNR; second, the various opinions which advocated or opposed JNR's privatization; third, the process of the privatization; fourth, its managerial effects; and, finally, the influence of JNR's privatization on the land transportation markets. The purpose of this chapter is to estimate the effects in the short term, to clarify the problems which JR faces now, and to conclude provisionally as to whether JNR's privatization was successful or not.

THE BACKGROUND

We will first define Japanese-style privatization. The word 'privatization', which reminds Japanese people of the transfer of government companies to the private sector in the Meiji era, means basically the selling off or the transfer of public corporations or government enterprises to private companies within the framework of the Commercial Code. In contrast to Britain's privatization, which includes three concepts – denationalization, liberalization or deregulation, and contracting out – it can be said that Japanese-style privatization is much narrower in scope. Privatization in Japan can be compatible with regulation as seen in the case of NTT. It is also different from contracting out, which is expressed in Japan by the word *minkatsu* (the injection of private sector competitiveness or vitality into the public sector).

Now to the question of what significance the privatization measure holds in the wide range of administrative reforms of the mid-1980s. It could be evaluated as the representative policy among many measures suggested by Rincho. In fact privatization of the three public corporations became a key problem in terms of inefficiency, the impediments of monopolies, and diseconomies of scale. The proposal of JNR's privatization was especially seen as the focus of Rincho/Doko because of its huge financial deficits and fierce objections against the privatization.

Next, we examine the background and the factors which acted as a catalyst to privatization. Japan has previously experienced booms of privatization twice in modern history. The first wave of privatizations occurred during the early 1880s – the so-called *Kangyo Haraisage* in the Meiji era. At that time the government, urged to reconstruct fiscal conditions, found itself forced to sell of a number of infant enterprises to the private sector. As a result of *Shokusan Kogyo* (policy for promoting industry and increasing production), the government had owned and managed many enterprises in the major industries. The second wave was realized as part of the American Occupation policies which compelled the Japanese government to scrap or sell off most of the state-owned enterprises, and as part of the Dodge Line shift from 1949–52 which aimed to make the Japanese economy more efficient and to reduce the continuing costs of supporting Japan. For example, the Japan Electric Power Company, owned by the state, was divided and privatized in this period.

The boom in the mid-1980s can be seen as the third wave of privatization in Japan. We can pick out the following factors as the background of recent privatizations:

1 *Socioeconomic change.* Rapid technological changes in the field of hi-tech industries and their diffusion into nearly all industries, not only brought about environmental changes in market conditions and structures where government's monopolistic services were hitherto deemed indispensable, but also required the improvement of efficiency and service in the fields of industrial infrastructure.

2   *Fiscal crisis and rising financial costs of the public corporations.* Between 1974 and 1979, Japan's national deficit rose from 1.6 to 6.1 per cent of GNP, with the national debt service burden also increasing from 5.3 per cent of general account expenditures in 1975 to 11 per cent in 1979. Without tax reform, including a reduction in corporate tax, the government could not increase military spending as it was compelled to do by the Reagan adminis-tration. The government examined the fiscal conditions to reduce expendi-tures and was inclined to sell off the government-affiliated enterprises. In particular JNR's financial losses, non-profitability and inefficiency, which tended to eat up public money, were regarded as one reason for the national fiscal deficits.

3   *Maturity of conditions.* The government failed to improve the performance of the public sector in the 1960s. The Ikeda Cabinet advocated public sector retrenchment as a means of unshackling the private sector and established the first *ad hoc* Council on Administrative Reform in 1960. But the Japan Socialist Party (JSP) and the Sohyo (the largest federation of trade unions at that time) objected to the government's proposals; the bureaucracy resisted the reforms too. The conditions for privatization were not mature yet. But through the 1970s the surroundings were altered. Rincho's chairman Doko, who put forward the reforms, and Prime Minister Nakasone, who orchestrated the process of privatization, took the initiative and people who made complaints against the inefficiency of the public sector supported their activities. With regard to the circumstances, various factors such as socio-economic changes, the rapid progress of new technologies, and fiscal crisis, all required administrative reforms. It should be noted that the decline of the JSP and trade unions in the 1980s facilitated the reforms.

These factors, however, were not sufficient to realize the privatizations. There also existed other catalysts which stimulated the process of privatization:

1   *Foreign pressure.* In determining the profile of privatization in the 1980s, the role of foreign pressure should not be underestimated. The US in particular felt that privatization could open new opportunities by increasing competition and accelerating market growth – this in turn increasing demand for imports. Japan had to concede to America's pressure in order to alleviate escalating trade friction.

2   *Boom in the capital markets.* In the mid-1980s Japanese capital markets developed rapidly and sales of public assets promised to be highly profitable to the state, as well as to the financial intermediaries involved in under-writing them. In fact, the proceeds to the government by selling off 12.5 per cent of NTT shares came to more than 11 per cent of the total fiscal 1987 national revenue.

OPINIONS FOR AND AGAINST THE PRIVATIZATION OF JNR

In the Third Report of Rincho, the special panel chaired by Hiroshi Kato, pointed out that public corporations had difficulties in certain areas of operation. First there was the special principal–agent relationship, the Diet and government interventions, the ambiguity of managerial responsibility, and a lack of ability to deal with labour problems, etc. Second, there existed a lack of self-awareness on the part of labour as to their role as public servants. Third, there were the excessive demands from the people made on the public corporations and, finally, the difficulty of managerial control due to the large scale of the organization.

The Report insisted that the public corporations could not control themselves or promote the reforms within the existing framework, further suggesting that the public corporations should be privatized and effective competition be introduced in this field. It highlighted JNR's problems, which were identified as external interference; uniform management which disregarded different regional conditions concerning transport demands and regional economy; and the unstable relationship between management and labour, etc. To remedy the faults, the report suggested that the Diet intervention should be abolished and that government regulations be decreased to the same level as those affecting the private sector, concluding that JNR should be divided into seven special corporations and privatized completely through a selling off of its shares to the public after five years.

With regard to the clearance of the huge liabilities, the Report suggested that Japan Railways (JR) should inherit a level of debts consistent with being able to repay the amount with interest included, subject to the implementation of rationalization and cost reduction. It also suggested that the remaining debts should be kept in the JNR Settlement Corporation and subsidized by the government. Following these suggestions, the JNR Reconstruction Supervision Commission was set up in 1983 and it considered privatization measures to solve the problems of the debts and inefficiency.

Opinions against the privatization

After the announcement of the Third Report, an anti-privatization campaign was promoted by the JSP and the Kokuro (the largest trade union in JNR which played an important role in the Sohyo labour movement) and many critical opinions were expressed. In 1986, when the drafts of JNR's privatization laws were submitted to the Diet, the controversies reached their height. A number of different opinions were voiced.

1   The possibility of impeding the 'public interest'. If the abolition of unprofitable rural lines was permitted it would enlarge the gap among regional economies. Accordingly, privatization would be likely to destroy 'equity'.

2   The influence on labour problems. Privatization would bring about mass

unemployment and worsen the labour conditions, thus threatening passenger safety.

3 Division into regional companies would not only make it impossible to supply a universal service, but would also induce managerial inequality in the six regional passenger companies. It would give advantages to one or two companies (JR Higashi and JR Tokai) and drive the other companies into a hopeless condition.

Despite these opinions, the proposal for privatization was supported by most of the people and the mass media in the hope that train fares would be stabilized and bad service eradicated.

Opinions for privatization

In Japan there were no academic groups or research institutes which influenced policy formation like the Chicago School in the US or IEA in Britain. However, some academics, who believe in neo-liberalism and public choice theory, participated in Rincho as commissioners; others, who imported the contestability theory and principal–agent relation theory, were drawn to the ministries for policy formation (seisaku chosei kancho) such as the Economic Planning Agency.

Although they played a role in enlightening the people, it is doubtful whether the government applied the theories of these academics to the mechanics of Japanese privatization. For example, in the case of JNR, the theory of contestability may have been ineffectual because JNR competed with the private railway companies and underground railroads in the urban areas and had lost its monopolistic position: the market structure was more competitive than the contestability theory had supposed. Though the regional monopoly would be maintained in the countryside, the hypothesis of 'sunk cost = zero' would not be developed here. A lease or second-hand market had not developed because of the nature of the industry (the difficulty of separating the base structure from the superstructure) and the decreasing number of passengers, many of whom had abandoned the railway and made use of cars. The 'hit and run' strategy of the new entrants does not work in the railway industry.

It is wrong, however, to say that there was no place for theory in the privatizing of the public corporations. Several previous failures to reconstruct JNR required consideration of the following problems: government failure; comparison of performance between the public corporations and private enterprises; principal–agent relationships; management accountability; and the relationship between management and labour. These factors were studied pragmatically. Thus, privatization in Japan was implemented on the basis of analyses obtained from domestic experiences rather than from imported theories.

THE PROCESS OF THE PRIVATIZATION

Japan's first railway line, between Tokyo and Yokohama, was opened under government auspices in 1872. But the state did not suppress the construction of private railways. Its model was the mixed public–private railway system of Prussia. At the turn of the century, the private companies became much larger than the national railway in terms of the length of track lines and the volume of passenger transport. In 1906, the government nationalized the Japanese railway industry by acquiring seventeen private companies under the National Owner-ship of Railways Law. It was mainly motivated by military objectives (the efficient operation of a nation-wide transport system). After that it established a monopolistic position in land transportation and its management developed favourably till 1944, when the air raids of the US Army disrupted its operations.

In 1949, JNR was created in order to improve organizational efficiency in response to the demands of industry and to weaken the nascent labour movement, General Douglas MacArthur's design being to strengthen Japan as a bulwark against Communism and to disrupt the power of the militant public sector unions. JNR became a *kohsha*, or public corporation, whose model was based on the Anglo-American public corporation.

JNR maintained its monopolistic power in the 1950s and in 1955 accounted for 55 per cent of the passenger transport market and 52 per cent in the freight market. But its share began to decrease gradually in the 1960s because of the rapid development of motorization and urbanism. When automobiles and aircraft became the most efficient means of transportation, the railways lost their dominant position. In competition with private railways, JNR could not maintain the advantage, either. In 1964 JNR recorded operating losses of ¥30 billion and faced financial problems in the late 1960s. Its conditions became worse in the 1970s and its deficit reached ¥100 billion in 1980 alone. The company's share of transportation decreased to 24.7 per cent (passenger) and 8.4 per cent (freight) in the same year.

In order to revive JNR's share of the market, a kind of 'equal-footing' policy such as Kennedy's transport policy which aimed to equalize the base structure and secure a fair competition between railways and automobiles was examined. But such a policy was not adopted. One reason was that the 'equal-footing' policy had not stopped the decline of railways in the US and West Germany; another was that JNR's failure was thought to exist in management itself rather than in the disadvantageous position that railways found themselves in when competing against automobiles.

The causes of JNR's decline were:

1   *External intervention.* JNR was subjected to excessive government inter-vention, particularly by politicians with various 'local' concerns. Faced with these pressures, it was forced to engage in large-scale investment for which tariffs and fares were to be set by the government to cross-subsidize one line

by another. The result was that JNR was compelled to operate a number of deficit rural lines.

2   *Organizational inefficiency.* Management's accountability was not as firmly established as in the private sector. Management's concern with efficiency was lessened by its expectation that whatever financial loss it made was likely to be made up for by the government. Management failed to meet the socioeconomic changes and to control its relationship with labour (over-manning, wage scale).

3   *Lack of the market principle of the survival of the fittest.* In spite of monopolistic rights ceasing, JNR relied upon them and tried to be free from the competitive pressures of market forces.

The sixth (final) draft for reconstructing JNR, suggested the downsizing of management and an increase inefficiency by means of a reduction of employees (420 to 350 thousand); a revision of tariffs and fares; the abolition of deficit rural lines; and subsidies by the government to pay for the interests. This reconstruction attempt resulted in failure owing to the poor relations between management and labour. Indeed, JNR's financial deficits increased year by year. Though JNR had more than 358,000 employees and revenues exceeding ¥3 trillion in 1984, it also had huge operating deficits which required subsidies of ¥648.8 billion. In the same year, JNR borrowed ¥836 billion and the government issued public bonds of ¥620 billion for JNR.

Throughout the early 1980s, JNR was known as one of the '3K's (Kome – rice, Kokutetsu – JNR, Kenpo – National Health Service)' – one of the largest contributors to national budgetary deficits. In 1986 the pure operating loss approximated to ¥1,800 billion. The company's debt exceeded ¥25 trillion and pension fund deficits of the mutual aid association were ¥4.9 trillion, making a total debt of about ¥30 trillion in all.

Faced with the financial crisis, the JNR Reconstruction Supervision Commission submitted a 'report of JNR's reconstruction' to the Prime Minister after two years of investigation. Following this proposal, the government presented the drafts relating to JNR's reform to the Diet in 1986. The bills were passed and became law in 1987. JNR was dissolved and split into seven successor firms.

In privatizing JNR, the following steps were adopted as transitory measures: the establishment of rules in the workshop (abolition of implicit agreement); a reduction of employees; the discontinuance of capital investment; rationalization of the freight sector; the adjustment of special rural lines; entrance into profitable businesses; control of wage increases; and the freezing of tariffs and fares.

Thus, JNR was split up and privatized in 1987. The regional division was decided on the following criteria: to realize the appropriate size of management; to respond to the demand of regional economies; to introduce competition; and to guarantee accountability in each region.

With regard to the long-term liabilities, the JNR Settlement Corporation

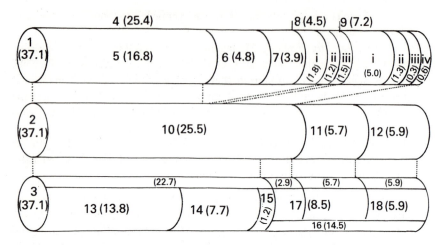

Figure 15.1 Disposal of Japan National Railways' long-term liabilities and other debts (in ¥ trillion)

Source: JNR Settlement Corporation 1990.
Notes: 1 Long-term liabilities total; 2 Transferred liabilities total; 3 Resources for repayment total; 4 JNR's long-term liabilities etc.; 5 Others; 6 Transferred to JR (passenger companies in Honshu, the freight company, etc.); 7 Equivalent of Tohoku, Tokaido and Sanyo Shinkansen assets (book price); 8 Railway Construction Public Corporation liabilities: i – for Joetsu Shinkansen facilities, ii – for conventional line facilities in Honshu, iii – for Seikan Tunnel facilities etc.; 9 Other liabilities: i – Pension obligations etc., ii – Financial stabilization funds for JR companies in the three smaller islands, iii – Cost for re-employment promotion, iv – Honshu–Shikoku Bridge Authority's liabilities; 10 Transferred to JNR SC; 11 Transferred to Shinkansen Holding Corporation; 12 Transferred to other JR organizations; 13 Borne by the public; 14 Revenue from land sales; 15 Revenue from stock sales, etc.; 16 Borne by JR organizations; 17 Shinkansen rent; 18 Operating revenue.

Table 15.1 Japan Railways: stocks owned by JNR SC

Company	Face value (yen)	Number of stocks (thousands)	Amount (¥ bn)
Hokkaido Railway Co.	50,000	180	9
East Japan Railway Co.	50,000	4,000	200
Central Japan Railway Co.	50,000	2,240	112
West Japan Railway Co.	50,000	2,000	100
Shikoku Railway Co.	50,000	70	3.5
Kyushu Railway Co.	50,000	320	16
Japan Freight Railway Co.	50,000	380	19
Total	–	9,190	459.5

Source: JNR Settlement Corporation 1990.

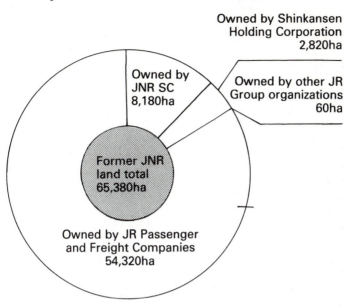

Figure 15.2 Land taken over by Japan National Railway SC

Source: JNR Settlement Corporation 1990.
Notes: 1 Of the land owned by JNR SC, the area reported to the national Diet as available for sales is 3.350 ha; 2 In addition to the land shown in this figure, JNR SC has about 630 ha of land transferred from the Japan Railway Construction Public Corporation; 3 All figures are as of 1 April 1987

assumed the burden of ¥25.5 trillion of the total debt amount of ¥37.1 trillion (as of April 1987). The seven companies and the Shinkansen Holding Corporation took over ¥5.9 trillion and ¥5.7 trillion respectively (see Figure 15.1).

As for the problem of overmanning, a measure to suspend recruitment was adopted. Surplus workers were gathered to the JNR Settlement Corporation, which was responsible for promoting re-employment through activities such as job-training. It also held shares of the seven companies (9.19 million shares, the value of each unit share ¥50 thousand, making a total of ¥459.5 billion) and a part of the railway lands (see Table 15.1, Figure 15.2).

The Shinkansen Holding Corporation was established to deal with the debts related to the Shinkansen. It owned four Shinkansen lines (Tokaido, Sanyo, Joetsu, and Tohoku) and began to lease them to JR. The debts related to the Shinkansen are expected to be made up for by the lease proceeds (see Figure 15.1).

The privatization of JNR was implemented from the viewpoint of overcoming management problems, because the causes of deficits were seen to exist in the public corporation system itself. But in a wide sense, the factors which deteriorated JNR's management were thought to lie hidden in a series of implicit

Table 15.2 Japan Railways: revenue and expenditure in 1989 (billion yen)

	JR Hokkaido	JR East	JR Central	JR West	JR Shikoku	JR Kyushu	Total (passenger companies)	Freight company	Overall total
(A) Part of ordinary revenue and expenditure									
(A.1) Section of operating account									
(1.1)	80.9	1672.8	999.5	823.1	41.0	129.7	3747.0	192.1	3939.1
(1.2)	131.7	1395.5	887.1	734.4	51.1	152.9	3352.7	182.2	3534.9
(1.3)	− 50.7	277.3	112.4	88.6	−10.0	− 23.2	394.4	9.8	404.2
(1.4)	18.9	62.6	3.6	11.2	2.8	14.2	113.3	–	113.3
(1.5)	20.8	58.8	2.3	8.9	4.4	19.7	114.9	–	114.9
(1.6)	− 1.9	3.7	1.3	2.2	− 1.6	− 5.5	− 1.8	–	1.8
(1.7)	− 52.7	281.1	113.7	90.9	−11.6	− 28.7	392.7	9.8	402.5
(A.2) Section of non-operating account									
(2.1)	3.4	− 177.6	− 5.3	− 50.6	2.5	4.4	− 223.2	− 3.4	− 226.6
(2.2)	49.5	–	–	–	15.1	28.2	92.8	–	92.8
(A.T.)	0.2	103.4	108.3	40.2	6.1	3.8	262.0	6.4	268.4
(B) Part of extraordinary revenue and expenditure									
(B.1)	0	1.7	16.6	1.9	0	0.7	20.9	0.1	21.0
(C)	0.3	105.2	124.9	42.1	6.0	4.5	283.0	6.5	289.5
(D)	0.1	47.9	58.2	16.4	2.4	0.7	125.7	3.5	129.2
(E)	0.2	57.2	66.7	25.7	3.6	3.8	157.2	2.9	160.1

Source: The White Paper on Transportation 1990.

Notes:

(1.1) operating revenues of railway business
(1.2) operating expenses of railway business
(1.3) operating revenue and expenditure of railway business
(1.4) operating revenues of the other businesses
(1.5) operating expenses of the other businesses
(1.6) operating revenue and expenditure of the other businesses
(1.7) Total operating revenues and expenditure

(2.1) non-operating revenues and expenditure
(2.2) revenue and expenditure from employing fund for stabilizing management
(A.T.) Total ordinary revenue and expenditure
(B.1) extraordinary revenue and expenditure
(C) income for this term before taxes
(D) corporation tax and like
(E) income for this term

agreements between the Liberal Democratic Party (LDP) and the JSP – especially concerning JNR's budget in the Diet – and in the failure to separate base-structure from superstructure. The former enabled the employees to increase wage scales above the level of productivity. As for the latter, the creation of the Japan Railway Construction Corporation (1964) did not work well because of the political interventions. For example, JNR's routeing decisions were exposed to greater political influence than before. Throughout the late 1960s and 1970s, JNR continued to increase salaries and benefit packages, and to expand its network of unprofitable rural lines, leading to an accumulation of deficits that attracted growing opposition from the government and the business world.

THE EFFECT OF THE PRIVATIZATION ON JR'S MANAGEMENT

It is said that the industrial behaviour of JR has changed remarkably since 1987. Some economists have analysed these changes by employing the principal–agent theory of Vickers and Yarrow (1988). For example, Okano divided these relationships into two stages (Diet–bureaucracy, bureaucracy–JNR) and analysed the effects of privatization on their management. He argued that privatization could improve the existing principal–agent relationships which inevitably caused inefficiency. The others were critical that JR's profits after privatization were artificially created by the Transport Ministry's plan and that JR's management was inferior to that practised by JNR.

Which opinion is right? Five years have passed since privatization and it is now possible to analyse the performance of JR. According to our observation, the principal–agent relationships have changed to some degree and the financial conditions of the corporation have improved gradually.

As for the volume of passenger transport (person/kilometre), this has been increased by the three inland companies of JR by 1–3 per cent yearly. However, the three island companies of JR have either maintained the same level or volume has fallen by 4 per cent in the Hokkaido company. With regard to freight transport, despite a decrease in the volume transported by freight car the annual growth rate was increased by 3–7 per cent as a result of the increase in cost of container transport.

Reflecting the gradual increase of the volume, the conditions of profit and loss have improved to some extent. Since the privatization, the three inland JR companies have recorded operating profits of ¥100–300 billion. As for the three island companies these have continued to operate in the red. Making up for the losses by the proceeds obtained from the use of the Fund for Stabilizing Management, the three island JR companies have barely maintained profits. Overall, the total operating profits of JR reached ¥268.4 billion in 1989, an increase of 26.7 per cent. The Japan Freight Railway Company has also secured ordinary profits through the increase of container transport and rationalization such as cost-cutting and the reduction of employees (see Table 15.2).

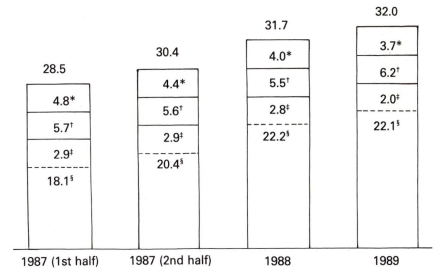

Figure 15.3 Japan Railways: situation of long-term liabilities, 1987–9 (in ¥ trillion)

Source: The White Paper on Transportation 1990.
Notes: *Liability of JR; †Liability of Shinkansen Holding Corporation; ‡Burden of Shinkansen Holding Corporation; §Liability of JNR Settlement Corporation. Increase of liabilities of JNR Settlement Corporation in 1987 and 1988 was due to taking over the debts of the Seikan Tunnel and the Seto Bridge.

The good performance of JR has been supported by the growth of the land transportation market accompanied by domestic prosperity and the effects of big projects such as the Seikan Tunnel and the Seto Bridge. Much of this is due, however, to the endeavour of JR's management to develop positive profit-earning policies (operation of extra trains, expansion of section operations, speed-up, improvement of train connections, provision of diversified services, introduction of new trains, improvement of stations and facilities), and to the retrenchment policy through rationalization (reduction of operating costs such as adjustment of deficit rural lines, constraint of personnel expenses and management costs).

At the level of JR's management, it can be said that the privatization has been successful. Some serious problems still remain, however. The largest problem is that the primary plan of eliminating the long-term liabilities has not proceeded according to schedule (see Figure 15.3). The JNR Settlement Corporation had a responsibility to sell the railway lands on a large scale through competitive tendering. But it could not do this because the government was worried that there might be a sudden rise of land prices, particularly in the metropolitan areas (see Table 15.3). In addition, it was unable to sell off the shares of JR (the inland companies). The share sale is likely to be postponed for some time owing to the current decline of the Japanese stock-market. Furthermore, the deficit of pension

349

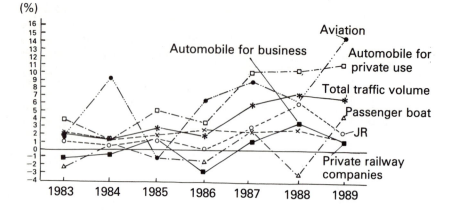

Figure 15.4 Japan Railways: trend of domestic passenger transport by means of transportation, 1983–9 (person/kilometre)

Source: Kohtsu Nenkan 1991.

funds became one of the factors that accelerated the financial crisis at JR, though this problem is expected to be solved by integrating this fund into the general pension fund for civil servants.

The second problem is related to the sources from which JR's profits stem. In gaining profits, JR depends on the Shinkansen and the metropolitan transport too heavily. This may cause an imbalance in services to users should rural lines grow worse as a result. The third problem is that JNR's privatization has hardly brought about deregulation. Regulation by the *Tetsudo Kyoku* (railroad office) in the Transport Ministry continues in the field of fares and entry into new businesses as well as in the appointment of managers.

Table 15.3 Japan Railways: disposal of land

	Open competitive bidding		Free contract		Total	
	Area (ha)	Price (¥100m)	Area (ha)	Price (¥100m)	Area (ha)	Price (¥100m)
Fiscal 1987	21	213	250	1,116	271	1,329
Fiscal 1988	94	281	872	1,760	966	2,041
Fiscal 1989	71	374	448	2,394	519	2,768
	(1.2)	(24)				

Source: JNR Settlement Corporation 1990.
Notes:
1 Figures in parentheses show the scales in areas under special surveillance, and are included in the upper figures.
2 Prices include those of depreciation assets such as buildings.

Table 15.4 Japan Railways: traffic volume

1 Domestic passenger

	Person/kilometre*		Compared with previous year (%)	
Means of transportation	1988	1989	88/87	89/88
Total traffic volume	1,190.60	1,267.04	107.5	106.4
Railway	361.80	368.82	105.0	101.9
JR	217.59	222.67	106.3	102.3
Private companies	144.21	146.15	103.0	101.3
Automobile	782.03	845.12	108.8	108.1
Bus	107.22	109.13	104.2	101.8
Bus for business	73.36	74.93	104.7	102.1
Bus for private use	33.86	34.20	103.2	101.0
Car for business	16.06	15.92	100.0	99.2
Car for private use	465.90	519.35	110.5	111.5
Light car	117.20	123.50	110.0	105.4
Freight car	75.65	77.22	106.2	102.1
Aviation	41.10	47.14	106.7	114.7
Passenger boat	5.67	5.96	97.0	105.0

2 Domestic freight

	Ton/kilometre†		Compared with previous year (%)	
	1988	1989	88/87	89/88
Total traffic volume	482.94	513.44	107.6	106.3
Railway	23.48	25.14	114.7	107.1
JR	23.03	24.67	115.0	107.1
Private companies	0.45	0.46	99.7	103.1
Automobile	246.14	262.86	108.7	106.8
for business	170.66	184.26	109.9	108.0
for private use	75.48	78.60	106.5	104.2
Domestic shipping	212.63	224.69	105.6	105.7
Aviation	0.69	0.75	108.9	109.1

Source: Kotsu Nenkan 1991.
Notes:
* hundred million passengers per kilometre.
† hundred million tons per kilometre.

THE EFFECT OF PRIVATIZATION ON THE TRANSPORT MARKET

First, we will examine the effect of the privatization on the transport market. From 1987–9 the total volume of JR's passenger traffic (person/kilometre) increased by 2–6 per cent year by year (see Figure 15.4 and Table 15.4) – a growth rate exceeding that achieved by any private railway company since 1987. It is probable that the introduction of competition resulted in a synergy effect, both on increasing demand and on enlarging the traffic market (see Table 15.5).

Second, we will analyse the influence of privatization on the transport industry from the view of microeconomics. We don't adopt the SCP (structure, conduct, performance) paradigm of the industrial organization theory. One reason is that I think the paradigm has some theoretical problems; for example, regarding market conduct as a 'black box' on the assumption of concentration-profit, also the mismatch between the spectrum of market structure (measured by concentration) and market performance (measured by efficiency of resource allocation). Another reason is simply that we don't have enough data to complete the work. Therefore, our analysis is based on the following criteria: efficiency; equity; transformation of the system or stability of supply; and safety.

Efficiency

This can be estimated using two criteria: the total productivity and the allocation of resources. With regard to the former it is labour productivity which is the most important factor.

Labour productivity

JR has achieved a substantial increase in labour productivity. The total number of employees has decreased from about 350,000 in 1984 to below 200,000 in 1989, meaning that half the number of employees are now handling intensified work in comparison with the labour situation in 1980. In general it is said that little labour rationalization was undertaken in Japan prior to privatization. However, this was not so in the case of JNR. As JNR's workers union (Kokuro) and its political party (the JSP) lost their strength and declined rapidly in the 1980s, the labour rationalization proceeded. Furthermore, the relationship between management and labour has been improving for the past few years. The wage

Table 15.5 Japan Railways: rural lines planned to be transformed

| | Transformed rural lines* | | |
	Bus	Railway	Total
First planned lines	22	18	40
Second planned lines	20	11	31
Third planned lines	3	9	12
Total	45	38	83

Source: The White Paper of Transportation 1990.
Note: *As at 1 April 1990.

scale has been restricted and no labour disputes such as strikes and walk-outs have taken place.

It should be noted that the reduction of employees did not lead to a problem of unemployment in Japan. The JNR Settlement Corporation, under a special law designed to promote recruitment (1987), took care of the employment of those who had lost their jobs, the shortage of workers in a prosperous Japanese economy greatly assisting this. Though the special law ended in 1990, by that time the number of surplus workers had been reduced from about 19,000 in 1987 to about 1,000; these were finally dismissed by the corporation in that year.

Allocation of resources

The division and reform have enabled JR to secure managerial autonomy to some extent and to reduce operating costs. Allocation of resources has become efficient due to retrenchment policies such as the revision of investment policy and the strategy of revitalizing manpower. Concerning the efficiency of allocation, the most important reform is that the adjustment policy of deficit rural lines, which the JNR was forced to keep on running, has been implemented under a special law designed to accelerate the reconstruction of JNR's management. According to this plan (see Table 15.5), 83 rural lines have been abolished and replaced by bus services or transferred to the third sector (mixed enterprise). The plan was enforced in 1983 under the special law relating to the reconstruction of JNR management. At the time of privatization 30 rural lines remained and these were not to be transferred. Later, the scheme was accelerated and the plan fully achieved in 1990.

Furthermore, it is important that the super-base structure ('base' means, essentially, the fixed capital such as railway lines, stations and railway lands; 'super' means the operations and services which use the 'base') has been separated clearly as seen in the case of the Shinkansen. The separation of ownership and use would not only make JR's management more efficient, but also avoid the risk of fixing capital for a long time.

The Japan Railway Construction Corporation (JRCC) might face a deterioration in its financial conditions, however, if it is unable to avoid political intervention. The JRCC has constructed new railway lines under various pressures, which were not necessarily viable. Although the deficit of the JRCC (¥4.5 trillion) was taken over by the JNRSC, the JRCC has reviewed its plan and strengthened its market behaviour by means of leasing its lines to the private railway companies. After privatization, the railway business, under the Railway Activity Act 1987, was divided into three kinds of enterprises (Type 1, Type 2, Type 3) based on the separation of the super-base structure. As a result of this, new management forms (the third sector and so on) have arisen. Allocation of resources has become more efficient as a whole.

Equity

In the case of the railway industry, the equity can be examined in terms of fares and services. As for the former, JR maintains fares which are traditionally based on an equal nation-wide rate system (fare depends on distance travelled). This serves the public interest – a state which the government is determined should continue. Taking into consideration the fact that JR supplies a large number of people with stable and safe traffic services and that its dominant position, especially in the countryside, would allow it to abuse that position, it is natural that the Transport Ministry continues substantially to regulate JR in the field of fares etc. Otherwise, if JR fixed its fares freely in accordance with the fluctuations of demand (business cycle, season, regional conditions), some customers would become losers. Though the system of setting railway fares was changed to the permission system, by which the Department of Transport had to approve JNR fares, in effect the legal system has continued to work. Required to constrain the increase of fares, JR has attempted to gain profits by diversifying its business or by putting on extra trains.

As for the latter, the problem is related to the opportunity of enjoying a universal service. It can be said that universal service, including alternatives supplied by other means of transportation (for example bus), is almost guaranteed: the government subsidized the rural small private railway companies (¥1.0 billion), regional bus companies (¥10.4 billion), and the companies managed by the third sector (¥1.4 billion) in 1989. If the service of the Shinkansen express were included in a 'universal service', however, equity is not satisfied in the three islands. For the purpose of correcting this inequality, the new Shinkansen (the so-called Seibi Shinkansen), which was discontinued for a time, is to be constructed. In this, many politicians of the LDP and JSP have played an important role. None the less it is doubtful that the new Shinkansen will bring about profits to JR.

Generally speaking, we can evaluate the consumer benefits positively. The services of passenger transport have been diversified in response to the demands of customers and shifted in accordance with the actual needs of the regional economies. The staff attitude towards customers has improved rapidly. The largest benefit for consumers is that JR has not raised train fares since the privatization. This has enabled JR to reduce the price gap in relation to the private railway companies and to recapture customers in urban areas.

Tranformation of the system

The privatization did not cause much confusion in the market for land transportation. The transaction cost, which was accompanied by transforming the trade mechanism, has not been great – even if the costs of judicial cases and organizational reforms (managerial cost, retirement funds, etc.) were included.

Safety

With regard to safety, the number of railway accidents, especially those at crossing points which account for almost 90 per cent of all the accidents, has decreased gradually. This is due to the promotion of safety policy (for example, the improvement of railroad crossings) and technological progress.

The effect from the viewpoint of macroeconomics cannot be evaluated at the present time. Nevertheless, it should be noted that a range of rationalizations, especially the tariff policy and cost-reduction tactics, have had a good effect on the Japanese economy if we consider the fact that JR still constitutes one of the main industrial infrastructures.

THE UNSOLVED PROBLEMS

The most difficult problem in privatizing the public sector is to harmonize economic efficiency with the public interest. External intervention, often in the name of the public interest, stifles efficiency and creates an irresponsible attitude towards profitability. Contrary to this, market economy, if it is implemented freely and thoroughly, could cause a market failure which damages the public interest.

The JNR's reform has overcome this dilemma to some degree. Under the leadership of Nakasone and Doko, the effort to reconcile the public interest with efficiency was pursued. Though the LDP supported this process, it did not forget to placate the JSP. Judging from the political side, JNR's privatization was a product of compromise between the government, the LDP, the business world (Keidanren), and the JSP.

This was the reason why the privatization did not lead to liberalization or deregulation in Japan. At the same time the problem casts a doubt over the future of JR if it remains unsolved. Competition should be promoted through deregulation. In order to compete with the private railway companies and other transport industries it is required that JR should be transformed into a number of complete private companies which make themselves responsible for their own management. In this respect we must pay attention to the continuous decline of JR's market share in relation to the competition with automobiles and aeroplanes.

JR's share of passenger transport has decreased annually and is likely to fall to under 20 per cent – what is worse, that of freight transport, despite a slight recovery since 1987, has been stagnant at the 4 per cent level (see Figure 15.5). If the Japanese economy should fall into recession in the near future, it is doubtful that JR could enhance market share by increasing volume.

The second remaining problem is related to long-term liabilities, which grow worse and worse. The White Paper on Transportation in 1990 proposed that JR should finalize privatization by tackling its long-term liabilities, as well as endeavouring to modernize management and clear the pension fund deficit. Following this, the JNR Settlement Corporation reacted by developing various

1.

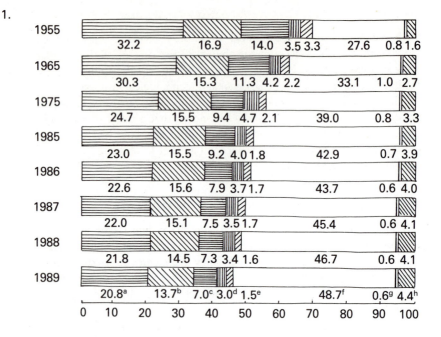

1955	32.2	16.9	14.0 3.5 3.3	27.6	0.8 1.6	
1965	30.3	15.3	11.3 4.2 2.2	33.1	1.0 2.7	
1975	24.7	15.5	9.4 4.7 2.1	39.0	0.8 3.3	
1985	23.0	15.5	9.2 4.0 1.8	42.9	0.7 3.9	
1986	22.6	15.6	7.9 3.7 1.7	43.7	0.6 4.0	
1987	22.0	15.1	7.5 3.5 1.7	45.4	0.6 4.1	
1988	21.8	14.5	7.3 3.4 1.6	46.7	0.6 4.1	
1989	20.8[a]	13.7[b]	7.0[c] 3.0[d] 1.5[e]	48.7[f]	0.6[g] 4.4[h]	

0 10 20 30 40 50 60 70 80 90 100

Figure 15.5 Japan Railways: trend of market shares, 1955–89 (%)
1 Domestic passenger transport (person/kilometre)

Source: Kotsu Nenkan 1991.
Notes: [a]JR; [b]Private railway companies; [c]Bus for business; [d]Bus for private use; [e] Automobile for business; [f]Automobile for private use; [g]Passenger boat; [h]Aviation.

2.

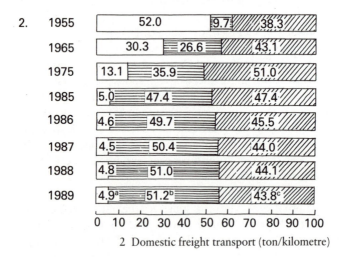

1955	52.0	9.7	38.3
1965	30.3	26.6	43.1
1975	13.1	35.9	51.0
1985	5.0	47.4	47.4
1986	4.6	49.7	45.5
1987	4.5	50.4	44.0
1988	4.8	51.0	44.1
1989	4.9[a]	51.2[b]	43.8[c]

0 10 20 30 40 50 60 70 80 90 100

2 Domestic freight transport (ton/kilometre)

Source: Kotsu Nenkan 1991.
Notes: [a]Railway; [b]Automobile; [c]Domestic shipping.

356

methods of selling railway lands (for example, including the introduction of a land-trust system). But these plans have not yet come to fruition.

The third problem, related to the sale of the state assets, is that the share sale of JR has not been realized on schedule because of the decline of the stock-market. Despite the market trend, however, it is important that the shares of JR Tohkai and JR Higashi be sold as fast as possible. If this can't be achieved, the principal–agent relationship would not change in the direction of enhancing efficiency and of promoting deregulation.

Last, we need to understand a style specific to JNR's privatization. The delay of JR's transformation into private companies caused some misunderstandings in this respect. Some economists, who refute the introduction of a 'profitability' concept into the public sector, regard it as not *Mineika* but *Shieika* (complete ownership and control by private capital). Others, who support Thatcher-style privatization, regard it as *Tokushu Kaishaka* (changing to a special company only).

The former group of economists neglect the public character of a network industry such as that of JR. The JR companies would be regulated by the government even if the necessary conditions of the privatization (share sale, control of shareholders) were satisfied completely. The latter group of econo-mists disregard the fact that the shares of JR will be floated and sold out to the public in the near future, interpreting the meaning of the privatization only in a narrow sense. Certainly the privatization of JNR was not accompanied by selling its shares at once, and lacked some factors (liberalization or deregulation) in comparison with a Thatcher-style privatization. In spite of this difference, JNR's reform should be interpreted as a Japanese-style privatization where the concept of public interest (in particular equity) was thought much of and share sale was decided to be postponed deliberately till after the success of management (see Table 15.6). The latter school of thought has a fault in that JNR's privatization is attempted to be understood by applying the criteria of Britain directly to it.

This chapter has presented an opinion founded on the basis of several years' observation. If we try to estimate what developments are likely to occur in the long term, the conclusion may be different from this. In fact, two serious problems which may cause some concern about the future of JR happened in autumn 1991. The first is that the Shinkansen Holding Corporation was dissolved and absorbed into a new organization named the Railway Develop-ment Fund (*Tetsudo Seibi Kikin*) on 1 October 1991. It is feared that this reform, motivated by the construction of Seibi Shinkansen, may impede efficiency by destroying the clear-cut separation which is the main feature of the super-base structure. The second problem is that the largest trade union (JR Soren) was disbanded, with a new militant trade union which insisted on strikes in the wage struggle (*shunto*) being created. This factor will also have a negative influence on the performance of JR's management. It can be concluded that the success of the privatization will depend on the extent to which the JR can solve the above difficulties in the early 1990s.

Table 15.6 Differences between the old system and the new system of Japan National Railways

Item	Old system	New system
Management form	Public corporation	• Special companies (six passenger companies one freight company) • Shinkansen Holding Corporation • The other private successors of JNR's businesses • JNR Settlement Corporation
Investment	All capital invested by the government	As for special companies, the capital of which was invested in kind by JNR Settlement Corporation. However, JR will be transformed into purely private companies through share-sales to the public as soon as the management is stabilized.
Scope of business	• Railway business • Ferry business connected with railway • Oil-pipeline business where JNR made use of its railway lands • Generation and transmission of electric power • Incidental business • Other business	• Passenger (Freight) railway business • Incident business • Transportation by automobile (bus) • Travel agent • Other business Some businesses related to JNR were transferred to the private sector through divestment.
Regulation	• Budget decided through the Diet • President of JNR was nominated by the Prime Minister, and commissioners of JNR-RSC were appointed by the Secretary of the Transport Ministry • Authorization of constructing the new railroad etc. came under JNR Act.	• Approval of business plan • Approval of election of a representative director and inspectors • Approval of the businesses and activities under the Railway Activity Law Regulation for JR is to be at the same level as that of private railway companies.

Fares and tariff	Principle of legal price system (by 1977)	Approval system
Labour relations	Application of National Public Service Law	Application of the so-called Three Labour Laws (the Labour Standard Law, the Trade Union Law, and the Labour Mediation Law)

NOTES

This chapter would not have been completed without the co-operation of Ian Smith (visiting researcher of the Institute of Business Research, Daito University) and Etsuo Kozawa (Associate Professor of Waseda University).

BIBLIOGRAPHY

Calder, K. E. (1990) 'Public corporations and privatization in modern Japan', in E. N. Suleiman and J. Watebury (eds), *The Political Economy of Public Sector Reform and Privatization*, Boulder, Colo.: Westview Press.

Gow, I. (1989) 'Government–industry relations: Japanese-style public corporations and privatization', *Japan Forum* 1(2).

Hirotaka Yamauchi (1990) 'Kokutetesu Kaikaku to Atarashii Tetsudo Seisaku', in Toshihiko Hayashi (ed.) *Koeki Jigyo to Kiseikanwa*, Tokyo: Keizai Shinposha.

Hurl, B. (1988) *Privatization and the Public Sector*, London: Heinemann.

JNR-SC (1990) *Nihon Kokuyu Tetsudo Seisan Jigyodan '90*, JNR-SC.

Kay, J., Mayer, C. and Thompson, D. (1986) *Privatisation and Regulation*, Oxford: Clarendon Press.

Kazuaki Tanaka and Masahiro Horie, *Mineika to Kiseikanwa*, Kokyo Sentaku no Kenkyu, no. 16 (1990), no. 17 (1991).

Kotsu Nenkan, Kotsu Kyoryokukai, 1987, 1988, 1989, 1990, 1991.

Rinji Gyosei Chosakai (1982) *Rincho Kihon Teigen*, Gyosei Kanri Kenkyu Centre.

Seizaburo Sato (1985) *The Experience of Japan's Privatization: Policies, Methods and Procedures*, Manila: Asian Development Bank.

Unyusho, *Unyu Hakusho* (The White Paper on Transportation), 1987, 1988, 1989, 1990.

Veljanovsky, C. (ed.) (1989) *Privatisation and Competition*, London: Institute of Economic Affairs.

Vickers, J. and Yarrow, G. (1988) *Privatisation: An Economic Analysis*, Cambridge, Mass.: MIT Press.

Yataro Fujii (1989) 'Tetsudo', in Masahiro Okuno *et al.* (ed.), *Koutsu Seisaku no Keizai gaku*, Nihon Keizai Shinbunsha.

Yukihide Okano (1989) 'Kisei to Kigyo Katsudo' (Tokyou University), *Keizaigaku Ronshu* 55(2).

16

RATIONALE AND OPTIMAL IMPLEMENTATION OF PRIVATIZATION POLICIES

The case of Greece

Yannis Katsoulacos

INTRODUCTION

Privatization, or the selling of public enterprises, has become one of the most significant economic policy issues in many countries in recent years (see, for example, Bos 1991a or Vickers and Yarrow 1988 for extensive discussions). Another important policy, pursued in conjunction or in the absence of privatization when markets are not considered natural monopolies, has been deregulation or market liberalization – the removal of state impediments, barriers or constraints to the operation of markets. In this chapter I will first of all examine the reasons and rationale of privatization and deregulation policies, and then, in the probably more original, second part of the chapter, I discuss issues of optimal privatization strategy.

BACKGROUND AND RATIONALE TO PRIVATIZATION AND DEREGULATION POLICIES

Both privatization and deregulation signify the removal or reduction of state involvement in an economy's productive process. The need for such policies requires some explanation despite their recent widespread acceptance among policy-makers in a large number of countries. This is because more than ever before, modern economic theory teaches that, in a large number of cases, the unimpeded operation of a market composed of profit-maximizing firms will not result in the maximization of social welfare. Even when competitive conditions are perfect, free markets may not produce satisfactory results when, as is often the case, there are externalities. If we assume, more realistically, that markets seldom approach the perfectly competitive ideal (for example, because of entry barriers or product differentiation) then in relation to the social optimum the market equilibrium outcome can result in:

- Too small production and too high a price (for some goods or services the market may be unable to produce at all, if the maximum profit is negative even in the absence of competition). This is still the most widely discussed example of market failure, even though it is now well known that the following market failures may be responsible for much larger welfare losses (see, for example, Beath and Katsoulacos 1991).

- Sub-optimal quality and/or number of products or brands (Beath and Katsoulacos 1991).
- An excessive number of firms (Beath and Katsoulacos 1991, Mankiw and Whinston 1986, Perry 1984).
- Non-optimal expenditures on R&D and sub-optimal technical change (Beath *et al.* 1989, Dasgupta and Stiglitz 1980a, 1980b).

These results, that are now well established in the Theory of Industrial Organization, are not really surprising. There is no reason to expect, except under special conditions, that a free market will generate optimal results given that firms act as profit maximizers and not as social welfare maximizers. Those cases where the market equilibrium seemed to be furthest away from the optimum, especially when account was taken of the distribution of welfare, led, in most countries of the industralized world in the post-Second World War period, to the establishment of the Welfare State that is directly responsible for the production and distribution of a number of 'necessary services' (such as health and education) and goods that are produced and distributed by large public monopolies. Later on, in several countries, by a logical extension of the argument that profit maximization does not generally generate satisfactory results, direct state intervention (that is, state ownership) was extended to various other sectors of economic activity through the creation of state organizations of direct state involvement, such as OAE in Greece (see Xanthakis 1989). The role of such organizations has been to take over, under state ownership, a large number of 'problematic' firms in various industrial sectors.

It should be emphasized now that whilst the above considerations provide a rationale for state involvement in the productive process they do not provide a justification for such involvement. Such justification would require showing that state intervention leads to more satisfactory outcomes than those that emerge in its absence. However, the original expectations from direct public involvement in production and distribution were not fulfilled. The objectives from public involvement would have been achieved if, by replacing the profit motive of the private firm, public firms not only achieved an immediate reduction in prices and increase in output, but, over time, did not fall behind in internal efficiency and the pursuit of innovations that lead to cost reductions and improvements in quality. This is, however, exactly what seems to have happened in at least a large number of cases (for discussions on evidence of the relative performance, see MacAvoy *et al.* 1990, especially Chs 2 and 4). This can be explained by referring to the following set of factors:

- The fact that in practice, the state (and hence public firms), will often not advocate the objective of long-run welfare maximization since this often conflicts with the government's priority to maximize the probability of electoral success (see, for example, the discussion in Vickers and Yarrow 1988, Ch. 2).

- Given the above, the state's involvement in public enterprises is often counter-productive and can result in inefficiency and lack of motivation in pursuing innovation and growth.
- The relatively great expansion of bureaucracies or hierarchical levels in public firms that limits internal efficiency (see, for example, Estrin and Perotin 1991).
- The fact that, in oligopolistic markets with public and private firms, under some circumstances, profit maximization by the public firm is preferable to other objectives (see, for example, Cremer *et al.* 1989, De Fraja and Delbono 1989) and may lead to greater incentives for cost reductions (Katsoulacos 1991).

These factors are clearly not sufficient to prove that in all countries and in all cases a large reduction in the extent of direct state involvement in the productive process, below the levels we have been accustomed to up to the mid-1980s (the time we start to get a rise in the popularity of privatization policies), will be desirable. Determining the optimal size of the public sector is an extremely complicated matter. This is because it is likely to be country- and time-specific and cannot be determined by taking into account just economic considerations: country-specific sociological and cultural factors, that to a large extent condition the objectives and style of state intervention, must be taken into account too. However, the above factors do suggest quite strongly that, at least in those countries in which direct state involvement in the economic process has been used over long periods of time as a means of satisfying political objectives and engaging in political patronage, a (perhaps drastic) reduction in state involvement below those levels is desirable. This is *because this will lead to an improvement in efficiency and innovativeness of the privatized enterprises*, and hence will directly aid the economy's development.

Having said this we must now stress two factors. First, one should stress the importance of market liberalization, irrespective of whether or not there is a shift in ownership. Market liberalization is very important, mainly as a means of allowing the forces of potential competition (the Schumpeterian 'threat of competition') to become effective in providing incentives for internal efficiency and as a spurt to innovation. An increase in actual, in contrast to potential, competition post-privatization may not always be desirable (see Katsoulacos 1990) though in considering previously monopolistic markets an increase in actual competition will be helpful as a mechanism of effective information collection that will allow comparisons in performance and hence will allow effective control of public or regulation of privatized firms (see, for example, Hart 1983, Hayek 1945, Kirzner 1984).

With respect to the effect of privatizations and market liberalization on firms previously privately owned, it has been argued (De Fraja 1991) that privatizations in oligopolistic markets, even assuming that they will increase the efficiency of privatized firms, could reduce average industry efficiency by increasing the slack rates of the privately owned firms that now face less severe competitive pressure (from 'unfair competition' or the social welfare related objectives of the public firms). This prediction, however, is unlikely to occur in reality because it ignores the impact of privatization and removal of state controls and constraints on potential competition and the ability of new firms to enter the market: this is likely to be positive and will tend to reverse any tendency of existing private firms to increase their slack rates following privatizations. Further, the improvement in the provision of, and/or quality of, goods and services previously produced by public firms should have a beneficial effect on the private sector consuming these goods and services as productive inputs and hence on the growth of this sector. That is, all other things being equal, privatizations and deregulation are likely to have a twofold beneficial impact on efficiency and hence on economic welfare: a direct one by leading to an increase in the efficiency of the privatized firms, and an indirect one by improving the efficiency of firms previously privately owned.

Coming to the second factor that should be stressed. In order for this beneficial impact to materialize in all cases in which the privatized firm is a public monopoly or the dominant firm (transportation services, telecommunications, electricity generation and distribution, water), if the public monopoly is privatized this should be done in a way that, as already noted, maximizes the potential role of competitive pressures, but *also* by establishing a means of indirect state control or state regulation (by setting up regulatory bodies), whose primary function is to protect the interests of users from monopolistic price exploitation and a deterioration in product or service quality. This has been done in the UK, and the experience of this country with setting up and implementing a regulatory process has been reviewed recently (see, Veljanovski 1991). The general consensus of the reviewers seems to be that despite the problems with regulation, having an extra group of agents – the shareholders – between the government and the corporation's managers, as is the situation with privatized regulated firms, improves the performance of these corporations without seriously jeopardizing the regulator's social objectives.

Related to this point, any reduction in the share of the public sector in the education and health sectors, via market liberalization in these sectors, should be accompanied by readiness by the state to support the consumption of these services (independently of who provides them) on the grounds of maximizing the country's human capital development.

OPTIMAL PRIVATIZATION STRATEGIES

We now turn to the following question: assuming that privatizations can result in an increase in the efficiency of privatized firms how can a government *maximize* the potential benefits from privatizations and market liberalization? We should here point out that in defining the potential benefits from these policies we will not only take into account their effect on efficiency and economic growth (discussed above) but also their effect on the distribution of the country's wealth and income (which should be a dimension of social welfare). The distributional aspect of privatization policies is important for the following reason. Empirical evidence suggests that whilst privatizations are usually followed by improvements in efficiency they do not result in lower prices. Indeed, the British experience indicates that the prices of privatized firms have often risen quite considerably post-privatization, though this has often been accompanied by improvements in service and product quality. Thus, overall, privatizations have resulted in large increases in profits and in wealth for the new owners (relatively few in number) of the privatized firms. The marginal increase in social welfare that would result from a government policy that redistributes some of the benefits of privatizations is in all likelihood going to be positive.

We will concentrate on two important aspects of government strategy that have a direct bearing on the long-term impact of a privatization programme. The first concerns the optimal timing of privatizations. Here I will concentrate on two broad choices: the first is to privatize public firms by allowing quite a long delay between the time the commitment to privatize is made and the date the firm is put up for sale. During this time the currently inefficient but potentially viable state enterprises can be restructured. Further, whilst logically distinct, I will assume that another feature of this option is that privatizations occur sequentially. The second is to proceed with rapid privatizations on a massive scale (as, for example, the current Greek government is attempting to do).

The second aspect of government strategy we will discuss is how the government should use the privatization proceeds. Here, we will again concentrate on two broad choices: the first is to use the proceeds to reduce public debt in an attempt to reduce taxes; the second is to use the proceeds to increase investment in infrastructure or public capital that is used by, and an improvement in the quality of which will increase the efficiency of, the private and the remaining public sectors (see Christodoulakis and Katsoulacos 1992).

Now, generally speaking, in formulating its strategy a government must take into account a number of fundamental factors:

1   The size of the deficit of public enterprises and the size of the public debt.
2   The issue of whether there are asymmetries in the extent of inefficiency of capital markets that imply that domestic firms or investors cannot compete effectively with foreign firms or investors in bidding for the firms to be privatized. This is especially important to countries such as Greece and those of Eastern Europe given that, in these countries, a large number of the firms to be privatized are likely to operate in tight oligopolistic conditions characterized by entry barriers and a potential for high rents: if privatized firms are sold to foreign firms, the domestic economy could lose the future share of these rents that cannot be captured at the time of sale by the

government, and this could have adverse effects on investment and hence on economic development.[1]

3 The extent to which the improvements in efficiency expected from privatization will be associated with large-scale redundancies and a big increase in unemployment.

4 The availability of human capital – especially of the management skills required – for the potential growth and improvement in profits of the privatized firms to be realized.

Now, these factors, should not, in principle, affect the decisions of a government interested only in the potential efficiency benefits resulting from privatizations, though of course the last factor could considerably constrain the speed with which the potential efficiency benefits are realized. However, as already noted in a different context above, efficiency considerations, whilst often stressed by the proponents of privatization policies, cannot form the sole basis of the privatization strategy of a populist government interested in its electoral prospects. We are going to assume that the government under consideration is a 'populist' one that maximizes the expected utility of a typical citizen or household. Given this we would like to put forward two propositions in relation to the two aspects of this strategy mentioned above.

Proposition 1

A populist government wishing to implement a rapid privatization programme without any prior restructuring of inefficient public firms, and using the government proceeds to reduce the public debt, may well find that the optimal number of privatizations is less than the maximum possible, even if the latter is what is required on social welfare grounds (as measured by the sum of the producers' and consumers' surplus in the industry). This is more likely the *larger* the size of the public debt, the smaller the anticipated profits of the privatized firms, the less efficient currently the public firms to be privatized, and the higher the (structural) unemployment created by privatizations. The reason is that privatizations increase unemployment but also can lead to a reduction in the tax rate: if the public debt is very large relative to the privatization proceeds whilst unemployment increases a lot, the expected income utility of the average citizen will be affected adversely by privatizations after a certain point. In this case, sequential selling, by first selling the most efficient and profitable public firms and restructuring (possibly using the proceeds of the previous privatizations) the less efficient ones which are sold at a later stage, could increase the optimal number of privatizations to a populist government to the extent that through sequential selling the government can increase its net revenue proceeds, and thus it can result in higher long-term efficiency gains. Independently of sequencing, the government should allow quite a long period of time between making a credible commitment to privatize (for example, by passing an Act of Parliament) and the actual sale date of a firm, during which the firms' managers are, under the threat of an increase in competitive pressures once privatized, instructed to restructure the firm and redirect its objectives: again, this could increase the government's proceeds from privatization.

One should also note that the option of rapid privatizations on a massive scale is inferior to that of slow and/or sequential selling with restructuring on social welfare grounds if distributional considerations are taken into account. This is because, as just noted and as will be explained below, the second option can result in higher revenue proceeds to the government and lower proceeds to the buyers of the privatized firms, and these higher revenues can be used for redistributive purposes. Also, the second option has the advantage of reducing the average duration of unemployment by allowing the private sector to respond and absorb some of the unemployed as privatizations proceed.

It may be worth while, in this respect, to compare the situation in two countries undergoing extensive privatization programmes: Greece and Eastern Germany. In the latter, it now seems that the option of restructuring will not be used to any great extent, even though it was one of the original options formally adopted by the government privatization agency, along with liquidation and immediate privatization. Further, this has been the recommendation of at least one eminent commentator (see Bos 1991b). In our view this should not be the recommendation in the Greek case because, whilst Greece shares with Eastern Germany the feature of a very inefficient set of firms to be privatized, the similarities end there. In particular, Greece has a much more serious public debt problem than that of Germany as a whole and, very importantly, the ability of the private sector in the Greek economy to absorb through growth the unemployment created by privatizations is much more limited than that of the German economy. As noted above, both of these factors, in conjunction with the inefficiency of the firms to be privatized, should limit the appeal of immediate large-scale privatizations to a populist or a social-welfare-maximizing government (to the extent that the latter takes into account distributional considerations too). It is important, finally, to note that the slow and/or sequential selling/restructuring option has been followed by the very initiator of the privatization policies: the Thatcher governments. The fact that in Greece the public firms to be privatized are even more inefficient than those in the UK, and public debt problems are more serious, increases the desirability of this option. It is also worth noting the procedure followed in the UK case: for each privatization the government made clear its commitment to privatize; passed a White Paper in Parliament specifying its objectives, rationale, the timing and other details of the future sale; and allowed two or more years before actually privatizing, during which time the firm was instructed to restructure with government assistance (see Walters's comment in MacAvoy *et al.* 1990: 249) and to move towards commercial principles of operation.

Discussion of proposition 1

We will here consider a very simple example to justify the claim, made in Proposition 1, that the restructuring–sequential selling option may be preferable because it could lead to higher government net revenue proceeds and thus result in a higher optimal number of privatizations. Assume that P is the capitalized value of *expected* net profit flow after restructuring and privatizing a public firm, as estimated by the *best placed* potential buyer (the buyer who can best exploit the assets of the firm given the firm's environment – position of rivals, market structure, etc.). Also let I indicate the investment outlay required for restructuring. Clearly, $P-I$ is the *maximum* that a potential buyer would be prepared to pay for the firm. However, even the best-placed buyer will make a bid smaller than $P-I$ if P is not known with certainty (as it is unlikely to be) and he is risk-averse. Taking this into account the government can only expect to obtain $kP-I$ from selling the firm, where $0 < k < 1$.

Now it is reasonable to assume that for any given expected P the variability of future profit flows fall after the firm is restructured if, as is likely to be the case, the cost reductions associated with restructuring are the result of a large number of production and organizational (cut in bureaucracies) changes the potential extent and impact of which cannot be known prior to restructuring. Further, it is reasonable to assume that the more efficient and profitable has been the public firm to be privatized, the smaller the magnitude of the required restructuring and, because of this, the smaller the uncertainty about the magnitude of potential cost reductions. Hence the smaller the variability of future profits, the smaller will be the gap in information concerning the firm's prospects between the government and private investors. These factors imply that: (a) the value of k is larger the more efficient (relative to potential maximum) is the firm to be privatized, and (b) the value of k is higher after the firm is restructured. Note that the value of k could increase even without any major restucturing if, during the period between the commitment to privatize and putting the firm up for sale, the adoption of commercial objectives by the firm allows potential investors to become better informed about the relative extent to which the firm's observed lack of profitability is the result of genuine inefficiency or of pursuing social objectives.

Assume that, after restructuring $k=k_1$, whilst before restructuring, $k=k_0$, and $k_1 > k_0$. Assume also that if the government does the restructuring the investment outlay will be I_1, whilst if it is done by the private buyer of the firm it will be I_0, where $I_1 > I_0$ (that is, I assume that the government is likely to be less efficient in restructuring). Then it is easy to see that as long as

$$P(k_1-k_0) > (I_1-I_0)$$

the government will maximize its revenue proceeds by first restructuring and then selling the public firm.

Proposition 2[2]

A populist government may find that the optimal number of privatizations is higher when privatization proceeds are used to invest in infrastructure, thus increasing the profitability of all firms (Option 1), than when the proceeds are used directly to reduce the existing public debt (Option 2). Thus, to the extent that privatizations increase the efficiency of the privatized firms, there will be greater efficiency gains from following the former option. Further, Option 1 may result in a higher expected utility for the average citizen than Option 2 for any given number of privatizations. Given the size of the public debt, the profitability of privatized firms and the unemployment created from privatizations, these results are more likely to hold the lower the quality of public capital and hence the greater the benefit to the corporate sector of infrastructural investment. Note, however, that a populist government may prefer Option 2 to Option 1, even if in the latter case the optimal number of privatizations is higher, if Option 2 results in greater tax reductions and thus increases more expected utility of the average citizen for any given number of privatizations. Figure 16.1 illustrates this case.

It would appear that the use of Option 1 in countries such as Greece and those of Eastern Europe will result in a higher optimal number of privatizations, given the particularly low quality of infrastructure, and hence must be favoured on social welfare grounds. It is worth while stressing here that, for *any given number of privatizations*, even if Option 2 is preferable to Option 1 to a populist

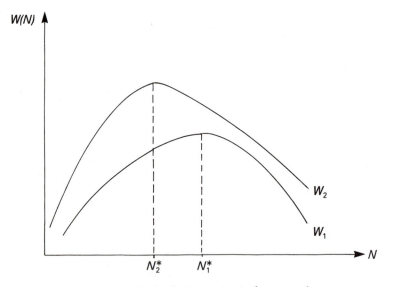

Figure 16.1 Optimal privatization in the two options

Notes: W = expected utility of the typical citizen; N = number of firms to be privatized; N_i^* = optimal privatizations under Option i (i = 1, 2).

government, Option 1 will be preferable on efficiency grounds since under Option 1 any privatization, apart from its impact effect on the efficiency of the privatized and possibly other privately owned firms (common under both options), leads to a *further* improvement in the efficiency of all firms as a result of permitting an increase in infrastructural investment. Further, provided the government can tax and redistribute the extra oligopolistic rents that result from its investment in infrastructure, Option 1 may well be preferable in the long-term on distributional grounds too. Finally, Option 1 is preferable on the grounds that investment in infrastructure, especially that which results in an improvement in transportation and communication services, will make the country more attractive to foreign investors and so will result in an increase in the amount of foreign capital inflows to the country.

NOTES

1 Of course, this last point involves assuming that foreign firms retain a smaller proportion of their profits for investment in the domestic economy than domestic firms would do and that the size of retained profit *is* an important determinant of firms' rates of investment. We do believe that these are the appropriate assumptions to make.
2 The technical details relating to this proposition are contained, or are corollaries of the discussion, in Christodoulakis and Katsoulacos (1992).

REFERENCES

Beath, J. and Katsoulacos, Y. (1991) *The Economic Theory of Product Differentiation*, Cambridge: Cambridge University Press.
——— , ——— and Ulph, D. (1989) 'The game theoretic analysis of innovation: a survey', *Bulletin of Economic Research*, 42, 163–84.
Bos, D. (1991a) *Privatisation: A Theoretical Treatment*, Oxford: Oxford University Press.
——— (1991b) *Privatisation Policy in Eastern Germany*, IMF Discussion Paper.
Christodoulakis, N. and Katsoulacos, Y. (1992) *Privatisation and Public Deficit Finance: An Investigation of Alternative Proposals*, Mimeo, Athens University of Economics and Business.
Cremer, H., Marchand, M. and Thisse, J-F. (1989) 'The public firm as an instrument for regulating an oligopolistic market', *Oxford Economic Papers*, 41, 283–301.
Dasgupta, P. and Stiglitz, J. (1980a) 'Industrial structure and the nature of innovative activity', *Economic Journal*, 90, 266–93.
——— (1980b) 'Uncertainty, industrial structure and the speed of R&D', *Bell Journal of Economics* 11(1), 1–28.
De Fraja, G. (1991) 'Efficiency and privatisation in imperfectly competitive industries', *Journal of Industrial Economics* XXXIX(3), 311–21.
——— and Delbono, F. (1989) 'Alternative strategies of a public enterprise in oligopoly', *Oxford Economic Papers*, 41, 302–11.
Estrin, S. and Perotin, V. (1991) 'Does ownership always matter?', *International Journal of Industrial Organisation* 9(1), 55–73.
Hart, O. (1983) 'The market mechanism as an incentive scheme', *Bell Journal of Economics*, vol. 14, 366–82.
Hayek, F. A. (1945) 'The use of knowledge in society', *American Economic Review*, 35, 519–30.

Katsoulacos, Y. (1990) 'Privatisation, competition and welfare', Paper presented at the European Economic Association Conference, Cambridge, 1–3 September 1991, and at the Conference of the European Association for Research in Industrial Economics, Ferrara, 2–4 September 1991.

—— (1991) *Ownership Arrangements and Incentives for Cost Reductions*, University of Liverpool, Discussion Paper in Economics.

Kirzner, I. M. (1984) *Prices, the Communication of Knowledge and the Discovery Process*, Mimeo, New York University, Department of Economics.

MacAvoy, P. W., Stanbury, W. T., Yarrow, G. and Zeckhauser, R. J. (1990) *Privatisation and State-Owned Enterprises*, London: Kluwer Academic Publishers.

Mankiw, N.G. and Whinston, M.D. (1986) 'Free entry and social inefficiency', *Rand Journal of Economics* 17(1), 48–58.

Perry, M. K. (1984) 'Scale economies, imperfect competition and public policy', *The Journal of Industrial Economics* XXXII(3), 313–33.

Veljanovski, C. (ed.) (1991) *Regulators and the Market: An Assessment of the Growth of Regulation in the UK*, London: Institute of Economic Affairs.

Vickers, J. and Yarrow, G. (1988) *Privatisation: An Economic Analysis*, London: MIT Press.

Xanthakis, M. (1989) *The Crisis in Greek Manufacturing and State Regulation*, Athens: Papazisis Editions (in Greek).

Part V

PRIVATIZATION IN EASTERN EUROPE

17

PRIVATIZATION OF SOCIALIST ECONOMIES

General issues and the Polish case[1]

D. Mario Nuti

INTRODUCTION

Today all the socialist economies of Central and Eastern Europe are restoring or expanding forms of private ownership and enterprise. The process involves all these 'transitional' economies, regardless of the pace and achievements of their economic reform, including the former Soviet Union and excluding only Albania: differences are only of speed, mode and degree. There is privatization in a broad sense (the permission and encouragement of private enterprise and ownership), and in the narrow sense (the sale, gift or rental of state assets to private individuals and companies). This chapter considers the general case for privatization in the narrow sense and in the light of the system-specific characteristics of socialist economies; additional reasons are offered for the resilience of private ownership in socialist economies and the mounting pressure for its extension. Some more general issues are considered in the current process of privatization in the transitional economies of Central and Eastern Europe, with a more specific focus on the privatization process in Poland.

THE GENERAL CASE FOR PRIVATIZATION

To a great extent the drive towards privatization in Central and Eastern Europe has the same basis as a similar process also seen in the last ten years in Europe, North America, Japan and the Third World (see Hemming and Mansoor 1988, Vickers and Yarrow 1988). The strongest reason for this development is the expectation that privatization can raise efficiency through changed incentives.

This expectation is found in the recent economic literature on principal–agent relations. Company managers, as agents of owners, are subject to contractual discipline enforced by shareholders; to take-over discipline enforced by potential bidders; and to bankruptcy discipline enforced by creditors. Managers of state enterprises are not subject to any such discipline, as they are subordinated to political authority and not to economically motivated shareholders; they are not subject to take-overs; and their losses are absorbed by automatic grants from the state budget (see Vickers and Yarrow 1988). Further arguments for privatization have been the adoption of a deflationary fiscal stance less austere than it would be if implemented through fiscal means, and the promotion of diffused owner-ship patterns associated with the 'property-owning democracy' model as an alternative to socialism.

These arguments for privatization may have to be modified. Public enterprises sometimes can be more efficient than their private counterparts (in practice, see South Korean state steel; in theory, see Sappington and Stiglitz 1987, Stiglitz 1989). Privatization of management might achieve the same effects as privatiz-ation of ownership without divesting the state of its assets (that is, the state could hold shares in private companies; see Meade 1989). In western market economies, privatization has not been accompanied by significant progress towards property-owning democracy. In the case of transitional economies, however, privatization not only raises the share of national assets held by private owners, it also extends the scope of ownership rights from absent or limited ownership to full-fledged private ownership. This qualitative aspect of privatiz-ation in transitional economies provides additional system-specific, supportive arguments.

SYSTEM-SPECIFIC ARGUMENTS FOR PRIVATIZATION IN SOCIALIST ECONOMIES

First, there is a presumption that privatization will inject life into the inert traditional system. With the benefit of hindsight the main drawback of central planning and state ownership has been its inability to respond to change (whether in technology, domestic demand, or world trade opportunities); the appropriation of the benefits that economic agents might obtain from faster response can only enhance the vitality and viability of those economies.

Second, privatization is bound to weaken the opportunity for political inter-ference in economic life, especially in those economies still dominated by the Communist Party and its all-pervasive *nomenklatura*. In principle it should be possible to cut the links between the centre and enterprises by inserting an intermediate layer of independent state holdings representing state interests. In this context privatization may not be necessary, but it is an effective, well-tested institution and therefore more appealing than more controversial and less well-tried state holdings.

Third, privatization of enterprises and commercial banks together is bound to harden the 'soft' budget constraint of enterprises, which has been one of the main sources of the endemic excess demand typical of centrally planned economies everywhere. Again, it is conceivable that the budget of a state enterprise might be hardened as a result of a change in government policy, but in the light of experience there is little – if any – support for this expectation.

Whatever the validity and strength of the general justification, these three arguments strengthen the case for the privatization now occurring in transitional economies. But there is more: privatization appears also as the consequence of the resilience of private ownership in socialist economies, and there is a strong case for the further extension of the limited property rights which already have existed.

THE RESILIENCE OF PRIVATE OWNERSHIP

Private ownership seems to have a built-in resilience in the socialist economies, where it was never completely eradicated. Moreover, regimes of limited ownership seem to suffer from a certain institutional instability: whenever private ownership is even minimally present, the system tends naturally towards its further extension.

Let us consider what is the necessary and sufficient condition for complete abolition of private ownership. Imagine an economy where individuals have access to instant consumption of goods and services, whether freely (in unlimited amounts or within predetermined limits for each good and service) or subject to money prices and a maximum money budget per unit of time. In either case we stipulate that in this economy individuals do not have any other access to consumption and are not able to transfer their consumption claims to others or over time – that is, they cannot save in the sense of accumulating that part of their maximum consumption entitlement which they do not actually consume. This is the kind of partial or temporary arrangement familiar from expense accounts, communal kibbutz consumption or participation in academic confer-ences but – with the possible though unproved exception of Stone Age economies – such an arrangement has never been a basis for the lasting economic organization of entire communities. Free unlimited consumption, the ultimate full Communist model,[2] belongs to this category but has never been implemented anywhere; 'realized socialism' has never organized consumption on that basis.

The lack of a generalized system of consumption allocation of this kind is a necessary and sufficient condition for private property to arise. Namely, it is a necessary condition because otherwise property could not be transferred, rented or used without violating our stipulations. It is a sufficient condition because a possible private property right on consumption goods arises as soon as claims to consumption can be transferred to others (creating the possibility of future reciprocity, whether through market exchange or possibly through a deferred exchange of reciprocal gifts) or to oneself over time through production or through storage of either the goods or the claims.

It is interesting to note that money is a sufficient but not a necessary condition for private ownership to arise: even in a system without either money or voucher claims and with short-lived goods only (the least favourable set up for property rights to consumption to arise), a stock of consumption goods can be carried and owned within the constraints set by the rate of durability and by the storage space available, the actual stock being determined possibly as the result of an optimization process leading to the equalization of rates of time preference and expected rates of return on each consumption good accumulated.[3] Once there is money – at least in the limited role of a means of distributing consumption goods – and this money is non-perishable,[4] the possibilities of amassing potential command over a stock of consumption goods become virtually unlimited even if all goods were perishable and no storage space were available. The actual stock of money held will be limited, though, by the same optimization process, whereby the real rate of time preference is set equal to the real rate of return on money holdings – that is, the percentage cost of money storage[5] minus the expected rate of money price increase, for all goods.

This reasoning presumes that 'markets' clear, though it does not necessarily imply a supply schedule, only that given quantities of dated consumption goods are available and distributed at state-fixed prices. Market clearing is an inappropriate assumption for traditional socialist economies, which are inordinately prone to permanent excess demand due to the unreasonable overambition of planned targets, combined with an unsustainable commitment to stable prices. However, a claim to a stock of consumption goods can be held in real terms and (through money) even in conditions of persistent shortages except that the relevant prices are official money prices plus a premium for queuing or for random access to goods. Secondary retrading of shortage goods, whether it exists legally or illegally, will necessarily tend towards this relevant price level.

It follows from these reflections on theoretical consumption behaviour that, when we discuss private property under models of socialism other than the (unrealized) full Communist model, we cannot bring into question the possibility of private property, which is always there at least in the form of some property rights to a stock of consumption goods, nor the existence of a rate of return (negative though it may be in real terms) on that stock. We can only discuss the scope of those property rights and the way that rate of return is determined. Namely, we can discuss who can own what for what purpose, the unbundling of property into its constituent rights (as simultaneous *jus utendi, fruendi ac abutendi* in Roman law, with possible finer distinctions in modern times), their yield and their transferability to whom, and how the efficiency implications of private property respond to progressively increasing extensions of the scope of private property. We can also discuss the set of possible limitations or obligations which may be attached to property rights. Finally, we can discuss whether and to what extent the effects of private property might be simulated by alternative arrangements.

THE CASE FOR EXTENSION OF LIMITED PROPERTY RIGHTS

The presence of property rights to consumption goods is an apparently harmless consequence of permitting individual choice of how to allocate consumption over time, an arrangement which is both efficient and, arguably, a basic freedom.

However, once this limited scope of property rights is established there are very strong logical arguments on efficiency grounds, and in response to actual economic pressures, for their extension to a full-fledged capitalist regime of property rights – where anybody can own and trade anything except drugs and slaves, and rights can be unbundled and transferred at will.[6]

In fact, if I am allowed to save real consumption and retain its ownership at a real rate of interest implicit in storage conditions, obviously I should be given the opportunity to save instead in the form of cash and interest-yielding deposits and bonds at a nominal monetary rate of interest equivalent to the same real rate, thus releasing real resources for productive use. Indeed, if I am willing to save more and more at progressively higher interest rates, and there are correspondingly profitable productive uses for those resources, I should be given that opportunity for the sake of efficiency. This multiplies the possibility of accumulating private property by relaxing storage and perishability constraints and of receiving a *rentier* income.

Any investment in consumption goods has an element – albeit small – of risk-taking, depending on current conditions (should I invest in an umbrella or in sunglasses?) affecting the course of relative prices. Financial claims broaden the scope of potential exposure to risk and to its rewards or penalties; loans can be at fixed or variable interest rates; borrowers' creditworthiness will be reflected in their cost of finance. Even in the absence of risk-taking in financial markets, lotteries may and usually do exist in any socialist economy.[7] Moreover employment contracts even under socialism often carry performance-related bonuses, uncertain and lottery-like, broadening further the scope of risk-taking. But now, if I am allowed to draw an interest on financial claims and to expose myself to risk for the sake of a higher expected return, why should I be barred from owning a stake in the present value of an 'enterprise' (defined broadly as a set of productive activities and contractual rights and obligations)? In a world where there are interest rates and risk premia the introduction of private shares and capital markets does not involve a qualitative change. At first shares may be issued to workers of the same enterprise and may not carry a vote; risk-spreading however suggests a reshuffling of stock across enterprises through generalized trade in a stock exchange, and managerial discipline requires the subjection of managers to the threat of an adverse majority vote (and the take-over threat of vote-acquiring bidders).

Finally, once I am allowed to hold an equity stake in an enterprise, and share in its success and failure, there is no qualitative change involved in my being allowed directly to found and run an enterprise and employ workers directly rather than through the mediation of managers.[8] Down the slippery slope of property rights, through Pareto-improving steps, one may quickly revert to full-fledged traditional capitalism.

Over time, the case for privatization mounts implacably with the accumulation of successive monetary gaps between income and expenditure, due to the excess demand systematically present in the socialist economy and the stubborn commitment to maintain stable prices in spite of it. The overhang takes the form of excess liquid assets and abnormally high levels of stocks, both by households and enterprises.[9] In the end the domestic overhang becomes so large as to suggest the selling of state assets to the population instead of alternatives which may be more unpalatable (currency confiscation, hyperinflation) or simply not available (additional domestic or international borrowing).

OWNERSHIP AND ENTREPRENEURSHIP

An interesting question is whether there is a natural breaking point in this chain: that is, where – if anywhere – do decreasing returns set in on the road to full capitalist ownership? According to Mises, private ownership of capital is a necessary precondition of capital markets and therefore of markets in general; without ownership, markets cannot even be simulated (see Mises 1951; Hanson 1989). Mises were certainly right in that private appropriability (including potential transferability and use/abuse) of at least a share of enterprise profits and capital gains must be essential to the very existence of entrepreneurship;[10] however this does not necessarily imply the private ownership of any of the actual means of production. In fact one could imagine a state ownership system in which state assets are leased on competitive leasing markets to private entrepreneurs who appropriate at least part of any residual income and who, by selling their lease to others, can realize the present value of their entrepreneurial activities without ever acquiring ownership of capital goods or, technically, of any enterprise. In such a system investment could remain a state function, whose efficiency would be monitored by comparing, *ex post*, the return on investment obtained from the rentals determined in competitive leasing markets, relative to the interest rates prevailing at the time of investing.

It is tempting to conjecture that there can be no markets without private property, nor economic planning with private property: however, this conjecture, though not rejected by experience, is still unproved on theoretical grounds. Once enterpreneurial rewards are at least partly appropriable it is possible to conceive a replication of competitive capital markets with or without the participation of private individuals but without private ownership of capital assets as such (see Nuti 1988, 1989). These kinds of arrangements (which would be actual markets and not just simulations), however, are not a case against private ownership but a case for economic reform; ideological obstacles against reform could be side-stepped, even if they were not to disappear as now seems the case. In practice, leasings of state property (as in the Soviet *arenda* and the Polish *dzierzawa*, and on an even larger scale in China) are one of the possible ways of implementing privatization of state assets – especially in special sectors such as agriculture, catering and small-scale production – but cannot represent a general exclusive alternative to the sale of assets and shares.

Another interesting question is whether entrepreneurship could be associated with forms of ownership other than state and private, such as municipal or co-operative. In the Soviet Union a great deal of emphasis has been placed on the growth of the co-operative sector, which in the 30 months since June 1987 had grown from 55,000 to 5.5 million employees (including members, full- and part-time dependent workers), and raised turnover from 29 million to 40 billion rubles. Soviet co-operatives are not subjected to the income- and capital-sharing restrictions typical of traditional co-operatives, and very often serve as shells for private enterprises. Therefore their growth is an indication of the potential role that might be played by ownership forms other than state or private under special conditions, but this growth cannot be taken at face value or simply extrapolated to other countries or periods. However, it is conceivable that privatization of state assets could help to transform dependent workers into partial entre-preneurs. This process seems to be making some progress in modern western capitalism with the introduction of income and capital sharing and worker participation in enterprise decision-making (see Nuti 1993).

GENERAL ISSUES: SUBJECTIVIZATION

In the current privatization experience of Central and Eastern European economies three general issues have arisen. The first is the danger that, in the early steps towards economic reform, decentralization of decision-making from central bodies to enterprises might divest the state of its assets without trans-ferring ownership rights to other subjects. In that case it is as if state ownership has become *res nullius*, and before privatization can take place it is necessary to undertake and complete a process of 're-subjectivization', re-uniting property rights under the same public holder before actually privatizing. This is what happened in Hungary with the 1984/5 legislation on state enterprises, which *de facto* acquired most of the rights associated with ownership on the unprece-dented and nonsensical theory that 'enterprises belong to themselves' (as officially stated by the Ministry of Justice). This unusual state was not remedied by the first attempts at privatization (Act VI 1988, Act XIII 1989, see Hare 1990).

A similar problem arises in those countries where workers have gained a measure of self-management: some of the new shares may have to be sold or granted to enterprise employees in order to trade off their full management rights (incompatible with shareholders' rights) with fuller ownership rights on a smaller scale (therefore embodying a smaller voice in enterprise management). Regard-less of this argument, or beyond the limits of this kind of 'conversion', shares may be sold to workers in order to strengthen popular support and to promote a property-owning democracy as an alternative system. Forms of workers' ownership abound in a capitalist economy: Employee Stock Ownership Plans (ESOPs, where workers acquire shares held collectively before they are distri-buted after a period or at retirement or departure) or Trusts (ESOTs, where workers are temporary co-owners and only enjoy a share of the revenue while they are employed), Personal Equity Plans (for regular savers, attracting tax exemption up to a maximum limit). Equity Holding Co-operatives, additional Pension Funds, Swedish-type collective investors, and so forth (see Uvalic 1990).

The new shares can be partly managed by state holdings and new pension funds. State holdings – as noted above – are often regarded with suspicion, as bearers of central interests dependent on and ultimately answering to the centre. There is, however, no reason why they should not respond to a policy commitment to make profits instead of being responsible for the achievement of government targets (the Italian state holding IRI, for instance, has responded to policy changes and has rapidly turned from an endemic loss-maker into a profit-oriented and profit-making entity, presiding over privatization). Pension funds (new, for there were none in Eastern European economies) are also credible collective investors, but they should only be given as much stock as they can reasonably need to take over pension liabilities; there is no justification in profits funding the consumption of pensioner *rentiers*, instead of being channelled to self-financed investment.

It is conceivable that the banking system might exercise control over companies through direct and indirect (namely, on behalf of clients) share-holdings and the associated voting rights. Such a role is typical of the German–Japanese model of financial markets and has been advocated for Poland by Gomulka (1989). However, banks in that model rely on a full-fledged stock exchange and do not replace it. Thus the ability of the banking system to hold and administer state ownership should not be overestimated.[11]

PRIVATE APPROPRIATION OF STATE PROPERTY

A phenomenon often practised and sometimes advocated in our 'transitional' economies is the private appropriation of state property, either as a public policy of free distribution or as the result of spontaneous, 'wild' auto-appropriation (in Polish *samouwlaszczenie*).

It has been suggested (for instance by Attila Soos in Hungary, Dusan Triska in Czechoslovakia, Jan Szomburg and Janusz Lewandowski in Poland) that shares in state enterprises or holdings may be given away freely to all citizens, directly or in the form of vouchers. This policy seems to have the advantage of creating an instant capital market, as well as the political advantage of generating instant capitalism and popular support for it. The needs of budgetary balance and monetary discipline, however, should strictly limit any privileged access to shares, as well as their free distribution (apart from the need of 'converting' self-management rights into ownership stakes, discussed in the previous section). Free distribution of shares would be costly (as it was in the only known case to date, in British Columbia in 1979).[12] It would add a wealth effect to consumption demand, worsening inflationary pressure whether open or repressed. It would have an urban bias (of a kind that would not be present in case of free distribution of the profits of state enterprises as citizens' income): peasants in remote rural areas would be unlikely to benefit as much as the inhabitants of the capital city. As soon as potential limits to disposal lapsed, free distribution would also likely lead to rapid retrading and concentration of assets in the hands of a few better-informed people with access to liquid means (if this is not a pre-occupation, perhaps a lottery with large bundles of shares would be preferable and cheaper to administer). The state is not withering away in the course of transition and will continue to tax: 'Daddy state ... is alive and well', as Kornai (1990: 82) graphically put it; privatization revenues could replace taxes, thereby avoiding their distortionary effects on economic efficiency (Newbery 1990).

Free share issues are often advocated on grounds of lack of sufficient domestic capital. However – depending on the policy towards debt/equity swaps – domestic credit may be granted on a large scale for the population to take part in privatization; as long as this credit is sterilized and is not recycled to government expenditure, it can create a useful buffer against possible subsequent loss of macroeconomic control, when the government might sell its credits rather than raise additional taxes. In a country like Poland, state revenue from privatization could be used to retire the hard currency credits of enterprises and households, via the state banking system, which are not backed by hard currency reserves and therefore limit central control over the money supply. Finally, the free gift of state assets seems an out-of-place largesse on the part of governments heavily indebted to international creditors, who would be justified in asserting a prior claim to those assets.[13]

The other form of private appropriation – spontaneous, or 'wild' auto-appropriation – is worse because it is selective: privatization without publicity and competition may result at least partially in divestiture, rather than sale, and in the parallel appropriation of state property by a few well-informed people in positions of power. In the early stages of privatization in Hungary and Poland (Hare 1990, Grosfield 1990, Chilosi 1990), then elsewhere, managers and party officials often converted their position into a share of state capital through semi-legal or outright illegal transactions tolerated because of their large scale and the offenders' positions. This type of transaction includes the subcontracting of profitable activities, reciprocal disposals between state enterprise managers to their personal advantage, personal deals in joint ventures with foreign partners, artificial liquidation of viable activities transferred to internal bidders, etc.[14] There is no conceivable justification for condoning these practices, which are equivalent to the worst cases of insider trading in western markets.

PRIVATIZATION IN THE REFORM SEQUENCE

A crucial general question is the position of privatization in the sequence of reform measures – that is, whether it should occur during or after stabilization, before or after de-monopolization, and financial and productive restructuring.

It seems most inappropriate to sell off shares in state enterprises before stabilization and fiscale reform. Here stabilization is understood as domes-tic market equilibrium in non-hyperinflationary or excessively inflationary conditions, at uniform prices; fiscal reform is understood as the termination of *ex post, ad hoc*, enterprise-specific taxes and subsidies levelling profitability throughout the economy. Without these prior achievements, trends in product and input prices (and therefore enterprise profitability) would be impossible to assess, and as a result assets would be underpriced and yet unattractive in conditions of uncertainty. Thus privatization cannot really contribute directly to the stabilization process (see Nuti 1990a, 1990b). An exception can be the privatization of housing (where the stream of future services is directly consumed by the owner), small plots of land and small-scale services (where future benefits are more strictly dependent on the owner-worker's effort supply). This kind of 'small' privatization can contribute to stabilization.

The very announcement of a firm decision to proceed with privatization on a clearly predetermined schedule and procedure can itself make a contribution to stabilization (the opposite happened in the USSR where announcement of future price increases destabilized domestic markets and aggravated shortages). The announcement can be particularly effective if it is followed by the issue of special bonds, at low or zero nominal interest but carrying an option to purchase without restriction any state asset which will be privatized subsequently – pending the determination of asset prices. In Poland in November 1989 this instrument was used, but bonds redeemable through privatization were indexed and the timing and pattern of privatization were not specified; thus the bonds cost the government much more than other forms of bond financing and even so, in the uncertainty about privatization terms, were not very attractive to the public at the time of issue.[15]

De-monopolization is also a necessary precondition of privatization: without it asset prices would include a capitalization of monopoly power, which would be either unduly validated or – from the viewpoint of buyers – unfairly removed later on. A firm commitment to subsequent de-monopolization still leaves a strong element of uncertainty; foreign trade liberalization may alleviate the problem by raising the degree of competition.

The transformation of state enterprises into joint-stock companies presupposes the valuation of their net assets and their recapitalization (as the Czechs put it, 'the bride has to be endowed before being given away'). Or, if necessary, excess liquid resources may be drained away before privatization; at least some rationalization of output structure and input outlays (including labour employment) must take place. To proceed otherwise implies the likely underselling of state assets. If, before privatization, an active capital market has been organized, valuation and financial restructuring can be left to competitive mechanisms; otherwise some competitive redeployment of assets has to be stimulated among state enterprises. In any case it seems important that labour redundancies and redeployments should be handled before, rather than after, privatization, both to ensure fair compensation of workers and to make assets more attractive to potential alternative users.

THE POLISH ECONOMIC FRAMEWORK

In the ten years preceding 1990 Poland experienced stagnation in real output, while consumption levels fell by 10 per cent over the ten years to the end of 1989. Polish external debt reached $42 billion (of which $28 billion was owed to other governments), too large an amount to be fully serviced in spite of recurring trade surpluses (about $1 billion per year from 1985–9). Shortages were endemic and inflation accelerated, reaching the yearly rate of 740 per cent in 1989 when output declined by 1.7 per cent (see Kolodko 1989).

The economic framework of the 1990 drive towards privatization is that of a drastic stabilization programme, launched by the new Mazowiecki government on 1 January 1990, aimed at restoring market equilibrium, introducing resident convertibility for current transactions, and promoting net exports, while at the same time making progress towards reform and restructuring (see Kolodko 1990, Frydman *et al.* 1990, Nuti 1990a).

The stabilization package envisaged the abolition of subsidies and the reduction of the budget deficit to 1 per cent of GNP (down from 8 per cent in the previous year); monetary discipline and an increase in real interest rates to positive levels (the interest rate was raised also on old contracts, amounting to a tax); almost complete price liberalization (except for energy, pharmaceuticals and fertilizers, the price increases of which were diluted in subsequent months); very mild wage indexation of wage guidelines (at 30 per cent of inflation in January; 20 per cent in February to April; 60 per cent in May to December, except for July when indexation was 100 per cent to compensate for energy price increases) and penal taxation over that level; trade liberalization; 32 per cent devaluation of the zloty, made convertible and held at 9,500 zlotys per dollar, with the backing of external assistance provided by international agencies and the Group of 24 (a $700 million IMF stand-by credit, a $1 billion stabilization fund, $300 million from the World Bank, CEC-co-ordinated assistance under the PHARE programme, and credits and gifts by individual countries) and the rescheduling of debt service.

The programme was successful in establishing domestic market equilibrium: net exports rose to $1.7 billion over the first seven months; inflation exploded going up to the monthly (point-to-point) rate of 105 per cent in January 1990 then settled down to 4–6 per cent per month, which is still much too high on a yearly basis; and the exchange rate was held at the target rate, in spite of hyper-inflation and continued inflation differentials with hard currency countries (which just goes to show how grossly undervalued it must have been in January 1990). However, the real purchasing power of wages (formerly overestimated by statistics because of permanent shortages) fell by a third; output in mid-year stagnated after a fall of over one-third; and unemployment, around 10,000 at the end of 1989, grew fast and at the end of July 1990 had reached 700,000, rising at a rate of over 25,000 per week – government forecasts expected 1.3 million unemployed by the end of 1990.

In brief, the stabilization programme has overshot its output, employment and real wages targets, and yet there is hardly a sign of 'supply response'. Against this background the advantages expected of privatization – demand, deflation, efficiency, entrepreneurship – become particularly important.

POLISH PRIVATIZATION: DEBATES AND PRACTICE

In Poland there is a long-standing tradition of private enterprise, both in agriculture (following the decollectivization of 1956, with about 4 million employees in 1990) and outside agriculture as well – especially in 1984–9 (private manufacturing, transport and other services, including joint ventures, with over 1 million employees). This makes up almost one-third of the labour force, and grew in 1988 at 11 per cent while state employment was falling at 1–2 per cent; these trends have accelerated in 1989/90. By early 1990 there were 845,677 private enterprises (though mostly of very small size) attracting the best employees away from the public sector (Chilosi 1990). Official forecasts for 1990 expect state industrial output to fall by 28 per cent and private output to grow by 5 per cent, bringing the relative shares of the two sectors in industry from 92 to 87–88 per cent and from 8 to 12–13 per cent, respectively.

The privatization of Polish state assets and the setting up of a stock exchange where they could be sold and retraded were already under consideration by the last Communist-dominated Polish government, and naturally were revamped by the Mazowiecki-led coalition (see Grosfeld 1990). Finance Minister Leszek Balcerowicz, speaking at the IMF assembly in Washington in October 1989, stated that: 'The government of Poland intends to transform the Polish economy to a market economy. This process is to be accompanied by a gradual change in the pattern of ownership towards that which prevails in countries with advanced economies.'

Privatization has been generally regarded as a deflationary instrument to avoid or reduce hyperinflation, a guarantee of enterprise independence from central organs and, most importantly, a way of enhancing productivity and entrepreneurship.

The main difficulty faced by both the former and the present government has been the reconciliation of privatization schemes with the self-management institutions set up in Polish enterprises by the legislation of September 1981 (see Nuti 1981 for a comparison of the legislation with the more militant draft law submitted by Solidarity at that time). This legislation gave workers collectively some, indeed most, of the rights usually exercised by shareholders (such as managerial appointments and dismissals, verification of current performance, distribution of profit, and investment plans). Therefore the transformation of state enterprises into joint-stock companies to be sold off to the public implies the cancellation or substantial dilution of those rights which, especially at times of drastic reductions in real wages, have to be compensated and negotiated. But there were also other difficulties, in part indirectly related to the modification of self-management.

The starting position of workers before privatization is that of part entrepreneurs – not having ownership rights but having extensive decision-making rights and some profit-related benefits – for 100 per cent of the enterprise. An obvious trade-off is that of giving workers the position of full entrepreneurs – that is, 100 per cent owners, decision-makers and residual claimants – as shareholders in the enterprise with a much smaller stake. But how much smaller? And should it not be an equal absolute stake in all enterprises rather than a percentage which would unduly favour capital-intensive sectors? But then how are shares to be valued before a capital stock is set up? Should one start with the ailing enterprises or with the viable ones? And why limit the share-out to workers in state enterprises, excluding for instance workers in government services, or the unemployed; should everybody not have an equal share of state assets financed by past consumption sacrifices on the part of the whole population? Current savings could not afford to buy more than a small fraction of the whole national capital anyway. Why not give everybody a free share in all state enterprises, or rather in a number of state holding companies, thus solving at a stroke problems of capital valuation, equality and low size of the market? Or perhaps free equal vouchers should be offered to the whole adult population to convert into a portfolio of their choice as privatization proceeds. But then, why dilapidate state assets when the state budget deficit must be eliminated and there are pressing welfare needs, not to speak of the burden of external debt? Should sales and debt–equity swaps not be explored first? Could workers in state enterprises be satisfied by a combination of lesser involvement in decision-making and stronger participation in enterprise profit, instead of having to be paid off with a capital stake?

These questions were hotly debated in Poland and arguments somewhat impeded the progress of privatization.

THE NEW POLISH LAW ON PRIVATIZATION (JULY 1990)

The office of the Government Plenipotentiary for questions of Property Transformations – a new ministerial post in the new government, held by Krzysztof Lis – prepared a number of successive versions of draft laws on 'The Privatization of State Enterprises' and on 'The Council of National Capital and the Agency for Ownership Transformations' (Biuro 1990a, 1990b). In April 1990 the fifteenth version was presented to the Polish Parliament, with a counter-draft law being submitted by a group of Trade Union deputies close to Andrzej Mikowski of OKP (Solidarity's Citizen Parliamentary Committee; see OKP 1990). The government project, somewhat modified to take into account suggested amendments, was approved in July 1990 by impressive majorities (328 votes to 2 with 39 abstentions in the lower house; 60 votes to 7 with 2 abstentions in the Senate), but it left many issues still unresolved.

The new law establishes a Ministry of Property Transformation, to oversee the transformation of state enterprises into share companies initially held by the Treasury as single shareholder, followed within two years by the sale of shares to domestic and foreign investors, mostly by public offer at a prefixed price. The initiative to privatize a given enterprise can be taken by management, workers, or the 'founding organs' (that is, the central body or bodies exercising authority on the enterprise to date) and is subject to governmental authorization.

Up to 20 per cent of shares are reserved for workers of the privatized enterprise at a 50 per cent discount on the price of issue; the discount however cannot exceed half of the buyer's salary over the last six months. This is an ingenious constraint which broadly equalizes access to capital by employees in enterprises characterized by different amounts of capital per person.

This reserve creates a potential class of 4 million small investors but excludes from the discount the other 13 million working in state agencies other than enterprises and in the private sector; however, a portion (expected to be 10–20 per cent) of the shares of companies undertaking privatization is to be distributed freely and equally to the general public. Moreover, access to capital ownership is facilitated by the fact that shares can be purchased on credit, if so decided by the Minister of Property Transformation and the Minister of Finance. In order to limit *nomenklatura* acquisitions only physical persons can acquire shares at the time of privatization. As long as an enterprise is in state hands, one-third of the board of directors is to be elected by workers.

Foreign investors can freely purchase state company shares subject to an overall ceiling of 10 per cent, which can be raised by the Agency for Foreign Investments (transferred to the Ministry of Property Transformations from the Foreign Trade Ministry). Dividends and the proceeds of subsequent share sales may be repatriated abroad without special permits.

An alternative form of ownership transformation is through liquidation – that is, selling or leasing all or part of the enterprise assets to employees or external entrepreneurial groups, preferably at public auction, with a view to facilitate the creation of new private enterprises.

Several hundred enterprises are expected to close in the next year, and their assets will be sold or leased. Privatization of some companies (out of over 7,000 potential candidates) started in September 1990; some leading enterprises will be included – for example, the Kielce construction conglomerate Exbud and a cable factory in Czechowice. Foreign assistance is providing funds to pay the fees of western consultants and banks involved in this operation.

Opposition to earlier government plans had been voiced primarily on the grounds of infringement of workers' self-management rights, neglect of workers' ownership schemes and excessive concentration of power in the hands of the CNC president. The proposed counter-project left greater scope for ESOP-type schemes of employee ownership and for access to finance by domestic investors, and envisaged greater social control over privatization, at the risk however of bureaucratizing the process. The law approved in July 1990 made some concessions in this direction, introducing some free shares and the possibility of purchases on credit.

A central question remains: that of the role of foreign capital might play in Polish privatization, and therefore the weight of implicit or explicit 'debt–equity swaps'. Capital inflows to date have been fairly small (a cumulative amount of

$200 million to March 1990 for joint ventures – over one-third from West Germany – compared with a Soviet total of $600 million). On the one hand foreign participants are needed to secure competition, to provide know-how and fresh hard currency capital; on the other hand Poland has little incentive to repay the extant debt ($41.4 billion at the end of 1989, or 4.8 times total Polish yearly exports) out of national capital assets, other than as part of an international exercise in debt relief or at a discount comparable to that at which Polish commercial debt retrades in 1990 in secondary markets (over 80 per cent). In any case, the result of any privatization targeted to foreign buyers is indeterminate without stipulating the associated credit policy (determining the zloty credit available to domestic buyers for the purchase of state assets) and exchange rate policy (determining the domestic value of foreign bids).

The new law leaves the scale and time schedule of privatization to governmental discretion; Parliament is to set only 'basic directions' for privatization once a year and decides on the uses to which sales revenues are to be put. The law also leaves to future governmental decisions the scale of free distribution, the scale of credit sales, and the size of foreign acquisitions; is also leaves to subsequent legislation the institution and regulation of financial markets – a step which is obviously out of sequence. Until these questions are resolved, the progress of privatization is bound to continue to be controversial and to be delayed.

NOTES

1 An earlier version of this chapter was presented at the OECD Conference on 'The Transformation of Planned Economies', Paris, on 20–22 June 1990. Acknowledgements for useful comments and suggestions are due to Grzegorz Kolodko and to Conference participants, in particular to Willem Evers as discussant, and to the *Proceedings* editors Hans Blommestein and Michael Marrese. Responsibility for opinions, errors and omissions rests solely with the author.

2 According to Strumilin a sufficient condition of full Communism is that free consumption should be the larger share. However, in order to measure the relative shares of free and non-free goods – unless all goods are subject to a two-tier (free and non-free) regime – it is necessary to use a set of weights (that is, actual or shadow prices), and it is not clear from where the necessary price system would come. In principle prices could come from a system of marginal valuations with reference to a central body, were it not for the fact that under full Communism presumably central bodies 'wither away' with the state.

3 If I consume a quantity $c(i)$ of good i per unit of time and that good has durability $T(i)$, I can carry a revolving stock of $c(i)^*T(i)$; if $v(i)$ is the storage volume required per unit of consumption good i and I have a maximum storage space V, then I will have a maximum command on a stock of consumption goods given by a vector c with elements $c(i)^*T(i)$ subject to the scalar product of c and v (the corresponding vector of storage requirements per unit of consumption) being equal to or less than V. Here 'durability' means 100 per cent conservation for a period of time $T(i)$, which is equivalent to a zero real own rate of return on storage; this already gives rise to an optimization problem, in that the rational consumer, given his expected future claims to consumption $c(i, t)$ will equate his real rate of time preference, implicit in his rate of intertemporal substitution, to the zero own rate of return on storage. As a result of this

maximization problem actual stocks of goods $C(i, t)$ may well be lower than the maximum allowed by storage space and durability characteristics. In practice the consumption goods stored have a rate of decay $d(i)$ which is a function of storage time – that is, $d(i) = d[i, T(i)]$, giving rise to a more complex optimization problem simultaneously determining $d(i)$ and $T(i)$ as well as $C(i, t)$; now there can be different real rates of time preferences for each good, being equated to the rate of decay which is an implicit negative rate of (own) real interest.

4 Even paper money could be made perishable if an early enough date were fixed by which it had to be spent, or its liquidity could be reduced if its validity as legal tender were subject to some inconvenient procedure of official validation. Keynes (1936), for instance, suggested that cash should be stamped at frequent intervals; for a history of the idea of money 'melting' or 'reabsorbing', see Morley-Fletcher (1980–1).

5 This cost is virtually equal to zero, or a small amount taken with negative sign; if interest-earning liquid deposits are possible, they are treated here as financial assets different from money.

6 Except for contracts involving the delivery of future labour services, which would not be capitalistic but feudal, as they would imply the compulsory subjection of individuals to other individuals or firms.

7 China appears to have been an exception, at least until recently.

8 The March 1990 Soviet legislation on property prohibits one-man-owned enterprises employing wage labour but allows joint-stock companies, somehow regarded as 'collective' forms of ownership. This is an absurd distinction, co-ownership being no less private than one-man ownership of a whole asset. Soviet legislators are literally preventing 'exploitation of man' by one other man but allow it when it is done by several men together.

9 In the Soviet economy in 1990 excess liquid assets in the hands of the population are estimated to be of the order of an average four months' wage bill; enterprises inventories were 82 per cent of national income in 1985, compared with 31 per cent in the United States (Shmelev and Popov 1989: 305).

10 In this respect my own views have radically altered with respect to Nuti (1974), where the possibility of group entrepreneurship in the traditional socialist model was considered with excessive optimism.

11 Gomulka envisages a special role for banks in the privatization process: public share-holdings in state enterprises would be entrusted to the management of banks, which would earn a share of dividends and realized capital gains; Gomulka regards privatization of those banks as equivalent to the privatization of the public assets entrusted to them, but this is a misconception: if I buy shares in Merrill Lynch I do not acquire a stake in the portfolio of their clients. Moreover, emphasis on realized capital gains rather than on the increase of portfolio evaluation is bound to unduly inflate turnover (by encouraging a special case of so-called 'bed and breakfast' transactions – that is, sales followed by quick repurchases).

12 In early 1979 the provincial government of British Columbia set up a new Crown Corporation, the British Columbia Resources Investment Corporation, with $151.5 million assets, and distributed five free shares to any citizen who asked for them, plus additional shares at $6 each; 170,000 persons were involved. However the new company made some bad investments and soon incurred substantial losses; the operation is not judged to have been a success (see Stanbury 1989: 282–3).

13 The loss of potential collateral on the part of creditors may be thought to be over-compensated by the greater potential productivity which could derive from privatiz-ation and the further impulse to economic reform. Certainly no international creditor has publicly argued against free distribution of state assets in debtor countries.

14 The auto-appropriation of state assets by the *nomenklatura* has been facilitated in Poland by the extraordinary growth of joint-stock and limited liability companies

founded in Poland, which numbered almost 30,000 in 1989. Some transactions, in which managers appeared on both sides as sellers on behalf of their state enterprises and as buyers for their own companies or even joint ventures, naturally have been declared void by the Supreme Court, but the bulk of this kind of transaction is unlikely to be challenged, especially when foreign buyers are also involved (Chilosi 1990).

A famous case is that of Igloopol, the largest Polish agro-industrial complex, valued at 145 billion zlotys and artificially liquidated and transferred for 55 billion zlotys to a joint-stock company with the same board of directors, whose shares – transferable at their discretion – were sold mostly to Party organizations and activists. The Ministry of Agriculture (of which the Igloopol Managing Director was Deputy Minister) approved the liquidation procedure in spite of a Ministry of Finance report which declared it illegal and economically unjustified (Grosfield 1990). A recent decree of the Mazowiecki government has now made illegal the participation of state enterprise managers and workers' councils in the companies founded by their own enterprise (Chilosi 1990).

15 Kolodko (1990) reports that a million zlotys invested in these bonds at the end of 1989 were worth by the end of the first quarter of 1990 2.5 million zlotys, compared with 1.3 million zlotys if invested in three-month deposits at the National Savings Bank (PKO) and 1.06 million zlotys if invested in dollar-denominated deposits. This is an indication of the lack of credibility of government policies.

BIBLIOGRAPHY

Act VI (1988) On *Economic Associations* [companies], Budapest: HungaroPress (Special issue, October).

Act XIII (1989) On the *Transformation of Organizations Carrying on Economic Activity and Economic Associations*, June, Budapest.

Aslund, A. (1985) *Private Enterprise in Eastern Europe*, London: Macmillan.

Balcerowicz, L. (1989) *Economic Reforms in Poland and the Role of Financial Aid*, Mimeo, Warsaw: Ministry of Finance.

Biuro P. R. S. P. W. (1990a) 'Zalozenia rzadowego programu prywatyzacji przedsie-biorstw panstwowych', Warsaw.

——— (1990b) 'Ustawa (Projekt) o prywatyzacji przedsiebiorstw panstwowych', April, Warsaw.

Chilosi, A. (1990) 'L'economia polacca tra stabilizzazione e trasformazione istituzionale', Conference Paper, Pisa.

Frydman, R., Kolodko, G. W. and Wellisz, S. (1990) 'Stabilisation in Poland: a progress report', Second International Monetary Conference, FU and Landeszentralbank Berlin, Berlin, 10–12 May.

Gomulka S. (1989) 'How to create a capital market in a socialist country and how to use it for the purpose of changing the system of ownership', Conference Paper, LSE Financial Markets Group, 13 December.

Grosfeld, I. (1990) 'Prospects for privatisation in Poland', *European Economy*, no. 43, CEC Brussels, March.

Hanson, P. (1989) 'Von Mises' revenge', Paper for the Conference on Perestroika: A Socioeconomic Survey, Radio Free Europe/Radio Liberty, Munich, 7–10 July.

Hare, P. G. (1990) 'Reform of enterprise regulation in Hungary – from "tutelage" to market', Seminar Paper, PHARE Group, EC-DG-II, Brussels, November.

Hemming, R. and Mansoor, A. M. (1988) *Privatisation and Public Enterprise*, IMF Occasional Paper No. 56, Washington, D.C., January.

Keynes, J. M. (1936) *The General Theory of Employment, Interest and Money*, London: Macmillan.

Kolodko, G. W. (1989) *Reform, Stabilisation Policies, and Economic Adjustment in*

Poland, WIDER Working Papers No. 51, Helsinki, January.

—— (1990) *Polish Hyperinflation and Stabilisation 1989–1990*, Working Papers of the Institute of Finance No. 10, Warsaw.

Kornai, J. (1990) *The Road to a Free Economy – Shifting from a Socialist System: The Example of Hungary*, New York and London: W.W. Norton & Co.

MacAvoy, P. W. (1989) *Privatisation and State Owned Enterprises*, Boston: Kluwer Academic Publishers.

Meade, J. (1989) *Agathotopia: The Economics of Partnership*, London: The Hume Institute.

Mises, L. von (1951) *Socialism – An Economic and Sociological Analysis*, Translated by J. Kahane, Indianapolis: Liberty Classics.

Morley-Fletcher, E. (1980–1) 'Per una storia dell'idea di "minimo sociale garantito"', *Rivista Trimestrale*, nos 64–66. October 1980–March 1981, pp. 297–321.

Newbery, D. M. (1990) 'Reform in Hungary: sequencing and privatisation', Paper presented at the EEA Fifth Annual Conference, Lisbon, September.

Nuti, D. Mario (1974) 'Socialism and ownership', in L. Kolakowski and S. Hampshire (eds),*The Socialist Idea*, Proceedings of a Conference at Reading University 1973, London: Weidenfeld and Nicolson.

—— (1981) 'Poland: socialist renewal and economic collapse', *New Left Review*, November.

—— (1988) 'Competitive valuation and efficiency of capital investment in the socialist economy', *European Economic Review* 32, 2–6.

—— (1989) 'Feasible financial innovation under market socialism', in C. Kessides, T. King, D. M. Nuti and K. Sokil (eds), *Financial Reform in Centrally Planned Economies*, Washington: EDI-World Bank.

—— (1990a) 'Internal and international implications of monetary disequilibrium in Poland', *European Economy*, no. 43, March, 169–82.

—— (1990b) 'Stabilisation and reform sequencing in the Soviet economy', *Recherches Economiques de Louvain* 56(2), 1–12.

—— (1993) 'Alternative employment and payment systems', in S. Bowles, H. Gintis and B. Gustafsson (eds) *Democracy and Markets: Participation, Accountability and Efficiency*, Cambridge: Cambridge University Press.

OKP (1990) 'Kontr-Ustawa (Projekt) o przeksztalceniach wlasnosciowych przedsie-biorstw panstwowych', Warsaw. (Polish Ministry of Finances, 'Holding companies as a means of accelerating privatization in Poland', Warsaw, 7 March.)

Sappington, D. and Stiglitz, J. E. (1987) 'Privatisation, information, and incentives', *Journal of Policy Analysis and Management* 6(4), 567–82.

Shmelev, N. and Popov, V. (1989) *The Turning Point: Revitalising the Soviet Economy*, New York: Doubleday.

Stanbury, W. T. (1989) 'Privatisation in Canada: ideology, symbolism or substance?', in P. W. MacAvoy *Privatisation and State Owned Enterprises*, Boston: Kluwer Academic Publishers.

Stiglitz, J. E. (1989) 'On the economic role of the state', in J. E. Stiglitz, *The Economic Role of the State*, Oxford: Blackwell.

Uvalic, M. (1990) *The PEPPER Report: Promotion of Employee Participation in Profits and Enterprise Results in the Member States of the European Community*, Florence and Brussels: EUI and CEC.

Vickers, J. and Yarrow, G. (1988) *Privatisation: An Economic Analysis*, Cambridge, Mass.: MIT Press.

18

SELLING OFF THE STATE
Privatization in Hungary[1]
Peter Lawrence

This chapter traces the development of the privatization of state-owned assets in Hungary since 1989. It is principally concerned with two issues: the first, that of appropriate techniques of privatization in the context of state socialist economies, including the question of who buys the state-owned assets being sold off; the second, that of control over the privatization process, and on whose behalf it is, or it should be, exercised.

The chapter is not concerned with the issue of whether privatization of state assets confirms the economic benefits claimed for it by its proponents. There is a substantial literature on this question (see, for example, Vickers and Yarrow, 1988) and in this writer's view the jury is still out on whether ownership matters in the case of large-scale enterprises' performance, or at least whether it is a relevant issue in the case of the former state socialist economies.

The large-scale sale of state-owned assets may, however, be infeasible as an option: first, because they may have no market value at all, and second, because the western industrial enterprises that may be able to mobilize the capital necessary may not be prepared to take the risk inherent in investing in an economy in transition which may be considered both economically and politically unstable. For these economies, transforming state enterprises into commercial forms with largely state shareholdings, rationalizing them and stimulating the growth of a small- and medium-size manufacturing and service private sector, may form the most appropriate means of 'privatizing' the economy.

The first section of this chapter begins with a summary of Hungary's economic performance during the 1980s which led to the pressure for enterprise ownership reform. There follows a description of the mechanisms, some legal and some illegal, of the 'spontaneous' or 'wild' privatizations of 1989 prior to the establishment of the State Privatization Agency in 1990. The second section describes the government's subsequent programme of ordered privatization. The final section assesses the progress of that programme and looks at the pressures to return to 'spontaneity' as a means of accelerating the process of state divestment of assets.

PRIVATIZATION: THE FIRST PHASE

The nature of the old system and its deficiencies is well documented, as have been the economic reforms which were attempted in order to make them good (see, for example, Hare *et al.* 1981). It became clear throughout the 1980s that the system, even in its 'reformed' state, did not work. The Hungarian economy, though one of the better supplied in the old CMEA bloc in terms of the availability of goods, the development of the small-scale service sector and the relative success of its agriculture (Swain 1987), began to show signs of stagnation and even negative growth after 1987. GDP in real terms fell between 1988 and 1989, and industrial output, which fell by 1 per cent over the same period, fell a further 8 per cent in 1990 (*Statisztikai Havi Kozlemenyek* 1991). This picture of stagnation and decline is presented in Figure 18.1.

The economic system was effectively geared to the fulfilling of contracts with the Soviet Union, Hungary's main energy supplier. Ministries ensured these contracts were fulfilled by a mixture of economic incentives – subsidies, bonuses for managers, preferential access to hard currency – which allowed ministries to keep control over production while reforms tinkered with enterprise autonomy and the introduction of the profit motive. The 1984 Enterprise Act attempted to strengthen autonomy by making 80 per cent of enterprises self-managing through enterprise councils. The council, which was effectively nominated by the general manager, comprised 50 per cent management and 50 per cent workers' representatives.

Firms governed by enterprise councils were officially not under state control but the pre-existing non-market mechanisms tied production plans of enterprises to state requirements. Firms were encouraged to fulfil plan requirements for intra-CMEA trade by being paid the Hungarian currency equivalent into their Hungarian bank account on commencement of contracts agreed with other CMEA enterprises and governments. In the case of hard currency contracts, of course, payment was only completely made when the contract had been fulfilled. The resulting incentive to trade with CMEA partners, and the inability of the Soviet Union in particular to fulfil its side of the contract because of its own supply-side difficulties, resulted in Hungary building up a surplus of transferable roubles which it could not set against its dollar account deficits. By 1989 Hungary was running a deficit on its dollar payments account of $1476 million, while running a surplus on its rouble account of $898 million (IMF, *Financial Statistics*, 1992).[2]

The system therefore provided weak incentives to compete in hard currency markets and therefore weak incentives to raise technological and labour productivity levels. Indeed, the existence of state subsidies and other incentives to fulfil production plans, and administered price setting in intermediate and final goods markets, meant that enterprise profit and loss accounts were meaningless in terms of international accounting practice.

Enterprise autonomy, therefore, was meant to increase efficiency, but it

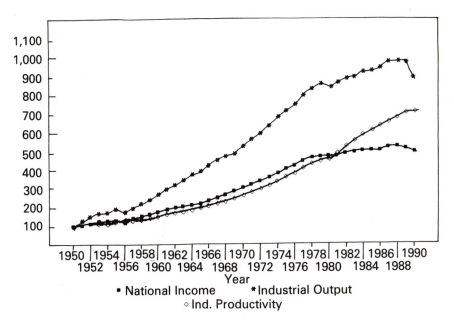

Figure 18.1 Hungary: selected economic indicators, 1950–90 (1950 = 100)

existed within a system which was geared to fulfilling administered plans and the contracts which went with them, rather than to satisfying market demand. Privatization was therefore seen by the reform economists as a means of separating enterprises from the control of the parent ministries by removing from them subsidies and other incentives, and, as part of a wider price reform and market liberalization process, forcing them to compete in open markets and to operate more competitively and efficiently in the course of which they would be switching trade away from rouble towards dollar markets.

Further attempts to generate increased enterprise autonomy and sow the seeds both for privatization and for a capital market, came with the 1988 Company Act and the 1989 Transformation Act. The Company Act on Economic Associations, *inter alia*, created the equivalent of the limited company. Foreign participation without restriction was permitted by the Act, but 30 per cent of any foreign capital stake had to be in the form of liquid assets. The Transformation Act allowed the companies run by enterprise councils to be transformed into public joint-stock companies. Twenty per cent of the asset capital had to come from outside the company, usually from foreign sources, and 20 per cent of the shares had to go to the State Property Fund; 80 per cent of the share of sales receipts was to go to the State Property Fund while 20 per cent was to go to the company as an incentive to privatize. Any shares still unsold after three years were to go to the State Property Fund.

There was very little incentive to an already supposedly autonomous company to privatize in this way since the company would get such a small share of the sale of its assets. The absence of a capital market also meant that floating shares presented problems and so it was hardly surprising that one year after the Transformation Act had been introduced only one company had been transformed in this way.

Other ways could be found to maintain control in the hands of those who managed the enterprise, by using the Company Act; these are discussed in the next section.

'SPONTANEOUS' PRIVATIZATION – THE PRACTICE

'Spontaneous' or 'wild' privatization was the initial means by which a form of divestment of state assets was undertaken – not by the state, but by the enterprises themselves. These methods to a greater or lesser extent involved some bending of the rules of the Company Act and in some cases were quite fraudulent.

There were two main ways in which spontaneous privatization took place – one semi-legal and one legal. In one celebrated case, that of the Apisz stationery distribution company, the privatization worked in this way:[3]

1   The Enterprise Council of Apisz creates Apisz Ltd.
2   Apisz values its assets at a book value of 300 million forints (fts).
3   Apisz Ltd issues bonds at a nominal rate of interest of 15 per cent with which it pays Apisz for the assets it has acquired from the original company.
4   Apisz Ltd takes on the whole workforce of 1,000 with the exception of 10 who nominally work for Apisz, which is now an 'empty shell'.
5   Apisz Ltd then issues shares to the value of 700 million fts. The managers and workers buy 8.5 per cent, 20 per cent are bought by an Austrian entrepreneur, and Citibank Budapest takes the rest.
6   Apisz Ltd then restructures its share issue by buying back 600 million fts-worth of shares, so that the value of the remaining shares increases from 100 million fts to 700 million fts.

The illegality involved here was the effective asset stripping of the enterprise. In theory the enterprise was being sold for its book value, but in practice it was sold for one-seventh of that because of the share restructuring which took place afterwards. In all other major respects, the Apisz route to transformation was followed in a more legal fashion by other Enterprise Council-'owned' enterprises.[4] Enterprise Councils used the Company Act to transfer assets to one, or where enterprises were broken up, several, limited companies, each of which was able to sell shares to partners (including foreign partners) with the original Enterprise Council-owned enterprise as an empty shell. The major question associated with this process is that of the valuation of the enterprise or that part of it which becomes the new limited company and is partially sold off.

Who gained from these forms of transformation? First, at least in the Apisz case had the deal been allowed to go through, the managers would have gained a substantial shareholding for a relatively small sum of money largely derived from awarding themselves huge bonuses before this transformation took place. As they were appointed under the old system, this would have been a clear case of the *nomenklatura* seeking to preserve their position under the new order. Second, the foreign shareholder was to acquire a stake in a highly profitable company on the cheap with minimum investment under the law and with profit repatriation and tax holidays thrown in. More generally, because of the lack of supervision over valuations – something which is inherent in spontaneous privatization – investors, domestic or foreign may well have been getting assets at below market valuation. Third, the employees' position was preserved, or at least time was being bought before rationalization and restructuring meant unemployment for some of them.

Who were the losers? The answer to this is not at all clear. Potentially the state was a loser. It was clearly losing the receipts from the sale of the enterprises so transformed. However, it was not clear who owned the enterprise and therefore whether the state was legally entitled to the receipts. Ownership was vested in the Enterprise Council in 85 per cent of enterprises as a result of the 1984 legislation on enterprise autonomy. So legally the enterprise owned itself and could presumably dispose of itself. Then there was the potential loss of revenue from taxing the enterprise profits (in the Apisz case, almost 300 million fts in 1988) because of the concessions made to the foreign private shareholder. It is conceivable that the state would have had to make similar concessions to other foreign entrepreneurs to lure them into Hungary, so that this 'loss' might be regarded as an investment incentive, yielding a stream of future social benefits in the form of higher productivity enterprises generating more employment than would have been the case if they had not been restructured by foreign capital. It is not clear that this is what was happening in the spontaneous privatization cases, but rather that foreign investors saw a way of acquiring assets in order to make high untaxed short-run profits with little investment.

However, much of this discussion hinged on the question of valuation. To be sure, the profits of Apisz, for example, were 270 million fts according to the accounts, which on an asset value of 700 million fts looks good. But, as observed earlier, all this profit-making took place in a non-competitive environment, with, for many enterprises, government subsidies and administered price-setting. The question of how much Hungarian enterprises were worth, even if they were profitable in Hungarian terms, was not settled until their accounts could be restructured according to international convention. The state could still gain from spontaneous privatization even if it received nothing for the assets of the enterprise to compensate for the loss of future income streams. If enterprises were, in international accounting terms, really making losses as was often the case, then no longer having to subsidize them to disguise these losses would be a gain to the state budget. Still, the fact that an enterprise made a loss did not mean that with effective restructuring it could not yield profits in the future. In that sense, effectively giving away rights to receipts from enterprise sales was clearly a loss to the public purse, although this could be recovered in the future by an appropriately set profits tax. In the Hungarian case the overvaluation of assets and the indebtedness of enterprises could mean that their net worth was negative in international terms and strengthens the argument for giving them away in the hope of receiving a stream of revenue from profits tax on restructured enterprises in the future (see Newbery 1990 for a discussion of this issue).

One answer to the question of how much the enterprises were really worth, was to put them up for public auction. One such enterprise, producing fertilizers, was auctioned in 1989. The state valued the enterprise at 4 billion fts, while the highest bid was 600 million fts from an agricultural co-operative. The government decided this bid was too low, and so decided to repeat the exercise. In the second auction there emerged a Swiss bidder who offered 500 million fts. There followed bid and counter-bid until the Swiss firm bid 1.75 billion fts, topping the final co-operative bid by 500,000 fts. The lesson of this story was that however highly enterprises were valued under the old accounting system, when put to the test of the market there were only two bidders of substance and their maximum valuations ended up at around 44 per cent of that of the state. The purchaser was certainly made to pay a higher percentage of book value than the buyers of Apisz, but the fertilizer enterprise was earning $80 million of exports per year, so that the purchase price of $28.3 million might be considered to be generously low.

This becomes a little clearer when another method of privatization is examined. This involved joint venture bids from foreign enterprises who wanted to buy substantial shareholdings in Hungarian companies. One such agreement involved the purchase of 50 per cent plus one of the shares of Tungsram (the large Hungarian lighting company) by the US General Electric Lighting Company, the rest being held by the Hungarian Credit Bank which, together with the Austrian Girozentrale Bank, had bought Tungsram shares the year previously. General Electric paid $150 million (9 billion fts), mainly for Girozentrale's portfolio which had cost that bank $110 million in 1988. Girozentrale received $130 million with the other $20 million going back to Tungsram. General Electric had the option of purchasing another 20 per cent of the shares if it doubled the company's west European turnover within five years (Hungarian Chamber of Commerce, 1989).

Tungsram has been a highly successful company with sales in 1988 of $300 million (18 billion fts), 85 per cent of which were exports. The deal involved the introduction of modern management techniques and equipment, and the training of Hungarian staff in the USA. Nevertheless, it might be argued that paying $150 million for a company with annual dollar earnings of $255 million was a good deal for General Electric. While it was true that they were expected to increase these dollar earnings by joint marketing of their products in Western Europe, it was not clear how effectively net dollar earnings would be monitored. Transnational companies have complex accounting systems as difficult to disentangle as those operating under state socialism. Although more was paid for this company than for the fertilizer plant, the potential for transfer pricing and other accounting manipulation may have made it a much better deal for the US company than for the Hungarian government.

SPONTANEOUS PRIVATIZATION – THE DEBATE

The initial wave of spontaneous privatizations was the subject of sharp debate in Hungary. On the one side there were the defenders of the nation led by the Hungarian Democratic Forum which now forms the government, who believed that this kind of privatization was selling off national assets on the cheap and leaving them in the hands of the old Communist bureaucratic management. Foreign investors were being given the opportunity to asset-strip the Hungarian economy, without any commitment to it, and all this was being done over the heads of the employees of the enterprises. The main advantage of privatization to governments with foreign and domestic debt and large budget deficits – namely, that of deficit and debt reduction through privatization proceeds – was not even available.

On the other hand, there were the economic liberals who believed that if large-scale privatization was required to establish a market economy – and they believed it was – then spontaneity was probably the quickest and most effective means of doing this. Of course, it should be achieved legally, but state control over privatization had to be kept at a minimum in order to prevent the bureaucratization of the economy by a different route. Foreign investment was essential, the risks to such investment would be seen to be high unless market liberalism was strictly operative. Barriers to entry and rules of behaviour should be minimized. As to the return of the *nomenklatura*, one informant suggested to the writer that this was exaggerated and that 50 per cent of the old managers had been replaced by younger managerial cadres, less tainted by the past and better trained in 'western' managerial techniques. For the economic liberals, there was no alternative.

However, alternatives were suggested (see Tardos 1989). Enterprises 'owned' by enterprise councils could be 'renationalized' and then privatized by a State Privatization Agency. Enterprises could be encouraged to engage in debt–equity swaps. Shares could be given to employees under ESOPs (employee share ownership plans). Self-management enterprises could be preserved but subject to 'hard-budget constraints' (see Kornai 1980). Other proposals involved shares in enterprises being taken by financial trusts – banks, insurance companies, by local authorities, by academic institutions (as a way of increasing their income) – some of these proposals being along the lines proposed for some other former state socialist economies (cf. Blanchard and Layard 1990).

None of these alternatives appealed. Renationalization was not on the political agenda since it appeared to be a step backward on the march to the free privatized market economy. Debt–equity swaps might prove impossible under the rules whereby all creditors would have to agree in every case. The implementation of ESOPs begged the question of how workers would pay for their shares. It would be wrong to give the shares away because this would be transferring assets which were technically owned by the people to the employees of enterprises. Workers could be given loans to buy the shares or they could pay for the shares out of future profits by forgoing dividends. As for self-management under hard budget constraints, this begged the question of how strongly motivated the state would be to enforce these constraints and how much it would be willing to shore up enterprises in order to satisfy Soviet contracts (at that time still a delicate issue), or avoid large-scale unemployment and political instability. The other question regarding self-management was that of ownership. If enterprises were self-managed, would they effectively be owned by their management? If so, this would be open to the same objection as that presented against spontaneous privatization – the old managers would retain power. Whether this mattered or not under a different economic system, where they would have to prove their efficiency, was not really the issue. Rightly or wrongly such a move was impossible because it was politically unpopular.

In the event, the government settled on the establishment of an agency, the State Privatization Agency, which would oversee privatizations proposed by enterprises. The nature of this agency and its activities are presented in the next section.

THE STATE PRIVATIZATION AGENCY

The State Privatization Agency (SPA) was set up in March 1990 consequent to the public disquiet about the path being taken by the spontaneous privatizations (Hare and Grosfeld 1991). Its board of directors is appointed by the Prime Minister and its general manager is appointed by the government. It employs around 120 people. Yet its task is to privatize around 2,200 enterprises with assets estimated at 2,000 billion fts ($26 billion). Of these enterprises, 32 per cent were state-run and 56 per cent self-managed. The other 12 per cent have been transformed into joint-stock companies, but are 100 per cent state owned. In the year since its inception approximately 9 per cent of these enterprises had been fully or partially privatized in various ways (SPA 1991).

The SPA has several channels through which it can oversee privatizations. Transformation and privatization can take place through a process initiated by enterprises themselves. The SPA can itself initiate privatization through establishing its own programme. Private investors (both foreign and domestic) can make proposals to the SPA to buy state property. Finally the state enterprises involved in retail trading, catering and consumer services are subject to the Preprivatization Act of September 1990 which regulates the sale of shops owned by state companies to individual entrepreneurs, partnerships, an unlimited liability company or a limited liability company operated by these sets of buyers.

In April 1991 the SPA reported that sixty-six transformations of enterprises with a book value of 71.3 billion fts had been started with the assistance of the Agency. In many cases foreign transnationals were involved in taking minority shareholdings in the transformed enterprises (SPA 1991). By the middle of 1991, although thirty-nine enterprises had been transformed and privatized through the SPA, the average state shareholding in these enterprises was still 70.5 per cent; foreign capital's share averaged 16.5 per cent, while the rest was in the hands of local authorities and other Hungarian institutions. Even Ibusz, after its 'successful' privatization, is still 61 per cent state owned (interview with an SPA director, June 1991).

In overseeing these privatizations, the SPA is charged with ensuring that various pre-privatization conditions are satisfied. In particular the agency is required to ensure that proper balance sheets in accordance with international standards are produced by the agent initiating privatization. It is also required to ensure that the valuation of the enterprise is a fair reflection of its market value so as to obtain for the state the maximum proceeds from the sale of state sector enterprises. Of the sale proceeds of those enterprises which had become self-managed companies under the Act on Economic Associations 80 per cent was to go to the SPA, while for fully state-owned enterprises, 20 per cent was to go to the SPA under Act VII of 1990. The state budget would have the first call on privatization receipts. By the end of 1991, the state expected to receive about 19 billion fts ($260 million) from the privatization of about 15 per cent of its assets; this compares with a budget deficit in 1989 of 49 billion fts (SPA 1991; *Statistical Yearbook* 1989; IMF, *Financial Statistics*, April 1992).

The SPA was also empowered to initiate its own programme of privatization. In the first privatization programme launched in September 1990, twenty companies were to be privatized by open tender through sealed bids. The best known among these companies (see Table 18.1) was the Ibusz travel agency, shares in which were subsequently floated on the Vienna Stock Exchange. This is hardly surprising given the profits/assets ratio of this company. Even allowing for the distortions of valuation and profit levels embodied in the economic system as a whole, this company was clearly the best performer of the twenty listed and as of June 1991 was the only one to have been privatized. The other companies were having their accounts disentangled and rewritten. A further programme of privatization involving another twelve state-owned enterprises, mainly some of the 'empty shells' described earlier, was announced early in 1991. While all the twenty enterprises in the first programme were profitable to a greater or lesser degree on paper, half of the twelve companies listed in the first phase of the second programme were loss-makers under the old system of accounting (see Table 18.2). The objective of this second round of privatization was to claw back the newly transformed economic associations formed out of the Enterprise Council-managed companies, so that the sale proceeds of subsequent privatization could accrue to the state and to be used to repay state debt.

In all these thirty-two cases tenders have been awarded to private foreign and Hungarian financial advisers to restructure that balance sheets and oversee the

Table 18.1 Hungary: first privatization programme

Enterprise	Asset value	Turnover (million forints)	Profits	Profits as per cent of asset value	Profits as per cent of turnover
Centrum Dept Store	5,219	18,621	401	7.7	2.2
Danubius Hotel and Spa	6,640	3,900	468	7.0	12.0
Forest Machinery	146	164	1.4	1.0	0.9
Gamma Works (medical instruments, computers, etc.)	1,754	1,598	51	2.9	3.2
Hollohazi Porcelain Works	484	425	39	8.1	9.2
Hungarhotels	10,936	7,537	932	8.5	12.4
Hungexpo (fairs, exhibitions)	1,654	2,072	118	7.1	5.7
Ibusz (tourist agency)	2,144	9,428	1,139	53.1	12.1
Idex (engineering exports)	4,400	2,200	89	2.0	4.0
Interglob (road freight)	1,062	1,427	21	2.0	1.5
Kner Printing	1,566	2,318	168	10.7	7.3
Kunep (construction)	515	638	12	2.3	0.9
MEH Scrap Processing	3,769	8,862	831	22.0	9.4
Pannonia Hotels	6,201	5,213	589	9.5	11.3
Pannonplast (plastics)	4,122	5,470	413	10.0	7.6
Pietra Building Ceramic	973	991	56	5.8	5.6
Richter Gedeon	17,481	15,576	935	5.4	6.0
Salgotarjan Plate Glass	1,724	1,909	155	9.0	8.1
Tritex Trading	694	1,670	86	12.4	5.2
Volantefu (freight transport)	2,405	3,681	161	6.7	4.4

Source: Hungarian Chamber of Commerce (1991).

privatization process for the SPA. The total number of enterprises scheduled to be privatized under the second privatization programme is around 100, though some of these include historic vineyards and country castles (SPA 1991).

The process of privatization is clearly very slow when compared to the distance it still has to travel. The criteria for choosing the thirty-two enterprises have also been queried and there is some suggestion that some successful enterprises managed to avoid being on the list while others were too close to bankrupty to be ready to be privatized (Kiss 1991: 5). The SPA has been criticized for being too cautious and bureaucratic in the demands it makes of enterprises wanting to privatize. The understaffed SPA is charged with ensuring

Table 18.2 Hungary: the second privatization programme, first phase

Enterprise (no. of economic associations)	Asset value	Turnover (million forints)	Profits (loss)	Profits as per cent of asset value	Profits as per cent of turnover
Machine Tool Works (17)	1,376	1,780	(110)	–	–
Szatmar Furniture (6)	77	968	13	16.9	1.3
Information Technique (33)	133	860	18	13.5	2.1
Screw Manufacturing Co. (12)	690	1,288	58	8.4	4.5
Building Machinery Mfg (3)	10	407	(101)	–	–
Food Processing Machinery (7)	381	2,631	(150)	–	–
Elegant Dressmaking (4)	69	1,175	15	21.7	1.3
Ganz Tool Mfg (5)	314	151	9	2.9	6.0
Hungarian Optical Works (14)	1,329	2,651	(83)	–	–
Grabocenter (cotton/ artificial leather) (4)	1,517	5,273	302	19.9	5.7
Csepel Bicycles and Dressmaking Mfg (10)	520	1,658	(108)	–	–
Chair and Upholstery Co. (11)	447	184	(10)	–	–

Source: Hungarian Chamber of Commerce (1991).

that enterprises are sold off to buyers who will not strip its assets, but whose very pursuit of this goal increases its degree of intervention. As a result two proposals have been made for speeding up the process. First, it is proposed to 'privatize the privatization'. Second, there are pressures to return to less closely supervised spontaneity.

SPONTANEITY AGAIN: THE PRESSURE TO GO FASTER

Privatizing the privatization was foreseen in the Act establishing the SPA. In any case the Agency subcontracts the management of privatization sales to private enterprises. It now proposes to subcontract its own work to consultancy firms, both domestic and foreign, so that it speeds up the process of privatization. Tenders have been put out for the work and this offers the opportunity to develop the activities of financial consultancies on the back of the privatization process. This in itself will be of particular benefit once the fledgling stock exchange becomes established and a capital market demands the services of such financial agents. Privatizing privatization is one way of speeding up the process of selling state assets. The other is to allow enterprises to sell themselves off without state intervention even at one remove.

However, it is not clear that the critics of the SPA are right about its speed of action or its slow bureaucratic procedures. In the recent case of refrigerator makers, Lehel, the SPA responded quickly to the evident pressure from Electrolux, the Swedish domestic appliance manufacturer, to buy the Hungarian company outright. The move was a logical one, both companies having co-operated with each other for the previous eleven years. However, the SPA was mindful of political pressures not to sell to foreign companies, while at the same time recognizing the need to speed up the privatization process. In the end, probably not wanting to risk the withdrawal of the only likely buyer, the SPA allowed the sale to go ahead, without a price being agreed, since the formal valuation of the company was not complete (Szep 1991).

A further problem facing the agency, which is anyway short staffed, is the time it takes to discover not only the 'true' balance sheet, but also the true ownership of the land on which the enterprise stands. Given the changes which have taken place in property rights law, care has to be exercised in case the buyer of the enterprise subsequently finds out it has obligations to landowners. Insecurity about property rights and the absence of proper land registry records is in itself a substantial deterrent to private investment. An attempt to buy out one enterprise ran into difficulty because records revealed that the land was owned by the Zoological Gardens. Who owned the Zoological Gardens was another matter. What was evident was that the deal could not go through without property rights being clarified (interview with an SPA Director, June 1991).

Finally, militating against any quick-fix approach is the problem of enterprise indebtedness. In some cases the liabilities of the enterprise are greater than its asset valuation. This is currently the case with the electronics firm, Videoton, whose hitherto secure markets in the Soviet military have collapsed. First the enterprise needs restructuring, but restructuring needs money and state-organized restructuring is too close to state renationalization for comfort. Videoton has split up into over twenty companies, some of which have become joint ventures with western firms – all this under the Company Act. A large part of the losses of Videoton are held by the 'empty shell' holding company. Part of the plant has been colonized by Philips as a video-recorder assembly line. This is a Transnational Corporation – host enterprise deal examples of which flooded the literature on TNCs in the 1970s. Philips charges its Videoton plant three times the price it normally charges for its inputs and pays its largely female labour force one-eighth the wage it was paying in Austria (interview with Videoton manager, June 1991).

The current state of Videoton and the attempts to rescue it by joint venture deals with foreign companies precisely illustrates the difficulty faced by the SPA: allow the companies to arrange their own deals with the risk of asset stripping on a large scale, or act as watchdog and incur the charge that a back-door form of state control is in evidence. Clearly though, some of the joint ventures appear to generate little benefit to the Hungarian economy.

PRIVATIZATION: THE DEVELOPMENT OF A PRIVATE SECTOR

The process of privatization of the Hungarian economy should not be viewed solely from the standpoint of the sale of the large-scale enterprises. The rapid increase in the number of corporations and limited liability companies, especially joint ventures (over 5,000 of these), in Hungary in the recent period has been accompanied by a rapid change in the size distribution of enterprises in favour of those employing smaller numbers (see Figures 18.2, 18.3, 18.4) and parallels growth in the number of private craft workers and of small shops and catering outlets which began much earlier than the late 1980s (see Figure 18.5). Indeed this kind of privatization was well advanced in the agricultural sector. The processes of decentralization and subcontracting in agricultural co-operatives and the growth of household plot production and other private smallholder activity gave rise to estimates as early as 1977 that 40 per cent of national food supply was produced on household plots and smallholder farms (Swain 1987: 64). Although these estimates were always unofficial, even the official figure for the value of agricultural production deriving from small-scale producers in 1989 was 36.5 per cent (*Statistical Yearbook* 1989).

This expansion in the size of the small trader sector can be expected to accelerate with the passing of the 'Pre-privatization Law' in late 1990. This law governs the privatization of the assets of state companies engaged in retail trade, catering, and consumer services, with under ten employees in the case of the first category and under fifteen in the case of the latter two. Excluded from this list are the hard currency shops, travel agencies, chemists, pawn shops, and shops which are in hotels, a part of chain stores or the retail outlet for a company's own products. The SPA's function is to take over the enterprise and to set the parameters for its sale, especially the starting price. The sale is organized by another company. Foreigners cannot bid for these businesses, although they can of course bid for the chain stores, travel agencies, and hotel chains which have a substantial part of service sector activity.

The problem associated with this process is that it comes into conflict with the results of the leasing and contractual arrangements entered into with shop managers as part of earlier economic reforms. These managers had often made investments in their business on the assumption that it was theirs. Under the Pre-privatization Law those already running a leased or contractual business would be able to bid for the ownership of the business alongside new bidders. If the management of a contractual business does not win the bid, it will be compensated by the SPA and given the value of any investments made, in cash and within eight days. The new owner will rent the property in which the business is carried out with an option to buy if the property is privatized. The

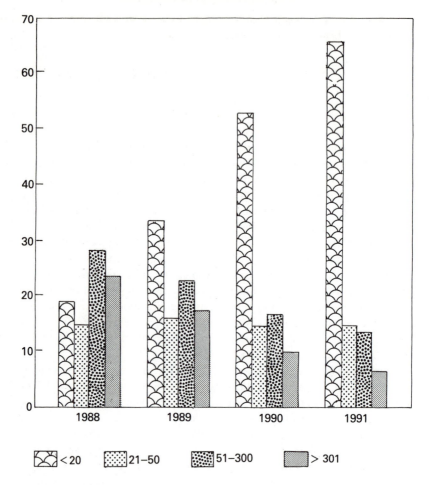

Figure 18.2 Hungary: enterprise size, 1988–91 (by number of employees, %)

minimum letting period is ten years and the owner of the business cannot change the nature of the activity without reference to the municipality (Hungarian Chamber of Commerce, 1991a).

The original number of 50,000 shops due to be privatized was then reduced to 10,000, and by mid-1991 186 had been sold (Kiss 1991: 6). Kiss further reports that 2,000 of the shops were already in private ownership and 3,000 were still subject to leasing contracts not due to run out until after the whole programme had been completed. This left 5,000 shops to be disposed of by the end of the programme in late 1992. The SPA *Newsletter* (February 1992) stated that 3,560 shops had been auctioned and 2,579 businesses had been privatized, a somewhat smaller number than originally foreseen. The failure to sort out the property

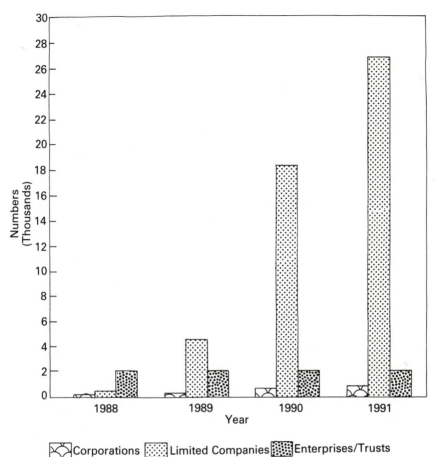

Figure 18.3 Hungary: economic organizations, 1988–91

ownership issue is a clear disincentive to prospective entrepreneurs taking a long-term view since they cannot be sure what rent they will be paying and to which owner. All they know with certainty is that except in extraordinary circumstances they will be secure in the property for ten years.

The alleged slow pace of privatization in both the large- and the small-scale sectors highlights an apparent contradiction between a public rhetoric of rapid privatization and an actuality of maintaining controls over the process in such a way as to slow it down – the usual contradiction between forces for change and forces for continuity. There have been observations about the Ministry of Finance's pressure for more rapid privatization, governed by its objective of reducing deficits and maintaining its commitments to the IMF and the World

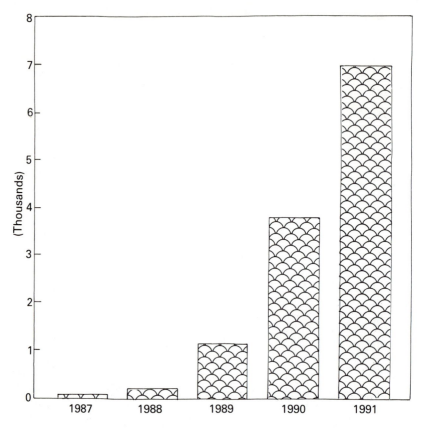

Figure 18.4 Hungary: joint ventures, 1987–91

Bank on increasing liberalization and privatization. These pressures are counter-acted by more 'conservative' or nationalist forces within the Ministry of Industry, anxious to maintain as much of its controlling relationship with large-scale industry. Implicit in this view of the process is the belief that some of those who benefited from the old cosy relationships are still in prominent positions of power within the bureaucracy, and while mouthing the rhetoric retain their old habits (see Kiss 1991: 7).

Setting so much store by state asset privatization potentially ignores another element in the fostering of a larger private sector – namely, the setting up of agencies to promote the development of small- and medium-sized enterprises as a means of creating jobs in a situation where restructuring is going to result in large-scale redundancy. In Szekesfehervar, the home of the Videoton electronics companies, a Regional Enterprise Agency has been set up with European Community assistance under the PHARE programme with a three-year budget of around $2 million. The objectives of the agency include training prospective

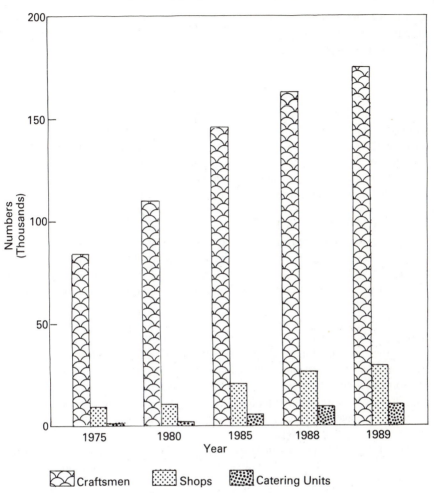

Figure 18.5 Hungary: small private activities, 1975–89

entrepreneurs, assisting them to find sources of finance for their enterprise, and helping them with the preparation of a business plan.

The major obstacle to successful implementation of these initiatives revolves around the supply of credit by the banks. Banks require collateral to the value of 1.5 times the credit given. To establish a medium-sized enterprise would require credits of approximately $0.5 million and finding the collateral for that in the form of personal property of the entrepreneurs is scarcely possible. So it would appear that although the small- and medium-sized business sector in industry and services can be expected to grow, its growth may well be stunted by the institutional constraints in property law and the credit market. This means in particular that the transformation of the entrepreneurial talent thrown up by the

407

growth of the second economy under the old regime into truly capitalist entrepreneurs functioning in a competitive capitalist system could be blocked. This would be an irony indeed.

CONCLUSIONS

Hungary has chosen a privatization route that avoids many of the more radical proposals for selling the state (see Borensztein and Kumar 1991). Having witnessed the disadvantages of spontaneity in the privatization process, the government has opted for closely monitored privatization and the parallel encouragement of small- and medium-sized enterprises. It has done this alongside the development of a small capital market, and various market liberalization reforms. However, it has still only privatized a small proportion of the enterprises under its control because of the difficulties outlined above.

The pressures to speed up the process are a reflection of frustrations on the part of the radical transformers with the almost inevitable continuities from the old regime with its well-connected networks of bureaucrats and managers. The changes the reformers are trying to implement by involving a 'market system' have to confront the coincidence of interest between a bureaucracy with established ways of working and a managerial class which wants to retain its power and therefore slow down the process of losing it.

Whether privatization would go any faster if the process was less controlled is questionable. The recessionary phase of the world economy, the risks of investing in countries whose political systems are too recently transformed to encourage faith in their stability, and the parlous state of many of the enterprises on offer all combine to suggest that privatization will not be a panacea for the solution of Hungary's economic problems.

Indeed, most enterprises will require substantial restructuring measures before they can be put up for sale. The indebtedness of many of these enterprises means that at some point any Hungarian government is going to be faced with the prospect of mass bankruptcy of state enterprises. They will have to make a choice between restructuring through large infusions of cash, or allowing bankruptcy and large-scale unemployment. Under this scenario restructuring through initial bailing out is probably the only answer. The criticism voiced against this is that there are costs of supervision and regulation to ensure that hard budget constraints are enforced and companies meet performance targets in addition to the bailing out and restructuring costs, and there is the danger that old loyalties and relations will lead to a slackening of the constraints. It will be interesting to see in which direction the government move on this issue in the future.

NOTES

1 Paper presented to Conference on 'International Privatisation: Strategies and Practices', University of St Andrews, Scotland, 12–14 September 1991. Research on which this paper is based was supported by a British Academy Exchange Fellowship at the Institute of Economics, Budapest in November 1989. Further research was undertaken in June 1991 as part of a project funded by the Nuffield Foundation. The writer wishes to thank the many Hungarian practitioners and academics who helped him understand the intricacies of privatization Hungarian-style.

2 The situation improved dramatically through 1990 and 1991 with Hungary first achieving a dollar payments surplus, reducing the amount of rouble trade, and moving towards a transition from rouble settlements to dollar settlements between the former CMEA countries. Convertible currency balance of payments surpluses resulted, though at the cost of severely restricting personal hard currency allowances for foreign travel (*Statistical Yearbook* 1989, Hungarian Chamber of Commerce 1991).

3 This account is based on interviews with government officials, and on Tardos (1989).

4 In fact the Apisz deal was stopped and the eventual state-approved sale was reportedly less advantageous to the state than the original one (Kiss 1991: 15).

REFERENCES

Blanchard, O. and Layard. R. (1990) *Economic Change in Poland*, Discussion Paper No. 3, Centre for Economic Performance, LSE (May).

Borensztein, E. and Kumar, M. S. (1991) 'Proposals for privatisation in Eastern Europe', *IMF Staff Papers*, June.

Hare, P., Radice, H. and Swain, N. (1981) *A Decade of Economic Reform*, London: Allen & Unwin.

—— and Grosfeld, I. (1991) *Privatisation in Hungary, Poland and Czechoslovakia*, Discussion Paper No. 544, Centre for Economic Policy Research, April.

Hungarian Chamber of Commerce (1989) *Economic Information* 23–4, Budapest.

—— (1991) *Investors' Guide to Hungary*, Budapest.

—— (1991a) 'Shops for Sale', *Hungarian Economic Review*, 1 (April).

International Monetary Fund (1992) Financial Statistics, Washington: IMF (May).

Kiss, J. (1991) 'Privatization in Hungary: wishful thinking or economic way-out?', Paper presented to Conference on International Privatisation, St Andrews University, 12–14 September.

Kornai, J. (1980) *The Economics of Shortage*, Amsterdam: North-Holland.

Newbery, D. (1990) 'Reform in Hungary: sequencing and privatisation', Paper presented to Fifth Annual Congress of the European Economic Association, Lisbon, September.

SPA (State Privatization Agency) (1991) *Privatization and Foreign Investment in Hungary*, Budapest (April).

Statistical Yearbook 1989, Budapest: Central Statistical Office.

Statisztikai Hari Közlemenyek (Monthly Statistical Bulletin) (1991), Budapest: Central Statistical Office (No. 4, May).

Swain, N. (1987) *Collectives that Work?* Cambridge: Cambridge University Press.

Szep, I. (1991) 'The Lehel breakthrough', *Hungarian Economic Review*, June.

Tardos, M. (1989) 'Reform of property rights', Paper presented to Conference on Attempts at Liberalisation: Hungarian Economic Policy and International Experience', Budapest, November.

Vickers, J. and Yarrow, G. (1988) *Privatisation: An Economic Analysis*, Cambridge, Mass.: MIT Press.

19

RESTRUCTURING EASTERN EUROPE

The case of buy-outs in the USSR

Igor Filatotchev, Trevor Buck, and Mike Wright[1]

INTRODUCTION

The period since the upheavals of 1989 have seen the beginnings of the transformation to market economies of the countries of Central and Eastern Europe. The privatization of state enterprises has slowly begun amidst considerable problems in developing appropriate institutional frameworks and debate as to the appropriate speed and method of transfer of assets from public ownership (see, for example, Lipton and Sachs 1990 for discussion).

Restructuring and moves to a market economy in what was the USSR (hereafter referred to as the 'USSR' for convenience) began a little after such moves elsewhere in Central and Eastern Europe. The problems of transition are compounded by the fragmentation of the USSR as the constituent republics pursue their moves towards independence and begin the process of implementing their own legislation in this area. Such fragmentation introduces the possibility of not only different approaches and speeds of privatization but also problems concerning the restructuring of the various activities of all-Union enterprises which are located in newly independent republics. For example, by late 1991 Estonia had selected seven large 'experimental' enterprises to privatize, three of which had been privatized, but had still to introduce a bankruptcy law and had still to resolve the problem of privatizing the all-Union enterprises on its territory.

The applicability of privatization experience in the west for Central and Eastern Europe has received considerable attention (Vickers and Yarrow 1988, Estrin 1991, Buck *et al.* 1991, etc.). An important form of privatization in the west, especially for small- and medium-sized enterprises, has been employee and management buy-outs. The definition of a buy-out is necessarily vague and subjective. A management buy-out (MBO) occurs when incumbent managers acquire a controlling interest in the firm that employed them, and an employee buy-out (EBO) exists when a controlling interest is acquired by employees outside the management. Buy-outs (BOs) can play a role in gradual or rapid privatization and they may also be attractive in that they fit in with the ideological distaste of many citizens for 'absentee' shareholders, who have no

410

significant link with the enterprise beyond the shares they hold. BOs can also be a particularly controversial form of privatization since they may also suit the interests of incumbent enterprise employees and Ministry officials. A reconciliation of these problems is important if privatization is to progress from policy formulation to implementation.

This chapter[2] analyses the role of BOs in the context of the wider problems of restructuring the USSR and of transferring state-owned assets to the private sector. The first section outlines the general context of restructuring and privatization in what was the USSR. The second analyses the issues involved in BOs and privatization in the west and their implications for the USSR. The third section discusses the actual problems of privatization in the USSR, and the fourth deals with the specific issues of BOs. Finally, some conclusions are drawn.

RESTRUCTURING AND PRIVATIZATION IN THE USSR

The transition from a central planning system towards a market economy in the USSR simultaneously raises problems of institutional and industrial restructuring. Institutional and microeconomic reforms should transform the economic structure and the legal system, dismantle the monopolistic organization of the economy and stimulate development of market mechanism. The task of microeconomic restructuring is gigantic. In the Soviet industrial sector there are 46,000 state-owned firms producing 90 per cent of total output and employing 92 per cent of the total labour force. The share of firms with more than 500 workers amounted to 30 per cent of all industrial enterprises. They account for 85.3 per cent of total output, 85 per cent of total industrial employment and almost 90 per cent of fixed assets in the industrial sector as a whole. It is clear now that the restructuring of these giant, basically inefficient and highly-polluting monopolist enterprises using traditional command methods of centralized industrial policy is almost impossible, and the failure of previous Soviet reforms confirms it.

In the newly emerged democracies in the different republics of the USSR, considerable interest has developed in the use of privatization as a means of transition from central planning to market economy. The ambition of the newly elected governments in the post-Union sovereign states is to create market economies as soon as possible. This is why privatization has become their top priority. Generally speaking, the problems of wide-scale privatization in the USSR are similar to those in Central and East European countries: the enormity of privatizing so many companies so quickly, the non-existence of capital markets and the tiny savings of the population (in comparison with the state assets to be sold). But in the USSR the reforming process gave rise to very specific problems, which contributed to the development of the very peculiar Soviet model of privatization.

First, the process of disintegration of the USSR and the declaration of sovereignty by different previously Union republics – and even different

411

autonomous regions – has caused the erosion of the very notion of 'state property'. Almost all these new 'sovereign states' have declared an exclusive republican or regional ownership of all assets on their territory, especially of so-called 'all-Union' enterprises. As a result, it is not clear today who is the owner of a particular enterprise: former Ministry, local authorities or regional 'privatization agency' (if any exist). This situation has been worsened by the 'war of laws', when different sovereign regions as well as the USSR in general adopted privatization and other laws related to market reforms, which are in contra-diction with each other. Consequently, in the present situation in the USSR a serious gap occurred between the legal framework of privatization and the real practice of 'denationalization' of state property.

Another specific characteristic of the Soviet economy is the enormous size of the military-industrial complex, which includes thousands of enterprises in different parts of the former Soviet Union. The top priority given to the defence sector under the Communist regime resulted in over-concentration of high-tech production in its industries and the technological backwardness of the rest of the economy. As a result, branches of the military-industrial complex and related industries concentrated in their hands more or less advanced equipment, potentially suitable to produce competitive goods (but at the expense of the other parts of the Soviet economic system). The loss of centralized control of the performance of the defence sector enterprises increased the role of their managers substantially. They started the process of 'conversion' of military enterprises into the production of civil goods, the 'commercialization' of their activities through the foundation of independent joint-stock companies and affiliated commercial banks, and the participation in capital of different commodity exchanges, etc.

The disintegration of the all-Union system of centralized management, certain legal vacua, and the foundation and rapid development of strong, independent, monopolistic structures, 'the hard core' of which very often consists of the enterprises from the defence sector industries, substantially weakened the role of the state as an 'owner' of assets in the USSR. The responsibility for the adminis-tration of the state-owned enterprises shifted recently to managers and employees' collectives, which received the right to make strategic decisions including profits distribution. In fact, managers of the state-owned firms received all the rights of private entrepreneurs without many of their responsibilities. As a result, state privatization agencies could face a very serious problem: soon there will be very little left to privatize. When firms come up for sale, they will have already been plundered. Controlling a large amount of the state assets through a cross-ownership system, managers have a good opportunity for privatizing profits if not all the assets.

Bearing in mind the general passivity of the Soviet population with respect to privatization, it is quite possible to predict that managers of state-owned enterprises will play a leading role in the process of the 'denationalization' of the enterprises, probably in coalition with representatives of previous *nomenklatura*. As a result, MBOs and EBOs could become a most common technique of privatization in different regions of the USSR. The supporters of 'collective ownership' usually assert that buy-outs may have an important role to play because they introduce active owners and appropriate incentives into the state-owned sector of the economy. The problem of 'collective ownership' also has a political meaning: in the USSR management and employee buy-outs are considered to be an illusory 'middle way' between capitalism and Communism. Moreover, populist governments in newly independent states in the former USSR urgently need to secure the support of workers' unions which have often built up powerful positions within the enterprises. They induce local authorities to grant them various privileges, and to give protection from the central regulation of production, profits distribution, etc. The development of MBOs and EBOs in the USSR may be one way of buying this support in order to form a symbiosis of bureaucracy, workers' collectives, managers and political leaders.

BUY-OUTS AND PRIVATIZATION IN THE WEST

The privatization of central and local government activities is advancing in Western, Eastern and Central Europe as governments seek to reduce state supervision costs and spending on deficit activities, raise revenue through the sale of assets, and raise the efficiency of operations by exposing them to capital market competition. The privatization of natural monopolies usually involves state regulation, but elsewhere it is possible to divide and sell off state enterprises. In Central and Eastern Europe, buy-outs may contribute to either gradual or rapid privatization. With gradual privatization, the enterprise is seen to evolve through a life-cycle, usually from state enterprise to leased enterprise, to buy-out or co-operative, and then flotation. On the other hand, BOs can enable the rapid privatization of small- and medium-sized enterprises in agriculture, industry, and services, and spin-offs from the largest state monopolies can be achieved through BOs.

Although stock-market flotation has been the main form of privatization in value terms, it is no surprise, given the amount of human capital in managers and other state employees, that BOs by incumbents have been a popular privatization device in the west. Up to mid-1991 in the UK, there had been forty-four stock-market privatizations (including secondary share sales in firms already floated and the multiple sales of water companies and electricity regions). At the same time, there had been 151 MBOs and EBOs from the public sector (see Chiplin *et al.* 1991), but these BOs were relatively small, accounting for only about 7 per cent of the total value of privatizations, which itself amounted to approximately £40 billion (excluding the sale of the second tranche of BT which was in progress at the time of writing). The buy-outs range from the EBO of a whole state firm (National Freight Consortium, NFC) to the sale by MBO and EBO of 39 of the 73 operating units of National Bus and include various small and large subsidiaries of state-owned firms (such as Travellers Fare catering from British Rail, and Allied Steel and Wire from British Steel, as well as local authority services –

413

(see Wright *et al.* 1989 and Paddon 1991 for full listing of these buy-outs). Table 19.1 shows the state firms and local authorities from which the buy-outs occurred. In addition, most of the conventional flotations included employee shares.

The general attraction of buy-outs as a means of privatizing public sector assets is as follows.[3] Public sector firms may be characterized by an absence of managerial incentives and sanctions related to performance, no sanction of potential take-over and no effective bankruptcy threat. Monitoring by means of the political process and sponsoring ministries may be successful in exposing gross misconduct but runs the risk of regulatory capture, together with problems of monitoring when social obligations enter the firm's objective function. As in corporations quoted on a stock-market, the effective separation of ownership and control in state firms is also problematical where the nature of the business demands significant amounts of entrepreneurial *judgement* from managers in an environment of great uncertainty. In these circumstances it is very difficult to meter the inputs (efforts) or outputs of managers, and 'agency' problems are inevitable.[4]

In principle, privatization by a stock-market flotation resolves some of these problems, but not all.[5] In a buy-out equity ownership and management control is concentrated in the hands of incumbent managers and their financial supporters. The buy-out thus re-unites ownership and control and sharpens the effort–reward relationship for managers who are motivated by a share of residual profits and losses in a way that is appropriate in many circumstances where vertical control is not.[6] The typical use of outside finance with significant servicing demands produces a bonding effect on managers being required to meet tight financing targets.

A wider spread of employee share ownership may provide a greater degree of horizontal monitoring to supplement the increased incentive of management to

Table 19.1 UK public sector buy-outs, excluding local authorities, to December 1990

Source	Number
British Aerospace	1
BL/Austin Rover	13
British Rail	7
British Shipbuilding	11
British Steel	10
BTG/NEB	12
National Bus Company	39
NFC	1
Scottish Bus Group	3
Total	97

Source: CMBOR, an independent research centre founded by Touche Ross & Co and Barclays Development Capital Limited at the University of Nottingham.

Table 19.2 Status of privatization buy-outs in the UK, 1991

Flotations	7
Trade sales	25
Secondary buy-out/buy-in	2
Failure	4
MBO continuing	59
Total	97

Source: CMBOR an independent research centre founded by Touche Ross & Co and Barclays Development Capital Limited at the University of Nottingham.

engage in vertical monitoring, and may be most effective where it is difficult to measure and monitor employee agents directly.

Two further aspects of western MBOs are of importance for their application to former CPEs (centrally planned economies). First, the incentive effect deriving from the concentration of equity ownership in the hands of managers is supplemented by other institutional control devices. Lenders usually demand business plans from managers and *apply vertical control* by comparing planned and actual performance. Indeed, the release of successive tranches of loan are often performance-related, and 'ratchet' schemes reward above-plan performance with higher equity stakes for managers. Some managers see the MBO as simply replacing one kind of vertical control with another.

Second, the emergence of MBOs should not be regarded as the end of an evolutionary process. Many BOs go on to stock-market flotations, and it is probably wise to see the MBO as one stage within a *life-cycle* of firms. This conclusion especially applies to BOs as part of the process of privatization. Table 19.2 shows that only 59 of the original 97 buy-outs shown in Table 19.1 survived as BOs in 1991. The 32 firms that went to flotation or trade sale only lasted for an average of less than four years as a BO. Indeed, fifteen of the trade sales involved bus buy-outs where the average time to exit was only 2.02 years (Wright, Dobson, Thompson and Robbie 1991).[7]

The third point about BOs is that, in contributing to wider share ownership, they help prevent a reversion to the old system (Estrin 1991). However, as will be seen below, in possibly being seen to favour members of the old regime in Eastern Europe BOs may contribute to social problems.

The problems experienced in British privatization BOs that are relevant to the plans for economic reform in Central and Eastern Europe can be summarized under the general heading of *incumbent advantages*, with particular difficulties in the form of *property under-valuations*.

A feature of most enterprises is that formal and on-the-job training financed by the enterprise makes the human capital in managers a major enterprise asset.[8] If managers are free to resign and relocate, or even threaten to do so upon privatization, this gives them a strong advantage in a BO situation over would-be external buyers whose bids must be reduced by payments to secure their retention.[9] Such an *incumbent advantage* is reinforced by the 'insider' knowledge of managers about the potential costs and revenues of a privatized activity that probably existed only as a cost centre under state ownership. These advantages put privatizing governments in a quandary: a major purpose of privatization is to encourage the entrepreneurship that will increase operating efficiency and seek to give consumers the type, quantity and quality of goods and services that they demand. Entrepreneurs seize profit opportunities by diverting resources from lower- to higher-yield uses.

On the other hand, such opportunistic behaviour by managers *before* privatization and *during* the negotiation of a BO sale may be against the short-term interests of the state. In the case of Britain, Table 19.2 shows that 32 privatization MBOs had gone to flotation or trade sale by 1991, although it must not be forgotten that 4 had failed and a further 2 had been the subject of a secondary buy-out or buy-in, indicating trading difficulties. Of the 32 principal exits, research by the CMBOR (Buck *et al.* 1991) showed that in the case of those 18 for which purchase and exit prices could be estimated, assets had appreciated threefold in an average period of 3.5 years. In the case of Britain's only large EBO, the National Freight Consortium (NFC), a net purchase price of £6.5 million in 1982 can be compared with a company valuation of £681 million in 1990 after flotation in 1989, a single year in which pre-tax profits alone were £90 million.

With these figures it is of course impossible to disentangle the effects of opportunism before BO and post-privatization improvements in efficiency. In any case, a number of devices have been employed by West European governments and lenders to minimize the advantages of incumbent managers before and during the BO. Two of these devices ('ratchet' equity stakes for managers and the performance-related release of successive loan tranches) have been referred to previously. In addition, governments or other lenders can insist upon independent valuations of enterprise assets, representation on the board, or they can retain a veto on large investments and divestments (Wright 1987).

The obvious danger with all these precautions is that they may discourage BO bids (and therefore reduce sale proceeds) before privatization, and/or lead managers to the conclusion after privatization that there is no point in improving profitability. Thus, privatizing governments must *either* walk a fine line between the prevention of 'unfair' opportunism before and during privatization and its encouragement thereafter, *or* they may decide to live with the early abuses of 'insider' advantages in the belief that in the longer term they will be reduced by more competition at the bidding stage. In the case of the USSR, this competition will be slower to emerge, and incumbent managers have access to information and influence within the vertical hierarchies of the economic system of industries and Ministries *and* of the political system, with the Communist Party and its associated forms. This issue will be addressed on pp. 418–21 and 426–8.

One particular manifestation of this general problem of incumbent advantages relates to *undervaluation of assets*. UK privatization experience demonstrates the existence of a wide range of general valuation problems, not all of which were resolved through the learning process as privatization programmes have developed. Moreover, the whole valuation process may be affected by an inter-related set of factors which may be grouped under the headings of 'presenta-tional', 'institutional', 'economic', and 'accounting' (Valentiny *et al.* 1991). Many of those factors relevant to the UK apply also to Central and Eastern Europe, but in addition there are factors specific to these economies such as major uncertainties, absence of asset markets, and accounting conventions which bear little if any relation to rational economic valuations, etc. As a result it is difficult if not impossible to apply valuation techniques traditionally used in western economies such as discounted cash-flow techniques, price-earnings multiples, etc. (Young 1991).

The introduction of new technologies and products and reductions in manning levels by privatized firms may be considered legitimate sources of entrepreneurial profit and consumer satisfaction. The disposal of unwanted buildings and land after privatization, however, raises particular difficulties, since the conversion of buildings and land to alternative uses requires so little entrepreneurial effort, and, in a bureaucratic system, implicit planning permis-sion for change-of-use may have been secured before privatization.

Certainly, land sales have accounted for a high proportion of the post-BO privatization gains listed above. In the case of NFC, the closure and sale of a number of freight depots in locations close to city centres contributed to profits of £24.6 million on property sales in just one year, 1990. In a similar industry, the privatization of the National Bus Company has produced similar experiences, with some buy-outs making substantial gains from property development. The Committee of Public Accounts (CPA) noted favourably that claw-back arrange-ments had been used in some instances to permit the government to recoup some of these gains. However, the CPA also commented that the Department of Transport made insufficient use of claw-backs, that it should have made a bench-mark valuation for each sale, that it should have done more to identify and value alternative uses for properties, and that it should have made more use of specific marketing of subsidiaries for sale. These deals echo the controversial closure of facilities and sale of land by British Aerospace following its acquisition of Royal Ordnance.

The usual response to such land-related opportunism in the west has been to introduce more vertical control into the privatization process, though this brings costs as well as benefits. The reports by the NAO, the independent audit agency, show that there is a need to demonstrate that those who are implementing privatization policy have taken reasonable care to deal with the problems of uncertainty, etc. A variety of techniques have been introduced in an attempt to take account of valuation problems, such as tender offers and partial sales involving stock-market flotations, and claw-back mechanisms and competitive bidding in respect of other forms of privatization.

In this context, Central and Eastern Europe have the dubious advantage of a

417

legacy of Marxist-Leninist ideology. This means that in the past, markets in land have been forbidden in order to prevent the 'unearned' incomes of landlords. The result today is that the *leasing* of land and buildings, rather than outright sale, is typical of the privatization process. This causes problems in the long-term allocation of land from lower- to higher-yield activities, but in the short term it presents the more blatant abuse of 'insider' advantages by incumbents in BOs. This theme will be returned to in the analysis of BOs in the USSR (see pp. 424–30).

PRIVATIZATION IN THE USSR

At the beginning of the 1990s, the USSR is still poised on the brink of significant market reforms, though some progress has been made within certain Republics already. The reasons why these reforms are needed have been well documented elsewhere. This section will concentrate on the special problems of privatization in the USSR, and the general forms that privatization might take.

Problems with USSR privatization

As in the rest of Central and Eastern Europe, privatization will be relatively easy to achieve in relation to small- and medium-sized enterprises and in those 'high technology' branches of state industries that have enjoyed priority status since the death of Stalin in 1953, usually close to the military-industrial complex. Privatization will be difficult in what used to be called the 'commanding heights' of Soviet industry with monopoly power at least at the Republican level – that is, 'Group A' heavy industry, including the capital goods industries that constituted Marx's Department II'. These industries continued to grow extensively after 1953, but tended to replicate old technologies in new locations rather than replace obsolete machines.

A number of problems in privatizing these industries may be identified.

Obsolete plant and buildings would combine with other factors to produce a dearth of bidders upon privatization. For example, over-manning accompanies over-investment in old technologies, and the Soviet heavy industrial plant is burdened with many associated activities that in the west would be provided by municipal or private suppliers. These usually include 'palaces of culture', housing, polyclinics, sanatoria, kindergartens and can even extend to professional sports teams.

The likely absence of serious buyers for these industries should not be confused with their current financial status. The dominance of *artificial* state prices means that asset valuations for privatization purposes are quite arbitrary, and in practice 'base values' (arbitrary, historic-cost, 'book' values less arbitrary depreciation) are adjusted in the best traditions of central planning through multiplication by a 'correction coefficient', established under Decree No. 763 of the State Pricing Committee, 13 November 1990. This decree provides a range of

Table 19.3 Capital value of the state enterprises, 1989 (billions of roubles)

	Balance value of fixed assets	Net income	Estimated capital value	
			P/E = 5	P/E = 8
All industries, total including:	920.7	136.8	684.0	1054.4
Fuel and power complex	275.7	20.4	102.0	163.2
Metallurgy	126.6	15.7	78.5	125.6
Machine building	92.0	44.1	220.5	352.8
Chemistry and forestry	115.3	16.5	82.5	132.0
Construction material production	34.5	4.0	20.0	32.0

Source: 'Promyshlennost SSSR' (Industries in the USSR), Goskomstat, 1990.

coefficients from 1.1 for laboratory equipment to 4.8 for automobiles. These valuations are then to be adjusted according to the most recent financial performance of the enterprise.

Unfortunately, financial performance is itself determined by artificial prices, and many enterprises are 'unprofitable-by-plan'. For example, many coal-mines in the USSR are destined to make financial losses under any feasible pricing structure, but it is difficult to identify mines with a long-term future since fuels are considered by the state to be essential inputs to be provided cheaply, while miners' wages, despite protestations in recent strikes, are relatively high. 'Unprofitable-by-plan' enterprises proliferate throughout the fuel sector and in the wood-pulp and paper industries – some of the USSR's major exporters. In Table 19.3 we have assumed that the firms are valued as a multiple of annual earnings, with a price-earning ratio of 5 and 8.[10] These 'market values' of assets in different industries are compared with their book value. As one can see in Table 19.3, the book value of the fuel-and-power complex assets is far higher than even the most optimistic estimation of their 'market value'. On the other hand, the book value of the machine-building sector assets is far below both 'market value' estimations. The basic explanation of this paradox is the low prices of output of the fuel-and-power complex (and, consequently, the low profits of its enterprises). At the same time, the prices of production of machine-building industries (including almost all enterprises of the military-industrial complex) are artificially high to ensure profitability of this privileged sector of the Soviet economy.

The problem of arbitrary profits and losses throughout Central and Eastern Europe can only be solved by the application of world prices to an input–output model of the economy (see, for example, Hare and Hughes 1991). Such studies reveal that a large proportion of Soviet enterprises are 'value-subtractors' in the sense of achieving negative value added at world prices. Such firms are incapable

Table 19.4 Fixed capital ownership structure in the Russian Republic, 1990 (percentages)

Private	Total (bn roubles)	State	Union	Republican	Cooperatives	Kolkhoses	Other
Fixed capital including:	1,828.7	92	56	36	1	5	2
Industries	614.9	99	85	14	–	1	–
Construction	67.4	99	56	43	–	1	–
Agriculture	297.8	66	4	62	–	30	–
Transport	243.7	100	67	33	–	–	–
Communications	19.0	96	30	66	–	4	–
Wholesale trade	11.6	100	51	49	–	–	–
Retail trade	41.9	80	42	38	19	1	–
Housing	340.1	83	38	45	4	4	9
Services	85.2	98	22	76	–	2	–

Source: Goskomstat SSSR, 1991.

Table 19.5 State ownership or privatization?: a survey of Soviet workers' opinions

Enterprise should:	Percentage of all interviewed
Continue to be in state ownership	40.2
Be reorganized as:	
• collectively owned enterprise	14.0
• leased enterprise	8.7
• joint venture with foreign capital	4.5
• joint-stock company	4.2
• private enterprise with unknown buyer	4.1
• co-operative	3.5

Source: Goskomstat SSSR, press issue no. 42, 8 February 1991.

of private sale as entities, although BOs could have a role in relation to the potentially profitable sections of larger firms.[11]

Even if valuations were realistic, however, the problem of the *imprecise ownership* of 'state' enterprises would remain. Table 19.4 shows the most recently available figures on ownership in the Russian Republic of the USSR, a Republic that includes more than 60 per cent of the industrial employment in the USSR. This table disregards claims by City Soviets, trade unions and even the Communist Party on state assets, but even so demonstrates the complicated task for privatization agencies.

With realistic valuations and clear ownership established, a successful programme of privatization must rely on an available stock of *investible funds*. The subject of private managerial contributions and ploughed-back profits for MBOs will be discussed later (see pp. 426–8). It is necessary at this stage to note however that there is unlikely to be a torrent of finance from overseas, that there is a lack of any private capital market in the USSR that could permit institutional investment, and that savings of enterprises and individuals in the USSR are insufficient to support large-scale privatization: even if *all* disposable income plus the stock of savings in 1990 (700 billion roubles) were available this would be less than one-quarter of the (adjusted) base-value of fixed and current assets (2,700 billion roubles). In any case, a sociological survey reported in Table 19.5 gives some indication of the public hostility that confronts privatization in the USSR: 40.2 per cent of Soviet workers favour the continuation of state ownership, and as few as 4.1 per cent support 'privatization with an unknown buyer'.

The final problem with privatization in the USSR concerns the power that has accumulated within enterprises in the hands of managers and trade unions, particularly *nomenklatura* placements. Incumbent managers have always caused problems for western privatizations, but in the USSR they have access to *two* vertical hierarchies (one economic, the other political) that can be used to divert resources in their direction.[12]

The form of privatization

Reference has already been made in the introduction of this chapter to the pace of privatization and to the ideological hostility of many citizens of the USSR to 'absentee' shareholders making negligible contributions to the enterprise beyond their capital contributions for the shares they hold. Economists can add to this hostility by pointing to other barriers between ownership and control. It is well known, for example, that over two-thirds of British industrial capital is held by financial institutions such as pension funds and insurance companies who, on the face of it, apply little control to the firms they own.

It is not possible, however, to conclude that unified ownership and control, or the ownership of enterprises by incumbent managers or other employees who *directly* control the firm through their 'voice', provides a more effective form of corporate governance in all circumstances. Indeed, the finance literature – see, for example, Fama and Jensen (1983) – demonstrates that shares unrestricted to internal controllers are relatively effective in many circumstances where shareholders can *indirectly* control managers and other employees by simply exercising their right to 'exit' from the firm by selling their shares. Such action may be based on press reports or share price movements, but its effect is to make incumbents fearful of take-over or liquidation.

The dilemma is made explicit in Table 19.6. Shares held by employees and managers improve direct enterprise control, since shareholders (principals) and employees (agents) are the same persons motivated by a share of residual income. On the other hand, shares held by employees amount to a restriction on the tradeability of shares, providing a barrier to indirect control, and increase the likelihood of asset under-valuation.

Within this framework, the various possible forms of private enterprise and privatization for the USSR can be considered briefly: individual and family enterprises, co-operatives, open share sales, citizens' shares, and institutional shareholdings. The leasing of enterprises by managers and other employees and BOs are discussed later (see pp. 424–6).

Under the Law on Individual and Family Enterprise in November 1986, private enterprise was permitted for certain activities. Such activities had mostly been carried out unlawfully, so the Law legitimized and taxed these businesses. Despite 'extended' families in Georgia and other southern Republics, the Law only gave rise to small-scale firms, since families had to live together to qualify. The employment of hired labour was thus forbidden.

Small firms which wanted to grow could convert into co-operatives under another 1986 law. The original rules again forbade hired labour and permitted a maximum of fifty members. Taxation and control by licences issued by City Soviets constrained the growth of co-operatives, however. Successful firms often bore little resemblance to genuine co-operatives with equal shares and control among members. Indeed, it could be argued that many co-operatives in the USSR have effectively been equivalent to MBOs of sections of state enterprises, with

422

Table 19.6 Alternative privatization share distribution and governance

	Likely number of bidders	Likelihood of asset under-valuation	Direct shareholder control (agency)	Indirect shareholder control (tradeability)
Shareholdings by incumbents:				
MBO	Few	Likely	High	Low
EBO	Few	Less likely	Quite high	Low
Shareholdings by absentees:				
Trade sale	Few	Quite likely	Medium	Quite high
Flotation	Large	Likely with fixed price flotation. Unlikely with tenders and successive sales of tranches	Medium	High
Free distribution to all citizens	Infinitely large, but overseas bids excluded?		Insignificant	High if shares immediately tradeable

Source: Buck *et al.* (1991).

non-managers exercising little control. In any case, high prices and profits brought hostility from citizens and the classic centrally planned response of regulation and higher taxation rather than the encouragement of competition. Co-operatives have found it difficult to survive outside the service sector, and their growth has been limited by the capital resources of their members and their inability to sell equity outside the firm.

To date, state firms in the USSR have not been able to sell equity without restriction. Certainly firms have been able to sell fixed-interest bonds, and employees have been able to buy non-tradeable shares, but otherwise state firms have so far only been able to share ownership and control with outsiders through the joint venture. Gradually, the permissible degree of foreign control and ability to repatriate profits in joint ventures has been increased, but from the perspective of this section the joint venture does not offer the kind of indirect control available to a public company with its own share price. Control is hidden from public scrutiny within the committees of the venture.

So why not distribute shares (or vouchers to buy shares at a subsidized price) in state enterprises to all citizens?[13] Such a proposal would appear to allay the suspicion of the Soviet citizen that 'their' assets may be 'given away' to foreigners and other capitalists through privatization. From the viewpoint of corporate governance, such a proposal would raise indirect control (see Table 19.6), though not by as much as the sale of shares unrestricted by the need for equal distributions to each citizen. Many Soviet enterprises would be unlikely to support a high share price, and where citizens' shares *do* have a significant value, their existence must reduce the value of the firm to other potential owners – for example, to managers considering an MBO.

Finally, there is the possibility of intermediate share ownership through state holding companies on the Italian model or through competing mutual funds.[14] Such proposals are too complex to discuss here, but it should be noted that the latter would seem to offer the potential for more indirect control by private shareholders and less state interference, though this of course depends on the legal framework.

BUY-OUTS IN THE USSR

On the face of it, BOs have much to contribute to Soviet economic reform. They offer close direct enterprise control, they allay hostility in the USSR towards 'absentee' shareholders and, from the viewpoint of lenders and western governments, they aid the rejuvenation of the small- and medium-sized firm sector (the so-called 'black hole' of socialism) and can be applied to the potentially profitable segments of the large state monopolies.

This potential should, however, be assessed after consideration of the actual pattern of BOs in the USSR to date. These developments are discussed for the first time in this chapter. They can be understood only after an appreciation of the evolution of BOs out of industrial *leases*, and the performance of BOs and their constraints, the precautions that must be taken if serious social unrest in the future is not to be provoked by the BO phenomenon.

Leased enterprises

The notion of managers and other employees leasing plant and equipment from a state enterprise in order to produce goods for sale on a market is simple in theory. In practice, however, the frequently reformed nature of the Soviet firm complicates matters.

At the risk of over-simplification, since 1961 enterprises in related activities have been integrated into larger entities. These could be production associations (groups of similar firms), industrial associations (effectively whole branches of Ministries), research-industrial associations (industrial branches plus research institutes) and territorial production complexes. The intention of these mergers was to internalize many transactions, bringing buyers and sellers closer together and reducing the need for vertical control from the centre – for example, by encouraging horizontal quality monitoring between firms within the association. The result has usually taken the form of vertically integrated associations still subject to a great deal of central control.

The 1989 Law on State Enterprises introduced the right of any enterprise to

Table 19.7 Comparative performance of leased enterprises in the USSR, 1990

	Rates of growth of output (%)		Fulfilment of contracts (%)	
	All enterprises	Leased enterprises	All enterprises	Leased enterprises
Total in industries, including:	99.2	103.5	98.0	99.0
Fuel-and-power complex	98.8	105.0	98.2	99.6
Machine-building complex	102.1	109.0	98.1	99.0
Metallurgy complex	97.4	99.4	97.2	98.7
Chemical-forestry complex	99.2	103.9	96.7	98.6
Agro-industrial complex	99.3	103.5	98.9	99.5
Light industries	100.1	104.7	97.5	98.9

Source: *Economica i gizn*, no. 51, December 1990, p. 5.

choose, as a legal entity, its own affiliation to an association, supposedly without Ministerial attachment or interference. This meant, for example, that a supplier of fabrics could associate with any one of its principal customers (for example, a clothing manufacturer). Thus, the typical Soviet enterprise is part of a vertically integrated association of enterprises which exchange commodities at state prices.

Finally, in 1989, article 7 of the 'Principles of Leasing Legislation of the USSR and Union Republics' gave the right to managers and other employees in any unit (for example, plant or workshop) of an enterprise to lease its assets. Ultimately, leased assets could be bought by the collective, at once or by instalments. After this BO stage, goods produced could be sold at uncontrolled prices, and the Soviet view of the BO as a stage in the life-cycle of the firm is now explained: from the traditional state enterprise, to supposed independence from Ministries to leased enterprise, to BO with possible flotation or sale to another group in the longer term.

Leasing has proved rather successful in relation to the objectives set for it. By the beginning of 1991, 2,400 leased enterprises were operating in the USSR, with 1.5 million employees, producing 5.2 per cent of total industrial output. In service industries, employees leased about 2,000 retail organizations and trusts 33,000 shops, and more than 2,000 dressmaking and tailoring workshops, etc. During a period of industrial crisis in the USSR, with industrial output falling by almost 1 per cent in 1990, leased activities increased output by 3.5 per cent. Furthermore, Table 19.7 shows a stronger contracting discipline in leased enterprises.

It is suggested that leased enterprises are effectively MBOs, since the stake of other employees is usually much lower than their relative wages would imply, but of course they are MBOs without full ownership, since plant, buildings and land are only rented from the parent firm. This prevents the worst kinds of insider abuse experienced in the west, since the under-pricing of leases can be rectified when the lease expires in the light of enterprise performance.

However, leasing is the main route to MBOs with assets controlled and owned by managers in the USSR, and the only other procedure for an MBO involves the liquidation of an enterprise or part thereof, the placing of liquidated assets into the administration of a state holding company, and the subsequent BO of assets by managers using a mixture of bank credit and plough-back funds from the old enterprise. The latter procedure is notorious for providing sinecures for Ministerial officials employed by the holding company.

The performance of MBOs in the USSR

Although the enabling legislation is very new (for example, in 1991 'Guidelines of Deregulation and Privatization in the USSR' were issued for the USSR, and for the Russian Republic 'Privatization of State-run and Municipal Enterprises in RSFSR') the BO process has advanced rapidly, especially in the Russian Republic and further acceleration is expected in 1992. According to this legislation, the employees of a state enterprise have first priority for a BO upon privatization, but they cannot prevent the privatization itself. If no BO is forthcoming, Soviet citizens are given priority over overseas bidders for shares.

Information presented here is derived from the State Committee of Statistics of the Russian Republic and the authors' own monitoring of developments. Table 19.8 shows the latest information on the first batch of industrial BOs in Russia. (In services, the numbers of MBOs are greater, but each is smaller on average. At the beginning of 1991, there had been 107 MBOs in services, with total sales of 5 million roubles.)

Although it is too early for published accounts, it seems clear that the majority of MBOs are trading profitably. This is not surprising when one understands their role within industrial associations. As with western BOs, MBOs in Russia have shown no shortage of entrepreneurial talent. Essentially, Russian BOs have been set up to exploit through arbitrage the difference between state input prices (secured through the association) and uncontrolled prices for the finished goods and services of the MBOs. With good reason, therefore, they have been named *nomenklatura* BOs, since the old hierachy assumes controlling positions in the new enterprise, and at the same time secures inputs at (subsidized) state prices.

If new MBOs do *not* offer benefits to *nomenklatura* in the associations and Ministries, they can be disciplined, despite their alleged independence. For example, Minelectrotechpribor SSSR (the USSR Ministry of Electro-technical Equipment) allowed managers and employees to lease and then buy-out the assets of unprofitable enterprises. A new leased enterprise 'Orgtechnica' was therefore created for the production of 'deficit' commodities like computer plotters, ball-point pens with silicon rollers, etc. With assets arbitrarily valued at 17 million roubles, the leased enterprise recorded profits of 15 million roubles in its first year alone. Predictably, however, the Ministry was able to confiscate 65 per cent of these profits by unilaterally increasing the leasing charge, and when a

Table 19.8 Buy-outs in the industries of the Russian Republic at the beginning of 1991

Name	Location (region)	Output (m. roubles)	Fixed capital (m. roubles)	Number of employees
Electric-mechanical plant	Vladimir	9.5	2.1	321
Chemical factory	Moscow	7.5	4.8	521
Factory N5 (canning equipment	Dmitrov	2.2	0.3	43
Construction plant	Volocolamsk	3.5	7.9	252
Construction polymers plant	Moscow	25.9	8.5	555
Confectionery factory	Yaroslavl	21.3	2.4	534
'Tveris' (retailing)	Tver	13.9	9.7	929
Confectionery factory	Rybinsk	21.2	1.8	538
'Vtorchermet' (scrap metal)	Ulyanovsk	5.8	4.4	212
'People's Enterprise'	Ulyanovsk	13.3	5.9	548
Bread production factory	Ufa	1.6	0.2	71
Turf processing plant	Kamchatka	1.0	2.2	46
'People's Enterprise'	Kaliningrad	37.3	43.4	1,736
Ventilator factory	Moscow	17.1	6.5	490
Total		181.1	100.1	646
Average		12.9	7.15	485

Source: Privatization data bank, Filatotchev.

BO was attempted, the asset valuation was multiplied by a factor of three. The BO did not take place and this emphasizes the need for a coalition of *nomenklatura* support for a successful BO.

Nevertheless, the MBO may, with proper precautions (for these, see pp. 429–30), makes a significant contribution to privatization in the USSR, whether rapid or gradual. There are, though, a number of constraints on this process.

First, managerial talent. Contrary to the intentions of the central planners who are supposed to achieve the *ex ante* co-ordination of demand and supply across all markets, the Soviet economy is characterized by a high degree of uncertainty. Soft budget constraints (Kornai 1986) generated by central planning produce excess demands for most usable inputs and outputs, and the average Soviet manager knows that his output targets may be threatened at any time by the non-delivery of inputs, by the 'poaching' or non-appearance of labour, or even by sudden increases in the output targets themselves.

All this uncertainty demands a high degree of judgement from the manager regarding proper levels of reserves and restraint in planning bargains. In emergencies, the manager needs contacts to survive, and the kinds of barter deals needed to secure scarce inputs informally are widely understood. Such managerial ability is human capital, and when combined with power in the hands of workers, it has prompted the cynical suggestion that BOs in the USSR are the *reverse* of their western counterparts. In the west, privatization BOs are a familiar device whereby managers and employees can buy assets from the state. In the

USSR, however, there is the possibility that the BO enables the state to buy-out the human capital and employees' rights threatened by privatization.

Therefore it seems likely that in future most Soviet managers will soon learn to direct their opportunistic talents towards the pursuit of profit in a market economy. The only reservations concern the lack of experience in relation to hard penalties for failure, minimal knowledge of the marketing function, and unfamiliarity with financial markets.

Second, this lack of financial understanding is likely to prove a serious constraint on the growth of MBOs. So far, a cosy relationship between *nomenklatura* managers and Ministerial officials has ensured that assets have been undervalued using arbitrary formulas, and finance has largely been available from trade credits obtained from associated customers and from the *khozraschot-dohod*, or self-accounting income of the old enterprise, which after payment of bank interest, taxes and other costs is by Soviet law available to the managers and other employees for salaries, bonuses, investment and BOs of leased enterprise assets.

Personal borrowing and contributions from incumbent managers have not been significant, and a survey conducted in October 1990 by the All-Union Research Institute for the Economics of (Retail) Trade found that only 30 per cent of managers would borrow to finance a BO, and 89 per cent of this number would not contemplate credit costing more than 5 per cent per annum.

A typical example of a Russian MBO is provided by the Moscow Ventilator Factory (see Table 19.8). This factory was leased and then bought-out at an arbitrary price of 6.5 million roubles in 1990. Besides a little personal savings, the BO team (led by the incumbent director, an ex-Communist *apparatchik* appointed to the factory in 1987) was able to borrow the bulk of the finance from the factory's major customer: the 'Svetlana' association in Leningrad. The loan comprised an interest-free credit repayable over ten years, and in return the customer was promised a reliable supply of fans at a negotiated price. (For further details, see *The Economist*, 18 May 1991: 78.)

Too many stories like 'Svetlana's will discredit the BO movement in the USSR and contribute to serious social unrest, as citizens see those responsible for the current economic crisis benefiting unfairly from market reforms. It is this point that has been raised with most force in privatization buy-outs in Central and Eastern Europe, since employees stand to make gains or losses simply as an 'accident' of where they happen to be employed, with the potential for bribery and corruption in the process being considerable as employees in profitable firms may well be able to transfer assets illicitly into their own hands. Widespread resentment to members of the former regime benefiting from privatization is cause for considerable concern. However, it may be possible to install precautions to prevent the worst kinds of abuse.

The future for BOs in the USSR

The USSR seems to be moving towards a market economy. Since market economies include markets in capital, it looks inevitable that some kind of capitalism will emerge, with all the benefits that are inherent in a regime of hard penalties and rewards, like productive and allocative efficiency and rapid technological progress, together with all the costs, including unemployment and inequality.

The BO is often seen by managers and workers as a means of preventing capitalism proper, but western experience suggests that many MBOs and EBOs evolve fairly quickly into conventional capitalist firms with 'absentee' shareholders. Managers and other employees with their employment prospects *and* their savings invested in one firm inevitably feel vulnerable and will often seek to diversify their holdings at the first profitable opportunity. Thus, many British privatization MBOs have quickly gone to a trade sale or flotation, and in the case of the large privatization EBO known as NFC, subsidized loans to employees to buy NFC shares have failed to prevent the share of equity held by NFC workers, pensioners and their families falling from 84 per cent in 1982 to 55 per cent after flotation in 1990 to 48.6 per cent in March 1991.[15]

This view of the BO as part of a life-cycle of firms, however, still gives it a potentially significant role in the economic reform of the USSR. The outstanding issues are the pace of change and its regulation, to be chosen by the state under the influence of overseas governments and lenders.

If the objective of these reforms is a competitive market economy, then *in the long term* the regulation of BOs is unnecessary. In this long term, sophisticated financial markets will be developed in which lenders impose terms upon BO borrowers to prevent the exploitation of lenders by incumbents, and BO teams will face competition from other firms (including other successful BOs) at the bidding stage to prevent under-valuations.

The question is: how can this long-run state be achieved, and how quickly?

The answer must involve value-judgements and political ideology. For example a 'neo-Austrian' economist following the philosophy of Friedrich von Hayek would advocate the immediate marketization of virtually all state assets. Of course the neo-Austrian would concede that this could result in speculation and incumbent abuse on a large scale, especially in the short term, but would insist that such speculation is at the very heart of the capitalist system: speculation involves guesses about uncertain states of the world, and the profits and losses of successful and unsuccessful entrepreneurs are the signals that lead others to compete and follow. Governments are seen as incapable of creating or even encouraging competition, except through the reduction of government-supported entry barriers. So, for example, if incumbent managers in BO firms make excess profits from the conversion of state inputs into products selling for high prices, then *laissez-faire* is the appropriate reaction, not the regulated distribution of inputs or controls on BOs. Successive entrepreneurs, lured by excess profits, will drive up the demand for state inputs until price increases become inevitable and profits from this form of speculation are competed away. On this view, it is irrelevant whether those who profit are foreigners, criminals or communists, so long as the signals are observable, thus making competition inevitable.

Such a philosophy has never been adopted in the west, however, in relation to privatization. Some state industries will involve monopoly that requires some kind of regulation, at least in the short term, and such extreme liberal policies would probably cause significant unpopularity within one electoral cycle. It is therefore even more unlikely to receive support in the USSR, where ideological hostility to the dreaded speculation is combined with a virtual absence of financial market, property market and product market competition. Unconstrained BOs could lead to serious social unrest.

In these circumstances, various forms of regulation must probably be used to simulate a competitive outcome, and western experience with BOs has many lessons to offer. Some of these possible regulations are:

- independent valuations of enterprise assets before a BO;
- open advertisement and a minimum number of bids before a BO is permitted;
- claw-back arrangements for 'excessive' profits, and the release of successive loan tranches according to BO performance;
- minimum levels of re-investment of profits after the BO;
- lenders' controls over large investments, divestments and diversification, perhaps including board representation for the lender;
- continued leasing of buildings and land rather than outright sale;
- the banning of purchases of inputs at state prices by BOs;
- the recruitment only of local managers to BOs, with the exclusion of any related Ministry or association official within the last, say, five years.

Such regulations would be difficult to enforce, would encourage the 'capture' of regulators by the enterprises, and, if successful, would deter many BO bids, thus reducing the proceeds from privatization sales. This kind of outcome is the fate of all regulation, but it might ease the process of privatization in the face of citizen's hostility. The danger is that controlled privatization will be slower, allowing opponents the opportunity to regroup and organize their obstructive tactics.

CONCLUSIONS

From 1991, the rapid privatization of small- and medium-sized enterprises, especially in the services sector, began to occur in many Republics of the USSR. It seems likely that the majority of these privatizations will be some form of BO.

BOs are probably infeasible for the USSR's massive state enterprises. They are too big, too unprofitable (at world prices, with the exception of parts of the military-industrial complex and of fuel and power branches) and carry enormous social obligations in the forms of pollution control, employees' housing, health care and even entertainment.

These same factors will deter foreign buyers as well as BOs, so the wholesale closure of large state enterprises seems inevitable followed by privatizations upon break-up. This process will take a long time, but BOs are again likely to play a significant role. BOs, especially EBOs, are seen to play a special role in the USSR, an ideologically acceptable 'middle way' between outright capitalism (with 'absentee' shareholders) and the old philosophies of collective control. It is also undeniable that the BO has a distinctive potential in the USSR as citizens observe the main beneficiaries of Communism enjoying the advantages of a market economy while the citizens pay for its costs.

For this reason, it is vital that the USSR learns the lessons so painfully acquired by the British government since 1979. Specifically, a list of regulations for BOs in the USSR was proposed at the end of the previous section. In the special circumstances of the USSR, such regulations probably require the involvement of western lenders and consultants, if corruption is to be kept to acceptable levels.

Despite such regulations, it cannot be denied that enterprise disinvestment by opportunist *nomenklatura* managers is likely on a large scale. Such costs will probably have to be tolerated, at least in the short term, if the long-term goal of voluntary investment in those privatized firms offering the highest rates of return is to be achieved. This investment alone can produce technological progress and genuine job creation.

NOTES

1   The authors gratefully acknowledge financial support for the Centre for Management Buy-Out Research, University of Nottingham, from Barclays Development Capital and from Touche Ross Corporate Finance.
2   An earlier version of this chapter appeared as Filatotchev *et al.* (1992).
3   For detailed discussion relating to buy-outs in general see Jensen (1989) and Wright, Thompson, Chiplin and Robbie (1991).
4   These arguments apply both to the rationale for buy-outs of complete firms or of divisions of larger organizations. In respect of the latter there are the added problems of monitoring and incentives in a vertical hierarchy which are exacerbated by greater organizational complexities, conflicts of culture, etc. For a detailed discussion of the rationale for divestment and buy-out in particular, see Thompson and Wright (1987). The nature of the problems of control in vertical hierarchies in CPEs is analysed in Buck and Wright (1990).
5   Privatization introduces the clear specification of profit objectives, the introduction of bankruptcy and take-over threats, and the potential for improved managerial incentives. However, if the newly privatized firm retains product market power and if shareholdings are diffuse there may be little pressure for internal improvements (Vickers and Yarrow 1988). Large privatizations may effectively be immune from take-over bids, especially where 'golden shares' are retained by government.
6   The post-deal performance of BOs generally seems to have been satisfactory, at least in the short term. On average buy-outs from the private sector have proved relatively

profitable, productively efficient and responsive to new market situations. Redundancies have been inevitable during the early rationalization of operations, but there has been significant subsequent re-employment (See Palepu 1990 for a review of the US evidence, and Wright, Thompson, Chiplin and Robbie 1991 for the UK position). In respect of buy-outs from the public sector, evidence is more limited but detailed individual case study evidence relating to the National Freight Corporation (Bradley and Nejad 1989), surveys of the privatized bus industry (Wright, Dobson, Thompson and Robbie 1991) and analyses of the change in value from buy-out to flotation or sale to a third party (Thompson *et al.* 1991) indicate significant improvements.

7   This exit rate in privatization buy-outs is about twice as high as that recorded for all buy-outs (Chiplin *et al.* 1991).

8   This point will be developed later in relation to the expertise and contacts of Soviet managers.

9   If managers have negative net productivities, of course, the reverse is true.

10 For the purpose of the analysis here we have taken the earnings figures of USSR enterprises as given, although it is well recognized that to be comparable with western enterprises major changes in accounting treatment are required.

11 Detailed discussion of the restructuring and vertical, horizontal and conglomerate separation of state-owned firms is contained in Wright, Dobson, Thompson and Robbie (1991).

12 This subject is returned to below. It is worth noting here that unions and workforces have also accumulated decision rights during the gradual economic reforms of the 1970s and 1980s.

13 For detailed general discussion of this point see, for example, Lipton and Sachs (1990), Estrin (1991). Its application in Czechoslovakia and Poland is discussed in Hare and Grosfeld (1991).

14 For discussion in relation to Poland see Blanchard and Layard (1990).

15 It should be noted, however, that employee shares have double votes in the event of a hostile take-over bid, so that employee ownership can be maintained.

BIBLIOGRAPHY

Blanchard, O. and Layard, R. (1990) *Economic Change in Poland?* London: Centre for Economic Policy Research, May.

Bleaney, M. (1990) Some Trade Policy Issues in Eastern Europe', *World Economy* 13(2) 250–62.

Bradley, K. and Nejad, A. (1989) *Managing Owners – The Case of NFC*, Cambridge: Cambridge University Press.

Buck, T. and Wright, M. (1990) Control in vertical hierarchies, soft budgets and employee buy-outs, *Economic Analysis* XXIV(4), 377–94.

——— , Thompson, S. and Wright, M. (1991) 'Post-Communist privatisation and the British experience', *Public Enterprise* 11(2–3), 185–200.

Chiplin, B., Wright, M. and Robbie, K. (1991) *UK Management Buy-outs in 1991: Annual Review from CMBOR*, Nottingham: CMBOR.

Estrin, S. (1991) *Privatization in Central and Eastern Europe: What Lessons Can Be Learnt From Western Experience*, Centre for Economic Policy Research, Working Paper 99, London School of Economics.

Fama, E. F. and Jensen, M. C. (1983) 'The separation of ownership and control', *Journal of Law and Economics*, vol. XXVI, 302–24.

Filatotchev, I., Buck, T. and Wright, M. (1992) 'Privatisation and buy-outs in the USSR', *Soviet Studies* 44(2) 265–82.

Hare, P. (1990) 'From central planning to market economy: some microeconomic issues', *Economic Journal*, vol. 100, 581–95.

—— and Grosfeld, I. (1991) 'Privatization in Hungary, Poland and Czechoslovakia', Centre for Economic Policy Research, Discussion Paper 544, April.

—— and Hughes, G. (1991) *Competitiveness and Industrial Restructuring in Czechoslovakia, Hungary and Poland*, Discussion Paper 543, Centre for Economic Policy Research.

Jensen, M. C. (1989) 'The eclipse of the public corporation', *Harvard Business Review*, 89(5), 61–74.

Kornai, J. (1986) 'The Soft Budget Constraint', *Kyklos*, 39(1), 3–30.

Lipton, D. and Sachs, J. (1990) *Creating a Market Economy in Eastern Europe: The Case of Poland*, Brookings Papers on Economic Activity, No. 1, Washington DC: Brookings Institution.

Paddon, M. (1991) 'Management buy-outs of local authority services', *Local Government Studies* 17(3) 27–52.

Palepu, K. G. (1990) 'Consequences of leveraged buy-outs', *Journal of Financial Economics*, vol. 27, 247–62.

Public Accounts Committee (1991) *Ninth Annual Report*, 'Sale of the National Bus Company', HC 119, 1990/91.

Thompson, S. and Wright, M. (1987) 'Markets to hierarchies and back again: the implications of management buy-outs for factor supply', *Journal of Economic Studies*, 14(3), 5–22.

——, —— and Robbie, K. (1991) *Corporate Restructuring and the Role of Management and Employee Buy-Outs: an Overview of the Issues and Evidence in the UK and Europe*, Centre for Management Buy-Out Research, Occasional Paper 21.

Valentiny, P., Buck, T. and Wright, M. (1991) *The Pricing and Valuation of Public Assets: Experiences in the UK and Hungary* Centre for Management Buy-out Research Occ. Paper, November.

Vickers, J. and Yarrow, G. (1988), *Privatization: An Economic Analysis*, Cambridge, Mass.: MIT Press.

Wright, M. (1987) 'Divestment and the regulation of natural monopolies in the UK: the case of British Gas', *Energy Policy* 15(3), 193–216.

——, Thompson, S. and Robbie, K. (1989) 'Management and employee buy-outs and privatisation: analysis and UK experience', *Annals of Public and Cooperative Economy* 60(4), 399–430.

——, Dobson, P., Thompson, S. and Robbie, K. (1991) 'How well does privatisation achieve government objectives? The case of the buy-outs in the UK bus industry', Conference on Privatisation, University of St Andrews, September.

——, Thompson, S. Chiplin, B. and Robbie, K. (1991) *Buy-ins and Buy-outs: New Strategies in Corporate Management*, London: Graham & Trotman.

Young, D. (1991) 'The role of business valuation in the privatisation of Eastern Europe', *Public Enterprise* 11(2–3), 201–8.

Part VI

PRIVATIZATION IN DEVELOPING COUNTRIES

20

PRIVATIZATION IN MALAYSIA
For what and for whom?
Jomo K.S.

The growth of the public sector since the 1930s has occurred in varied circumstances internationally. In the advanced industrial capitalist economies of Europe and, to a lesser extent, in North America, the growth of the public sector has been largely associated with the growth of the Welfare State, especially under the influence of social democratic movements and Keynesian economic ideas. However, in the Third World, the public sector has developed most under so-called 'intermediate regimes' often established by populist nationalist movements (for example, Sukarno's Indonesia, Nasser's Egypt, Nehru's India), statist capitalist governments using state intervention and ownership to achieve rapid economic growth in favour of the ruling interests (for example, Suharto's Indonesia, Marcos's Philippines, and Malaysia under the NEP in South-East Asia), as well as politically beleaguered resource-poor regimes which intervened to ensure rapid industrialization for economic and political survival (for example, Park Chung Hee's South Korea, Taiwan under the Kuomintang, and Lee Kuan Yew's Singapore).

While different factors have contributed to the growth, nature and role of the public sector in these different contexts, there are also important similarities. This is especially true for public utilities and services, which sometimes involve natural monopolies not priced strictly according to cost or profit-maximizing criteria. Important considerations of social welfare, political legitimacy and patronage have often been very influential in their development. But perhaps most importantly, the inability or even the failure of the private sector to meet needs and expectations encouraged and legitimized government intervention and the growth of the public sector to compensate. Ironically, with the recent swing of the ideological pendulum, the private sector, once seen as the problem, is now promised as the solution.

By the early 1980s, the generally lacklustre performance of the Malaysian public sector, including many public enterprises, required a policy response. The key question, however, should be whether such inefficiencies are necessarily characteristic of the public sector, and hence cannot be overcome except through privatization. If the current record of the Malaysian public enterprises is primarily due to the nature, interests and abilities of those in charge, rather than to the consequences of public ownership, then privatization in itself cannot and will not overcome the root problem. Also, while privatization may improve enterprise profitability for the private owners concerned, such changes may not necessarily benefit the public or consumers.

Since a significant portion of such activities are public monopolies, privatization will hand over such monopoly powers to private interests which are likely to use them to maximize profits. The privatization of public services tends to burden the people, especially if charges are raised for the privatized services. Obviously, private interests are only interested in profitable or potentially profitable activities and enterprises. This may mean that the government will be left with unprofitable and less profitable activities. And this will worsen public sector performance, already considered less than efficient. Public sector inefficiencies and other problems need to be overcome, but privatization in Malaysia has primarily enriched the few with strong political connections to secure many of these profitable opportunities, while the public interest increasingly becomes vulnerable to private capitalists' powers and interests.

While most affected public sector employees have felt threatened by privatization, many other Malaysians fed up with the waste, inefficiency and corruption usually associated with the public sector have been indifferent to, if not supportive of this policy. Many Malaysians also associate the growth of the public sector with increased state intervention and the ascendancy of Malay hegemony under the New Economic Policy (NEP), and see privatization as a desirable policy change that would reverse these trends which have apparently discouraged private investment and thus slowed down growth. Some others identify state intervention with socialism and support privatization as a measure to restore capitalist hegemony. While statist capitalism (Jomo 1985) is not socialism, undermining the public sector – especially public services – through privatization has important welfare implications for the people, especially public sector employees, consumers and the poor.

However, the current campaign for privatization internationally goes back to the beginning of the 1980s, especially after the election of Margaret Thatcher in Britain in 1979 and Ronald Reagan to the United States presidency in 1980, with the accompanying swing to conservative and right-wing economic thinking (for example, monetarism and supply-side economics) in the west, and the promotion of privatization by powerful international agencies such as the World Bank and the Asian Development Bank (1985), usually as part of a larger structural adjustment package favouring private (and often foreign) capitalist interests.

The Malaysian government was among the first to climb on this privatization bandwagon, enthusiastically endorsed and promoted by the Bretton Woods institutions, particularly the World Bank. Two years after becoming Prime Minister in 1981, Dr Mahathir Mohamad announced the Malaysian government's own commitment to privatization in 1983. Unlike the 'Look East' policy and the 'Malaysia Incorporated' concept – also associated with Mahathir's administration – which had faded in significance by the mid-1980s, privatization achieved new vigour, especially after the appointment of Daim Zainuddin as Finance Minister in mid-1984 and the deepening economic crisis of 1985/6. To be sure, Mahathir's own commitment to private – rather than public – enterprise began much earlier, being reflected in his *The Malay Dilemma* (1970) and especially his *Menghadapi Cabaran* (1976; published in English translation as *The Challenge* in the mid-1980s). This unwavering commitment is all the more remarkable because of the commitment of his two predecessors to public enterprise as the main vehicle for furthering national, especially ethnic, Malay communal business interests.

From 1971, the Malay elite-dominated Malaysian government's New Economic Policy was committed to reducing poverty and inter-ethnic economic disparity, ostensibly to achieve national unity, which was understood primarily in terms of reduced inter-ethnic resentment. New statutory bodies, government corporations, government-owned or controlled publicly listed companies as well as government-owned or controlled private companies all became means to achieve government objectives, including the NEP's corporate wealth re-distribution target of increasing indigenous (Bumiputera) ownership of shares to 30 per cent by 1990 from 2.4 per cent in 1970. The NEP's Outline Perspective Plan for 1971–90 also envisaged the creation of a Bumiputera commercial and industrial community (BCIC), while the Fourth Malaysia Plan for 1981–5 expected Bumiputera 'trust agencies' to account for 83 per cent of Bumiputera share capital in 1990 – that is, only 17 per cent (or 5.2 per cent of total share capital) was to be held by Bumiputera individuals. By 1990, however, Bumiputera share capital had risen to 20.3 per cent of total share capital, with trust agencies accounting for 6.3 per cent and individuals for 14 per cent – that is, 31 per cent and 69 per cent of the Bumiputera share respectively!

However, it should also be pointed out that various criticisms have been made about official share distribution data (Jomo *et al.* 1989). Besides the valuation problem raised by using nominal or par values – which, it is claimed, especially underestimates the market value of Bumiputera corporate wealth – and under-estimation owing to the use of nominee companies, the Malaysian government has not explained how share capital owned directly by the government and other bodies, such as Bank Negara Malaysia (the central bank) or the Employees Provident Fund, is categorized.

Two years after the privatization policy was announced, and possibly in response to public criticisms, the Privatization Section of the powerful Economic Planning Unit (EPU) of the Prime Minister's Department issued its *Guidelines on Privatization* which outlined policy aims, modes of privatization and the means for implementation. Since then, various laws have been reformed to facilitate the incorporation of government departments and agencies as public limited companies and to facilitate privatization more generally.

The government also commissioned the drafting of a privatization master plan, the main elements of which were announced in various forums in 1989 (see, for example, Sheriff 1991). The EPU finally published the *Privatization*

Masterplan (*PMP*) document in February 1991 (EPU 1991a). Claiming success for its privatization programme thus far, the *PMP* announced the government's intention to 'expand and accelerate further the pace of privatization process' [*sic*].

THE MEANING OF PRIVATIZATION

Privatization – or denationalization – refers to changing the status of a business, service or industry from state, government or public to private ownership or control. The term sometimes also refers to the use of private contractors to provide services previously rendered by the public sector. In Malaysia, privatization has referred to:

1   Sale or divestment of state concerns. The public service concerned usually has to first be incorporated legally as a public limited company to facilitate such a sale – for example, the establishment of Syarikat Telekom Malaysia Berhad on 1 January 1987 to take over the activities of the Telecoms Department (Jabatan Telekom) or the incorporation of Tenaga Nasional Berhad, taking over the National Electricity Board (Lembaga Letrik Negara).

2   Public issue or sale of a minority or even a majority of shares in a state-owned public company – for example, Malaysian Airlines System (MAS) in 1985 and the Malaysian International Shipping Corporation (MISC) in 1987.

3   Placement of shares with institutional investors – for example, the sale of about 5 per cent of MAS stock to the Brunei government in 1986.

4   Sale or lease of physical assets – for example, the lease of the Lady Templer Hospital to Rampai Muda in 1984.

5   Joint public/private sector ventures – for example, the establishment of Perbadanan Otomobil Nasional (Proton) in 1983, with 70 per cent held by HICOM, the Heavy Industries Corporation of Malaysia, and 15 per cent each by two Mitsubishi companies, the Mitsubishi Corporation and the Mitsubishi Motor Corporation (see Jomo 1985).

6   Schemes to draw private financing into construction projects – for example, North Port Kelang toll road bypass, the Jalan Kuching toll flyover and the North–South Highway as well as the low-cost housing scheme 'privatized' since the mid-1980s.

7   'Contracting out' public services previously provided within the public sector – for example, the contracting out of various local government authorities' activities, such as parking services and garbage disposal, Telecoms' $2.5 billion telecommunications development projects (Kennedy 1991), Port Kelang's container terminal services.[1]

8   Allowing private competition where the public sector previously enjoyed a monopoly – for example, the launching of a third television channel (TV3) in 1984 owned by Sistem Televisyen Malaysia Berhad, now controlled by

the New Straits Press Berhad, and controlled in turn by the UMNO-owned Fleet Group, and now by the UMNO-controlled Renong Bhd.

TYPES OF PRIVATIZATION

The *PMP* only considers four main modes of implementing privatization, namely:

- sale of assets or equity;
- lease of assets;
- management contract;
- 'build–operate–transfer' (BOT) or 'build–operate' (BO) new infrastructure.

However, the document also cites other examples of privatization which have nothing to do with any of these – for example, the so-called privatization of TV3 through issue of a licence for a private television broadcasting company, and contracting-out services.

The *PMP* mentions broad alternative methods, considerations and criteria for the valuation of assets for sale or lease – net tangible assets (NTA), price-earning (PE) ratios, discounted cash flows (DCF) – emphasizing that only the latter two take account of potential earnings, which the *PMP* favours. However, there is no evidence that any of these methods have been strictly adhered to in determining the actual price (or lease rate) of privatized government assets. On the contrary, very substantial discounts (in the case of sales) and premiums (in the case of privatized infrastructure projects) seem to have been the norm, with the proportion apparently not unrelated to the political influence of the beneficiary.

It is believed that the predominance of the (politically more influential) Malays among public sector employees, the presence of relatively large unions in the major public utilities earmarked for privatization, and the virtual public sector wage freeze since 1980 (despite considerable inflation, especially in the early 1980s) encouraged the government to ensure employment security for five years and to offer better service terms and conditions as carrots to induce workers not to resist privatization. Hence, though workers have the option of not joining the privatized entity most do; the vast majority have yet another option of continuing with the government's scheme of service or accepting the new company's scheme, which the majority tend to pick.

The government has had to legislate many changes to existing laws to facilitate privatization. However, the primary concern has been with overcoming legal obstacles to privatization. Little attention has gone to ensuring greater competition or public or consumer accountability, which are matters of considerable concern since many of the privatized entities remain virtual monopolies. Since the *PMP* acknowledges that there is not much scope for increasing competition with natural monopolies, it promises an appropriate regulatory framework to protect consumer interests, particularly in terms of price, quality and availability of services, as well as 'commercial freedom' for private

441

monopolies. Implicit in this formulation is the acknowledgement that such regulation does not yet exist, and, if introduced, is unlikely to threaten enterprise autonomy.

While privatization undoubtedly exerts heavy demands on private sector financial resources to mobilize both debt and equity capital, it is not self-evident that deepening and broadening the Malaysian capital market are desirable in themselves. On the contrary, it has been suggested that with privatization, capital resources – which might otherwise have been invested into expanding productive capacity – have instead been diverted into acquiring or transferring existing public sector assets.

The *PMP* reiterates the government's intention to advance Bumiputera corporate participation through ethnically preferential privatization. This is expected to include collaboration between Bumiputera institutional investors and others as well as management buy-outs (MBOs) and employee share ownership plans (ESOPs). The *PMP* also promises an institutional mechanism to ensure sustained Bumiputera participation after privatization.

Anticipating public objections, the *PMP* advocates minority (no more than 25 per cent) foreign investments in privatized entities where:

- foreign expertise is needed and local expertise is not available;
- foreign participation is crucial for export market access and promotion;
- international linkages and exposure are required by the business;
- the supply of local capital is not sufficient to buy up the shares offered.

Until 1992, there had been no significant increase in foreign ownership due to privatization except in the case of the sale of MAS shares to the Brunei government in the mid-1980s to ameliorate pressures associated with Malaysia's foreign debt burden then. Instead, it appears that foreign interests were better secured and advanced through contractual arrangements with politically influential *rentiers* requiring technical and managerial expertise. However, in 1992, the government announced the proposed sale of shares in Tenaga Nasional Berhad (TEN) to foreign investors; ironically, the British Central Electricity Generating Board (CEGB) has been envisaged as the most likely candidate to take up a quarter of TEN's share capital.

An interesting innovation proposed by the *PMP* is the establishment of a special fund to finance related expenses such as feasibility studies, preparing candidates for privatization and disbursing compensation related to privatization.

To motivate staff, the *PMP* recommends employee share ownership as well as other incentives. However, it acknowledges that such schemes have not benefited poorer employees very much, while loyalty and commitment to the company has been undermined by the subsequent sale of shares. To overcome these problems, the *PMP* recommends that ESOPs for future privatizations involve the establishment of a trust to hold shares for employees, who will be able to sell them only when they retire or resign. The *PMP* also recommends management as well as management-cum-employee buy-outs – that is, MBOs and MEBOs.

The *PMP* proposes a privatization action plan (PAP) consisting of a two-year 'rolling plan' reviewed at the end of each year, identifying the targets for privatization and for preparing for eventual privatization in the following years. According to *PMP*, 424 government-owned entities (GOEs) were studied by private consultants to determine the desirability and suitability of their privatization. The consultants identified 246 as privatizable, with 69 to be privatized within two years, 107 in two to five years and the balance after five years. However, the government has deemed some of these 246 not suitable for privatization on various grounds. It also claims to be considering others not covered by the study for possible privatization. Such government-initiated privatizations are supposed to be subject to competitive bidding.

However, according to the *PMP*, the government is still prepared to consider private-sector-initiated privatization if it is convinced that no other private sector party can privatize a particular project, as in the following circumstances:

- the proposer offers a unique cost-effective solution to an economic problem or potential savings to the government;
- the proposer has unique possession of certain technical know-how or patent rights essential to the proposal;
- the privatization would not be viable on its own as its viability is dependent on another component possessed by the proposer.

Although still open to abuse, if strictly interpreted these criteria represent a significant departure from the earlier 'first come, first served' policy, which has still not been unequivocally rejected.

The *PMP* claims to be influenced by both feasibility and desirability criteria in determining priorities for privatization. Feasibility is, in turn, said to be determined by both ease of privatization and attractiveness to the private sector, whereas desirability seems to be defined by the government's perception of private sector superiority. Using a 2 by 2 matrix, the *PMP* distinguishes four categories:

- *immediate privatization* candidates will be the main focus in the early years of the *PAP* as they rank highly on the feasibility and desirability criteria;
- *priority restructuring* candidates are deemed to require preparation (for example, restructuring) for privatization despite the government's desire to privatize them;
- *back-burner* candidates are deemed feasible for privatization, though the benefits of privatization are considered to be less than self-evident;
- the *consider future* candidates rank poorly on both feasibility and desirability criteria.

The *PAP* distinguishes six different categories of candidates for privatization requiring different treatment, namely:

- flagships' – comprising GOEs of national importance in terms of size and complexity, thus meriting special treatment (such as JTM and LLN) – are to be privatized over several years, usually one annually;
- 'easily privatizable government majority-owned companies', especially in manufacturing and agricultural production, are most likely to be given priority for privatization;
- 'restructuring candidates' mainly refers to unprofitable companies needing financial and operational restructuring; however, the government prefers to minimize pre-privatization restructuring, which usually involves financial aspects;
- 'services' previously protected from commercial competition are to be deregulated and privatized in the consumer interest;
- listed and minority shareholdings are to be given low priority since the private sector is already quite involved;
- 'new projects' – usually involving infrastructural development – are to be privatized on a BOT basis.

To facilitate implementation, the *PAP* distinguishes those ready for privatization from those requiring preparation – for example, most flagships. The stages required for their preparation may include:

- commercialization (for example, user charges, commercial accounting and commercial performance criteria);
- legal corporatization.

Other changes at this stage before actual divestment may include:

- replacing bureaucratic administration with profit-oriented management;
- replacing centralized production-oriented decision-making with market-driven consumer preferences;
- introducing clear financial and operational performance criteria and commercial accounting.

The main divestment options considered by the *PMP* include:

- public flotation;
- private sale;
- management buy-out (MBO);
- employee share ownership plan (ESOP).

THE RATIONALE FOR PRIVATIZATION

The Malaysian government summed up its arguments for privatization as follows in its *Guidelines on Privatization*:

> Privatization has a number of objectives. First, it is aimed at relieving the financial and administrative burden of the government in undertaking and

maintaining a vast and constantly expanding network of services and investments in infrastructure. Second, privatization is expected to promote competition, improve efficiency and increase the productivity of the services. Third, privatization, by stimulating private entrepreneurship and investment, is expected to accelerate the rate of growth of the economy. Fourth, privatization is expected to assist in reducing the presence and size of the public sector, with its monopolistic tendencies and bureaucratic support, in the economy. Fifth, privatization is also expected to contribute towards meeting the objectives of the New Economic Policy (NEP), especially as Bumiputera entrepreneurship and presence have improved greatly since the early days of the NEP and they are therefore capable of taking up their share of the privatized services.

(EPU 1985)

These arguments in favour of privatization have been refuted on the following grounds:

1   The public sector can be more efficiently run, as has been demonstrated by some other public sectors – for example, in Singapore (Rodan 1989), Taiwan (Wade 1990) and South Korea (Amsden 1989). Also, privatization is not going to provide a miracle cure for all the problems (especially the inefficiencies) associated with the public sector, nor can private enterprise guarantee that the public interest is most effectively served by private interests taking over public sector activities. Also, by diverting private sector capital from productive new investments to buying over public sector assets, economic growth would be retarded rather than encouraged.

2   Greater public accountability and a more transparent public sector would ensure greater efficiency in achieving the public and national interest while limiting public sector waste and borrowing.

3   The government would only be able to privatize profitable or potentially profitable enterprises and activities because the private sector would be interested only in these.

4   Privatization may postpone a fiscal crisis by temporarily reducing fiscal deficits, but it would not necessarily resolve it because the public sector would lose income from the more profitable public sector activities and would be stuck with financing the unprofitable ones, which would undermine the potential for cross-subsidization within the public sector.

5   Privatization tends to affect the interests of the public sector employees and the public adversely, especially poorer consumers, which the public sector is more sensitive to.

6   Privatization would give priority to profit maximization at the expense of social welfare and the public interest, except on the rare occasions when the former and the latter coincide; hence, for example, only profitable new services would be introduced, rather than services needed by the people, especially the poor and politically uninfluential.

7   Privatization exercises in Malaysia may not even pretend to achieve their other alleged advantages and benefits by invoking NEP restructuring considerations, supposedly to increase Bumiputera wealth ownership and business opportunities. With increased Bumiputera competition, where prior collusion cannot be arranged, it seems that political influence and connections have become increasingly decisive.

As of the end of 1990, according to the *PMP*, thirty-seven privatizations had taken place since the announcement of the policy, of which twenty-seven involved private interests taking over existing government entities, while the other ten involved the construction of new infrastructure. The government had also approved another eighteen privatizations, of which seven are new infrastructure projects. This did not include government divestments since 1981 to transfer government equity to Bumiputeras, involving some thirty companies transferred to Permodalan Nasional Berhad and another 120 or so to private Bumiputera interests – which remain to be systematically documented. Also, minor privatizations – such as contracting out of services (such as security, cleaning and laundry) – are not included.

Of the twenty-seven privatizations, seventeen involved ownership divestment by sale of equity or assets to the public, or by way of private placement and management buy-out; two involved leasing arrangements, five involved management contracts and two more a combination of sale and lease; also, the Lembaga Letrik Negara (LLN, or National Electricity Board) was corporatized as Tenaga Nasional Berhad (National Power Ltd) as a step towards privatization. Of the ten new infrastructure projects, eight involved 'build–operate–transfer' (to government after some time), while the other two involved 'build–operate' (for perpetuity).

The advocates of privatization in Malaysia have not been honest in presenting a full and balanced record of what has happened with privatization. Instead, anecdotal claims have been selectively advanced to imply that the Malaysian experience has been an unqualified success, as in the *PMP*. The existence of mistakes or negative consequences and implications is not even acknowledged in order to avoid their recurrence. While the policy-makers or those in charge presumably know better, the *PMP*'s failure to publicly consider these bears ominous implications about how the policy has been formulated, adopted and implemented. While the *PMP* undoubtedly represents an advance, at least on paper, over some of the most blatant abuses of early Malaysian privatization policy, especially the 'first come, first served' policy, it offers little grounds for comfort about the future of privatization in Malaysia, especially in the light of what has taken place or seems likely to occur in the foreseeable future.

Despite the *PMP*'s claim that privatization is 'premised on the superiority of market over administrative directives in governing economic activity to achieve efficiency' and that the 'Government's intervention in the economy will be minimal', efforts at deregulation are well behind those of privatization. While there has been a great deal of rhetoric about deregulation accompanying privatization, such efforts have been quite limited and mainly oriented to inducing foreign investments. And in many instances, especially with public utilities, the government has retained effective control despite changes in ownership. Privatization in itself only involves the transfer of property rights, and in many instances in Malaysia (for example, the privatization of major public utilities and management buy-outs), management personnel have not even been significantly changed.

Improvements in management generally reflect management initiatives encouraged by increased enterprise and administrative autonomy as well as new incentive systems – that is, changes which do not require privatization as a pre-requisite but can alternatively be achieved by greater decentralization, devolution or administrative authority – long advocated by trade unions (see, for example, Mustapha Johan Abdullah and Shamsulbahriah 1987) and others in the public sectors, which became increasingly centralized in the early 1980s with the Cabinet Committee Report on new salary structures for the public sector, chaired by the then Deputy Prime Minister Mahathir, and the later centralization of authority over the public sector, in the Prime Minister's Department under Mahathir, especially through the strengthening of the Public Services Department (JPA). Also, the so-called Non-Financial Public Enterprises (NFPEs), or Off-Budget Agencies (OBAs), were removed from the Treasury's purview after the then Finance Minister, Tengku Razaleigh Hamzah, challenged Mahathir's preferred candidate (Musa Hitam) for the ruling party's deputy leadership, and traditionally, the deputy prime ministership as well.

If one accepts the view that it is competition – rather than mere changes in ownership status – which is likely to induce greater enterprise efficiency, then it becomes difficult to conclude that economic efficiency has been improved because of privatization in Malaysia. Some of the often exaggerated efficiency gains have been brought about by greater employee and managerial motivation with new incentive systems and greater scope for managerial initiatives with administrative autonomy (that is, enterprise reform).

In many cases of privatization in Malaysia, it is popularly believed that there are strong influences from private interests which try to determine what is to be privatized, in what manner and to whom. For example, Sapura Holdings commissioned a consultancy report by Arthur D. Little of Boston entitled 'The Advantages and Feasibility of Privatizing Jabatan Telekom Malaysia' in 1983 for the attention of the Malaysian government; with the benefit of hindsight, it is generally acknowledged that Sapura is undoubtedly the main beneficiary of the privatization of telecommunications in Malaysia (Kennedy 1991).

Often, privatization in Malaysia does not even involve the formalities of an open tender system, as sanctioned by the official 'first come, first served' policy by which the government justifies awarding privatization opportunities to those who have supposedly first proposed the privatization of a government property or activity. Instead, many beneficiaries are believed to have been chosen on the basis of political and personal connections. For example, in 1986 it was announced that M$1.4 billion worth of water supply projects involving 174 schemes had been awarded to Antah Biwater without open tender. Though hailed as the nation's first privatized water supply project, the government will remain responsible for the operation and maintenance of the schemes. Antah Biwater – which is 51 per cent owned by the Negeri Sembilan royal family's Antah Holdings Berhad and 49 per cent owned by the British water supply and treatment group, Biwater Ltd – had in fact secured a turnkey contract with a British government financing arrangement thrown in as an aid package. It is anticipated that all the design and engineering work will be handled by Biwater (since Antah has no relevant engineering track record) at the expense of Malaysian engineers and consultants who have long handled such projects. Disgruntled Malaysian civil engineering firms claim that Antah Biwater is charging much more than they would have, while senior Malaysian government officials point to the British aid package as the inducement which secured the deal for Biwater.

In December 1986, the Malaysian Parliament passed amendments to the Official Secrets Act (OSA) which extended the definition of official secrets to include, among other things, government tender documents (even after completion of the tender exercise) and any other documents or material which Ministers and public officials may arbitrarily deem secret or confidential. The classification of a document or material as an official secret cannot be challenged in any court of law, while the amendments impose a mandatory minimum one-year jail sentence for any OSA offence. Such legislation, accompanying the privatization drive, further limits the already limited scope for meaningful governmental transparency and public accountability.

In the increasingly authoritarian and centralized Malaysian polity, with public accountability and governmental transparency considerably diminished deliberately by those in power, the strengthening of private business interests, especially of those which are politically well-connected, is very likely to influence, and even increase, rather than eliminate the opportunities for rent appropriation. Ironically, the remaining democratic features of the system in such a context may well serve to sustain rent-seeking behaviour and costs. This is not intended to legitimize further authoritarianism to reduce such waste. Rather, it serves to emphasize that enhanced public accountability, governmental transparency and other democratic safeguards are crucial for reducing rents (which can still be productively deployed) and, more importantly, rent-seeking behaviour in the context of privatization.

Privatization is also supposed to free market forces and encourage competition in the economy generally, especially in the sectors concerned. But this is negated by the fact that potential beneficiaries have a common interest in getting the public sector to privatize services, which can be far more important. Not surprisingly, with the limited experience of privatization thus far, there is already widespread concern about and even evidence of:

- the existence of formal and informal collusion (for example, cartel-like agreements);
- possible patterns in bidding for contracts, suggesting collusion among bidders;
- some companies enjoying special influence and privileged information, thus consistently being able to bid successfully for profitable opportunities from privatization.

While privatization undoubtedly reduces the role of the public sector in the economy, it is not clear whether this is meant to be an end in itself or merely the means to an end. If the former, then the policy is essentially intended to aggrandize its politically influential beneficiaries, or is clearly ideological in inspiration, or else is meant to please the ideologically motivated governments and powerful international economic institutions (such as the World Bank and the Asian Development Bank) that the Malaysian government seeks to find favour with. There is evidence that all three factors may be relevant in the Malaysian case.

Advocates of privatization in Malaysia, including the *PMP*, also claim that it will reduce the government's financial and administrative burden. Hence, the massive foreign debt burden which mounted quickly in the first half of the 1980s (see Jomo 1990) may well have encouraged such sales. (Much of this debt was incurred to finance new heavy industries of dubious feasibility enjoying heavy protection, which may be privatized after enjoying massive subsidization.) While there undoubtedly are one-off revenues for the government from the sale of public assets, it is not self-evident that the retention of such assets would not have been in the government's and the public's medium- and long-term interest for a variety of reasons mentioned above. Perhaps most importantly, the considerable evidence of heavy discounting in asset prices for sale or lease suggests otherwise. Also, the sale of the government's most valuable assets, while it is obliged to retain those less profitable activities and assets of little interest to the profit-seeking private sector, contributes to the self-fulfilling prophecy of the unprofitability of public sector economic activities. The diminution of the public sector also reduces the scope for government intervention – for example, for equity reasons or in support of industrial policy. There is also no clear evidence that additional recurrent revenues from leases or taxation come anywhere near to compensating for the loss of recurrent revenue from the government's more profitable investments, especially when tax holidays and other inducements associated with privatization are taken into consideration.

The *PMP*'s claim that privatization contributes to growth is vague and even spurious. After the announcement of the policy in 1983, Malaysia went through a deep recession in 1985 and 1986 before experiencing rapid manufacturing-led growth in the late 1980s. Although the mid-1980s recession was exacerbated by the deflationary consequences of public spending cuts, which can be analytically distinguished from privatization *per se*, there is also no clear evidence that privatization in particular has significantly contributed to recent economic growth. No claim has yet been made that privatization is a necessary and indispensable ingredient for the broader economic liberalization measures of the mid-1980s which probably induced the foreign investment increase associated with the recent boom. On the contrary, however, it may be argued that private acquisition of public assets has probably diverted potential investment funds, while it is now generally agreed that the stock-market – undoubtedly expanded by privatization – has not been important for the corporate financing of the dynamic foreign-dominated manufacturing sector.

Perhaps of greatest concern, privatization in Malaysia appears to have strengthened the *rentier* rather than the Entrepreneurial elements and tendencies among Malaysian capitalists, though this does not mean that they are mutually exclusive. While allowing that rent appropriation and deployment can be crucial to supporting and strengthening entrepreneurs and productive investors – with one exception which seems to prove the rule (Kadir Shamsuddin's Sapura Holdings) – there is little evidence that privatization has strengthened domestic capital accumulation in export-oriented manufacturing or other progressive capitalist elements.

Some other adverse consequences of privatization to be considered include:

- increased 'costs' to the public of reduced, inferior or costlier services – for example, the unit charge for local telephone calls was increased by 30 per cent just before STMB was incorporated;
- the implications of two sets of services: that is, one for those who can afford privatized services and the other for those who cannot, and hence have to continue to rely on public services (for example, medical services and education);
- the effects of minimal investments by private contractors concerned with short-term profits;
- increased costs of living and poorer services and utilities – especially in remote and rural areas – due to 'economic costing' of services (for example, telephone, water supply and electricity);
- reduced jobs, overtime and real wages for employees of privatized concerns;
- the deflationary consequences of fewer jobs or lower wages, or both.

While the *PMP* admits that 'it is still too early to make an assessment of the effectiveness of the privatization programme', it none the less claims several major achievements, including efficiency gains, stimulation of economic growth, a reduction of governmental responsibilities, and wealth redistribution.

The *PMP* cites four examples of *efficiency gains*:

- reduction of average vessel turnaround time at the Kelang container terminal from 11.7 hours to 8.9 hours two years after privatization;
- improvements in television broadcasting with greater competition after the licensing of a private third television channel, TV3;

- improved telecommunication services since the corporatization of STMB in 1987;
- completion of the Labuan water supply project ahead of schedule.

The *PMP* claims privatization has *stimulated economic growth* by providing greater opportunities to (and thus motivating) the private sector, generating multiplier effects (for example, TV3's stimulus to the domestic film-making and advertising industries), compensating for the decline in public expenditure and encouraging private entrepreneurship.

Also claimed is a significant *reduction of governmental responsibilities* – both administrative and financial – due to privatization, citing the cutting of the public sector workforce by 54,000, of whom 29,000 were Telecom's employees. One-off proceeds from the sale of government properties came to M$1.18 billion, while recurrent revenues are expected from taxation and leases (for example, the Kelang container terminal); meanwhile, the government's tax burden has been reduced as privatized companies take over loan refinancing. The *PMP* also claims that privatizing new infrastructure projects has saved the government M$8.2 billion, while other capital spending (development expenditure) commitments have been significantly reduced.

Since most privatizations have involved at least 30 per cent Bumiputera participation, the policy is said to have furthered the NEP's inter-ethnic *wealth redistribution* objectives. The *PMP* also claims that privatization has enabled the government to spend more on poverty alleviation.

Privatization in Malaysia has probably been most successful in contributing to the government's NEP objective, particularly Bumiputera wealth acquisition. One might even argue that the prioritization of this objective has probably seriously undermined achievement of the other stated aims of its privatization policy. However, it is unclear how the creation and distribution of substantial economic rents through ethnically biased privatization has been in the national interest, whether this is understood in developmentalist or equity terms. There is now official acknowledgement that most of these rents have not been efficiently deployed through productive investments to accelerate industrialization significantly or to consolidate genuine Bumiputera entrepreneurship. Instead, much has been wasted on rent-seeking costs associated with political involvement in business, while the very source of such rents and the limited abilities of those who control them have contributed to their deployment in real property, construction, finance and other investments with a short-term time horizon, thus adversely affecting investment priorities and activities generally in an economy officially committed to sustained manufacturing-led growth.

The foregoing analysis also implies that privatization is unlikely to enhance the NEP's other equity objectives (inter-ethnic parity in occupational and employment distribution, poverty reduction), and may instead undermine public welfare as a result of the strengthening of private monopolistic interests. The privatization policy has put increasing pressure on the predominantly Bumiputera public sector employees and sectors of the population more reliant

451

on public services. However, some of the costs of privatization have been softened by related policies to ameliorate adverse effects, especially on those sectors of the electorate considered supportive of the government – for example, workers in the privatized utilities have been guaranteed employment security as well as higher wages in the short term. Also, despite its claim to be assimilating Islamic values, the government has ignored Islamic objections against the privatization of properties Muslims are enjoined to share or own commonly or through the state, rather than privately.

APPENDIX: THE NORTH–SOUTH HIGHWAY PRIVATIZATION

Owing to disclosure in Parliament by the then Minister of Works, Datuk Samy Vellu, and subsequent information disclosed in connection with a civil court case brought by the head of the Parliamentary opposition, Lim Kit Siang, as well as other civic groups, several serious abuses in awarding the privatization of the North–South Highway (NSH) to United Engineers Malaysia (UEM) have come to public attention which conflict with the government's own justification for its privatization policy.

UEM was unable to provide the most competitive bid in several crucial regards, such as construction costs, the financial burden on government involved, the toll rates to be levied, the period of toll collection and the total amount of toll expected. Also, other bidders were given less time to prepare their tenders (less than three months) compared to UEM; nevertheless UEM's tender was less attractive than at least some of the others pre-selected. Details of the tender document are not publicly available as they are deemed secret by the amended Official Secrets Act (OSA).

Prior to being awarded the NSH project, UEM had never built any roads and had a dismal record in many other respects. UEM had been a virtually insolvent company for some years, suspended from trading on the Kuala Lumpur Stock Exchange (KLSE), with accumulated losses of M$90 million in 1985; half of its shares were believed to have been taken over just before the NSH privatization by Hatibudi Sendirian Berhad, whose trustees included the President, Deputy President, Secretary-General and Treasurer of UMNO. The UMNO Treasurer was then also the Finance Minister responsible for tender decisions, while the Attorney-General – who should investigate and prosecute malpractices as well as prepare government contractual agreements – was answerable to the Prime Minister, who is also UMNO President. Remarkably, the Prime Minister explained that UMNO needed to settle debts incurred in building its new headquarters, the Putra World Trade Centre – costing over M$300 million – by securing the NSH privatization. The Works Minister who was also President of MIC, also acknowledged his sale of two million MIC-sponsored lottery tickets to UEM!

According to the Works Minister, UEM will be able to collect M$34 billion in tolls over a 25-year period! This sum had been scaled down from UEM's original demand for M$54 billion over 30 years, after this became public knowledge. UEM is to be guaranteed minimum traffic volume and toll collections for 17 years by the government, and will even be compensated for shortfalls in toll collection! This is despite the fact that on justification for the privatization policy is that private entrepreneurs, and not the government, ought to bear the risks involved, especially in view of the vast differences in the forecasts of UEM, the project consultants (Rendel, Palmer and Triton), and the Malaysian Highway Authority (Lembaga Lebuhraya Malaysia, LLM).

The government also argued that UEM deserved to be awarded the NSH project over other bidders despite not being able to come up with the most attractive proposal as it had originally proposed the privatization of the highway. Not only were there differences of several billion ringgit between the competing tenders concerned, but such an argument is especially dubious when some of the same people are involved in both UEM and the government. Also, many UEM shares were held by a foreign company, United Engineers Ltd of Singapore, while most other shortlisted bidders for the tender were local companies, including Bumiputera companies apart from UEM.

The NSH privatization will fail to achieve the government's privatization aims for a number of reasons. First, due to UEM's conditions, apparently accepted by the government, the financial burden on the government will increase in several ways:

- The government has agreed to advance credit facilities to UEM at government-subsidized interest rates to the tune of M$750 million (reduced from M$1,650 million in mid-July 1987, after the public outcry).
- The Malaysian Highway Authority (LLM) will hand over highways – for which it spent M$3,320 million – to UEM, which will then charge higher toll rates on them, while the government will still have to pay off the remaining loans of M$1,600 million incurred by the LLM for their construction.
- UEM will be exempted from various taxes, estimated to cost the government about M$2,650 million in forgone revenue. (The government had reportedly also been prepared to offer some guarantees against currency devaluation, rising interest rates, delays and appreciating costs – worth about M$1,150 million – to UEM. However, when these became public knowledge, they were withdrawn.)

Second, there is no evidence that the NSH privatization will encourage competition and increase efficiency with the government's virtual monopoly of the highways falling into private hands, with all its attendant implications and consequences. Third, it is clear that the privatization of the NSH to UEM will raise living costs, particularly for transport. Fourth, as UEM had no direct experience in highway construction, UEM has been heavily dependent on its foreign partners – Mitsui and Co. (Japan), Taylor Woodrow International Ltd (UK) and Societe Française de Dragages et de Travaux Publics (France). In fact,

UEM's subsidiary, Projek Lebuhraya Utara Selatan (PLUS), has awarded contracts for actual road construction of different sectors to other domestic and foreign companies as well.

UEM has also procured several other lucrative tenders, such as the pharmaceutical stores and services project for the Ministry of Health (even though this was reportedly opposed by the then Director-General of Health), the National Sports Complex and the Peninsular Malaysia Utilization Project natural gas pipeline consultancies and the second link to Singapore. In most instances, it appears that UEM lacks relevant experience and staff competence and serves as a front for foreign companies, collecting handsome commissions for its connections.

BIBLIOGRAPHY

Amsden, A. (1989) *Asia's Next Giant: South Korea and Late Industrialization*, New York: Oxford University Press.

Asian Development Bank (1985) *Privatization: Policies, Methods and Procedures*, Manila: ADB.

EPU (1985) *Guidelines on Privatization*, Kuala Lumpur: Economic Planning Unit.

—— (1991a) *Privatization Masterplan*, Kuala Lumpur: Economic Planning Unit.

—— (1991b) *The Second Outline Perspective Plan, 1991–2000*, Kuala Lumpur: Economic Planning Unit.

—— (1991c) *Sixth Malaysia Plan, 1991–1995*, Kuala Lumpur: Economic Planning Unit.

Jomo K. S. (1985) *The Sun Also Sets: Lessons in 'Looking East'* (2nd edn), Kuala Lumpur: INSAN.

—— (1986) *A Question of Class: Capital, The State and Uneven Development in Malaya*, Singapore: Oxford University Press.

—— (1990) *Growth and Structural Change in the Malaysian Economy* London: Macmillan.

—— *et al.* (1989) *Mahathir's Economic Policies* (2nd edn), Kuala Lumpur: INSAN.

Kennedy, L. (1991) 'Liberalization, privatization and the politics of patronage in Malaysian telecommunications', Paper presented at the 41st Annual Conference of the International Communications Association, Chicago, Illinois, 24 May.

Mahathir Mohamad (1970) *The Malay Dilemma*, Singapore: Donald Moore.

—— (1976) *Menghadapi Cabaran*, Kuala Lumpur: Penerbit Utusan Melayu.

—— (1991) *The Way Forward*, Kuala Lumpur: ISIS.

Mustapha Johan Abdullah and Shamsulbahriah, K. A. (eds) (1987) *Penswastaan: Kebajikan Pekerja atau Untung Kapitalis*, Kuala Lumpur: MBPBK.

Nankani, H. (1988) *Techniques of Privatization of State-owned Enterprises, Volume II: Selected Country Case Studies*, Washington, DC: World Bank.

Rodan, G. (1989) *The Political Economy of Singapore's Industrialization*, Singapore: Macmillan.

Sheriff, Kassim, Mohd. (1991) 'Privatization: performance, problems and prospects', in Lee Kiong Hock and Shyamala Nagaraj (eds), *The Malaysian Economy Beyond 1990*, Kuala Lumpur: Malaysian Economic Association.

Wade, R. (1990) *Governing The Market: Economic Theory and the Role of Government in East Asian Industrialization*, Princeton: Princeton University Press.

21

PRIVATIZATION IN AFRICA
Prospects for Tanzania
John S. Henley

INTRODUCTION

Tanzania presents some interesting challenges to policy-makers concerned with developing strategies for rehabilitating and regenerating African agricultural processing and manufacturing capacity. Between 1967 and 1986, the Tanzanian government pursued a strong interventionist industrialization policy. This included nationalization of the majority of existing productive capacity, and state promotion, financing and management of new large-scale projects. Until the adoption of the Economic Recovery Programme in June 1986, the private sector was crowded out of official thinking, access to loan capital and foreign exchange allocations. Moreover, the majority of new state investment initiatives were financed through official loans from bilateral and multilateral agencies. Foreign lending agencies must, then, accept some of the responsibility for the subsequent performance of many of these investments.[1]

PRIVATIZATION ISSUES

Revenue benefits

One of the principle benefits to be obtained from privatization in a developed market economy is the transfer of funds from the private sector to augment public revenues when state assets are sold. This benefit is unobtainable in a poor socialist economy such as Tanzania where the financial market is undeveloped and domestic private savings are limited and dispersed. Gains to public revenues are more likely to arise because public enterprises which are presently a drain on expenditure cease to be so. In due course, if privatization is successful, the firms should generate surpluses and pay income taxes. At the very least, bankruptcy becomes politically feasible if an enterprise continues to lose money.

This raises a key policy issue. Should further public revenues be spent on rehabilitating state enterprises prior to privatization? Generally, private investors are only interested in taking over a state enterprise that can be said to be viable according to conventional commercial appraisal techniques. However, there is considerable scope for bargaining over the value of assets, various forms of tariff and non-tariff protection, the availability of loan finance, the provision of additional infrastructure, dispensations from a variety of other government controls, and so on. Each concession needs to be carefully evaluated by both parties. The government is liable to be at a relative disadvantage in these negotiations, particularly in dealing with foreign investors. This is because it will usually not have access to as much expertise or detailed commercial information as the private investor. Indeed, senior managers of state enterprises will be tempted to try to secure their position in advance of privatization by assisting potential private investors.

The ownership question

While financial considerations tend to be uppermost in a government's mind, the ownership question also needs to be settled. The 'property rights' school of institutional economists bases its case for privatization on the argument that it is the incentive effect of a change in the beneficial ownership of enterprises which results in enhanced economic efficiency (Commmander and Killick 1988: 91–124). The change to private ownership, it is argued, creates an interest group with a direct and strong interest in efficiency. The new owners therefore insist on introducing a system of managerial controls and incentives that ensures all employees are dedicated to economic efficiency. This, it is maintained, is the obverse of the managerial culture that typically prevails in enterprises operating in a classical socialist economy.

Under socialism, the state is the 'good father' with an obligation to protect the livelihoods of its citizens so that bankruptcy is politically inconceivable. As a consequence, financial constraints are ultimately 'soft' to the extent that a minimum level of resources will always be found to prevent an enterprise going under. Management is thus partially insulated from the harsh discipline of the market place and the constant need to improve efficiency and responsiveness to changing patterns of consumer demand. It is production-oriented rather than market-oriented.

The 'property rights' school predicts that efficiency gains are not simply a product of the transfer of ownership rights from the public to the private sector but that they depend crucially on the extent to which the new owners have a direct interest in managerial efficiency. In short, something more is required to secure improved efficiency than merely the conversion of a public monopoly into a private monopoly. Unfortunately, Tanzania has a relatively small economy which is oligopolistic in structure and heavily protected. This presents the economic policy adviser with a dilemma. In order to attract private buyers for ailing state enterprises, it may be necessary to offer 'sweeteners' in the form of protection from competing imports or tax breaks. However, high effective rates of protection may create a policy environment in which private investors have no more interest in economic efficiency than had their predecessors.

Of course, in many African countries in the 1990s, the ability of policy-makers to offer concessions to private investors is fairly tightly constrained by the requirements of a World Bank/IMF SAP (structured adjustment programme). This is certainly true of Tanzania. Under Tanzania's programme all that is supposed to be on offer to investors is the prospect of a 'realistic' and progressively lower local exchange rate, tariff neutrality, real local interest rates and access to foreign exchange for the purchase of essential inputs. This kind of policy environment is unlikely to be attractive to foreign investors interested in manufacturing consumer goods for the domestic market. This is perhaps just as well, given the lack of obvious comparative advantage in the manufacture of goods that rely on extensive use of imported materials. In any case, the property rights school would have a clear policy preference for local private ownership over a joint venture arrangement or direct foreign investment involving a multinational corporation. This is because it is hypothesized that the efficiency gains of privatization depend on the strength of the direct financial incentive available to owners and managers. From this perspective, portfolio investment by a local financial institution might also be expected to suffer some efficiency loss from excessive attenuation of property rights. However, Tanzania is deficient on both counts. There are very few indigenous entrepreneurs nor venture capital fund managers.

The provision of finance

The place of equity finance, or its equivalent, in the capital structure is clearly affected by issues such as whether privatized units are to be transformed into companies with shareholders or into some form of mutual organization owned by employees and/or customers. The ownership question is also linked to the kind of financial sector that develops. The absence of organized capital markets is typical of sub-Saharan African economies. There are formal stock-markets in Côte d'Ivoire, Kenya, Nigeria and Zimbabwe but these markets are only in the incipient stage of development. In these markets new issues are rare and trading is thin. Stocks are normally bought for dividend yield rather than the expectation of capital appreciation. There is no formal stock-market in Tanzania. Unsurprisingly, debt financing is presently the most common method of raising funds.

The questions then arise as to who will hold the equity of enterprises after privatization and what relationship will equity holders have with the financial institutions that lend to these enterprises. Tanzania currently adopts the British or US methods of industrial finance requiring equity to be held by non-banking institutions. However, there are no private banks. By contrast, promoters of the German or Japanese 'universal banking' approach to finance might expect banks to retain cross-holdings in major enterprises in order to create a captive customer base and provide a basis for close monitoring of performance of major borrowers. This latter approach is said to encourage lenders to adopt a long-term view of investments which, in turn, enables enterprise managements to adopt longer-term strategies for developing the business. The British/US private system of banking fosters greater specialization of function and a more competitive market for capital but is claimed to promote a short-term view of investment.

The most likely transitional arrangement on the road to privatization is the formation of financial institutions that hold the capitalized government debt of different state enterprises. When investors are eventually invited to tender for equity, the problem then arises as to how to stimulate demand in the absence of substantial concentrations of private savings in politically acceptable hands. Not only do investors need capital to acquire the assets of a state enterprise, most also require substantial additional resources to finance rehabilitation. Inevitably, further loan finance will have to be provided by state financial institutions, unless firms can be sold in their entirety direct to foreign investors. However, most foreign investors are likely to prefer some form of joint venture arrangement at least until they are confident about the new policy environment.

In the transition from lending according to the priorities set through a planning mechanism to lending through a capital market, there is likely to be a continuing need for an 'honest broker' between state, private foreign, and private local interests. Clearly, expectations about the profitability of the enterprises concerned enter into considerations. Where a state enterprise has a well-established record of profitability there should be few difficulties in raising loan finance but these may not be the first candidates for privatization. The capacity of financial institutions to assess risk and supervise loan disbursement will be critical in ensuring good money is not thrown after bad. There is presently a chronic shortage of such personnel in Tanzania.

The record of development finance institutions (DFIs) in Africa has so far not been good. Part of the poor performance of DFIs is undoubtedly attributable to the consequences of inappropriate national macroeconomic policies. In particular, the sharp adjustment of unrealistic exchange rates and negative to positive interest rates in the 1980s caused havoc in the loan portfolios of Tanzanian DFIs lending to local firms against foreign exchange borrowings. Even so, their technical capacity to evaluate bankable projects was sometimes inadequate and investment decision-making processes may have been overly influenced by political considerations. The increased donor-dependence of Tanzania since the onset of the 1981–3 world economic recession has introduced a range of additional external administrative and political factors into the decision-making process.

International banks will continue to be reluctant to re-establish commercial foreign lending operations in Africa. The combination of political risk and the high overhead costs of making loans in unfamiliar markets will remain a powerful deterrent in the medium term and Tanzania is no different from the majority of African countries in this respect. By contrast, it should be relatively easy to privatize retail banking by inviting in foreign banks with the necessary expertise and capital base. The security implied by an international reputation should attract sufficient domestic deposits to generate surpluses to more than cover local administrative overheads associated with trade financing, supplier credit operations and aid flows. From the perspective of the corporate head-quarters of international banks, the main interest in a country such as Tanzania is in the access that retail banking gives to commercial foreign exchange trans-actions. The prospect of dividend remissions generated from local operations will be a relatively minor consideration.

The effect of privatization on innovation

Much of the debate about privatization in Africa is understandably preoccupied with the productivity of existing assets. However, in a world increasingly dominated by accelerating rates of technical change, shorter product life-cycles and rising research and development costs per unit of output, it is also important to consider the impact of ownership on sources and rates of innovation. Here the evidence is unclear. Overall, Africa has a dismal record of expenditure on research and development and its dependence on OECD economies for its technology requirements needs no further elaboration. If, as is likely, techno-logical dependence will continue at least in the medium term, the policy issue then becomes the capacity of public sector enterprises to adopt and adapt imported technology.

It is difficult to believe that Tanzanian state enterprises in their present form can be effective innovators as they have so often been net consumers of state revenues. A critical constraint on the development of innovative capacity is the availability of high-level scientific and engineering manpower. Once Tanzanian state enterprises became locked into a downward spiral based on insufficient working capital and rates of reinvestment, low-capacity utilization and over-manning, they inevitably had difficulty in rewarding their high-level manpower sufficiently to retain them. The rigidities of the Tanzanian centralized state wages and salaries structure compounded the problem.

Dynamic efficiency gains, particularly through improved human resource management, are difficult to estimate. None the less, they are likely to be the most important source of improved economic efficiency to be obtained from privatization. Improved human resource management depends crucially on the competence and quality of managers and skilled technical personnel. With shortages and low levels of capacity utilization widespread in Tanzanian enter-prises, the priority for management has, of necessity, been to keep production going. Product and process development, marketing, and financial management skills are likely to have been neglected in the struggle for survival. On the positive side, there is some evidence that Tanzanian state enterprises spent more on human resource development than comparable firms in the private sector, especially on management and technical training. However, it is difficult to establish the extent to which this training was economically justified. Sometimes it seems to have been distributed as a reward for loyal service and/or was provided as highly subsidized or 'free' technical assistance from aid agencies.

Disposal of public assets

Disposal of publicly owned assets is complicated by technical and political factors. In Tanzania's quasi-administered economy, there were no 'real' measures of the costs of inputs and outputs at least until the late 1980s. There were substantial distortions in the pricing of capital, labour and material inputs. Output prices were subject to manipulation. Domestic production was highly concentrated, if not monopolistic. Consequently, the benefits to be obtained from increasing the influence of market-determined prices are difficult to estimate and diffuse. By contrast, the losers from the short-run income distributional effects of privatization are likely to be a narrowly defined section of the community and can be expected to resist strongly.

It is also important to remember that any move towards privatization is superimposed on existing underlying structural problems. In Tanzania's case, these are derived from previous policies such as the Basic Industrial Strategy (BIS) which aimed to promote self-reliant industrialization based on import substitution. The cumulative effect of these policies has been increased import dependence. As a result, Tanzania is likely to face severe foreign exchange constraints for some time to come. Yet foreign investors want guarantees that it will always be possible to repatriate interest payments, dividends and royalties. Without prior and substantial structural adjustment, private production will remain dependent on government licensing and therefore exposed to the possibilities of political interference. Will this vitiate the dynamic effects of increased managerial autonomy?

Experience of privatization in mature industrial economies, such as the United Kingdom, suggests that it is difficult to maintain a commitment to the promotion of competition. It is easier of sell off monopolies, while it takes time and is complicated to prepare monopolies for competition. Perhaps more importantly, the Tanzanian government depends on the senior management of state enterprises for information, expertise and co-operation in formulating the privatization arrangements. While Tanzanian managers may be keen to reduce government interference in their affairs, they are unlikely to be so enthusiastic about exposing their newly privatized industry to competition.

Ultimately, the Tanzanian government is also dependent on the co-operation of senior management in implementing a privatization policy. Hence, there is a real danger that the newly privatized public sector will be dependent on political connections for a wide variety of monopolistic privileges. To help forestall this possibility, the Tanzanian government is encouraging the formation of institutions which can represent the interests of the private sector, such as the Tanzanian Chamber of Commerce, for the political system lacks people with commercial experience or knowledge. The more pressure is applied to try to speed up the process of privatization without due attention to liberalization and competition policy, the greater the risk that opportunities to improve the performance of many industries will be missed.

THE TANZANIAN CASE: BARRIERS TO ECONOMIC LIBERALIZATION AND PRIVATIZATION

In order to assess the true potential for privatization in Tanzania it is important to have a clear understanding of current barriers to both economic liberalization and privatization. Many barriers stem from the socialist programme adopted in the Arusha Declaration of February 1967 and its resulting implications for ownership and control of industry, the discouragement of privatized enterprises and non-individual ownership of land, subsidization and support of inefficient public enterprises, compression of public sector salaries and the collapse of work incentives, public sector retrenchment, and the negative attitude of trade unions towards liberalization and privatization.

The Arusha Declaration: background to the socialization programme

Until independence in 1961, Tanganyika was administered by the British colonial government with relatively little intervention in economic matters. Unlike its neighbour, Kenya, which was governed very much as a European settler political economy with various economic privileges carefully parcelled out amongst settler and foreign business interests, Tanganyika had a relatively shallow state structure. Britain had never intended it to be a settler economy so there was no pressing need to create an elaborate system of internal redistribution. Such economic development that did occur was largely the product of private initiative, particularly by migrants from South Asia. Foreign investments were generally managed as an adjunct of regional operations headquartered in Nairobi, Kenya. Thus the brewery, the cigarette factory, the cement works, the oxygen plant, a major shoe manufacturer and the metal can plant, among others, were incorporated as subsidiaries of Kenyan-based operations. Even five years after independence, only 10 per cent of parastatal assets were in manufacturing, while the majority were in mining and electricity with scattered investments in financial services, tourism and plantation agriculture. The First Five-Year Plan (1964–9) assumed a private investment share of 75 per cent of the industrial sector albeit with the anticipation of a substantial public sector investment programme.

The first interventionist programme, moderate by 1960s' standards, was superseded by the publication of the Arusha Declaration of February 1967 which heralded the adoption of a full socialist programme of economic development. The influence of Soviet and Chinese thinking of the 1950s and 1960s on Tanzanian economic development policy is reflected in the emphasis on self-reliant industrialization. It is sometimes forgotten that the Arusha Declaration also called for greater emphasis on rural development though, in the event, priority was assigned to industrial self-reliance. A process of substantial resource transfer to the manufacturing sector was started in 1967 relying on public investment in state-owned enterprises. This policy continued until the economic

461

crisis of the early 1980s. The manifest absence, in 1967, of an educated and skilled industrial class or indigenous technological capabilities embodied in a capital goods industry does not seem to have deterred policy-makers. Indeed, policy-makers seem to have simply assumed that the expansion of the public sector would stimulate the creation of these missing social formations and, moreover, that there would be no significant efficiency losses while they were being created.

Ownership and control of industry

An attraction of state ownership was the expectation that profits would no longer go to private sector shareholders, most of whom were either non-indigenous residents or residents abroad, but would be available for domestic investment. In an attempt to ensure that accumulation was restricted to the state and there would be no conflict between private and public interests, the government introduced a Leadership Code. This officially forbade public employees from having second sources of income from private businesses or from renting property. Tanzania's economic development strategy thus became sharply distinct from that of Kenya which was pursuing a vigorous policy of attracting foreign investors through joint venture arrangements with government DFIs. Kenyan civil servants were openly encouraged by President Kenyatta to have sideline businesses.

The subsequent economic history of Tanzania has demonstrated that far from generating a re-investable surplus, state-owned enterprises have been net consumers of resources – TSh 7.8 billion between 1981/2 and 1985/6, if corporate taxes are deducted from current account transfers.[2]

There has been a significant shift in the composition of imports towards intermediates and capital goods – the share of consumer goods in imports has declined from around 30 per cent in 1970 to below 20 per cent in the 1980s. However this trend reflects increased import dependency and probably hides considerable repressed demand for imported consumer goods. According to the World Bank (1989a), imports minus exports as a percentage of GDP have been above 9 per cent for eleven of the past fifteen years; it was 10.5 per cent in 1985 and 14.5 per cent in 1986. Value added and production in the manufacturing sector, where investments by parastatals have been concentrated, actually declined between 1976 and 1986, from TSh 3.1 to TSh 1.0 billion (in 1976 prices), a decline of 68 per cent. In addition, the composition of output has not changed significantly towards capital and intermediate goods production despite heavy investment in chemicals, fertilizers, rubbers, plastics and metals.

The politics of manufacturing under government licence and the discouragement of private enterprise

While the economic consequences of Tanzania's development policy between

1967 and 1986 may have been poor, the experience might be expected to have stimulated the search for alternatives. Unfortunately, a programme of national-ization also has its social impact. One of its effects is to discourage, and in extreme cases, criminalize private accumulation.[3] What was left of the private sector was suddenly placed at a disadvantage relative to the public sector over a whole range of business relationships. This is of particular importance in countries such as Tanzania where the government is pursuing a policy of industrialization through import substitution. Under these conditions, investors rely on the domestic market and a wide range of licences negotiated with the government for their profitability – from quotas on competing imports and favourable treatment by the price controller to import licences and foreign exchange allocations for the purchase of essential inputs. Overnight, hard-won concessions may be lost to the public sector which, by definition, usually has superior political support. People are encouraged to believe that private ownership is suspect, and if anyone is clever enough to accumulate capital, the state is liable to expropriate it. This in turn discourages entrepreneurial invest-ment. As might be expected, there are very few local industrialists today in Tanzania. Equally, there are very few civil servants who have any experience of negotiating with private sector business interests – local or foreign.

The disruption of agriculture: villagization and non-individual ownership

Another argument advanced in support of the Arusha Declaration and, in particular, the policy of villagization or *ujamaa vijijini*, was that the traditional landholding systems of communal farming prevalent in Tanzania did not involve individual ownership of land. Cultivation was a man's right within the vicinity of his home village. Therefore, it was argued, greater efficiency could be achieved in agricultural production with little social disruption by the expedient of moving the dispersed rural population into villages with new communal landholdings, now designated by the state. This concentration of the rural population was supposed to facilitate the delivery of extension and social services. On the contrary this policy led to a progressive decline in agricultural production in the 1970s – the annual growth rate of agricultural GDP declined from 2.4 per cent during 1970–5 to 1 per cent during 1976–80.

The poor performance of parastatal marketing boards, expanded to rationalize the marketing and distribution of crops, exacerbated the social disruption caused by villagization by further undermining individual incentives. Fortunately, Tanzanian farmers seem to be resilient. With a series of good harvests in the mid-1980s, the transfer of responsibility for crop purchases to primary co-operative unions and the licensing of private traders in agricultural produce, agricultural output has increased sharply to an annual growth rate of 5.4 per cent during 1984–7. The lesson from agriculture seems to be clear – centralized direction of production and marketing does not work well in a large country with a scattered population.

463

While there has been a retreat from forced villagization, all land is held on a leasehold basis from the state, either 33 or 99 years. This would seem to be one barrier to the development of a freehold property market that could be used for collateral for industrial investments. In its favour, the land tenure system probably discourages over-investment in land and reduces inflationary pressures. Another factor in Tanzania and in many other African countries that inhibits the development of an active property market is the complexity and political sensitivity of property law and its application. This often discourages banks from accepting land titles as collateral for commercial loans.[4]

The political significance of state employees and reduced incentives for efficiency

Another result of state socialism was the creation of a major political constituency – the bureaucratic bourgeoisie – that is dependent on the state and its political leadership (Shivji 1976). The adoption of state socialism also justifies the incorporation of the trade union movement as a subordinate wing of the ruling party, achieved in 1964 in Tanzania.[5] Paradoxically, one of the features of state socialism, namely the tendency of state institutions in the absence of a price mechanism to suck in scarce resources until physical limits are reached, has worked to undermine the dependency of employees on the state.

Under socialism, the paternalistic state cannot permit a state-owned enterprise to go bankrupt, so there is a tendency for financial constraints to be what Kornai refers to as 'soft' (Kornai 1980). In theory, more resources will always be found to underwrite the solvency of state institutions, so the rational manager continues to accumulate resources, human and material, until physical scarcities are encountered. In Tanzania, shortages of imported inputs and machinery were invariably encountered before those of human resources. There were, however, often shortages of skilled and experienced manpower and attempts by managers to substitute inferior human capital resulted in additional inefficiencies.

Public sector salary compression and the collapse of work incentives

What has happened in Tanzania, as in many other developing countries, has been severe compression of public sector wages in parallel with substantial expansion of the number of employees. Figure 21.1 demonstrates this effect graphically. In 1984, public sector employment totalled some 302,000 or 77 per cent of formal sector wage employment. While employment in the public sector has increased at around 5 per cent per annum since 1970, the index of real average wages has declined from 100 to 1969 to 19 in 1986. The index for top salaries has declined even more dramatically, to 6. Differentials have also been compressed sharply. A top salary that was nearly thirty times the minimum wage in 1969 was only about six times the minimum wage on the 1987/8 pay scale, and only four times after tax (World Bank 1989b: 55).

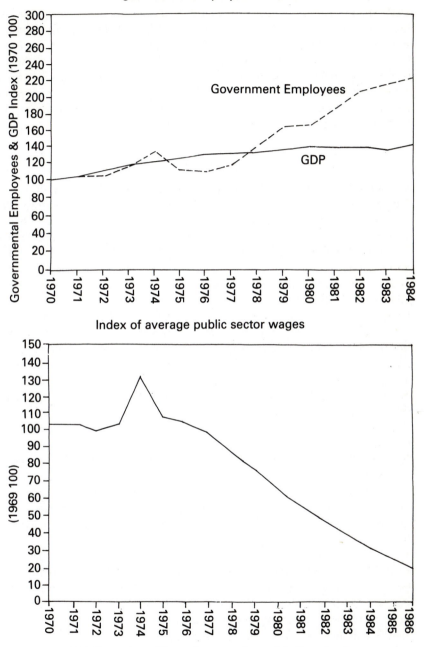

Figure 21.1 Tanzania: public service expansion and decline of real pay

Source: World Bank, *PER*, 1989: 56.

Unsurprisingly, the World Bank's Tanzanian *Public Expenditure Review* (PER) found random evidence of departmental supply votes being used to compensate for low pay through benefits in kind. Evidence was also found of attempts to supplement pay of more senior public employees with increased fringe benefits. Middle-level officials seemed to have suffered most over the last ten years. As might be expected, many public servants have alternative sources of income, notwithstanding the Leadership Code. The World Bank's PER proposed a 30 per cent reduction in the number of staff on the payroll of both central and local government (World Bank 1989b: 20).

Public sector retrenchment and possible political resistance

Without substantial retrenchment, it is not clear how the efficiency of the Tanzanian civil service or parastatals can be improved for there is no prospect of a rapid expansion of the government's revenue base. Also, without sufficient supporting expenditures proper levels of efficiency cannot be obtained. Yet the government's ambitious plans for an expanding role for the private sector implies increased competition for scarce managerial and technical skills and substantial increases in income inequality generally. Without adequate incentives, those public servants with scarce skills will leave to join the expanding private sector or will increase the effort they put into income generation from secondary employment to achieve what they consider to be a reasonable income level. Clearly, privatization without retrenchment is also not viable. Doing nothing to reduce public sector employment and failure to increase wage levels will result in increased loss of talent, inefficiency and corruption as those who remain seek to 'tax' those who quit. Policy-makers are thus caught between a rock and a hard place.

In considering possible forms of resistance to liberalization and privatization, it is also necessary to take account of political structures and processes in Tanzania. While a broad analysis of the political debate is beyond the scope of this chapter, and political factors may be very important, one arena in which argument and resistance may be fierce is in the enterprise itself. It is here that the social consequences of retrenchment are going to be felt and where the losers and winners are going to be concentrated. While real wages may have declined very sharply over the last ten years, *some* guaranteed income is better than no income and where primary employment often forms a basis of secondary sources of income. Primary employment provides a buffer to absorb the shocks of the more uncertain and competitive secondary labour market. Some argue, however, that because most people already have a 'second line' in the private sector, there is very little ideological attachment to the public sector.[6] The latter, in the popular mind, is synonymous with queues and shortages.

Public sector management are not insensitive to disparities in the labour market and will indulge valued skilled tradesmen in various ways. For example, they may permit them to use the company's machine shop facilities to earn extra income carrying out work on behalf of private companies or individuals. Again where production in Tanzanian parastatal enterprises is subject to sharp fluctuations in capacity utilization with periods of forced idleness due to shortages of energy, water, components or raw materials, management are probably only too willing to relieve the obvious hardship of their workers by turning a blind eye to secondary employment. In other words, Tanzanian public sector employment cannot be assumed to be an individual employee's sole source of income. While those most wanted by newly privatized enterprises will probably have the widest range of secondary sources of income, the poorly educated, young, inexperienced and unskilled workers and, therefore, most dispensable will have few alternatives.[7] Moreover, the unskilled are also most likely to have been hired on the basis of the personal recommendations of influential politicians and officials.

Management retrenchment and management skills

The quality and skills of management undertaking specific privatization exercises will be an important factor in minimizing the political backwash from the process of disposing of parastatals. The government will have to place heavy reliance on particular enterprise management to oversee the transfer of assets and oversee the restructuring of the labour force. Unfortunately, the World Bank's PER is not very encouraging on the matter of the quality of Tanzanian parastatal management.

> Enterprise management is weak as evidenced by the fact that a substantial percentage of managers cannot run their firms with a minimal level of financial discipline. In 1985–86, a third of the parastatals were delinquent in producing basic accounts and of those that did, three-fifths were deficient; of those with clean audits, one-fourth were making losses. Few Tanzanian parastatals carry out regular inventories of their assets, controls over use of credit and cash are weak, records on procurement and transactions with subsidiaries are often missing or incomplete, internal auditing procedures are often weak or non-existent, and allegations and proven instances of fraud, corruption and theft are common.... Good managers exist in Tanzania, but they appear few in numbers.
>
> (World Bank 1989b: 125)

Apparently, twenty years after the Arusha Declaration and the creation of over 410 parastatals, the public sector management cadre is still very weak. Clearly, if the World Bank's PER is correct, a major management development programme is required in support of any privatization programme. The rehabilitation survey of Tanzania by UNIDO (1989: 156–8) also supports the World Bank's findings about the weaknesses in enterprise management. In addition to an absence of real managerial skills, the UNIDO survey found that many plants had a large number of vacancies in key management positions and at the intermediate level. This is particularly so with respect to production and accounting functions.

Alternatively, the management cadre may be more competent than the World Bank gives it credit for. Present behaviour could be a consequence of the prevailing system of incentives and level of managerial rewards. Being rational people, Tanzanian managers may have decided to devote their energies to other income-generating activities to the detriment of their primary employment. There is some evidence to suggest that the bureaucratic and hierarchical management structure in parastatals discourages initiative and decision-making. However, in the absence of reliable empirical evidence of public sector management motivation and time budgets, it would be foolhardy to make predictions as to the likely outcome of a radical change in the incentive system. More to the point, what evidence there is available does raise some very serious questions about the capacity and motivation of existing managers to carry through an effective privatization programme without substantial investment in management training and incentives.

Trade union attitudes to privatization

Every public corporation employing more than ten workers has to have a Worker's Council that is serviced by JUWATA, the workers' organization affiliated to the Party. Any privatization or retrenchment proposal for a parastatal would have to be considered, at enterprise level, by the Workers' Council and debated within the Management Committee. The functions of the Workers' Council are formally limited to advising a Management Committee. Sixty per cent of committee members are drawn from senior management and outside appointees and up to 40 per cent of members are workers' representatives elected by the Workers' Council. Parastatal management and government appointees normally command a majority on the enterprise Management Committee, but with the prospect of serious retrenchment, some managers might be tempted to side with workers' representatives or even organize the opposition.

Theoretically, JUWATA is bound to uphold Chama Cha Mapinduzi (CCM) Party policy. However, workers may sidestep institutions which do not receive their support. At the present point in time, the general opinion is that JUWATA is not a very significant organization at enterprise level, but it does provide a possible base for organizing opposition to major changes, particularly if policy reforms do not receive full backing from key Party members. At least in formal terms the Arusha Declaration still forms the bedrock of government policy and acts in various ways to inhibit the trend towards liberalization and privatization.

The textile industry: an example of the legacy of public ownership

Prior to independence in 1961 Tanzania had only one textile mill. The state holding company, TEXCO, established by Presidential order in 1973 to 'clothe the nation', has expanded its role and now has fourteen subsidiary companies that own eighteen mills. By 1988, of the total process capacities between 85 per cent and 90 per cent lay in the public sector.

The strategy adopted by TEXCO reflected its mandate to supply the domestic market and to use locally grown cotton. Only one mill does not rely on domestically produced cotton. The local market was protected from foreign competition until 1986, when the government acceded to popular pressure to allow imports. The consequential flood of very low-cost, second-hand clothing with which no conventional garment maker could compete, even with a 60 per cent tariff protection, virtually destroyed the local ready-made clothing industry.

The small private sector responded to the increasingly liberal market after 1986 by altering its product mix. It began manufacturing both towels and bed linen and exporting some of these items together with knitted fabrics and garments, mainly T-shirts. By contrast, TEXCO companies have generally continued to supply the local market with Khanga and Kitenge cloth. While TEXCO companies are attempting to change their product range and orientation towards exports, they are locked into past decisions by poorly maintained machines, very low productivity, weak management and working-capital problems caused by low-capacity utilization and by the need to service a large foreign debt burden. The total nominal annual capacity of Tanzania's textile industry is 49,000 tonnes of yarn and 278 million square metres of woven cloth. In 1988 annual utilization of capacity was 34 per cent in spinning, 17 per cent in weaving and 24 per cent in wet processing. The normal overall minimum level of capacity utilization that should be expected is 75 per cent in spinning and processing and 68 per cent in weaving. In short, utilization of national capacity was at a level that is financially unsustainable.

Some of the causes of the low level of performance were outside the control of mill management, in particular shortages of electrical power and water. However, capacity utilization statistics suggest that private sector managers were much more successful coping with the problems of operating in Tanzania than their public sector counterparts. Thus the private sector achieves 60 per cent utilization in spinning and processing compared with around 18 per cent in the public sector. For weaving the public sector achieved only 13.5 per cent while the private sector obtained 46 per cent. The prima-facie case for privatizing the textile sector would seem to be very strong.

The move towards economic liberalization, privatization, and the promotion of private investment

The path to economic liberalization has not been smooth. At the same time as the Party and a section of the government have continued to assert their belief in national plans, the government, with the Ministry of Finance as the lead Ministry, has been engaged in developing a progressive liberalization programme since 1982. To be sure, it has taken some time to build up the political and administrative momentum behind this reform programme, as evidenced by the protracted negotiations over the SAP with the IMF/World Bank from 1982–5. However, the launch of the Economic Recovery Programme in June 1986, and subsequent events, would seem to indicate the ascendancy of liberalization and reformism over state control and socialism.

Despite the government's espousal of the Economic Recovery Programme, the CCM propounded its industrial development policy through the Party Programme (1987–2002). This was more or less a reiteration of the Basic Industrial Strategy (BIS) of 1975–8. The Party document proposed further development of basic industries such as iron and steel, coal, chemicals, metal and engineering. In response, the government produced the Second Union Five-Year Development Plan (1988/9–1992/3), but this seems to be already largely disregarded in the struggle for economic recovery. Nevertheless, there is some evidence of a continuing rearguard action, with the Ministry of Finance and the Bank of Tanzania (BOT) identified as bastions of economic liberalism and the Party as defender of the principles of the Arusha Declaration. The formation of the Planning Commission, in July 1989, outside the Ministry of Finance but in the Union President's Office, would seem to reflect the need to establish an arbiter between those who favour the public sector and those who favour the private sector. Further evidence of continuing debate about the direction of economic policy and its political sensitivity is provided in the 1990 Investment Promotion Policy.

The rediscovery of the virtues of private investment

In the opening paragraph, the Investment Promotion Policy (IPP) quotes the Arusha Declaration of 1967, and 'the Nation's commitment to the policy of Socialism and Self-Reliance, under which control of the commanding heights of the economy is vested to the public via the Government, parastatals and co-operative organizations'. It continues 'During the whole period following Independence, foreign investment had played a key role in the development of various sectors of the economy' almost as if the nationalization programme that followed from the Arusha Declaration had not been of any significance. Paragraph two reveals the government's recognition of the shift in bargaining power in favour of foreign investors' interests at the expense of host governments as a result of increased competition for inward investment. Tanzania, it would seem, has to make good for its post-independence history of nationalization, blocked compensation funds and dividends and reticence towards foreign investors. In the 1990s, the IPP promises that transparency and clarity of investment rules and regulations will characterize the new policy environment.

Import-substituting industrialization and indebtedness

In the debate about the failures of Tanzania's industrialization policy most attention has been focused on the role of public ownership and the quality of

470

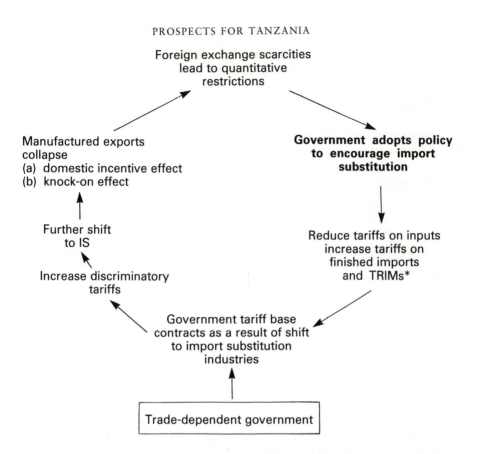

Foreign exchange scarcities
lead to quantitative
restrictions

Manufactured exports
collapse
(a) domestic incentive effect
(b) knock-on effect

**Government adopts policy
to encourage import
substitution**

Further shift
to IS

Increase discriminatory
tariffs

Reduce tariffs on inputs
increase tariffs on
finished imports
and TRIMs*

Government tariff base
contracts as a result of shift
to import substitution
industries

Trade-dependent government

Figure 21.2 Tanzania: consequence of felt need for 'industry'

Note: *Trade-related investment measures.

public sector management. Relatively little attention has been paid to the underlying policy of import-substitution-based industrialization (ISI) and the implications of that policy for liberalization and privatization. The limited available evidence on the private sector raises some rather disquieting questions about the supposed 'liberality' of the policy environment in which the private sector operates.

The causes of illiberality in an economy pursuing industrialization through ISI are straightforward. The dynamics of an import substituting industrialization policy are outlined in Figure 21.2. The diagram shows clearly the way in which an ISI policy creates its own shortages and pressures on the authorities to introduce discriminatory tariffs and, ultimately, rationing of import licences. These in turn encourage the growth of smuggling and corruption of licensing procedures.

At present the Open General Licensing (OGL) system financed under the SAP is relieving the pressure on the authorities. It is a matter of conjecture as to how long the OGL scheme is sustainable. If privatization proceeds on a significant scale, this implies substantial reinvestment in capital equipment and increased capacity utilization. While some of the re-equipment costs may be externally financed, the new private investment will also contribute to increased imports of raw materials and intermediates.

Moreover, the government is going to find it extremely difficult to persuade local or foreign investors to buy public sector enterprises without offering some concessions on import protection. Once these are conceded, privatization merely means the transfer of monopolistic privilege from public servants to private citizens. While private firms may be expected to exploit these privileges with greater vigour than their predecessors, the fundamental structural problems of industrialization based on import substitution will remain. The only way such a policy can be sustained is through expanding the export base, which is primarily agricultural, or through increased donor support. While there may be some opportunities for the development of domestic resource-based, export-oriented manufacturing industry, they are likely to be limited in the short- to medium-term.

Policies, privatization and the resource gap

One of the main political factors that contributed to the initial popularity of the Arusha Declaration was the way it was presented as a solution to the problem of establishing national control of the 'commanding heights' of the economy. The problem still remains. There are not enough indigenous Tanzanians with the financial resources to take over more than a very small proportion of parastatal enterprises. Most enterprises that are successfully privatized will be joint ventures between private interests (local and/or foreign) and quasi-public portfolio investors such as the National Insurance Company (NIC) – the state insurance monopoly – and the National Provident Fund (NPF) and the DFIs. Foreign investors are likely to insist on some Tanzanian-owned equity.

The more general question than that of privatization, then, is how to open up the public sector to new capital investment in a way that reflects whether a project is truly bankable. Ownership is, in the Tanzanian context, an important but a secondary issue. Where profitability of an import-substituting parastatal depends substantially on government protection and licences, valuation of assets is in any case going to be very difficult. It is essential that the project appraisal process is 'ring-fenced' from political interference yet existing institutions are organized for just that purpose, as all projects involving parastatals need ultimately to be approved by the Planning Commission and CCM. Experience in other African countries of DFIs lending to the private sector is not very encouraging. Too often, public investment, funds are squandered on 'privately sponsored' white elephants.

Generalizing from the Tanzanian case, it is clear that in considering privatization as a strategy for economic regeneration the key issue from the point of view of the government is one of finance. In the absence of any alternative way of rehabilitating industry, private share ownership is acceptable. If the financial requirements to turn an enterprise around are so large that the state's share declines below 50 per cent then, in present circumstances, loss of control is no longer an issue.

The priority is to develop mechanisms for refinancing illiquid but potentially viable firms and encouraging new private inward investment. This suggests there is a need for a greatly enhanced role for the development banks to act as 'honest brokers' between the public and the private sector. It also implies an enhanced technical and management consulting capacity, for successful rehabilitation depends on careful attention to technical factors, marketing and human resource development, as well as realistic financial provision. Tanzania is presently littered with derelict projects that have failed to take account of the totality of business enterprise. Ownership transformation, then, is only part of the process of revitalizing the economy. Without structural adjustment, old problems will merely change their form to reappear in their familiar guise of foreign exchange shortages, import quotas and inflation.

NOTES

1   Total foreign assistance flows to Tanzania were US$764.4 million in 1987 compared with total export earnings of around US$350 million. Bilateral technical assistance amounted to US$226.4 million and principal donors were Sweden (24.4 per cent), Denmark (12.2 per cent), Finland (11.1 per cent), Norway (9.7 per cent), West Germany (6.8 per cent) and Japan (6.6 per cent). Capital assistance amounted to US$492 million and principal donors were the World Bank (20.5 per cent), Sweden (10.4 per cent), The Netherlands (9.1 per cent), IMF (8.9 per cent), Norway (7.3 per cent) and Japan (6.9 per cent).

2   State-owned enterprises would, in all probability, have paid the same taxes if they were privately owned. The World Bank estimates a net transfer on the current account of only TSh991 million in the five years 1981/2–1985/6 (World Bank 1989a: 11–13).

3   The Leadership Code was introduced to prevent leaders having two incomes. This meant that members of the managerial and civil service elite were not supposed to participate in any private business. It was never very successful but it resulted in a stigma being attached to private sector activity. Officials who broke the Code were forced to employ all sorts of indirect means in pursuing their sideline interests.

4   For example, in Kenya and Zimbabwe, which otherwise have relatively well-developed financial institutions. Property and development companies make up a very important part of the smaller stock-markets of South-East Asia and, although often of a very speculative nature, are successful in mobilizing private savings for industrial development.

5   The National Union of Tanganyika Workers (Establishment) Act 1964 abolished the independent Tanganyika Federation of Labour and reconstituted the trade union movement as an affiliated organization of the ruling Party, TANU, with nine industrial sections.

6   In 1980, when the Bureau of Statistics last classified Central Government employees by whether they were 'regular' or 'casual' employees, over 14 per cent or 31,000 were classified as 'casuals'.

7   Some 7,000 civil servants were laid off between 1983/4 and 1984/5 without any major unrest and this was at a time when the economy was in deep recession. By contrast, Tanzania today is experiencing real per capita economic growth largely as a result of improved agricultural output so that the absorptive capacity of the rural economy should be much greater than in the mid-1980s. However, the World Bank's PER anticipates a reduction of 30 per cent of the public sector payroll of 291,841 – that is, nearly 90,000 people or over 10 per cent of the total formal sector labour force excluding the Armed Forces.

REFERENCES

Commander, S. and Killick, T. (1988) 'Privatization in developing countries: a survey of issues', in P. Cook and C. Kirkpatrick (eds), *Privatization in Less Developed Countries*, Brighton: Wheatsheaf.

Kornai, J. (1980) *The Economics of Shortage* Amsterdam: North-Holland.

Shivji, I. G. (1976) *Class Struggles in Tanzania*, New York: Monthly Review Press.

UNIDO (1989) *The Regeneration of the Tanzanian Manufacturing Industry with Emphasis on Agro-based Industries*, PRD/R 26, Vienna: UNIDO.

World Bank (1989a) *Parastatals in Tanzania Towards a Reform Program*, Report No. 7100-TA, Washington, DC: World Bank.

—— (1989b) *Tanzania Public Expenditure Review, Volume I: Executive Report*, Washington, DC: World Bank.

INDEX